TRANSLATOR AND EDITOR:
Rabbi David Strauss

MANAGING EDITOR:
Baruch Goldberg

EDITOR:
Rabbi Yehezkel Anis

ASSOCIATE EDITOR:
Dr. Jeffrey M. Green

COPY EDITOR:
Alec Israel

BOOK DESIGNER:
Ben Gasner

GRAPHIC ARTIST:
Michael Etkin

TECHNICAL STAFF:
Muriel Stein

Random House Staff

PRODUCTION MANAGER:
Richard Elman

DESIGN DIRECTOR:
Bernard Klein

MANAGING EDITOR:
Amy Edelman

The Talmud
The Steinsaltz Edition

Volume XI
Tractate Ketubot
Part V

Volume XI
Tractate Ketubot
Part V

Random House
New York

THE TALMUD

תלמוד בבלי

THE STEINSALTZ EDITION

Commentary by Rabbi Adin Steinsaltz (Even Yisrael)

This is an English translation of a work originally published in Hebrew by The Israel Institute for Talmudic Publications, Jerusalem, Israel.

Library of Congress Cataloging-in-Publication Data
(Revised for volume XI)
The Talmud.
English, Hebrew, Aramaic.
Includes bibliographical references.
Contents: v.1- Tractate Bava metzia-
v. 7. Tractate Ketubot, pt.1. v. 11. Tractate Ketubot, pt. 5.
Accompanied by a reference guide.
I. Title.
BM499.5.E4 1989 89-842911
ISBN 0-394-57665-9 (guide)
ISBN 0-394-57666-7 (v. 1)
ISBN 0-679-44397-5 (v. 11)

Random House website address: http://www.randomhouse.com/
Printed in the United States of America on acid-free paper

2 4 6 8 9 7 5 3

First Edition

לא עליך המלאכה לגמור,
ולא אתה בן־חורין להבטל ממנה
(אבות ב:כא)

You need not complete the task,
nor are you free to abandon it.
(Ethics of the Fathers 2:21)

Dedicated in loving memory of

Morris David Baker, z'l

משה דוד בן בן־ציון

who was tireless in his commitment and devotion
to the Jewish people and the Land of Israel

Beverly Franzblau Baker
Marc Samuel and Nenita Rachel, Adam Joseph and Joshua Benjamin

The Steinsaltz Talmud in English

The English edition of the Steinsaltz Talmud is a translation and adaptation of the Hebrew edition. It includes most of the additions and improvements that characterize the Hebrew version, but it has been adapted and expanded especially for the English reader. This edition has been designed to meet the needs of advanced students capable of studying from standard Talmud editions, as well as of beginners, who know little or no Hebrew and have had no prior training in studying the Talmud.

The overall structure of the page is similar to that of the traditional pages in the standard printed editions. The text is placed in the center of the page, and alongside it are the main auxiliary commentaries. At the bottom of the page and in the margins are additions and supplements.

The original Hebrew-Aramaic text, which is framed in the center of each page, is exactly the same as that in the traditional Talmud (although material that was removed by non-Jewish censors has been restored on the basis of manuscripts and old printed editions). The main innovation is that this Hebrew-Aramaic text has been completely vocalized and punctuated, and all the terms usually abbreviated have been fully spelled out. In order to retain the connection with the page numbers of the standard editions, these are indicated at the head of every page.

We have placed a *Literal Translation* on the right-hand side of the page, and its punctuation has been introduced into the Talmud text, further helping the student to orientate himself. The *Literal Translation* is intended to help the student to learn the meaning of specific Hebrew and Aramaic words. By comparing the original text with this translation, the reader develops an understanding of the Talmudic text and can follow the words and sentences in the original. Occasionally, however, it has not been possible to present an exact literal translation of the original text, because it is so different in structure from English. Therefore we have added certain auxiliary words, which are indicated in square brackets. In other cases it would make no sense to offer a literal translation of a Talmudic idiom, so we have provided a close English equivalent of the original meaning, while a note, marked "lit.," explaining the literal meaning of the words, appears in parentheses. Our purpose in presenting this literal translation was to give the student an appreciation of the terse and enigmatic nature of the Talmud itself, before the arguments are opened up by interpretation.

Nevertheless, no one can study the Talmud without the assistance of commentaries. The main aid to understanding the Talmud provided by this edition is the *Translation and Commentary,* appearing on the left side of the page. This is Rabbi Adin Steinsaltz's highly regarded Hebrew interpretation of the Talmud, translated into English, adapted and expanded.

This commentary is not merely an explanation of difficult passages. It is an integrated exposition of the entire text. It includes a full translation of the Talmud text, combined with explanatory remarks. Where the translation in the commentary reflects the literal translation, it has been set off in bold type. It has also been given the same reference numbers that are found both in the original text and in the literal translation. Moreover, each section of the commentary begins with a few words of the Hebrew-Aramaic text. These reference numbers and paragraph headings allow the reader to move from one part of the page to another with ease.

There are some slight variations between the literal translation and the words in bold face appearing in the *Translation and Commentary.* These variations are meant to enhance understanding, for a juxtaposition of the literal translation and the sometimes freer translation in the commentary will give the reader a firmer grasp of the meaning.

The expanded *Translation and Commentary* in the left-hand column is intended to provide a conceptual understanding of the arguments of the Talmud, their form, content, context, and significance. The commentary also brings out the logic of the questions asked by the Sages and the assumptions they made.

Rashi's traditional commentary has been included in the right-hand column, under the *Literal Translation.* We have left this commentary in the traditional "Rashi script," but all quotations of the Talmud text appear in standard square type, the abbreviated expressions have all been printed in full, and Rashi's commentary is fully punctuated.

Since the *Translation and Commentary* cannot remain cogent and still encompass all the complex issues that arise in the Talmudic discussion, we have included a number of other features, which are also found in Rabbi Steinsaltz's Hebrew edition.

At the bottom of the page, under the *Translation and Commentary*, is the *Notes* section, containing additional material on issues raised in the text. These notes deepen understanding of the Talmud in various ways. Some provide a deeper and more profound analysis of the issues discussed in the text, with regard to individual points and to the development of the entire discussion. Others explain Halakhic concepts and the terms of Talmudic discourse.

The *Notes* contain brief summaries of the opinions of many of the major commentators on the Talmud, from the period after the completion of the Talmud to the present. Frequently the *Notes* offer interpretations different from that presented in the commentary, illustrating the richness and depth of Rabbinic thought.

The *Halakhah* section appears below the *Notes.* This provides references to the authoritative legal decisions reached over the centuries by the Rabbis in their discussions of the matters dealt with in the Talmud. It explains what reasons led to these Halakhic decisions and the close connection between the Halakhah today and the Talmud and its various interpreters. It should be noted that the summary of the Halakhah presented here is not meant to serve as a reference source for actual religious practice but to introduce the reader to Halakhic conclusions drawn from the Talmudic text.

English commentary and expanded translation of the text, making it readable and comprehensible

Hebrew/Aramaic text of the Talmud, fully vocalized, and punctuated

Literal translation of the Talmud text into English

REALIA

קַלְתָּהּ Her basket. The source of this word is the Greek κάλαθος, kalathos, and it means a basket with a narrow base.

Illustration from a Greek drawing depicting such a basket of fruit.

CONCEPTS

פֵּאָה *Pe'ah.* One of the presents left for the poor (מַתְּנוֹת עֲנִיִּים). The Torah forbids harvesting "the corners of your field," so that the produce left standing may be harvested and kept by the poor (Leviticus 19:9).

The Torah did not specify a minimum amount of produce to be left as *pe'ah*. But the Sages stipulated that it must be at least one-sixtieth of the crop.

Pe'ah is set aside only from crops that ripen at one time and are harvested at one time. The poor are allowed to use their own initiative to reap the *pe'ah* left in the fields. But the owner of an orchard must see to it that each of the poor gets a fixed share of the *pe'ah* from places that are difficult to reach. The poor come to collect *pe'ah* three times a day. The laws of *pe'ah* are discussed in detail in tractate *Pe'ah*.

Marginal notes provide essential background information

TRANSLATION AND COMMENTARY

[1]**and her husband threw her a bill of divorce into her lap or into her basket**, which she was carrying on her head, [2]would you say **here, too,** that **she would not be divorced**? Surely we know that the law is that she *is* divorced in such a case, as the Mishnah (*Gittin* 77a) states explicitly!

אָמַר לֵיהּ [3]**Rav Ashi said** in reply **to Ravina**: The woman's **basket is** considered to be **at rest, and it is she who walks beneath it.** Thus the basket is considered to be a "stationary courtyard," and the woman acquires whatever is thrown into it.

MISHNAH הָיָה רוֹכֵב [4]**If a person was riding on an animal and he saw an ownerless object** lying on the ground, **and he said to another person** standing nearby, **"Give** that object **to me,"** [5]if **the other person took** the ownerless object **and said, "I have acquired it for myself,"** [6]he has **acquired it** by lifting it up, even though he was not the first to see it, and the rider has no claim to it. [7]But **if, after he gave** the object **to** the rider, the person who picked it up **said, "I acquired** the object **first,"** [8]**he** in fact **said nothing**. His words are of no effect, and the rider may keep it. Since the person walking showed no intention of acquiring the object when he originally picked it up, he is not now believed when he claims that he acquired it first. Indeed, even if we maintain that when a person picks up an ownerless object on behalf of someone else, the latter does *not* acquire it automatically, here, by *giving* the object to the rider, he makes a gift of it to the rider.

GEMARA תְּנַן הָתָם [9]**We have learned elsewhere** in a Mishnah in tractate *Pe'ah* (4:9): **"Someone who gathered *pe'ah*** — produce which by Torah law [Leviticus 23:22] is left unharvested in the corner of a field by the owner of the field, to be gleaned by the poor — **and said, 'Behold, this** *pe'ah* which I have gleaned **is** intended **for so-and-so the poor man,'** [10]**Rabbi Eliezer says:** The person who gathered the *pe'ah* **has acquired it**

בִּרְשׁוּת הָרַבִּים [1]וְזָרַק לָהּ גֵּט לְתוֹךְ חֵיקָהּ אוֹ לְתוֹךְ קַלְתָּהּ — [2]הָכָא נַמִּי דְּלָא מְגָרְשָׁה? [3]אֲמַר לֵיהּ: קַלְתָּהּ מֵינָח נַיְיחָא, וְאִיהִי דְּקָא מְסַגְּיָא מִתּוּתָהּ.

מִשְׁנָה [4]הָיָה רוֹכֵב עַל גַּבֵּי בְהֵמָה וְרָאָה אֶת הַמְּצִיאָה, וְאָמַר לַחֲבֵירוֹ "תְּנָה לִי", [5]נְטָלָהּ וְאָמַר, "אֲנִי זָכִיתִי בָּהּ", [6]זָכָה בָּהּ. [7]אִם, מִשֶּׁנְּתָנָהּ לוֹ, אָמַר, "אֲנִי זָכִיתִי בָּהּ תְּחִלָּה", [8]לֹא אָמַר כְּלוּם.

גְּמָרָא [9]תְּנַן הָתָם: "מִי שֶׁלִּיקֵּט אֶת הַפֵּאָה וְאָמַר, 'הֲרֵי זוֹ לִפְלוֹנִי עָנִי', [10]רַבִּי אֱלִיעֶזֶר

LITERAL TRANSLATION

in a public thoroughfare [1]and [her husband] threw her a bill of divorce into her lap or into her basket, [2]here, too, would she not be divorced?

[3]He said to him: Her basket is at rest, and it is she who walks beneath it.

MISHNAH [4][If a person] was riding on an animal and he saw a found object, and he said to another person, "Give it to me," [5][and the other person] took it and said, "I have acquired it," [6]he has acquired it. [7]If, after he gave it to him, he said, "I acquired it first," [8]he said nothing.

GEMARA [9]We have learned there: "Someone who gathered *pe'ah* and said, 'Behold this is for so-and-so the poor man,' [10]Rabbi Eliezer says:

RASHI

קלתה – סל שעל ראשה, שנותנת בה כלי מלאכתה וטווי שלה. הכי נמי דלא הוי גיטא – והאנן תנן במסכת גיטין (עז,א): זרק לה גיטה לתוך חיקה או לתוך קלתה – הרי זו מגורשת!

משנה לא אמר כלום – דאפילו אמרינן המגביה מציאה לחבירו לא קנה חבירו, כיון דיהבה ליה – קנייה ממה נפשך. אי קנייה קמא דלא מתכוין להקנות לחבירו – הא יהבה ניהליה במתנה. ואי לא קנייה קמא משום דלא היה מתכוין לקנות – הויא ליה הפקר עד דמטא לידיה דהאי, וקנייה האי כמאי דעקרה מידיה דקמא לשם קנייה.

גמרא מי שליקט את הפאה – אדם בעלמא שאינו בעל שדה. דאי בבעל שדה – לא אמר רבי אליעזר זכה. דליכא למימר "מגו דזכי לנפשיה", דאפילו הוא עני מוזהר הוא שלא ללקט פאה משדה שלו, כדאמר בשחיטת חולין (קלא,ב): "לא תלקט לעני" – להזהיר עני על שלו.

Hebrew commentary of Rashi, the classic explanation that accompanies all editions of the Talmud

Numbers link the three main sections of the page and allow readers to refer rapidly from one to the other

NOTES

מִי שֶׁלִּיקֵּט אֶת הַפֵּאָה If a person gathered *pe'ah*. According to *Rashi*, the Mishnah must be referring to someone other than the owner of the field. By Torah law the owner of a field is required to separate part of his field as *pe'ah*, even if he himself is poor, and he may not take the *pe'ah* for himself. Therefore the "since" (מגו) argument

Notes highlight points of interest in the text and expand the discussion by quoting other classical commentaries

HALAKHAH

קַלְתָּהּ A woman's basket. "If a man throws a bill of divorce into a container that his wife is holding, she thereby acquires the bill of divorce and the divorce takes effect." (*Shulḥan Arukh, Even HaEzer* 139:10.)

הַמְלַקֵּט פֵּאָה עֲבוּר אַחֵר A person who gathered *pe'ah* for someone else. "If a poor person, who is himself entitled to collect *pe'ah*, gathered *pe'ah* for another poor person, and said, 'This *pe'ah* is for X, the poor person,' he acquires the *pe'ah* on behalf of that other poor person. But if the person who collected the *peah* was wealthy, he does not acquire the *pe'ah* on behalf of the poor person. He must give it instead to the first poor person who appears in the field," following the opinion of the Sages, as explained by Rabbi Yehoshua ben Levi. (*Rambam, Sefer Zeraim, Hilkhot Mattenot Aniyyim* 2:19.)

On the outer margin of the page, factual information clarifying the meaning of the Talmudic discussion is presented. Entries under the heading *Language* explain unusual terms, often borrowed from Greek, Latin, or Persian. *Sages* gives brief biographies of the major figures whose opinions are presented in the Talmud. *Terminology* explains the terms used in the Talmudic discussion. *Concepts* gives information about fundamental Halakhic principles. *Background* provides historical, geographical, and other information needed to understand the text. *Realia* explains the artifacts mentioned in the text. These notes are sometimes accompanied by illustrations.

The best way of studying the Talmud is the way in which the Talmud itself evolved - a combination of frontal teaching and continuous interaction between teacher and pupil, and between pupils themselves.

This edition is meant for a broad spectrum of users, from those who have considerable prior background and who know how to study the Talmud from any standard edition to those who have never studied the Talmud and do not even know Hebrew.

The division of the page into various sections is designed to enable students of every kind to derive the greatest possible benefit from it.

For those who know how to study the Talmud, the book is intended to be a written Gemara lesson, so that, either alone, with partners, or in groups, they can have the sense of studying with a teacher who explains the difficult passages and deepens their understanding both of the development of the dialectic and also of the various approaches that have been taken by the Rabbis over the centuries in interpreting the material. A student of this kind can start with the Hebrew-Aramaic text, examine Rashi's commentary, and pass on from there to the expanded commentary. Afterwards the student can turn to the Notes section. Study of the *Halakhah* section will clarify the conclusions reached in the course of establishing the Halakhah, and the other items in the margins will be helpful whenever the need arises to clarify a concept or a word or to understand the background of the discussion.

For those who do not possess sufficient knowledge to be able to use a standard edition of the Talmud, but who know how to read Hebrew, a different method is proposed. Such students can begin by reading the Hebrew-Aramaic text and comparing it immediately to the *Literal Translation*. They can then move over to the *Translation and Commentary*, which refers both to the original text and to the *Literal Translation*. Such students would also do well to read through the *Notes* and choose those that explain matters at greater length. They will benefit, too, from the terms explained in the side margins.

The beginner who does not know Hebrew well enough to grapple with the original can start with the *Translation and Commentary*. The inclusion of a translation within the commentary permits the student to ignore the *Literal Translation*, since the commentary includes both the Talmudic text and an interpretation of it. The beginner can also benefit from the *Notes*, and it is important for him to go over the marginal notes on the concepts to improve his awareness of the juridical background and the methods of study characteristic of this text.

Apart from its use as study material, this book can also be useful to those well versed in the Talmud, as a source of additional knowledge in various areas, both for understanding the historical and archeological background and also for an explanation of words and concepts. The general reader, too, who might not plan to study the book from beginning to end, can find a great deal of interesting material in it regarding both the spiritual world of Judaism, practical Jewish law, and the life and customs of the Jewish people during the thousand years (500 B.C.E.–500 C.E.) of the Talmudic period.

Contents

THE TALMUD
THE STEINSALTZ EDITION

VOLUME XI
TRACTATE KETUBOT
PART V

Introduction to Chapter Six

מְצִיאַת הָאִישָּׁה

Although this chapter opens with a discussion of a husband's rights to what his wife finds and to her handiwork, and to the compensation paid if she is injured, it deals for the most part with the regulations governing the dowry brought by the wife to the husband upon their marriage.

The dowry that a woman receives from her father and brings to her husband is not required by Torah law, nor is it an essential component of the marriage agreement. Over the course of time, however, fixed customs regarding a woman's dowry developed, and the Rabbis endowed those customs with Halakhic authority. One of the principal questions arising with respect to a dowry relates to the very essence of the obligation falling upon the father of the bride: Is his obligation to provide his daughter with a dowry personal in nature, or is a lien attached to his estate in favor of his daughter's dowry? Another major topic of discussion relates to the size of the dowry: Must the father provide his daughter with a dowry of some minimal size? And is there any relationship between the extent of the father's assets and the size of the dowry he must give his daughter?

Just as it became customary for a woman to bring her husband a dowry at the time of their marriage, so too did it become customary for the husband to obligate himself to restore a certain sum of money to his wife upon the dissolution of their marriage as the equivalent of the dowry that she originally brought into the marriage. The sum that the husband undertook to restore to his wife was recorded in the ketubah deed in addition to the main ketubah — the minimum amount that the wife is entitled to receive should her marriage end in divorce or the death of her husband — and the additional amount that the husband may add of his own free will to the main ketubah. The amount that the husband would render himself liable to return to his wife depended not only on the size of his wife's dowry but also on the nature of the assets she brought into the marriage. If she brought a dowry of money with which the husband could do business and earn a profit, he would accept liability to restore to his wife a sum exceeding the value of the dowry. And if she brought a dowry of movable goods with which the husband could not do business, and which would depreciate in value over time, he would accept liability for a sum that was less than the assessed value of the dowry. Establishing the husband's liability was further complicated by the fact that it was customary to inflate the value of the assets comprising the dowry when assessing their value at the time of the marriage.

Another issue which is discussed in our chapter relates to the daughter's control over assets that her father deposits on her behalf into the hands of a trustee.

The clarification of these and related issues comprises the subject matter of this chapter.

TRANSLATION AND COMMENTARY

MISHNAH מְצִיאַת הָאִשָּׁה [1]The Mishnah opens with a discussion of a husband's right to his wife's earned and unearned income. **The things that a wife finds and the handiwork** she produces while she is married **belong to her husband.** [2]If, after her marriage, a wife acquires property by way **of inheritance,** she retains ownership of it, but her husband **enjoys the usufruct during her lifetime.** All benefits deriving from the property in a manner that leaves the principal intact, such as the natural or legal fruits (e.g., rent), belong to the husband. Only if the wife dies before her husband does the principal of the property pass to him together with the rest of her estate.

A person who inflicts bodily harm on another may be obligated to reimburse him under the following five headings: (1) Damage (נֶזֶק, also known as פְּגָם — literally "blemish"), meaning the decrease in the value of the injured party. This is assessed by determining how much the injured person would have been worth on the slave market before his injury, taking into account his professional qualifications, compared to what he is now worth. (2) Pain (צַעַר). This is assessed by estimating what a person like the injured party would be willing to pay to avoid the pain resulting from the injury. (3) Medical expenses (רִיפּוּי). (4) Loss of livelihood (שֶׁבֶת), reimbursement for loss of earnings while the injured party was unable to work. (5) Humiliation (בּוֹשֶׁת — literally "shame"), which is assessed according to the social standing of both the person who suffered the humiliation and the person who caused it. Payment for humiliation is required even if no physical injury was inflicted, provided that the humiliation was caused by a physical act. Now, if a person inflicts bodily harm on a married woman, he must compensate her husband for her medical costs, for it is the husband who must pay his wife's medical expenses. Similarly, the husband must be compensated for his wife's loss of earnings, for it is the husband who is entitled to her handiwork. The wife herself receives the payment for pain, for it is she who suffered the pain resulting from her injury. There is a difference of opinion between the Tannaim about the compensation that must be made for the wife's humiliation and her loss of value.

מְצִיאַת

[1] הָאִשָּׁה וּמַעֲשֵׂה יָדֶיהָ לְבַעְלָהּ. [2] וִירוּשָּׁתָהּ הוּא אוֹכֵל פֵּירוֹת בְּחַיֶּיהָ.

LITERAL TRANSLATION

MISHNAH [1]What a wife finds and her handiwork [belong] to her husband. [2]And [of] her inheritance he enjoys the usufruct during her lifetime.

RASHI

משנה מציאת האשה. וירושתה – אם נפלה לה ירושה, הוא אוכל פירות בחייה והקרן שלה. לישנא אחרינא: ואם מתה בחייו — יורשה.

NOTES

מְצִיאַת הָאִשָּׁה **What a wife finds.** Not all the sources agree as to the order of the chapters of our tractate. According to the Jerusalem Talmud, the Tosefta, and most Rishonim (*Rabbenu Ḥananel, Tosafot, Ramban,* and others), our chapter, מְצִיאַת הָאִשָּׁה, "What a woman finds," is the sixth chapter of tractate *Ketubot,* and it is followed by הַמַּדִּיר אֶת אִשְׁתּוֹ, "If someone forbids his wife with a vow," and this is how they appear in most editions. Our chapter, which opens with a regulation regarding a wife's handiwork, continues the detailed discussion at the end of the fifth chapter regarding a wife's obligation to produce handiwork for her husband. However, according to the Talmudic text before *Rashi* (see *Tosafot*), our chapter is the seventh chapter of the tractate, coming after the chapter, "If someone forbids his wife with a vow."

וִירוּשָּׁתָהּ **And her inheritance.** *Rashi* offers two explanations of the expression, "and her inheritance." Our commentary follows the first, according to which that expression begins the clause which continues, "he enjoys the usufruct during her lifetime." Thus the Mishnah is informing us that if a woman inherits landed property during her marriage, her husband may enjoy the usufruct of that property while they are married.

According to *Rashi's* second explanation, the expression "and her inheritance" constitutes a separate regulation. After stating that what a wife finds and her handiwork

HALAKHAH

מְצִיאַת הָאִשָּׁה **What a wife finds.** "What a wife finds belongs to her husband," following the Mishnah. (*Rambam, Sefer Nashim, Hilkhot Ishut* 12:3; *Shulḥan Arukh, Even HaEzer* 69:3, 84:1.)

מַעֲשֵׂה יָדֶיהָ **And her handiwork.** "A wife's handiwork belongs to her husband," following the Mishnah. (*Rambam, Sefer Nashim, Hilkhot Ishut* 12:3; *Shulḥan Arukh, Even HaEzer* 69:3.)

יְרוּשָּׁתָהּ **And of her inheritance.** "If a wife dies before her husband, her entire estate passes to her husband," following the Mishnah. (*Rambam, Sefer Nashim, Hilkhot Ishut* 12:3, 22:1; *Shulḥan Arukh, Even HaEzer* 90:1.)

אוֹכֵל פֵּירוֹת **He enjoys the usufruct.** "During a wife's lifetime, her husband is entitled to the usufruct of all her property, both her *tzon barzel* property and her *melog* property." (*Rambam, Sefer Nashim, Hilkhot Ishut* 12:3, 22:7; *Shulḥan Arukh, Even HaEzer* 85:1.)

SAGES

רַבִּי יְהוּדָה בֶּן בְּתֵירָא Rabbi Yehudah ben Beterah. See *Ketubot,* Part I, pp.189-190.

BACKGROUND

וּבִזְמַן שֶׁבַּגָּלוּי And when in an exposed place. When the amount of compensation is determined, consideration is naturally given to the difference between a hidden defect and a visible one. However, regarding the division of the compensation between husband and wife, the rationale of the Mishnah is that a visible defect causes the husband double grief, both because his wife becomes unpleasant to him and also because others see her defect and this causes him additional humiliation.

TRANSLATION AND COMMENTARY

בּוֹשְׁתָּהּ וּפְגָמָהּ שֶׁלָּהּ [1] According to the anonymous first Tanna of the Mishnah, **the payments for** the wife's **humiliation and loss of value belong** entirely **to her.** [2] **Rabbi Yehudah ben Betera** disagrees and **says:** If a woman suffers a bodily injury resulting in her humiliation or loss of value, her husband also suffers humiliation and is distressed by the damage caused her. He is therefore entitled to part of the compensation for humiliation and loss of value. [3] **If** the injury resulting in the wife's humiliation or loss of value was inflicted **on a part** of her body **which is** ordinarily **covered,** she herself **is entitled to two-thirds** of the compensation, and her husband **is entitled to one-third.** [4] **But if** the injury was inflicted **on a part** of her body **which is** ordinarily **exposed,** her husband suffers greater humiliation and distress. [5] He **is** therefore **entitled to two-thirds** of the compensation, and the wife **is entitled to one-third. The husband's** part of the payments for humiliation and loss of value **is given** to him **immediately,** and he may do with the money as he pleases. [6] **But the wife's part** of those payments **is used for buying land.** [7] This land remains in the wife's ownership until she dies, **and** her husband **enjoys the usufruct** during her lifetime, just as he enjoys the usufruct of any other property which comes into her possession during their marriage.

[1] בּוֹשְׁתָּהּ וּפְגָמָהּ שֶׁלָּהּ. [2] רַבִּי יְהוּדָה בֶּן בְּתֵירָא אוֹמֵר: [3] בִּזְמַן שֶׁבַּסֵּתֶר, לָהּ שְׁנֵי חֲלָקִים וְלוֹ אֶחָד. [4] וּבִזְמַן שֶׁבַּגָּלוּי, לוֹ שְׁנֵי חֲלָקִים וְלָהּ אֶחָד. [5] שֶׁלּוֹ יִנָּתֵן מִיָּד. [6] וְשֶׁלָּהּ יִלָּקַח בָּהֶן קַרְקַע, [7] וְהוּא אוֹכֵל פֵּירוֹת.

LITERAL TRANSLATION

[1] [The payments for] her shame and her blemish [belong] to her. [2] Rabbi Yehudah ben Betera says: [3] When in a hidden place, she has two parts and he has one. [4] And when in an exposed place, he has two parts and she has one. [5] His [share] is given immediately. [6] But [with] her [share] land is bought, [7] and he enjoys the usufruct.

RASHI

ופגמה — נזק חבלה אם יחבלו בה. **ובזמן שבגלוי** — שהבושת שלו. ועוד: שנמאסת עליו והוא סובל. **ילקח בהן קרקע** — שהרי זה כשאר נכסים הנופלים לה, שהן תלויין. **אוכל פירות בחייה** — והקרן שלה, אם יגרשנה או ימות. **ואם תמות היא** — יורשה.

NOTES

belong to her husband, the Mishnah teaches that her inheritance also belongs to the husband, if she dies before him. The Mishnah then continues with the regulation that the husband enjoys the usufruct of his wife's property during her lifetime.

Tosafot and others argue that the Gemara's discussion of why our Mishnah was necessary supports the first explanation, for according to the second explanation, the Gemara should have said that our Mishnah was needed to teach that a husband is his wife's heir. The second explanation is supported by two alternative readings cited by some of the Rishonim and found in some Talmudic manuscripts: (1) "And her inheritance, *and* he enjoys the usufruct during her lifetime"; (2) "and he inherits her." *Talmidei Rabbenu Yonah* and others argue that according to the first explanation the Mishnah should not have limited the regulation that the husband enjoys the usufruct of his wife's property to the case where the wife inherits property during her marriage, but should have taught that in general a man is entitled to the usufruct of his wife's property! Some commentators answer that the purpose of the Mishnah was to teach us that the husband's right to the usufruct of his wife's property is not limited to property she brought into the marriage. It even applies to the property she acquires during her marriage by way of inheritance or gift.

Meiri suggests that the expression "and her inheritance" should be understood as "*but* her inheritance." The sense of the Mishnah would then be: What a wife finds and her handiwork belong entirely to her husband even during her lifetime, but regarding property she inherits during her marriage, the husband may enjoy the usufruct of such property immediately, but he does not acquire the property itself during her lifetime.

וּבִזְמַן שֶׁבַּגָּלוּי And when in an exposed place. Most Rishonim explain that Rabbi Yehudah ben Betera disagrees with the anonymous first Tanna both about the compensation that must be made for the wife's humiliation and about the compensation that must be made for her loss of value. Rabbi Yehudah ben Betera maintains that when a wife suffers a bodily injury resulting in her humiliation or loss of value, her husband is entitled to part of the compensation because he too suffers humiliation and is distressed by the damage caused her. The Gemara's statement, "It was necessary for him to teach about her shame and her

HALAKHAH

בּוֹשְׁתָּהּ וּפְגָמָהּ Her shame and her blemish. "If someone causes bodily injury to a married woman, he must compensate her husband for her loss of earnings, as well as for her medical costs. Compensation for pain must be made to the wife herself. Regarding the payments made for her humiliation and her loss of value, if the injury was inflicted on a part of her body that is ordinarily exposed (such as her hands or face), one-third of the payment must be made to the wife, and two-thirds to her husband. If the injury was inflicted on a part of her body which is ordinarily covered, two-thirds of the payment must be made to the wife, and one-third to her husband. The husband's part of the payment is given to him immediately. Land is bought with the wife's portion, and the husband is entitled to the usufruct of that property during her lifetime," in accordance with the viewpoint of Rabbi Yehudah ben Betera. (*Rambam, Sefer Nezikin, Hilkhot Ḥovel U'Mazzik* 4:15; *Shulḥan Arukh, Even HaEzer* 83:1.)

גמרא [1]מַאי קָא מַשְׁמַע לָן? [2]תָּנֵינָא: [3]״הָאָב זַכַּאי בְּבִתּוֹ בְּקִידּוּשֶׁיהָ, [4]בְּכֶסֶף, בִּשְׁטָר וּבְבִיאָה. [5]זַכַּאי בִּמְצִיאָתָהּ, וּבְמַעֲשֵׂה יָדֶיהָ, וּבַהֲפָרַת נְדָרֶיהָ. [6]מְקַבֵּל אֶת גִּיטָּהּ, [7]וְאֵינוֹ אוֹכֵל פֵּירוֹת בְּחַיֶּיהָ. [8]נִישֵּׂאת, יָתֵר עָלָיו הַבַּעַל, [9]שֶׁהוּא אוֹכֵל פֵּירוֹת בְּחַיֶּיהָ״.

[10]בּוֹשְׁתָּהּ וּפְגָמָהּ אִיצְטְרִיכָא לֵיהּ, [11]פְּלוּגְתָּא דְּרַבִּי יְהוּדָה בֶּן בְּתֵירָא וְרַבָּנַן.

TRANSLATION AND COMMENTARY

GEMARA מַאי קָא מַשְׁמַע לָן [1]The Gemara begins its analysis of the Mishnah by arguing that the Mishnah is superfluous, and asks: **What is** the Tanna of our Mishnah **teaching us?** [2]**We have already learned** the regulations taught in our Mishnah in another Mishnah found earlier in our tractate (46b), which stated: [3]**"A father has authority over his daughter's betrothal** while she is a minor (under the age of twelve) and also while she is a *na'arah* (between twelve and twelve-and-a-half years of age). A woman may be betrothed in one of three ways: (1) By the transfer of money or something worth money (such as a ring) from the bridegroom to the bride; (2) by a document that the bridegroom hands over to the bride, in which he attests that he is betrothing her; and (3) by sexual intercourse. A father is entitled to arrange his daughter's betrothal while she is a minor or a *na'arah* in one of these three ways. [4]He may accept **money** from the bridegroom for his daughter's betrothal, and he may keep the money for himself. He may, alternatively, receive **a deed** of betrothal from the bridegroom on his daughter's behalf. **And** he may hand his daughter over to the bridegroom for betrothal by sexual **intercourse.** [5]The father **is** also **entitled to objects that his** daughter finds while she is a minor or a *na'arah*, **as well as to the handiwork** she produces before she reaches full adulthood. The father is also authorized to **annul the vows** made by his daughter before she reaches full adulthood or marries. If a father has arranged his daughter's betrothal, and the bridegroom wishes to dissolve the relationship, [6]the father **receives the bill of divorce** on his daughter's behalf, provided that she has not reached full adulthood (at the age of twelve-and-a-half) or married. If a girl who is a minor or a *na'arah* has inherited property from one of her mother's relatives, and the girl then dies, her father inherits the property from her. [7]**But he does not enjoy the usufruct** of that property **during her lifetime.** [8]**If** the girl **marries, her husband** is entitled to all those things to which her father was previously entitled — to whatever she finds, and to her handiwork; and he is authorized to annul her vows. In fact, the husband **has more rights than the father,** [9]**in that** not only does he inherit his wife's property when she dies, but **he** also **enjoys the usufruct during her lifetime."** Thus, we see that the matters taught in our Mishnah regarding the husband's right to what his wife finds, to her handiwork, and to the usufruct of her landed property, have already been taught earlier in the tractate. What, then, does our Mishnah come to teach us?

בּוֹשְׁתָּהּ וּפְגָמָהּ [10]The Gemara answers: **It was necessary for** the Tanna of our Mishnah **to teach** it **on account** of the laws pertaining to the payments for the wife's **humiliation and loss of value,** [11]**which are** the subject of **the dispute between Rabbi Yehudah ben Betera and the Rabbis.**

LITERAL TRANSLATION

GEMARA [1]What is he teaching us? [2]We have [already] learned: [3]"A father has authority over his daughter regarding her betrothal, [4][whether it is] by money, by deed, or by intercourse. [5]He is entitled to what she finds, and to her handiwork, and to the annulment of her vows. [6]He receives her bill of divorce, [7]but he does not enjoy the usufruct during her lifetime. [8][If] she marries, the husband has more [rights] than [the father], [9]in that he enjoys the usufruct during her lifetime."

[10]It was necessary for him [to teach about] her shame and her blemish, [11][which is] a dispute between Rabbi Yehudah ben Betera and the Rabbis.

RASHI

גמרא תנינא – בפרק ״נערה״. יתר עליו הבעל – אלמא בעל זכאי בכולן.

NOTES

blemish, which is a dispute between Rabbi Yehudah ben Betera and the Rabbis," supports this understanding of Rabbi Yehudah ben Betera's position.

Meiri explains that a Tosefta (*Bava Kamma* 9:14) implies that the Tannaim disagree only about the compensation paid for a wife's humiliation (see also *Rashi*). According to *Tosafot* and others, Rabbi Yehudah ben Betera maintains that the husband is entitled to compensation for his wife's humiliation even if no physical injury was inflicted. If she was humiliated in private, the husband is entitled to one-third of the compensation; if she was humiliated in public, he is entitled to two-thirds of the payment. *Talmidei Rabbenu Yonah* argues that Rabbi Yehudah ben Betera maintains that the husband is entitled to compensation for his wife's humiliation only if it results from a physical injury. If she was injured in a place that is usually covered, her husband is entitled to one-third of the compensation; if she was injured in a place that is visible to all, he is entitled to two-thirds of the payment. But if the wife did not suffer any physical injury, and she was humiliated in private, her husband is not entitled to any compensation, because he did not suffer any damage.

TRANSLATION AND COMMENTARY

תָּנֵי תַּנָּא [1]The Gemara now relates that **a Tanna** — a reciter of Baraitot — **recited** the following Baraita **before Rava: "What a wife finds** during the course of her marriage **belongs to her.** [2]**Rabbi Akiva** disagrees and **says:** What she finds belongs **to her husband."**

אֲמַר לֵיהּ [3]Rava posed a question before the Tanna, **saying to him: Now, if regarding the surplus** earnings that a wife produces in excess of the minimum required of her by law, [66A] **which** certainly come under the general category of **handiwork,** so that it could be argued that the surplus earnings should belong to her husband, because he enjoys the right to his wife's handiwork in return for his obligation to maintain her, [4]**Rabbi Akiva** nevertheless **said that** such surplus earnings **belong to** the wife **herself,** then does it not stand to reason that regarding **what she finds,** which certainly does not come under the category of handiwork, **how much more so** should Rabbi Akiva say that it belongs to the wife herself and not to her husband! [5]**For we have learned** elsewhere in a Mishnah (*Nedarim* 85a; also see above, 59a): **"If a wife says** to her husband: **'Whatever I produce is forbidden to you as a** ***konam*** [the word *konam* is used in vows as a substitute for the word *korban* — "sacrifice" — in order to avoid using the word *korban* itself],' [6]**he does not need to annul** the vow, because a wife is obligated to produce handiwork for her husband, and she cannot make a vow forbidding him from benefiting from her handiwork. Nor can she forbid her surplus earnings to her husband by a vow, for they belong to him. [7]**Rabbi Akiva** disagrees and **says:** The husband **must annul** the vow, in case his wife **produces more** handiwork **than is due to him.** The wife's surplus earnings do not belong to her husband, and therefore they are subject to her vow. Thus the husband must annul the vow, in order to prevent his wife's surplus earnings from becoming forbidden to him." We see from this Mishnah that Rabbi Akiva maintains that a wife's surplus earnings belong to her. Hence she should also be entitled to what she finds, as was argued above. How, then, can Rabbi Akiva maintain that what a wife finds belongs to her husband?

אֶלָּא אֵיפּוּךְ [8]The Gemara answers: **Rather,** it is necessary to **reverse** the viewpoints recorded in the Baraita, so that it reads as follows: **"What a wife finds** during her marriage **belongs to her husband.** [9]**Rabbi Akiva** disagrees and **says:** What she finds **belongs to her."**

וְהָא כִּי אֲתָא רָבִין [10]The Gemara objects: **But surely when Ravin came** to Babylonia from Eretz Israel, **he said in the name of Rabbi Yoḥanan:** [11]**Regarding the surplus** earnings that a wife **gains without** undue **exertion,**

[1]תָּנֵי תַּנָּא קַמֵּיהּ דְּרָבָא: "מְצִיאַת הָאִשָּׁה לְעַצְמָהּ. [2]רַבִּי עֲקִיבָא אוֹמֵר: לְבַעְלָהּ". [3]אֲמַר לֵיהּ: הָשְׁתָּא, וּמָה הַעֲדָפָה, [66A] דְּמַעֲשֵׂה יָדֶיהָ הִיא, [4]אָמַר רַבִּי עֲקִיבָא לְעַצְמָהּ, מְצִיאָתָהּ לֹא כָּל שֶׁכֵּן! [5]דִּתְנַן: "'קוֹנָם שֶׁאֲנִי עוֹשָׂה לְפִיךָ', [6]אֵינוֹ צָרִיךְ לְהָפֵר. [7]רַבִּי עֲקִיבָא אוֹמֵר: יָפֵר, שֶׁמָּא תַּעְדִּיף עָלָיו יוֹתֵר מִן הָרָאוּי לוֹ". [8]אֶלָּא אֵיפּוּךְ: "מְצִיאַת הָאִשָּׁה לְבַעְלָהּ. [9]רַבִּי עֲקִיבָא אוֹמֵר: לְעַצְמָהּ". [10]וְהָא כִּי אֲתָא רָבִין אֲמַר רַבִּי יוֹחָנָן: [11]בְּהַעֲדָפָה שֶׁלֹּא עַל יְדֵי

LITERAL TRANSLATION

[1]A Tanna taught before Rava: "What a wife finds belongs to herself. [2]Rabbi Akiva says: [It belongs] to her husband."

[3]He said to him: Now, if [regarding] the surplus, [66A] which is her handiwork, [4]Rabbi Akiva said [that] it belongs to herself, how much more so what she finds! [5]For we have learned: "[If a wife says:] 'What I produce (lit., "do") is [forbidden] to you (lit. "to your mouth") [as] a *konam*,' [6]he does not need to annul [it]. [7]Rabbi Akiva says: He must annul [it], lest she do more work than is due to him."

[8]Rather, reverse [it]: "A woman's find belongs to her husband. [9]Rabbi Akiva says: It belongs to herself."

[10]But surely when Ravin came he said in the name of Rabbi Yoḥanan: [11]Regarding the surplus [achieved] without

RASHI

העדפה — אם תעשה מלאכה יותר ממה שפסקו לה חכמים. **דמעשה ידיה** — ושייך למימר שיהא שלו, דמעשה ידיה תחת מזונות. **קונם שאני עושה לפיך** — מה שאני עושה — יהא קונם לפיך. **אינו צריך להפר** — דמשעבדא ליה, ואפילו לשמא תעדיף נמי לא חיישינן, דאי מעדפה — נמי לבעל הוא. **שמא תעדיף** — והעדפה דידה הוא, וחייל עלה קונם. **שלא על ידי הדחק** — כגון שהיא עירנית ובעלת מלאכה.

SAGES

רָבָא Rava. A Babylonian Amora of the fourth generation. See *Ketubot,* Part I, p. 14.

רַבִּי עֲקִיבָא Rabbi Akiva. A Tanna of the fourth generation. See *Ketubot,* Part II, p. 206.

CONCEPTS

קוֹנָם ***Konam.*** This is a term for a type of vow and it is explained as a euphemism for the word קָרְבָּן — "sacrifice." The thing which one has forsworn with a *konam* is forbidden to one as though it were intended for sacrifice, though it is not truly sanctified or sacrificed but is merely forbidden to the person who made the vow. Some authorities maintain that a *konam* is more severe than other forms of oaths, as though a real prohibition were placed on the forsworn object.

NOTES

וְהָא כִּי אֲתָא רָבִין But surely when Ravin came. Our translation and commentary follow the reading of *Rashi:* "*But surely* [וְהָא] when Ravin came," according to which Ravin is arguing that if Rabbi Akiva agrees with the Rabbis that a wife's surplus earnings achieved without undue exertion belong to her husband, he should also agree with them that what a wife finds belongs to him. Most Rishonim reject this reading, arguing that the Gemara assumed earlier that there is more reason to say that a married woman is entitled to what she finds than there is to say that she is

TRANSLATION AND COMMENTARY

[1]**both** the anonymous first Tanna of the Mishnah in *Nedarim* and Rabbi Akiva **agree that** such earnings **belong to the husband.** [2]**Where they disagree is regarding surplus** earnings **gained** by the wife **as a result of exertion.** [3]**The** anonymous **first Tanna** of the Mishnah **maintains** that even such surplus earnings **belong to the husband.** [4]**But Rabbi Akiva maintains** that they **belong to the wife.** Surely what a wife finds should be treated in the same manner as surplus earnings acquired by her without undue exertion, because what a person finds is ordinarily something that a person comes across by chance without having to invest any special effort in its acquisition! If both the Tannaim agree that surplus earnings acquired by a wife without undue exertion belong to her husband, why are they in dispute about what she finds?

אָמַר רַב פַּפָּא [5]**Rav Pappa said** in reply: Actually, **What** a wife **finds is similar to** her **surplus** earnings

הַדְּחָק, [1]כּוּלֵּי עָלְמָא לָא פְּלִיגִי דְּבַעַל הָוֵי. [2]כִּי פְּלִיגִי בְּהַעֲדָפָה שֶׁעַל יְדֵי הַדְּחָק. [3]תַּנָּא קַמָּא סָבַר: לְבַעְלָהּ. [4]וְרַבִּי עֲקִיבָא סָבַר: לְעַצְמָהּ!
[5]אָמַר רַב פַּפָּא: מְצִיאָתָהּ

LITERAL TRANSLATION

exertion, [1]all agree (lit., "the whole world does not disagree") that it belongs to the husband. [2]Where they disagree is regarding surplus [acquired] through exertion. [3]The first Tanna maintains: It belongs to her husband. [4]But Rabbi Akiva maintains: It belongs to her!

[5]Rav Pappa said: What she finds

RASHI

על ידי הדחק — כגון שדחקה עצמה, והעדיפה. הכי גרסינן: **והא כי אתא רבין כו׳** — וקא סלקא דעתך מציאתה כהעדפה שלא על ידי הדחק היא, והיכי פליגי בה? ומשני: **אמר רב פפא מציאתה כהעדפה שעל ידי הדחק היא** — דרוב מציאות צריך לחזור אחריהם, כגון דגים שנשארו ביבשה, או צבי שבור, או לחפש סימא בקרקע.

SAGES

רַב פַּפָּא **Rav Pappa.** A Babylonian Amora of the fifth generation. See *Ketubot*, Part III, p. 11.

NOTES

entitled to her surplus earnings, whereas here, according to *Rashi*, the Gemara assumes the opposite — that if a wife's surplus earnings acquired without undue exertion belong to her husband, then surely what she finds should belong to him as well. Most Rishonim therefore prefer the reading of *Rabbenu Ḥananel:* "When Ravin came," according to which Ravin's statement is an independent remark intended to clarify the scope of the dispute between the Rabbis and Rabbi Akiva (see *Tosafot, Rashba, Ritva,* and others; *Rabbenu Tam* in his *Sefer HaYashar* notes that *Rashi* himself had this reading before he emended it by adding the words "but surely"). The Gemara then continues with Rav Pappa's ruling that what a wife finds is comparable to her surplus earnings acquired as a result of exertion, and is therefore, according to Ravin's distinction, subject to the dispute between Rabbi Akiva and the Rabbis.

Rid explains the whole passage in an entirely different manner: Ravin's purpose is to rebut the argument that the attributions recorded in the Baraita must be reversed. The Rabbis maintain that a wife's surplus earnings belong to her husband, but what she finds belongs to her, for a married woman is governed by the same rule as a Jewish maidservant whose surplus earnings belong to her master while what she finds belongs to her. Rabbi Akiva disagrees and maintains that what a wife finds belongs to her husband for a different reason. The Rabbis enacted that a husband is entitled to what his wife finds in order to avoid the enmity that might arise between husband and wife if the husband does not receive what his wife finds. This does not contradict Rabbi Akiva's own position that a wife's surplus earnings belong to her, for when Rabbi Akiva said that a wife's surplus earnings belong to her, he was referring to the surplus earnings acquired as a result of exceptional exertion. Regarding such earnings there is no concern lest enmity arise between husband and wife if the wife is allowed to keep them for herself. But as for surplus earnings acquired by the wife without exertion, Rabbi Akiva agrees that they belong to the husband, and they are comparable to what she finds. Rav Pappa rejects Ravin's reconciliation of the contradiction between Rabbi Akiva's two rulings, arguing that what a wife finds is comparable to her surplus earnings acquired as a result of exertion, and so the attributions recorded in the Baraita must indeed be reversed as the Gemara suggested above.

מְצִיאָתָהּ **What she finds.** *Tosafot* infers from the Gemara's comparison between what a wife finds and her surplus earnings that the husband was granted the right to what his wife finds in return for his duty to maintain her, just as he was given the right to her handiwork in exchange for that same obligation. This does not contradict what the Gemara states elsewhere (*Bava Metzia* 12b) that the Rabbis granted the husband what his wife finds in order to prevent enmity from arising between them, for elsewhere (above, 58b) the Gemara states that the Rabbis granted the husband his wife's handiwork for the very same reason — in order to avoid enmity between husband and wife. The Jerusalem Talmud offers another explanation for the Rabbinic enactment entitling the husband to what his wife finds, arguing that it was to prevent a wife from taking something belonging to her husband and then claiming that she had found it.

מְצִיאָתָהּ כְּהַעֲדָפָה שֶׁעַל יְדֵי הַדְּחָק דָּמֵי **What she finds is similar to surplus acquired through exertion.** Our commentary follows *Rashi*, who explains that what a wife finds may be compared to surplus earnings gained by exertion,

HALAKHAH

הַעֲדָפָה שֶׁעַל יְדֵי הַדְּחָק **Surplus acquired through exertion.** "If a wife exerts herself and produces more than is required of her, her surplus earnings belong to her husband," following the anonymous Tanna of the Mishnah. (*Rambam, Sefer Nashim, Hilkhot Ishut* 21:2; *Shulḥan Arukh, Even HaEzer* 80:1.)

TRANSLATION AND COMMENTARY

achieved as a result of exertion, for in most cases lost property comes into a person's possession only after a search has been conducted and considerable energy expended in its recovery. [1]Just as **Rabbi Akiva and the Rabbis are in disagreement** about who is entitled to a wife's surplus earnings acquired as a result of exertion, so too do they disagree about who is entitled to what a wife finds.

בָּעֵי רַב פַּפָּא [2]**Rav Pappa asked: If** a wife **performs** two different **tasks at the same time, what is the law?** Is she regarded as having produced surplus earnings as a result of exertion, in which case according to Rabbi Akiva she may keep such earnings for herself?

כְּהַעֲדָפָה שֶׁעַל יְדֵי הַדְּחָק דָּמֵי, [1]פְּלוּגְתָּא דְּרַבִּי עֲקִיבָא וְרַבָּנַן. [2]בָּעֵי רַב פַּפָּא: עָשְׂתָה לוֹ שְׁתַּיִם בְּבַת אַחַת, מַהוּ?

LITERAL TRANSLATION

is similar to surplus [achieved] through exertion, [1][which is the subject of] a dispute between Rabbi Akiva and the Rabbis.

[2]Rav Pappa asked: If she performed two [tasks] for him at the same time, what [is the law]?

RASHI

שתים שלש וארבע בבת אחת – שומרת קישואים, וטווה פשתן, ומלמדת שיר לנשים בשכר, ומחממת ביצים בחיקה, או בילי תולעים העושים משי, שהנשים מחממות אותן בחיקן, והם נולדים. **מהו** – מי הוי כעל ידי הדחק או לא.

NOTES

because people do not usually acquire lost property without first conducting a search for it and expending considerable energy in its recovery. *Rabbi Crescas Vidal* explains that what a wife finds is similar to surplus earnings attained by exertion in that both are unusual gains. *Shittah Mekubbetzet* cites another explanation in the name of *Rashi:* When a wife is involved in acquiring lost property, she must pause, if only for a short time, from the work she is obliged to perform for her husband. Therefore, after she has taken possession of the lost property, she must work harder than usual to make up for lost time. Hence, what a wife finds may be compared to surplus earnings gained by exertion.

הָעֲדָפָה Surplus. *Rabbenu Ḥananel* explains that surplus earnings attained without undue exertion are those that the wife gains by chance — for example, if she happens to come across flax of particularly fine quality which enables her to produce more fabric than is required of her, or if she happens to receive food that is unusually filling, so that her appetite is satisfied with less food than she is entitled to. Surplus earnings acquired as a result of exertion are those that the wife gains, for example, by working harder than she has to, or by going hungry and eating less than she is entitled to. *Rav Hai Gaon* explains that surplus earnings acquired as a result of exertion include earnings gained by working at night when ordinary people are asleep.

עָשְׂתָה לוֹ שְׁתַּיִם בְּבַת אַחַת If she performed two tasks for him at the same time. *Rabbenu Ḥananel* explains that Rav Pappa and Ravina posed their questions in accordance with the viewpoint of Rabbi Akiva — that a wife's surplus earnings attained by exertion belong to her and not to her husband. If she performs several tasks at once, are the surplus earnings viewed as having been acquired as a result of exertion, so that they belong to the wife, or are they seen as having been acquired without exertion, so that they belong to the husband? For according to the Rabbis who maintain that even surplus earnings gained by a wife by exertion belong to the husband, surely the surplus earnings from her performing several tasks at once belong to him! *Rabbenu Ḥananel* concludes that, since the Gemara discusses the matter in accordance with the viewpoint of Rabbi Akiva, the law must be in accordance with him, and surplus earnings gained by a wife as a result of exertion belong to her.

Rif and *Rambam* seem to have understood the Gemara's questions in the same way, but they maintain that the passage has no Halakhic ramifications, because the Halakhah is in accordance with the viewpoint of the Rabbis that even surplus earnings achieved by a wife through exertion belong to her husband.

Rav Hai Gaon explains Rav Pappa's question in accordance with the viewpoint of the Rabbis, that surplus earnings gained by a wife through exertion belong to her husband. Perhaps, suggests Rav Pappa, the Rabbis maintain that position only when a wife exerted herself in the performance of a single task, by working longer hours than was required of her, for example. But if she exerted herself by performing two tasks at once, even the Rabbis might agree that her surplus earnings belong to her. Ravina asked further: If a wife's surplus earnings do belong to her husband if she performs two tasks at the same time, what is the law in the highly unusual case that she performs three or four tasks at the same time? *Rav Hai Gaon* concludes that the law is in accordance with the viewpoint of the Rabbis, that a wife's surplus earnings belong to her husband, but if she performs several tasks at the same time her surplus earnings belong to her, for the matter was left unresolved in the Gemara.

HALAKHAH

עָשְׂתָה לוֹ שְׁתַּיִם בְּבַת אַחַת If she performed two tasks for him at the same time. "According to *Rif* and *Rambam,* all of a wife's surplus earnings, even those achieved by exertion, belong to her husband. According to *Rav Hai Gaon,* if the wife exerts herself and works extra hours (if, for example, she works at night), her surplus earnings belong to her husband. But if she performs several tasks at the same time, her surplus earnings belong to her. According to *Rabbenu Ḥananel,* a wife's surplus earnings achieved without undue exertion belong to her husband, but all surplus earnings acquired by her as a result of exertion, whether she worked extra hours or performed several tasks at the same time, belong to the wife herself." (*Tur, Even HaEzer* 80; *Shulḥan Arukh, Even HaEzer* 80:1, in *Bet Shmuel,* note 2.)

TRANSLATION AND COMMENTARY

[1]And similarly, **Ravina asked:** If a wife **performs three or four** different tasks **at the same time, what is the law?** Are her surplus earnings regarded as having been acquired through undue exertion, or not?

תֵּיקוּ [2]The Gemara offers no solutions to the problems raised by Rav Pappa and by Ravina, and concludes: **These questions remain undecided.**

בּוֹשְׁתָּהּ וּפְגָמָהּ [3]We learned in the Mishnah: **"The payments for** a wife's **humiliation and her loss of value** belong entirely to her. Rabbi Yehudah ben Betera disagrees and says: The woman's husband is entitled to part of the compensation for her humiliation and loss of value." [4]**Rava bar Rav Ḥanan objected to** the viewpoint put forward by Rabbi Yehudah ben Betera: **If it is true** that a person is required to compensate the husband for the humiliation he caused the man's wife, then it should follow that **if someone humiliated another person's horse** by spitting on it or the like, [5]**he too should be required to pay** the owner of the horse **for** the animal's **humiliation!** But a person is surely not entitled to compensation for the humiliation suffered by his animal!

וְסוּס [6]The Gemara is puzzled by the question: How can a comparison be drawn between a man's wife and his horse? **Is a horse subject to humiliation** if it is spat upon or the like, and can it be said that its owner shares this humiliation? Surely a person is not entitled to compensation for humiliation unless he suffers some degree of humiliation himself.

אֶלָּא [7]**Rather,** says the Gemara, Rava bar Rav Ḥanan's objection should be formulated as follows: If it is true that a person must compensate a husband for humiliation caused to his wife, then it should follow that **if someone spits on another person's garment, he too should be required to pay** the garment's owner **for the humiliation** he suffered! Granted that a person does not suffer humiliation if someone spits on his horse; but he surely suffers humiliation if someone spits on his garment! [8]**And if you say** that **it is indeed true** that a person is entitled to compensation for humiliation if someone spits on his garment, there is a diificulty.

[1]בָּעֵי רָבִינָא: שְׁלֹשָׁה אוֹ אַרְבָּעָה בְּבַת אַחַת, מַהוּ?
[2]תֵּיקוּ.
[3]"בּוֹשְׁתָּהּ וּפְגָמָהּ". [4]מַתְקִיף לַהּ רָבָא בַּר רַב חָנָן: אֶלָּא מֵעַתָּה, בִּיֵּישׁ סוּסָתוֹ שֶׁל חֲבֵירוֹ, [5]הָכִי נַמִי דְּבָעֵי לְמֵיתַן לֵיהּ בּוֹשֶׁת!
[6]וְסוּס בַּר בּוֹשֶׁת הוּא?
[7]אֶלָּא, רָקַק בְּבִגְדוֹ שֶׁל חֲבֵירוֹ, הָכִי נַמִי דְּבָעֵי לְמֵיתַן לֵיהּ בּוֹשֶׁת! [8]וְכִי תֵּימָא הָכִי נַמִי,

LITERAL TRANSLATION

[1]Ravina asked: [If she performed] three or four at the same time, what [is the law]?
[2]Let [these questions] remain [undecided]!
[3]"[The payments for] her shame and her blemish."
[4]Rava bar Rav Ḥanan objected to this: If so, [if] someone shamed his fellow's horse, [5]he too should be required to pay him [for the] shame!
[6]But is a horse subject to shame?
[7]Rather, [if] someone spat on his fellow's garment, he too should be required to pay him [for the] shame! [8]And if you say it is indeed so,

RASHI

מתקיף לה רבא בר רב חנן — אדרבי יהודה בן בתירא.

SAGES

רָבִינָא Ravina. A Babylonian Amora of the fifth and sixth generations. See *Ketubot,* Part II, p. 18.

רָבָא בַּר רַב חָנָן Rava bar Rav Ḥanan. A Babylonian Amora of the fourth generation. See *Ketubot,* Part I, p. 70.

BACKGROUND

בִּיֵּישׁ סוּסָתוֹ שֶׁל חֲבֵירוֹ If someone shamed his fellow's horse. This refers to some action taken against a person's horse, such that if it were done to a human being, it would be a humiliating act. The main point in question is whether, since the horse belongs to someone who rides on it, if a humiliating act is committed against the horse, it is indirectly committed against the horse's owner.

NOTES

שְׁלֹשָׁה אוֹ אַרְבָּעָה בְּבַת אַחַת Three or four at the same time. *Rashi* (and similarly *Arukh*) constructs the following case to illustrate Ravina's question: What is the law in a case where a wife is guarding gourds, spinning flax, teaching other women to sing, and warming eggs in her lap?

בִּיֵּישׁ סוּסָתוֹ שֶׁל חֲבֵירוֹ If someone shamed his fellow's horse. According to most Rishonim, a person is not required to pay compensation for spitting on someone's horse or garment, even if the injured person was riding on the horse or wearing the garment when the spittle landed. But *Meiri* records a view according to which a person is indeed liable to compensate another for humiliation, if he spat on the horse he was riding or on the garment he was wearing. Thus, the Gemara must be referring to a case where one person spat on another's horse or garment when it was not being ridden or worn, or when it was being ridden or worn by a person other than its owner.

וְסוּס בַּר בּוֹשֶׁת הוּא? But is a horse subject to shame? At first glance, the Gemara's whole discussion is difficult to understand, because it is obvious that a horse is not subject to humiliation. How, then, could Rava bar Rav Ḥanan have thought to draw a comparison between a man's wife and his horse? (Some Aḥaronim suggest that Rava bar Rav Ḥanan actually asked about a person's garment, but his question was misunderstood as referring to a person's horse; see *Ḥaver ben Ḥayyim.*) *Rashba* explains (and *Shittah Mekubbetzet* understands the position of *Tosafot* in the same way) that Rava bar Rav Ḥanan never meant that a person is entitled to compensation for the humiliation suffered by his horse. He was asking whether a man can claim compensation when his horse is humiliated, for in such a case he too suffers humiliation. The Gemara interjects: But is a horse subject to humiliation — in other words, is a horse so closely identified with its owner that its owner would suffer humiliation if someone spat on it or otherwise insulted it?

TRANSLATION AND COMMENTARY

For surely we have learned otherwise in the following Mishnah (*Bava Kamma* 90a): **"If** someone **spits** on another person, **and the spittle lands on him, or if** someone **uncovers a woman's head,** exposing her hair, **or if** someone **strips** another **person of his** outer **garment,** leaving him improperly dressed, [1]in all these cases the injuring party **is required to pay** the injured party the fixed sum of **four hundred zuz** as compensation for the humiliation suffered." [2]**And** in clarification of this Mishnah, **Rav Pappa said: They only taught this** law, that someone who spits on another person must pay compensation for humiliation if the spittle lands on the injured party **himself.** [3]**But** if it lands on the injured party's **garment,** the offender **is exempt.** Now, if a person is not entitled to compensation for humiliation if someone spits on his garment, why is a husband entitled to part of the compensation paid for the humiliation of his wife?

בְּבִגְדוֹ [4]The Gemara answers: There is no comparison between a person's garment and his wife. If someone spits on another **person's garment,** the owner of the garment **does not** actually **suffer** any **humiliation,** and therefore he is not entitled to any compensation. [5]But if someone embarrasses **a man's wife,** her husband too **suffers humiliation** and is therefore entitled to part of the compensation.

אֲמַר לֵיהּ רָבִינָא [6]**Ravina said to Rav Ashi: If it is true** that a husband is entitled to compensation for humiliation caused to his wife, [7]then it should follow that **if someone humiliates a poor man from a respectable family, in which case humiliation is suffered by all the members of his family,** [8]**he too should be required to pay compensation to all the members of the family for the humiliation** they have suffered!

אֲמַר לֵיהּ [9]Rav Ashi **replied to** Ravina: **There,** it is the poor relative who has been put to shame, and **he is not** so closely identified with the wealthier members of his family that they can argue that it was **they themselves who suffered humiliation** for which they are entitled to compensation. [10]But **here,** in the case of the Mishnah, **a man's wife is** virtually the same as **the man himself.** Thus, when a married woman is put to shame, her husband himself is regarded as having been humiliated, and he is therefore entitled to part of the compensation.

וְהָתְנַן: "רָקַק וְהִגִּיעַ בּוֹ הָרוֹק, וּפָרַע רֹאשׁ הָאִשָּׁה, וְהֶעֱבִיר טַלִּיתוֹ מִמֶּנּוּ, [1]חַיָּיב לִיתֵּן לוֹ אַרְבַּע מֵאוֹת זוּז". [2]וְאָמַר רַב פַּפָּא: לֹא שָׁנוּ אֶלָּא בּוֹ, [3]אֲבָל בְּבִגְדוֹ פָּטוּר!

[4]בְּבִגְדוֹ, לֵית לֵיהּ זִילוּתָא. [5]אִשְׁתּוֹ, אִית לֵיהּ זִילוּתָא.

[6]אֲמַר לֵיהּ רָבִינָא לְרַב אַשִׁי: אֶלָּא מֵעַתָּה, [7]בִּיֵּישׁ עָנִי בֶּן טוֹבִים, דְּאִית לְהוּ זִילוּתָא לְכוּלְּהוּ בְּנֵי מִשְׁפָּחָה, [8]הָכִי נַמִי דְּבָעֵי לְמִיתַּן לְהוּ בּוֹשֶׁת לְכָל בְּנֵי מִשְׁפָּחָה!

[9]אֲמַר לֵיהּ: הָתָם, לָאו גּוּפַיְיהוּ. [10]הָכָא, אִשְׁתּוֹ גּוּפֵיהּ הֲוַאי.

LITERAL TRANSLATION

surely we have learned: "[If] he spat and the spittle reached him, or [if] he uncovered a woman's head, or [if] he removed his garment from him, [1]he is required to give him four hundred zuz." [2]And Rav Pappa said: They only taught [this] regarding him, [3]but regarding his garment he is exempt!

[4]Regarding his garment, there is no humiliation for him. [5][Regarding] his wife, there is humiliation for him.

[6]Ravina said to Rav Ashi: If so (lit., "but from now"), [7][if] he shamed a poor man from a respectable family, where there is humiliation for all the members of the family, [8]he too should be required to give all the members of the family [compensation for] humiliation!

[9]He said to him: There, it is not their own persons [that are humiliated]. [10]Here, his wife is [like] his own person.

SAGES

רַב אַשִׁי **Rav Ashi.** A Babylonian Amora of the sixth generation. See *Ketubot,* Part I, p. 14.

BACKGROUND

אִשְׁתּוֹ גּוּפֵיהּ הֲוַאי **His wife is like his own person.** In various areas of the Halakhah a man and his wife are regarded as a single unit. From this it follows that all the wife's relatives become relatives of the husband the moment the couple marry (with respect to incapacity to bear witness in matters concerning them). Since we say that a man's wife is like his own person, she is not considered merely close to him, but identical to him. Thus one honors a Torah scholar's wife just as one honors the scholar himself. This principle also applies to the issue of humiliation. Embarrassing a wife is tantamount to striking her husband's person.

NOTES

בְּבִגְדוֹ, לֵית לֵיהּ זִילוּתָא **Regarding his garment, there is no humiliation.** *Ra'ah* explains this passage differently (reading בִּגְדוֹ, "his garment," rather than בְּבִגְדוֹ, "regarding his garment"): The garment itself is not subject to humiliation when spittle lands on it, and therefore its owner is not entitled to compensation for humiliation, even if he himself was humiliated by the act, because the injuring party spat on the garment and not on its owner. But a wife is indeed subject to humiliation, and therefore her husband is entitled to part of the compensation.

HALAKHAH

רָקַק וְהִגִּיעַ בּוֹ הָרוֹק **If he spat and the spittle reached him.** "If a person spits at someone, and the spittle lands on the other person, or if someone strips another person of his outer garment, or if someone uncovers a woman's head, he must pay the injured party four hundred zuz. But if he spits on another person and the spittle lands on the other person's garment, he is exempt," following the Mishnah and Rav Pappa. (*Rambam, Sefer Nezikin, Hilkhot Ḥovel U'Mazzik* 3:9; *Shulḥan Arukh, Ḥoshen Mishpat* 420:38, 41.)

TRANSLATION AND COMMENTARY

MISHNAH הַפּוֹסֵק מָעוֹת לַחֲתָנוֹ [1]**If someone undertakes to give** a certain amount of **money to his** future **son-in-law** as his daughter's dowry, **and the son-in-law dies** before receiving it, so that the deceased husband's brother is now required either to take his sister-in-law as his wife in levirate marriage, or to absolve her from this obligation through the ceremony of *ḥalitzah*, and the husband's brother demands the dowry promised to his late brother, [2]**the Sages say:** The father **can say** to his deceased son-in-law's brother: **"I was willing to give** the dowry to **your brother,** [3]**but I am not willing to give you** anything. Take my daughter in levirate marriage without the dowry, or free her from the levirate bond by granting her *ḥalitzah*."

משנה [1]הַפּוֹסֵק מָעוֹת לַחֲתָנוֹ, וּמֵת חֲתָנוֹ, [2]אָמְרוּ חֲכָמִים: יָכוֹל הוּא שֶׁיֹּאמַר: "לְאָחִיךָ הָיִיתִי רוֹצֶה לִיתֵּן, [3]וּלְךָ אִי אֶפְשִׁי לִיתֵּן".
[4]פָּסְקָה לְהַכְנִיס לוֹ אֶלֶף דִּינָר, הוּא פּוֹסֵק כְּנֶגְדָּן חֲמֵשׁ עֶשְׂרֵה

LITERAL TRANSLATION

MISHNAH [1][If] someone undertakes to give money to his son-in-law, and his son-in-law dies, [2]the Sages said: He can say: "To your brother I was willing to give, [3]but to you I am not willing to give."

[4][If] she undertook to bring him a thousand dinarim, he undertakes corresponding to them [to give her] fifteen

RASHI

משנה ומת חתנו – ונפלה לפני יבם, והוא תובע מה שפסקו לאחיו. יכול הוא שיאמר כו' – או חלוץ או ייבם. אבל אחיו – או יתן, או תשב עד שילבין ראשה. הוא פוסק כנגדן חמשה עשר מנה – שליש יותר יקבלם עליו לכתוב בכתובתה, לבד תוספת שהוא מוסיף, לפי שמשתכר בהן. אלף דינר הן עשרה מנה.

פָּסְקָה לְהַכְנִיס לוֹ [4]In addition to the basic ketubah that a wife is entitled to receive in the event of divorce or widowhood (two hundred zuz for a virgin, and one hundred zuz for a non-virgin), and any additional amount that the husband may add to it if he wishes, the ketubah also records the amount that the husband is obliged to give his wife upon the dissolution of their marriage in return for the dowry she brought into the marriage. Our Mishnah teaches that the amount recorded in the ketubah does not always correspond to the actual or assessed value of the wife's dowry. **If** a woman **undertakes to bring** her husband a dowry of **a thousand dinarim** in cash, her husband **undertakes to restore** to his wife at the time her ketubah becomes due the sum of **fifteen maneh** (one thousand five hundred dinarim), **as the equivalent** of that dowry. Since the husband is permitted to use the dowry in his business, he must accept liability for an increment

NOTES

הַפּוֹסֵק מָעוֹת לַחֲתָנוֹ If someone undertakes to give money to his son-in-law. The Jerusalem Talmud asks: According to the Halakhah, the dowry obligation is effected by mere verbal agreement. Thus the son-in-law acquired the dowry at the moment his father-in-law promised to give it to him. Why, then, does the brother not inherit the late bridegroom's right to the dowry together with the rest of his estate, when he takes his sister-in-law in levirate marriage?

The Jerusalem Talmud answers that the father-in-law's undertaking to give the dowry was made on condition that his son-in-law actually married her, but the prospective son-in-law died before doing so.

Rif notes that this condition is presumed, even if it was not expressly stipulated at the time the dowry undertaking was made. *Rav Hai Gaon* explains that the Jerusalem Talmud means to say that the Mishnah is referring to a case in which the father stipulated explicitly that his undertaking would be binding only if the marriage process was completed. But if no such stipulation was made, the brother-in-law would indeed be entitled to the dowry promised to his late brother, for the brother acquired it during his lifetime. *Rav Hai Gaon* also observes that if the father obligated himself to his daughter (rather than to his son-in-law) to provide her with a dowry, the daughter is entitled to the dowry even if her bridegroom dies and she marries his brother.

פּוֹסֵק כְּנֶגְדָּן חֲמֵשׁ עֶשְׂרֵה מָנֶה He undertakes corresponding to them to give her fifteen maneh. The Jerusalem Talmud explains that in return for the right to do business with the money his wife has brought into the marriage as her dowry, the husband is willing to undertake to return to his wife a sum that is fifty percent greater than the amount

HALAKHAH

הַפּוֹסֵק מָעוֹת לַחֲתָנוֹ If someone undertakes to give money to his son-in-law. "If someone undertakes to give his son-in-law a certain amount of money as his daughter's dowry, and the prospective son-in-law dies before the wedding, and the bridegroom's brother comes to take his sister-in-law as his wife in levirate marriage, the bride's father is entitled to say to the second bridegroom: 'I was willing to give your brother that sum of money, but I am not willing to do so to you,'" following the Mishnah. (*Rambam, Sefer Nashim, Hilkhot Ishut* 23:15; *Shulḥan Arukh, Even HaEzer* 52:2.)

פָּסְקָה לְהַכְנִיס לוֹ If she undertook to bring him. "There are many different customs regarding a wife's dowry. Unless specified otherwise, a man must accept liability for his wife's dowry in accordance with the local custom, and a woman who undertakes to bring into the marriage a dowry of a certain value must provide her husband with property of that value in accordance with the local custom regarding the manner of assessment. According to *Maggid Mishneh,* in a new community that has no fixed custom regarding a wife's dowry, we follow the custom described in the Talmud: If a woman brings in a dowry of cash, the

TRANSLATION AND COMMENTARY

to the dowry. According to custom, the amount of the increment was fixed at one-half of the amount specified as the dowry. Thus the husband would record in the ketubah as the amount of his wife's dowry a sum fifty percent greater than the amount she actually brought into the marriage. [1]**But corresponding to** the movable goods that a wife brings her husband as part of her dowry and which require **an assessment** before being recorded in the ketubah — for example, her clothing, jewelry, and household utensils — **her husband undertakes to restore** to his wife at the time her ketubah becomes due a sum that is **one-fifth less** than the assessed value of those goods. The husband cannot use his wife's personal property in his business, so he is not expected to increase their value. Instead, he records in the ketubah a sum that is one-fifth less than the assessed value of those goods, because it is customary to inflate the value of those goods by twenty-five percent when assessing their value. Thus, if the dowry composed of the wife's personal property is assessed at the sum of one thousand dinarim, her husband records in the ketubah the sum of eight hundred dinarim.

שׁוּם בְּמָנֶה [2]If a woman wants her husband to undertake liability for a dowry that **is assessed at a maneh, and** the movable goods she brings into the marriage as her dowry **are** indeed **worth a maneh,** the assessment having been made in accordance with the true market price, [3]the husband **is only entitled to** goods worth **a maneh.** He cannot argue that since he is undertaking liability for a maneh, his wife must bring in goods assessed at a maneh-and-a-quarter, because the husband is entitled to record in the ketubah a sum that is one-fifth less than the assessed value of the dowry only if the assessment has indeed been inflated by twenty-five percent.

LITERAL TRANSLATION

maneh. [1]But corresponding to an assessment, he undertakes [to give her] a fifth less.

[2][If] the assessment is a maneh, and it is worth a maneh, [3]he only has a maneh.

מָנֶה. [1]וּכְנֶגֶד הַשּׁוּם, הוּא פּוֹסֵק פָּחוֹת חוֹמֶשׁ.

[2]שׁוּם בְּמָנֶה, וְשָׁוֶה מָנֶה, [3]אֵין לוֹ אֶלָּא מָנֶה.

RASHI

וכנגד השום — אם בא חתן לכתוב קבלה עליו, כנגד אלף דינר של שום שמכניס לו בגדים או כלים המשתמשין בהן, והן פוחתין, או פרקמטיא. ודרך הנועדים למזמוטי חתן לשום יותר משויים לכבוד הכלה ולחבבה על בעלה. **הוא פוסק פחות חומש** — לא מיבעיא דלא מוסיף, אלא שפוחת. שאם הכניסה שום של אלף דינר — הוא כותב שמונה מאות זוז. **שום במנה ושוה מנה אין לו אלא מנה** — הכניסה שום לקבלו עליו בשטר הכתובה במנה, והוא שוה מנה בשוק לכל אדם — אין לו לומר: תנו לי עוד חמישיתו שהרי אמרו לפחות חומש מן השום — לפי שלא נאמרו דברים הללו אלא בשום ששמאוהו בבית חתנים והנשואים. ומיהו תוספת שליש לא יוסיף שלא אמרו להוסיף שליש אלא לכספים, שהן ראויים להשתכר מיד.

NOTES

she actually brought into the marriage, if the marriage is dissolved. A number of Rishonim ask: Why is the additional sum paid by the husband not regarded as forbidden interest, for the prohibition against interest applies whenever a person pays back a larger sum of money than he originally received?

According to *Rambam* (*Hilkhot Ishut* 23:11) there is no difficulty, because he maintains that the husband would record in the ketubah a sum fifty percent greater than the amount his wife actually brought into the marriage, in order to make her dowry appear more impressive, but when the wife came to collect her ketubah, she would only collect the amount she actually brought into the marriage (see *Leḥem Mishneh* who questions this position).

Talmidei Rabbenu Yonah explains that the prohibition against interest does not apply here, because the addition to the dowry that the husband promises his wife is regarded as a gift, and not as interest. *Mordekhai* argues that the addition to the wife's dowry does not involve a violation of the prohibition against interest, because that prohibition applies only to a payment compensating one party for leaving money in the hands of another party for a certain length of time, and here the husband undertakes to pay the additional sum even if he divorces his wife immediately after they are married. *Tosefot Yom Tov* maintains that the prohibition against interest does not apply here, because the prohibition does not apply if the debtor may not have to repay the loan, and here the husband does not have to pay back anything if his wife dies before him.

פּוֹסֵק פָּחוֹת חוֹמֶשׁ He undertakes to give her a fifth less. Our Commentary follows *Rashi,* who explains that the husband undertakes to restore to his wife at the time her ketubah becomes due a sum one-fifth less than the assessed value of the goods, because it was the common custom to inflate the value of those goods by twenty-five percent when assessing their value at the time of the wedding. Thus the husband would in fact undertake to restore to his wife a sum equal to the true value of the goods she brought into the marriage as her dowry. *Rav Hai Gaon* and most Rishonim maintain that the husband undertakes to give his wife one-fifth less than the assessed value of the dowry, because the wife will use the goods during the course of her marriage and will cause them to wear out and depreciate in value (see also Jerusalem Talmud).

שׁוּם בְּמָנֶה, וְשָׁוֶה מָנֶה If the assessment is a maneh, and it is worth a maneh. Following his explanation of the

HALAKHAH

husband must accept liability for an addition to the value of one-half of the amount of the dowry. And if she brings in a dowry of personal goods, the husband can undertake to restore a sum that is one-fifth less than the assessed value of those goods." (*Rambam, Sefer Nashim, Hilkhot Ishut* 23:11; *Shulḥan Arukh, Even HaEzer* 66:11.)

TRANSLATION AND COMMENTARY

שׁוּם בְּמָנֶה [1]If a woman wants her husband to write in her ketubah that she has brought into the marriage a dowry of movable goods **assessed at a maneh** (1 maneh = 100 dinarim), **she must give** him movable goods assessed at **thirty one sela'im** (1 sela = 4 dinarim) **plus a dinar,** which is one hundred and twenty-five dinarim, for her husband will record her dowry in the ketubah at one-fifth less than the assessed value of those goods, as was explained above. [2]Similarly, if a woman wants her husband to write in her ketubah that she has brought into the marriage a dowry of movable goods assessed at **four hundred dinarim, she must give him** movable goods assessed at **five hundred dinarim.** [66B] **Whatever** sum **the bridegroom undertakes** in the ketubah to return to his wife in place of the movable goods she brought into the marriage as her dowry, [3]**he** need only **undertake** to return a sum **a fifth less** than the assessed value of the goods, as was explained above.

GEMARA תָּנוּ רַבָּנַן [4]We learned in the Mishnah that the bride's father is not obliged to provide the second bridegroom with the dowry he promised to the first bridegroom. **Our Rabbis taught** a Baraita clarifying the scope of this ruling: **"There was no need to say** that the bride's father does not have to provide the second bridegroom with the dowry he promised to the first bridegroom in a case **where the first** bridegroom **was a Torah scholar and the second** bridegroom **is an ignorant man.** [5]**Rather,** the ruling was stated specifically to teach that **even if the first** bridegroom **was an ignorant man and the second is a Torah scholar,** the

[1]שׁוּם בְּמָנֶה, הִיא נוֹתֶנֶת שְׁלֹשִׁים וְאֶחָד סֶלַע וְדִינָר; [2]וּבְאַרְבַּע מֵאוֹת, הִיא נוֹתֶנֶת חֲמֵשׁ מֵאוֹת. מַה [66B] שֶׁחָתָן פּוֹסֵק, [3]הוּא פּוֹסֵק פָּחוֹת חוֹמֶשׁ.

גמרא [4]תָּנוּ רַבָּנַן: "אֵין צָרִיךְ לוֹמַר רִאשׁוֹן תַּלְמִיד חָכָם וְשֵׁנִי עַם הָאָרֶץ. [5]אֶלָּא אֲפִילוּ רִאשׁוֹן עַם הָאָרֶץ וְשֵׁנִי תַּלְמִיד

LITERAL TRANSLATION

[1][If] the assessment is a maneh, she gives thirty-one sela'im and a dinar; [2]and [if it is] four hundred [dinarim], she gives five hundred. Whatever [66B] a bridegroom undertakes, [3]he undertakes less a fifth.

GEMARA [4]Our Rabbis taught: "It is not necessary to say [this where] the first is a Torah scholar and the second is an ignorant man. [5]Rather, even if the first is an ignorant man and the second is a Torah scholar,

RASHI

שום במנה היא נותנת שלשים ואחד סלע ודינר — שום שהוא מקבלו במנה, שאמרו לו: כתוב מנה בכתובה, והיא תכניס לך שום של מנה — צריך שישומו אותו בבית של חתונה שלשים ואחד סלע ודינר, דהוי מנה וחומשו. **ובארבע מאות** — שום שיקבל עליו לכתוב ארבע מאות. **היא נותנת חמש מאות** — לפי שומת הנועדים שם. **וכשחתן פוסק כו'** — ואם שמו הם תחלה, והכניסה לו, בין שום קטן בין שום גדול — הוא כותב בשטר פחות חומש. ובגמרא מפרש לה למה לי כל הני.

NOTES

previous clause of the Mishnah, *Rashi* explains that this clause teaches that if the wife brings her husband a dowry to be recorded in her ketubah as having been assessed at a maneh, and the goods are actually worth a maneh, the husband is only entitled to goods worth a maneh. He cannot argue that if he is to undertake liability for a maneh, she must bring in goods assessed at a maneh-and-a-quarter, because the dowry is assessed at its true value without any inflation.

Rabbenu Ḥananel and many others maintain that this clause refers to a case in which the wife stipulated explicitly that she would bring into the marriage a dowry assessed at a maneh and actually worth a maneh. Consequently the husband is only entitled to goods worth a maneh, since any stipulation regarding a money matter is binding. But if she stipulated that she would bring into the marriage a dowry assessed at a maneh, she must provide her husband with goods worth twenty-five percent more, a dowry worth one hundred and twenty-five dinarim.

Meiri (who had a different reading of the passage) distinguishes between a case where the wife stated שׁוּם מָנֶה and a case where she stated שׁוּם בְּמָנֶה. In the former case she must provide her husband with a dowry of a maneh, and he undertakes liability for eighty dinarim. In the latter case she must bring him goods that will be assessed in her ketubah at a maneh, and so she must provide him with a dowry of one hundred and twenty-five dinarim.

Rav Hai Gaon explains this clause as referring to a case where a wife agreed to provide her husband with a dowry assessed at a maneh, and she brought him goods that do not wear out or depreciate in value. In such a case, the wife is not required to provide her husband with goods worth twenty-five percent more, since he is only entitled to goods worth a maneh.

מַה שֶּׁחָתָן פּוֹסֵק **Whatever a bridegroom undertakes.** Our commentary follows *Rashi,* who explains that the last clause of the Mishnah teaches that if the woman has already brought in her dowry, when the husband records the sum that he undertakes to restore to her upon the dissolution of their marriage, he need obligate himself only to one-fifth less than the assessed value of the dowry

HALAKHAH

אֲפִילוּ רִאשׁוֹן עַם הָאָרֶץ **Even if the first is an ignorant man.** "If someone undertakes to give his son-in-law a certain sum of money as his daughter's dowry, and the prospective son-in-law dies before the wedding, the father is not obligated to provide that dowry to the bridegroom's brother who comes to take his sister-in-law as his wife in levirate marriage,

חָכָם, יָכוֹל לוֹמַר: [1]'לְאָחִיךָ הָיִיתִי רוֹצֶה לִיתֵּן, לְךָ אִי אֶפְשִׁי לִיתֵּן'".
[2]"פָּסְקָה לְהַכְנִיס לוֹ אֶלֶף דִּינָר, כו'". [3]הַיְינוּ רֵישָׁא! [4]תָּנָא שׁוּמָא רַבָּה, [5]וְקָתָנֵי שׁוּמָא זוּטָא. [6]תָּנָא שׁוּמָא

LITERAL TRANSLATION

he can say: [1]'To your brother I was willing to give, [but] to you I am not willing to give.'"

[2]"[If] she undertook to bring him a thousand dinarim, etc." [3]This is [the same as] the first clause!

[4]He taught a large assessment, [5]and he taught a small assessment. [6]He taught his assessment,

TRANSLATION AND COMMENTARY

bride's father **can** still **say:** [1]**'I was willing to give your brother** that sum of money as my daughter's dowry, **but I am not willing to give you** anything.'" Even if the second bridegroom is greater than the first in Torah learning, since he obligated himself only to the first bridegroom, that obligation does not pass automatically to the second.

פָּסְקָה לְהַכְנִיס לוֹ [2]We **learned in the Mishnah: "If** a woman **undertakes to bring** her husband a dowry of **a thousand dinarim** in cash, her husband undertakes to restore to her the sum of fifteen maneh as the equivalent of that dowry. But if she brings him movable goods which require an assessment before being recorded in the ketubah, her husband undertakes to restore to her a sum that is one-fifth less than the assessed value of those goods." The Gemara now asks about apparent redundancies in the Mishnah, which continues with a series of additional rulings, namely, that if a woman wants it recorded in her ketubah that she brought a dowry assessed at a maneh, she must give him movable goods assessed at thirty-one sela'im and a dinar, and that when the bridegroom undertakes to restore his wife's dowry when her ketubah becomes due, he need only undertake to return a sum one-fifth less than the assessed value of the goods. [3]Surely, says the Gemara, **these** rulings **are** the same as the one found in **the earlier clause** of the Mishnah, that if a wife brings her husband a dowry of movable goods that require an assessment, her husband undertakes liability for a sum one-fifth less than the assessed value of those goods!

תָּנָא שׁוּמָא רַבָּה [4]The Gemara answers: The earlier clause, where the dowry is a thousand dinarim, **teaches** the law in a case where **the assessment is large,** whereas the later clause, [5]which refers to a dowry assessed at a maneh, **teaches** the law in a case where **the assessment is small.** And both rulings are necessary to avoid the mistaken conclusion that only in the case of a large assessment or only in the case of a small assessment does the husband record in the ketubah a sum that is one-fifth less than the assessed value, for only in that case would the value of the dowry be inflated when being assessed for the ketubah. Furthermore, the last clause of the Mishnah, which states that the husband has only to obligate himself to a sum one-fifth less than the assessed value of the dowry, [6]**teaches** the law in a case where the woman brought her husband the dowry and **he then assessed** its value. Since it was customary to inflate the value of such goods by twenty-five percent when assessing them, the husband would then obligate himself to a sum that was one-fifth less than the assessed value when he recorded the amount in his wife's ketubah. The earlier clause in the Mishnah, which stated that the woman must give her husband goods assessed at

RASHI

גמרא תנא שומא רבה — דפחות חומש, רישא דתנא "וכנגד השום" דקאי א"אלף דינר". **וקתני שומא זוטא** — "שום במנה היא נותנת שלשים ואחד סלע ודינר". דלא תימא שומא רבה הוא דדרך השמאים להעלותו על שוויו. אי נמי, שומא זוטא — איכא דמעלו ליה טפי, שלא תתבזה בעיני הנועדים. **תנא שומא דידה וקתני שומא דידיה** — היכא

TERMINOLOGY

הַיְינוּ **This is [the same as].** A term usually used to express astonishment at the repetition of something which has already been mentioned, either in the previous discussion or by another scholar.

NOTES

property. *Rabbenu Ḥananel* maintains that this clause refers to the goods belonging to the husband that he adds to his wife's dowry on his own initiative. When he records their value in his wife's ketubah, he need only obligate himself to one-fifth less than their assessed value.

תָּנָא שׁוּמָא רַבָּה, וְקָתָנֵי שׁוּמָא זוּטָא He taught a large assessment and he taught a small assessment. *Rashi* maintains that "a large assessment" refers to the ruling found in the first clause of the Mishnah regarding a dowry of a thousand dinarim, whereas "a small assessment" refers to the ruling regarding a dowry of a maneh. *Rabbenu Ḥananel* (cited by *Tosafot* and others) explains that "a large assessment" refers to the ruling regarding a dowry of four hundred dinarim, whereas "a small assessment" refers to the ruling regarding a dowry of a maneh.

Rav Hai Gaon offers a completely different explanation: "A large assessment" refers to a dowry of money to which the husband must contribute an additional sum. "A small assessment" refers to a dowry of movable goods, regarding which the husband undertakes to restore a sum that is one-fifth less than the assessed value of the goods. "His assessment" refers to the dowry that the wife brings into her marriage; "her assessment" refers to what the husband adds of his own to his wife's dowry.

HALAKHAH

even if the first bridegroom was an ignorant man and his brother is a Torah scholar, and even if the bride wishes to marry the second bridegroom." (*Rambam, Sefer Nashim, Hilkhot Ishut* 23:15; *Shulḥan Arukh, Even HaEzer* 52:2.)

דִּידֵיהּ, [1]וְקָתָנֵי שׁוּמָא דִּידָהּ.

מִשְׁנָה [2]פָּסְקָה לְהַכְנִיס לוֹ כְּסָפִים, [3]סַלְעָהּ נַעֲשָׂה שִׁשָּׁה דִּינָרִין.

[4]הֶחָתָן מְקַבֵּל עָלָיו עֲשָׂרָה דִּינָרִים לְקוּפָּה לְכָל מָנֶה וּמָנֶה. [5]רַבָּן שִׁמְעוֹן בֶּן גַּמְלִיאֵל אוֹמֵר: הַכֹּל כְּמִנְהַג הַמְּדִינָה.

גְּמָרָא [6]הַיְינוּ: [7]״פּוֹסֵק כְּנֶגְדָּם חֲמִשָּׁה עָשָׂר מָנֶה״! [8]תָּנָא עִסְקָא רַבָּה, [9]וְתָנָא

LITERAL TRANSLATION

[1]and he taught her assessment.

MISHNAH [2][If] she undertook to bring him money, [3]her sela becomes six dinarim.

[4]The bridegroom must undertake [to give] ten dinarim for the basket for each and every maneh.

[5]Rabban Shimon ben Gamliel says: Everything is in accordance with local custom.

GEMARA [6]This is [the same as]: [7]"He undertakes corresponding to them [to give her] fifteen maneh!"

[8]He taught a large transaction, [9]and he taught

TRANSLATION AND COMMENTARY

thirty-one sela'im and a dinar, [1]**teaches** the law in a case where the husband has already written in the ketubah that his wife has brought into the marriage a dowry of a certain sum, and now **she** must **assess** movable goods and hand them over to her husband. Since it was customary to inflate the value of the dowry when assessing it, the woman would have to provide her husband with property assessed at twenty-five percent more than the sum recorded in her ketubah.

MISHNAH פָּסְקָה לְהַכְנִיס לוֹ [2]If a woman **undertakes to bring** her husband a dowry that consists of **money**, [3]each **sela** (1 sela = 4 dinarim) that she brings him **is treated as six dinarim** when the husband undertakes liability for the dowry.

הֶחָתָן מְקַבֵּל עָלָיו [4]**The bridegroom must** undertake **to provide** his wife with **ten dinarim for the basket** (this term will be explained in the Gemara) **for each maneh** that she brings into the marriage as her dowry, whether in cash or in movable goods.

רַבָּן שִׁמְעוֹן בֶּן גַּמְלִיאֵל [5]**Rabban Shimon ben Gamliel says: All** matters relating to the way in which the dowry is recorded in the ketubah **must be in accordance with local custom.**

GEMARA הַיְינוּ [6]We learned in our Mishnah that when the husband undertakes liability for his wife's dowry in the ketubah, he treats each sela received from her in cash as six dinarim. The Gemara asks: Surely **this is identical with** what was taught in the previous Mishnah: "If a woman undertakes to bring her husband a dowry of a thousand dinarim in cash, [7]her husband **undertakes to restore** to his wife at the time her ketubah becomes due the sum of **fifteen maneh as the equivalent** of that dowry?"

תָּנָא עִסְקָא רַבָּה [8]The Gemara answers: The previous Mishnah, which refers to the case of a woman who brings her husband a dowry of a thousand dinarim, **teaches** that the law of recording the dowry in the ketubah at one-and-a-half times its actual value applies when the **amount of money is large.** [9]Our Mishnah, which states that each sela the woman brings is treated as six dinarim, **teaches** that the law also applies

RASHI

דקתני ״חתן פוסק״ – הרי שומא דידיה, כגון שהיא הכניסה קודם השום, והוא שם אותו בחמש מאות. כשבא לכתוב – יכתוב ארבע מאות, שאף הוא שם אותו חומש יותר על שוויו. **שומא דידה** – היכא דקתני ״היא נותנת״, שהוא כתב הכתובה קודם שבא השום, ועכשיו היא מביאתו וקרוביה שמין אותו. ו״חתן פוסק״ דתנא תרי זימני – חד לשומא רבה וחד לשומא זוטא.

משנה **פסקה להכניס לו כספים** – שהן מוכנים לשכר מיד. **סלעה נעשה** – לכתוב בשטר הכתובה בששה דינר, יותר שליש, כדתנן לעיל. ובגמרא מפרש הא תו למה לי. **לקופה** – בגמרא מפרש: שיתן לה עשרה זוז לכל מנה ומנה שהיא מביאה לו, ויקנו לה מהם בשמים לרחוץ בהם בתמרוקי הנשים. שכך שיערו שהאשה המביאה לבעלה מנה ראויה היא לבשמים של עשרה זוז. ולא פירשו במשנה אם לכל יום, אם לכל שבת, אם לכל חדש, אם לכל שנה.

גמרא **עסקא** – כספים קרי עסקא, שהם עומדים להשתכר בהם, להתעסק בהן תמיד. **תנא עסקא רבה** – אלף דינר, שיוסיף שליש ויכתוב חמשה עשר מנה.

SAGES

רַבָּן שִׁמְעוֹן בֶּן גַּמְלִיאֵל **Rabban Shimon ben Gamliel.** See *Ketubot*, Part I, pp.120-1.

BACKGROUND

הַכֹּל כְּמִנְהַג הַמְּדִינָה **Everything in accordance with local custom.** This principle applies in many areas of Jewish law. In the opinion of various Sages, it is an inherent part of any contract or agreement. Regarding all the details that are not explicitly stated in an agreement, it is assumed that the parties accept local custom, and this tacit agreement is sufficient to oblige each party to act according to that custom.

NOTES

הַכֹּל כְּמִנְהַג הַמְּדִינָה **Everything is in accordance with local custom.** Most Rishonim explain that Rabban Shimon ben Gamliel's statement refers to all the regulations found in this and the previous Mishnah. Rabban Shimon ben Gamliel teaches that all matters relating to the way the dowry is recorded in the ketubah follow local custom, whether to add an additional sum to the ketubah or to record in the ketubah a sum that is less than the assessed value of the dowry, or to record in the document the precise sum that the wife brought into the marriage as her dowry. According to most Rishonim, there is no dispute between the first Tanna of the Mishnah and Rabban Shimon ben Gamliel. And if they do disagree, it is only about a place where it was not customary to add to the dowry or to record a sum

HALAKHAH

הַכֹּל כְּמִנְהַג הַמְּדִינָה **Everything is in accordance with local custom.** "All matters relating to the way in which the dowry is recorded in the ketubah follow local custom, both with respect to the assessment of the dowry and with respect to the addition that the husband makes to the dowry, following Rabban Shimon ben Gamliel (whose

BACKGROUND

קוּפָּה **Basket.** This is the main meaning of the word, usually one woven of palm leaves or willow branches, in which various things were placed. Some baskets were quite large, with several interior sections, while small baskets were used by women to carry jewelry or cosmetics.

עִסְקָא זוּטָא. [1]וּצְרִיכָא, דְּאִי תְּנָא עִסְקָא רַבָּה, דְּנָפֵישׁ רַוְוחָא, [2]אֲבָל עִסְקָא זוּטָא, דְּזוּטַר רַוְוחָא, [3]אֵימָא לָא. [4]צְרִיכָא. [5]וְאִי אַשְׁמְעִינַן עִסְקָא זוּטָא, דְּזוּטַר זִיוּנָא, [6]אֲבָל עִסְקָא רַבָּה, דְּנָפֵישׁ זִיוּנָא, אֵימָא לָא. [7]צְרִיכָא.

[8]"הֶחָתָן מְקַבֵּל עָלָיו עֲשָׂרָה דִּינָר לְקוּפָּה". [9]מַאי קוּפָּה? [10]אָמַר רַב אַשִׁי: קוּפָּה שֶׁל בְּשָׂמִים.

[11]וְאָמַר רַב אַשִׁי: לֹא נֶאֶמְרוּ

LITERAL TRANSLATION

a small transaction. [1]And it was necessary [to do so], for if he had taught a large transaction, [I might have said that it was] because the profit is great, [2]but [regarding] a small transaction, where the profit is small, [3]I might have said no. [4][Therefore] it was necessary [to state the second case]. [5]And if he had taught us [about] a small transaction, [I might have said that it was] because the expenses are small, [6]but [regarding] a large transaction, where the expenses are great, I might have said no. [7][Therefore] it was necessary [to state the first case].

[8]"The bridegroom must undertake [to give] ten dinarim for the basket." [9]What is the basket?

[10]Rav Ashi said: The basket of perfumes.

[11]And Rav Ashi said: These things were said

RASHI

עסקא זוטא – סלעה נעשה ששה דינר. זיונא – יליאה ואחריות.

TRANSLATION AND COMMENTARY

when the **amount of money is small.** [1]**And it was necessary** for the Tanna to teach the law in both cases, **for if he had** only **taught** the law when **the amount of money involved is large, I might** mistakenly **have said that** the law applies then, **because** there **the profit** that the husband may derive from the dowry **is** also **great,** and this is why the husband is willing to undertake liability for an addition to the dowry. [2]**But** if **the amount of money involved is small,** and thus **the profit** that the husband may derive from the dowry **is** also **small,** [3]**I might have said** that this law does **not** apply. [4]**Therefore, it was necessary** for the Tanna **to teach** in **the second** Mishnah that the law applies even when the amount of money involved is small. [5]**And if** the Tanna **had** only **taught** the law when **the amount of money is small, I might** mistakenly **have said that** the law applies only then, **because** there the **expenses** incurred in the management of that amount of money **are** also **small,** and this is why the husband is willing to undertake liability for an addition to the dowry. [6]**But** when **the amount of money is large,** and thus **the expenses** of managing it **are great, I might have said** that the law does **not** apply. [7]**Therefore it was necessary** for the Tanna **to teach** in **the first** Mishnah that the law applies even in a case where the amount of money involved is large.

הֶחָתָן מְקַבֵּל עָלָיו [8]We learned in the Mishnah: **"The bridegroom must undertake to provide** his wife with **ten dinarim for the basket** for each maneh that she brings into the marriage as her dowry." [9]The Gemara asks: **What is** meant by **"a basket"?**

אָמַר רַב אַשִׁי [10]Rav Ashi said in reply: The basket mentioned here in the Mishnah refers to **the basket of perfumes.** For each maneh that a woman brings into her marriage, she is entitled to receive from her husband ten dinarim for the purchase of perfumes and cosmetics.

וְאָמַר רַב אַשִׁי [11]**And Rav Ashi added: This regulation applied only in Jerusalem,** where the women were

NOTES

in the ketubah that is less than the assessed value of the dowry. But where the custom is not to add to the dowry or not to record a sum that is less than the assessed value of the dowry, there is certainly no disagreement between the Tannaim (see *Ramban, Rashba,* and others).

דְּזוּטַר זִיוּנָא **Because the expenses are small.** Several different explanations have been offered for the term זיונא. Our commentary follows *Rashi,* who interprets the term as referring to expenses: The Tanna needed to teach the case where the transaction is large, for in such a case the expenses of managing the money are also large, and so I might have thought that the husband would be unwilling to undertake liability for an addition to the dowry.

Ri Migash explains the term זִיוּנָא as referring to losses. The Tanna needed to teach the case where the transaction is large, for in such a case the possible losses are great, and so I might have thought that the husband would be unwilling to accept liability for any more than his wife brought into the marriage. *Meiri* interprets the term to mean effort: The Tanna needed to teach the case where the transaction is large, for then the husband must make a greater effort to take care of the goods, and so I might have thought that he would be unwilling to accept liability for an addition to the dowry.

HALAKHAH

position may not be disputed by the anonymous first Tanna of the Mishnah, and whose views when recorded in the Mishnah are always accepted as law; *Maggid Mishneh*)." (*Rambam, Sefer Nashim, Hilkhot Ishut* 23:11-12; *Shulḥan Arukh, Even HaEzer* 66:11.)

TRANSLATION AND COMMENTARY

accustomed to using large quantities of perfume.

בָּעֵי רַב אַשִׁי [1] **Rav Ashi** also **asked** a series of questions on this subject: The Mishnah stated that the husband must provide his wife with ten dinarim to be spent on perfumes for each maneh that she brings into the marriage as her dowry. How is the dowry measured for this purpose? [2] **Must the husband give his wife ten dinarim for** each **maneh of the assessed** value of her dowry, **or for** each **maneh that he undertook** to restore to his wife when the ketubah became due? If, for example, the woman's dowry was assessed at ten maneh, the husband would record in the ketubah document the sum of eight maneh, one-fifth less than the assessed value of the goods. Would he be required to provide her with a hundred dinarim for her perfumes, or only eighty dinarim? [3] **If you say** that the husband must provide his wife with ten dinarim **for** each **maneh for which he undertook liability,** does this mean that he must provide her with that money only on **the first day** of their marriage, **or** must he pay that sum **each and every day?** [4] **And if you say** that the money must be paid **every day,** does this mean that he must provide her with that sum only during **the first week** that they are married, **or** must he pay that amount **each and every week?** [5] **And if you say** that the money must be paid **every week,** does this mean that the husband must provide his wife with an allowance for her perfumes only during **the first month** of their marriage, **or** must he pay her that money **each and every month?** [6] **And if you say** that the allowance must be paid **every month,** does this mean that he must provide money for her perfumes only during **the first year** that they are married, **or** must he pay the said amount **each and every year?**

LITERAL TRANSLATION

only in Jerusalem.

[1] Rav Ashi asked: [2][Does this apply] to the maneh that was assessed or to the maneh for which responsibility was accepted? [3]If you say to the maneh for which responsibility was accepted, [does it apply to] the first day or [to] each and every day? [4]If you say [to] every day, [does it apply to] the first week or [to] each and every week? [5]If you say [to] every week, [does it apply to] the first month or [to] each and every month? [6]If you say [to] every month, [does it apply to] the first year or [to] each and every year?

דְּבָרִים הַלָּלוּ אֶלָּא בִּירוּשָׁלַיִם. בָּעֵי רַב אַשִׁי: [2] בְּמָנֶה הַנִּישׁוֹם אוֹ בְּמָנֶה הַמִּתְקַבֵּל? [3] אִם תִּמְצָא לוֹמַר מָנֶה הַמִּתְקַבֵּל, יוֹם רִאשׁוֹן אוֹ כָּל יוֹם וָיוֹם? [4] אִם תִּמְצָא לוֹמַר כָּל יוֹם וָיוֹם, שַׁבָּת רִאשׁוֹנָה אוֹ כָּל שַׁבָּת וְשַׁבָּת? [5] אִם תִּמְצָא לוֹמַר כָּל שַׁבָּת וְשַׁבָּת, חֹדֶשׁ רִאשׁוֹן אוֹ כָּל חֹדֶשׁ וָחֹדֶשׁ? [6] אִם תִּמְצָא לוֹמַר כָּל חֹדֶשׁ וָחֹדֶשׁ, שָׁנָה רִאשׁוֹנָה אוֹ כָּל שָׁנָה וְשָׁנָה?

RASHI

בירושלים — הָיוּ נוֹהֲגוֹת לְהִתְקַשֵּׁט בִּבְשָׂמִים. במנה הנישום או במנה המתקבל — הַאי ״לְכָל מנה ומנה״ דְּקָאמַר — לְפִי חֶשְׁבּוֹן הַשּׁוּמָא קָאמַר, אוֹ לְפִי חֶשְׁבּוֹן שֶׁהוּא מְקַבְּלָן עָלָיו, דְּהַיְינוּ פָּחוֹת חוֹמֶשׁ. שבת ראשונה בו׳ — אֵינִי יוֹדֵעַ לְיַשֵּׁב סֵדֶר בְּעָיוֹת הַלָּלוּ לְפִי שִׁיטַת הַתַּלְמוּד. וְנִרְאֶה בְּעֵינֵי שֶׁכֵּן סִידְרָן: יוֹם רִאשׁוֹן, אוֹ כָל יוֹם יוֹם, וְאִם תִּמְצָא לוֹמַר כָל יוֹם וָיוֹם — שַׁבָּת רִאשׁוֹנָה אוֹ כָל שַׁבָּת וְשַׁבָּת, וְאִם תִּמְצָא לוֹמַר כָל שַׁבָּת וְשַׁבָּת — חֹדֶשׁ רִאשׁוֹן אוֹ כָל חֹדֶשׁ וָחֹדֶשׁ. וְאִם תִּמְצָא לוֹמַר כָל חֹדֶשׁ וָחֹדֶשׁ — שָׁנָה רִאשׁוֹנָה אוֹ כָל שָׁנָה וְשָׁנָה?

NOTES

אֶלָּא בִּירוּשָׁלַיִם **Only in Jerusalem.** *Rashi* explains that the regulation that the bridegroom must undertake to provide his wife with a perfume allowance of ten dinarim for each maneh that she brings into the marriage applies only in Jerusalem, because there the women were accustomed to using large quantities of perfume. *Rid* and others add that Jerusalem women used such large quantities of perfume because they were particularly wealthy. Some Rishonim maintain that outside Jerusalem the perfume allowance was smaller, in accordance with local custom. Others maintain that outside Jerusalem the husband would not provide his wife with any special allowance for perfumes (*Talmidei Rabbenu Yonah*).

Tosafot points out that elsewhere (*Yoma* 39b) the Gemara states that a Jerusalem bride would not have to use perfume because the scent of the Temple incense was so strong. Why, then, did the women of Jerusalem need a special allowance for perfumes? *Rabbenu Tam* explains that while the Jerusalem women did not use perfume, they were still in need of other types of cosmetics to treat their skin and hair. Others argue that because the scent of the

incense was so strong, the Jerusalem women had to use larger quantities of perfume so that their husbands would take notice of their sweet smell, and so that they would not violate the prohibition against deriving benefit from the Temple incense (*Rabbi Ya'akov Emden*).

יוֹם רִאשׁוֹן אוֹ כָּל יוֹם וָיוֹם **Does it apply to the first day or to each and every day?** The questions asked by Rav Ashi present a number of difficulties. *Tosafot* notes that the first use of the expression "if you say" is imprecise, because the questions that follow may be asked even if we say that the husband must give his wife ten dinarim for each maneh of the assessed value of her dowry. More difficult are the questions themselves. They can certainly not be understood according to their plain sense — that Rav Ashi accepts as a possibility that the husband may be required to provide his wife with ten dinarim for each maneh of her dowry every day, every week, every month, every year that they are married, for if that were the case, the capital of the dowry would be used up very quickly. *Tosafot* suggests that it was clear to Rav Ashi that the ten dinarim that the husband must provide his wife for each maneh she brings

[1] תֵּיקוּ.

[2] אָמַר רַב יְהוּדָה אָמַר רַב: [3] מַעֲשֶׂה בְּבִתּוֹ שֶׁל נַקְדִּימוֹן בֶּן גּוּרְיוֹן שֶׁפָּסְקוּ לָהּ חֲכָמִים אַרְבַּע מֵאוֹת זְהוּבִים לְקוּפָּה שֶׁל בְּשָׂמִים לְבוֹ בַּיּוֹם. [4] אָמְרָה לָהֶם: ״כָּךְ תִּפְסְקוּ לִבְנוֹתֵיכֶם״. [5] וְעָנוּ אַחֲרֶיהָ: ״אָמֵן״.

[6] תָּנוּ רַבָּנַן: ״מַעֲשֶׂה בְּרַבָּן יוֹחָנָן בֶּן זַכַּאי שֶׁהָיָה רוֹכֵב עַל הַחֲמוֹר, וְהָיָה יוֹצֵא מִירוּשָׁלַיִם, [7] וְהָיוּ תַּלְמִידָיו מְהַלְּכִין אַחֲרָיו. רָאָה רִיבָה אַחַת שֶׁהָיְתָה מְלַקֶּטֶת שְׂעוֹרִים מִבֵּין גְּלָלֵי בְהֶמְתָּן שֶׁל עֲרָבִיִּים. [8] כֵּיוָן שֶׁרָאֲתָה אוֹתוֹ, נִתְעַטְּפָה בִּשְׂעָרָהּ וְעָמְדָה לְפָנָיו. אָמְרָה לוֹ: ׳רַבִּי, פַּרְנְסֵנִי!׳ [9] אָמַר לָהּ:

LITERAL TRANSLATION

[1] Let [these questions] remain [undecided].

[2] Rav Yehudah said in the name of Rav: [3] It once happened regarding the daughter of Nakdimon ben Guryon that the Sages granted her four hundred gold coins for the basket of perfumes for that day. [4] She said to them: "Grant the same to your daughters." [5] And they answered after her: "Amen."

[6] Our Rabbis taught: "It once happened that Rabban Yoḥanan ben Zakkai was riding an ass, and he was leaving Jerusalem, and his disciples were walking after him. [7] He saw a young woman who was gathering barley from among the dung of animals belonging to Arabs. [8] When she saw him, she covered herself with her hair and stood before him. She said to him: 'Master, support me!' [9] He said to her:

TRANSLATION AND COMMENTARY

תֵּיקוּ [1] The Gemara offers no solutions to the problems raised by Rav Ashi, and it concludes: **The problems** raised here **remain unresolved**.

אָמַר רַב יְהוּדָה [2] **Rav Yehudah related** the following story **in the name of Rav:** [3] **It once happened that the Sages awarded four hundred gold coins to the daughter of Nakdimon ben Guryon,** one of the wealthiest men living in Jerusalem at the end of the Second Temple period, **for** her to spend on **the basket of perfumes for that day.** [4] Pleased with their decision, Nakdimon's daughter blessed the Sages, **saying to them: "May the same be awarded to your** own **daughters."** [5] And the Sages **responded "Amen."**

תָּנוּ רַבָּנַן [6] **Our Rabbis taught** a Baraita which describes the poverty to which Nakdimon's daughter was later reduced: **"It once happened that Rabban Yoḥanan ben Zakkai was riding an ass, and he left** the city of **Jerusalem, and his disciples followed after him** on foot in order to watch their master and learn from him. [7] As he was riding, **he saw a young woman who was gathering barley from among the dung of cattle belonging to** the local **Arabs.** She was apparently so poor and desperate for food that she was searching through the animals' dung for undigested barley grains so that she would have something to eat. [8] **When** she **saw** Rabban Yoḥanan ben Zakkai, **she covered her** face in shame **with her hair, and stood before him and begged: 'Master,** please **support me!'** Rabban Yoḥanan ben Zakkai sensed that the young woman knew him, even though he did not recognize her, [9] and so **he asked her: 'My daughter, who**

RASHI

שפסקו לה חכמים — שמת בעלה, ובאת לבית דין לפסוק לה צרכיה מנכסיו. **לבו ביום** — לצורך יום אחד.

NOTES

into the marriage are paid only once. What Rav Ashi is asking is whether the husband must give the money to his wife in one payment at the beginning of their marriage or in small payments over an extended period of time in accordance with her actual needs.

According to *Ra'ah*, Rav Ashi's question is as follows: For how long must the ten dinar per maneh allowance for perfumes last the woman — a day, a week, or a month? The answer to this question has practical ramifications, because as long as the wife still has money left from her perfume allowance, her husband is exempt from providing her with the weekly allowance of a silver ma'ah for her personal needs (see above, 64b).

Meiri suggests yet another explanation of Rav Ashi's questions: For how long may the woman come and demand her allowance? Must she ask for it on the first day of her marriage; or, perhaps, during the first week of marriage while the wedding celebrations are still continuing; or, perhaps, during the first month of marriage, while she is still regarded as a newlywed bride regarding matters of mourning; or, perhaps, during the first year, while the couple are still regarded as newlyweds regarding certain matters; or, perhaps, even during the following years?

שֶׁפָּסְקוּ לָהּ חֲכָמִים That the Sages granted her. *Rashi* explains that the daughter of Nakdimon ben Guryon had recently been widowed, and that she had come before the court so that they would award her maintenance from the estate of her late husband. According to *Tosafot*, her husband was still alive, but he had asked the court to award his wife an allowance that would fit her personal needs, because she did not need the allowance to which she would have been entitled according to the formula of the Mishnah (ten dinarim per maneh).

כָּךְ תִּפְסְקוּ לִבְנוֹתֵיכֶם Grant the same to your daughters. The Tosefta (*Ketubot* 5:9) and the Jerusalem Talmud (*Ketubot* 5:11) record a different version of this story, according to which Nakdimon's daughter was dissatisfied with the award and cursed the Sages, saying: "May the same [i.e., so little] be awarded to your daughters." But the Sages nevertheless responded with "Amen," for they thought that the award was in fact very generous.

LANGUAGE

רִיבָה A young woman. This word refers to a maiden. The masculine form is רוֹבֶה. Some authorities believe that the source of the word is the Aramaic רַבְיָא, meaning a child. Others believe that it is a term of respect for a maiden from an important family.

SAGES

רַב יְהוּדָה Rav Yehudah. A Babylonian Amora of the second generation. See *Ketubot,* Part I, p. 8.

רַב Rav. A Babylonian Amora of the first generation. See *Ketubot,* Part I, pp. 42-43.

רַבָּן יוֹחָנָן בֶּן זַכַּאי Rabban Yoḥanan ben Zakkai. The Nasi of the Sanhedrin after the destruction of the Temple, he was one of the greatest Jewish leaders of all time. Rabban Yoḥanan ben Zakkai (the Priest) was one of the youngest students of Hillel the Elder. He lived a long life and led the Jewish people for many years. Before the destruction of the Temple he lived in the town of Beror Ḥayil and later in the city of A'rav.
He was held in high esteem for his greatness: "He ignored nothing, either great or small, in his studies, from the account of the Chariot [mysticism] to the debates of Abaye and Rava, the conversation of the palm trees and the conversation of laundrymen and fables about foxes." It is said of him that he never held an idle conversation in his life, and that he wore tefillin constantly. He was extremely humble in his ways and greeted everyone, even gentiles in the market.
He was already one of the greatest Sages of his generation while the Temple still stood, and most of the Sages at that time were his students. After the outbreak of the great rebellion, he consistently expressed his opinion against the rebellion and acted to bring peace. When, from within the besieged city, he saw that the end of Jerusalem was near, with the help of his nephew, a leader of the rebels, he managed to leave the city with some of his students. He was received with great honor by Aspasianus (Vespasian, the Roman general), and prophesied that

TRANSLATION AND COMMENTARY

are you?' [1]**She said to him: 'I am the daughter of Nakdimon ben Guryon.'** [2]Rabban Yoḥanan then **asked her: 'My daughter, where has** all **the wealth of your father's house gone**, that you have reached this state of destitution?' [3]The young woman **explained: 'Master, do not** the people **in Jerusalem have the popular saying: "The salt of wealth is diminution** [חֶסֶר]"?' In other words, the only way to preserve one's wealth is by diminishing it through acts of charity, for the more one gives to charity, the wealthier one becomes. [4]**(And some say** that the adage was phrased slightly differently: **'The salt of wealth is loving-kindness** [חֶסֶד].' In other words, wealth can only be preserved through the performance of acts of loving-kindness.) 'Apparently,' continued Nakdimon's daughter, 'my father did not perform sufficient acts of charity and loving-kindness, and this is why his wealth has disappeared.' Rabban Yoḥanan ben Zakkai asked Nakdimon's daughter one more question: [5]**'And where is the wealth** that you should have received **from your father-in-law's house?'** [6]**She answered: 'This one,** my father, **came and caused the loss of the other one's** money, that of my father-in-law. They combined their assets and went into business together, and all the money was lost.' [7]Nakdimon's daughter then **said to** Rabban Yoḥanan ben Zakkai: **'Master, do you remember** years ago **when you signed my ketubah** at my marriage?' [8]Rabban Yoḥanan ben Zakkai **said to his disciples: 'I remember** well **that when I signed this woman's ketubah, I read from it:** [9]She shall receive a dowry of **a million golden dinarim from her father's house, apart from** the addition to her dowry that was to come **from** the house of **her father-in-law.'** Remembering the wealth of Nakdimon's family at the time of his daughter's wedding, and witnessing the abject poverty to which that daughter had now been reduced, [10]**Rabban Yoḥanan ben Zakkai wept and said: 'Happy are** the Children of **Israel.** [11]**When they act in accordance**

'בִּתִּי, מִי אַתְּ?' [1]אָמְרָה לוֹ: 'בַּת נַקְדִּימוֹן בֶּן גּוּרְיוֹן אֲנִי'. [2]אָמַר לָהּ: 'בִּתִּי, מָמוֹן שֶׁל בֵּית אָבִיךְ הֵיכָן הָלַךְ?' [3]אָמְרָה לוֹ: 'רַבִּי, לָא כְּדֵין מַתְלִין מַתְלָא בִּירוּשָׁלַיִם: "מֶלַח מָמוֹן חֶסֶר"?' [4](וְאָמְרִי לָהּ: 'חֶסֶד'.) [5]'וְשֶׁל בֵּית חָמִיךְ הֵיכָן הוּא?' [6]אָמְרָה לוֹ: 'בָּא זֶה וְאִיבֵּד אֶת זֶה'. [7]אָמְרָה לוֹ: 'רַבִּי, זָכוּר אַתָּה כְּשֶׁחָתַמְתָּ עַל כְּתוּבָּתִי?' [8]אָמַר לָהֶן לְתַלְמִידָיו: 'זָכוּר אֲנִי כְּשֶׁחָתַמְתִּי עַל כְּתוּבָּתָהּ שֶׁל זוֹ, וְהָיִיתִי קוֹרֵא בָּהּ: [9]אֶלֶף אֲלָפִים דִּינְרֵי זָהָב מִבֵּית אָבִיהָ, חוּץ מִשֶּׁל חָמִיהָ'. [10]בָּכָה רַבָּן יוֹחָנָן בֶּן זַכַּאי וְאָמַר: 'אַשְׁרֵיהֶם יִשְׂרָאֵל. [11]בִּזְמַן שֶׁעוֹשִׂין רְצוֹנוֹ

LITERAL TRANSLATION

'My daughter, who are you?' [1]She said to him: 'I am the daughter of Nakdimon ben Guryon.' [2]He said to her: 'My daughter, where has the wealth of your father's house gone?' [3]She said to him: 'Master, is this not the saying which they say in Jerusalem: "The salt of wealth is diminution"?' [4](And some say: '[The salt of wealth is] loving-kindness.') [5]'And where is [the wealth] of your father-in-law's?' [6]She said to him: 'This came and destroyed that.' [7]She said to him: 'Master, do you remember when you signed my ketubah?' [8]He said to his disciples: 'I remember when I signed this one's ketubah, and I read in it: [9]A thousand thousand gold dinarim from her father's house, apart from [the amount from] her father-in-law's.' [10]Rabban Yoḥanan ben Zakkai wept and said: 'Happy are Israel. [11]When they act in accordance with the will

RASHI

ולא כדין מתלין מתלא – ולא כך היו מושלין משל בירושלים? **מלח ממון חסר** – הרוצה למלוח ממונו, כלומר לגרום לו שיתקיים – יחסרנו לצדקה תמיד, וחסרונו זהו קיומו. **ואמרי לה חסד** – יעשה ממנו חסד. ושל בית אבא לא עשו צדקה כראוי, וכלה ממונן. **בא זה ואיבד זה** – לפי שנתערב בו. **חוץ משל חמיה** – תוספת שהוסיף לה החתן.

NOTES

Nakdimon's daughter's anger is understandable in the light of *Tosafot's* observation (see previous note) that according to the Mishnah's formula (ten dinarim of perfumes per maneh of dowry) she should have been entitled to a larger award, but her husband persuaded the Sages to reduce his obligation.

מֶלַח מָמוֹן חֶסֶר **The salt of wealth is diminution.** Our commentary follows *Rashi, Arukh,* and others, who understand the word *ḥeser* in the sense of diminution, and explain the proverb as saying that the salt of wealth, the way to preserve it, is by diminishing it through charitable deeds. *Maharal* adds that wealth is like a fountain, about which it may be said that the more that one removes from it, the more it is replenished.

Maharam Schiff explains that the two versions of the proverb disagree about whether wealth may be preserved by diminishing it through all sorts of good deeds, or only through the performance of acts of loving-kindness. Alternatively, the first version may be explained as follows: Wealth lacks salt, the word *ḥeser* being understood in the sense of deficiency. There is no salt for wealth, no way to guarantee its preservation. Thus, argued Nakdimon's daughter, it is not surprising that her father's great wealth was reduced to nothing.

אַשְׁרֵיהֶם יִשְׂרָאֵל **Fortunate are Israel.** At first glance, Rabban Yoḥanan ben Zakkai's remarks are difficult to understand, for his introductory words, "Fortunate are Israel," appear to apply to everything he said, including his

he would soon be the Roman Emperor. The fulfillment of this prophecy advanced Rabban Yoḥanan's prestige in the eyes of the emperor, who acceded to Rabban Yoḥanan's request to be permitted to establish a new Torah center in Yavneh, which was to be the seat of the Sanhedrin and the national leadership. He also saved Rabban Gamliel (of Yavneh), although his father, Rabban Shimon ben Gamliel, had been a leader of the rebellion, so that he could transfer the inherited presidency of the Sanhedrin to the House of Hillel.

In Yavneh Rabban Yoḥanan performed acts of major importance by instituting various rulings which were intended, on the one hand, to preserve the memory of the Temple and hopes for its speedy rebuilding, and, on the other hand, to provide the basis for the Jewish people's spiritual existence without dependency on the Temple. In these actions he was very successful, and in some respects it may be said that in every subsequent generation the Jewish people continues to follow in the course mapped out by Rabban Yoḥanan in Yavneh.

The Sages of that generation, Rabbi Eliezer, Rabbi Yehoshua, and others, were all his students, and from them the Torah spread throughout the Jewish world. He also fostered Rabban Gamliel and prepared him to take his place as the Nasi after his death, and some say even during his lifetime. Hence it is no wonder that his students spoke of him in terms of great admiration.

Rabban Yoḥanan ben Zakkai dedicated most of the years of his long life to the needs of the people. He had a son, Rabbi Yehudah, who was also a Sage.

BACKGROUND

אוּמָּה שְׁפָלָה A lowly nation. The Arabs at that time and in later generations were regarded as a lowly nation because they were nomads who lived in poverty in the desert, appearing in settled places as robbers. Even members of tribes that settled permanently in various countries in the East engaged in small-scale trade and were not averse to thievery. The Arab tribes were not united, nor did they have a kingdom of their own, except in southern Arabia. For all these reasons they were regarded as a lowly nation.

LANGUAGE

מֵילַת A basket. This word seems to be derived from the Greek, perhaps by extension from the word μηλοτη (*myloti*), meaning wool. Others believe that it derives from the name of the Greek island Μίλητος (*Milytos*), where fine woolen goods were manufactured. When used by the Sages, the word always means the finest and most expensive clothing.

TRANSLATION AND COMMENTARY

with the will of God, no nation or tongue has power over them. [1]**But when they do not act in accordance with the will of God, He delivers them into the hand of a lowly nation,** making them the lowliest of peoples. When they rebel against Him, [2]He **not only delivers them into the hand of the lowly nation** itself, **but into the hand of the cattle of the lowly nation,** just as Nakdimon's daughter has been reduced to searching through the dung of animals belonging to Arabs so that she may find something to eat.'"

וְנַקְדִּימוֹן בֶּן גּוּרְיוֹן [3]The Gemara raises a question about the story that was just related: **But isn't it true** that **Nakdimon ben Guryon performed acts of charity?** How could Nakdimon's daughter have attributed his downfall to his failure to act charitably? [4]**Surely it was taught** in a Baraita: **"It was said about Nakdimon ben Guryon that whenever he would leave his house** to go to **the Academy,** [5]**carpets of fine wool would be** [67A] **spread out beneath him,** so that his feet would not have to touch the ground, [6]**and poor people would come and roll them up** and keep them **after he** passed." Thus we see that Nakdimon contributed generously to the poor!

אִיבָּעֵית אֵימָא [7]The Gemara answers: **If you wish,** you can **say** that Nakdimon **acted** in that way not for the sake of the poor but **for his own glory,** in order to display his own great wealth. [8]**And if you wish,** you can **say** that Nakdimon's motives may indeed have been pure, and that he was truly concerned to assist the poor, [9]but **he** still **did not act as he should have acted.** A man of his means should have given even more to charity, [10]**as the popular saying goes: According to the camel is the load.** The stronger the camel, the heavier is the burden he is expected to bear. Similarly, the wealthier the person, the greater is his responsibility toward the poor.

שֶׁל מָקוֹם, אֵין כָּל אוּמָּה וְלָשׁוֹן שׁוֹלֶטֶת בָּהֶם. [1]וּבִזְמַן שֶׁאֵין עוֹשִׂין רְצוֹנוֹ שֶׁל מָקוֹם, מוֹסְרָן בְּיַד אוּמָּה שְׁפָלָה, [2]וְלֹא בְּיַד אוּמָּה שְׁפָלָה, אֶלָּא בְּיַד בְּהֶמְתָּן שֶׁל אוּמָּה שְׁפָלָה׳״.

[3]וְנַקְדִּימוֹן בֶּן גּוּרְיוֹן לָא עֲבַד צְדָקָה? [4]וְהָתַנְיָא: ״אָמְרוּ עָלָיו עַל נַקְדִּימוֹן בֶּן גּוּרְיוֹן כְּשֶׁהָיָה יוֹצֵא מִבֵּיתוֹ לְבֵית הַמִּדְרָשׁ, [5]כְּלֵי מֵילָת הָיוּ [67A] מַצִּיעִין תַּחְתָּיו, [6]וּבָאִין עֲנִיִּים וּמְקַפְּלִין אוֹתָן מֵאַחֲרָיו״!

[7]אִיבָּעֵית אֵימָא: לִכְבוֹדוֹ הוּא דַּעֲבַד. [8]וְאִיבָּעֵית אֵימָא: [9]כִּדְבָעֵי לֵיהּ לְמֶיעֱבַד לָא עֲבַד, [10]כִּדְאָמְרִי אֱינָשֵׁי: לְפוּם גַּמְלָא שִׁיחֲנָא.

LITERAL TRANSLATION

of God, no nation or tongue has power over them. [1]But when they do not act in accordance with the will of God, He delivers them into the hand of a lowly nation, [2]and not [only] into the hand of a lowly nation, but into the hand of the animal of a lowly nation.'"

[3]But did not Nakdimon ben Guryon perform acts of charity? [4]But surely it was taught: "They said about Nakdimon ben Guryon that when he used to go out of his house to the Academy, [5]fabrics of fine wool would be [67A] spread out beneath him, [6]and poor people would come and fold them up after him"!

[7]If you wish, say: He acted for his own glory. [8]And if you wish, say: [9]He did not act as he should have acted, [10]as people say: According to the camel is the load.

RASHI

ערביים — קרי אומה שפלה, שׁשוכני אהלים הם במדבר. **מציעין תחתיו** — תחת רגליו להלך עליהם. **לפום גמלא שיחנא** — לפי כח הגמל יטעינוהו משא.

NOTES

statement that when the people of Israel do not act in accordance with God's will, He hands them over to a lowly nation. How does that situation reflect the good fortune of Israel?

Maharsha and *Maharal* explain that both the elevation of the people of Israel above all other nations when they comply with God's will, and their degradation below all other peoples when they rebel against Him, testify to the unique relationship between God and Israel, for they both bear witness to the special divine providence that controls the destiny of the Jewish people.

בְּיַד אוּמָּה שְׁפָלָה Into the hand of a lowly nation. In order to reconcile the statement that God hands His people over to lowly nations with other Talmudic passages which state otherwise, *Rabbi Ya'akov Emden* suggests that when the people of Israel as a whole are handed over to the nations of the world, they are handed over only to mighty nations, but when individual members of the people of Israel are made subordinate to other peoples, they are made dependent upon the members of lowly nations.

לִכְבוֹדוֹ הוּא דַּעֲבַד He acted for his own glory. It is taught elsewhere in a Baraita (*Pesaḥim* 8a) that a person is rewarded for giving charity, even if he makes his donation for some ulterior motive — for example, so that his son may recover from an illness. How, then, can our Gemara argue that Nakdimon was liable for punishment because he did not make his charitable contributions for the sake of the poor, but only for his own glory?

Maharsha explains that giving charity for one's personal glory is worse than giving it for other ulterior motives. *Ḥafetz Ḥayyim* understands our passage in the light of the Gemara's statement (*Menaḥot* 41a) that when God is angry,

TRANSLATION AND COMMENTARY

תַּנְיָא [1]Another Baraita dealing with the desperate situation of Nakdimon's daughter **taught** as follows: **"Rabbi Elazar the son of Rabbi Tzadok said: [2]May I not witness the consolation** of the people of Israel, **if I did not see** Nakdimon's daughter **gathering barley from between the hooves of horses in Akko. [3]I applied to her the verse** [Song of Songs 1:8] which says: **'If you do not know, you fairest among women, go your way forth by the footsteps of the flock, and feed your kids beside the shepherds' tents.' [4]Do not read** the word **'your kids** [גְּדִיּוֹתַיִךְ],' with the letter dalet, as it is written, [5]**but rather** read the word as if it contained the letter vav as **'your bodies** [גְּוִיּוֹתַיִךְ].' By changing a single letter of the word an important moral lesson may be derived from the verse: If you do not observe the commandments of the Torah, Israel, you will be forced to go forth in the footsteps of the animals and feed yourselves ['your bodies'] on the grains of barley that you find between their hooves."

אָמַר רַב שֶׁמֶן בַּר אַבָּא [6]The Gemara now records additional regulations regarding the manner in which a woman's dowry is recorded in her ketubah. **Rav Shemen bar Abba said in the name of Rabbi Yoḥanan: [7]If** a woman **brings** her husband nuggets of **gold** as her dowry, the gold **is assessed and is** recorded in her ketubah in accordance **with its** assessed **value.**

מֵיתִיבֵי [8]**An objection was raised** against Rabbi Yoḥanan's ruling from the following Baraita, which stated: "Regarding the manner in which a woman's dowry is recorded in her ketubah, **gold** nuggets **are** treated **like utensils."** The Gemara asks: [9]**Does not** the Baraita mean to say that gold nuggets **are** treated **like silver utensils, which wear out** over time? If a woman brings a dowry of silver utensils, one-fifth less than the assessed value of the utensils is recorded in her ketubah, because such utensils wear out. Now, if the Baraita rules that gold nuggets are similar to silver utensils, it follows that they too should be recorded in a woman's

LITERAL TRANSLATION

[1]It was taught: "Rabbi Elazar the son of Rabbi Tzadok said: [2]May I [not] see the consolation [of Zion] if I did not see her gathering barley from between the hooves of horses in Akko. [3]I applied to her this verse: 'If you do not know, you fairest among women, go your way forth by the footsteps of the flock, and feed your kids [beside the shepherds' tents]. [4]Do not read 'your kids,' [5]but 'your bodies.'" [6]Rav Shemen bar Abba said in the name of Rabbi Yoḥanan: [7][If] she brought him gold, we assess it, and it is as its value. [8]They raised an objection: "Gold is like utensils." [9]Is it not like silver utensils,

[1]תַּנְיָא: ״אָמַר רַבִּי אֶלְעָזָר בְּרַבִּי צָדוֹק: [2]אֶרְאֶה בְּנֶחָמָה אִם לֹא רְאִיתִיהָ שֶׁהָיְתָה מְלַקֶּטֶת שְׂעוֹרִים מִבֵּין טַלְפֵי סוּסִים בְּעַכּוֹ. [3]קָרָאתִי עָלֶיהָ מִקְרָא זֶה: ׳אִם לֹא תֵדְעִי לָךְ, הַיָּפָה בַּנָּשִׁים, צְאִי לָךְ בְּעִקְבֵי הַצֹּאן, וּרְעִי אֶת גְּדִיּוֹתַיִךְ׳. [4]אַל תִּקְרֵי ׳גְּדִיּוֹתַיִךְ׳, [5]אֶלָּא ״גְּוִיּוֹתַיִךְ׳״. [6]אָמַר רַב שֶׁמֶן בַּר אַבָּא אָמַר רַבִּי יוֹחָנָן: [7]הִכְנִיסָה לוֹ זָהָב, שָׁמִין אוֹתוֹ, וַהֲרֵי הוּא כְּשָׁוְויוֹ. [8]מֵיתִיבֵי: ״הַזָּהָב הֲרֵי הוּא כְּכֵלִים״. [9]מַאי לָאו כְּכֵלִים שֶׁל

RASHI

אם לא תדעי – אם לא תתני לב כנסת ישראל לשמור את התורה, ״צאי לך וגו׳״ – סופך לצאת בעקבי הצאן ולרעות את גדיותיך. **זהב** – חתיכות זהב. **והרי הוא כשוויו** – לא יוסיף שליש ולא יפחות חומש. **זהב הרי הוא ככלים** – זהב שבור הרי הוא ככלים ומפרש ואזיל מאי ״כלים״.

NOTES

punishments are meted out for even slight infractions, which in other times would go unpunished. Thus Nakdimon, who lived during the period of the destruction of the Second Temple, when God's anger against His people came to the fore, was not saved by his charitable activities, for they were tainted by his desire for personal glory.

אַל תִּקְרֵי ׳גְּדִיּוֹתַיִךְ׳ **Do not read "your kids."** *Ritva* explains that the Gemara understands that Scripture used the expression "your kids" as a euphemistic substitute for the expression "your bodies." *Ḥokhmat Manoaḥ* explains that the homiletical interpretation of the verse is based on the rule of *atbaḥ*, according to which one letter (in this case the letter vav of the word גְּוִיּוֹתַיִךְ) may be exchanged for another letter (in this case the letter dalet of the word גְּדִיּוֹתַיִךְ), when the sum of the numerical values of the two letters is ten or a hundred (the numerical value of vav is six, and that of dalet is four). It may also be suggested that according to the Midrashic interpretation of the verse, the word רְעִי — "feed" — is understood as having the meaning of another word with the same spelling, "dung."

הִכְנִיסָה לוֹ זָהָב **If she brought him gold.** Our commentary follows *Rashi,* who explains that Rabbi Yoḥanan's ruling that gold "is as its value" refers to nuggets of gold, which are used neither as ornaments nor as currency. Since they have no day-to-day use, they do not depreciate in value as a result of wear, and are therefore recorded in a woman's ketubah in accordance with their assessed value. According to *Rabbenu Ḥananel* (cited by *Tosafot*), Rabbi Yoḥanan's ruling refers to gold ornaments. Such ornaments are recorded in a woman's ketubah in accordance with their assessed value, because they do not depreciate with wear. The Baraita teaches that they are like other gold utensils, for example, cups or plates, which do not depreciate in value as a result of use because they are not used frequently.

כֵּלִים שֶׁל כֶּסֶף, דְּפָחְתִי **Silver utensils that wear out.** *Rashi* explained above (66a), that when a woman brought her

SAGES

רַבִּי אֶלְעָזָר בְּרַבִּי צָדוֹק **Rabbi Elazar the son of Rabbi Tzadok.** He lived at the time of the destruction of the Temple, and was the son of a Sage of the previous generation who was famous for his piety and many fasts, in addition to being one of the important priests in the Temple. The family of Rabbi Tzadok were extremely important to the Sages, and Rabban Yoḥanan Ben Zakkai tried to save them when the Temple was destroyed. Rabbi Elazar the son of Rabbi Tzadok was one of the friends of the Nasi, Rabban Gamliel of Yavneh, and was active in the Great Assembly of Sages that met in Yavneh. His teachings and personal memories are found in many places in the Mishnah among the important testimonies of the Sages. He was apparently a merchant by profession, and his righteous behavior and piety are regarded in the Talmud as exemplary. He appears to have lived a long life and was active for many years. There were two Sages of this name, and the second of them was one of the last of the Tannaim, a member of the generation of Rabbi Yehudah HaNasi.

רַב שֶׁמֶן בַּר אַבָּא **Rabbi Shemen bar Abba.** This is Rav Shemen bar Abba the Priest (Shemen is a nickname for Shimeon), who belonged to the second generation of Amoraim of Eretz Israel. Rav Shemen bar Abba was born in Babylonia and was a student of Shmuel's there. But he immigrated to Eretz Israel while still a young man and was privileged to become a student of Rabbi Ḥanina. However, he was mainly the close disciple of Rabbi Yoḥanan, whom he served with particular affection. Much has been said in praise of his great righteousness and wisdom. Nevertheless his life was extremely hard, and the Biblical saying was applied to him, "To the wise there is no bread," not only because of his poverty but also because as a result of all his vicissitudes, Rabbi Yoḥanan did not manage to ordain him, though he was certainly one of the greatest scholars of his generation.

It is mentioned that Rav Shemen bar Abba married the

כֶּסֶף, דְּפָחֲתֵי? ¹לָא, כִּכְלִים שֶׁל זָהָב, דְּלָא פָּחֲתֵי. ²אִם כֵּן, "כִּכְלָיו" מִיבָּעֵי לֵיהּ! ³וְעוֹד, תַּנְיָא: "זָהָב הֲרֵי הוּא כְּכֵלִים. ⁴דִּינָרֵי זָהָב הֲרֵי הֵן כִּכְסָפִים. ⁵רַבָּן שִׁמְעוֹן בֶּן גַּמְלִיאֵל אוֹמֵר: בְּמָקוֹם שֶׁנָּהֲגוּ שֶׁלֹּא לְפוֹרְטָן, ⁶שָׁמִין אוֹתָן, וַהֲרֵי הֵן בְּשָׁוְויֵהֶן". ⁷רַבָּן שִׁמְעוֹן בֶּן גַּמְלִיאֵל אַהַיָּיא? ⁸אִילֵימָא אַסֵּיפָא, מִכְּלָל דְּתַנָּא קַמָּא סָבַר אֲפִילּוּ בְּמָקוֹם שֶׁנָּהֲגוּ שֶׁלֹּא לְפוֹרְטָן. ⁹הָא לָא נָפְקִי! ¹⁰אֶלָּא לָאו אַרֵישָׁא, ¹¹וְהָכִי קָאָמַר:

LITERAL TRANSLATION

that wear out?

[1] No, it is like gold utensils, that do not wear out.

[2] If so, it should have [stated]: "Like utensils [made] of it"! [3] Moreover, it was taught: "Gold is like utensils. [4] Gold dinarim are like money. [5] Rabban Shimon ben Gamliel says: In a place where it is customary not to change them, [6] we assess them, and they are as their value." [7] To which [clause] is Rabban Shimon ben Gamliel [referring]? [8] If we say to the last clause, [this proves] by implication that the first Tanna maintains [that they are like money] even in a place where it is customary not to change them. [9] [But] surely they do not circulate! [10] Rather [must he] not [be referring] to the first clause, [11] and this is what he said:

TRANSLATION AND COMMENTARY

ketubah at less than their assessed value, and this contradicts the ruling of Rabbi Yoḥanan!

לָא [1] The Gemara rebuts this objection: **No,** the Baraita means to say that gold nuggets **are** treated **like gold utensils, which do not wear out.** Just as gold utensils are recorded in a woman's ketubah at their assessed value, since they do not depreciate as a result of wear, so too are gold nuggets recorded in a woman's ketubah at their assessed value, in accordance with the ruling of Rabbi Yoḥanan.

אִם כֵּן [2] The Gemara now challenges this interpretation of the Baraita: But **if it is true** that the Baraita means to liken gold nuggets to gold utensils, **it should have stated** explicitly: "Gold nuggets are treated **like utensils made of** the same material"! By changing one letter of one word (כֵּלָיו rather than כֵּלִים), the Baraita could have made it clear that gold nuggets are like gold utensils, which are recorded in a woman's ketubah at their assessed value, rather than like silver utensils, which are recorded at less than their assessed value. [3] **Moreover, it was taught** in another Baraita: "Regarding the manner in which a woman's dowry is recorded in her ketubah, **gold** nuggets **are** treated **like utensils** [what sort of utensils will be explained below]. [4] **Gold dinarim are** treated **like money,** so that a sum fifty percent greater than the amount his wife has actually brought into the marriage is recorded in her ketubah. [5] **Rabban Shimon ben Gamliel says: In a place where it is customary not to change** the gold dinarim that a woman brings as her dowry into silver or copper coins so that her husband can use them in business (silver and copper coins, being much less valuable, circulate much more easily than gold coins), [6] **an assessment is made and** the dowry is recorded in the woman's ketubah in accordance **with its** assessed **value,** no more and no less." The Gemara first seeks to clarify the position of Rabban Shimon ben Gamliel, and asks: [7] When **Rabban Shimon ben Gamliel** says that an assessment is made and the dowry is recorded in the woman's ketubah at its assessed value, **to which** ruling of the anonymous first Tanna is he referring? To his first ruling regarding gold nuggets or to his second ruling regarding gold dinarim? [8] **If you say** that he is referring **to the** first Tanna's **second** ruling, that gold dinarim are treated like money, then surely **this proves by implication that the first Tanna maintains that they are like money.** Hence her husband records in her ketubah a sum greater than the amount she has actually brought into the marriage. This is true **even where it is customary not to change** the gold dinarim into smaller silver and copper coins. [9] **But surely** this cannot be the position of the first Tanna, because the money the woman brings into the marriage **does not circulate!** [10] **Rather,** says the Gemara, Rabban Shimon ben Gamliel **must have been referring to the** first Tanna's **first ruling,** that gold nuggets are treated like utensils, [11] **and this is what** the Baraita **said: Gold** nuggets **are** treated

RASHI

דינרי זהב – שהן טבועין. **הרי הן כבספים** – להוסיף שליש, לפי שמזומנים לשכר. **לפורטן** – שיש להן קלבת מטבע להחליפן תמיד בדינרי כסף ובפרוטות להוצאה ולסחורה. **דפחתי** – לפי שמשתמשין בהן, והוא מקבלן בפחות חומש. **אי נימא אסיפא** – אדינרי זהב.

NOTES

husband movable goods as her dowry, he would undertake to restore to her at the time that her ketubah became due a sum that was one-fifth less than their assessed value, because it was customary to inflate the value of those goods by twenty-five percent when assessing them. Many Rishonim (see *Rashba, Ritva,* and others) raise an objection against *Rashi* from our passage, since it implies that in the case of silver utensils the husband would undertake to restore to his wife a sum less than the assessed value of the utensils, because the woman would use the utensils during her marriage and thus they would wear out and depreciate in value.

daughters (one after the other) of his first teacher, Shmuel, after they were captured and redeemed in Eretz Israel. All of Rabbi Yoḥanan's students were colleagues of Rav Shemen, and members of the succeeding generation transmit teachings in his name. He had a son who was also a Sage, Rav Amram, and who transmitted teachings in his father's name.

BACKGROUND

כֵּלִים שֶׁל כֶּסֶף, דְּפָחֲתֵי Silver utensils, that wear out. Silver does not generally combine with other elements, although exposure to the hydrogen sulfide (H_2S) in the air may precipitate a chemical reaction, causing it to combine with the sulfur and form a thin black layer of silver sulfide (Ag_2S). This black layer can only be removed by scraping the silver away, which causes the utensil to decrease in weight and value.

TRANSLATION AND COMMENTARY

like utensils. [1]To **what** sort of **utensils** may the gold nuggets be likened? [2]To **silver utensils**, which are recorded in the woman's ketubah at less than their assessed value. This is the viewpoint of the anonymous first Tanna. [3]But **Rabban Shimon ben Gamliel** disagrees and **says:** Gold nuggets **are** treated **like gold dinarim in a place where it is customary that they not be changed** into smaller silver or copper coins. They are recorded in the woman's ketubah at their assessed value. Thus we see that the Tanna who maintains that gold nuggets are treated like utensils compares the nuggets to silver utensils and not to gold utensils.

לָא [4]The Gemara answers: **No,** gold nuggets may **in fact** be treated like gold utensils, and the second Baraita poses no difficulty, for Rabban Shimon ben Gamliel is referring **to the** first Tanna's **second** ruling, regarding gold dinarim. [5]**And the** Tannaim disagree about a case **where** gold dinarim **circulate with difficulty.** Because of their great value, gold dinarim are ordinarily not used in business transactions, but exceptions may be dictated by special circumstances. [6]**And it is about** the following point **that** the Tannaim **disagree:** [7]**One Sage,** the anonymous first Tanna of the Baraita, **maintains** that **since** the gold dinarim do in fact **circulate,** even if only with difficulty, the husband **must add to their** value when he records the dowry in the ketubah, just as he would have to add to a dowry made up of silver coins. [8]**And the other Sage,** Rabban Shimon ben Gamliel, says: **Since** the gold dinarim **only circulate with difficulty,** so that the husband cannot conduct his business with them in an orderly manner, [9]**he does not have to add to their** value when he records his wife's dowry in her ketubah.

אִיבָּעֵית אֵימָא [10]The Gemara now proposes an alternative interpretation of the Baraita. **If you wish,** you can **say** as follows: The objection raised earlier was based on the assumption that there is an anonymous first Tanna in the Baraita who disagrees with Rabban Shimon ben Gamliel. [11]In fact, however, **the entire Baraita** can be interpreted as reflecting the viewpoint of **Rabban Shimon ben Gamliel,** as the Gemara now explains: [12]The text of **the Baraita is defective** — a clause is missing from it — **and it should read as follows:** [13]**"Gold** nuggets **are** treated **like utensils** made of gold. [14]**Gold dinarim are** treated **like money,** so that the husband records in his wife's ketubah a sum that is fifty percent greater than the amount his wife has actually brought into the marriage. The Gemara now cites the crucial clause that was omitted from the Baraita: [15]**When does this** last ruling that gold dinarim are treated like money **apply?** [16]**Where it is customary to change** gold dinarim into smaller coins. [17]**But where it is customary not to change** gold dinarim into coins that circulate more easily, [18]**an assessment is made and** the dowry is recorded in the woman's ketubah at **its** assessed **value.** [19]**This is the opinion of Rabban Shimon ben Gamliel, for Rabban Shimon ben Gamliel says:** [20]**Where it is customary not to change** gold dinarim into coins that circulate more easily, [21]**an assessment is**

[1]זָהָב הֲרֵי הוּא כְּכֵלִים. מַאי כֵּלִים? [2]כֵּלִים שֶׁל כֶּסֶף. [3]רַבָּן שִׁמְעוֹן בֶּן גַּמְלִיאֵל אוֹמֵר: הֲרֵי הוּא כְּדִינָרִין שֶׁל זָהָב בְּמָקוֹם שֶׁנָּהֲגוּ שֶׁלֹּא לְפוֹרְטָן.

[4]לָא, לְעוֹלָם אַסֵּיפָא, [5]וּדְנָפְקִי עַל יְדֵי הַדְּחָק. [6]וּבְהָא קָמִיפַּלְגִי: [7]מָר סָבַר: כֵּיוָן דְּנָפְקִי, מַשְׁבְּחִינַן לַהּ. [8]וּמָר סָבַר: כֵּיוָן דְּלָא נָפְקִי אֶלָּא עַל יְדֵי הַדְּחָק, [9]לָא מַשְׁבְּחִינַן לַהּ.

[10]אִיבָּעֵית אֵימָא: [11]כּוּלָּהּ רַבָּן שִׁמְעוֹן בֶּן גַּמְלִיאֵל הִיא, [12]וְחַסּוּרֵי מִיחַסְּרָא, וְהָכִי קָתָנֵי: [13]"זָהָב הֲרֵי הוּא כְּכֵלִים. [14]דִּינָרֵי זָהָב הֲרֵי הֵן כִּכְסָפִים. [15]בַּמֶּה דְּבָרִים אֲמוּרִים? [16]בְּמָקוֹם שֶׁנָּהֲגוּ לְפוֹרְטָן. [17]אֲבָל בְּמָקוֹם שֶׁנָּהֲגוּ שֶׁלֹּא לְפוֹרְטָן, [18]שָׁמִין אוֹתָם, וַהֲרֵי הֵן בְּשָׁוְויֵהֶן. [19]דִּבְרֵי רַבָּן שִׁמְעוֹן בֶּן גַּמְלִיאֵל, שֶׁרַבָּן שִׁמְעוֹן בֶּן גַּמְלִיאֵל אוֹמֵר: [20]בְּמָקוֹם שֶׁנָּהֲגוּ שֶׁלֹּא לְפוֹרְטָן, [21]שָׁמִין אוֹתָם, וַהֲרֵי הֵן בְּשָׁוְויֵהֶן".

LITERAL TRANSLATION

Gold is like utensils. [1]What utensils? [2]Silver utensils. [3]Rabban Shimon ben Gamliel says: It is like gold dinarim in a place where it is customary not to change them.

[4]No, in fact [he is referring] to the last clause, [5]and where they circulate with difficulty. [6]And [it is] about this [that] they disagree: [7]One [Sage] maintains: Since they circulate, we add to them. [8]And one [Sage] maintains: Since they only circulate with difficulty, [9]we do not add to them.

[10]If you wish say: [11]All of it is Rabban Shimon ben Gamliel, [12]and [the Baraita] is defective, and it teaches as follows: [13]"Gold is like utensils. [14]Gold dinarim are like money. [15]In what [case] are these things said? [16]In a place where it is customary to change them. [17]But in a place where it is customary not to change them, we assess them, [18]and they are as their value. [19][These are] the words of Rabban Shimon ben Gamliel, for Rabban Shimon ben Gamliel says: [20]In a place where it is customary not to change them, [21]we assess them and they are as their value."

TRANSLATION AND COMMENTARY

made and the dowry is recorded in accordance with its assessed value."

מִכָּל מָקוֹם [1]The Gemara continues: Granted that the second Baraita can be reconciled with the viewpoint that gold nuggets are treated like gold utensils, nevertheless a difficulty **still** remains, for if the Baraita had meant to say that gold nuggets are treated like gold utensils, **it should have stated** explicitly: "Gold nuggets are treated **like utensils** made **of** the same material"!

קַשְׁיָא [2]The Gemara answers: If it is true that gold nuggets are treated like gold utensils, the formulation of the Baraita **is** indeed **difficult** to understand.

אִיבָּעֵית אֵימָא [3]The Gemara now offers another refutation of the objection raised against Rabbi Yoḥanan. **If you wish,** you can **say** that the Baraita does indeed teach that gold is treated like silver utensils that depreciate with the passage of time and are therefore recorded in a woman's ketubah at one-fifth less than their assessed value. Nevertheless the Baraita does not contradict Rabbi Yoḥanan's ruling that gold is assessed and recorded in the woman's ketubah at its assessed value. For Rabbi Yoḥanan was referring to large gold nuggets, which are recorded in a woman's ketubah in accordance with their assessed value, [4]whereas **what we are dealing with here** in the Baraita **are broken nuggets of gold,** which do indeed wear out over time and are therefore recorded in a woman's ketubah at less than their assessed value.

רַב אַשִׁי אֲמַר [5]**Rav Ashi said:** Alternatively, it can be argued that the Baraita is referring **to gold leaf,** which also wears out.

אָמַר רַבִּי יַנַּאי [6]**Rabbi Yannai said: Perfumes from Antioch are** treated **like money,** and are recorded in the ketubah at a sum fifty percent greater than their actual value. Since these perfumes were a commodity with which the husband could conduct business and earn a profit, he would accept liability for an addition to a dowry consisting of such merchandise.

אָמַר רַבִּי שְׁמוּאֵל בַּר נַחְמָנִי [7]**Rabbi Shmuel bar Naḥmani said in the name of Rabbi Yoḥanan:** [8]If **a woman** brings her husband **Arabian camels** as her dowry, she is entitled to **collect her dowry,** when her ketubah

[1]מִכָּל מָקוֹם, ״כְּכֵלָיו״ מִיבָּעֵי לֵיהּ!
[2]קַשְׁיָא.
[3]אִיבָּעֵית אֵימָא: הָכָא בְּמַאי עָסְקִינַן? [4]בְּדַהֲבָא פְּרִיכָא.
[5]רַב אַשִׁי אֲמַר: בִּמְמָלָא.
[6]אָמַר רַבִּי יַנַּאי: בְּשָׂמִים שֶׁל אַנְטוֹכְיָא הֲרֵי הֵן כִּכְסָפִים.
[7]אָמַר רַבִּי שְׁמוּאֵל בַּר נַחְמָנִי אָמַר רַבִּי יוֹחָנָן: [8]גְּמַלִּים שֶׁל עֲרַבְיָא אִשָּׁה גּוֹבָה פַּרְנָא מֵהֶם.

LITERAL TRANSLATION

[1]Nevertheless, it should have [stated]: "Like utensils [made] of it"!
[2]It is difficult.
[3]If you wish, say: With what are we dealing here? [4]With broken [pieces of] gold.
[5]Rav Ashi said: With gold leaf.
[6]Rabbi Yannai said: Perfumes of Antioch are like money.
[7]Rabbi Shmuel bar Naḥmani said in the name of Rabbi Yoḥanan: [8]A woman collects her dowry from Arabian camels.

RASHI

ואיבעית אימא — ככלים של כסף דפחתי, ולא תקשי לרבי יוחנן, דכי אמר רבי יוחנן בגרוטאות גדולות, ומתניתין בדהבא פריכא: גרוטאות דקות שנופל מהן כשממשמשין בהן. **בממלא** — דק דק של זהב שקורין *פלאל״א. **בשמים של אנטוכיא** — הוא עיקר סחורתן, ואשה שהכניסה לבעלה שום מהם הרי הן ככספים להוסיף שליש. **פרנא** — ריוח שליש.

NOTES

דַּהֲבָא פְּרִיכָא **Broken pieces of gold.** According to *Rashi,* the Gemara answers that the Baraita is referring to small nuggets of gold or to gold leaf, which do indeed lose value over time and are therefore treated like silver utensils which are recorded in the woman's ketubah at less than their assessed value. *Tosafot* explains that the Gemara's answer is that the Baraita is referring to broken pieces of gold or to gold ore, and it teaches that gold in those forms is treated like gold utensils, which are recorded in the woman's ketubah at their assessed value.

גְּמַלִּים שֶׁל עֲרַבְיָא **Arabian camels.** *Rashi* explains that the term *parna* (translated here as "dowry") used with respect to Arabian camels, garments of Be Mikhse, sacks of Rodya and ropes of Kimḥonya refers to the fifty percent addition to a wife's dowry that a husband would undertake to pay upon the dissolution of the marriage. If a woman brought her husband such items as her dowry, she would be entitled to collect her dowry when her ketubah became due together with a fifty percent additional sum, as if she had brought her husband a dowry of money. The last time that the term is used in our passage — with respect to the moneybags of Meḥoza — *Rashi* maintains that it refers to the ketubah in general. While the general rule is that a widow can collect her ketubah only from the immovable property of her husband's estate, Rava first thought that in Meḥoza a woman should be able to collect it from movable

HALAKHAH

גְּמַלִּים שֶׁל עֲרַבְיָא **Arabian camels.** "According to Talmudic law, a widow may collect her ketubah only from the landed property of her husband's estate. But with the decrease of landholding and the increase in the reliance upon movable goods for the repayment of debts, the Geonim enacted that a widow can also collect her ketubah from the movable

BACKGROUND

בְּשָׂמִים שֶׁל אַנְטוֹכְיָא **Perfumes of Antioch.** Apparently caravans used to reach the city of Antioch with spices from Arabia and the Far East. From Antioch (which was an important port) the spices would be shipped elsewhere, to Syria and Babylonia and overseas to Rome and other parts of Europe.

גְּמַלִּים שֶׁל עֲרַבְיָא **Arabian camels.** A number of Talmudic passages suggest that there were Jewish settlements in Arabia during the Talmudic period. The reference in the Gemara here implies that the Jews there earned their livelihood from the camel trade, like the native Arabs.

SAGES

רַבִּי שְׁמוּאֵל בַּר נַחְמָנִי **Rabbi Shmuel bar Naḥmani.** A Palestinian Amora of the second generation, Rabbi Shmuel bar Naḥmani was an important teacher of the Aggadah. He was a disciple of Rabbi Yonatan and transmitted many teachings in his name. He also studied with Rabbi Yehoshua ben Levi. He lived in Lydda in central Palestine.

LANGUAGE

פַּרְנָא **Dowry.** From the Greek φερνή, *pherne,* which means the dowry brought by the wife from her father's house. In Rabbinic literature, this word denotes any additional sum that the wife receives in excess of the standard ketubah payment.

LANGUAGE (RASHI)

פלאל״א* From the Old French *pailole,* meaning "slivers" or "pieces."

TRANSLATION AND COMMENTARY

becomes due, together with a fifty percent addition, for Arabian camels are also a commodity with which the husband can trade profitably.

אָמַר רַב פַּפִּי 1 Similarly, **Rav Pappi said:** If **a woman** brings her husband **garments from Be Mikhse** as her dowry, she is entitled to **collect her dowry** with an addition of one-half of its actual value, because such garments are business merchandise.

וַאֲמַר רַב פַּפִּי 2 **Rav Pappi said further:** If **a woman** brings her husband **sacks from Rodya or ropes from Kimḥonya** as her dowry, she is entitled to **collect her dowry** together with a fifty percent addition when her ketubah becomes due, for sacks from Rodya and ropes from Kimḥonya are also regarded as commodities with which the husband can conduct business and earn a profit.

אֲמַר רָבָא 3 **Rava said: At first I thought that a woman** is entitled to **collect her ketubah from the moneybags of Meḥoza. 4 What was my reasoning?** The Talmudic rule is that a widow may collect her ketubah only from the immovable property of her late husband's estate, because in general it is only upon property that cannot be carried away or spoiled that a woman relies to receive payment of her ketubah. Thus I thought that in Meḥoza a woman can also collect her ketubah from the cash portion of her husband's estate, because most Meḥozan Jews earned their livelihood from trade and not from real estate. 5 Therefore the women of Meḥoza would also **rely upon** their husbands' liquid assets for the recovery of the ketubah that was owed them. 6 But **when I saw that** the widows **would collect** payment of their ketubah from the cash portion of their husbands' estates, **and** then **go out** and look for a suitable venture in which to invest their money, **and when they found land** for sale, **they would buy** the land **with** their ketubah money, 7 I changed my mind and **said:** Even in a place like Meḥoza, women **rely** only **on land,** and therefore a woman may collect her ketubah only from immovable property.

1 אֲמַר רַב פַּפִּי: הָנֵי תּוֹתְבֵי דְּבֵי מִכְסֵי אִשָּׁה גּוֹבָה פָּרְנָא מֵהֶם. 2 וַאֲמַר רַב פַּפִּי: הָנֵי שַׂקֵּי דְּרוֹדְיָא וְאַשְׁלֵי דְּקִמְחוֹנְיָא אִשָּׁה גּוֹבָה פָּרְנָא מֵהֶן. 3 אֲמַר רָבָא: מֵרֵישׁ הֲוָה אָמִינָא הָנֵי אַרְנָקֵי דִּמְחוֹזָא אִשָּׁה גּוֹבָה פָּרְנָא מֵהֶם. 4 מַאי טַעֲמָא? 5 אַסְמַכְתַּיְיהוּ עֲלַיְיהוּ. 6 כֵּיוָן דַּחֲזַאי דְּשָׁקְלֵי לְהוּ וְנָפְקֵי, וְכִי מַשְׁכְּחֵי אַרְעָא, זַבְנֵי בְּהוּ, 7 אָמִינָא: אַסְמַכְתַּיְיהוּ אַאַרְעָא הוּא.

LITERAL TRANSLATION

1 Rav Pappi said: From the garments of Be Mikhse a woman collects her dowry.

2 And Rav Pappi said: From the sacks of Rodya and the ropes of Kimḥonya a woman collects her dowry.

3 Rava said: From the moneybags of Meḥoza at first I said [that] a woman collects her dowry. 4 What is the reason? 5 Their reliance is on them. 6 When I saw that they were taking them and going out, and when they found land, they would buy [it] with them, 7 I said: Their reliance is on land.

RASHI

תותבי דבי מכסי – שמלות של אותו מקום. **אשלי** – חבלים. **ארנקי דמחוזא** – כיסין מלאין מעות. **פרנא** – לזה שמעתי כתובה מנכסי יתומים, ולא אמרינן מטלטלי דיתמי לא משתעבדי לבעל חוב. **אסמכתייהו עלייהו** – וגביין מטלטלי כי הני, שהן להן במקום קרקעות, לפי שבעלי סחורה הם. **דשקלי להו** – הנשים האלמנות והגרושות שגובות כתובתן. **אארעא הוא** – ואין גובות אלא מן הקרקע מן היתומים.

BACKGROUND

תּוֹתְבֵי דְּבֵי מִכְסֵיי From the garments of Be Mikhse. This list shows that in those places (Be Mikhse, Rodya, and Kimḥonya) the people engaged in small manufacturing or trade and were not farmers, like most Jews at that time.

רוֹדְיָא Rodya. Some commentators maintain that רוֹדְיָא refers to the Greek island of Rhodes (Ῥόδος, *Rhodos*), while others explain that it was a Babylonian city.

LANGUAGE

תּוֹתְבֵי Garments. The Aramaic word תּוֹתְבָא is a translation of the Hebrew word שִׂמְלָה, meaning "clothing" or "garment." It usually refers to men's clothing.

NOTES

goods as well. Most Rishonim (from *Rav Natronai Gaon* to the disciples of *Ramban*) maintain that the term is used uniformly throughout the passage and refers to the woman's ketubah. The Amoraim ruled that a woman may collect her ketubah from Arabian camels, Be Mikhse garments and the like, because it had become common for people to earn their livelihood from trade in such merchandise, and they would rely on these assets for the recovery of their debts. A number of Rishonim explain these rulings as the basis for the Geonic enactment that a widow may collect her ketubah from the movable property of her husband's estate (see Halakhah).

אַרְנָקֵי דִּמְחוֹזָא The moneybags of Meḥoza. According to *Rashi,* Rava considered the possibility that the women of Meḥoza should be entitled to collect their ketubot from the money found in their husbands' moneybags. Since most Meḥozan Jews earned their livelihood from trade, the women should be entitled to collect their ketubot from the cash portion of their husbands' estates. *Meiri* maintains that Rava first thought that the Meḥozan women should be entitled to collect their ketubot from the moneybags themselves, for the Meḥozans used to trade in moneybags, just as the people of Be Mikhse used to trade in garments, and therefore people would rely on those assets for the recovery of their debts.

HALAKHAH

property of her husband's estate. This enactment was accepted in all places, and it became customary to include in the ketubah a clause stating that the amount of the ketubah payment could be collected from the husband's movable property. *Maggid Mishneh* and others argue that the Geonic enactment is based on the Talmudic ruling regarding Arabian camels. The Geonim extended this ruling so that all movable goods were to be treated like Arabian camels." (*Rambam, Sefer Nashim, Hilkhot Ishut* 16:7; *Shulḥan Arukh, Even HaEzer* 100:1.)

BACKGROUND

פָּסַק לְהַכְנִיסָהּ עֲרוּמָה If he undertook to take her in without clothing. The father used this expression to say that he would give his daughter nothing, and that all the obligations to provide for her needs, even her clothing, fell upon the husband.

LITERAL TRANSLATION

MISHNAH [1] [If] someone marries off his daughter without specifying, [2] he may not give her less than fifty zuz.

[3] [If] he undertook to take her in without clothing (lit., "naked"), the husband may not say: [4] "When I bring her into my house, I will clothe her with my clothing." [5] Rather, he must clothe her while she is still in her father's house.

משנה [1] הַמַּשִּׂיא אֶת בִּתּוֹ סְתָם, [2] לֹא יִפְחוֹת לָהּ מֵחֲמִשִּׁים זוּז.

[3] פָּסַק לְהַכְנִיסָהּ עֲרוּמָה, לֹא יֹאמַר הַבַּעַל: [4] "כְּשֶׁאַכְנִיסֶנָּה לְבֵיתִי, אֲכַסֶּנָּה בִּכְסוּתִי". [5] אֶלָּא מְכַסָּהּ וְעוֹדָהּ בְּבֵית אָבִיהָ.

TRANSLATION AND COMMENTARY

MISHNAH הַמַּשִּׂיא אֶת בִּתּוֹ סְתָם [1] It was stated earlier in the tractate (above, 52b) that a father is instructed to fit his daughter out, dress her appropriately, and give her a sizable dowry, so that prospective bridegrooms will be eager to marry her. There is no fixed amount which a father must give his daughter as her dowry. If the father commits himself to provide a dowry of a certain size, he must fulfill his commitment. **If he marries off his daughter without specifying** the amount of her dowry, [2] **he must give her** a dowry worth **not less than fifty zuz.**

פָּסַק [3] If the prospective son-in-law agreed **that he would accept** his bride **without any dowry at all, he may not say** later: [4] **"When I bring her into my house** after we are married **I will clothe her with clothing** that befits her dignity, in compliance with my marital obligation to provide my wife with clothing. But before that time I will not provide her with anything." [5] **Rather, he must clothe her** with clothing that befits her dignity **while she is still in her father's house,** so that she may enter her husband's house in a dignified manner.

NOTES

הַמַּשִּׂיא אֶת בִּתּוֹ סְתָם If someone marries off his daughter without specifying. *Rambam* (*Hilkhot Ishut* 20:1) explains the Mishnah's ruling as referring specifically to the father's obligation to provide his daughter with clothing. The father must provide his daughter with at least as much clothing as the poorest man in Israel is obliged to provide his wife, which the Mishnah teaches us elsewhere (above, 64b) is valued at fifty zuz. According to *Rambam,* the Mishnah's ruling is limited to a case where the father is a poor man; but if the father is wealthy, it is fitting that he provide his daughter with a dowry in accordance with his wealth. *Shiltei Gibborim* writes that a wealthy man cannot be compelled to provide his daughter with a larger dowry. According to *Tur,* a wealthy person is required to give his daughter a dowry commensurate with his means.

אֲכַסֶּנָּה בִּכְסוּתִי I will clothe her with my clothing. The Jerusalem Talmud notes that the Mishnah's ruling seems to be contradicted by the Tosefta (6:7), which states: "If someone marries off his daughter, and stipulates with his son-in-law that he must stand naked and dress his wife, we do not say that he must stand naked and dress her, but rather that he should dress her as befits her." Why does the Mishnah rule that the stipulation made between the father and his son-in-law is binding, whereas the Tosefta rules that the son-in-law is not bound by a similar stipulation?

The Jerusalem Talmud answers that the son-in-law's undertaking that he would stand naked in order to dress his wife in expensive clothing was not mere exaggeration intended to demonstrate his devotion to his wife. Thus the son-in-law is not required to go naked or to dress in rags in order that his wife may be able to dress expensively. But the stipulation discussed in our Mishnah was meant as a real stipulation, and therefore binds the son-in-law to provide his bride with clothing while she is still in her father's house.

Meiri infers from the Jerusalem Talmud's discussion that the husband's argument in the Mishnah, "When I bring her into my house I will clothe her with *my* clothing," should be understood as follows: "After she is married, I will clothe her with my own clothing and I myself will go naked or in rags."

Melekhet Shlomo understands the emphasis on *my* clothing differently: The husband argues that if he clothes his wife only after she comes into his house, he will clothe her in accordance with his means and social standing. But if he clothes her while she is still in her father's house, he will dress her only in accordance with the father's means and social standing.

HALAKHAH

הַמַּשִּׂיא אֶת בִּתּוֹ סְתָם If someone marries off his daughter without specifying. "The Rabbis instructed that a person should provide his daughter with a dowry so that she might find a suitable husband. If someone marries off his daughter without specifying otherwise, he must provide her with at least as much clothing as the wife of the poorest person in Israel is entitled to receive from her husband. This ruling applies only if the father is himself a poor man; but if he is wealthy, it is fitting that he provide her with a dowry commensurate with his means." (*Rambam, Sefer Nashim, Hilkhot Ishut* 20:1; *Shulḥan Arukh, Even HaEzer* 58:1.)

פָּסַק לְהַכְנִיסָהּ עֲרוּמָה If he undertook to take her in without clothing. "If the bride's father stipulates that he is giving his daughter in marriage without any dowry at all, the husband may not say that he will clothe his wife only after she is brought into his house, but rather he must clothe her while she is still in her father's home." (*Rambam, Sefer Nashim, Hilkhot Ishut* 20:2; *Shulḥan Arukh, Even HaEzer* 58:2.)

TRANSLATION AND COMMENTARY

וְכֵן [1] **And similarly, if** a charity administrator **marries off an orphan girl,** providing her with a dowry from charity funds, **he must give her** a dowry worth **not less than fifty zuz.** [2] **If there is** enough money **in the purse, she must be supported** and given a dowry from those funds **in accordance with her dignity.**

GEMARA אָמַר אַבַּיֵי [3] The Gemara first clarifies what the Mishnah meant when it spoke of fifty zuz. **Abaye said:** The fifty zuz mentioned in the Mishnah are **fifty provincial zuz,** each provincial zuz being worth one-eighth of a Tyrian zuz. During the time of the Mishnah and the Talmud, a number of different coins shared the same name, because two different systems of coinage were in use: (1) Tyrian money, which was roughly equivalent to the coins mentioned in the Torah, and according to which the values mentioned in the Torah were calculated. (2) Provincial money, which had units bearing the same names as Tyrian coins, but whose value was only one-eighth of that of the corresponding Tyrian money. According to Abaye, the fifty zuz that the father is required to give his daughter as her dowry are calculated in provincial zuz. [4] **How do we know this? From what is taught in the last clause** of the Mishnah, which stated: [5] **"If there is** enough money **in the purse, she must be supported** and given a dowry from those funds **in accordance with her dignity."** [6] **And** regarding this passage **we asked: What is** the meaning here of **"the purse"?** [7] And **Raḥavah said:** The Mishnah is referring to **the charity purse.** If there is extra money in the charity fund, the orphan girl is given a larger dowry from that fund. [8] **Now if it should enter your mind** to say that when the Mishnah speaks of fifty zuz, it means **fifty** Tyrian **zuz literally,** there is a difficulty; [9] for **if there were extra** money **in the** charity **purse, how much** more **would** the orphan girl **be given?** Surely fifty Tyrian zuz (which are the equivalent of four hundred provincial zuz) are a substantial amount. [10] **Rather, infer from this** that when the Mishnah speaks of fifty zuz, it means **fifty provincial zuz.**

תָּנוּ רַבָּנַן [11] **Our Rabbis taught** a Baraita, which stated: **"If an orphan boy and an orphan girl came** before the charity administrators **for support,** and there is not enough money in the charity fund to provide for

[1] וְכֵן הַמַּשִּׂיא אֶת הַיְּתוֹמָה, לֹא יִפְחוֹת לָהּ מֵחֲמִשִּׁים זוּז. [2] אִם יֵשׁ בַּכִּיס, מְפַרְנְסִין אוֹתָהּ לְפִי כְבוֹדָהּ.

גמרא [3] אָמַר אַבַּיֵי: חֲמִשִּׁים זוּזֵי פְּשִׁיטֵי. [4] מִמַּאי? מִדְּקָתָנֵי סֵיפָא: [5] "אִם יֵשׁ בַּכִּיס, מְפַרְנְסִין אוֹתָהּ לְפִי כְבוֹדָהּ". [6] וְאָמְרִינַן: מַאי "כִּיס"? [7] אָמַר רַחֲבָה: אַרְנָקִי שֶׁל צְדָקָה. [8] וְאִי סָלְקָא דַעְתִּין חֲמִשִּׁים זוּזֵי מַמָּשׁ, [9] אִם יֵשׁ בַּכִּיס כַּמָּה יָהֲבִינַן לָהּ? [10] אֶלָּא שְׁמַע מִינָּהּ: חֲמִשִּׁים זוּזֵי פְּשִׁיטֵי.

[11] תָּנוּ רַבָּנַן: "יָתוֹם וִיתוֹמָה

LITERAL TRANSLATION

[1] And similarly, [if] someone marries off an orphan girl, he may not give her less than fifty zuz. [2] If there is [enough] in the purse, they support her in accordance with her dignity.

GEMARA [3] Abaye said: Fifty provincial (lit., "simple") zuz. From where [do we know this]? [4] From what [the Mishnah] teaches in the last clause: [5] "If there is [enough] in the purse, they support her in accordance with her dignity." [6] And we said: What is the purse? [7] Raḥavah said: The charity bag. [8] And if it were to enter our mind [that it means] the fifty zuz literally, [9] how much do we give her if there is [enough] in the purse? [10] Rather, deduce from this: Fifty provincial zuz.

[11] Our Rabbis taught: "[If] an orphan boy and an orphan girl

RASHI

משנה וכן המשיא את היתומה – גבאי צדקה.

גמרא זוזי פשיטי – זוזי מדינה שמונה מהן זוז צורי.

LANGUAGE

אַרְנָקִי **Moneybags.** The source of this word is the Greek Αρνακις, *arnakis*, a type of leather garment. In Rabbinic literature the word usually means "purse" or "moneybag" (perhaps made of leather).

NOTES

אִם יֵשׁ בַּכִּיס **If there is enough in the purse.** The Jerusalem Talmud records an Amoraic dispute about whether or not the charity administrators must borrow money if there is not enough in the charity fund to provide the orphan girl with even a minimal dowry. *Rav Hai Gaon* was in doubt about how to rule in such a situation (see Halakhah).

HALAKHAH

הַמַּשִּׂיא אֶת הַיְּתוֹמָה **If someone marries off an orphan girl.** "When the charity administrators marry off an orphan girl, they must provide her with a dowry worth not less than fifty zuz (i.e., fifty provincial zuz, which are the equivalent of six-and-a-quarter Tyrian zuz). If there is extra money in the charity coffers, the orphan girl should be given a larger dowry in accordance with her dignity. The amount specified here applied during the Talmudic period, but today an orphan girl is given a dowry in accordance with local custom. If there is not enough money in the charity fund to provide her with a minimal dowry, the charity administrators must borrow money for that purpose, but they are not required to borrow money in order to provide her with a larger dowry than is customary (*Shakh* in the name of *Ran*)." (*Rambam, Sefer Zeraim, Hilkhot Mattenot Aniyyim* 8:16; *Shulḥan Arukh, Yoreh De'ah* 250:2; see also 253:2.)

יָתוֹם וִיתוֹמָה שֶׁבָּאוּ לְהִתְפַּרְנֵס **If an orphan boy and an orphan girl came to be supported.** "If a man and a

TRANSLATION AND COMMENTARY

both of them, [1]**we** first provide **support** for **the orphan girl, and** only **afterwards** do **we** provide **support** for **the orphan boy** with the money that is left, or with what will be collected in the future. [2]The girl is given precedence, **because it is a man's way to go around at the doors begging** for charity, [3]**but it is not a woman's way to go around** from door to door begging. [4]Similarly, **if an orphan boy and an orphan girl** [67B] **have come** before the charity administrators, each of them asking for financial assistance **to be married off,** and there is not enough money to provide for both of them, [5]**we** first use the available funds to **marry off the orphan girl, and** only **afterwards** do **we marry off the orphan boy** with what remains. [6]The orphan girl is married off first, **because the humiliation** that **a** single **woman** suffers **is greater than** the humiliation suffered by **an** unmarried **man."**

תָּנוּ רַבָּנַן [7]Our Rabbis taught a related Baraita: **"If an orphan boy comes** asking for financial help **to be married off, we** first provide him with all of his basic needs. **We rent a house for him, and prepare a bed**

שֶׁבָּאוּ לְהִתְפַּרְנֵס״, [1]מְפַרְנְסִין אֶת הַיְּתוֹמָה, וְאַחַר כָּךְ מְפַרְנְסִין אֶת הַיָּתוֹם, [2]מִפְּנֵי שֶׁהָאִישׁ דַּרְכּוֹ לַחֲזוֹר עַל הַפְּתָחִים, [3]וְאֵין אִשָּׁה דַּרְכָּהּ לַחֲזוֹר. [4]יָתוֹם וִיתוֹמָה [67B] שֶׁבָּאוּ לִינָּשֵׂא, [5]מַשִּׂיאִין אֶת הַיְּתוֹמָה וְאַחַר כָּךְ מַשִּׂיאִין אֶת הַיָּתוֹם, [6]מִפְּנֵי שֶׁבּוּשְׁתָּהּ שֶׁל אִשָּׁה מְרוּבָּה מִשֶּׁל אִישׁ״.
[7]תָּנוּ רַבָּנַן: ״יָתוֹם שֶׁבָּא לִישָּׂא, שׂוֹכְרִין לוֹ בַּיִת וּמַצִּיעִין לוֹ

LITERAL TRANSLATION

have come to be supported, [1]we support the orphan girl, and afterwards we support the orphan boy, [2]because it is a man's way to go around [begging] at the doors, [3]but it is not a woman's way to go around [in this manner]. [4][If] an orphan boy and an orphan girl [67B] have come to be married off, [5]we marry off the orphan girl and afterwards we marry off the orphan boy, [6]because a woman's shame is greater than a man's."
[7]Our Rabbis taught: "[If] an orphan boy has come to marry, we rent a house for him and prepare

RASHI

להתפרנס — מזונות של צדקה. **שבאו לינשא** — משל צדקה, דאמרינן לקמן: ״אשר יחסר לו״ — זו אשה.

NOTES

שֶׁבָּאוּ לְהִתְפַּרְנֵס **Have come to be supported.** Elsewhere (*Horayot* 13a), the Mishnah states: "A man is given precedence over a woman with respect to keeping him alive and restoring his lost property. A woman is given precedence over a man with respect to clothing her and redeeming her from captivity." *Rashba* (see also *Meiri*) concludes from this that our Baraita, which states that an orphan girl is given precedence over an orphan boy regarding support, must be referring to a case where the two orphans came asking for clothing. But if they came asking for maintenance, the orphan boy is given precedence over the orphan girl, for the Mishnah in *Horayot* states explicitly that a man is given precedence over a woman with respect to keeping him alive. But most authorities explain that our Baraita refers even to a case where the two orphans came asking for maintenance. *Rid* explains that the Mishnah in *Horayot* refers to a case where nobody can go out to beg for food — for example, when the choice must be made whether to feed a starving man or a starving woman found in the desert or the like. In such a case the man is given precedence, for he is under greater obligation with regard to the performance of the commandments. But our Baraita refers to a case where the one who is not given money from the charity fund can go out and beg for his food. In such a case an orphan girl is given precedence over an orphan boy, because she is too embarrassed to go begging at other people's doors. (*Bet Yosef* [*Yoreh De'ah* 251] demonstrates that this is *Rambam's* position as well.)

הָאִישׁ דַּרְכּוֹ לַחֲזוֹר **It is a man's way to go around.** *Meiri* suggests that the simple understanding of the Baraita's explanation that "it is a man's way to go around begging at the doors" supports the view that the Baraita is referring to a case where the two orphans came asking for maintenance (see previous note). The orphan girl is given precedence over the orphan boy because it is a man's way to go around begging for his food at other people's doors. According to those who maintain that the Baraita is referring to a case where the two orphans came asking for clothing, it means to say that the orphan girl is given precedence because it is a man's way to go around and find a way to earn enough for his clothing needs.

An entirely different explanation is cited in the name of the Geonim. It is not a woman's way to go around in search of a husband, and therefore if an orphan girl receives an offer of marriage, the charity managers must provide her with all her needs without delay, so that the bridegroom will

HALAKHAH

woman come before the charity administrators asking for food or clothing, and there is not enough money in the charity fund to provide for both of them, the woman is given precedence." (*Rambam, Sefer Zeraim, Hilkhot Mattenot Aniyyim* 8:15; *Shulḥan Arukh, Yoreh De'ah* 251:8.)

יָתוֹם וִיתוֹמָה שֶׁבָּאוּ לִינָּשֵׂא **If an orphan boy and an orphan girl have come to be married off.** "If an orphan boy and an orphan girl come before the charity administrators for support so that they may be married off, precedence is given to the orphan girl." (*Rambam, Sefer Zeraim, Hilkhot Mattenot Aniyyim* 8:16; *Shulḥan Arukh, Yoreh De'ah* 251:8.)

יָתוֹם שֶׁבָּא לִישָּׂא **If an orphan boy has come to marry.** "If an orphan boy comes before the charity administrators to be married off, they must rent a house for him, and prepare

TRANSLATION AND COMMENTARY

for him and all the other **household utensils** he needs, [1]and only **afterwards** do **we marry him off to a wife,** [2]**for the verses state** [Deuteronomy 15:7-8]: 'If there is a poor man among you... you shall open your hand wide to him, and shall surely lend him **sufficient for his need, that which is lacking to him.'** And the end of the last verse is to be explained as follows: [3]The expression **'sufficient for his need'** refers to **a house,** a person's primary need; [4]the expression **'that which is lacking'** refers to **a bed and a table,** a person's secondary needs; the expression [5]**'for him** [לוֹ]**'** refers to **a wife.** [6]**And similarly the verse says** [Genesis 2:18]: **'I will make for him** [לוֹ] **a helpmeet to him.'"**

תָּנוּ רַבָּנַן [7]Our Rabbis taught another Baraita, which expounds the verse in a different manner: "The expression **'sufficient for his need'** teaches us that **we are commanded to support** a poor man and provide him with his essential needs, **but we are not commanded to make him wealthy** and to provide him with luxuries. [8]But the expression **'that which is lacking to him'** teaches us that we are commanded to give a poor man **even a horse to ride upon and a servant to run before him,** if he was accustomed to such luxuries. Need is a relative concept. Thus, if a person was once wealthy but now is poor, so that he cannot afford a horse or a servant, he is entitled to receive his special needs from charity funds. [9]**The story is told about Hillel the Elder that he bought for a certain poor man from a respectable family a horse to ride upon and a servant to run before him.** [10]It once happened that Hillel **did not find a servant to run before** the poor man, **and** so Hillel **himself ran before him** a distance of **three miles,** so that the poor man should not feel that he was in need."

מִטָּה וְכָל כְּלֵי תַּשְׁמִישׁוֹ, [1]וְאַחַר כָּךְ מַשִּׂיאִין לוֹ אִשָּׁה, [2]שֶׁנֶּאֱמַר: ׳דֵּי מַחְסֹרוֹ, אֲשֶׁר יֶחְסַר לוֹ׳. [3]׳דֵּי מַחְסֹרוֹ׳ — זֶה הַבַּיִת. [4]׳אֲשֶׁר יֶחְסַר׳ — זֶה מִטָּה וְשֻׁלְחָן. [5]׳לוֹ׳ — זוֹ אִשָּׁה. [6]וְכֵן הוּא אוֹמֵר: ׳אֶעֱשֶׂה לּוֹ עֵזֶר כְּנֶגְדּוֹ׳״.

[7]תָּנוּ רַבָּנַן: ״׳דֵּי מַחְסֹרוֹ׳ — אַתָּה מְצוּוֶּה עָלָיו לְפַרְנְסוֹ, וְאִי אַתָּה מְצוּוֶּה עָלָיו לְעַשְּׁרוֹ. [8]׳אֲשֶׁר יֶחְסַר לוֹ׳ — אֲפִילּוּ סוּס לִרְכּוֹב עָלָיו וְעֶבֶד לָרוּץ לְפָנָיו. [9]אָמְרוּ עָלָיו עַל הִלֵּל הַזָּקֵן שֶׁלָּקַח לְעָנִי בֶּן טוֹבִים אֶחָד סוּס לִרְכּוֹב עָלָיו וְעֶבֶד לָרוּץ לְפָנָיו. [10]פַּעַם אַחַת לֹא מָצָא עֶבֶד לָרוּץ לְפָנָיו, וְרָץ לְפָנָיו שְׁלֹשָׁה מִילִין״.

LITERAL TRANSLATION

a bed and all his household utensils for him, [1]and afterwards we marry him off to a wife, [2]for it is said: 'Sufficient for his need, that which is lacking for him.' [3]'Sufficient for his need' — this is a house. [4]'That which is lacking' — this is a bed and a table. [5]'For him' — this is a wife. [6]And similarly it says: 'I will make for him a helpmeet to him.'"

[7]Our Rabbis taught: "'Sufficient for his need' — you are commanded to support him, but you are not commanded to make him wealthy. [8]'That which is lacking to him' — even a horse to ride upon and a servant to run before him. [9]They said about Hillel the Elder that he bought for a certain poor man from a respectable family a horse to ride upon and a servant to run before him. [10]Once he did not find a servant to run before him, and he [himself] ran before him three miles."

NOTES

not retract his offer. But there is no similar concern regarding an orphan boy, for it is a man's way to search for a wife, and if his first marriage proposal is unsuccessful, he can always find another wife. (The last two explanations seem to be based on the reading: "It is a man's way to go around," the expression "at the doors" being omitted.)

אֲפִילּוּ סוּס לִרְכּוֹב עָלָיו Even a horse to ride upon. *Talmidei Rabbenu Yonah* notes that this obligation to provide a poor man with a horse and a servant applies only in the case of someone who was once wealthy, for such a person is accustomed to such luxuries. The Geonim further restrict this regulation, arguing that the obligation to provide a once-wealthy man with a horse and a servant applies only if his present financial situation is not yet a matter of public knowledge. In such a case, the poor man must be provided with the luxuries to which he has always been accustomed, so that his present situation may not become known and cause him humiliation. But if everybody already knows that he is no longer wealthy, he is entitled to no more support than any other poor person.

רָץ לְפָנָיו שְׁלֹשָׁה מִילִין He ran before him three miles. We find elsewhere (*Bava Metzia* 30b) that a Torah scholar is exempt from the obligation to restore lost property to its rightful owner if fulfilling that obligation is considered undignified. *Rosh* (*Bava Metzia* 2:21) adds that a Torah scholar is forbidden to go beyond the letter of the law and

HALAKHAH

a bed and all other necessary household utensils for him, and afterwards they marry him off." (*Rambam, Sefer Zeraim, Hilkhot Mattenot Aniyyim* 7:4; *Shulhan Arukh, Yoreh De'ah* 250:1.)

״דֵּי מַחְסֹרוֹ״ "Sufficient for his need." "A poor man must be given charity in accordance with his needs: If he is hungry, he must be given food; if he has nothing to wear, he must be given clothing; if he lacks household utensils,

LANGUAGE

לִיטְרָא Pound. From the Greek λίτρα, *litra*, a type of coin, or a unit of weight (about 327 grams) or volume (less than 300 cc). The "pound of meat" mentioned here was very small, though expensive.

SAGES

רַבִּי נְחֶמְיָה Rav Neḥemyah. Regarding Rav Neḥemyah the Exilarch (or, according to manuscripts, "Rabbana," which was the title given to Sages of the family of the Exilarch), various details are recorded which are difficult to reconcile. According to one source, Rabbana Neḥemyah was the Exilarch's brother. From another source we learn that Rabbana Neḥemyah and Rabbana Ukva were members of the family of the great Amora, Rav, and studied with Rav Ḥisda. Chronologically, and also according to the list of Exilarchs dating from the Geonic period, it does not seem that Rabbana Neḥemyah was himself an Exilarch, but that he belonged to that family. The difficulty in explaining the long generation gap between the time of Rav Ḥisda and that of Rav Ashi can be resolved if we assume that Rabbana Neḥemyah lived to a great age, and take into consideration that even in his youth Rav Ashi was regarded as the foremost Sage of his generation. Another possibility is that this question was asked by the descendants of Rabbana Neḥemyah.

TRANSLATION AND COMMENTARY

תָּנוּ רַבָּנַן [1]**Our Rabbis taught** another Baraita illustrating the principle that a poor man is to be maintained from charity in the manner to which he is accustomed: **"It once happened that the people of Upper Galilee bought for a certain poor man from a respectable family from** the city of **Sepphoris a pound of meat every day."**

לִיטְרָא בָּשָׂר [2]The Gemara asks: **What is the novelty in** their buying **a pound of meat?** Is this an example of maintaining a poor man in an extravagant manner?

אָמַר רַב הוּנָא [3]**Rav Huna said:** The people of Upper Galilee provided the poor man with **a pound of fowl's meat,** an unusually expensive delicacy. [4]**And if you wish,** you can **say:** What the Baraita means is that **for the value of a pound** of silver the people of Upper Galilee bought the poor man **ordinary meat,** which is indeed an example of extravagance.

רַב אַשִׁי אָמַר [5]**Rav Ashi explained** the Baraita in yet another manner. The place where the incident took place **was a small village.** In order to provide the poor man with a pound of fresh meat every day, an animal had to be slaughtered; and because the local population was so small, buyers could not be found for all the meat; thus **every day** the better part of **an animal would go to waste on account of** the poor man.

הַהוּא דַּאֲתָא [6]It was related that **a certain man** once **came before Rabbi Neḥemyah** and asked for charity. Rabbi Neḥemyah **asked him: "On what** foods **do you dine?"** [7]The poor man **said to** Rabbi Neḥemyah: "I am used to eating **fat meat and old wine."** Thinking that this was inappropriate fare for a person supported by charity, Rabbi Neḥemyah said to him: [8]**"Are you willing to join me for** one of my regular meals of **lentils?"** [9]The poor man **joined him for lentils and,** not being accustomed to eating such food, **died** soon afterwards. [10]Rabbi Neḥemyah **commented: "Woe to him whom Neḥemyah killed."**

אַדְּרַבָּה [11]The Gemara objects: **On the contrary,** Rabbi Neḥemyah **should have said: "Woe to Neḥemyah who killed this man"!** He should have fed the poor man in the manner to which he was accustomed.

[1]תָּנוּ רַבָּנַן: "מַעֲשֶׂה בְּאַנְשֵׁי גָּלִיל הָעֶלְיוֹן שֶׁלָּקְחוּ לְעָנִי בֶּן טוֹבִים אֶחָד מִצִּיפּוֹרִי לִיטְרָא בָּשָׂר בְּכָל יוֹם". [2]לִיטְרָא בָּשָׂר מַאי רְבוּתָא? [3]אָמַר רַב הוּנָא: לִיטְרָא בָּשָׂר מִשֶּׁל עוֹפוֹת. [4]וְאִיבָּעֵית אֵימָא: בְּלִיטְרָא בָּשָׂר מַמָּשׁ. [5]רַב אַשִׁי אָמַר: הָתָם כְּפַר קָטָן הָיָה, בְּכָל יוֹמָא הֲוָה מַפְסְדֵי חֵיוָתָא אַמְּטוּלְתֵיהּ. [6]הַהוּא דַּאֲתָא לְקַמֵּיהּ דְּרַבִּי נְחֶמְיָה, אֲמַר לֵיהּ: "בַּמֶּה אַתָּה סוֹעֵד"? [7]אָמַר לוֹ: "בְּבָשָׂר שָׁמֵן וְיַיִן יָשָׁן". [8]"רְצוֹנְךָ שֶׁתְּגַלְגֵּל עִמִּי בַּעֲדָשִׁים"? [9]גִּלְגֵּל עִמּוֹ בַּעֲדָשִׁים וָמֵת. [10]אָמַר: "אוֹי לוֹ לָזֶה שֶׁהֲרָגוֹ נְחֶמְיָה". [11]אַדְּרַבָּה, "אוֹי לוֹ לִנְחֶמְיָה שֶׁהֲרָגוֹ לָזֶה" מִיבְּעֵי לֵיהּ!

LITERAL TRANSLATION

[1]Our Rabbis taught: "It once happened that the people of Upper Galilee bought for a certain poor man from a respectable family from Sepphoris a pound of meat every day."

[2]What is the novelty (lit., "greatness") [in] a pound of meat?

[3]Rav Huna said: [It was] a pound of fowl's meat. [4]And if you wish, say: With a pound [they bought] actually meat.

[5]Rav Ashi said: There it was a small village, [and] every day they would waste an animal on his account.

[6]A certain man came before Rabbi Neḥemyah, [who] said to him: "On what do you dine?" [7]He said to him: "On fat meat and old wine." [8]"Do you wish to put up with lentils with me?" [9]He put up with lentils with him and died. [10]He said: "Woe to this man whom Neḥemyah killed."

[11]On the contrary, he should have [said]: "Woe to Neḥemyah who killed this man"!

RASHI

משל עופות — שדמיהן יקרים והוא היה מעונג. **בליטרא בשר** — שהיה בשר ביוקר והיה צריך בשר בדמי ליטרא מעות. **כפר קטן היה** — ואין המותר נמכר. **אמטולתיה** — בשבילו, והיינו רבותא, ולעולם במשקל ליטרא בשר קאמר. **ההוא דאתא** — עני המבקש פרנסה. **במה אתה סועד** — מה אתה רגיל לאכול בסעודתך.

NOTES

treat his elevated status lightly by restoring the property. *Ramban* extends the exemption stated with respect to the return of lost property to all obligations that one person has to another. It is therefore surprising that Hillel ran before the poor man, acting in a manner unbefitting the leading Torah figure of his day. *Rabbi Elḥanan Wasserman* suggests that Hillel may have been in a place where nobody recognized him and was therefore permitted to serve the poor man.

HALAKHAH

he must be given what he needs. If he was once wealthy and was accustomed to riding a horse or having a servant run before him, he must now be provided with a horse and a servant. Even though there is an obligation to provide a poor man with his needs, there is no need to make him wealthy." (*Rambam, Sefer Zeraim, Hilkhot Mattenot Aniyyim* 7:3; *Shulḥan Arukh, Yoreh De'ah* 250:1.)

TRANSLATION AND COMMENTARY

אֶלָּא [1]**Rather,** says the Gemara, this is what Rabbi Neḥemyah meant to say: "Woe to him whom Neḥemyah killed, for **it was he who should not have indulged himself so much,** letting himself grow accustomed to luxuries."

הַהוּא דַּאֲתָא [2]It was further related that **a certain man came before Rava** and asked for charity. And Rava **asked him: "On what** foods **do you dine?"** [3]The poor man **said to him:** "I am accustomed to eating **a fattened chicken and old wine."** [4]Rava **said to him: "Are you not concerned about the burden** you place **on the** other members of the **community,** by expecting to be fed delicacies which many of those who support you cannot afford?" [5]The poor man defended himself against Rava's criticisms and **said to him:** "**Do I eat from** anything belonging to **them?** [6]Surely **I eat from** what belongs to **the Merciful One,** [7]**for we have learned** in the following Baraita: 'The verse states [Psalm 145:15]: **"The eyes of all wait upon You, and You give them their food in his season."** [8]The verse **does not read,** as one might have expected, "You give them their food **in *their* season," but rather** "You give them their food **in *his* season."** [9]**This** formulation **teaches us that the Holy One, blessed be He, gives each and every person his support in his** own **season,** according to his individual needs and the manner in which he is accustomed to being maintained.' Thus we see that the true source of my support is God Himself, and the members of the community merely serve as His earthly agents." [10]**Meanwhile,** as Rava and the poor man were discussing the issue, **Rava's sister, who had not seen** her brother **for thirteen years, came and brought him** a present of **a fattened chicken and old wine.** [11]Considering the significance of this unexpected gift, Rava **said** to himself: **"Why was this** fattened chicken and old wine brought **before me** just now?" Interpreting the gift as a sign from Heaven, [12]Rava **said to him: "I apologize to you. Arise and eat** the chicken and wine."

[1]אֶלָּא, אִיהוּ הוּא דְּלָא אִיבָּעֵי לֵיהּ לְפַנּוּקֵי נַפְשֵׁיהּ כּוּלֵּי הַאי.
[2]הַהוּא דַּאֲתָא לְקַמֵּיהּ דְּרָבָא, אָמַר לוֹ: "בַּמֶּה אַתָּה סוֹעֵד"?
[3]אָמַר לוֹ: "בְּתַרְנְגוֹלֶת פְּטוּמָה וְיַיִן יָשָׁן". [4]אָמַר לֵיהּ: "וְלָא חָיֵישַׁתְּ לְדוּחֲקָא דְּצִיבּוּרָא"?
[5]אֲמַר לֵיהּ: "אַטּוּ מִדִּידְהוּ קָאָכֵילְנָא? [6]מִדְּרַחֲמָנָא קָאָכֵילְנָא, [7]דְּתַנְיָא: '"עֵינֵי כֹל אֵלֶיךָ יְשַׂבֵּרוּ, וְאַתָּה נוֹתֵן לָהֶם אֶת אָכְלָם בְּעִתּוֹ". [8]"בְּעִתָּם" לֹא נֶאֱמַר, אֶלָּא "בְּעִתּוֹ".
[9]מְלַמֵּד שֶׁכָּל אֶחָד וְאֶחָד נוֹתֵן הַקָּדוֹשׁ בָּרוּךְ הוּא פַּרְנָסָתוֹ בְּעִתּוֹ'". [10]אַדְּהָכִי אֲתַאי אַחְתֵּיהּ דְּרָבָא, דְּלָא חַזְיָא לֵיהּ תְּלֵיסְרֵי שְׁנֵי, וְאָתְיָא לֵיהּ תַּרְנְגוֹלֶת פְּטוּמָה וְיַיִן יָשָׁן.
[11]אֲמַר: "מַאי דְּקַמָּא"? [12]אֲמַר לֵיהּ: "נַעֲנֵתִי לָךְ. קוּם אֱכוֹל".

LITERAL TRANSLATION

[1]Rather, it was he who should not have indulged himself so much.

[2]A certain man came before Rava, [who] said to him: "On what do you dine?" [3]He said to him: "On a fattened chicken and old wine." [4]He said to him: "But are you not concerned about the burden on the community?" [5]He said to him: "Do I eat from them? [6]I eat from the Merciful One, [7]for we have learned: '"The eyes of all wait upon You, and You give them their food in his season." [8]"In their season" is not said, but rather "in his season." [9][This] teaches that the Holy One, blessed be He, gives each and every person his support in his season.'" [10]Meanwhile Rava's sister, who had not seen him [for] thirteen years, came and brought him a fattened chicken and old wine. [11]He said: "What is [this] before me?" [12]He said to him: "I have sinned toward you. Arise [and] eat."

RASHI

בעתו — הכל לפי מה שהוא צריך, כל יחיד ויחיד לפי לימודו. **אמר רבא מאי דקמא** — מה דבר זה שאירע לפני עתה שלא הייתי רגיל בכך, שבאת זו לכאן ותרנגולת ויין ישן בידה. **נענתי לך** — דברתי יותר מדאי.

LANGUAGE

נַעֲנֵתִי לָךְ **I have sinned toward you.** In Rabbinic literature, this expression generally means "I apologize," "I beg your pardon." *Rashi* derives it from the root ענה, "to answer." Thus, by extension, נַעֲנֵתִי means "I spoke [=answered] too much." Others derive it from the root ענה, "to afflict," and explain it as meaning "I have sinned toward you."

NOTES

לְפַנּוּקֵי נַפְשֵׁיהּ **Have indulged himself.** *Maharsha* and others distinguish between this case involving Rabbi Neḥemyah and the two previously mentioned cases involving Hillel the Elder and the people of Upper Galilee. In each of the first two cases, the poor man came from a wealthy family and was accustomed to certain luxuries. Such a person must be maintained in the manner to which he was accustomed, in compliance with the Biblical directive to provide a poor person with "that which is lacking to him," as was explained in the Gemara above. But the man who appeared before Rabbi Neḥemyah acquired his expensive tastes while being maintained by charity. In such a case, there is certainly no obligation to continue providing him with the luxuries to which he has grown accustomed.

"בְּעִתָּם" לֹא נֶאֱמַר **"In their season" is not said.** *Maharsha* explains that the poor man who came before Rava did not always dine on fattened chicken and old wine, but only when such foods were necessary for his health. Thus Rava did not say that the poor man should not have indulged himself so much (as Rabbi Neḥemyah said about the poor man who came before him), but rather that he should consider whether or not he was placing the community under an unnecessary burden. The poor man responded with the verse, "You give them their food *in his season*,"

TRANSLATION AND COMMENTARY

תָּנוּ רַבָּנַן [1]**Our Rabbis taught** another Baraita dealing with the laws of charity: **"If someone has no** money of his own upon which to subsist **and does not wish to support himself from charity** because he is too proud to take charity, **he should** at first **be given** money **as a loan, and afterwards,** when the loan becomes due, the money **should be given to him** to keep **as a gift.** [2]This is **the viewpoint of Rabbi Meir.** [3]**But the Sages** disagree and **say: He should** at first **be given** money **as a gift, and afterwards** the money **should be given to him as a loan."**

לְשׁוּם מַתָּנָה [4]The Gemara interrupts its presentation of the Baraita with the following question: How do the Sages really maintain that the poor man should first be given money **as a gift?** [5]But **surely** this person is too proud to accept charity and **will** therefore **not take** a gift!

אָמַר רָבָא [6]**Rava said:** The Sages meant that the poor man should **first be offered** the money **as a gift.** If he refuses the gift, he should then be offered the money as a loan, and afterwards the loan should be waived and converted into a gift.

יֵשׁ לוֹ [7]The Baraita continues: **"If someone** is a miser who **has resources of his own but does not wish to support himself from them,** preferring to live on charity received from others, [8]**he may be given money as a gift, and afterwards** the money **can be collected from him** as if it had been given to him as a loan."

חוֹזְרִין וְנִפְרָעִין הֵימֶנּוּ [9]Once again the Gemara interrupts its presentation of the Baraita with a question: How can you say that such a person should be given money as a gift, and that **afterwards** the money **can be collected from him** as if it had been given to him as a loan? But **surely** we are dealing here with a person who is too miserly to spend his own money! [10]**He will** certainly **not take** a gift if he knows that it will later be collected from him!

אָמַר רַב פַּפָּא [11]**Rav Pappa said:** The Baraita means that the money given to the miser is eventually collected from his estate **after** his **death.**

רַבִּי שִׁמְעוֹן אוֹמֵר [12]The Baraita continues: **"Rabbi Shimon** disagrees with the Sages and **says: If someone has resources of his own but does not wish to support himself from them,** the community is **not bound to**

[1]תָּנוּ רַבָּנַן: ״אֵין לוֹ וְאֵינוֹ רוֹצֶה לְהִתְפַּרְנֵס, נוֹתְנִין לוֹ לְשׁוּם הַלְוָאָה, וְחוֹזְרִין וְנוֹתְנִין לוֹ לְשׁוּם מַתָּנָה. [2]דִּבְרֵי רַבִּי מֵאִיר. [3]וַחֲכָמִים אוֹמְרִים: נוֹתְנִין לוֹ לְשׁוּם מַתָּנָה, וְחוֹזְרִין וְנוֹתְנִין לוֹ לְשׁוּם הַלְוָאָה״.
[4]לְשׁוּם מַתָּנָה? [5]הָא לָא שָׁקֵיל!
[6]אָמַר רָבָא: לִפְתּוֹחַ לוֹ לְשׁוּם מַתָּנָה.
[7]״יֵשׁ לוֹ וְאֵינוֹ רוֹצֶה לְהִתְפַּרְנֵס, [8]נוֹתְנִין לוֹ לְשׁוּם מַתָּנָה, וְחוֹזְרִין וְנִפְרָעִין מִמֶּנּוּ״.
[9]חוֹזְרִין וְנִפְרָעִין הֵימֶנּוּ? [10]תּוּ לָא שָׁקֵיל!
[11]אָמַר רַב פַּפָּא: לְאַחַר מִיתָה.
[12]״רַבִּי שִׁמְעוֹן אוֹמֵר: יֵשׁ לוֹ וְאֵינוֹ רוֹצֶה לְהִתְפַּרְנֵס, אֵין

LITERAL TRANSLATION

[1]Our Rabbis taught: "[If] he has nothing and does not wish to support himself [from charity], we give him [money] as a loan, and afterwards we give [it] to him as a gift. [2][These are] the words of Rabbi Meir. [3]But the Sages say: We give him [money] as a gift, and afterwards we give [it] to him as a loan."

[4]As a gift? [5]Surely he does not take!

[6]Rava said: To begin with [we offer it] to him as a gift.

[7]"[If] he has [resources of his own] but does not wish to support himself [from them], [8]we give him [money] as a gift, and afterwards we collect [it] from him."

[9]Afterwards we collect [it] from him? [10]He will not take [it] again!

[11]Rav Pappa said: After death.

[12]"Rabbi Shimon says: [If] he has [of his own] but does not wish to support himself [from them], we are not

RASHI

אין לו – משלו. **ואינו רוצה להתפרנס** – משל צדקה. **יש לו ואינו רוצה להתפרנס** – משלו אלא משל צדקה ומסגף עצמו ברעב.

NOTES

which teaches that God supports each and every person according to his needs of the moment. Since the poor man was then in need of certain delicacies, he was entitled to ask that they be supplied to him from charity.

HALAKHAH

אֵין לוֹ וְאֵינוֹ רוֹצֶה לְהִתְפַּרְנֵס **If he has nothing and does not wish to support himself from charity.** "If someone needs charity but does not wish to accept it, it is permissible to mislead him into accepting charity under the pretense that he is being given a gift or a loan." (*Rambam, Sefer Zeraim, Hilkhot Mattenot Aniyyim* 7:9; *Shulḥan Arukh, Yoreh De'ah* 253:9.)

יֵשׁ לוֹ וְאֵינוֹ רוֹצֶה לְהִתְפַּרְנֵס **If he has resources of his own but does not wish to support himself from them.** "If a wealthy man is starving himself because he is too miserly

TRANSLATION AND COMMENTARY

help him. [1]**If** the poor man **has no** money of his own **and does not wish to support himself from charity,** because he sees it as a humiliation, [2]**he should be told: 'Bring a pledge and take** the money as a loan,' **in order that his spirits may be uplifted."**

תָּנוּ רַבָּנַן [3]**Our Rabbis taught** a related Baraita, which records the Biblical sources of the rulings found in the Baraita just cited: "The verse [Deuteronomy 15:8] which commands us to lend money to a poor person uses a double verb form: 'You shall surely lend him — *ha'avet ta'avitennu* [הַעֲבֵט תַּעֲבִיטֶנּוּ].' The first expression, **'Lend'** [הַעֲבֵט], [4]**refers to someone who has no money** of his own but is proud **and does not wish to be supported from charity.** Such a person **should** first **be given** money **as a loan, and afterwards,** when the loan becomes due, the money **should be given to him** to keep **as a gift.** [5]The second expression, **'Surely lend him'** [תַּעֲבִיטֶנּוּ], [6]refers to someone who has resources of his own but is a miser and **does not wish to support himself from them,** preferring to live on charity received from others. Such a person **should be given** money **as a gift, and eventually** the money **can be collected from his** estate **after** his death as if it had been given to him as a loan. [7]This is **the viewpoint of Rabbi Yehudah.** [8]**The Sages** disagree and **say: If someone has resources of his own but does not wish to support himself from them,** the community is **not bound to help him.** [9]**But then how do I explain** the second expression, **'Surely lend him'?** [10]According to the Sages, **the Torah speaks in the** ordinary **language of people.** Thus the use of the double verb form is purely stylistic, with no special Halakhic significance."

נִזְקָקִין לוֹ. [1]אֵין לוֹ וְאֵינוֹ רוֹצֶה לְהִתְפַּרְנֵס, [2]אוֹמְרִים לוֹ: ׳הָבֵא מַשְׁכּוֹן וְטוֹל׳, כְּדֵי שֶׁתָּזוּחַ דַּעְתּוֹ עָלָיו״.

[3]תָּנוּ רַבָּנַן: ״׳הַעֲבֵט׳. [4]זֶה שֶׁאֵין לוֹ וְאֵינוֹ רוֹצֶה לְהִתְפַּרְנֵס, שֶׁנּוֹתְנִים לוֹ לְשׁוּם הַלְוָאָה, וְחוֹזְרִין וְנוֹתְנִין לוֹ לְשׁוּם מַתָּנָה. [5]׳תַּעֲבִיטֶנּוּ׳. [6]זֶה שֶׁיֵּשׁ לוֹ וְאֵינוֹ רוֹצֶה לְהִתְפַּרְנֵס, שֶׁנּוֹתְנִין לוֹ לְשׁוּם מַתָּנָה, וְחוֹזְרִין וְנִפְרָעִין הֵימֶנּוּ לְאַחַר מִיתָה. [7]דִּבְרֵי רַבִּי יְהוּדָה. [8]וַחֲכָמִים אוֹמְרִים: יֵשׁ לוֹ וְאֵינוֹ רוֹצֶה לְהִתְפַּרְנֵס, אֵין נִזְקָקִין לוֹ. [9]וְאֶלָּא מָה אֲנִי מְקַיֵּים ׳תַּעֲבִיטֶנּוּ׳? [10]דִּבְּרָה תּוֹרָה כִּלְשׁוֹן בְּנֵי אָדָם״.

LITERAL TRANSLATION

bound to [help] him. [1][If] he has nothing and does not wish to support himself [from charity], [2]we say to him: 'Bring a pledge and take,' in order that his mind may be uplifted."

[3]Our Rabbis taught: "'Lend' [הַעֲבֵט]. [4]This [refers to someone] who has nothing and does not wish to be supported [from charity], to whom we give [money] as a loan, and afterwards we give [it] to him as a gift. [5]'Surely lend him' [תַּעֲבִיטֶנּוּ]. [6]This [refers to someone] who has [resources of his own] but does not wish to support himself [from them], to whom we give [money] as a gift, and afterwards we collect [it] from him after death. [7][These are] the words of Rabbi Yehudah. [8]But the Sages say: [If] he has [resources of his own] but does not wish to support himself [from them], we are not bound to [help] him. [9]But then how do I explain [lit., 'establish'] 'surely lend him'? [10]The Torah spoke in the language of people."

RASHI

שתזוח דעתו עליו — יגבה לבו לומר: דעתס לחזור ולגבות הימני, הואיל ותבעוני משכון אין זו אלא הלואה, ויטול בלא בושת. שיאמר: אין לי משכון, והם יאמרו: טול בלא משכון.

NOTES

דִּבְּרָה תּוֹרָה כִּלְשׁוֹן בְּנֵי אָדָם The Torah spoke in the language of people. In medieval Jewish philosophical literature, this statement is used for a different purpose — to explain that some of the difficult passages in the Torah, especially the use of anthropomorphisms, are examples of "the ordinary language of people" in which the Torah speaks. Hence it is important to note that in the Gemara this statement is *never* used to make a general statement on the Torah's style. As used in the Gemara, it refers only to the Torah's use of double verbs, and occasionally to double pronouns.

There is a Tannaitic dispute as to whether the use of double verbs was intended to convey additional Halakhic information, informing us of a case that we might otherwise not have included, or whether it has no Halakhic significance and was used merely for stylistic reasons, as "in the ordinary language of people." The position that the Torah speaks in ordinary human language is attributed here to the Sages.

HALAKHAH

to spend his money on food and drink, the community is under no obligation to help him." (*Rambam, Sefer Zeraim, Hilkhot Mattenot Aniyyim* 7:9; *Shulḥan Arukh, Yoreh De'ah* 253:10.)

¹מָר עוּקְבָא הֲוָה עַנְיָא בְּשִׁיבָבוּתֵיהּ דַּהֲוָה רָגִיל כָּל יוֹמָא דְּשָׁדֵי לֵיהּ אַרְבָּעָה זוּזֵי בְּצִינּוֹרָא דְּדַשָּׁא. ²יוֹם אֶחָד אֲמַר: ״אֵיזִיל אֶיחֱזֵי מַאן קָעָבֵיד בִּי הַהוּא טִיבוּתָא״. ³הַהוּא יוֹמָא נַגְהָא לֵיהּ לְמָר עוּקְבָא בְּבֵי מִדְרָשָׁא, אָתְיָא דְּבֵיתְהוּ בַּהֲדֵיהּ. ⁴כֵּיוָן דְּחָזָא דְּקָא מַצְלֵי לֵיהּ לְדַשָּׁא, נְפַק בָּתְרַיְיהוּ. ⁵רְהוּט מִקַּמֵּיהּ, עָיְילֵי לְהַהוּא אַתּוּנָא דַּהֲוָה גְּרוּפָה נוּרָא. ⁶הֲוָה קָא מִיקַלְיָין כַּרְעֵיהּ דְּמָר עוּקְבָא. ⁷אָמְרָה לֵיהּ דְּבֵיתְהוּ: ״שְׁקוֹל כַּרְעֵיךְ אוֹתֵיב אַכַּרְעַאי״. ⁸חֲלַשׁ דַּעְתֵּיהּ. ⁹אָמְרָה לֵיהּ: ״אֲנָא שְׁכִיחְנָא בְּגַוֵּיהּ דְּבֵיתָא, וּמִקַּרְבָא אַהֲנָיָיתִי״.
¹⁰וּמַאי כּוּלֵּי הַאי?

LITERAL TRANSLATION

¹In Mar Ukva's neighborhood there was a poor man into whose door socket he was accustomed each day to toss four zuz. ²One day he said: "I will go [and] see who is doing for me this kindness." ³That day Mar Ukva stayed late in the Academy, [and] his wife came with him. ⁴When he saw that the door was being moved, he went out after them. ⁵They ran away from him, [and] entered a furnace from which the fire had been swept. ⁶Mar Ukva's feet were burned. ⁷His wife said to him: "Lift up your feet [and] put [them] on my feet." ⁸He became distressed. ⁹She said to him: "I am found at home, and the benefit I provide is immediate."
¹⁰And what was [the reason for] all this?

TRANSLATION AND COMMENTARY

מָר עוּקְבָא ¹It was related that **a certain poor man** lived **in Mar Ukva's neighborhood.** Mar Ukva did not wish to humiliate him by offering him charity directly, and so **each day he would toss** the poor man **four zuz through** the hole in his door next to **the door socket,** and the poor man never knew the identity of his benefactor. ²**One day** the poor man **said** to himself: "Today **I will go and see who is doing me this kindness.**" ³**That day Mar Ukva** happened to **stay late in the Academy,** and since he did not wish to go out alone at that late hour, Mar Ukva's **wife accompanied him** when he went out to distribute charity to the poor. ⁴**When** the poor man **saw that his door was being moved,** he quickly **went out after them** to see who was leaving him money. ⁵Mar Ukva and his wife **ran away from him,** and, to avoid discovery, **entered a furnace from which the fire had** already **been swept** but which was still very hot. ⁶**Mar Ukva burned his feet** on the floor of the furnace. ⁷**His wife,** who did not sustain similar burns, **said to him: "Lift up your feet** from the floor of the furnace **and put them on** top of **my feet** so that they will not suffer any further injury." ⁸Mar Ukva did as she said, but **he was distressed** because he had been injured by the heat of the furnace whereas his wife had not been hurt. He took this as a sign from Heaven that his wife was regarded as being more righteous than he. ⁹Mar Ukva's wife **said to him:** "Do not be distressed. **I am** usually **found at home,** so that I can give charity to the poor who come begging at the door in the form of food which is ready to be eaten. Thus **the benefit I provide is immediate.** But you give charity in the form of money. The charity you give cannot be enjoyed until the recipient buys something with it. I was spared injury not because I am any more righteous than you, but rather in reward for the immediate benefit I provide the poor when I give them charity."

וּמַאי כּוּלֵּי הַאי ¹⁰The Gemara raises a question about this incident: **And what was the reason for all this?** Why were Mar Ukva and his wife so concerned that the poor man should not learn their identity that they entered a furnace in order to escape detection?

RASHI

צינורא דדשא — חור שבמפתן, וציר הדלת סובב בו. **ההוא יומא** — אותו היום, שנתן העני לבו לדעת מי נותנם לו. **כיון דחזא** — העני. **אנא שכיחנא בגו ביתא** — ועניים מוצאין אותי, לפיכך זכותי גדול. **ומקרבא הנייתי** — הנאתי מזומנת, שאני מחלקת לחם ובשר ומלח, אבל אתה נותן מעות לעניים והם טורחים וקונים סעודה. **מאי כולי האי** — למה להם לברוח ולכנס לתנור?

SAGES

מָר עוּקְבָא **Mar Ukva.** The Exilarch in Babylonia during the first generation of Amoraim, Mar Ukva was a political leader and a distinguished scholar. His main teacher was Shmuel (who was apparently not much older than he), and Mar Ukva may thus be considered a student-colleague of Shmuel. Mar Ukva lived in the Exilarch's residence in Kafri, where his court was located.

Mar Ukva is mentioned frequently in the Talmud. He engaged in Halakhic discourse with his contemporaries, and his teachings are cited by many Amoraim of later generations. He maintained close relations with the Sages of Eretz Israel, with whom he corresponded on Halakhic matters.

Mar Ukva was renowned not only for his great learning but also for his piety, and particularly for his deeds of kindness and charity. Two other scholars mentioned in the Talmud, Rav Natan bar Mar Ukva and Mari bar Mar Ukva, may have been his sons.

BACKGROUND

צִינּוֹרָא דְּדַשָּׁא **Door socket.** This apparently refers to the hole in the threshold of the house through which the pivot of the door was inserted. In order to make it easier to attach the door to the building (or remove it), there was usually a small slit near the door socket. Through this, small objects could be passed inside.

NOTES

אָתְיָא דְּבֵיתְהוּ בַּהֲדֵיהּ **His wife came with him.** *Meiri* explains that Mar Ukva's gift to the poor man could still be considered a gift of charity given in secrecy, even though Mar Ukva's wife accompanied him when he slipped the money under the poor man's door, for a man's wife is regarded as sharing a single identity with her husband.

HALAKHAH

דַּהֲוָה רָגִיל כָּל יוֹמָא דְּשָׁדֵי לֵיהּ אַרְבָּעָה זוּזֵי בְּצִינּוֹרָא דְּדַשָּׁא **Into whose door socket he was accustomed each day to toss four zuz.** "The third most virtuous way of giving charity is in such a manner that the donor knows who is the recipient, but the recipient does not know who is the donor. This was the practice of Mar Ukva, who would clandestinely leave charity at a poor man's door." (*Rambam, Sefer Zeraim, Hilkhot Mattenot Aniyyim* 10:9; *Shulḥan Arukh, Yoreh De'ah* 249:8.)

[1]דְּאָמַר מָר זוּטְרָא בַּר טוֹבִיָּה אָמַר רַב; וְאָמְרִי לָהּ אָמַר רַב הוּנָא בַּר בִּיזְנָא אָמַר רַבִּי שִׁמְעוֹן חֲסִידָא; וְאָמְרִי לָהּ אָמַר רַבִּי יוֹחָנָן מִשּׁוּם רַבִּי שִׁמְעוֹן בֶּן יוֹחַי: [2]נוֹחַ לוֹ לְאָדָם שֶׁיִּמְסוֹר עַצְמוֹ לְתוֹךְ כִּבְשַׁן הָאֵשׁ, וְאַל יַלְבִּין פְּנֵי חֲבֵרוֹ בָּרַבִּים.

[3]מְנָא לָן? [4]מִתָּמָר, דִּכְתִיב: "הִיא מוּצֵאת".

[5]מָר עוּקְבָא הֲוָה עַנְיָא בְּשִׁיבָבוּתֵיהּ דַּהֲוָה רָגִיל לְשַׁדּוּרֵי לֵיהּ אַרְבַּע מְאָה זוּזֵי כָּל מַעֲלֵי יוֹמָא דְכִיפּוּרָא. [6]יוֹמָא חַד שַׁדְּרִינְהוּ נִיהֲלֵיהּ בְּיַד בְּרֵיהּ. [7]אֲתָא אֲמַר לֵיהּ: "לָא צְרִיךְ". [8]אֲמַר: "מַאי חֲזֵית"? [9]"חֲזַאי דְּקָא מְזַלְּפֵי לֵיהּ יַיִן

LITERAL TRANSLATION

[1]For Mar Zutra bar Toviyyah said in the name of Rav; and some say: Rav Huna bar Bizna said in the name of Rabbi Shimon Ḥasida; and some say: Rabbi Yoḥanan said in the name of Rabbi Shimon ben Yoḥai: [2]It is better for a man to cast himself into a fiery furnace and not to put his fellow to shame in public.

[3]From where do we [know this]? [4]From Tamar, for it is written: "She was brought forth."

[5]In Mar Ukva's neighborhood there was a poor man to whom he was accustomed to send four hundred zuz every eve of Yom Kippur. [6]One day he sent them to him by the hand of his son. [7]He came [back and] said to him: "He does not need [the money]." [8]He said: "What did you see?" [9]"I saw that they were sprinkling old wine

RASHI

היא מוצאת — "והיא שלחה וגו'" אף על פי שנאתה לישרף לא גילתה הדבר אלא אם כן יגלה הוא, ואם לא יגלה — נשרפת.

TRANSLATION AND COMMENTARY

דְּאָמַר מָר זוּטְרָא בַּר טוֹבִיָּה [1]The Gemara answers: **It was according to what Mar Zutra bar Toviyyah said in the name of Rav; and some say: Rav Huna bar Bizna said in the name of Rabbi Shimon Ḥasida; and some say: Rabbi Yoḥanan said in the name of Rabbi Shimon ben Yoḥai:** [2]**It is better for a man to cast himself into a fiery furnace than to put another person to shame in public.**

מְנָא לָן [3]The Gemara asks: **From where do we know this?** What is the Biblical source for that statement? [4]The Gemara answers: It is learned **from** the case of **Tamar** (Genesis, chapter 38). Tamar had been married to two of Judah's sons, each of whom died without issue. Under the law of levirate marriage as it existed in those times, she was required to marry another member of Judah's family. Judah seemed reluctant to allow her to marry his only remaining son, so Tamar disguised herself as a prostitute, seduced Judah himself, and persuaded him to give her his signet. She became pregnant, and Judah accused her of adultery. The punishment for that crime was death by burning. **The verse** (Genesis 38;25) **records** Tamar's response: "When **she was brought forth** [to be executed], she sent to her father-in-law, saying: I am pregnant by the man to whom this signet, cord and staff belong." Tamar did not clear herself by publicly declaring that Judah himself was the father of her unborn child. She left the matter to Judah's own conscience. Thus we see that she was willing to be burned to death, rather than publicly humiliate her father-in-law. Accordingly, we may infer that it is better to be cast into a fiery furnace than to put another person to shame in public.

מָר עוּקְבָא [5]It was further related that **in Mar Ukva's neighborhood there lived a poor man to whom** Mar Ukva **was accustomed to send** a charitable gift of **four hundred zuz every** year on the **eve of Yom Kippur.** [6]**One year** Mar Ukva **sent him** the money **by way of his son.** [7]Mar Ukva's son **came back** to his father **and said to him:** "The man to whom you send four hundred zuz every year **does not need** to be given **money** from charity." [8]Mar Ukva **asked** his son: **"What did you see** that led you to this conclusion?" [9]His son answered: **"I saw that they were sprinkling old wine** on the floor so that the room would be filled with its fragrance. Surely, if he can afford such extravagances, he does not need to receive charity."

SAGES

מָר זוּטְרָא בַּר טוֹבִיָּה **Mar Zutra bar Toviyyah.** A second-generation Babylonian Amora, Mar (or Rav) Zutra bar Toviyyah was an outstanding disciple of Rav, and in many Talmudic passages he transmits Rav's Halakhic and Aggadic teachings. After Rav's death, Mar Zutra studied in the yeshivah of Rav Yehudah, where he became a student-colleague of that scholar. His own teachings are also cited in a number of places.

NOTES

שֶׁיִּמְסוֹר עַצְמוֹ לְתוֹךְ כִּבְשַׁן הָאֵשׁ **To cast himself into a fiery furnace.** *Maharal* explains that it is preferable that a person cast himself into a fiery furnace rather than put another person to shame publicly, because the spiritual injury suffered by a person who is publicly humiliated is even greater than the physical injury suffered by a person whose body is consumed by the flames of a furnace.

הִיא מוּצֵאת **She was brought out.** *Rabbenu Ḥananel* (cited by *Tosafot* and others) reads הִיא מוּצֶּתֶת, "she was set on fire" (rather than הִיא מוּצֵאת, "she was brought forth"). According to this reading the verse teaches us that even after Tamar was already set on fire, she was unwilling to humiliate Judah in public. *Ritva* argues that there is no such reading in Scripture. *Arukh* and others cite *Rabbenu Ḥananel's* derivation as part of a "Do not read" (אַל תִּקְרֵי) argument: Do not read the word as it is written, מוּצֵאת, but rather as מוּצֶּתֶת, and in this way you can derive an important moral lesson from the verse.

LANGUAGE

סִיאַנְקֵי **Sian.** Sian was a Persian town in the district of Shiraz. Some scholars suggest that the dinarim of Sian were worth about half a dram (=2.9 grams) of silver. The coins of Sian are mentioned elsewhere as having been of gold.

SAGES

רַבִּי אִילְעַאי **Rabbi Il'ai.** A Palestinian Amora of the third generation. See *Ketubot,* Part III, p.63.

רַבִּי אַבָּא **Rabbi Abba.** An Amora of the third generation. See *Ketubot,* Part II, p.112.

BACKGROUND

אַל יְבַזְבֵּז יוֹתֵר מֵחוֹמֶשׁ **Spend no more than a fifth.** See *Ketubot,* Part IV, p.118.

TRANSLATION AND COMMENTARY

[1]After considering the matter, Mar Ukva **said:** "If this man is so **fastidious,** he needs to be given an even larger gift of charity." [2]Mar Ukva **doubled** the poor man's grant **and sent** the money **to him.**

כִּי קָא נִיחָא נַפְשֵׁיהּ [3]**When** Mar Ukva **was dying, he said** to those attending to him: **"Bring me my charity accounts,** so that I can review them." [4]After going through the accounts, Mar Ukva **found that** gifts to the value of **seven thousand Sian gold dinarim were recorded in them.** [5]Dissatisfied, Mar Ukva **said** to himself: **"My provisions are light, and my journey is long.** The good deeds I performed during my lifetime are not sufficient." [6]He immediately **got up and gave away half his money** to charity.

הֵיכִי עָבֵיד הָכִי [7]The Gemara now asks: **How could** Mar Ukva **have acted in this way?** [8]**Surely Rabbi Il'ai said:** When the Sanhedrin was sitting **in Usha,** the Sages **enacted** that even if [9]**someone** wishes to **give** money to charity, he **should not give away more than one-fifth** of his assets. How, then, could Mar Ukva have given away half his assets to charity?

הָנֵי מִילֵּי [10]The Gemara answers: **This** regulation limiting the amount that a person may give to charity **applies** only **during his lifetime, lest he lose** the rest of **his property** and become dependent on other people. [11]**But after** a person's **death, there is no** such **concern.**

רַבִּי אַבָּא [12]The Gemara now relates another incident to illustrate how the Sages would give charity. **Rabbi Abba used to tie coins in his scarf, and cast** the scarf **behind his** back; **he would then go among the poor,** so that they could take the money and he would not know who had done so. [13]**But** Rabbi Abba would **glance behind him** from time to time **in order to prevent swindlers,** who were not deserving of charity, from coming and taking the money for themselves.

יָשָׁן״. [1]אֲמַר: ״מְפַנַּק כּוּלֵּי הַאי״? [2]עַיְיפִינְהוּ וְשַׁדְרִינְהוּ נִיהֲלֵיהּ.

[3]כִּי קָא נִיחָא נַפְשֵׁיהּ, אֲמַר: ״אַיְיתוּ לִי חוּשְׁבְּנַאי דִּצְדָקָה״. [4]אַשְׁכַּח דַּהֲוָה כְּתִיב בֵּיהּ שִׁבְעַת אַלְפֵי דִּינָרֵי סִיאַנְקֵי. [5]אֲמַר: ״זְוַודַאי קַלִּילֵי, וְאוֹרְחָא רְחִיקְתָא״. [6]קָם בַּזְבְּזֵיהּ לְפַלְגֵּיהּ מָמוֹנֵיהּ.

[7]הֵיכִי עָבֵיד הָכִי? [8]וְהָאָמַר רַבִּי אִילְעַאי: בְּאוּשָׁא הִתְקִינוּ: [9]הַמְבַזְבֵּז אַל יְבַזְבֵּז יוֹתֵר מֵחוֹמֶשׁ!

[10]הָנֵי מִילֵּי מֵחַיִּים, שֶׁמָּא יֵרֵד מִנְּכָסָיו. [11]אֲבָל לְאַחַר מִיתָה, לֵית לָן בָּהּ.

[12]רַבִּי אַבָּא הֲוָה צָיֵיר זוּזֵי בְּסוּדָרֵיהּ וּשְׁדֵי לֵיהּ לַאֲחוֹרֵיהּ, וּמַמְצֵי נַפְשֵׁיהּ לְבֵי עֲנִיֵּי. [13]וּמְצַלֵּי עֵינֵיהּ מֵרַמָּאֵי.

LITERAL TRANSLATION

for him." [1]He said: "Is he so fastidious?" [2]He doubled them and sent them to him.

[3]When he was dying, he said: "Bring me my charity accounts." [4]He found that seven thousand Sian dinarim were recorded in it. [5]He said: "My provisions are light and the journey is long." [6]He arose [and] gave away half of his money.

[7]How did he act that way? [8]But surely Rabbi Il'ai said: In Usha they enacted: [9]Someone who gives away [to charity] should not give away more than a fifth!

[10]This applies (lit., "these words") during [his] lifetime, lest he lose (lit., "go down from") his property. [11]But after [his] death, we have no [concern] about it.

[12]Rabbi Abba used to tie coins in his scarf, and cast it behind him, and would place himself among the poor. [13]But he would glance (lit., "turn his eyes") [behind him] on account of swindlers.

RASHI

עייפינהו = כפלינהו. **סיאנקי** — שם מקום. **זוודאי קלילי** — צידה קלה הכינותי לדרך רחוקה שאני יוצא לה. **ומצלי עיניה** — ומטה עיניו כלפי אחוריו, לראות שלא יבא רמאי ויתירה, שעושה עצמו עני, והעניים באים ומתירים אותם.

NOTES

עַיְיפִינְהוּ וְשַׁדְרִינְהוּ נִיהֲלֵיהּ **He doubled them and sent them to him.** *Meiri* adds that a poor man should be given charity even if the donor sees that he allows himself certain luxuries, for he may be indulging himself in order to hide his true financial situation from others, and thus preserve a facade of respectability for himself and his family.

HALAKHAH

אַל יְבַזְבֵּז יוֹתֵר מֵחוֹמֶשׁ **Should not give away more than a fifth.** "A person should not give away to charity more than one-fifth of his assets, so that he himself does not become dependent upon the charity of others. This limitation applies only during a person's lifetime; but a dying person may give as much charity as he desires, as we learn from the case of Mar Ukva." (*Rambam, Sefer Hafla'ah, Hilkhot Arakhin* 8:13; *Rema, Shulḥan Arukh, Yoreh De'ah* 249:1.)

הֲוָה צָיֵיר זוּזֵי בְּסוּדָרֵיהּ **Used to tie coins in his scarf.** "The fourth most virtuous way of giving charity is in such a

[1]רַבִּי חֲנִינָא הֲוָה הַהוּא עַנְיָא דַּהֲוָה רָגִיל לְשַׁדּוּרֵי לֵיהּ אַרְבָּעָה זוּזֵי כָּל מַעֲלֵי שַׁבְּתָא. [2]יוֹמָא חַד שָׁדְרִינְהוּ נִיהֲלֵיהּ בְּיַד דְּבֵיתְהוּ. [3]אֲתַאי אָמְרָה לֵיהּ: "לָא צְרִיךְ". [4]"מַאי חָזֵית"? [5]"שְׁמָעִי דַּהֲוָה קָאָמְרִי לֵיהּ: 'בַּמֶּה אַתָּה סוֹעֵד? [68A] בִּטְלֵי כֶסֶף אוֹ בִּטְלֵי זָהָב?'" [6]אֲמַר: "הַיְינוּ דַּאֲמַר רַבִּי אֶלְעָזָר: [7]בּוֹאוּ וְנַחֲזִיק טוֹבָה לָרַמָּאִין, שֶׁאִלְמָלֵא הֵן, הָיִינוּ חוֹטְאִין בְּכָל יוֹם, שֶׁנֶּאֱמַר: [8]'וְקָרָא עָלֶיךָ אֶל ה׳, וְהָיָה בְךָ חֵטְא'". [9]וְתָנֵי רַבִּי חִיָּיא בַּר רַב מִדִּיפְתִּי: "רַבִּי יְהוֹשֻׁעַ בֶּן קָרְחָה אוֹמֵר: כָּל הַמַּעֲלִים עֵינָיו מִן

LITERAL TRANSLATION

[1]There was a certain poor man to whom Rabbi Ḥanina was accustomed to send four zuz every Friday. [2]One day he sent them to him by the hand of his wife. [3]She came [back and] said to him: "He does not need [the money]." [4]"What did you see?" [5]"I heard them saying to him: 'On what will you dine? [68A] On silver cushions or gold cushions?'" [6]He said: "This is what Rabbi Elazar said: [7]Come, let us be grateful to the swindlers, for were it not for them, we would sin every day, for it is said: [8]'And he will cry against you to the Lord, and it shall be reckoned to you as a sin.'" [9]And Rabbi Ḥiyya bar Rav of Difti taught: "Rabbi Yehoshua ben Korḥah says: Whoever closes his eyes against

RASHI

בטלי כסף או בטלי זהב — במפות של פשתן לבנות או בשל משי צבועות. **היינו חוטאים** — שאנו מעלימין עין מן העניים אבל עכשיו הרמאים גורמים לנו.

TRANSLATION AND COMMENTARY

רַבִּי חֲנִינָא [1]The Gemara now relates that **there was a certain poor man to whom Rabbi Ḥanina was accustomed to send** a charitable gift of **four zuz every Friday.** [2]**One week** Rabbi Ḥanina **sent** the money **to** the poor man **by way of his wife.** After seeing the poor man in his home, [3]Rabbi Ḥanina's wife **came back** to her husband **and said to him: "The** man to whom you send money each week **does not need** to be given charity." [4]Rabbi Ḥanina asked his wife: **"What did you see** that you should say such a thing?" [5]His wife answered: **"I overheard** people **saying to him: 'On what will you dine?** [68A] **On cushions** embroidered with **silver or on cushions** embroidered with **gold?'** Surely, a person who is asked such a question is not in need of charity!" Accepting his wife's judgment that the man he had been accustomed to support was merely pretending to be poor, [6]Rabbi Ḥanina **commented: "This is what Rabbi Elazar said:** [7]**Come, let us be grateful to the swindlers** who ask for charity even though they are not in need, **for were it not for** such people, **we would sin every day, as the verse says** [Deuteronomy 15:9]: 'And your eye will be evil against your poor brother, and you will give him nothing, [8]**and he will cry against you to the Lord, and it shall be reckoned to you as a sin.'"** Withholding charity is a serious transgression, which many people violate regularly. Fortunately, swindlers who pretend to be poor provide those who withhold charity with a rationalization for their callous behavior, because they allow them to argue that many of those who beg for alms are not really in need.

וְתָנֵי [9]The Gemara continues with a Baraita that elaborates on the seriousness of withholding charity. **Rabbi Ḥiyya bar Rav of Difti taught** the following Baraita: **"Rabbi Yehoshua ben Korḥah says: Whoever closes**

LANGUAGE

טְלֵי Cushions. The meaning and etymology of this word are not fully clear. Some authorities claim that it refers to a kind of table cloth or table utensils. Others derive the word from the Greek τύλη, *tyle,* meaning "cushion," or "sofa."

NOTES

בִּטְלֵי כֶּסֶף אוֹ בִּטְלֵי זָהָב On silver cushions or gold cushions. According to *Rabbenu Ḥananel,* we are dealing here with bowls made of silver or gold. *Rashi* and *Tosafot* explain that the poor man was asked whether he wished to use linen cloths as white as silver or silk cloths as brightly colored as gold. Others explain that we are dealing here with cushions embroidered with silver or gold threads.

Many commentators ask: Why did Rabbi Ḥanina not respond like Mar Ukva (see above, 67b) when the latter heard that the poor man whom he was supporting was accustomed to sprinkling old wine on the floor? In other words, why did Rabbi Ḥanina not conclude that the poor man had fastidious tastes and therefore had to be given an even larger gift of charity?

Tosafot and *Ritva* suggest that such extravagances cannot be attributed to the poor man's having been spoiled by indulgence; instead, they testify to great wealth and disqualify him from receiving charity. *Talmidei Rabbenu Yonah* explains that if the poor man had indeed been accustomed to using gold utensils exclusively, he would not have been required to sell them before accepting charity. Here, however, where he was accustomed to using both silver and gold utensils, he should have sold the more expensive gold utensils before taking charity. *Meiri* suggests

HALAKHAH

manner that the recipient knows who the donor is, but the donor does not know who the recipient is. This was the practice of Rabbi Abba, who would tie coins in his scarf and cast the scarf behind his back, and the poor would come and take the money." (*Rambam, Sefer Zeraim, Hilkhot Mattenot Aniyyim* 10:10; *Shulḥan Arukh, Yoreh De'ah* 249:9.)

הַמַּעֲלִים עֵינָיו מִן הַצְּדָקָה Whoever closes his eyes against charity. "Whoever closes his eyes to those who are in need

TRANSLATION AND COMMENTARY

his eyes to those who are in need of **charity is treated as if he were worshiping idols.** [1]**The verse here,** which refers to a person who will not give to charity, **says** [Deuteronomy 15:9]: **'Beware that there not be a *base* thought in your heart**...and your eye will be evil against your poor brother, and you will give him nothing.' [2]**And a verse elsewhere,** which refers to a city whose inhabitants were guilty of idolatry, **says** [Deuteronomy 13:14]: **'Certain men, *base* persons, have gone out.'** [3]The similar expressions used in these two verses teaches us that **just as there it refers to** people who are guilty of **idolatry,** [4]**so too here it refers to** people who refrain from giving charity and thus are considered guilty of **idolatry."**

תָּנוּ רַבָּנַן [5]**Our Rabbis taught** a Baraita describing what will happen to those who pretend to be poor and who ask for charity when they are not in need: **"Someone who pretends to be blind, or who causes his belly to swell** as if he were seriously ill, **or who distorts his leg** as if he were a cripple, so as to elicit people's compassion and benefit from their charity, [6]**will not leave this world until he** actually **arrives at such a state** — of blindness, illness, or being crippled. [7]Similarly, **someone who receives charity when he does not** really **require** other people's help **will not in the end leave this world until he** actually **arrives at such a state** of poverty."

תְּנַן הָתָם [8]The Gemara now discusses a Mishnah that establishes the poverty level with respect to the various agricultural gifts that must be made to the poor — gleanings, forgotten sheaves, and the produce left in the corner of the field. **We have learned elsewhere** in the Mishnah (*Pe'ah* 8:8): [9]"If someone has two hundred

הַצְּדָקָה כְּאִילּוּ עוֹבֵד עֲבוֹדָה זָרָה. [1]כְּתִיב הָכָא: ׳הִשָּׁמֶר לְךָ פֶּן יִהְיֶה דָבָר עִם לְבָבְךָ בְלִיַּעַל, וגו׳׳ [2]וּכְתִיב הָתָם: ׳יָצְאוּ אֲנָשִׁים בְּנֵי בְלִיַּעַל׳. [3]מַה לְּהַלָּן עֲבוֹדָה זָרָה, [4]אַף כָּאן עֲבוֹדָה זָרָה״.

[5]תָּנוּ רַבָּנַן: ״הַמְסַמֵּא אֶת עֵינוֹ, וְהַמַּצְבֶּה אֶת בִּטְנוֹ, וְהַמְקַפֵּחַ אֶת שׁוֹקוֹ, [6]אֵינוֹ נִפְטָר מִן הָעוֹלָם עַד שֶׁיָּבֹא לִידֵי כָּךְ. [7]הַמְקַבֵּל צְדָקָה וְאֵין צָרִיךְ לְכָךְ״ סוֹפוֹ אֵינוֹ נִפְטָר מִן הָעוֹלָם עַד שֶׁיָּבֹא לִידֵי כָּךְ״.

[8]תְּנַן הָתָם: [9]״אֵין מְחַיְּיבִין

LITERAL TRANSLATION

charity [is considered] as if he worships idols. [1]It is written here: 'Beware that there not be a base thought in your heart, etc.' [2]And it is written there: 'Certain men, base persons, have gone out.' [3]Just as there [it refers to] idolatry, [4]so too here [it refers to] idolatry."

[5]Our Rabbis taught: "One who pretends to be blind [lit., 'who blinds his eye'], or causes his belly to swell, or distorts his leg, [6]does not pass from the world until he arrives at such [a state]. [7]One who receives charity and does not require it does not in the end pass from the world until he arrives at such [a state]."

[8]We have learned elsewhere: [9]"We do not require

RASHI

המסמא את עינו — מראה את עצמו כאילו עינו סמויה. **מקפח שוקו** — כאילו שוקו נכוולת. **אין מחייבין אותו למכור כו׳** — רישא

NOTES

that Rabbi Ḥanina was the administrator of the communal charity fund, which, unlike a private person, is not required to support a poor man until he sells his expensive utensils. Alternatively, Rabbi Ḥanina discovered that the poor man had always been poor, and had grown accustomed to his luxuries while receiving charity.

כְּאִילּוּ עוֹבֵד עֲבוֹדָה זָרָה As if he worships idols. A person who recognizes that all his worldly possessions are a gift from God is willing to share his wealth with those who are less fortunate than he is. A person who refrains from giving charity to the poor demonstrates that he views himself as having acquired his wealth entirely on his own, without any divine assistance. Thus he is guilty of worshiping an idol of sorts — himself.

וְהַמְקַפֵּחַ אֶת שׁוֹקוֹ Or distorts his leg. The Rishonim record several different readings and interpretations of this line, according to all of which the swindler presents himself as having something wrong with his leg. The standard text of the Talmud reads מְקַפֵּחַ, meaning "breaks," and is best understood according to *Talmidei Rabbenu Yonah* who explains that the Baraita is dealing with someone who pretends that his leg is broken. According to *Rashi,* the Baraita speaks of someone who pretends that his leg has shrunk. This interpretation fits in well with the reading

HALAKHAH

of charity is considered a wicked person and is placed in the same category as someone who worships idols. A person must be very careful about giving charity, for a delay in responding to a poor man's request for charity may possibly lead to the man's death." (*Rambam, Sefer Zeraim, Hilkhot Mattenot Aniyyim* 10:3; *Shulḥan Arukh, Yoreh De'ah* 247:1.)

הַמְסַמֵּא אֶת עֵינוֹ One who pretends to be blind. "Any person who does not need to be supported by others, but feigns poverty and takes charity, will not live out his life without experiencing a real need to rely on others." (*Rambam, Sefer Zeraim, Hilkhot Mattenot Aniyyim* 10:19; *Shulḥan Arukh, Yoreh De'ah* 255:2.)

אֵין מְחַיְּיבִין אוֹתוֹ לִמְכּוֹר אֶת בֵּיתוֹ We do not require him to sell his house. "Even if a poor man owns a house or possesses household utensils of gold or silver, if he does

TRANSLATION AND COMMENTARY

dinarim, he is not entitled to the various agricultural gifts that are made to the poor. A person who does not have that sum of money in cash **is not required to sell his house or his household utensils** in order to raise the money and thus make himself ineligible for those gifts."

וְלָא [1]The Gemara now queries: **Is** it true that a person is **not** required to sell his property in order not to take charity? [2]**But surely it was taught** in a Baraita: **"If** a person who has been reduced to poverty **was** previously **accustomed to using gold utensils, he should** sell his gold utensils and begin to **use silver utensils.** [3]And if he was accustomed to using **silver utensils, he should** sell the silver utensils and begin to **use copper utensils."** Thus we see that a person is required to sell at least some of his household utensils before accepting charity, and this contradicts the Mishnah just quoted!

אֲמַר רַב זְבִיד [4]**Rav Zevid said** in reply: **There is no difficulty,** because the Baraita and the Mishnah refer to two different matters. The Baraita, which rules that before a person accepts charity, he must sell his more expensive utensils and replace them with cheaper ones, [5]**refers to** the person's **bed and table.** Whereas the Mishnah, which rules that a person is not required to sell his household utensils, [6]**refers to** the person's **cups and bowls.**

מַאי שְׁנָא [7]The Gemara objects to this distinction: **What is** so **different about** a person's **cups and bowls that he is not required to sell them** before taking charity? [8]It must be **because he can say:** The cheaper cups and bowls **are** so **repulsive to me** that I am unable to eat from them. [9]But if this is his argument, then **he should also be able to say regarding his bed and his table:** A cheaper bed and table **are not acceptable to me,** because I find them too uncomfortable for use!

אֲמַר רָבָא בְּרֵיהּ דְּרַבָּה [10]**Rava the son of Rabbah said:** The Baraita, which states that a person must sell his more expensive utensils rather than take charity, refers to items like **a strigil of silver,** a comb-like instrument used to scrape one's skin during a bath. A person must surely sell such a luxury utensil and replace it if necessary with a cheaper one. But a person is not required to sell his house or essential household utensils in order to avoid taking charity, as is stated in the Mishnah.

אוֹתוֹ לִמְכּוֹר אֶת בֵּיתוֹ וְאֶת כְּלֵי תַשְׁמִישׁוֹ".

[1]וְלָא? [2]וְהָתַנְיָא: הָיָה מִשְׁתַּמֵּשׁ בִּכְלֵי זָהָב, יִשְׁתַּמֵּשׁ בִּכְלֵי כֶסֶף; [3]בִּכְלֵי כֶסֶף, יִשְׁתַּמֵּשׁ בִּכְלֵי נְחוֹשֶׁת"!

[4]אֲמַר רַב זְבִיד: לָא קַשְׁיָא. [5]הָא בְּמִטָּה וְשׁוּלְחָן; [6]הָא בְּכוֹסוֹת וּקְעָרוֹת.

[7]מַאי שְׁנָא כּוֹסוֹת וּקְעָרוֹת דְּלָא? [8]דְּאָמַר: מְאִיסֵי לִי. [9]מִטָּה וְשׁוּלְחָן נַמִי אָמַר לָא מְקַבַּל עִילָוַאי!

[10]אֲמַר רָבָא בְּרֵיהּ דְּרַבָּה: בְּמַחֲרֵישָׁה דְּכַסְפָּא.

LITERAL TRANSLATION

him to sell his house or his household utensils."

[1]But [do we] not? [2]But surely it was taught: "[If] he used to use gold utensils, he should use silver utensils; [3]silver utensils, he should use copper utensils"!

[4]Rav Zevid says: There is no difficulty. [5]This [refers] to a bed and a table; [6]this [refers] to cups and bowls.

[7]What is different [about] cups and bowls that he is not [required to sell them]? [8]Because he can say: They are repulsive to me. [9][Regarding] a bed and a table he can also say: They are not acceptable to me!

[10]Rava the son of Rabbah said: [It refers] to a strigil of silver.

RASHI

דמתניתין מי שיש לו מאתים זוז לא יטול לקט שכחה ופאה. אין מחייבין אותו למכור כו' – להשלים מאתים זוז כדי שלא יטול.

NOTES

מַקְפֶּה (or מַקְפָּא) meaning "raises," i.e., he lifts up his leg, pretending that it does not reach the ground. The Geonim read מְעַבֶּה, meaning "thickens," and explain that the Baraita refers to someone who causes his leg to swell as if he were suffering from some disease. *Arukh* reads מַקְבֶּה, meaning "puts on a wooden leg."

בְּמַחֲרֵישָׁה דְּכַסְפָּא **It refers to a strigil of silver.** Most Rishonim explain that the silver implement (מַחֲרֵישָׁה) mentioned here is not an agricultural tool used for plowing fields, for a silver plow would be too soft to be effective. Rather, the Gemara is referring here to a strigil, a comb-like instrument used to scrape one's skin during the bath,

HALAKHAH

not have two hundred zuz in cash, he may nevertheless accept charity, and he is not obliged to sell his house or utensils. This ruling applies only to eating utensils, clothing, linen, and the like, but he must sell an item like a silver strigil and replace it with a cheaper substitute, rather than take charity, in accordance with Rava's ruling. This ruling is also restricted to a case where the poor man accepts donations from individuals, not from the charity fund. He may not be supported by the communal charity fund before he sells all his expensive utensils, in accordance with Rav Pappa, who does not disagree with Rava." (*Rambam, Sefer Zeraim, Hilkhot Mattenot Aniyyim* 9:14: *Shulḥan Arukh, Yoreh De'ah* 253:1.)

[1]רַב פַּפָּא אֲמַר: לָא קַשְׁיָא. [2]כָּאן קוֹדֶם שֶׁיָּבֹא לִידֵי גִיבּוּי; כָּאן לְאַחַר שֶׁיָּבֹא לִידֵי גִיבּוּי.

מִשְׁנָה [3]יְתוֹמָה שֶׁהִשִּׂיאָתָהּ אִמָּהּ אוֹ אַחֶיהָ מִדַּעְתָּהּ, וְכָתְבוּ

LITERAL TRANSLATION

[1]Rav Pappa said: There is no difficulty. [2]Here it is before it comes to collection; here it is after it comes to collection.

MISHNAH [3]An orphan girl whom her mother or her brothers married off with her consent, and they wrote

TRANSLATION AND COMMENTARY

רַב פַּפָּא אֲמַר [1]**Rav Pappa suggested** another resolution of the apparent contradiction between the Mishnah in *Pe'ah* and the Baraita: **There is** really **no difficulty.** [2]**Here** in tractate *Pe'ah* the Mishnah **is** teaching the law that applies **before** the courts **come to collect** from the poor man because he has taken charity illegally. If a poor man does not have two hundred dinarim in cash, so that he is entitled to the agricultural gifts that are made to the poor, but he does have assets which if sold would place him outside the category of poverty, he is not required to sell his house or his household utensils in order to avoid taking charity. But **there** in the Baraita it teaches the law that applies **after** the courts **come to collect** from the poor man because he has accepted charitable gifts after feigning poverty. The Baraita teaches us that if he does not have any money then, he is indeed required to sell expensive utensils to pay back the money he owes.

MISHNAH יְתוֹמָה שֶׁהִשִּׂיאָתָהּ אִמָּהּ [3]As was explained earlier in this chapter, a father is obliged to provide his daughter with a dowry in accordance with his means, so that she may find a suitable husband. If a man dies and leaves an unmarried daughter, the girl's mother and brothers are entitled to marry her off, and the girl is entitled to receive a fitting dowry from her father's estate. **If an orphan girl** under the age of twelve **was married off by her mother or her brothers,** even if she gave **her consent, and they obligated**

RASHI

כאן קודם שיבוא לידי גיבוי — הא דתנן אין מחייבין מעיקרא קאי כשבא ליטול לקט ולא היו לו מאתים זוז ואם היה מוכר כלי תשמישו היה משיג למאתים זוז אין מחייבין אותו למכור והא דתנן מחייבין לאחר שבא לידי גיבוי לאחר שהביא עצמו לידי כך שבית דין גובין הימנו כגון שהיה לו מאתים זוז ונטל לקט שכחה ופאה ונודע שעשיר היה ב״ד באין וגובין הימנו מה שנטל ואם אין לו כדי לשלם מוכר כלי תשמישו היקרים ומשתמש בפחותים. **לידי גיבוי** — שבית דין גובין הימנו.

משנה מדעתה — רבותא קמ״ל דאע״פ שנתרצית אין מחילתה מחילה.

NOTES

which the wealthy would make out of silver (*Arukh, Rif* in the name of the Geonim). A luxury item like this must be sold before a person takes charity, but he is not required to sell his more essential utensils. *Talmidei Rabbenu Yonah* explains, however, that the silver implement mentioned here is a small plow used in the garden. An agricultural implement like this must be sold before a person takes charity, but he is not required to sell his personal utensils.

לְאַחַר שֶׁיָּבֹא לִידֵי גִיבּוּי **After it comes to collection.** Our commentary follows *Rashi,* who distinguishes between the law that applies before the court comes to collect from the poor man who has taken charity illegally, and the law that applies after the court has come to collect from the poor man who has received charitable gifts after feigning poverty. *Tosafot* distinguishes between a poor man who takes charity from ownerless property, such as gleanings and what's left in the corner of the field, who is not required to sell his more expensive utensils before taking the gifts, and a poor man who receives money that has been collected for the communal charity fund, who must indeed sell his more expensive utensils before accepting the charity. *Rif, Rid,* and others argue that a poor man who discreetly receives charity from private individuals is not required to sell his more expensive utensils first. But he cannot take money that has been collected for the communal charity fund until he first sells his more expensive utensils.

Ra'ah and *Ritva* maintain that the poor man is not required to sell utensils that were in his possession before a collection was made on his behalf, but he is required to sell more expensive utensils that came into his possession after he started to receive charity. *Rosh* (in the name of *Rabbenu Tam*) argues the reverse — that before the poor man comes to take money from the communal charity fund, he must first sell his more expensive utensils, but if such utensils came into his possession after he had already received the charity, he is not required to sell them.

יְתוֹמָה שֶׁהִשִּׂיאָתָהּ אִמָּהּ אוֹ אַחֶיהָ מִדַּעְתָּהּ **An orphan girl whom her mother or her brothers married off with her consent.** *Rid* explains that the Mishnah mentions that the orphan girl gave her consent to the marriage, because if she did not give her consent, the marriage contracted on her behalf by her mother or brothers would not be legally binding. The Mishnah teaches us that even if the orphan girl consented to the marriage, so that the marriage is valid, she did not forfeit the dowry to which she was entitled. *Rashi* argues that the consent mentioned here refers to the size of the dowry. The Mishnah teaches us that even if the orphan girl consented to the dowry arrangements, she may later collect the full amount to which she is entitled, for a minor's waiver has no legal validity. (*Shittah Mekubbetzet* points out that, according to

HALAKHAH

יְתוֹמָה שֶׁהִשִּׂיאָתָהּ אִמָּהּ אוֹ אַחֶיהָ **An orphan girl whom her mother or her brothers married off.** "If an orphan girl was married off by her mother or her brothers while she was still a minor (even if she gave her consent), and they provided her with a meager dowry, she may, when she reaches majority, collect from her father's estate a dowry befitting

לָהּ בְּמֵאָה אוֹ בַּחֲמִשִּׁים זוּז, [1]יְכוֹלָה הִיא מִשֶּׁתַּגְדִּיל לְהוֹצִיא מִיָּדָן מַה שֶּׁרָאוּי לְהִנָּתֵן לָהּ.

[2]רַבִּי יְהוּדָה אוֹמֵר: אִם הִשִּׂיא אֶת הַבַּת הָרִאשׁוֹנָה [3]יִנָּתֵן לַשְּׁנִיָּה כְּדֶרֶךְ שֶׁנָּתַן לָרִאשׁוֹנָה. [4]וַחֲכָמִים אוֹמְרִים: פְּעָמִים שֶׁאָדָם עָנִי וְהֶעֱשִׁיר, [5]אוֹ עָשִׁיר וְהֶעֱנִי. [6]אֶלָּא שָׁמִין אֶת הַנְּכָסִים וְנוֹתְנִין לָהּ.

גמרא [7]אָמַר שְׁמוּאֵל: לְפַרְנָסָה שָׁמִין בָּאָב.

LITERAL TRANSLATION

for her a hundred or fifty zuz, [1]may when she reaches majority collect from them what is fitting to be given to her.

[2]Rabbi Yehudah says: If someone has married off his first daughter, [3]the second one should be given in the manner that he gave to the first one. [4]But the Sages say: There are times when a person is poor and becomes wealthy, [5]or is wealthy and becomes poor. [6]Rather, we assess the property and give to her [accordingly].

GEMARA [7]Shmuel said: For the dowry we assess the father.

RASHI

מה שראוי ליתן לה – עישור נכסים. **אם השיא** – האב בחייו את הבת הראשונה. **ינתן כו'** – בין שהוא עישור בין שהוא פחות בין שהוא יותר.

גמרא לפרנסה שמין באב – הבת יתומה שבאת לינשא נותנים לה נדוניא כפי אומד שאנו בקיאין באביה וותרן או קמצן.

TRANSLATION AND COMMENTARY

themselves to provide her with a dowry of **a hundred or fifty zuz,** and, given the size of her father's estate, she ought to have received a much larger dowry, [1]**when she reaches majority** the girl **may collect from** her father's heirs an amount **that is fitting to be given to her.**

רַבִּי יְהוּדָה אוֹמֵר [2]**Rabbi Yehudah says: If someone has married off his first daughter** during his lifetime and has provided her with a dowry, and he then dies leaving another daughter unmarried, [3]**the second** daughter when she marries **must be given** a dowry from the father's estate **that is similar** to the dowry **that** he **gave to his first** daughter. [4]**But the Sages say:** The size of the first daughter's dowry does not determine the size of the dowry to be given to the second daughter, for **sometimes a person may have been poor but** later **became wealthy,** [5]**or may** originally **have been wealthy but** later **became poor.** [6]**Rather,** the court **assesses the property** of the father's estate and **gives** his daughter an appropriate dowry.

GEMARA אָמַר שְׁמוּאֵל [7]**Shmuel said:** In order to determine the amount that an orphan girl may collect **as her dowry** from her father's estate, **we assess** how much **the father** would have been willing to give his daughter as a dowry. We consider the father's means, his social standing, and his character.

NOTES

Rashi, the Mishnah should have been formulated: "And they wrote with her consent.") *Rabbenu Barukh* explains that the Mishnah refers to a case where the girl consented to the marriage, but did not explicitly waive the dowry to which she was entitled. In such a case, she may later collect the dowry, even if at the time of her marriage she had sufficient understanding to appreciate the significance of a waiver, and even though an explicit waiver on her part would have been binding.

בְּמֵאָה אוֹ בַּחֲמִשִּׁים A hundred or fifty. *Tosefot Yom Tov* explains the significance of both figures mentioned in the Mishnah. Even if the girl's mother or brothers obligated themselves to only the most minimal dowry, a dowry of fifty dinarim (see previous Mishnah), she cannot collect from them the full sum to which she is entitled until she reaches majority. And even if they obligated themselves to a sizable dowry, i.e., a dowry of one hundred dinarim, they did not fulfill their obligation to provide the girl with a fitting dowry, if she was fit to receive an even larger dowry.

יְכוֹלָה הִיא מִשֶּׁתַּגְדִּיל May when she reaches majority. The Tosefta (*Ketubot* 6:7) adds that even if the girl's husband signed away his right to demand a larger dowry, the girl herself upon reaching majority may collect the dowry that she is entitled to from her father's estate.

לְהוֹצִיא מִיָּדָן מַה שֶּׁרָאוּי לְהִנָּתֵן לָהּ Collect from them what is fitting to be given to her. According to *Rashi, Tosafot,* and *Rid,* there are only two opinions in the Mishnah and Gemara about the manner in which the size of the orphan girl's dowry is determined. According to Rabbi Yehudah, we assess how much the father would have been willing to give his daughter as a dowry. And according to the Sages, we assess the father's estate, so that we can award the daughter a tenth of the assets as her dowry, as is explained by Rabbi Yehudah HaNasi in the Baraita cited below in the Gemara. *Ramban, Ra'ah, Ritva, Meiri* and others maintain that we are dealing here with three opinions. According to Rabbi Yehudah, we assess the father's personal disposition, and according to Rabbi Yehudah HaNasi, we award the girl a tenth of her father's estate. In addition, the Sages of our Mishnah maintain that we assess the father's estate and give the orphan girl a dowry of the same size as the dowries given by other people of similar economic standing.

לְפַרְנָסָה שָׁמִין בָּאָב For the dowry we assess the father. *Rabbenu Ḥananel* explains that, according to Shmuel, we

HALAKHAH

her. *Rema* (in the name of *Tur* and others) adds that even if she said nothing about the matter for an extended period of time after reaching majority, she may still demand the dowry to which she is entitled." (*Rambam, Sefer Nashim, Hilkhot Ishut* 20:12; *Shulḥan Arukh, Even HaEzer* 113:7.)

לְפַרְנָסָה שָׁמִין בָּאָב For the dowry we assess the father. "If a man died and was survived by a daughter, we assess how much the father would have been willing to give his

TRANSLATION AND COMMENTARY

מְתִיבֵי [1]**An objection** against Shmuel's ruling **was raised** from a Baraita, which stated: "Orphan **daughters are maintained and supported from their father's property.** [2]**How** is the amount of the daughter's maintenance and support determined? [3]**We do not** ask ourselves how the father himself would have acted and **say: If** the girl's **father had been alive, he would have given** her **such-and-such.** [4]**Rather,** the court **assesses the property** of the father's estate **and gives** the daughter a certain amount irrespective of what the father's personal inclination might have been." Now, says the Gemara, when the Baraita speaks of the daughter's support, [5]**is it not** referring to the **support** in the form of a dowry to which she is entitled when she is given away in marriage **to her husband?** And the Baraita states explicitly that the court assesses the father's property, and not his character. Surely this contradicts Shmuel's ruling!

אֲמַר רַב נַחְמָן בַּר יִצְחָק [6]The Gemara rebuts this objection. **Rav Naḥman bar Yitzḥak said: No,** the Baraita is referring to the **support** in the form of maintenance to which the orphan girl is entitled while she is still by **herself** without a husband. Orphan daughters are entitled to maintenance from the estate of their deceased father until they reach the age of majority or become betrothed (see above, 53b). The Baraita teaches us that the level of that maintenance is determined in accordance with the father's estate. But regarding the dowry to which an orphan girl is entitled, it may well be that we must assess how much the father would have been willing to give his daughter, as maintained by Shmuel.

הָא "נִיזּוֹנוֹת וּמִתְפַּרְנְסוֹת" [7]The Gemara now questions this interpretation of the Baraita. But **surely** the Baraita **states:** "Orphan daughters **are maintained and supported** from their father's property." [8]Since the Baraita speaks both of maintenance and of support, **is it not referring both to the support** to which the orphan girl is entitled when she is given away in marriage **to her husband,** i.e., her dowry ("orphan girls are supported"), **and** to the support to which the orphan girl is entitled while she is still by **herself** without a husband, i.e., maintenance ("orphan girls are maintained")? Regarding both types of support the Baraita rules that the court assesses the father's property, and this contradicts Shmuel's ruling!

[1]מֵתִיבֵי: "הַבָּנוֹת נִיזּוֹנוֹת וּמִתְפַּרְנְסוֹת מִנִּכְסֵי אֲבִיהֶן. [2]כֵּיצַד? [3]אֵין אוֹמְרִים: אִילּוּ אָבִיהָ קַיָּים, כָּךְ וְכָךְ הָיָה נוֹתֵן לָהּ. [4]אֶלָּא שָׁמִין אֶת הַנְּכָסִים וְנוֹתְנִין לָהּ". [5]מַאי לָאו פַּרְנָסַת הַבַּעַל?

[6]אֲמַר רַב נַחְמָן בַּר יִצְחָק: לָא. בְּפַרְנָסַת עַצְמָהּ.

[7]הָא "נִיזּוֹנוֹת וּמִתְפַּרְנְסוֹת" קָתָנֵי. [8]מַאי לָאו אַחַת פַּרְנָסַת הַבַּעַל וְאַחַת פַּרְנָסַת עַצְמָהּ?

LITERAL TRANSLATION

[1]They raised an objection: "Daughters are maintained and supported from their father's property. [2]How so? [3]We do not say: If her father had been alive, he would have given her such-and-such. [4]Rather, we assess the property and give to her." [5]Is it not [referring to] the support of the husband?

[6]Rav Naḥman bar Yitzḥak said: No it is [referring] to the support of herself.

[7]Surely it states: "They are maintained and supported." [8]Is it not [referring to] both the support of the husband and the support of herself?

RASHI

פרנסת הבעל – נדוניא של נשואין.
פרנסת עצמה – מזונות בעודה אצל אחין.

NOTES

assess how much the father would be willing to give his daughter as a dowry, only in order to reduce the size of the orphan daughter's dowry and to give her less than a tenth of her father's estate. But the daughter may never collect as her dowry more than a tenth of her father's estate, even if it is clear that the father would have been willing to give her more. According to *Rashi,* Shmuel maintains that we assess how much the father would have been willing to give his daughter as a dowry, whether to increase the size of her dowry and give her more than a tenth of the father's estate or to reduce the size of her dowry and give her less than a tenth of the estate. The Rishonim treat these two positions at length, adducing support for and raising objections against each position.

HALAKHAH

daughter as a dowry, and we give her a dowry of that amount from her father's estate. How do we make such an assessment? On the basis of the reports of his friends and acquaintances, on the basis of his business activities, and on the basis of his social standing. If the father had married off another daughter before he died, we base our assessment on what he gave that daughter as her dowry, in accordance with the ruling of Rabbi Yehudah whose viewpoint is accepted in the Gemara. *Rema* adds that if the father had once been wealthy but later became impoverished, or if he had once been generous but later became miserly, our assessment of the father's intentions must reflect the later period, in accordance with the ruling of the Sages. If the court is unable to assess how much the father would have given his daughter as a dowry, we assess his estate, and award the daughter a tenth of her father's property as her dowry, in accordance with Rava's understanding of Rabbi Yehudah HaNasi's viewpoint." (*Rambam, Sefer Nashim, Hilkhot Ishut* 20:3; *Shulḥan Arukh, Even HaEzer* 113:1.)

בְּפַרְנָסַת עַצְמָהּ **It is referring to the support of herself.** "An orphan daughter is awarded maintenance, clothing, and

[1]לָא. אִידִי וְאִידִי בְּפַרְנָסַת עַצְמָהּ. [2]וְלָא קַשְׁיָא. [3]הָא בַּאֲכִילָה וּבִשְׁתִיָּה, וְהָא בִּלְבוּשָׁא וְכִיסוּיָא.
[4]תְּנַן: ״וַחֲכָמִים אוֹמְרִים: פְּעָמִים שֶׁאָדָם עָנִי וְהֶעֱשִׁיר, [5]אוֹ עָשִׁיר וְהֶעֱנִי. [6]אֶלָּא שָׁמִין הַנְּכָסִים וְנוֹתְנִין לָהּ״. [7]מַאי עָנִי וּמַאי עָשִׁיר? [8]אִי נֵימָא עָנִי בִּנְכָסִים, עָשִׁיר בִּנְכָסִים, [9]מִכְּלָל דְּתַנָּא קַמָּא סָבַר אֲפִילּוּ עָשִׁיר וְהֶעֱנִי, [10]כִּדְמֵעִיקָּרָא יָהֲבִינַן לָהּ. [11]הָא לֵית לֵיהּ! [12]אֶלָּא לָאו עָנִי בְּדַעַת, [13]עָשִׁיר עָשִׁיר בְּדַעַת. [14]וְקָתָנֵי:

TRANSLATION AND COMMENTARY

לָא [1]The Gemara answers this objection as well. **No,** both **the term** "maintained" **and the term** "supported" refer to **the support** that the orphan girl must be given while she is still by **herself** before she is married. [2]**And** the apparent redundancy poses **no difficulty.** [3]The first expression refers to the support to which she is entitled **for food and drink, and** the second expression refers to the support to which she is entitled **for clothing and** other **coverings.** It can still be argued that in order to determine the size of an orphan girl's dowry it is necessary to assess how much the father would have been willing to give his daughter, in accordance with Shmuel's ruling.

תְּנַן [4]The Gemara now raises another objection against Shmuel, this time from our Mishnah, where **we have learned: "But the Sages say:** The size of the first daughter's dowry does not determine the size of the dowry to be given to the second daughter, for **sometimes a person may have been poor but** later **became wealthy,** [5]**or may** originally **have been wealthy but** later **became poor.** [6]**Rather,** the court **assesses the property** of the father's esate and **gives her** an appropriate dowry." The Gemara first clarifies the meaning of this ruling: [7]**What** do the Sages mean here when they speak of **a poor man, and what** do they mean when they talk about **a wealthy man?** [8]**If we** take these terms literally and **say that "a poor man" refers** here **to a person who is poor in property, and "a wealthy man" refers** here **to a person who is wealthy in property,** there is a certain difficulty. For if the Sages argue that the size of the first daughter's dowry does not determine the size of the second daughter's dowry because the father's financial situation may have changed in the meantime, [9]**this proves by implication that the first Tanna** — Rabbi Yehudah, whose position the Sages are disputing — **maintains that even if** a person married off a daughter during his lifetime, when **he was wealthy, and** later **became poor,** and then died leaving an unmarried daughter, [10]the second daughter **must be given** a dowry from the father's estate that is **as** large as the **first** dowry, which her father gave her sister when he was wealthy. [11]**But** surely the father ended his life as a poor man, and so **he did not leave** enough to give the second daughter a dowry equal to the one given to her sister when their father was wealthy! [12]**Rather,** continues the Gemara, **it must be that** the term **"a poor man" refers** here **to a person who is poor in his mind,** ungenerous, [13]**and** the term **"a wealthy man" refers** here **to a person who is wealthy in mind,** generous. According to this interpretation the Sages argue as follows: We cannot assume that a father would have wanted to give his second daughter a dowry equal to the one he gave his first daughter, for it is possible that he wanted to be mean with his first daughter and generous with his second, or generous with his first daughter and mean with his second. [14]**And** the Mishnah **teaches** us

LITERAL TRANSLATION

[1]No. This and that [refer] to the support of herself. [2]And there is no difficulty. [3]This [refers] to food and drink, and this [refers] to clothing and coverings.

[4]We have learned: "But the Sages say: There are times when a person is poor and becomes wealthy, [5]or is wealthy and becomes poor. [6]Rather, we assess the property and give to her [accordingly]." [7]What is poor and what is wealthy? [8]If we say [that] poor [refers to a person who is] poor in property, [and] wealthy [refers to a person who is] wealthy in property, [9][this proves] by implication that the first Tanna maintains [that] even if he is wealthy and becomes poor, [10]we give her as at first. [11]Surely he does not have! [12]Rather, must it not be that poor [refers to a person who is] poor in mind, [13][and] wealthy [refers to a person who is] wealthy in mind. [14]And it teaches:

RASHI

הא באכילה ושתיה כו׳ — שמין הנכסים אם עני הוא נותנין לה כפי מה ששנינו ב״אף על פי״ (כתובות סד) במשרה את אשתו על ידי שליש ואם הנכסים מרובים הכל לפי הכבוד. **עני בדעת** — אין בדעתו ליתן לה נדוניית עשיר אלא נדוניית עני.

HALAKHAH

housing from her father's estate, just as a widow is awarded these things from the estate of her late husband. To maintain the orphan daughter the court may sell estate assets without previous announcement, just as it may do to maintain a widow. A widow is awarded maintenance in accordance with her social standing and that of her husband, whereas an orphan daughter is awarded maintenance according to what she needs." (*Rambam, Sefer Nashim, Hilkhot Ishut* 19:11; *Shulḥan Arukh, Even HaEzer* 112:6.)

"שָׁמִין אֶת הַנְּכָסִים וְנוֹתְנִין לָהּ". [1]אַלְמָא לָא אָזְלִינַן בָּתַר אוּמְדָּנָא, וּתְיוּבְתָּא דִשְׁמוּאֵל!
[2]הוּא דְּאָמַר כְּרַבִּי יְהוּדָה, דִּתְנַן: [3]"רַבִּי יְהוּדָה אוֹמֵר: אִם הִשִּׂיא בַּת הָרִאשׁוֹנָה, [4]יִנָּתֵן לַשְּׁנִיָּה כְּדֶרֶךְ שֶׁנָּתַן לָרִאשׁוֹנָה".
[5]וְנֵימָא הֲלָכָה כְּרַבִּי יְהוּדָה! [6]אִי אָמַר הֲלָכָה כְּרַבִּי יְהוּדָה, [7]הֲוָה אָמִינָא דַּוְקָא הִשִּׂיאָהּ, דְּגַלֵּי דַּעְתֵּיהּ. [8]אֲבָל לֹא הִשִּׂיאָהּ, לָא. [9]קָא מַשְׁמַע לַן טַעְמָא דְּרַבִּי יְהוּדָה דְּאָזְלִינַן בָּתַר אוּמְדָּנָא, [10]לָא שְׁנָא הִשִּׂיאָהּ וְלָא שְׁנָא לֹא הִשִּׂיאָהּ. [11]וְהַאי דְּקָתָנֵי: "הִשִּׂיאָהּ", [12]לְהוֹדִיעֲךָ כֹּחָן דְּרַבָּנַן, דְּאַף עַל גַּב דְּהִשִּׂיאָהּ וְגַלֵּי דַּעְתֵּיהּ, [13]לָא אָזְלִינַן בָּתַר אוּמְדָּנָא.

LITERAL TRANSLATION

"We assess the property and give to her." [1]Hence we do not follow an estimation, and [this is] a refutation of Shmuel!

[2]He ruled (lit., "said") in accordance with Rabbi Yehudah, for we have learned: [3]"Rabbi Yehudah says: If someone has married off his first daughter, [4]the second one should be given in the manner that he gave to the first one."

[5]Then let him say [that] the Halakhah is in accordance with Rabbi Yehudah!

[6]If he said [that] the Halakhah is in accordance with Rabbi Yehudah, [7]I might have said [that this applies] only if he married her off, where he revealed his intention. [8]But [if] he did not marry her off, no. [9][Hence] he informs us [that] Rabbi Yehudah's reason is that we follow an estimation, [10][and] it makes no difference whether he married her off or he did not marry her off. [11]And the reason why it stated: "If he married her off," [12]was to inform you of the extent (lit., "power") of the Rabbis' [ruling], that even though he married her off and revealed his intention, [13]we do not follow an estimation.

TRANSLATION AND COMMENTARY

that the Sages say: "The court **assesses the property** of the father's estate **and gives** the orphan girl an appropriate dowry. **Hence** we see that in order to determine how much an orphan girl can collect from her father's estate **we do not assess** how much **the father** would have been willing to give his daughter as a dowry. Instead, the court assesses the father's property, and gives the girl a certain fixed amount. [1]Surely **this is a** conclusive **refutation of** the position **of Shmuel!**

הוּא דְּאָמַר [2]No, the Gemara answers: This difficulty, too, can be resolved. It is true that Shmuel's ruling cannot be reconciled with the viewpoint of the Sages, but in maintaining that we assess the father's property, **Shmuel agrees with Rabbi Yehudah,** whose viewpoint **we have learned** in our Mishnah: [3]**"Rabbi Yehudah says: If someone has married off his first daughter** during his lifetime and has provided her with a dowry, and he then dies leaving another daughter unmarried, [4]**the second** daughter **must be given** a dowry from the father's estate **that is similar** to the dowry **that** he **gave to his first** daughter, for we assume that her father would have acted in that manner."

וְנֵימָא הֲלָכָה [5]The Gemara objects: But if this so, **then** Shmuel **should have stated** simply **that the Halakhah is in accordance with** the viewpoint of **Rabbi Yehudah!**

אִי אָמַר הֲלָכָה [6]The Gemara resolves this difficulty. **If** Shmuel **had said that the Halakhah is in accordance with** the viewpoint of **Rabbi Yehudah,** [7]**I might have said that** his ruling **applies only when** the father actually **married off** his first daughter, for in such a case the father **revealed his** true **intentions** as to how large a dowry he wished to provide for his daughter. [8]**But if** the father **did not** actually **marry off** his first daughter, I might have thought that we do **not** assess the father's intentions. [9]**Hence** Shmuel **informs us that the reasoning of Rabbi Yehudah is that** in determining the size of an orphan girl's dowry **we follow an estimation** of how much the father would have been willing to give her, [10]**and** that **it makes no difference whether he has married off** his first daughter **or he has not married her off.** [11]**And the reason why** the Mishnah **stated:** "Rabbi Yehudah says: **If someone has married off** his first daughter, the second daughter must be given a dowry from the father's estate that is similar to the dowry the father gave to his first daughter," was not to imply that Rabbi Yehudah's ruling applies only when the father has married off his first daughter. The Mishnah chose that particular case in order to emphasize the far-reaching consequences of the viewpoint of the Rabbis who disagree with Rabbi Yehudah. [12]That case was chosen **to inform us of the extent of the Rabbis' ruling, that even where** the father **has married off** his first daughter **and has revealed his intentions** as to how large a dowry he wishes to provide for his daughter, [13]**we do not follow an estimation** of how much the father would have been willing to give his second daughter as a dowry. Instead, the court assesses the father's estate and gives the orphan girl a dowry of a certain size irrespective of the father's personal inclination to be mean or generous.

[1] אֲמַר לֵיהּ רָבָא לְרַב חִסְדָּא: "דָּרְשִׁינַן מִשְּׁמָךְ הֲלָכָה כְּרַבִּי יְהוּדָה". [2] אֲמַר לֵיהּ: "יְהֵא רַעֲוָא כָּל כִּי הָנֵי מִילֵּי מַעַלְיָיתָא תִּדְרְשׁוּ מִשְּׁמַאי". [3] וּמִי אֲמַר רָבָא הָכִי? [4] וְהָתַנְיָא: "רַבִּי אוֹמֵר: בַּת הַנִּיזּוֹנֶת מִן הָאַחִין נוֹטֶלֶת עִישּׂוּר נְכָסִים". [5] וַאֲמַר רָבָא: הִלְכְתָא כְּרַבִּי! [6] לָא קַשְׁיָא. [7] הָא דַּאֲמִידְנֵיהּ; [8] הָא דְּלָא אֲמִידְנֵיהּ. [9] הָכִי נַמִי מִסְתַּבְּרָא, דַּאֲמַר רַב אַדָּא בַּר אַהֲבָה: [10] מַעֲשֶׂה וְנָתַן לָהּ רַבִּי אֶחָד מִשְּׁנֵים עָשָׂר

TRANSLATION AND COMMENTARY

אֲמַר לֵיהּ [1] **Rava said to Rav Ḥisda: "We** are accustomed to **teach in your name that the Halakhah is in accordance with** the viewpoint of **Rabbi Yehudah** that an orphan girl is given a dowry of the same size as that received by her sister during her father's lifetime." Pleased with the way that his position was being presented, [2] Rav Ḥisda **said to** Rava: **May it be God's will that you will teach all such good things in my name.**

וּמִי אֲמַר [3] The Gemara asks: **But did Rava** really **say** that the Halakhah is in accordance with Rabbi Yehudah? [4] **Surely it was taught** in a Baraita: **"Rabbi** Yehudah HaNasi **says: An** orphan **daughter who is being maintained by her brothers** from her father's estate **takes a tenth of the property** as her dowry." [5] **And** in connection with this, **Rava said: The Halakhah is in accordance with** the viewpoint of **Rabbi** Yehudah HaNasi! Thus we see that, according to Rava, we do not assess the father's intentions, but we give the orphan daughter a dowry of a fixed amount.

לָא קַשְׁיָא [6] The Gemara answers: **There is no difficulty.** [7] **Rava's ruling** that the Halakhah is in accordance with Rabbi Yehudah applies in a case where the father has already provided one of his daughters with a dowry and **we can assess** how much he would have wished to give his second daughter. [8] And **Rava's ruling** that the Halakhah is in accordance with the viewpoint of Rabbi Yehudah HaNasi applies in a case where the father did not provide one of his daughters with a dowry, and **we cannot assess** how much he would have wished to give as a dowry. In such a case, the orphan daughter is given a tenth of her father's estate.

הָכִי נַמִי מִסְתַּבְּרָא [9] The Gemara adds: **It also stands to reason** that Rabbi Yehudah HaNasi agrees with Rabbi Yehudah in a case where it is possible to assess the father's intentions, **for Rav Adda bar Aḥavah said:** [10] **It once happened that Rabbi** Yehudah HaNasi **gave** an orphan girl **a twelfth of the property** of her late father's estate as her dowry. At first glance Rabbi Yehudah HaNasi's statement in the Baraita, that an orphan

LITERAL TRANSLATION

[1] Rava said to Rav Ḥisda: "We expound in your name [that] the Halakhah is in accordance with Rabbi Yehudah." [2] He said to him: "May it be [God's] will [that] you will expound all such good things in my name."

[3] But did Rava say this? [4] But surely it was taught: "Rabbi says: A daughter who is being maintained by her brothers takes a tenth of the property." [5] And Rava said: The Halakhah is in accordance with Rabbi!

[6] There is no difficulty. [7] This is where we have assessed him; [8] this is where we have not assessed him.

[9] This also stands to reason, for Rav Adda bar Ahavah said: [10] It once happened that Rabbi gave her a twelfth

RASHI

נוטלת עישור נכסים — ולא שמין באב. **הכי גרסינן לא קשיא הא דאמידניה הא דלא אמידניה** — הא דאמר רבי עישור נכסים בדלא אמידניה לאב שלא גר בינינו ולא עמדנו על סוף דעתו אם וותרן אם קמצן. **הכי נמי מסתברא** — דהיכא דאמידניה מודה רבי דשמין באב.

NOTES

דָּרְשִׁינַן מִשְּׁמָךְ **We expound in your name.** Elsewhere (*Betzah* 28a) *Rashi* explains the same expression to mean that Rava came to ask Rav Ḥisda whether he could rely on the tradition that he had heard in Rav Ḥisda's name and publicize his view as the normative law. Rav Ḥisda's response was intended to confirm that the tradition being reported in his name was indeed his view.

הָכִי נַמִי מִסְתַּבְּרָא **This also stands to reason.** *Ritva* notes that the expression, "This also stands to reason," is well chosen, since there is no absolute proof that Rabbi Yehudah HaNasi agrees with Rabbi Yehudah that we assess the father's intentions whenever it is possible to do so. Rabbi Yehudah HaNasi's ruling, awarding the orphan daughter as her dowry a twelfth of her father's estate, can be explained differently: He may first have maintained that an orphan girl is entitled to a tenth of her father's estate as her dowry, and may later have thought that she should be given only a twelfth of the estate. Alternatively, Rabbi

HALAKHAH

עִישּׂוּר נְכָסִים **A tenth of the property.** "If a father is survived by several daughters, each daughter takes a tenth of the property of his estate as her dowry when she marries. The first daughter to marry takes a tenth of the estate, and each successive daughter takes a tenth of what is left over. If all the daughters are married at the same time, each daughter takes her portion in this manner, and then the property is redivided equally between all the daughters, in accordance with the Gemara's conclusion." (*Rambam, Sefer Nashim, Hilkhot Ishut* 20:4; *Shulḥan Arukh, Even HaEzer* 113:4.)

בַּנְּכָסִים. [1]קַשְׁיָין אַהֲדָדֵי! [2]אֶלָּא לָאו שְׁמַע מִינָּהּ הָא דַּאֲמִידְנֵיהּ; [3]הָא דְּלָא אֲמִידְנֵיהּ. [4]שְׁמַע מִינָּהּ.

[5]גּוּפָא: [6]״אָמַר רַבִּי: בַּת הַנִּיזּוֹנֶת מִן הָאַחִין נוֹטֶלֶת עִישּׂוּר נְכָסִים. [7]אָמְרוּ לוֹ לְרַבִּי: ׳לִדְבָרֶיךָ, מִי שֶׁיֵּשׁ לוֹ עֶשֶׂר בָּנוֹת וּבֵן, אֵין לוֹ לַבֵּן בִּמְקוֹם בָּנוֹת כְּלוּם׳. [8]אָמַר לָהֶן: ׳כָּךְ אֲנִי אוֹמֵר: רִאשׁוֹנָה נוֹטֶלֶת עִישּׂוּר נְכָסִים, [9]שְׁנִיָּה בְּמַה שֶּׁשִּׁיְּירָה, [10]וּשְׁלִישִׁית בְּמַה שֶּׁשִּׁיְּירָה, [11]וְחוֹזְרוֹת וְחוֹלְקוֹת בְּשָׁוֶה׳״.

[68B] [12]כָּל חֲדָא וַחֲדָא דְּנַפְשָׁהּ שָׁקְלָה!

LITERAL TRANSLATION

of the property. [1][Surely] they contradict each other! [2]Rather, is it not to be inferred from here [that] this is where we have assessed him; [3]this is where we have not assessed him? [4]Infer from this.

[5]Returning to the statement quoted above (lit., "the thing itself"): [6]"Rabbi said: A daughter who is being maintained by her brothers takes a tenth of the property. [7]They said to Rabbi: 'According to your words, [if] someone has ten daughters and a son, the son does not have anything in the place of the daughters.' [8]He said to them: 'This is what I say: The first [daughter] takes a tenth of the property, [9]the second [a tenth] of what she left over, [10]and the third [a tenth] of what she left over, [11]and they redivide [the property] equally.'"

[68B] [12]Each and every one took her own!

RASHI

ראשונה — קא סלקא דעתין השתא ראשונה לינשא. **כל חדא וחדא דנפשה שקלה** — וחכמים תקנו להם נדוניית נשואין עישור נכסים. והנישאת ראשון ראשון זכתה בעישור שבפניה, ולמה יחזרו ויחלקו עישוריהן שוב בשוה?

TRANSLATION AND COMMENTARY

girl receives a tenth of her father's estate as her dowry and the ruling he issued according to which an orphan girl received a twelfth of her father's estate seem to [1]**contradict each other!** [2]**Rather, it can be inferred from here** that Rabbi Yehudah HaNasi agrees that a distinction must be made between the different cases: The ruling that the orphan girl was to receive a twelfth of her father's estate was issued in a case **where we** we were able to **assess** that the father would have wished his daughter to receive a twelfth of his property as her dowry, for Rabbi Yehudah HaNasi agrees that when it is possible to assess the father's intentions, we follow that assessment; [3]and **the other** ruling, that an orphan daughter receives a tenth of her father's estate, applies in a case **where we cannot assess** how large a dowry the father would have given his daughter. [4]The Gemara concludes: **Infer from this** that Rabbi Yehudah HaNasi agrees that where it is possible to assess the father's intentions, we follow that assessment.

גּוּפָא [5]The Gemara now proceeds to quote at length the Baraita of which a portion was cited above: **Returning to the statement quoted above,** the Baraita stated: [6]"**Rabbi** Yehudah HaNasi **said: An** orphan **daughter who is maintained by her brothers** from her father's estate **takes a tenth of the property** as her dowry. [7]The Sages **said to Rabbi** Yehudah HaNasi: By Torah law, a son excludes a daughter from inheriting any of their father's property, and it is only by Rabbinic enactment that a daughter is entitled to receive a dowry from the property. Now, **according to you,** it turns out that **if a person has ten daughters and a son, the son will be left with nothing** of his father's property **when there are** orphan **daughters** who must each be given a tenth of the father's estate as a dowry. How could a Rabbinic enactment that was intended to better the position of orphan daughters completely cancel the Biblical laws of succession?' [8]Rabbi Yehudah HaNasi **said to them: 'This is what I say: The first daughter takes a tenth of the property** of her father's estate. [9]Then **the second** daughter **takes a tenth of what** her sister **left over.** [10]And then **the third** daughter **takes a tenth of what** her two sisters **left over.** After each of the daughters has taken a progressively smaller portion of the father's estate, [11]**they redivide** all the **property equally** between them, so that the dowry of the first daughter is no larger than that of the last. If the dowries are apportioned in this manner, the son will always retain part of his father's estate.'"

כָּל חֲדָא [68B] [12]The Gemara asks: Why should the daughters redivide the property equally between them after the last daughter has taken her dowry? Surely **each** daughter **has** already **taken her own** dowry, thereby acquiring a tenth of the property that remains from her father's estate!

NOTES

Yehudah HaNasi may have issued his ruling in a case where the father left explicit instructions that his daughter not be given more than a twelfth of his estate as her dowry.

כָּל חֲדָא וַחֲדָא **Each and every one.** *Tosafot*, *Rashba*, and others ask: While an orphan daughter's dowry is recoverable only at the time of her marriage, each of the daughters has a lien on her father's estate from the time of his death for the payment of her dowry. Why, then, should one daughter receive a larger dowry than another, merely

[1]הָכִי קָאָמַר: אִם בָּאוּ כּוּלָּם לְהִנָּשֵׂא כְּאַחַת, [2]חוֹלְקוֹת בְּשָׁוֶה.

[3]מְסַיַּיע לֵיהּ לְרַב מַתְּנָה, [4]דְּאָמַר רַב מַתְּנָה: אִם בָּאוּ לְהִנָּשֵׂא כּוּלָּם כְּאַחַת, נוֹטְלוֹת עִישּׂוּר אֶחָד. [5]״עִישּׂוּר אֶחָד״ סָלְקָא דַּעְתָּךְ? [6]אֶלָּא, נוֹטְלוֹת עִישּׂוּר כְּאֶחָד.

[7]תָּנוּ רַבָּנַן: [8]״הַבָּנוֹת, בֵּין בָּגְרוּ עַד שֶׁלֹּא נִישְּׂאוּ וּבֵין נִישְּׂאוּ עַד שֶׁלֹּא בָּגְרוּ, אִיבְּדוּ מְזוֹנוֹתֵיהֶן, וְלֹא אִיבְּדוּ פַּרְנָסָתָן. [9]דִּבְרֵי רַבִּי. [10]רַבִּי שִׁמְעוֹן בֶּן אֶלְעָזָר

LITERAL TRANSLATION

[1]This is what he said: If they all came together to be married, [2]they divide [the property] equally.

[3][This] supports Rav Matenah, [4]for Rav Matenah said: If they all came together to be married, they take one-tenth. [5]Can "one-tenth" enter your mind? [6]Rather, they take a tenth as one.

[7]Our Rabbis taught: [8]"Daughters, whether they reached majority before they were married or were married before they reached majority, forfeited their maintenance, but did not forfeit their dowry. [9][These are] the words of Rabbi. [10]Rabbi Shimon ben Elazar

TRANSLATION AND COMMENTARY

הָכִי קָאָמַר [1]The Gemara offers the following clarification: **This is what** Rabbi Yehudah HaNasi meant to **say: If all** the daughters **come together to be married off** at the same time, one daughter takes a tenth of her father's estate, another daughter takes a tenth of what is left, a third daughter takes a tenth of what remains, and likewise the rest of the daughters. After the daughters have taken their portions, [2]**they redivide** all **the property equally** between them, so that each will receive a dowry of the same size.

מְסַיַּיע לֵיהּ [3]The Gemara notes: **This** interpretation of the position of Rabbi Yehudah HaNasi **supports** the viewpoint of **Rav Matenah,** [4]**for Rav Matenah said: If all** the orphan daughters **come together to be married off** at the same time, **they take one-tenth** of their father's estate. The Gemara explains what Rav Matenah meant to say: [5]**Can you** possibly **imagine** that all the daughters together take no more than **one-tenth** of their father's estate? [6]**Rather, they** each **take a tenth** of their father's estate **as one.** After each of the daughters takes a progressively smaller portion of the father's estate, they redivide all the property equally between them, so that each daughter receives a dowry of the same size. Thus the viewpoint of Rav Matenah is identical with that of Rabbi Yehudah HaNasi.

תָּנוּ רַבָּנַן [7]**Our Rabbis taught** a Baraita which stated: "By Torah law a daughter does not inherit any part of her deceased father's estate if he is also survived by a son. But the Rabbis enacted that an orphan daughter is entitled to maintenance from her father's estate until she reaches majority or until she is married, and she must be given part of her father's estate as her dowry upon her marriage. [8]Orphan **daughters, whether they have reached** full **majority** at the age of twelve-and-a-half **before they are married, or are married before they have reached** full **majority, have forfeited their** right to **maintenance** from their father's estate, **but have not forfeited their** right to a **dowry.** [9]**This is the viewpoint of Rabbi** Yehudah HaNasi. [10]**Rabbi Shimon ben Elazar**

RASHI

אם באו כולם לינשא כאחת חוזרות וחולקות עישוריהן בשוה — שאין כאן קודמת לזכות. הלכך, בשביל הראוי לישאר לפני הבן נוטלת האחת עישור, והשניה עישור במה ששיירה, וכן כולם, והמותר לבן. אם היו מאה מנה, האחת נוטלת עשר מנים והשניה תשע והשלישית שמונה מנה ועישור של מנה, וכן כולם, כדי לברר ירושת הבן. והן חוזרות וחולקות עישוריהן בשוה. **איבדו מזונותיהן** — שכן כתב להן: או עד דתבגרן או עד דתלקחון לגוברין.

NOTES

because she married first? The Rishonim answer: The sons are obligated to provide the orphan daughter with a dowry, just as the father would have provided his daughter with a dowry had he lived. Just as the father would have given each of his daughters a tenth of the property in his possession at the time she married, so too must the sons provide each of the daughters with a tenth of what remains of their father's estate at the time of her marriage.

אִם בָּאוּ כּוּלָּם לְהִנָּשֵׂא כְּאַחַת **If they all came together to be married off.** It may be asked: What is the novelty of Rav Matenah's ruling, for why would we think that when all the daughters come to be married off at the same time, one daughter is given a larger dowry than another? *Ayyelet Ahavim* suggests that Rav Matenah informs us that even if we can assess that the father would have given one daughter a larger dowry than the rest, the brothers must nevertheless provide each of the daughters with a dowry of equal size.

עַד שֶׁלֹּא נִישְּׂאוּ **Before they were married.** The Rishonim conclude from here that an orphan daughter is entitled to maintenance from her father's estate until she marries, and not, as is stated elsewhere (see above, 53b), only until she is betrothed.

Rabbi Yehudah HaNasi maintains that an orphan daughter is entitled to her dowry even if she reached full majority before she married, provided that she registered a protest at the time she reached majority that she was not waiving her right to her dowry. According to some authorities (*Rabbenu Yonah,* cited by *Shiltei Gibborim; Rosh*), this applies only if she reached majority after her father's death. But if she reached majority during her father's lifetime, even Rabbi Yehudah HaNasi agrees that she is not entitled to a dowry. *Rambam* and others do not recognize such a distinction.

אוֹמֵר: אַף אִיבְּדוּ פַּרְנָסָתָן. [1]כֵּיצַד הֵן עוֹשׂוֹת? [2]שׂוֹכְרוֹת לָהֶן בְּעָלִים וּמוֹצִיאִין לָהֶן פַּרְנָסָתָן״.

[3]אֲמַר רַב נַחְמָן: [4]אֲמַר לִי הוּנָא: הִלְכְתָא כְּרַבִּי.

[5]אֵיתִיבֵיהּ רָבָא לְרַב נַחְמָן: ״יְתוֹמָה שֶׁהִשִּׂיאָתָהּ אִמָּהּ אוֹ אַחֶיהָ מִדַּעְתָּהּ, [6]וְכָתְבוּ לָהּ בְּמֵאָה אוֹ בַּחֲמִשִּׁים זוּז, [7]יְכוֹלָה הִיא מִשֶּׁתַּגְדִּיל לְהוֹצִיא מִיָּדָם מַה שֶּׁרָאוּי לְהִנָּתֵן לָהּ״. [8]טַעֲמָא דִּקְטַנָּה, [9]הָא גְּדוֹלָה, וִיתְּרָה!

LITERAL TRANSLATION

says: They also forfeited their dowry. [1]How do they act? [2]They hire husbands for themselves and collect their dowry for themselves."

[3]Rav Naḥman said: Huna said to me: [4]The Halakhah is in accordance with Rabbi.

[5]Rava raised an objection against Rav Naḥman: "An orphan girl whom her mother or her brothers married off with her consent, [6]and they wrote for her a hundred or fifty zuz, [7]may when she reaches majority collect from them what is fitting to be given to her." [8]The reason is that she was a minor, [9]but [if she was] an adult, she waived [it]!

TRANSLATION AND COMMENTARY

disagrees and **says:** The orphan daughters **have also forfeited their** right to a **dowry** if they reach full majority before they marry. The Rabbis enacted a dowry for an orphan daughter who marries before she reaches full majority (twelve-and-a-half), because she is under her father's authority with respect to marriage and certain other matters. But they did not enact a dowry for an orphan daughter who marries after she reaches full majority, when she is no longer seen as being connected to her father's house. [1]**What should** orphan daughters **do** if they see that they are approaching the age of majority without having received offers of marriage, and they do not wish to forfeit their right to a dowry from their father's estate? [2]**They should hire husbands for themselves** before they reach the age of twelve-and-a-half, **and** should **collect their dowries for themselves."**

אָמַר רַב נַחְמָן [3]**Rav Naḥman said** in reference to this Tannaitic dispute: [4]Rav **Huna said to me: The Halakhah is in accordance with Rabbi** Yehudah HaNasi that an orphan daughter does not forfeit her right to a dowry from her father's estate even if she reaches the age of twelve-and-a-half before she marries.

אֵיתִיבֵיהּ [5]**Rava raised an objection against Rav Naḥman** from our Mishnah, which stated: **"If an orphan girl** under the age of twelve **was married off by her mother or her brothers,** even if the girl gave **her consent,** [6]**and they obligated** themselves to provide her with a dowry of **a hundred or fifty zuz,** and, given her father's substantial estate, she should have received a much larger dowry, [7]**when she reaches majority** the girl may **collect from** her father's heirs an amount **that is fitting to be given to her."** [8]It would appear from this Mishnah that **the reason** why the orphan daughter may later collect from her father's heirs the balance of the dowry to which she is entitled **is that she was a minor** when she was married; a minor's waiver has no legal validity. [9]**But** from this it follows that if the orphan daughter **was an adult** at the time of her marriage — having already reached the age of twelve-and-a-half — and her mother or her brothers obligated themselves to a dowry of only a hundred or fifty zuz, we say that **she waived** the rest of the dowry to which she would have been entitled. Thus our anonymous Mishnah follows the viewpoint of Rabbi Shimon ben Elazar.

RASHI

אף איבדו פרנסתן — עישור נכסים. דקסבר: לא תקון לה נדוניא אלא היכא דמינסבא בקטנות או בנערות, אבל בגרה — איסתלקא לה מההיא ביתא לגמרי. וכן נשאת בנערות, הואיל וגדולה היא ונתרצית — איבדה פרנסתה אלא מה שפסקו. אבל בניסת בקטנות — לא פליג. **שוכרות להן בעלים** — שישאו אותן עד שלא יבגרו, ומוציאים להם פרנסתם. **הא גדולה** — כגון נערה. **ויתרה** — מחלה על השאר ואבדתו. אלמא, סתם לן תנא כרבי שמעון בן אלעזר.

NOTES

שׂוֹכְרוֹת לָהֶן בְּעָלִים **They hire husbands for themselves.** *Rashash* explains that if an orphan daughter sees that she is approaching the age of majority and has not yet received a suitable offer of marriage, she should hire a man who will lie on her behalf and say that he intends to marry her, so that she can collect her dowry from her brothers, and she can then wait until she finds a fitting match. *Eshel Avraham* argues that if an orphan daughter acts in this manner, her brothers can reclaim the dowry which she has collected from them under false pretenses. Rather, the orphan daughter is advised here to hire a man who will actually marry her and will then grant her a divorce after the dowry is collected (see also *Rid, Talmidei Rabbenu Yonah,* and *Rivash*).

וּמוֹצִיאִין לָהֶן פַּרְנָסָתָן **And collect their dowry for themselves.** *Talmidei Rabbenu Yonah* explains that, according to Rabbi Shimon ben Elazar, the orphan daughter must collect her dowry before she marries, because once she marries she forfeits her right to collect it, even if she registered a protest at the time of the marriage.

Rashba proves from here that an orphan daughter may not collect her dowry before she is ready to be married, for if she were able to collect her dowry in advance, an orphan daughter approaching the age of majority would not have to hire a husband in order to safeguard her right to a dowry. But the assessment of the father's estate to determine the size of the orphan daughter's dowry is carried out at the time of the father's death.

¹לָא קַשְׁיָא. ²הָא דִּמְחַאי; ³הָא דְּלָא מְחַאי.

⁴הָכִי נַמִי מִסְתַּבְּרָא, ⁵דְּאִם כֵּן קַשְׁיָא דְּרַבִּי אַדְּרַבִּי, ⁶דְּתַנְיָא: ״רַבִּי אוֹמֵר: בַּת הַנִּיזּוֹנֶת מִן הָאַחִין נוֹטֶלֶת עִישּׂוּר נְכָסִים״. ⁷נִיזּוֹנֶת, אִין; ⁸שֶׁאֵינָהּ נִיזּוֹנֶת, לָא! ⁹אֶלָּא לָאו שְׁמַע מִינָּהּ: ¹⁰הָא דִּמְחַאי; הָא דְּלָא מְחַאי. ¹¹שְׁמַע מִינָּהּ.

¹²אֲמַר לֵיהּ רָבִינָא לְרָבָא: אֲמַר לָן רַב אַדָּא בַּר אַהֲבָה מִשְּׁמָךְ:

LITERAL TRANSLATION

[1]There is no difficulty. [2]This is when she protested; [3]this is when she did not protest.

[4]This also stands to reason, [5]for if so there is a contradiction between the two statements of Rabbi (lit., "a difficulty from Rabbi to Rabbi"), [6]for it was taught: "Rabbi says: A daughter who is being maintained by her brothers takes a tenth of the property." [7]If she is being maintained, yes; [8]if she is not being maintained, no! [9]Rather, is it not [correct to] infer from this: [10]This is where she protested; this is where she did not protest. [11]Infer from this.

[12]Ravina said to Rava: Rav Adda bar Ahavah said to us in your name:

TRANSLATION AND COMMENTARY

לָא קַשְׁיָא [1]The Gemara answers: **There is** really **no difficulty.** When Rabbi Yehudah HaNasi said that an orphan daughter who has reached full majority has not forfeited her right to her dowry, [2]he was referring to a case **in which** the orphan daughter **protested** against the dowry arrangements made on her behalf at the time of her marriage. By contrast, when the anonymous Mishnah said that an orphan daughter who was married off by her mother or her brothers while she was a minor without receiving a proper dowry may later collect from her father's estate, [3]it was referring to an orphan daughter who **did not protest** against the dowry arrangements at the time of her marriage.

הָכִי נַמִי מִסְתַּבְּרָא [4]The Gemara continues: **This** argument **also stands to reason,** [5]**for if** we do not accept this distinction, **there is a contradiction between two statements made by Rabbi** Yehudah HaNasi himself, [6]**for it was taught** in the Baraita cited earlier in the Gemara: "**Rabbi** Yehudah HaNasi **says: An** orphan **daughter who is being maintained by her brothers** from her father's estate **takes a tenth of the property** as her dowry." [7]It would appear from this Baraita that only if the orphan daughter is married off while she **is** still **being maintained** by her brothers from her father's estate, before she has reached full majority at the age of twelve-and-a-half, does Rabbi Yehudah HaNasi say that she is **indeed** entitled to receive a dowry from her father's estate. [8]But if the orphan daughter is married off when **she is no longer being maintained** by her brothers from her father's estate, after she has already reached full majority, Rabbi Yehudah HaNasi agrees that she does **not** receive a dowry from her father's estate. At first glance this contradicts what was taught in the other Baraita, that according to Rabbi Yehudah HaNasi the orphan daughter does not forfeit her right to a dowry, even if she has reached full majority before she marries. [9]**Rather,** says the Gemara, **is it not correct to infer from this** that a distinction must be made between two different cases: The Baraita that says the orphan daughter does not forfeit her right to a dowry from her father's estate even if she is married off after she has already reached full majority, [10]refers to an orphan daughter who **protested** against the dowry arrangements at the time of her marriage. The Baraita which implies that, according to Rabbi Yehudah HaNasi, the orphan daughter is entitled to a dowry from her father's estate only if she is married before reaching full majority, refers to an orphan daughter who **did not protest** against the dowry arrangements. [11]The Gemara accepts this line of reasoning and says: Indeed, **conclude from this** that a distinction must be made between a case where the orphan daughter protested, and a case where she did not protest.

אֲמַר לֵיהּ [12]The Gemara continues: **Ravina said to Rava: Rav Adda bar Ahavah said to us in your name:**

RASHI

הא דמחאי — הא דאמר רבי: לא איבדו, ואמר רב הונא הלכתא כוותיה — בשמיחתה על מותר עישור נכסיה. והא דקתני מתניתין: גדולה ויתרה — בשלא מיחתה. נזונית אין — אם באה לינשא בעודה ניזונית, דהיינו בקטנות או בנערות.

NOTES

הָכִי נַמִי מִסְתַּבְּרָא **This also stands to reason.** *Ritva* notes that the Gemara states that the distinction it has proposed "stands to reason," but it does not argue that it can be conclusively proven to be true. The Baraita that states that

HALAKHAH

הָא דִּמְחַאי; הָא דְּלָא מְחַאי **This is when she protested; this is when she did not protest.** "If an orphan daughter was married off after she reached adulthood (whether she was more than twelve years old or had already turned twelve-and-a-half), and she did not demand the dowry to which she was entitled, she forfeited the right to collect her dowry at some later time. But if, at the time of her marriage, she protested against the forfeiture of her dowry, she may collect the dowry to which she is entitled whenever she wants." (*Rambam, Sefer Nashim, Hilkhot Ishut* 20:13; *Shulḥan Arukh, Even HaEzer* 113:7.)

[1] בָּגְרָה, אֵינָהּ צְרִיכָה לִמְחוֹת. [2] נִישֵּׂאת, אֵינָהּ צְרִיכָה לִמְחוֹת. [3] בָּגְרָה וְנִישֵּׂאת, צְרִיכָה לִמְחוֹת. [4] מִי אֲמַר רָבָא הָכִי? [5] וְהָא אֵיתִיבֵיהּ רָבָא לְרַב נַחְמָן יְתוֹמָה, [6] וְשַׁנֵּי לֵיהּ: [7] הָא דְּמָחֵי; [8] הָא דְּלָא מָחֵי! [9] לָא קַשְׁיָא. [10] הָא דְּקָא מִיתְזְנָא מִינַּיְיהוּ; [11] הָא דְּלָא קָא מִיתְזְנָא מִינַּיְיהוּ.

LITERAL TRANSLATION

[1] [If] she has reached majority, she does not need to protest. [2] [If] she is married, she does not need to protest. [3] [If] she has reached majority and is married, she does need to protest.

[4] Did Rava say this? [5] But surely Rava raised an objection against Rav Naḥman [from the law of] an orphan girl, [6] and he answered him: [7] This is where she protested; [8] this is where she did not protest!

[9] There is no difficulty. [10] This is when she is being maintained by them; [11] this is when she is not being maintained by them.

TRANSLATION AND COMMENTARY

[1] **If** the orphan daughter has **reached** full **majority** at the age of twelve-and-a-half before she marries, **she does not need to protest** against forfeiture of her dowry. She can still demand the dowry to which she is entitled when she marries. [2] And similarly **if** the orphan daughter is **married** before she reaches full majority, **she does not need to protest** but at some later point can still demand the dowry to which she is entitled. [3] But **if** the orphan daughter **has reached** full **majority and is** then **married, she must protest** against the dowry arranged for her, and if she fails to do so, she forfeits the right to collect the dowry.

מִי אֲמַר [4] The Gemara asks: **Did Rava** really **say this?** [5] **Surely Rava raised an objection against Rav Naḥman**, who ruled in accordance with the viewpoint of Rabbi Yehudah HaNasi, **from the law of an orphan girl** who is married off by her mother or her brothers while she is a minor. If they obligate themselves to provide her with a dowry smaller than the one to which she is entitled, upon reaching adulthood she may collect from her father's heirs the balance of the dowry to which she is entitled. Rava argued that this implies that if the girl has already reached the age of twelve when she marries, she may not later demand the dowry to which she is entitled. This contradicts the viewpoint of Rabbi Yehudah HaNasi. [6] **And** Rav **Naḥman answered him** that a distinction is to be drawn between two cases: Rabbi Yehudah HaNasi's ruling, that an orphan daughter does not forfeit her right to her dowry even if she has reached full majority before she marries, [7] refers to a case **where she protested** against forfeiting her right to her dowry. And the Mishnah's implication that an orphan daughter who is married off by her mother or her brothers after she has reached adulthood is unable later to collect the dowry to which she is entitled, [8] refers to a case **where** the orphan daughter **did not protest.** And Rava silently accepted Rav Naḥman's distinction. But this contradicts what was reported by Rav Adda bar Ahavah in the name of Rava, that if an orphan daughter is married before she has reached full majority, she is not required to protest against forfeiture of her dowry!

לָא קַשְׁיָא [9] The Gemara answers: **There is** really **no difficulty.** When Rava said that an orphan daughter who is married before she has reached full majority does not need to protest, [10] he was referring to a case **where** the orphan daughter **is being maintained by** her brothers even after her marriage. In this case the orphan daughter's failure to protest is not treated as a waiver, for she is silent about her dowry because she is still receiving maintenance from her brothers. By contrast, when Rava agreed with Rav Naḥman that an orphan daughter who is married off after reaching adulthood has forfeited the right to her dowry, [11] he was referring to a case **where** the orphan daughter is **no longer being maintained by** her brothers. In such

RASHI

ושני ליה — דהא דתני: גדולה ויתרה דלא מחאי, אלמא ניסת בנערות ולא מיחתה אף על פי שאינה בוגרת, ויתרה, ואת אמרת ניסת אינה צריכה למחות, ואפילו נערה. **הא** — דאמר רבא: ניסת בנערות אינה צריכה למחות — כגון דקא מיתזנא מינייהו לאחר שניסת, דמשום דקא מיתזנא מינייהו הוא דקא שתקה, ולא מחלה על פרנסתה. והא דקתני: הא גדולה ויתרה — דלא קא מתזנא.

NOTES

an orphan daughter who is maintained by her brothers takes a tenth of the property as her dowry may not excludean orphan daughter who is no longer being maintained by her brothers because she has reached the age of full majority. Rather it may exclude an orphan daughter who is no longer being maintained by her brothers because they have died, and the surviving daughters have divided the estate between them (see below, 69a).

צְרִיכָה לִמְחוֹת **She does need to protest.** *Meiri* states that the orphan daughter must make her protest before a court.

HALAKHAH

הָא דְּקָא מִיתְזְנָא **This is when she is being maintained.** "If an orphan daughter reached full majority at the age of twelve-and-a-half, and her brothers stopped providing her with maintenance (for they were no longer obligated to

[1]אָמַר רַב הוּנָא אָמַר רַבִּי: פַּרְנָסָה אֵינָהּ כִּתְנַאי כְּתוּבָּה. [2]מַאי ״אֵינָהּ כִּתְנַאי כְּתוּבָּה״? [3]אִי נֵימָא דְּאִילּוּ פַּרְנָסָה טָרְפָא מִמְּשַׁעְבְּדֵי, [4]וּתְנַאי כְּתוּבָּה לָא טָרְפָא מִמְּשַׁעְבְּדֵי, [5]מַאי קָא מַשְׁמַע לָן? [6]הָא מַעֲשִׂים בְּכָל יוֹם מוֹצִיאִין לְפַרְנָסָה וְאֵין מוֹצִיאִין לִמְזוֹנוֹת!

LITERAL TRANSLATION

[1]Rav Huna said in the name of Rabbi: A dowry is not like a ketubah condition.

[2]What is [the meaning of] "is not like a ketubah condition"? [3]If we say that a dowry may be seized from mortgaged property, [4]whereas a ketubah condition may not be seized from mortgaged property, [5]what does it teach us? [6]Surely incidents [take place] every day [in which] we collect for a dowry but we do not collect for maintenance!

TRANSLATION AND COMMENTARY

a case, the orphan daughter's failure to protest is regarded as a waiver of her right to receive her dowry.

אָמַר רַב הוּנָא [1]The Gemara now proceeds to discuss another distinction between an orphan daughter's right to a dowry and her right to maintenance. **Rav Huna said in the name of Rabbi** Yehudah HaNasi: An orphan daughter's right to **a dowry** from her father's estate **is not like** her right to maintenance, to which she is entitled by virtue of **a ketubah condition.** A woman's ketubah ordinarily includes a clause which states: "The female daughters whom you will have from me will live in my house and will be maintained from my property after my death until they are taken by husbands." No similar stipulation is included in a woman's ketubah regarding her daughter's right to receive a dowry from her father's estate, because that right does not arise as a condition laid down by the Rabbis but rather from an assessment of what the father would have given his daughter as a dowry had he lived.

מַאי [2]The Gemara now attempts to clarify the meaning of Rabbi Yehudah HaNasi's statement: **What** did Rabbi Yehudah HaNasi mean when he said that an orphan daughter's right to a dowry from her father's estate **is not like** her right to maintenance, to which she is entitled by virtue of **a ketubah condition?** [3]**If we say that** Rabbi Yehudah HaNasi meant to teach us that, **whereas** the daughter **may seize** her **dowry from property** belonging to her father's estate **that** her brothers **have mortgaged** or sold to a third party, [4]**she may not seize** the maintenance to which she is entitled by virtue of **a ketubah condition from property that** her brothers **have mortgaged** or sold to a third party, there is a certain difficulty. Even though the orphan girl may collect her dowry from her father's estate only at the time of her marriage, a claim against the estate in favor of the daughter's dowry came into existence at the time of the father's death. Thus the daughter may seize for her dowry any of the assets of her father's estate that her brothers transferred to a third party during the time between the father's death and her marriage. Although a similar charge on the father's estate exists in favor of the daughter's maintenance, the Rabbis enacted that the daughter may only collect her maintenance from the free assets of her father's estate, and not from assets mortgaged or sold to a third party by her brothers. The Rabbis limited the daughter's right to collect her maintenance in the public interest, because the amount of the daughter's maintenance is not a fixed sum, and a buyer cannot know how much property must be left in the hands of the brothers for their sister's maintenance. But no such limitation was placed on the girl's right to a dowry, for the amount of an orphan girl's dowry is set at one-tenth of the value of her father's estate. Now, if this is what Rabbi Yehudah HaNasi meant when he said that the orphan daughter's right to a dowry is unlike her right to maintenance, [5]**what** novel ruling **did he teach us? Surely incidents take place every day in which we collect** from her father's estate which her brothers sold to a third party **for an** orphan girl's **dowry,** [6]**but we do not collect** from such property **for** her **maintenance!** Surely Rabbi Yehudah HaNasi did not seek to teach us something that was already well known and accepted!

RASHI

פרנסה – נדוניא. תנאי כתובה – מזונות של בת כדתנן בנן נוקבן כו׳.
ממשעבדי – שמשיעבדו אחין, ולא ששעבד האב. **לא טרפא ממשעבדי** – אפילו שיעבדו אחין, דתנן (גיטין מח,ג): אין מוציאין לאכילת פירות, ולשבח קרקעות, ולמזון האשה והבנות, מנכסים משועבדים מפני תיקון העולם. אבל פרנסתה – טרפא, דשויוה רבנן כבעל חוב בעישור נכסים משמת האב, דדבר קצוב הוא. אבל מזונות אין להם קצבה, ויש בהן מפני תיקון העולם.
מוציאין לפרנסה – ממשעבדי ששיעבדו אחין.

HALAKHAH

maintain her), and she was silent and did not demand her dowry, she forfeited her dowry. If she demanded her dowry, she did not forfeit it. But if her brothers continued to maintain her even after she reached full majority, then even if she did not raise an objection and demand her dowry, she did not forfeit it." (*Rambam, Sefer Nashim, Hilkhot Ishut* 20:13; *Shulḥan Arukh, Even HaEzer* 113:7.)

TRANSLATION AND COMMENTARY

וְאֶלָּא [1]The Gemara now suggests another interpretation of Rabbi Yehudah HaNasi's ruling. **Rather,** Rabbi Yehudah HaNasi meant to say that [2]**although** an orphan daughter **may collect her dowry even from the movable property** of her father's estate, [3]**she may collect** the maintenance to which she is entitled by virtue of **a ketubah condition only from the landed property** of his estate [4]**but she may not collect** it **from the movable property.** An orphan daughter's right to a dowry derives from an assessment of what the father would have wanted to give her, and if he did not have land, he would surely have provided her with a dowry of movable goods. But the maintenance to which an orphan girl is entitled by virtue of a stipulation in her mother's ketubah may be collected by her only from the landed property of her father's estate, just as a widow can claim her ketubah itself only from the landed property of her late husband's estate. But this interpretation of Rabbi Yehudah HaNasi's ruling is also difficult to accept, for [5]**according to Rabbi** Yehudah HaNasi an orphan girl **may collect both** her dowry and her maintenance **from the movable property** of her father's estate! [6]**For it was taught** in a Baraita: "If a man dies and his estate passes to his sons, **we collect maintenance for the widow and** maintenance and dowries **for the** orphaned **daughters, both from immovable property and from movable property,** because the widow and the daughters are entitled to maintenance even from the movable goods of the estate. And all the more so may the orphan daughter collect her dowry from the movable assets of her late father's estate. [7]This is **the opinion of Rabbi** Yehudah HaNasi."

[8]The Gemara now suggests yet another interpretation of Rabbi Yehudah HaNasi's statement. **Rather, what did** Rabbi Yehudah HaNasi **mean** when he said that an orphan daughter's right to **a dowry** from her father's estate **is not like** her right to maintenance, to which she is entitled by virtue of **a ketubah condition?** [9]The Gemara explains: They are different with respect to **what was taught** in the following Baraita: [10]**"If** a dying man **proclaims** on his deathbed: 'It is my wish that **my daughters not be maintained from my property** after my death,' **we do not follow his instructions.** Since the daughter's right to maintenance derives from a condition laid down in her mother's ketubah, the father's instructions that his daughter be deprived of that right are invalid.

[1]וְאֶלָּא, [2]דְּאִילּוּ פַּרְנָסָה גָּבְיָא נַמִי מִמִּטַּלְטְלֵי, [3]וּתְנַאי כְּתוּבָּה מִמְּקַרְקְעֵי גָּבְיָא [4]מִמִּטַּלְטְלֵי לָא גָּבְיָא. [5]לְרַבִּי, אִידִי וְאִידִי מִיגְבָּא גָּבְיָא, [6]דְּתַנְיָא: "אֶחָד נְכָסִים שֶׁיֵּשׁ לָהֶן אַחֲרָיוּת וְאֶחָד נְכָסִים שֶׁאֵין לָהֶן אַחֲרָיוּת מוֹצִיאִין לִמְזוֹן הָאִשָּׁה וְלַבָּנוֹת. [7]דִּבְרֵי רַבִּי"!

[8]אֶלָּא, מַאי "פַּרְנָסָה אֵינָהּ כִּתְנַאי כְּתוּבָּה"? [9]לְכִדְתַנְיָא: [10]"הָאוֹמֵר: 'אַל יִזּוֹנוּ בְּנוֹתָיו מִנְּכָסָיו', אֵין שׁוֹמְעִין לוֹ.

LITERAL TRANSLATION

[1]Rather, [2][let us say] that she may also collect a dowry from movable property, [3]whereas she may collect a ketubah condition [only] from landed property [4][but] she may not collect [it] from movable property. [5][But] according to Rabbi, she may collect both this and that [from movable property], [6]for it was taught: "We seize both immovable property [lit., 'property with responsibility'] and movable property [lit., 'property without responsibility'] for the maintenance of the wife and for the daughters. [7][These are] the words of Rabbi"!

[8]Rather, what is [the meaning of] "a dowry is not like a ketubah condition"? [9]For what was taught: [10]"[If] someone says: 'Let his daughters not be maintained from his property,' we do not listen to him.

RASHI

אידי ואידי — פרנסה ומזונות גביא ממטלטלי. **למזון האשה והבנות** — וכל שכן פרנסה. ולא מיבעיא פרנסה, אלא אפילו מזונות, דסלקא דעתך אמינא כיון דתנאי כתובה נינהו — ניהוו ככתובה, ולא ניגבו ממטלטלי — קא משמע לן. **האומר** — בשעת מיתתו. הכי גרסינן: **אל יזונו בנותיו מנכסיו אין שומעין לו** — דהא אישתעבד בתנאי כתובה.

NOTES

הָאוֹמֵר: ׳אַל יְזוּנוּ׳ If someone says: "Let his daughters not be maintained." Our translation and commentary follow the reading of *Rashi* and most Rishonim, according to which the Baraita reads: "If someone says: 'Let his daughters not be maintained from his property,' we do not listen to him. [But if he says:] 'Let his daughters not receive a dowry from his property,' we listen to him." A father cannot deprive his daughter of her right to maintenance from his estate, because she is entitled to such maintenance by virtue of a condition attached to her mother's

HALAKHAH

אַל יְזוּנוּ בְּנוֹתָיו מִנְּכָסָיו Let his daughters not be maintained from his property. "If someone proclaims on his deathbed that his daughters are not to be maintained from his estate, we do not listen to him. But if he stipulated at the time of his marriage that his daughters were not to be maintained from his estate after his death, the stipulation is valid just like any other stipulation regarding a monetary matter." (*Rambam, Sefer Nashim, Hilkhot Ishut* 19:13; *Shulḥan Arukh, Even HaEzer* 112:10.)

TRANSLATION AND COMMENTARY

[1] But if the father proclaims prior to his death: 'It is my wish that **my daughters not receive a dowry from my property** after my death,' **we follow his instructions,** [2] **for** an orphan daughter's right to **a dowry is not like** her right to maintenance, to which she is entitled by virtue of **a ketubah condition.** Therefore, if he states explicitly that he wants his daughter to be deprived of a dowry, his instructions have legal validity."

תָּלָה לֵיהּ [69A] [3] The Gemara now returns to the issue of whether an orphan can collect her dowry from property belonging to her father's estate that her brothers have mortgaged to a third party. **Rav** sent a letter **to Rabbi** Yehudah HaNasi and **inserted** the following question **between the lines:** If someone dies, and is survived by sons and a daughter, [4] and the **brothers mortgage** to a third party **the property** they inherited from their father, **what is the law** regarding their sister's dowry? Can the orphan daughter collect her dowry from the property that her brothers have mortgaged to a third party?

הֲוָה יָתֵיב [5] **Rabbi Ḥiyya was sitting before** Rabbi Yehudah HaNasi when Rav's letter arrived. On hearing Rav's

[1] 'אַל יִתְפַּרְנְסוּ בְּנוֹתָיו מִנְּכָסָיו', [2] שׁוֹמְעִין לוֹ, שֶׁהַפַּרְנָסָה אֵינָהּ כִּתְנַאי כְּתוּבָּה". [69A] [3] תָּלָה לֵיהּ רַב לְרַבִּי בֵּינֵי חִטֵּי: [4] הָאַחִין שֶׁשִּׁיעְבְּדוּ מַהוּ? [5] הֲוָה יָתֵיב רַבִּי חִיָּיא קַמֵּיהּ.

LITERAL TRANSLATION

[1] 'Let his daughters not receive a dowry from his property,' we listen to him, [2] for a dowry is not like a ketubah condition."

[69A] [3] Rav inserted [in a letter] to Rabbi between the lines: [4] [Regarding] brothers who mortgaged [property] what [is the law]?

[5] Rabbi Ḥiyya was sitting before him.

RASHI

אל יתפרנסו שומעין לו — שהפרנסה אינה חוב עליו כתנאי כתובה, אלא חוב על היתומים הוא, היכא דלא צוה האב שלא לפרנסם. **תלה ליה רב לרבי ביני חיטי** — שלח לו אגרת שלומים, ותלה שאלה זו בין השיטים. **הוה יתיב רבי חייא קמיה** — דרבי כשבאת שאלה זו לפניו.

LANGUAGE

בֵּינֵי חִטֵּי Between the lines. The Geonim associate the word חִטֵּי with the Hebrew חוּט, meaning "thread." According to this explanation our passage refers to writing on the seams between the threads used to tie sheets of parchment together.

NOTES

ketubah. But he can deprive her of her right to a dowry, because that right does not derive from a condition of her mother's ketubah but rather from an assessment of how her father would have acted had he still been alive.

Rav Hai Gaon, Rabbenu Ḥananel and others have the reverse reading: "If someone says: 'Let his daughters not be maintained from his property,' we listen to him. [But if he says:] 'Let his daughters not receive a dowry from his property,' we do not listen to him." *Rabbenu Ḥananel* explains that, since the father is not required to maintain his daughter during his lifetime, he can also deprive her of her right to maintenance from his estate, but since he is required to provide her with a dowry while he is alive, he cannot deprive her of her right to a dowry from his estate. Moreover, the daughter's right to a dowry from her father's estate is stronger than her right to maintenance. This is shown by the fact that the brothers can cancel her right to maintenance by selling the assets of the estate, but they cannot cancel her right to a dowry in that manner.

Rav Hai Gaon explains that the Baraita is referring to a case where, at the time of his marriage, the father stipulated that the daughters to be born to him would not be entitled to maintenance or a dowry from his estate. The father can attach such a stipulation regarding a daughter's right to maintenance, because that right derives from her mother's ketubah, but he cannot make such a stipulation regarding her right to a dowry, for that right is an independent obligation on the father and his estate. While most Rishonim reject this reading, many accept *Rav Hai Gaon's* ruling that an orphan girl is entitled to her dowry, even if her father stipulated at the time of his marriage that the daughters to be born to him were not to receive dowries from his estate (see Halakhah).

בֵּינֵי חִטֵּי Between the lines. Our commentary follows *Rashi,* who explains that Rav inserted his question between the lines of a letter he sent to Rabbi Yehudah HaNasi. Others (*Rav Hai Gaon, Arukh, Rabbenu Ḥananel*) suggest that Rav inserted his question between the stitches attaching the pages of the letter together. *Ri Migash* maintains that after Rav completed his letter to Rabbi Yehudah HaNasi, he added another question on a separate page which he then inserted between the other pages of the letter. *Hafla'ah* gives a novel explanation. Rav did not want to write his question in the ordinary manner, because of the prohibition against committing the Oral Law to writing. Thus he wrote a communication to Rabbi Yehudah HaNasi, leaving out certain letters and then inserting the missing letters between the lines. When taken together, the inserted letters yielded Rav's question. It has also been suggested that the Gemara mentions that Rav inserted his question between the lines in order that we should understand that it was on account of the lack of space in his letter that Rav did not adequately explain his question (*Ḥever ben Ḥayyim*).

HALAKHAH

אַל יִתְפַּרְנְסוּ בְּנוֹתָיו מִנְּכָסָיו Let his daughters not receive a dowry from his property. "If someone proclaims on his deathbed that his daughters are not to be given dowries from the assets of his estate, we listen to him, for the daughter's right to a dowry is not based on a condition of her mother's ketubah. *Rema* (based on *Tur* in the name of *Rav Hai Gaon*) adds that if the father stipulated at the time of his marriage that his daughters were not to receive dowries from his estate, the stipulation is not binding, for we assume that he would have changed his mind by the time his daughters reached the age of marriage." (*Rambam, Sefer Nashim, Hilkhot Ishut* 20:10; *Shulḥan Arukh, Even HaEzer* 113:10.)

TRANSLATION AND COMMENTARY

question, Rabbi Ḥiyya **said to** Rabbi Yehudah HaNasi: [1]"Was he referring to a case where the brothers **sold** the property **or** to a case where they **pledged** the property as security for a debt?" The Hebrew term used by Rav, *sheshi'bedu* (translated here as "mortgage"), is ambiguous and could refer either to a sale or to a lien. Which did Rav mean?

אֲמַר לֵיהּ [2]Rabbi Yehudah HaNasi **said to** Rabbi Ḥiyya: "**What difference does it make**? The law is identical in both cases. [3]**Whether** the brothers **sold** the property they had inherited from their father **or they pledged** the property as security for a loan they owed to a third party, [4]**we collect** from such property **for** the orphan girl's **dowry, but we do not collect** from such property **for** her **maintenance.**"

וְרַב [5]Returning to Rav's question, the Gemara asks: Why did **Rav** formulate his question in such an ambiguous manner? [6]**If he was in doubt about** the law in a case **where** the brothers **sold** the property they had inherited from their father, [7]**he should have written** explicitly that he was asking about a case where the brothers **sold** it! [8]And **if he was in doubt about** the law in a case **where** the brothers **pledged** the property belonging to their father's estate, [9]**he should have written to him** that he was inquiring about a case where the brothers **pledged** it!

רַב תַּרְוַיְיהוּ [10]The Gemara answers: In fact, **Rav was in doubt about** the law in **both** cases, **and** when formulating the question that he would pose before Rabbi Yehudah HaNasi **he thought** to himself as follows: [11]**If I write to him** asking only about a case where the brothers **sold** the property they had inherited from

[1]אֲמַר לֵיהּ: ״מָכְרוּ אוֹ מִשְׁכְּנוּ?״ [2]אֲמַר לֵיהּ: ״מַאי נָפְקָא מִינָּהּ? [3]בֵּין מָכְרוּ בֵּין שֶׁמִּשְׁכְּנוּ, [4]מוֹצִיאִין לְפַרְנָסָה וְאֵין מוֹצִיאִין לִמְזוֹנוֹת״. [5]וְרַב, [6]אִי מָכְרוּ קָמִיבַּעְיָא לֵיהּ, [7]נִכְתּוֹב לֵיהּ: ״מָכְרוּ״. [8]אִי מִשְׁכְּנוּ קָא מִיבַּעְיָא לֵיהּ, [9]נִכְתּוֹב לֵיהּ: ״מִשְׁכְּנוּ״. [10]רַב תַּרְוַיְיהוּ קָמִיבַּעְיָא לֵיהּ, וְסָבַר: [11]אִי כָּתֵיבְנָא לֵיהּ:

LITERAL TRANSLATION

[1]He said to him: "Did they sell [it] or did they pledge [it]?"

[2]He said to him: "What difference does it make? [3]Whether they sold [it] or they pledged [it], [4]they collect for a dowry but they do not collect for maintenance."

[5]And [as for] Rav, [6]if he was in doubt about [where] they sold [it], [7]let him write to him: "They sold [it]." [8]If he was in doubt about [where] they pledged it, [9]let him write to him: "They pledged [it]."

[10]Rav was in doubt about both of them, and he thought: [11]If I write to him:

RASHI

אמר ליה — רבי חייא: מאי שיעבדו דקא מיבעי ליה, מכרו או משכנו?

NOTES

מָכְרוּ אוֹ מִשְׁכְּנוּ? **Did they sell it or did they pledge it?** Some Rishonim (*Rabbenu Crescas Vidal, Rivash*) ask: What was Rabbi Ḥiyya's doubt with respect to Rav's query? Is there a case where the creditor's right of seizure is limited to property the debtor has *pledged* to a third party, to the exclusion of property *sold* to another person? *Shittah Mekubbetzet* answers that the orphan daughter's right to her dowry is unlike an ordinary debt, since a father can leave explicit instructions that his daughter should not be given a dowry from his estate — something that he cannot do to other creditors. Thus we might have thought that the daughter may collect her dowry only from property of her father's estate that her brothers have subjected to a lien, but not from property that the brothers have already transferred into the ownership of a third party.

אִי כָּתֵיבְנָא לֵיהּ: ״מָכְרוּ״ **If I write to him: "They sold it."** *Ritva* asks: Why did Rav have to ask Rabbi Yehudah HaNasi about a case in which the brothers sold the property they had inherited from their father? He could have asked him about a case in which they pledged the property, and then, depending on the tone of the answer, he could have inferred Rabbi Yehudah HaNasi's position about sale of the property. For if Rabbi Yehudah HaNasi had answered that we collect the orphan girl's dowry from the pledged property, and had delivered the answer in a pleasant manner, it would have been legitimate to infer that he was of the opinion that we may not collect the girl's dowry from property that has already been sold; for if he maintained that we may collect the girl's dowry even from property that has already been sold, he would have been angry that Rav had asked him

HALAKHAH

מוֹצִיאִין לְפַרְנָסָה **They collect for a dowry.** "If brothers sold or pledged assets of their father's estate, an orphan daughter is entitled to seize such property from the party who acquired it and to collect her dowry from it. When she seizes the property, she must take an oath that she has not already collected what she is entitled to, just like any other creditor who seizes property sold by his debtor to a third party." (*Rambam, Sefer Nashim, Hilkhot Ishut* 20:7; *Shulḥan Arukh, Even HaEzer* 113:5.)

וְאֵין מוֹצִיאִין לִמְזוֹנוֹת **But they do not collect for maintenance.** "Even today when a widow can collect her ketubah and conditions contained in it from the movable property of her late husband's estate, an orphan daughter may not collect her maintenance from mortgaged property, whether the property was mortgaged by the father during his lifetime or by her brothers after his death." (*Shulḥan Arukh, Even HaEzer* 112:7.)

TRANSLATION AND COMMENTARY

their father, all **will be well if he sends me the answer that we collect** from this property for the orphan girl's dowry, for then I will know the law in both cases. [1]**For** if we collect from property that the brothers have actually sold to a third party, then **all the more so** may we collect from property that the brothers have merely **pledged** to another person as security for a loan. [2]**But if** Rabbi Yehudah HaNasi **sends me the answer that we do not collect** the dowry from property that the brothers have sold to another person, [3]**I will still be in doubt about** the law in a case **where they pledged** the property to a third party. In that case perhaps we do collect. [4]And **if I write to him** asking only about a case where the brothers **pledged** the property they had inherited from their father, all **will be well if he sends me the answer that we do not collect** from this property for the orphan girl's dowry, for then, too, I will know the law in both cases. For if we do not collect from property that the brothers have merely pledged to a third party, [5]then **all the more so** may we not collect from property that the brothers have actually **sold** to another person. [6]**But if** Rabbi Yehudah HaNasi **sends me the answer that we do** indeed **collect** the orphan girl's dowry from property that the brothers have pledged to another person, [7]**I will still be in doubt about** the law in a case **where they** actually **sold** the property to a third party; perhaps we do not collect from the father's assets that have actually been sold. [8]Taking all this into consideration **I will write to** Rabbi Yehudah HaNasi that **"they mortgaged it," for** the expression "mortgaged" can be understood to **imply** that I am in doubt both about **the case** where the brothers actually sold the property **and** about **the case** where they only pledged it. Rabbi Yehudah HaNasi will then rule on both cases and I will receive a complete answer to my question.

וְרַבִּי יוֹחָנָן [9]The Gemara continues: **Rabbi Yoḥanan** disagreed with Rabbi Yehudah HaNasi and **said: Neither for** an orphan girl's dowry **nor for** her maintenance **do we collect** from property belonging to her father's estate which her brothers have sold or pledged as security to another person.

אִיבַּעְיָא לְהוּ [10]**The following problem arose** in discussion among the Sages regarding the viewpoint of Rabbi Yoḥanan: [11]**Was Rabbi Yoḥanan not aware of Rabbi** Yehudah HaNasi's ruling that we collect from mortgaged property for an orphan daughter's dowry but not for her maintenance? [12]**But if he had been aware** of Rabbi Yehudah HaNasi's ruling, **would he have accepted** it? [13]**Or was** Rabbi Yoḥanan **perhaps aware** that Rabbi Yehudah HaNasi had issued his ruling but **did not accept it?**

„מָכְרוּ", הָא נִיחָא אִי שָׁלַח לִי דְּמוֹצִיאִין, [1]כָּל שֶׁכֵּן מִשְׁכְּנוּ. [2]אִי שָׁלַח לִי אֵין מוֹצִיאִין, [3]אַכַּתִּי מִשְׁכְּנוּ קָמִיבַּעְיָא לִי. [4]אִי כָּתֵיבְנָא לֵיהּ: „מִשְׁכְּנוּ", אִי שָׁלַח לִי דְּאֵין מוֹצִיאִין, [5]כָּל שֶׁכֵּן מָכְרוּ. [6]אִי שָׁלַח לִי מוֹצִיאִין, [7]אַכַּתִּי מָכְרוּ קָא מִיבַּעְיָא לִי. [8]אֶכְתּוֹב לֵיהּ: „שִׁיעְבְּדוּ", דְּמַשְׁמַע הָכִי וּמַשְׁמַע הָכִי.

[9]וְרַבִּי יוֹחָנָן אָמַר: אֶחָד זֶה וְאֶחָד זֶה אֵין מוֹצִיאִין.

[10]אִיבַּעְיָא לְהוּ: [11]לְרַבִּי יוֹחָנָן, לָא שְׁמִיעַ לֵיהּ הָא דְּרַבִּי, [12]וְאִי שְׁמִיעַ לֵיהּ, הֲוָה מְקַבֵּל לֵיהּ. [13]אוֹ דִּלְמָא שְׁמִיעַ לֵיהּ וְלָא מְקַבֵּל לֵיהּ?

LITERAL TRANSLATION

"They sold [it]," it will be well if he sends me [the answer] that they collect, [1][for I can deduce that] all the more so [is this the case where] they pledged [it]. [2][But] if he sends me [the answer that] they do not collect, [3]I will still be in doubt [about where] they pledged [it]. [4]If I write to him: "They pledged [it]," [it will be well] if he sends me [the answer] that they do not collect, [5][for I can deduce that] all the more so [is this the case where] they sold [it]. [6][But] if he sends me [the answer that] they collect, [7]I will still be in doubt [about where] they sold it. [8]I will write to him: "They mortgaged [it]," which implies this and implies that.

[9]But Rabbi Yoḥanan said: [For] both this and that they do not collect.

[10]It was asked of them: [11]Did Rabbi Yoḥanan not hear that [ruling] of Rabbi, [12]but if he had heard it, would he have accepted it? [13]Or did he perhaps hear it and not accept it?

RASHI

דמשמע הכי ומשמע הכי – והוא כשישיב תשובתו יפרש אם שניהם שוים לו או (אם) יש חילוק ביניהן, ומהו אומר על שניהם.
אחד זה ואחד זה אין מוציאין – אחד לפרנסה ואחד למזונות.

NOTES

about the more simple matter. *Ritva* cites other authorities who explain that the case of sold property is not so different from the case of pledged property that Rabbi Yehudah HaNasi would have become angry that Rav had asked about the one and not about the other. *Ritva* himself explains that Rav would not have been able to know whether or not Rabbi Yehudah HaNasi was angry with Rav's question, for the correspondence between the two was conducted in writing, and it is difficult to detect anger in a written response.

TRANSLATION AND COMMENTARY

תָּא שְׁמַע [1]The answer to this question may be inferred from another statement of Rabbi Yoḥanan. **Come and hear, for it was stated** that the Amoraim disagree about the following matter: [2]**If someone died leaving two daughters and a son, and the first daughter went ahead and took a tenth of the property** of her father's estate as her dowry, **but the second** daughter **did not have time to collect** her own dowry **before the son** also **died,** so that the entire estate would now be shared by the two daughters, the Amoraim disagree about whether the second daughter is entitled to take a tenth of the estate as her dowry before it is divided between the two sisters. [3]**Rabbi Yoḥanan said:** Now that **the second daughter** is to receive half of the entire estate, she **waives** her right to receive a tenth of her father's estate as her dowry. [4]**Rabbi Ḥanina** disagreed and **said:** Surely the Sages **said something** much **greater than this:** [5]If brothers sell or pledge property they have inherited from their father, **we collect** from such property **for** an orphan girl's **dowry, but we do not collect** from such property **for** the girl's **maintenance.** Now if for her dowry the orphan daughter can seize from a third party assets belonging to her father's estate which her brothers have sold or pledged, how can **you say** that **the second daughter waived her right** to her dowry if the estate's assets have not even been sold or pledged, but are still in the heirs' possession?! [6]Now, **if it is true** that Rabbi Yoḥanan was not aware of Rabbi Yehudah HaNasi's ruling, **he should have said to** Rabbi Ḥanina: **"Who said** that an orphan daughter can collect her dowry from property which the brothers have sold or pledged?" Hence it follows that Rabbi Yoḥanan was well aware of Rabbi Yehudah HaNasi's ruling, but did not accept it.

[1]תָּא שְׁמַע, דְּאִתְּמַר: [2]מִי שֶׁמֵּת וְהִנִּיחַ שְׁתֵּי בָּנוֹת וּבֵן, וְקָדְמָה הָרִאשׁוֹנָה וְנָטְלָה עִישּׂוּר נְכָסִים, וְלֹא הִסְפִּיקָה שְׁנִיָּה לִגְבּוֹת עַד שֶׁמֵּת הַבֵּן, [3]אָמַר רַבִּי יוֹחָנָן: שְׁנִיָּה וִיתְּרָה. [4]אָמַר רַבִּי חֲנִינָא: גְּדוֹלָה מִזּוֹ אָמְרוּ: [5]מוֹצִיאִין לְפַרְנָסָה וְאֵין מוֹצִיאִין לִמְזוֹנוֹת, וְאַתְּ אָמְרַתְּ שְׁנִיָּה וִיתְּרָה?! [6]וְאִם אִיתָא, נֵימָא לֵיהּ: "מַאן אֲמָרָהּ?"

LITERAL TRANSLATION

[1]Come [and] hear, for it was stated: [2]If someone died, and left two daughters and a son, and the first [daughter] anticipated and took a tenth of the property, and the second did not have time to collect before the son died, [3]Rabbi Yoḥanan said: The second [daughter] waived [her tenth]. [4]Rabbi Ḥanina said: They said [something] greater than this: [5]They collect for a dowry, but they do not collect for maintenance, and you say [that] the second [daughter] waived [her tenth]!? [6]But if this is [the case], let him say to him: "Who said it?"

RASHI

עד שמת הבן – ונפלה הירושה לפני הבנות. **ויתרה** – עישור נכסים. ולא אמרינן: תיטול עישור נכסים תחלה כמו שנטלה זו, ואחר כך יחלוקו. אלא זו שקדמה ונשאת – זכתה. ובת על הבת אין לה עישור נכסים, שהרי שתיהן שוות בירושה. **גדולה מזו** – שאפילו שיעבדו אחין את הנכסים, יפה כח פרנסה לטרוף לקוחות, וזו שהנכסים בעין, אמרת: ויתרה. **נימא ליה מאן אמרה** – אלא לאו שמיע ליה ולא קבלה. ומשום הכי לא הדר נמי מהא דשתי בנות וכו׳.

NOTES

מוֹצִיאִין לְפַרְנָסָה **They collect for a dowry.** *Hafla'ah* asks: Why did Rabbi Yehudah HaNasi also rule about maintenance, when he was asked only about the dowry? *Hafla'ah* answers that when the father's assets have been sold, so that the daughter's maintenance cannot be collected from them, we might have argued that once one of the daughters collects her dowry, another daughter can then collect her maintenance from her sister, for the property

HALAKHAH

מֵת וְהִנִּיחַ שְׁתֵּי בָּנוֹת וּבֵן **If someone died, and left two daughters and a son.** "If someone died and was survived by two daughters and a son, and one daughter took a tenth of her father's estate as her dowry, but the second daughter did not have time to collect her dowry before the son died, the second daughter may no longer collect a tenth of the estate as her dowry. Instead, the two daughters divide what remains of the estate equally between them, following Rabbi Yoḥanan (whose viewpoint was discussed by the Amoraim, implying that it was accepted as law; *Maggid Mishneh*). *Rema* notes that some authorities (*Tur* in the name of *Rosh, Rashba,* and others) maintain that the second daughter may collect her tenth of the estate as her dowry before the estate is divided between the two sisters, following Rabbi Ḥanina (who was Rabbi Yoḥanan's teacher, and whose viewpoint was explicitly accepted as law in the Jerusalem Talmud)." (*Rambam, Sefer Nashim, Hilkhot Ishut* 20:9; *Shulḥan Arukh, Even HaEzer* 113:8.)

עִישּׂוּר נְכָסִים **A tenth of the property.** "An orphan daughter's right to a dowry does not derive from a condition of her mother's ketubah; and therefore even today after the Geonim enacted that a woman may enforce her ketubah and its conditions against the movable property of her husband's estate, an orphan daughter may collect her dowry only from the immovable property of her father's estate, or from rent generated by such property (if the brothers have not yet collected the rent; *Tur,* following *Tosafot*). The orphan daughter is regarded as a creditor with respect to her dowry, and therefore the brothers may dismiss her with money, in accordance with the Gemara's conclusion." (*Rambam, Sefer Nashim, Hilkhot Ishut* 20:5; *Shulḥan Arukh, Even HaEzer* 113:2.)

LITERAL TRANSLATION

[1]But perhaps in fact he did not hear it [initially], [2]but when he heard it he accepted [it], [3]and it is different there because there is ample provision in the house.

[4]Rav Yemar said to Rav Ashi: [5]If so, if she found some lost object, so that there is ample provision in the house, [6]would we likewise not give her a tenth of the property?

[7]He said to him: I meant (lit., "said") [that] there is ample provision in the house from that property.

[8]Amemar said: A daughter is an heir.

[1]וְדִלְמָא לְעוֹלָם לָא שְׁמִיעַ לֵיהּ, [2]וְכִי שְׁמִיעַ לֵיהּ קַבֵּיל, [3]וְשָׁאנֵי הָתָם דְּאִיכָּא רֶוַוח בֵּיתָא.
[4]אֲמַר לֵיהּ רַב יֵימָר לְרַב אַשִׁי: [5]אֶלָּא מֵעַתָּה, אַשְׁכַּחָה מְצִיאָה בְּעָלְמָא, דְּאִיכָּא רֶוַוח בֵּיתָא, [6]הָכִי נַמִי דְּלָא יָהֲבִינַן לָהּ עִישּׂוּר נְכָסִים?
[7]אֲמַר לֵיהּ: אֲנָא רֶוַוח בֵּיתָא מֵהָנֵי נִכְסֵי קָאָמִינָא.
[8]אֲמַר אַמֵימָר: בַּת יוֹרֶשֶׁת הָוְיָא.

RASHI

לעולם לא הוה שמיע ליה — מעיקרא, **וכי שמעה** — קיבלה. וכי אותביה רבי חנינא — כבר הוה שמיע ליה וקיבלה, ומשום הכי לא אמר ליה מאן אמרה. **ושאני התם** — הא דלא הדר ביה ממאי דאמר: שניה ויתרה. **משום רווח ביתא** — שהרי נשתכרה הרבה, שנוטלת חצי הירושה. **יורשת הויא** — עישור נכסים שתקנו לה — בתורת ירושה תקינו לה.

TRANSLATION AND COMMENTARY

וְדִלְמָא [1]The Gemara rejects this argument: **But perhaps** Rabbi Yoḥanan **was not** at first **aware** of Rabbi Yehudah HaNasi's ruling, **and when he heard** that Rabbi Yehudah HaNasi had in fact ruled in that way, [2]**he** too **accepted** the ruling. Rabbi Yoḥanan did not, however, accept Rabbi Ḥanina's argument that Rabbi Yehudah HaNasi's ruling that an orphan daughter may collect her dowry from mortgaged property is relevant to the case of the dowry rights of the second daughter, because he distinguished between the two cases. Where the brothers have sold or pledged property they inherited from their father, their orphan sister may indeed still collect from that property for her dowry, as argued by Rabbi Yehudah HaNasi. [3]And **there**, if the son died before the second daughter had time to collect her dowry, the law **is different, because** after the second daughter has received half of her father's estate as an inheritance, **there is ample provision in her house,** and she is ready to waive her right to a tenth of the estate as her dowry.

אֲמַר לֵיהּ [4]The Gemara now questions the validity of this distinction. **Rav Yemar said to Rav Ashi:** [5]**If** this is **so,** then it should follow that **if** an orphan daughter happens to **find some lost object** of particular value, **so that** now **there is ample provision in her house,** [6]**she would likewise not be given a tenth of her** father's **property** as her dowry! If an orphan daughter waives her right to a dowry when she comes into possession of her share of her father's estate, then she should also waive that right when she attains financial security in some other way. But since this is not the case, it follows that she does not waive her right to her dowry just because she inherited a portion of her father's estate.

אֲמַר לֵיהּ [7]Rav Ashi **said to** Rav Yemar: **I meant that** the orphan daughter waives her right to a dowry from her father's estate **when there is ample provision in her house from the property o**f that estate. But if she comes into possession of money in some other way, she is unwilling to give up her right to her dowry.

אֲמַר אַמֵימָר [8]The Gemara now considers the legal basis of the orphan daughter's right to a dowry from her father's estate. **Amemar said:** When the Rabbis enacted that **an** orphan **daughter** is entitled to a tenth of her father's estate as her dowry, they treated her as **an heir.** Although by Torah law daughters do not inherit their father's estate if he is survived by a son or sons, the Rabbis instituted that a daughter inherits part of her father's assets as her dowry.

NOTES

that the first daughter collected is no longer mortgaged. Thus Rabbi Yehudah HaNasi taught that we do not collect an orphaned daughter's maintenance from landed property that has been sold or pledged, even if the land has already been seized for her sister's dowry.

Regarding the difference between an orphan girl's maintenance and her dowry, *Rid* explains (in accordance with the Gemara in *Gittin* 51a) that her maintenance may not be collected from property that has been sold or pledged to a third party because there is no limit to the maintenance she may require. But there is a fixed limit to the size of a orphan girl's dowry, and it may therefore be collected even from property that has been sold or pledged, just like any other debt that can be collected from mortgaged property (see also *Ran* and *Nimmukei Yosef*).

דְּאִיכָּא רֶוַוח בֵּיתָא Because there is ample provision in the house. *Tosafot* and others raise a question that is ultimately left unresolved: What is the law if one of the surviving daughters takes a tenth of her father's estate as her dowry, and then the son dies, and there are ten other daughters who have not yet received their dowries? Is each of these daughters entitled to take a tenth of the estate as her dowry before the estate is divided between the eleven daughters, or not? This case is different from the one discussed in the Gemara, for here it can be argued that the ten daughters are not ready to waive their right to receive dowries, for each one's share of the estate is smaller than the dowry to which she is entitled.

[1]אֲמַר לֵיהּ רַב אַשִׁי לְאַמֵימָר: אִילּוּ בָּעֵי לְסַלּוּקָהּ בְּזוּזֵי, [2]הָכִי נַמִי דְּלָא מָצֵי לְסַלּוּקָהּ?

[3]אֲמַר לֵיהּ: אִין.

[4]אִי בָּעֵי לְסַלּוּקָהּ בַּחֲדָא אַרְעָא, [5]הָכִי נַמִי דְּלָא מָצֵי מְסַלֵּק לָהּ?

[6]אֲמַר לֵיהּ: אִין.

[7]רַב אַשִׁי אֲמַר: בַּת בַּעֲלַת חוֹב הָוְיָא.

[8]וְאַף אַמֵימָר הֲדַר בֵּיהּ, דַּאֲמַר רַב מַנְיוּמֵי בְּרֵיהּ דְּרַב נִיחוּמֵי: [9]״הֲוָה קָאֵימְנָא קַמֵּיהּ דְּאַמֵימָר, וַאֲתַאי הַאי אִיתְּתָא לְקַמֵּיהּ דַּהֲוַת קָא בָּעֲיָא עִישּׂוּר נְכָסִים. [10]וַחֲזִיתֵיהּ לְדַעְתֵּיהּ דְּאִי בָּעֵי לְסַלּוּקָהּ בְּזוּזֵי, הָוֵי מְסַלֵּק לָהּ, [11]דִּשְׁמַעִי מֵאַחֵי דְּהָווּ קָאָמְרִי לָהּ: ׳אִילּוּ הֲוָה לָן זוּזֵי, סָלֵיקְנָא בְּזוּזֵי׳.

LITERAL TRANSLATION

[1]Rav Ashi said to Amemar: If he wished to dismiss her with money, [2]would he likewise not be able to dismiss her?

[3]He said to him: Yes.

[4]If he wished to dismiss her with one [plot of] land, [5]would he not likewise be able to dismiss her?

[6]He said to him: Yes.

[7]Rav Ashi said: A daughter is a creditor.

[8]And Amemar also retracted, for Rav Manyumi the son of Rav Niḥumi said: [9]"I was standing before Amemar, and a certain woman came before him who was claiming a tenth of the property. [10]And I saw that he was of the opinion that if he had wished to dismiss her with money, he would have been able to dismiss her, [11]for I heard that the brothers were saying to her: 'If we had money, we would dismiss you with money.'

TRANSLATION AND COMMENTARY

אֲמַר לֵיהּ [1]**Rav Ashi said to Amemar:** If an orphan daughter is treated as an heir with respect to the property she receives as her dowry, does it not follow that **if** the brother **wished to dismiss** the girl **with money,** paying her a tenth of the value of her father's estate in cash, [2]**he would not be able to dismiss her** in that manner but would have to give her a tenth of the assets themselves?

אֲמַר לֵיהּ [3]Amemar **said to** Rav Ashi in reply: **Yes,** the brother is indeed barred from dismissing the orphan daughter with a cash settlement.

אִי בָּעֵי לְסַלּוּקָהּ [4]Rav Ashi posed a second question to Amemar: If an orphan daughter is treated as an heir with respect to the property she receives as her dowry, does it not follow that **if** the brother **wished to dismiss** the girl **with one plot of land,** paying her from one particular parcel of land, [5]**he would not be able to dismiss her** in that manner but would be required to give her, if she so desired, a tenth of each of the properties belonging to the estate?

אֲמַר לֵיהּ [6]Amemar **said to** Rav Ashi: **Yes,** the brother is indeed barred from dismissing the orphan daughter with one particular plot of land, if she wishes to take her share of each of the properties.

רַב אַשִׁי [7]**Rav Ashi** disagreed with Amemar and **said:** When the Rabbis enacted that **an** orphan **daughter** is entitled to a tenth of her father's estate as her dowry, they treated her as **a creditor.** Hence her brother, if he so desires, can settle her claim with money or with a particular plot of land, just as he can settle the claim of any other creditor with money and keep the rest of the estate for himself.

וְאַף אַמֵימָר [8]The Gemara notes that **Amemar also withdrew** from his original position that an orphan daughter is treated as an heir, **for Rav Manyumi the son of Rav Niḥumi said:** [9]**"I was** once **standing before Amemar, when a certain woman came before him claiming a tenth of the property** of her father's estate as her dowry. [10]**I could see that** Amemar **was of the opinion that if** a brother **had wished to settle** his orphan sister's **claim with money,** paying her a tenth of the value of their father's estate in cash, **he would have been able to settle her claim** in that manner. How did I know that this was his position? [11]**I heard the** woman's **brothers saying to her: 'If we had the money** with which to settle the matter of your dowry, **we would** indeed **settle your claim with money** and keep the property of our father's estate for ourselves.'

RASHI

אין – באמת לא מצו לסלוקה בזוזי, ולא בחדא ארעא. שאם רוצה נוטלת חלקה מכל קרקע וקרקע, ואין יכולין להקנות לה חלקה במקום אחד. **בעלת חוב הויא** – ומצי לסלוקה בזוזי, או בחדא ארעא.

HALAKHAH

בַּעֲלַת חוֹב הָוְיָא She is a creditor. "An orphan daughter is regarded as her brothers' creditor with respect to her dowry. Hence she may collect her dowry even from property of intermediate quality and even without taking an oath. If the brothers have died, she may collect her dowry from their heirs, but only from property of the poorest quality and only after taking an oath, just like any other creditor who recovers payment from his debtor's heirs," in accordance with the Gemara's conclusion. (*Rambam, Sefer Nashim, Hilkhot Ishut* 20:6; *Shulḥan Arukh, Even HaEzer* 113:3.)

[1]וְאִישְׁתִּיק וְלָא אֲמַר לְהוּ וְלָא מִידֵּי״.
[2]וְהָשְׁתָּא דְּאָמְרַתְּ בַּעֲלַת חוֹב הָוְיָא, דְּאַבָּא אוֹ דְּאַחֵי?
[3]לְמַאי נָפְקָא מִינָּהּ?
[4]לְמִיגְבָּא לְבֵינוֹנִית שֶׁלֹּא בִּשְׁבוּעָה, [5]וְזִיבּוּרִית בִּשְׁבוּעָה.
[6]מַאי?
[7]תָּא שְׁמַע, דְּרָבִינָא אַגְבֵּיהּ לִבְרַתֵּיהּ דְּרַב אַשִׁי מִמָּר בְּרֵיהּ דְּרַב אַשִׁי [8]בֵּינוֹנִית וְשֶׁלֹּא בִּשְׁבוּעָה, [9]מִבְּרֵיהּ דְּרַב סַמָּא בְּרֵיהּ דְּרַב אַשִׁי זִבּוּרִית בִּשְׁבוּעָה.

LITERAL TRANSLATION

[1]And he was silent and did not say anything to them."

[2]And now that you say [that] she is a creditor, [is she the creditor] of the father or of the brothers?

[3]What difference does it make (lit., "what comes out of it")?

[4]To collect from land of intermediate quality without an oath, [5]or from land of the poorest quality with an oath.

[6]What is the law?

[7]Come [and] hear, for Ravina collected for the daughter of Rav Ashi from Mar the son of Rav Ashi [8]from land of intermediate quality without an oath, [9][but] from the son of Rav Sama the son of Rav Ashi from land of the poorest quality with an oath.

TRANSLATION AND COMMENTARY

[1]Amemar **remained silent and did not say anything to them** in response." Thus it is reasonable to infer that Amemar must have adopted Rav Ashi's viewpoint that an orphan daughter is regarded as a creditor with respect to the property she receives as her dowry.

וְהָשְׁתָּא [2]The Gemara proceeds to clarify the matter further. **Now that we have said that** both Rav Ashi and Amemar agree that an orphan daughter is regarded as a creditor with respect to her dowry, a question remains: Is she regarded as the **creditor of her** late **father or** as the creditor **of her brothers?**

לְמַאי נָפְקָא מִינָּהּ [3]Before answering this question, the Gemara first inquires: **What is the** practical **difference** between these two possibilities?

לְמִיגְבָּא [4]The Gemara explains: The practical difference lies in whether the orphan daughter may **collect** her dowry even **from land of intermediate quality** and even **without an oath,** [5]**or** whether she may collect her dowry only **from land of the poorest quality** and only **with an oath.** If the orphan daughter is treated as her brothers' creditor, she may collect her dowry even from estate property of intermediate quality and even without taking an oath, just as she would recover a loan from any other debtor. But if she is treated as her father's creditor, and she now comes to collect from his heirs, she may collect only from estate property of the poorest quality, for when a creditor wishes to recover a loan from the heirs of a deceased debtor, he may collect payment only from the poorest land that the heirs inherited from the debtor (see *Gittin* 48b). Similarly, the orphan daughter may collect payment from the brothers only after she has taken an oath that she has not already received her dowry, for a creditor may not recover a loan from his debtor's heirs without first taking such an oath (see *Gittin* 34b).

מַאי [6]Having established that there is indeed a practical difference between the status of a creditor of brothers who have inherited their father's estate, the Gemara asks: **What is the law** in this case?

תָּא שְׁמַע [7]The Gemara resolves the problem from the following story: **Come and hear** the solution to the probem from the fact **that Ravina collected** part of the dowry of **the daughter of Rav Ashi from** her brother **Mar the son of Rav Ashi** [8]**from land of intermediate quality** that he had inherited from his father, and **without** requiring her to take **an oath** that she had not already received her dowry, [9]**and** he collected the rest of her dowry **from** her nephew **the son of Rav Sama the son of Rav Ashi from land of the poorest quality** that he had inherited from his father, and only **after** she took **an oath** that she had not already received her dowry. When Rav Ashi died he was survived by two sons, Mar and Rav Sama, and by a daughter. Thus the daughter was entitled to receive half her dowry from Mar and half from Rav Sama. But before she

RASHI

למיגבא בינונית ושלא בשבועה כו׳ – אי בעלת חוב דאבא הויא – אינה גובה אלא מן הזיבורית, ואינה נפרעת אלא בשבועה, שלא נטלה מנכסים הללו כלום. דקיימא לן (גיטין מח): אין נפרעין מנכסי יתומים אלא מן הזבורית, ואין נפרעים מהן אלא בשבועה. ואי בעלת חוב שלהן – אין כאן בא ליפרע מנכסי יתומין. רב אשי מת, ומת רב סמא בנו בחייו, וכשבאת בתו ליפרע נטלה מחלקו של מר בר רב אשי שהיה קיים, בינונית שלא בשבועה. אלמא: בעלת חוב דאחי הויא. **ומבריה דרב סמא זיבורית** – לפי שבעלת חוב של אביו היתה, שהיה אחיה.

NOTES

וְאִישְׁתִּיק וְלָא אֲמַר **And he was silent and did not say.** *Tosafot* and others conclude from here that a judge is obliged to issue a correction if one party to a lawsuit presents the other party with an erroneous argument, even if this argument is not presented directly to the court. *Ra'ah* explains that the brothers argued before the court that if they had the money they would have dismissed their sister with money, and Amemar should have raised an objection if he did not accept their argument.

[1] שְׁלַח לֵיהּ רַב נְחֶמְיָה בְּרֵיהּ דְּרַב יוֹסֵף לְרַבָּה בַּר רַב הוּנָא זוּטָא מִנְּהַרְדְּעָא: [2] ״כִּי אָתְיָא הָא אִיתְּתָא לְקַמָּךְ, אַגְבְּהּ עִישּׂוּר נְכָסִים אֲפִילּוּ מֵאִיצְטְרוּבְּלָא״.

[3] אֲמַר רַב אַשִׁי: כִּי הֲוֵינַן בֵּי רַב כָּהֲנָא, [4] הֲוָה מַגְבִּינַן אֲפִילּוּ מֵעֲמָלָא דְּבֵיתֵי.

[5] שְׁלַח לֵיהּ רַב עָנָן לְרַב הוּנָא: ״הוּנָא, חַבְרִין, שְׁלָם! [6] כִּי אָתְיָא הָא אִיתְּתָא לְקַמָּךְ, אַגְבְּהּ עִישּׂוּר נִכְסֵי״. [7] הֲוָה יָתֵיב רַב שֵׁשֶׁת קַמֵּיהּ. [8] אֲמַר לֵיהּ: ״זִיל אֵימָא לֵיהּ, [9] וּבְשַׁמְתָּא יְהֵא מַאן דְּלָא אֲמַר

LITERAL TRANSLATION

[1] Rav Neḥemyah the son of Rav Yosef sent to Rabbah bar Rav Huna Zuta of Neharde'a: [2] "When this woman comes before you, collect a tenth of the property even from the lower millstone."

[3] Rav Ashi said: When we were in the academy of Rav Kahana, [4] we would collect even from the rent of houses.

[5] Rav Anan sent to Rav Huna: "Huna, our colleague, greetings! [6] When this woman comes before you, collect a tenth of the property." [7] Rav Sheshet was sitting before him. [8] [Rav Huna] said to him: "Go [and] tell him, [9] and let him be under the ban who does not tell him:

RASHI

כי אתיא ההיא איתתא – אשה אחת באת לפני רבי נחמיה, שהיה לה ליטול עישור נכסים במקומו של רבה בר רב הונא, ובקשה ממנו לשלוח לו דבר מאתו, שישתדל בדינה. **אצטרובלא** – מושב אמת הרחים כמות שהן. ומקרקעי חשיב להו. **מעמלא דביתי** – שכירות הבתים ממקרקעי קא אתי. **הוה יתיב רב ששת קמיה** – כשבא השליח לפניו, ואיקפד רב הונא על דקרייה ״הונא חברין״. **אמר ליה** – רב הונא לרב ששת. **זיל אימא ליה** – בלשון גנאי, כאשר אומר לך. **ובשמתא** – תהיה, אם לא תאמר בלשון זה.

TRANSLATION AND COMMENTARY

actually collected her dowry, her brother Rav Sama died, so that now she would have to collect the second half of her dowry from her nephew, Rav Sama's son. From her brother Mar she collected from land of intermediate quality and without an oath, showing that a daughter is regarded as her brother's creditor with respect to her dowry. From the son of her second brother, Rav Sama, she collected from land of the poorest quality and with an oath, for she collected that part of her dowry from her debtor's heir.

שְׁלַח [1] The Gemara continues with another anecdote. A certain woman came before Rav Neḥemyah the son of Rav Yosef, asking him to help her collect her dowry from the property of her late father's estate which was located in Neharde'a. **Rav Neḥemyah the son of Rav Yosef sent** her off with a letter **to Rabbah bar Rav Huna Zuta of Neharde'a:** [2] **"When the woman** who bears this letter **comes before you, collect** on her behalf **a tenth of the** landed **property** of her father's estate for her dowry, **even from the lower millstone,** which is immovable and therefore regarded as landed property."

אֲמַר רַב אַשִׁי [3] **Rav Ashi said: When we were** studying **in the academy of Rav Kahana,** [4] **we used to collect** an orphan daughter's dowry **even from the rent** paid **for the houses** belonging to the father's estate, because the rental fees generated by real estate are treated as landed property.

שְׁלַח לֵיהּ [5] It was related that **Rav Anan sent** the following letter **to Rav Huna: "Huna, our colleague, greetings!** [6] **When the woman** who bears this letter **comes before you, collect** for her dowry **a tenth of the property** of her father's estate." [7] **Rav Sheshet was sitting before** Rav Huna when Rav Anan's letter arrived. Rav Huna was disturbed by the undue familiarity with which Rav Anan addressed him. [8] Rav Huna **said to** Rav Sheshet: **"Go and tell** Rav Anan as follows." Fearing that Rav Sheshet might be reluctant to fulfill the mission, [9] Rav Huna added: **"And let he who does not tell** what I am about to say precisely as I said it **be under the ban:**

NOTES

מֵאִיצְטְרוּבְּלָא **From the lower millstone.** *Arukh* cites two explanations of this term: (1) The lower millstone; (2) the receptacle upon which the millstones rest and into which the ground flour falls. Both are regarded as immovable property from which an orphan daughter may collect her dowry.

מֵעֲמָלָא דְּבֵיתֵי **From the rent of houses.** The Rishonim ask: To which rent does the Gemara refer? The Gemara cannot be talking about rent that has already been collected, for surely that money is movable property from which the orphan daughter cannot collect her dowry. And the Gemara also cannot be referring to the rent that will be generated in the future, for it is obvious that such rent is regarded as landed property from which the orphan daughter may collect her dowry. They answer that the Gemara is referring to a case where the brothers (*Tosafot*) or the father (*Ra'ah, Rashba*) had rented out the house and the orphan daughter came to collect her dowry before the rental period had come to an end. The Gemara teaches us that the orphan daughter may collect her dowry from the rent covering the period that has already passed. For rent may not be recovered until the end of the rental period. According to *Remah* and *Talmidei Rabbenu Yonah,* the orphan daughter may collect her dowry even from rent that has already been collected by the brothers. Since the rent was generated by real estate, it too is regarded as landed property from which the orphan daughter's dowry may be collected.

וּבְשַׁמְתָּא יְהֵא מַאן **And let him be under the ban.** *Ritva* infers from this story that a Torah scholar may place a ban

LANGUAGE

אִיצְטְרוּבְּלָא **The lower millstone.** This word is probably derived from the Greek στρόβιλος, *strobilos,* meaning "pine cone," and, by extension, "conical object," or "millstone."

TRANSLATION AND COMMENTARY

'Anan, Anan! When you asked me to collect the woman's dowry, [1]did you mean that I should collect it **from the landed property** of her father's estate **or** even **from the movable goods?** Answer me also about the following: [2]**Who sits at the head** of the table **in a house of** ***marzeḥa*****?'"** [3]**Rav Sheshet went to Rav Anan and said to him:** [4]"Do not be angry with me for what I am about to tell you, for while **you, Sir, are a master, Rav Huna is the master of the master,** [5]**and he has placed under the ban the person who does not tell** what Rav Huna had to say and precisely as he said it. [6]**And were it not for** the threat of **the ban, I would** certainly **not say** what I am about to say. Rav Huna sends you the following message: **'Anan, Anan!** When you asked me to collect the woman's dowry, [7]did you mean that I should collect it **from the landed property** of her father's estate, **or** even **from the movable goods?** [8]**And** answer me about the following: **Who sits at the head** of the table **in a house of** ***marzeḥa*****?'"** [9]**Rav Anan went to** the Exilarch **Mar Ukva** to complain about the way Rav Huna had treated him. Rav Anan **said to him:** [10]**"See, Sir, how Rav Huna sent me** a humiliating message, addressing me as **'Anan, Anan.'** [11]**And furthermore, as to the** ***marzeḥa*** **about which** Rav Huna **sent me** a question, I **do not know what it is** and I am therefore unable to answer him." [12]Mar Ukva **said to him: "Tell me, my friend,**

לֵיהּ: ׳עָנָן, עָנָן׳! [1]מִמְּקַרְקְעֵי אוֹ מִמְּטַלְטְלֵי? [2]וּמַאן יָתֵיב בֵּי מַרְזֵיחָא בְּרֵישָׁא?׳״ [3]אֲזַל רַב שֵׁשֶׁת לְקַמֵּיהּ דְּרַב עָנָן, אֲמַר לֵיהּ: [4]״מָר רַבָּה, וְרַב הוּנָא רַבֵּיהּ דְּרַבָּה, [5]וְשַׁמּוּתֵי שַׁמֵּית מַאן דְּלָא אָמַר לֵיהּ. [6]וְאִי לָאו דְּשַׁמֵּית, לָא הֲוָה קָאָמִינָא: עָנָן, עָנָן! [7]מִמְּקַרְקְעֵי אוֹ מִמְּטַלְטְלֵי? [8]וּמַאן יָתֵיב בֵּי מַרְזֵיחָא בְּרֵישָׁא?׳״ [9]אֲזַל רַב עָנָן לְקַמֵּיהּ דְּמָר עוּקְבָא, אֲמַר לֵיהּ: [10]״חֲזִי מָר הֵיכִי שְׁלַח לִי רַב הוּנָא: ׳עָנָן, עָנָן׳. [11]וְעוֹד מַרְזֵיחָא דִּשְׁלַח לִי לָא יָדַעְנָא מַאי נִיהוּ״. [12]אֲמַר לֵיהּ: ״אֵימָא לִי, אִיזִי,

LITERAL TRANSLATION

'Anan, Anan! [1]From landed property or from movable property? [2]And who sits at the head in a house of *marzeḥa*?'" [3]Rav Sheshet went to Rav Anan, [and] he said to him: [4]"You, Sir, are a master, but Rav Huna is the master of the master, [5]and he has placed under the ban he who does not tell you. [6]And had he not issued the ban, I would not say [this]: 'Anan, Anan! [7]From landed property or from movable goods? [8]And who sits at the head in a house of *marzeḥa*?'" [9]Rav Anan went to Mar Ukva, [and] he said to him: [10]"See, Sir, how Rav Huna sent to me: 'Anan, Anan.' [11]And furthermore, [as to] the *marzeḥa* about which he sent to me, I do not know what it is." [12]He said to him: "Tell me, my friend,

RASHI

ענן ענן — מהיכן אתה אומר להגבותה, ממקרקעי או אפילו ממטלטלי? ועוד שאלה אחרת השיבני. **מאן יתיב בי מרזיחא ברישא** — מי מיסב בבית אבל בראש הקרואים. כשהיו מסובים בסעודה, היה ניכר מסיבתן מי הוא הראש, שהגדול מיסב במטה אחת לראש השולחן, ושני לו במטה אחרת למטה הימנו. **אמר ליה מר רבה** — אתה, ורב הונא רבך. ולפייסו אמר לו כך, שלא יכעוס עליו על שנעשה שליח בדבר, ומראהו פנים שעל כרחו נעשה שליח לכך.

LANGUAGE

איזי My friend. Neither the meaning nor the etymology of this word is fully clear. Some scholars understand it to be an Aramaic word meaning "now then," while others derive it from the Persian word *aza*. *Rashi*, however, interprets the word as meaning "my friend."

SAGES

רַב עָנָן Rav Anan. A Babylonian Amora of the second generation, Rav Anan was a disciple of Shmuel, many of whose teachings he transmitted. He also transmitted teachings in the name of Rav. After Shmuel's death, Rav Anan became one of the judges of the city of Neharde'a. Rav Anan was a younger contemporary of Rav Huna and an older contemporary of Rav Naḥman. Rav Anan's teachings, both in the name of Shmuel and in his own name, are found in several places in the Talmud, and several Sages of the following generation cite teachings in his name.

NOTES

on his disciple for not complying with his instructions, for such noncompliance is regarded as an affront to the scholar's honor.

Rabbi Ya'akov Emden questions the conduct of Rav Huna and Rav Sheshet as reported in this story. How could Rav Huna have instructed Rav Sheshet to belittle Rav Anan, and how could Rav Sheshet have complied with the order? Surely Rav Anan himself was an important Sage, he too being a disciple of Rav and Shmuel, and one is absolutely forbidden to show disrespect to a Torah scholar!

וּמַאן יָתֵיב בֵּי מַרְזֵיחָא בְּרֵישָׁא? And who sits at the head in a house of ***marzeḥa*****?** Many commentators have asked why Rav Huna chose to ask Rav Anan about a house of *marzeḥa*. *Rabbenu Crescas Vidal* suggests that the word *marzeḥa* was meant to be taken by Rav Anan as a hint that he should not be so haughty (*zaḥuah*). Others say that Rav Huna meant to put Rav Anan in his place by implying that he would be unable to answer even a simple question like this. *Rivash* argues that Rav Huna meant to shame Rav Anan by saying that, just as a mourner sits at the head of the table, even though he is not necessarily the most distinguished person in the room, so too may Rav Anan have become the leading Rabbinic figure in his town, even though he is not a particularly distinguished scholar. *Rabbi Yoshiah Pinto* argues that there is an intrinsic connection between the two questions posed by Rav Huna. The question whether or not an orphan daughter may collect her dowry from the movable goods of her father's estate depends on whether she is regarded as an heir or as a creditor with respect to her dowry. Rav Huna meant to hint to Rav Anan that the daughter is not considered an heir, since the brothers and not the orphan daughter sit at the head of the table in a house of mourning.

TRANSLATION AND COMMENTARY

[69B] **what was the incident itself** that led Rav Huna to send you that disparaging message? Surely you must have done something to prompt Rav Huna's response!" [1]Rav Anan **said to** Mar Ukva: **"Such-and-such was the incident,"** and he told him about the letter he had sent to Rav Huna. After hearing the entire sequence of events, [2]Mar Ukva **said to** Rav Anan: "Can **a person who does not know** the meaning of the word ***marzeḥa*** **send** a letter **to Rav Huna,** addressing him as **'our colleague'?** He was right to reproach you for implying that you were his equal."

מַאי מַרְזֵיחָא [3]The Gemara asks: **What is** the meaning of the word ***marzeḥa?***

אֵבֶל [4]The Gemara answers: *Marzeḥa* means **mourning, as the verse says** (Jeremiah 16:5): **"Thus says the Lord, Do not enter the house of mourning** [מַרְזֵחַ *—marze'aḥ*]; neither go to lament nor bemoan them." Thus Rav Huna's question was: Who sits at the head of the table in a house of mourning when the comforters come to console the mourners?

אָמַר רַבִּי אַבָּהוּ [5]On this point **Rabbi Abbahu said: From where do we derive that the mourner reclines at the head** of the table when the comforters come to console him? [6]It is derived from **the following verse** (Job 29:25): **"I chose their way, and I sat as chief, and I dwelt as a king in the army, as one that comforts the mourners."**

יְנַחֵם [7]The Gemara raises a question about this proof text: Does the word ***yenaḥem*** (יְנַחֵם — "comforts") not **imply** that the verse refers to the **other people** who come to comfort the mourners? Thus those who console the mourners, and not the mourners themselves, sit at the head of the table!

אָמַר רַב נַחְמָן בַּר יִצְחָק [8]**Rav Naḥman bar Yitzḥak said** in reply: In the Bible the word **is written** without vocalization, so that it can be read as ***yinnaḥem*** (יִנָּחֵם — "is comforted"), teaching that the mourners sit at the head of the table.

[69B] גּוּפָא דְּעוּבְדָא הֵיכִי הֲוָה?״ [1]אֲמַר לֵיהּ: ״הָכִי וְהָכִי הֲוָה מַעֲשֶׂה״. [2]אֲמַר לֵיהּ: ״גַּבְרָא דְּלָא יָדַע מַאי נִיהוּ מַרְזֵיחָא שָׁלַח לֵיהּ לְרַב הוּנָא ׳הוּנָא חַבְרִין׳״? [3]מַאי מַרְזֵיחָא? [4]אֵבֶל, דִּכְתִיב: ״כֹּה אָמַר ה׳, אַל תָּבֹא בֵּית מַרְזֵחַ, וגו׳״. [5]אָמַר רַבִּי אַבָּהוּ: מִנַּיִן לְאָבֵל שֶׁמֵּיסֵב בָּרֹאשׁ? [6]שֶׁנֶּאֱמַר: ״אֶבְחַר דַּרְכָּם, וְאֵשֵׁב רֹאשׁ, וְאֶשְׁכּוֹן כְּמֶלֶךְ בַּגְּדוּד, כַּאֲשֶׁר אֲבֵלִים יְנַחֵם״. [7]״יְנַחֵם״ אֲחֵרִים מַשְׁמַע! [8]אֲמַר רַב נַחְמָן בַּר יִצְחָק: ״יִנָּחֵם״ כְּתִיב.

LITERAL TRANSLATION

[69B] how did the incident itself happen?" [1]He said to him: "Such-and-such was the incident." [2]He said to him: "A man who does not know what *marzeḥa* is addresses (lit., 'sends to') Rav Huna [as] 'our colleague'?"

[3]What is *marzeḥa*?

[4]Mourning, for it is written: "Thus says the Lord, Do not enter the house of mourning, etc."

[5]Rabbi Abbahu said: From where [do we derive] that a mourner reclines at the head?

[6]For it is said: "I chose their way, and I sat as chief, and I dwelt as a king in the army, as one that comforts the mourners."

[7]"*Yenaḥem*" [יְנַחֵם — "comforts"] implies [that he comforts] others!

[8]Rav Naḥman bar Yitzḥak said: It is written "*yinnaḥem*" [יִנָּחֵם — "will be comforted"].

RASHI

גופא דעובדא — תחלת הדברים, מה לשון שלחת לו? **ינחם כתיב** — אין לך לומר פתח בשוא אות אלא אם כן אל״ף או ה״א סמוכין לו, או על פי הנקודה שתחתיה והיא באה במקום אות, כאילו כתוב ״ינאחם״. וכיון שלא כתיב כאן אל״ף — על כרחך על פי מסורת הכתב אתה קורא יִנָּחֵם, וזהו המנוחם עצמו, כלומר: כאבל המתנחם.

LANGUAGE

מַרְזֵיחָא ***Marzeḥa.*** The Hebrew word מַרְזֵחַ appears twice in the Bible (in the verses cited in our passage), and the classical commentators had difficulty explaining it. Some claim that מַרְזֵחַ has two different meanings: בֵּית מַרְזֵחַ in Jeremiah meaning "a house of mourning," and מִרְזַח סְרוּחִים in Amos meaning "a banquet." Others (such as Rabbi Jonah ibn Janaḥ) suggest that the word means "sound" or "noise" in both verses (cf. Arabic مرزيح); in Amos the word refers to the sound of banqueting, whereas in Jeremiah it refers to the sound of wailing and lamentation. The word מַרְזֵחַ also appears in Canaanite inscriptions, where it means "banquet." Indeed, some commentaries explain that מַרְזֵחַ means "meal" or "banquet" in both Biblical verses: in Amos it denotes a wedding meal, and in Jeremiah the mourners' meal (this latter meaning is occasionally found in Rabbinic Hebrew).

NOTES

״יִנָּחֵם״ כְּתִיב It is written *"yinnaḥem."* Our commentary follows *Rashi,* who explains that since the Biblical text is not vocalized, the word יִנָּחֵם can be read as *yinnaḥem* ("is comforted"), rather than *yenaḥem* ("comforts"). Thus the verse can be understood as referring to the mourner, and not to the comforter, as one who sits as chief. *Tosafot* argues that the Gemara's derivation should be read as follows: "It is written *yenaḥem.*" The word יְנַחֵם must in fact be read as *yenaḥem;* but since the verse chose to use a word that can be misread as *yinnaḥem,* rather than to use the word *menaḥem,* which cannot give rise to such a mistake, it may be inferred that the person who is being comforted, the mourner, sits as chief at the head of the table.

HALAKHAH

מִנַּיִן לְאָבֵל שֶׁמֵּיסֵב בָּרֹאשׁ? From where do we derive that a mourner reclines at the head? "When people come to console a mourner, the mourner reclines at the head of the table." (*Rambam, Sefer Shofetim, Hilkhot Evel* 13:3; *Shulḥan Arukh, Yoreh De'ah* 376:1.)

TRANSLATION AND COMMENTARY

מָר זוּטְרָא אֲמַר [1]**Mar Zutra said:** The regulation that the mourner reclines at the head of the table when the comforters come to console him is derived **from the following** verse (Amos 6:7): **"And the feast of those who stretched themselves out shall pass away** [וְסָר מִרְזַח סְרוּחִים]." According to the plain sense of the verse, Amos is describing the disaster that awaits those who stretch themselves out at banquet tables and indulge themselves in merrymaking. Mar Zutra interprets the word מִרְזַח, translated here as "revelry," as if it were two words: מַר, "bitter," and זָח, "distracted." According to this interpretation the verse refers to a mourner, who is embittered and unsettled on account of the loss he has suffered. And Mar Zutra reads the word סָר, translated here as "shall pass away," as if it were spelled שַׂר, "shall be chief." Thus the verse, as interpreted by Mar Zutra, teaches: [2]**The one who is bitter and distracted shall be made the chief of those who stretch themselves out at the meal** of consolation. In other words, the mourner himself reclines at the head of the table when the comforters come to console him.

אָמַר רָבָא [3]The Gemara concludes its discussion of the orphan daughter's right to a dowry from her father's estate with the following ruling: **Rava said: The Halakhah is** that whenever we collect from the heirs of the deceased, we collect **from the landed property** of the estate **and not from the movable goods.** [4]This applies **whether** we are collecting **for the maintenance** of the widow or of the minor daughter, **or for the** widow's **ketubah, or for the** orphan daughter's **dowry.**

[1]מָר זוּטְרָא אֲמַר: מֵהָכָא: "וְסָר מִרְזַח סְרוּחִים". [2]מַר וְזָח נַעֲשָׂה שַׂר לִסְרוּחִים.

[3]אֲמַר רָבָא: הִלְכְתָא: מִמְּקַרְקְעֵי וְלָא מִמִּטַּלְטְלֵי, [4]בֵּין לִמְזוֹנֵי, בֵּין לִכְתוּבָּה, בֵּין לְפַרְנָסָה.

LITERAL TRANSLATION

[1]Mar Zutra said: [It is derived] from here: "And the feast of those who stretched themselves out shall pass away." [2]One who is bitter and distracted is made the chief of those stretched out [at the meal].

[3]Rava said: The Halakhah is: [Payment is made] from land and not from movable goods, [4]whether for maintenance, or for a ketubah, or for a dowry.

RASHI

מר וזח – מי שנפשו מרה, ודעתו זחה ומעותקת מעליו. **נעשה שר לסרוחים** – לגדולים הבאים לנחמו.

NOTES

לִסְרוּחִים Of those who stretched out. *Rashi* understands the word סְרוּחִים to mean "the great ones." Thus the mourner is made chief of the great ones who come to console him. *Rabbi Ya'akov Emden* suggests that this usage is found in the Biblical expression (Exodus 26:12): "[וְסֶרַח הָעֹדֵף], and the remnant that hangs over," that portion of the Tabernacle's curtain that extends past its frame and hangs over its back and sides. Alternatively, the word סְרוּחִים can mean "those who stretch themselves out on banqueting couches." Thus the mourner is made chief of those who recline with him at the meal of consolation.

בֵּין לְפַרְנָסָה Or for a dowry. Most authorities (*Rif, Rambam, Rosh, Rashba*) maintain that even after the Geonim enacted that a widow may collect her ketubah and its conditions from the movable property of her husband's estate, an orphan daughter may collect her dowry only from the immovable property of her father's estate, for the daughter's right to her dowry does not derive from a condition of her mother's ketubah.

Rav Sherira Gaon and *Rav Hai Gaon* write that the Geonim wanted to enact that the orphan daughter's dowry could be collected even from movable property, but the enactment was not accepted.

Tosafot (above, 51a), *Ritva* and others argue that Rava's ruling that an orphan daughter may collect her dowry only from the landed property of her father's estate is restricted to a case where we do not know whether the father would have been willing to have his daughter provided with a dowry from his movable property. But if we can assess that the father would have provided his daughter with movable goods as her dowry, she may indeed collect her dowry from the movable assets of his estate. Moreover, the Geonic enactment allowing a woman's ketubah and its conditions to be collected from movable goods applies also to the orphan daughter's right to a dowry, for today we assess all people as wishing their daughters to be provided with a dowry of movable property.

HALAKHAH

מִמְּקַרְקְעֵי וְלָא מִמִּטַּלְטְלֵי From land and not from movable goods. "Now that a widow may claim her ketubah from the movable property of her husband's estate, an orphan daughter may also collect her maintenance from the movable property of her father's estate, for her right to maintenance derives from a condition of her mother's ketubah." (*Rambam, Sefer Nashim, Hilkhot Ishut* 16:7; *Shulḥan Arukh, Even HaEzer* 112:7.)

לִכְתוּבָּה For a ketubah. "According to Talmudic law, a widow may collect her ketubah only from the landed property of her husband's estate. But the Geonim enacted that she can also collect her ketubah and its conditions from the movable property of his estate." (*Rambam, Sefer Nashim, Hilkhot Ishut* 16:7; *Shulḥan Arukh, Even HaEzer* 100:1.)

לְפַרְנָסָה For a dowry. "An orphan daughter's right to a dowry does not derive from a condition of her mother's ketubah, and so even today after the Geonim have enacted that a woman may collect her ketubah and its conditions from the movable property of her husband's estate, an orphan daughter may collect her dowry only from the immovable property of her father's estate, following Rava." (*Rambam, Sefer Nashim, Hilkhot Ishut* 20:5; *Shulḥan Arukh, Even HaEzer* 113:2.)

TRANSLATION AND COMMENTARY

MISHNAH הַמַּשְׁלִישׁ מָעוֹת לְבִתּוֹ [1]**If a father entrusts money to a third party on behalf of his daughter** and instructs him to buy her a field as her dowry when she marries, and the father dies, [2]**and** after her betrothal his daughter **says** to the trustee: **"My husband is trustworthy in my eyes.** Give him the money and he will buy the field for me," [3]**the trustee must do what he was entrusted to do.** He must buy the field for the daughter as he was instructed by her father. [4]**This is the viewpoint of Rabbi Meir.** [5]**Rabbi Yose** disagrees and **says:** What is gained by the trustee's going ahead and buying a field for the daughter with the money given to him by her father? **If** the money **were** no longer in the trustee's hands, but had already been spent on buying **a field, and** the daughter now **wished to sell** the field and give the proceeds to her husband, [6]**surely** she would be permitted to do so. Therefore we should **now** regard the money in the trustee's hands as if it has already been spent on a field, and as if the field **has been sold** by the daughter, and the proceeds are already in the daughter's hands so that she can now hand over the money to her husband. Thus we listen to the daughter's request and we transfer the money from the trustee to the husband. [7]**When does this apply? In a case** where the daughter is already **an adult.** [8]**But in a case** where the daughter is still **a minor,** we do not listen to her, for **the act of a minor is not valid.** In this case the trustee must buy a field for the daughter as he was instructed by her father.

מִשְׁנָה [1]הַמַּשְׁלִישׁ מָעוֹת לְבִתּוֹ, [2]וְהִיא אוֹמֶרֶת: ״נֶאֱמָן בַּעְלִי עָלַי״, [3]יַעֲשֶׂה הַשָּׁלִישׁ מַה שֶּׁהוּשְׁלַשׁ בְּיָדוֹ. [4]דִּבְרֵי רַבִּי מֵאִיר. [5]רַבִּי יוֹסֵי אוֹמֵר: וְכִי אֵינָהּ אֶלָּא שָׂדֶה וְהִיא רוֹצָה לְמוֹכְרָהּ, [6]הֲרֵי הִיא מְכוּרָה מֵעַכְשָׁיו. [7]בַּמֶּה דְּבָרִים אֲמוּרִים? בִּגְדוֹלָה. [8]אֲבָל בִּקְטַנָּה, אֵין מַעֲשֵׂה קְטַנָּה כְּלוּם.

LITERAL TRANSLATION

MISHNAH [1][If] someone entrusts money to a third party on behalf of his daughter, [2]and she says: "My husband is trustworthy to me," [3]the trustee must do what he was entrusted [to do]. [4][These are] the words of Rabbi Meir. [5]Rabbi Yose says: But if it [the trust] were a field and she wished to sell it, [6]surely it is sold from now. [7]In what [case] are these things said? In [the case of] an adult. [8]But in [the case of] a minor, the act of a minor is nothing.

RASHI

משנה המשליש מעות לבתו — מסר מעות ביד שליש לצורך בתו, לקנות שדה או נדוניא לכשתנשא. **והיא אומרת** — לאחר שנשאת. **נאמן בעלי עלי** — שלא יעכבם לעצמו, תנם לו והוא יקנה לי שדה כשארצה. **יעשה שליש כו׳** — יקנה השדה, ואין שומעין לה, דמצוה לקיים דברי המת. **וכי אינה אלא שדה** — וכי מה תועלת לו לקנות? אפילו אין כאן מעות, אלא כבר נקנה השדה והיא רוצה למוכרה — הרי היא מכורה, הלכך שומעין לה. **במה דברים אמורים** — בגמרא מפרש מאן קתני לה. **במה דברים אמורים** — ששומעין לה.

NOTES

הַמַּשְׁלִישׁ **If someone entrusts money to a third party.** *Melekhet Shlomo* explains the connection between this Mishnah and the previous one as follows: The previous Mishnah records the dispute between Rabbi Yehudah and the Sages regarding the sum that an orphan girl can extract from her brothers as her dowry — a tenth of her father's estate or some other amount determined in accordance with an assessment of her father's intentions. This Mishnah continues with the dispute between Rabbi Meir and Rabbi Yose about whether an orphan girl can extract from a trustee the sum of money that her father had entrusted to him on her behalf.

וְכִי אֵינָהּ אֶלָּא שָׂדֶה **But if it were a field.** The Rishonim object: Elsewhere (*Bava Batra* 155a), the Gemara states that a son must not, before he reaches the age of twenty, sell real estate that he has inherited from his father. Here, however, the Mishnah does not seem to recognize such a limitation, for Rabbi Yose argues that if the trustee had already bought a field with the money he had received from the father, the daughter could now sell the field and give the proceeds to her husband! *Rashba* understands from *Rashi* that a distinction is to be made between real estate received from the father and real estate bought with money received from him. *Ra'avad* argues that the limitation applies only to real estate received as an inheritance, but here the orphan daughter acquires the real estate as a gift from her father.

הֲרֵי הִיא מְכוּרָה מֵעַכְשָׁיו **Surely it is sold from now.** According to a straightforward reading of the Mishnah, Rabbi Yose accepts the principle that there is an obligation to carry out the wishes of the deceased (see below, 70a), but he argues that in this case it is useless to invoke that principle, for after the trustee buys a field in accordance with the father's instructions, the daughter can sell the field

HALAKHAH

הַמַּשְׁלִישׁ מָעוֹת לְבִתּוֹ **If someone entrusts money to a third party on behalf of his daughter.** "If someone entrusts money to a third party, instructing him to buy land for his daughter as her dowry, and the father dies and the money is still in the hands of the trustee, and the daughter asks that the money be given to her husband for him to do with as he pleases, the following distinctions apply: If she is an adult and already married, we listen to her. If she is betrothed, the trustee must do as he was instructed by the father. And if she is still a minor, then even if she is already married, the trustee must do as he was instructed by the father, following Rabbi Meir whose view was

TRANSLATION AND COMMENTARY

GEMARA תָּנוּ רַבָּנַן [1]**Our Rabbis taught** a related Baraita: **"If someone entrusts money to a third party on behalf of his son-in-law** and instructs the trustee to use the money **to buy a field for his daughter** when she marries, and the father dies, [2]**and** his daughter **says: 'Let** the money **be given to my husband,** for I have confidence in him,' the following distinction applies: [3]**If** the daughter is already **married, the authority is in her hands** to ask for the money entrusted to the third party to be handed over to her husband. [4]But **if** she **is** only **betrothed, the trustee must do what he was entrusted to do.** He must buy the field for the daughter as he was instructed by her father. [5]**This is the viewpoint of Rabbi Meir.** [6]**Rabbi Yose** disagrees and **says: If** the daughter is **an adult,** then **whether** she **is married or is** only **betrothed, the authority is in her hands** to ask that the money be given to her husband. [7]But **if** she **is** still **a minor,** then **whether** she **is married or** only **betrothed, the trustee must do what he was entrusted to do** and must accordingly buy the field for the daughter."

מַאי בֵּינַיְיהוּ [8]The Gemara asks: **What is the difference between** the viewpoint of Rabbi Meir and that of Rabbi Yose? About what case do the two Tannaim disagree? [9]**We can say that there is a difference between them** in the case of **a minor** who is already **married,** [10]**and that Rabbi Meir maintains** that if the daughter is already married, even if she is a minor, **the authority is in her hands** to ask that the money be handed over to her husband, [11]**and Rabbi Yose came to say that even if** the daughter is already **married,** if she is **an adult, she is indeed authorized** to ask that the money be given to her husband, **but if** she

LITERAL TRANSLATION

GEMARA [1]Our Rabbis taught: "If someone entrusts money to a third party on behalf of his son-in-law to purchase with it a field for his daughter, [2]and she says: 'Let it be given to my husband;' [3][if it is] after marriage, the authority is in her hand; [4][if it is] after betrothal, the trustee must do what he was entrusted [to do]. [5][These are] the words of Rabbi Meir. [6]Rabbi Yose says: [In the case of] an adult, whether after marriage or after betrothal, the authority is in her hand. [7][In the case of] a minor, whether after marriage or after betrothal, the trustee must do what he was entrusted [to do]."

[8]What is [the difference] between them? [9]If we say that [the difference] between them is [the case of] a minor after marriage, [10][and] that Rabbi Meir maintains [that] the authority is in her hand, [11]and Rabbi Yose came to say [that] even after marriage also an adult has the authority (lit., "yes") [but] a minor does not (lit., "no"),

גמרא [1]תָּנוּ רַבָּנַן: "הַמַּשְׁלִישׁ מָעוֹת לַחֲתָנוֹ לִיקַּח מֵהֶן שָׂדֶה לְבִתּוֹ, [2]וְהִיא אוֹמֶרֶת: 'יִנָּתְנוּ לְבַעְלִי', [3]מִן הַנִּשּׂוּאִין, הָרְשׁוּת בְּיָדָהּ; [4]מִן הָאֵירוּסִין, יַעֲשֶׂה הַשָּׁלִישׁ מַה שֶּׁהוּשְׁלַשׁ בְּיָדוֹ. [5]דִּבְרֵי רַבִּי מֵאִיר. [6]רַבִּי יוֹסֵי אוֹמֵר: הַגְּדוֹלָה, בֵּין מִן הַנִּשּׂוּאִין וּבֵין מִן הָאֵירוּסִין, הָרְשׁוּת בְּיָדָהּ. [7]קְטַנָּה, בֵּין מִן הַנִּשּׂוּאִין בֵּין מִן הָאֵירוּסִין, יַעֲשֶׂה הַשָּׁלִישׁ מַה שֶּׁהוּשְׁלַשׁ בְּיָדוֹ".

[8]מַאי בֵּינַיְיהוּ? [9]אִילֵימָא קְטַנָּה מִן הַנִּשּׂוּאִין אִיכָּא בֵּינַיְיהוּ, [10]דְּרַבִּי מֵאִיר סָבַר הָרְשׁוּת בְּיָדָהּ, [11]וַאֲתָא רַבִּי יוֹסֵי לְמֵימַר אֲפִילּוּ מִן הַנִּשּׂוּאִין נַמִי גְּדוֹלָה אִין קְטַנָּה לָא,

RASHI

גמרא מן הנשואין הרשות בידה — שאף האב לא עלה בדעתו למוסרם ביד שליש אלא עד שתנשא, דמשנשאת הבעל זכאי לאכול פירות. **מאי ביניהו** — בהי פליגי, בגדולה או בקטנה. **דרבי מאיר סבר הרשות בידה** — דהאי דקאמר רבי מאיר מן הנשואין הרשות בידה — אפילו בקטנה נמי אמר.

NOTES

and give the proceeds to her husband. *Rabbi Shimshon of Sens* and others note that the Gemara below implies that only Rabbi Meir maintains that there is an obligation to carry out the wishes of the deceased. Thus Rabbi Yose disagrees with Rabbi Meir's ruling because he maintains that the trustee is not required to act in accordance with the father's instructions. Hence we must understand that Rabbi Yose is not expressing his true opinion here, but rather raising an objection against Rabbi Meir on the basis of Rabbi Meir's own viewpoint.

אִילֵימָא קְטַנָּה מִן הַנִּשּׂוּאִין אִיכָּא בֵּינַיְיהוּ **If we say that the difference between them is the case of a minor after marriage.** *Tosafot* and others note that the Gemara cannot be suggesting that Rabbi Meir and Rabbi Yose disagree only about the case of a minor who is already married, for they surely disagree about the case of an adult who is betrothed. Rather, the Gemara is suggesting that the Tannaim also disagree about the case of a minor who is already married, and then, after demonstrating that they do not disagree about that case, it concludes that Rabbi Meir and Rabbi Yose disagree only about the case of an adult who is betrothed.

HALAKHAH

accepted as the Halakhah by Rava." (*Rambam, Sefer Nashim, Hilkhot Ishut* 20:14; *Shulḥan Arukh, Even HaEzer* 54:1.)

TRANSLATION AND COMMENTARY

is a minor, she is **not** authorized to make such a request. [1]But this leads to a difficulty if we **consider the last clause** of our Mishnah, which states: "When does this apply? When the daughter is already an adult. **But in a case where** the daughter **is** still **a minor,** we do not listen to her, for **the act of a minor is not valid.** In such a case the trustee must do as he was instructed by her father." [2]Now, continues the Gemara, **which** Tanna **taught this** ruling? [3]**If we say** that it was **Rabbi Yose** who taught this ruling, **surely we could have inferred** that **this** was his position **from the previous clause** of the Mishnah? [4]**For Rabbi Yose said: "If** the money had already been spent on buying **a field, and** the daughter now **wished to sell** the field and hand over the proceeds of the sale to her husband, surely she would be permitted to do so. Therefore we should **now** regard the money in the trustee's hands as if it had already been spent on a field which was **sold** by the daughter, and she can now give the proceeds to her husband. Thus we listen to the daughter's request and transfer the money from the trustee to the husband." [5]It follows from the reasoning offered by Rabbi Yose that this ruling applies only when the daughter is **an adult who has the legal capacity to sell** the field. **But** if the daughter is **a minor who does not have the legal capacity to sell** the field, we do **not** listen to the daughter, since we know from the previous clause that Rabbi Yose distinguishes between an adult and a minor, and there was no reason for Rabbi Yose to repeat that distinction in the last clause of the Mishnah. [6]**Rather,** says the Gemara, **it** must have been **Rabbi Meir** who taught the ruling found in the last clause of the Mishnah, [7]**and** the text of **the Mishnah is defective** and a sentence is missing from it. The Mishnah **should** actually **read as follows:** "If someone entrusts money to a third party on behalf of his daughter and instructs him to buy her a field as her dowry when she marries, and the father dies, and the daughter asks that the money be given over to her husband, **the trustee must do what he was entrusted to do.** He must buy a field for the daughter as he was instructed to do by her father." The Gemara now adds the critical clause that is missing in the Mishnah: [8]**"When does this** ruling **apply?** [9]It applies only in a case where the daughter is **betrothed** to her husband. **But** if she is already **married** to him, **the authority is in her hands** to ask that the money entrusted to the third party be handed over to her husband." And Rabbi Meir concludes with the qualification: [10]**"When does this** distinction **apply?** [11]When the daughter is **an adult.** In such a case we listen to the daughter and give the money to the husband. **But** when the daughter is still **a minor,** we do not listen to her even if she is married, for **the act of a minor has no legal force."** It follows from this that what Rabbi Meir stated in the Baraita — that if the daughter is married, she has the authority to ask that the money entrusted to the third party be handed over to her husband — applies only when she is an adult. But if she is still a minor, even Rabbi Meir agrees that the trustee must do what he was entrusted to do. Hence it cannot be argued that Rabbi Meir and Rabbi Yose disagree about the

[1]אֵימָא סֵיפָא: ״אֲבָל בִּקְטַנָּה, אֵין מַעֲשֵׂה קְטַנָּה כְּלוּם״. [2]הָא מַאן קָתָנֵי לָהּ? [3]אִילֵימָא רַבִּי יוֹסֵי, הָא מֵרֵישָׁא שָׁמְעַתְּ מִינָּהּ, [4]דְּאָמַר רַבִּי יוֹסֵי: ״וְכִי אֵינָהּ אֶלָּא שָׂדֶה וְהִיא רוֹצָה לְמוֹכְרָהּ, הֲרֵי הִיא מְכוּרָה מֵעַכְשָׁיו״. [5]גְּדוֹלָה דְּבַת זְבִינֵי אִין, קְטַנָּה דְּלָאו בַּת זְבִינֵי הִיא לָא! [6]אֶלָּא רַבִּי מֵאִיר הִיא, [7]וְחַסּוּרֵי מִיחַסְּרָא וְהָכִי קָתָנֵי: ״יַעֲשֶׂה הַשָּׁלִישׁ מַה שֶּׁהוּשְׁלַשׁ בְּיָדוֹ. [8]בַּמֶּה דְּבָרִים אֲמוּרִים? [9]מִן הָאֵירוּסִין, אֲבָל מִן הַנִּשּׂוּאִין הָרְשׁוּת בְּיָדָהּ. [10]בַּמֶּה דְּבָרִים אֲמוּרִים? [11]בִּגְדוֹלָה, אֲבָל בִּקְטַנָּה,

LITERAL TRANSLATION

[1]consider (lit., "say") the last [clause]: "But in [the case of] a minor, the act of a minor is nothing." [2]Who taught that? [3]If we say Rabbi Yose, surely you can infer this from the first [clause], [4]for Rabbi Yose said: "But if it were a field and she wished to sell it, surely it is sold from now." [5]An adult who is fit to sell has the authority (lit., "yes"), [but] a minor who is not fit to sell does not (lit., "no")! [6]Rather, it is Rabbi Meir, [7]and [the Mishnah] is defective and it teaches as follows: "The trustee must do what he was entrusted [to do]. [8]In what [case] are these things said? [9]After betrothal, but after marriage the authority is in her hand. [10]In what [case] are these things said? [11]In [the case of] an adult, but in [the case of] a minor,

RASHI

אימא סיפא — דמתניתין. **הא מרישא שמעינן מינה** — דלא אמר רבי יוסי. שומעין לה אלא בגדולה, מדקא מייתי טעמא למילתיה: וכי אינה אלא שדה והיא רוצה למוכרה — אלמא בגדולה הראויה למכור שדות קאמר. **אלא רבי מאיר** — ועל כרחך, כי אמר בברייתא נמי: מן הנשואין הרשות בידה — בגדולה אמר, ולא בקטנה.

אֵין מַעֲשֵׂה קְטַנָּה כְּלוּם".
[1]אֶלָּא, גְּדוֹלָה מִן הָאֵירוּסִין אִיכָּא בֵּינַיְיהוּ.
[2]אִיתְּמַר: רַב יְהוּדָה אָמַר שְׁמוּאֵל: [3]הֲלָכָה כְּרַבִּי יוֹסֵי. [4]רָבָא אָמַר רַב נַחְמָן: הֲלָכָה כְּרַבִּי מֵאִיר.
[5]אִילְפָא תְּלָא נַפְשֵׁיהּ בְּאִיסְקַרְיָא דְּמָכוּתָא, אֲמַר: [6]"אִיכָּא דְּאָתֵי דְּאָמַר לִי מִילְּתָא דְּבֵי רַבִּי חִיָּיא וְרַבִּי אוֹשַׁעְיָא וְלָא פְּשִׁיטְנָא לֵיהּ מִמַּתְנִיתִין, נָפֵילְנָא מֵאִסְקַרְיָא וְטָבַעְנָא". [7]אֲתָא הַהוּא סָבָא, תָּנָא לֵיהּ: [8]"הָאוֹמֵר: 'תְּנוּ שֶׁקֶל לְבָנַי בְּשַׁבָּת,'

LITERAL TRANSLATION

the act of a minor is nothing."

[1]Rather, [the difference] between them is [the case of] an adult after betrothal.

[2]It was stated: Rav Yehudah said in the name of Shmuel: [3]The Halakhah is in accordance with Rabbi Yose. [4]Rava said in the name of Rav Naḥman: The Halakhah is in accordance with Rabbi Meir.

[5]Ilfa suspended himself from the mast of a ship, [and] he said: [6]"[If] there is someone who will come and tell me something [that has been taught in] the Academy of Rabbi Ḥiyya and Rabbi Oshaya, and I will not derive it [from what has been taught in] our Mishnah, I will drop from the mast and drown." [7]A certain old man came, [and] repeated before him: [8]"[If] someone says: 'Give my sons a shekel a week,'

TRANSLATION AND COMMENTARY

case of a minor who is married. What, then, is the practical difference between the viewpoint of Rabbi Meir and that of Rabbi Yose?

אֶלָּא [1]**Rather,** answers the Gemara, we must say that **a difference between** the two Tannaim may be found in the case of **an adult** daughter who is **betrothed.** According to Rabbi Meir, the trustee must do what he was entrusted to do and must buy a field on behalf of the daughter. And according to Rabbi Yose, since the daughter is already an adult, she has the authority to ask that the money entrusted to the third party be handed over to her husband.

אִיתְּמַר [2]**It was stated** that the Amoraim disagree about the following matter: **Rav Yehudah said in the name of Shmuel:** [3]**The Halakhah is in accordance with Rabbi Yose.** [4]**Rava said in the name of Rav Naḥman: The Halakhah is in accordance with Rabbi Meir.**

אִילְפָא [5]The Gemara continues with an anecdote that includes a reference to a ruling found in our Mishnah. The Sage **Ilfa** immediately went and **suspended himself from the mast of a ship, and proclaimed:** "Even though I left the Academy in order to engage in business, I never abandoned my Torah studies. To prove this, I am ready to stake my life in the following test. [6]**If there is anyone who can ask me about** a matter discussed in a Baraita taught **in the Academy of Rabbi Ḥiyya and Rabbi Oshaya** [the Tosefta compiled by these two Sages on the basis of the traditions they had received from their teacher, Rabbi Yehudah HaNasi], **and I am unable** to **derive it from** a ruling found in **the Mishnah** itself, **I will drop from the mast** of this ship **and drown** myself." [7]**A certain old man came, and taught** the following Baraita **before** Ilfa: [8]**"If a person** on his deathbed deposits all his assets in the hands of a trustee and **says** to him: 'I do not want my entire estate to pass to my minor sons immediately upon my death. Instead, I want you to **give my sons a shekel** [half a sela] **a week** to cover their expenses until they reach majority,'

RASHI

אלא גדולה מן האירוסין איכא בינייהו – דקאמר רבי מאיר: מן האירוסין יעשה שליח שליחותו, ואפילו היא גדולה. וקא אמר ליה רבי יוסי: כיון דגדולה היא – שומעין לה. **הלכה כרבי מאיר** – טעמא משום דמצוה לקיים דברי המת. **אילפא** – שם חכם. **תלא נפשיה** – גופא דעובדא במסכת תענית. משום דאותבוהו לרבי יוחנן ברישא, כשהלך אילפא בסחורה, כי אתא אמרו ליה: אי הוה יתיב מר וגריס לא מר הוה מליך? אזל תלא נפשיה באיסקריא דמכותא = בכלונסות ארזים שתולים בה וילון הספינה. **מכותא** = וילון. **אמר כל מאן דאתי כו'** – כלומר, אף על פי שהלכתי בסחורה, לא שכחתי תלמודי, ויש בידי לתקן כל הברייתות שסידרו רבי חייא ורבי אושעיא [בתוספתא שלהן – אמינא להן סמך במשנתנו של הששה סדרים שסדר רבי. ולהכי נקט רבי חייא ורבי אושעיא] – לפי שהן עיקר, כדאמרינן בעלמא: כל מתניתא דלא מיתניא בי רבי חייא ורבי אושעיא – לא תותבו מינה בבי מדרשא. **תנא ליה** – שנה לפניו ברייתא זו, ושאלו למצוא לה סמך במשנה שסדר רבי. **שקל** – חצי סלע.

LANGUAGE

אִיסְקַרְיָא Mast. This word is probably derived from the Greek ἱστοκεραία, *histokeraia,* meaning "a mast."

מָכוּתָא Ship. This word, which is apparently derived from the Persian *makok* (or the shorter neo-Persian *mako*), meaning "ship" or "boat," is also found in Aramaic and other languages.

SAGES

אִילְפָא Ilfa. A first-generation Palestinian Amora, he is called Ḥilfai (חִילְפַי) in the Jerusalem Talmud. He was a disciple of Rabbi Yehudah HaNasi and studied under him and his senior disciples. Ilfa was also a friend of Rabbi Yoḥanan and they studied together. Because of the difficulty of sustaining themselves, the two men decided to engage in commerce. However Rabbi Yoḥanan changed his mind and continued to study Torah in poverty, and only Ilfa went into trade, apparently going overseas. In time the post of the head of the yeshiva fell vacant, and Rabbi Yoḥanan was chosen to fill it. When Ilfa returned, people said that he had not received the appointment because he was not learned in Torah. Therefore Ilfa wanted to prove the greatness of his knowledge. His Torah teachings are found in both the Babylonian and Jerusalem Talmuds, including remarks that he recorded in a notebook. He had an extremely sharp mind and was one of the greatest Torah authorities of his generation.

NOTES

נָפֵילְנָא מֵאִסְקַרְיָא וְטָבַעְנָא I will drop from the mast and drown. A slightly different version of the story is reported in the Jerusalem Talmud, according to which Ilfa sat on a river bank, and asked to be cast into the river if he failed to explain on the basis of the Mishnah a regulation recorded in the Tosefta. Some suggest that Ilfa's conduct is to be understood in the light of the Mishnah (*Avot* 3:8), which states that whoever forgets even one word of his study is regarded by Scripture as if he had forfeited his life (*Ramat Shmuel, Ḥever ben Ḥayyim*).

[1]וּרְאוּיִן לִיתֵּן לָהֶם סֶלַע, נוֹתְנִין לָהֶם סֶלַע. [2]וְאִם אָמַר: ׳אַל תִּתְּנוּ לָהֶם אֶלָּא שֶׁקֶל׳, [3]אֵין נוֹתְנִין לָהֶם אֶלָּא שֶׁקֶל. [4]וְאִם אָמַר: ׳אִם מֵתוּ, יִירְשׁוּ אֲחֵרִים תַּחְתֵּיהֶם׳, [5]בֵּין שֶׁאָמַר, ׳תְּנוּ׳, בֵּין שֶׁאָמַר, ׳אַל תִּתְּנוּ׳, [6]אֵין נוֹתְנִים לָהֶם אֶלָּא שֶׁקֶל״. [7]אֲמַר לֵיהּ: הָא מַנִּי?

LITERAL TRANSLATION

[1]and they are fit to be given a sela, we give them a sela. [2]But if he said: 'Give them only a shekel,' [3]we give them only a shekel. [4]And if he said: 'If they die, let others inherit in their place,' [5]whether he said, 'Give,' or he said, 'Give only,' [6]we give them only a shekel." [7]He [Ilfa] said to him: Whose [opinion] is this?

TRANSLATION AND COMMENTARY

[1]but it turns out that **they need to be given a** full **sela** each week, a shekel being insufficient to cover all their expenses, then **they must be given a sela.** We assume that the father intended to have his children maintained at a moderate level, and if they really did need more than a shekel for their basic subsistence, he would surely not have objected to their being given a larger allowance. [2]**But if** the father **says:** 'When I die, I wish you to **give** my sons *only* **a shekel** a week,' [3]**they are given only a shekel,** even if that amount does not suffice to provide for their needs. Since the father made use of the word 'only' in formulating his instructions, we assume that he meant his words to be followed strictly. [4]And **if** the father **says: 'When** my sons **die,** I do not want my estate to pass to their heirs, but I want **other** people to **inherit in their place,'** [5]then **whether he said, 'Give** my sons a shekel a week,' **or he said, 'Give** them **only** a shekel a week,' [6]the sons **are given only a shekel a week."** Since the father said that he wanted his estate to be transferred to people other than his grandchildren on the death of his sons, we assume that he meant to restrict his children's allowance, so that assets would remain after their deaths to be passed on to the other parties? Where, asked the old man, do we find a ruling in the Mishnah on which this Baraita is based? [7]Ilfa **said to him: Whose opinion does this** Baraita **follow?**

RASHI

וראוין — שאין נזונין בפחות. **נותנים להם סלע** — דאי הוה ידע שיתייקרו המזונות ויצטרכו לסלע — לא הוה אמר. **אל תתנו** — הרי מיחה בידם, ולא עשאן יורשים אלא בענין זה. **אם מתו** — בלא בנים. **אין נותנין להן אלא שקל** — שאין לנו להפסיד את הבאים אחריהם. והואיל ועשה את האחרים יורשים אחריהם — ודאי דווקא שקל קאמר, כדי שתפול ירושה אחריהם לאותן אחרים. **הא מני** — היכא דאמר להו: אל תתנו להם אלא שקל — אין נותנין להם אלא שקל. ואף על גב דסוף סוף כולהו נכסי דידהו נינהו — לא יהבינן להו בקוטנן אלא שקל בשבת והמוֹתָר יזונו מן הצדקה. וליכא לאקשויי עלה הא דאמר בפרק "נערה" (כתובות מח,א): לא כל כמיניה שיעשיר את בניו ויפיל עצמו על הצבור — דהתם הוא דאמר: אל תקברוהו מנכסיו, ונכסי דידיה נינהו — הלכך לא ציתינן ליה לקוברו מן הצדקה כדי להעשיר את בניו. אבל הכא — נכסי לאו דיתמי נינהו, כי אם לפי צוואתו.

NOTES

"אַל תִּתְּנוּ לָהֶם אֶלָּא שֶׁקֶל" "Give them only a shekel." *Rashi* and others maintain that if the father said: "Give my sons only a shekel a week," then under no circumstances may the sons be given more than a shekel a week, even if they cannot live on that amount and will have to accept charity. According to *Remah* and *Talmidei Rabbenu Yonah,* the sons may not be given more than a shekel a week, even if that means that they will have to live frugally. But if they cannot subsist on a shekel a week, they may be given a larger allowance, for we assume that even when the father said: "Give them only a shekel a week," he did not want them to starve or to be supported by charity.

"אִם מֵתוּ, יִירְשׁוּ אֲחֵרִים תַּחְתֵּיהֶם" "If they die, let others inherit in their place." The Rishonim ask: There is a general rule that an inheritance cannot be terminated (*Bava Batra* 129b). Therefore, if a person bequeathed his property to his legal heir, saying: "To you and afterwards to someone else," the property does not pass to the other person upon the heir's death, but rather to the heir's heirs. Why, then, does the Baraita rule that the father's instructions are effective when he says that, when his sons die, others are to inherit in their place?

Rambam (*Hilkhot Zekhiyyah U'Mattanah* 12:6) explains that the Baraita's ruling is restricted to a case where the father states explicitly that his heirs are not to receive his property as an inheritance, but as a gift, for a gift may indeed be terminated. *Ra'avad* maintains that the Baraita's ruling applies only in a case where the father deposited his assets in the hands of a trustee; but if the heirs actually received the property, the inheritance cannot be terminated. Others (see *Meiri*) explain that the Baraita's ruling is restricted to a case where the father limited his heirs to a shekel a week, for in such a case they never received the estate itself and so it can be passed on to others upon their death.

HALAKHAH

וְאִם אָמַר: "אִם מֵתוּ, יִירְשׁוּ אֲחֵרִים תַּחְתֵּיהֶם" And if he said: "If they die, let others inherit in their place." "If a person who was on his deathbed said: 'When my sons die, I wish my estate to pass to other people and not to my grandsons,' then whether he said: 'Give my sons a shekel a week,' or he said: 'Give them only a shekel a week,' they are given only a shekel a week, even if they need more." (*Rambam, Sefer Kinyan, Hilkhot Zekhiyyah U'Mattanah* 12:6; *Shulḥan Arukh, Ḥoshen Mishpat* 253:17.)

TRANSLATION AND COMMENTARY

[70A] [1]**It follows the opinion of Rabbi Meir, who said:** [2]**It is a** religious **duty to fulfill the words of the deceased,** as we learned in our Mishnah: "If a father entrusts money to a third party on behalf of his daughter and instructs him to buy her a field as her dowry when she marries, and the father dies, and after her betrothal the daughter asks the trustee to hand over the money to her bridegroom, for she trusts him to carry out her father's wishes, the trustee may not do so, but must himself execute the father's instructions as he received them." Our Baraita's rulings are based on the same principle, which finds expression in Rabbi Meir's statement: It is a duty to carry out the wishes of the deceased in the sense that they were intended. If the father's instructions may be interpreted so as to allow the sons to be given more than a shekel a week, they may be given a full sela. But if it is clear that the father meant that his instructions were to be followed strictly, or that his estate should pass to someone else on the death of his sons, the sons may not be given more than a shekel a week.

אֲמַר רַב חִסְדָּא [3]**Rav Ḥisda said in the name of Mar Ukva:** [4]**The Halakhah is** that **whether** the father **said** to the trustee: **"Give** my sons a shekel a week," **or he said** to him: **"Give** them **only** a shekel a week," [5]the sons **are given whatever they need** to cover their expenses.

הָא קַיְימָא לַן [6]The Gemara disputes this ruling: But **surely we maintain that the Halakhah is in accordance with Rabbi Meir, who said:** [7]**It is a** religious **duty to carry out the wishes of the deceased!**

הָנֵי מִילֵּי [8]The Gemara answers: The duty to carry out the wishes of the deceased **does** indeed **apply in**

[70A] [1]רַבִּי מֵאִיר הִיא, דְּאָמַר: [2]מִצְוָה לְקַיֵּים דִּבְרֵי הַמֵּת.

[3]אֲמַר רַב חִסְדָּא אֲמַר מָר עוּקְבָא: [4]הִלְכְתָא: בֵּין שֶׁאָמַר, "תְּנוּ", וּבֵין שֶׁאָמַר, "אַל תִּתְּנוּ", [5]נוֹתְנִין לָהֶם כָּל צוֹרְכָּם.

[6]הָא קַיְימָא לַן הֲלָכָה כְּרַבִּי מֵאִיר, דְּאָמַר: [7]מִצְוָה לְקַיֵּים דִּבְרֵי הַמֵּת!

[8]הָנֵי מִילֵּי בְּמִילֵּי אַחֲרָנִיתָא,

LITERAL TRANSLATION

[70A] [1]It is [that of] Rabbi Meir, who said: [2]It is a duty to fulfill the words of the deceased.

[3]Rav Ḥisda said in the name of Mar Ukva: [4]The Halakhah is: Whether he said, "Give," or he said, "Give only," [5]we give them all they need.

[6]Surely we maintain [that] the Halakhah is in accordance with Rabbi Meir, who said: [7]It is a duty to fulfill the words of the deceased!

[8]This applies (lit., "these words") to other things.

RASHI

רבי מאיר — דמתניתין היא, דאמר: יעשה שליש מה שהושלש בידו.

NOTES

מִצְוָה לְקַיֵּים דִּבְרֵי הַמֵּת It is a duty to fulfill the words of the deceased. *Tosafot* (here, and at greater length in *Bava Batra,* 149a; see also *Tosefot Rash*) and others raise a question regarding this duty to carry out the wishes of the deceased. If there is indeed such an obligation, why was it also necessary for the Rabbis to enact that the gift of a person on his deathbed is valid even if no act of acquisition was performed? Such a gift should be valid even without any special enactment on the basis of the general obligation to carry out the wishes of the deceased. It cannot be argued that the duty to carry out the wishes of the deceased is just a moral one, for elsewhere (*Gittin* 40a) the Gemara states that this obligation is a strict legal duty which the heirs can be compelled to fulfill.

Rivam argues that the obligation to carry out the wishes of the deceased is limited to an explicit command, such as, "Give such-and-such to So-and-so." The enactment regarding the gift of a dying person ensures that his gift is valid no matter how he expressed his intention, even if he only said, "Such-and-such to So-and-so."

Ri maintains that the obligation to carry out the wishes of the deceased applies only to a person who has the legal capacity to carry out the instructions of the deceased and who received those instructions from the dying man. However, the enactment regarding the gift of a dying man applies even if the dying man expressed his intentions to another party.

According to *Rabbenu Tam,* the obligation to carry out the wishes of the deceased applies only with respect to property that was deposited with a trustee for the purpose of carrying out his instructions. *Ran* suggests that the obligation to fulfill the wishes of the deceased does not apply if the instructions were given to a minor, for a minor has no legal obligations. Thus the Rabbis had to enact that the gift of a person on his deathbed is valid even if no act of acquisition was performed.

HALAKHAH

בֵּין שֶׁאָמַר, "תְּנוּ" Whether he said, "Give." "If a person who is on his deathbed says: 'Give my sons a shekel a week,' or if he says: 'Give them only a shekel a week,' and it turns out that they need more, they must be given as needed, following the Gemara's conclusion that there is no practical difference between the two formulations." (*Rambam, Sefer Kinyan, Hilkhot Zekhiyyah U'Mattanah* 11:23; *Shulḥan Arukh, Ḥoshen Mishpat* 253:17.)

TRANSLATION AND COMMENTARY

other cases. [1]**But here** the law is different, because we assume that the father **wanted** his children to have enough money to cover their basic needs. [2]**And when he said:** "Give my sons only a shekel a week," he formulated his instructions in that manner, because **he wished to encourage** his sons to live modestly and not to spend more than was absolutely necessary.

תְּנַן הָתָם [3]**We have learned elsewhere** in the Mishnah (*Gittin* 59a): **"Regarding young children** who appreciate the significance of a purchase or a sale, [4]**their purchases and their sales are valid in the case of movable property.** By Torah law, the sale or purchase of property by a minor is void. But the Rabbis enacted that a particularly intelligent child of six or seven, or a slightly older child of average intelligence, may buy or sell movable property. The Rabbis validated the purchases and sales of such children so that they would be able to conduct transactions and procure the basic necessities of life."

אָמַר רַפְרָם [5]**Rafram said** in connection with this Mishnah: **This** ruling that the purchases and sales carried out by a minor are valid **applies only** if **a guardian was not** appointed (by the father or by a court) to conduct

[1]אֲבָל בְּהָא, מֵינָח נִיחָא לֵיהּ. [2]וְהָא דַּאֲמַר הָכִי לְזָרוּזִינְהוּ הוּא דַּאֲתָא.

[3]תְּנַן הָתָם: "הַפָּעוֹטוֹת, [4]מִקָּחָן מִקָּח וּמִמְכָּרָן מֶכֶר בְּמִטַּלְטְלִים." [5]אָמַר רַפְרָם: לֹא שָׁנוּ אֶלָּא שֶׁאֵין שָׁם אַפּוֹטְרוֹפּוֹס.

LITERAL TRANSLATION

[1]But here he is pleased. [2]And the reason why he spoke thus is that he came to encourage them.

[3]We have learned elsewhere: "[Regarding] young children, [4]their purchase is a [valid] purchase and their sale is a [valid] sale in [the case of] movable property."

[5]Rafram said: They only taught [this] where there is no guardian.

RASHI

מינח ניחא ליה – שיתנו להן כל צורכן. **לזרוזינהו** – שיחזרו אחר מזונותיהן, ושלא יהו רעבתנין. **הפעוטות** – תינוקות בני תשע ושמונה, כדאמרינן ב"הניזקין". **במטלטלי** – דווקא. אבל במקרקעי – לא, עד שיביאו שתי שערות, או עד שיהא בן עשרים. **אפוטרופוס** – שמינהו אבי יתומים, או בית דין.

NOTES

הַפָּעוֹטוֹת מִקָּחָן מִקָּח **Regarding young children, their purchase is a valid purchase.** The primary discussion of the validity of transactions conducted by minors is found elsewhere (*Gittin* 59a). Though by Torah law the sale or purchase of property by a minor is not valid, the Rabbis enacted that a child who understands the significance of a sale or purchase may conduct such a transaction if it involves movable property. A child between the ages of six and ten must be tested to see whether he possesses such understanding. An older child is assumed to have such understanding unless we know that the opposite is true. The Gemara explains that the Rabbis validated the sales and purchases of such minors for the sake of their sustenance, so that they would be able to conduct certain transactions and thus acquire the things they needed. Once such minors were given the authority to sell and purchase property for the sake of their maintenance, they were entitled to conduct such transactions even if they involved larger sums and were not necessary for their maintenance. Since the enactment was made for the sake of the minor's sustenance, it applies only where a guardian has not been appointed to conduct the minor's affairs. But if there is a guardian looking after the minor, the minor's sales and purchases are void.

לֹא שָׁנוּ אֶלָּא שֶׁאֵין שָׁם אַפּוֹטְרוֹפּוֹס **They only taught this where there is no guardian.** The Gemara concludes that the presence of a guardian renders void the transactions conducted by a minor. The Rishonim infer from this that if the father appointed a guardian to conduct the affairs of his adult son, the son's transactions are valid even without the guardian's confirmation. Even if the father had deposited money with a trustee on behalf of his adult son, if the son seized the money from him, the transactions conducted with that money are valid (*Ritva, Rivash*).

HALAKHAH

הַפָּעוֹטוֹת מִקָּחָן מִקָּח **Regarding young children, their purchase is a valid purchase.** "The transactions conducted by a minor below the age of six are void. If a minor six years of age or older appreciates the significance of a purchase and a sale (i.e., he was tested and found to understand the meaning of such transactions), or if he was already ten, and not an imbecile (*Rema* in the name of *Tur*), his purchases, sales and gifts are valid, whether he performed a large transaction or a small one, whether the gift was made while he was healthy or was made while he was on his deathbed. These transactions are all valid by Rabbinic enactment. All these regulations apply only to movable property. *Rema* (in the name of *Ran*) adds that since these transactions are valid only by Rabbinic enactment, if they involve an impropriety, they are not valid." (*Rambam, Sefer Kinyan, Hilkhot Mekhirah* 29:6; *Shulḥan Arukh, Ḥoshen Mishpat* 235:1.)

לֹא שָׁנוּ אֶלָּא שֶׁאֵין שָׁם אַפּוֹטְרוֹפּוֹס **They only taught this where there is no guardian.** "The ruling that the purchases and sales conducted by a minor who appreciates the significance of such transactions are valid applies only if a guardian has not been appointed to conduct the minor's affairs. But if a guardian has been appointed (or the minor is being maintained by an adult who has the status of a guardian; *Rema*), the minor's purchases and sales are not valid, unless they are confirmed by the guardian." (*Rambam, Sefer Kinyan, Hilkhot Mekhirah* 29:7; *Shulḥan Arukh, Ḥoshen Mishpat* 235:2.)

[1]אֲבָל יֵשׁ שָׁם אַפּוֹטְרוֹפּוֹס, אֵין מִקְּחָן מִקָּח וְאֵין מִמְכָּרָן מֶכֶר. [2]מִמַּאי? [3]מִדְּקָתָנֵי: [4]"אֵין מַעֲשֵׂה קְטַנָּה כְּלוּם". [5]וְדִלְמָא הֵיכָא דְּאִיכָּא שָׁלִישׁ שָׁאנֵי? [6]אִם כֵּן לִיתְנֵי: [7]"אֲבָל בִּקְטַנָּה, יַעֲשֶׂה שָׁלִישׁ מַה שֶּׁהוּשְׁלַשׁ בְּיָדוֹ". [8]מַאי: "אֵין מַעֲשֵׂה קְטַנָּה כְּלוּם"? [9]שְׁמַע מִינָּהּ: אֲפִילּוּ בְּעָלְמָא.

הדרן עלך מציאת האשה

LITERAL TRANSLATION

[1]But where there is a guardian, their purchase is not a [valid] purchase, and their sale is not a [valid] sale.

[2]From what?

[3]From what is taught: [4]"The act of a minor is nothing."

[5]But perhaps where there is a trustee it is different?

[6]If so, let it teach: [7]"But in [the case of] a minor, the trustee must do what he was entrusted to do." [8]What is [the significance of]: "The act of a minor is nothing"? [9]Infer from this: Even in general.

TRANSLATION AND COMMENTARY

the affairs of the minor. [1]**But if a guardian was** appointed by the father or by a court, **the purchases and sales** carried out by the minor **are not valid.**

מִמַּאי? [2]The Gemara asks: **From where** does Rafram know this?

מִדְּקָתָנֵי [3]The Gemara explains: Rafram derives his ruling **from what is stated** in our Mishnah: "If the daughter is still a minor, we do not listen to **her** request to transfer the money from the trustee to her husband, [4]for **the act of a minor is not valid."** A trustee appointed by the father to buy a field on behalf of his daughter is similar to a guardian appointed by the father to conduct his child's affairs. Hence it follows that if a guardian has been appointed to conduct the affairs of a minor, the transactions carried out by that minor are void.

וְדִלְמָא [5]The Gemara asks: **But perhaps** the case **of a trustee is different?** In the case of our Mishnah, the father specifically appointed the trustee to buy a field on his daughter's behalf. If after her father's death the daughter asks that the money entrusted to the third party be handed over to her husband, we do not listen to her, because it is a religious duty to carry out the explicit wishes of the deceased. But a guardian who receives a general appointment to conduct the minor's affairs is authorized to conduct transactions on behalf of his ward whenever necessary. Perhaps, then, if the minor buys or sells property on his own initiative, his transactions are valid.

אִם כֵּן [6]The Gemara answers: **If it is true** that the law applying to a trustee appointed with a specific task is different, then the Mishnah **should have stated:** [7]**"But with respect to a minor, the trustee must do what he was entrusted to do."** [8]**What is** the significance of the Mishnah's comprehensive statement: **"The act of a minor is not valid"?** [9]The Gemara concludes: We can **infer from this** that **in general,** whenever a guardian is appointed to conduct a minor's affairs, the transactions conducted by the minor are void.

RASHI

מדקתני – במתניתין. **שאני הכא דאיכא שליש** – שנשתלש לכך, ופירשו לו מה יעשה בהן. אבל אפוטרופוס – אינו אלא לעשות צורכי יתומים לכל הצריך, והרי אם מכרו אלו הפעוטות – אין זה שינוי מצות המת, שאף האפוטרופוס ימכור לצורך מזונותיהם. **אם כן** – דשליש דווקא. וטעמא, לפי שפירשו לו לקנות שדה – ליתני: יעשה שליש כו׳. **דאפילו בעלמא** – במקום אפוטרופוס, דדמי קצת לשליש.

הדרן עלך מציאת האשה

NOTES

אֵין מִקְּחָן מִקָּח Their purchase is not a valid purchase. Here the Gemara states that the presence of a guardian invalidates the sales and purchases of a minor. Elsewhere (*Gittin* 59a), the Gemara concludes that the gifts of a minor who understands the significance of the transactions are valid. The Rishonim disagree about whether the presence of a guardian invalidates a minor's gifts. *Rav Hai Gaon* and *Rabbenu Ḥananel* argue that the minor's gifts are valid even if a guardian has been appointed to conduct his affairs. The Rabbis enacted that the minor's gifts are made in response to acts of kindness. Thus the validity of the minor's gifts should not be dependent on the presence or absence of a guardian. Others argue that a minor's gifts are just like his sales and purchases, and therefore the gifts of a minor who has a guardian are void.

Conclusion to Chapter Six

A wife's handiwork and what she finds belong entirely to her husband. If a wife inherits property during her marriage, her husband is entitled to enjoy the usufruct of the property during her lifetime, and he acquires ownership of it upon her death. If a wife is caused bodily injury, entitling her to compensation for shame and blemish, one-third of the payments for an injury inflicted on a part of her body which is ordinarily covered, and two-thirds of the payments for an injury inflicted on a part of her body which is ordinarily exposed, must be made to the husband, and the rest goes to the wife. If land is bought with the wife's portion of the payments, the husband is entitled to the usufruct of that property during his wife's lifetime.

While there is no obligation in Torah law to provide one's daughter with a dowry, and such an obligation does not derive from a ketubah condition, the Rabbis imposed this obligation on the father. Upon the father's death, his heirs are bound to give his daughter part of his estate as her dowry, as if the father were still alive. The amount that a father must give his daughter as her dowry is left to his discretion. The minimum that the daughter should be given is fifty zuz, the amount given to a woman who is supported by charity. A wealthy man should give his daughter a dowry in accordance with his means. The father's heirs are obligated to provide his orphan daughter with a dowry based on an assessment of what he would have given her had he still been alive. If such an assessment is not possible, the heirs must give the daughter a tenth of the father's estate as her dowry. If the father is survived by several daughters, each daughter receives a tenth of what remains of her father's estate at the time of her marriage. Since the obligation falling upon the heirs is based on an assessment of the father's disposition, the father's instructions to deprive his daughter of her dowry are legally valid.

The orphan daughter may collect her dowry only from the immovable property of her father's estate. This regulation remains in force even though the Geonim enacted that a woman may claim her ketubah and its conditions from the movable property of her husband's estate.

As for the sum that a husband obligated himself to return to his wife upon the dissolution of their marriage as the equivalent of her dowry, it is concluded that if the wife brought her husband a dowry of money, the husband accepts liability for an increment to the dowry fixed at half of the amount specified as the dowry. If she brought him a dowry of movable goods, he obligates himself to restore the assessed value of those goods, provided that they were assessed at their true value. But in places where it was customary to inflate the value of the assets a wife brought into the marriage as her dowry, the husband would accept liability for the true value of the goods.

If the father deposited money with a trustee so that after his death the trustee would buy real estate for his daughter's dowry, and the daughter later reached majority and married, she may ask that the money be transferred to her husband to buy the property on her behalf. But if the daughter is still a minor or only betrothed, the trustee is obligated to buy the real estate on her behalf in accordance with her father's instructions.

Introduction to Chapter Seven

הַמַּדִּיר

The relations between a man and his wife are based on a system of mutual rights and obligations, agreed upon by the two parties and recorded in the ketubah. This agreement is valid as long as it does not include a condition which runs contrary to Torah law. But there are instances where one of the parties violates a condition attached to the agreement (whether explicit or implicit) in such a fundamental way that the courts compel the couple to terminate their marriage.

The Rabbis imposed a penalty upon the party that violated the marriage agreement. If it is the woman who violated the agreement, she may be divorced without receiving her ketubah. If it is the husband who is guilty, the courts can compel him to divorce his wife and pay her her ketubah.

A violation of the basic marriage agreement may occur prior to the marriage (during the period of the couple's betrothal) or during the course of the marriage. The criteria that determine what is considered a fundamental violation of the marriage agreement and the consequences of such a violation are essentially the same, no matter when the violation occurred.

There are three categories of violations of the basic marriage agreement: Vows, misconduct, and physical defects. Our chapter defines and clarifies these three categories. Not every vow, or act of misconduct, or physical defect is regarded as a fundamental violation of the basic marriage agreement, even if in a particular instance the vow, misdeed, or defect makes it difficult for a man and a woman to continue living together. Objective standards must be set in order to determine what is considered a violation of the marriage agreement: Which vow adversely affects the relationship between man and wife? What is regarded as unseemly conduct? Which defect or blemish is reason for divorce? All these matters must be considered with respect to both the woman and the man, for there are recognizable differences between their respective obligations and expectations. It is also necessary to determine when and how divorce is imposed upon the couple.

The clarification of these and related issues is the subject matter of this chapter.

הַמַּדִּיר

[1]אֶת אִשְׁתּוֹ מִלֵּיהָנוֹת לוֹ, עַד שְׁלֹשִׁים יוֹם יַעֲמִיד פַּרְנָס; [2]יָתֵר מִיכָּן, יוֹצִיא וְיִתֵּן כְּתוּבָּה. [3]רַבִּי יְהוּדָה אוֹמֵר: בְּיִשְׂרָאֵל, חֹדֶשׁ אֶחָד, יְקַיֵּים; [4]וּשְׁנַיִם, יוֹצִיא וְיִתֵּן כְּתוּבָּה.

LITERAL TRANSLATION

MISHNAH [1][If] someone prohibits his wife with a vow from benefiting from him, up to thirty days, he must appoint an administrator; [2]more than that, he must divorce [her] and pay [her] ketubah. [3]Rabbi Yehudah says: In [the case of] a non-priest (lit., "an Israelite"), [if his vow was for] one month, he may keep [her]; [4]but [if it was for] two, he must divorce [her] and pay [her] ketubah.

TRANSLATION AND COMMENTARY

MISHNAH הַמַּדִּיר אֶת אִשְׁתּוֹ [1]**If someone makes a vow forbidding his wife to** derive any **benefit from him** for a period of **up to thirty days,** he is not required to divorce her but **must appoint an administrator** to maintain his wife in his stead. [2]But if he forbids her to derive any benefit from him for **more than** thirty days, and he takes no steps to secure an annulment of his vow, and his wife is unwilling to continue being supported by someone other than her husband, **he must grant her a divorce and pay** her **her ketubah.** [3]**Rabbi Yehudah** disagrees and **says:** If the husband **is a non-priest** and he forbids his wife to derive any benefit from him for a period of **one month, he may keep her** as his wife and must appoint an administrator to maintain her. [4]But if he forbids her to benefit from him for **two** months, and he takes no steps to have his vow annulled, and his wife is unwilling to continue receiving her support from the administrator, the husband **must grant her a divorce and pay** her

RASHI

משנה המדיר את אשתו מליהנות לו — אין הנאת תשמישו נאסר עליה — דהא משועבד לה. הלכך, בשביל תשמיש אין לנו לכופו להוציא וליתן כתובה. והנאת מזונות, בגמרא פריך: והא משועבד לה? **יעמיד פרנס** — שליח שיפרנסנה. **בישראל** — אם ישראל הוא, שיכול להחזיר את גרושתו.

CONCEPTS

נֶדֶר Vow. The main laws regarding vows are written in the Torah (Numbers, chapter 30) and presented in detail in tractate *Nedarim*.

In general when a person takes a vow, he forbids himself from deriving benefit from something for a specified period of time or forever. After taking on a vow, he is not permitted to derive benefit from the thing he has forsworn, and he receives lashes if he violates his oath. Tractate *Nedarim* states that there are various terms for vows, which differ slightly from each other. These include נֶדֶר, אִיסָּר, קוֹנָם and חֵרֶם.

The vows of a young girl (a קְטַנָּה or נַעֲרָה) or of a wife may be annulled by the father or husband, respectively. Other people can also be released from their vow by a Torah scholar or a Rabbinical Court.

NOTES

הַמַּדִּיר אֶת אִשְׁתּוֹ If someone forbids his wife with a vow. According to *Rashi,* someone who takes a vow forbidding his wife to "benefit" from him wishes not only to prevent her from deriving material benefit from him, but also to deprive her of enjoyment from sexual relations with him. But the vow, as far as it relates to sexual relations, is invalid, because the husband is obligated by law to cohabit with his wife.

Rabbenu Tam and others explain that a man who makes a vow forbidding his wife to "benefit" from him intends only to prevent her from deriving material benefit from him. He does not intend to forbid her to engage in sexual relations with him. The Rishonim consider these two positions in the light of the Gemara's discussion of our Mishnah below, as well as on the basis of other Talmudic sources. The Jerusalem Talmud notes the apparent contradiction between our Mishnah and the Mishnah found earlier in our tractate (61b), which states: "If someone forbids his wife with a vow from sexual relations, Bet Shammai say: Two weeks. Bet Hillel say: One week." The Jerusalem Talmud argues that there the husband is forbidding his wife to derive benefit from his body, whereas here he is forbidding her to derive benefit from his property. The Rishonim (see *Ramban, Rashba,* and *Ritva*) discuss whether the Jerusalem Talmud means to say that the term "benefit" necessarily implies material benefit (supporting *Rabbenu Tam*), or whether it has that meaning here because the husband states explicitly that he is forbidding his wife to derive benefit from his property.

יַעֲמִיד פַּרְנָס He must appoint an administrator. The Jerusalem Talmud asks: If the husband can appoint an administrator to maintain his wife in his stead, why can he not maintain her permanently by means of the administrator? It answers: A wife has the right to receive her maintenance directly from her husband. Earlier in the tractate (64b), the Mishnah speaks of a man who provides for his wife's support through a third party; but in that case, the wife willingly agreed to receive her maintenance from someone other than her husband. But if a wife is unwilling to be supported by an administrator, her husband cannot compel her to receive her maintenance in that manner, and she may demand a divorce and payment of her ketubah.

שְׁנַיִם יוֹצִיא But if it was for two, he must divorce her. Most commentators explain that if the vow has entered its second month, and the husband has taken no steps to secure an annulment, he can be compelled to divorce his wife and to pay her her ketubah. *Rashba* notes, however, that the Jerusalem Talmud and the Tosefta imply that the husband cannot be forced to divorce his wife until two full months have passed without his having secured a dispensation annulling his vow. Similarly, "three months" in the case of a priest refers to the end of the third month.

יוֹצִיא וְיִתֵּן כְּתוּבָּה He must divorce her and pay her ketubah. *Hafla'ah* asks: If the husband makes a vow

HALAKHAH

הַמַּדִּיר אֶת אִשְׁתּוֹ מִלֵּיהָנוֹת לוֹ If someone prohibits his wife with a vow from benefiting from him. "If someone takes a vow to prevent his wife from deriving any benefit from him, whether or not he specifies for how long she will be forbidden to derive such benefit, we wait thirty days. If during those thirty days his vow comes to an end, or the husband secures a Sage's dispensation annulling his vow, all is well. But if after thirty days the vow is still in force, the husband must divorce his wife and pay her her ketubah. During these thirty days, the wife can maintain herself with the handiwork she produces, and if that does not suffice, an acquaintance should provide her with whatever else she needs." (*Rambam, Sefer Nashim, Hilkhot Ishut* 12:23; *Shulḥan Arukh, Yoreh De'ah* 235:2; *Even HaEzer* 72.)

TRANSLATION AND COMMENTARY

her ketubah. [1]But **if** the husband is **a priest,** then even if he forbids his wife to benefit from him for a period of **two** months, **he may keep her** as his wife and appoint an administrator to maintain her. [2]Only if he forbids his wife to benefit from him for **three** months, and he makes no attempt to secure a dispensation annulling his vow, and his wife refuses to be maintained by someone other than her husband, **must he grant her a divorce and pay** her **her ketubah.** A priest is forbidden to marry a divorcee (Leviticus 21:7), even his own former wife. Thus, he is given an extra month to secure a Sage's dispensation annulling his vow before he is compelled to grant his wife a divorce, for once he has divorced her, he can never again take her back as his wife.

הַמַּדִּיר אֶת אִשְׁתּוֹ [3]**If someone makes a vow forbidding his wife to eat a** particular **kind of fruit,** and she is unwilling to continue living with him under such circumstances, **he must grant her a divorce** immediately **and must pay** her **her ketubah.** [4]**Rabbi Yehudah** disagrees and **says: If** the husband is **a non-priest** and he forbids his wife to eat a certain fruit for a period of **one day, he may keep her** as his wife. [5]But if he forbids her to eat that fruit for **two** days, **he must divorce her and pay** her **her ketubah.** [6]But **if** the husband is **a priest,** then even if he forbids his wife to eat that fruit for a period of **two** days, **he may keep her** as his wife. [7]Only if he forbids his wife to eat that fruit for **three** days, **must he grant her a divorce and pay** her **her ketubah.**

הַמַּדִּיר אֶת אִשְׁתּוֹ [8]**If someone makes a vow forbidding his wife to adorn herself with a** particular **kind of cosmetic,** and she is unwilling to live with him under such a restriction, **he must grant her a divorce** immediately **and must pay** her **her ketubah.** [9]**Rabbi Yose** disagrees and **says** that, **with** respect to **a poor woman,** who is not accustomed to using cosmetics, only **if** her husband **does not limit** the period of time during which she is forbidden to do so, must he divorce her immediately and pay her her ketubah. But if he forbids her the use of a certain perfume for a limited period of time, he cannot be compelled to divorce her and to pay her her ketubah, but rather she must wait out that period. [10]**With** respect to **a rich woman,** who is accustomed to wearing cosmetics, if her husband forbids her to use them for **thirty days** or more, he can be compelled to grant her a divorce and to pay her her ketubah.

[1]בְּכֹהֵן, שְׁנַיִם, יְקַיֵּים; [2]וּשְׁלֹשָׁה, יוֹצִיא וְיִתֵּן כְּתוּבָּה.

[3]הַמַּדִּיר אֶת אִשְׁתּוֹ שֶׁלֹּא תִּטְעוֹם אֶחָד מִכָּל הַפֵּירוֹת, יוֹצִיא וְיִתֵּן כְּתוּבָּה. [4]רַבִּי יְהוּדָה אוֹמֵר: בְּיִשְׂרָאֵל, יוֹם אֶחָד, יְקַיֵּים; [5]שְׁנַיִם, יוֹצִיא וְיִתֵּן כְּתוּבָּה. [6]וּבְכֹהֵן, שְׁנַיִם, יְקַיֵּים; [7]שְׁלֹשָׁה, יוֹצִיא וְיִתֵּן כְּתוּבָּה.

[8]הַמַּדִּיר אֶת אִשְׁתּוֹ שֶׁלֹּא תִּתְקַשֵּׁט בְּאֶחָד מִכָּל הַמִּינִין, יוֹצִיא וְיִתֵּן כְּתוּבָּה. [9]רַבִּי יוֹסֵי אוֹמֵר: בַּעֲנִיּוֹת, שֶׁלֹּא נָתַן קִצְבָּה; [10]וּבַעֲשִׁירוֹת, שְׁלֹשִׁים יוֹם.

LITERAL TRANSLATION

[1]In [the case of] a priest, [if his vow was for] two [months], he may keep [her]; [2]but [if it was for] three, he must divorce [her] and pay [her] ketubah.

[3][If] someone prohibits his wife with a vow from tasting one of all the fruits, he must divorce [her] and pay [her] ketubah. [4]Rabbi Yehudah says: In [the case of] a non-priest, [if his vow was for] one day, he may keep [her]; [5][if it was for] two, he must divorce [her] and pay [her] ketubah. [6]But in [the case of] a priest, [if his vow was for] two [days], he may keep [her]; [7][if it was for] three, he must divorce [her] and pay [her] ketubah.

[8][If] someone prohibits his wife with a vow from adorning herself with one of all the kinds [of cosmetics], he must divorce [her] and pay [her] ketubah. [9]Rabbi Yose says: In [the case of] poor women, [this applies] if he did not set a limit; [10]and in [the case of] rich women [if he set a limit of] thirty days.

RASHI

ובכהן – שאם יגרשנה לא יוכל להחזירה, ושמא סופו יתחרט, יהבו ליה רבנן זימנא טפי. **אחד מכל הפירות** – "קונם פרי פלוני עלי", והוא קיים לה. **שלא תתקשט באחד מכל המינין** – "קונם בושם פלוני עלי", והוא קיים לה. **בעניות שלא נתן קצבה** – באשה עניה, אם לא נתן קצבה לדבר עד מתי אסרו עליה – הוא דיוציא ויתן כתובה, אבל אם נתן קצבה – תמתין עד אותו זמן. ובגמרא מפרש עד כמה היא קצבתה. **ובעשירות** – שרגילות לכך. **עד שלשים יום** – אם לא הדירה יותר – אין כופין להוציא.

NOTES

forbidding his wife to derive any material benefit from him, how can he pay her her ketubah, thus allowing her to derive benefit from his property? *Ḥatam Sofer* answers that, since the husband's property is mortgaged for the payment of his wife's ketubah, it is not in his power to cancel his wife's lien on that property.

אֶחָד מִכָּל הַפֵּירוֹת **One of all the fruits.** The Rishonim explain that the husband took a vow forbidding his wife

HALAKHAH

שֶׁלֹּא תִּטְעוֹם אֶחָד מִכָּל הַפֵּירוֹת **From tasting one of all the fruits.** "If someone prevents his wife with a vow from eating

גמרא [1]וְכֵיוָן דִּמְשׁוּעְבַּד לָהּ, הֵיכִי מָצֵי מַדִּיר לָהּ? [2]כָּל כְּמִינֵיהּ דְּמַפְקַע לָהּ לְשִׁיעְבּוּדָהּ? [3]וְהָתְנַן: ״׳קוֹנָם שֶׁאֲנִי עוֹשָׂה לְפִיךְ׳, אֵינוֹ צָרִיךְ לְהָפֵר״. [4]אַלְמָא, כֵּיוָן דִּמְשַׁעְבְּדָא לֵיהּ, [5]לָאו כָּל כְּמִינָהּ דְּמַפְקַע לֵיהּ לְשִׁיעְבּוּדֵיהּ. [6]הָכָא נַמִי, כֵּיוָן דִּמְשׁוּעְבַּד לָהּ, [7]לָאו כָּל כְּמִינֵיהּ דְּמַפְקַע לָהּ לְשִׁיעְבּוּדָהּ!
[8]אֶלָּא, מִתּוֹךְ שֶׁיָּכוֹל לוֹמַר לָהּ: [9]״צְאִי מַעֲשֵׂה יָדַיִךְ בִּמְזוֹנוֹתַיִךְ״,

LITERAL TRANSLATION

GEMARA [1]But since he is obligated to her, how can he forbid her with a vow? [2]Is it in his power to cancel his obligation to her? [3]But surely we have learned: "[If a wife says:] 'What I produce (lit., "do") is [forbidden] to you (lit., "to your mouth") [as] a *konam*,' he does not need to annul [it]." [4]Consequently, since she is obligated to him, [5]it is not in her power to cancel her obligation to him. [6]Here too, since he is obligated to her, [7]it is not in his power to cancel his obligation to her!

[8]Rather, since he can say to her: [9]"Use your handiwork for your maintenance,"

RASHI

גמרא וכיון דמשועבד לה – למזונות.

TRANSLATION AND COMMENTARY

GEMARA וְכֵיוָן דִּמְשׁוּעְבַּד לָהּ [1]Our Mishnah discussed the regulations governing a man who makes a vow forbidding his wife to derive any material benefit from him. The Gemara questions the husband's authority to make such a vow. **Since** a man **is obligated by law to** maintain his wife — the obligation to provide one's wife with sustenance being one of the duties imposed upon a husband by his marriage — **how can he make a vow forbidding her** to derive any benefit from him? [2]**Is it in his power to cancel his obligation to her?** [3]**But surely we have learned** a Mishnah that implies otherwise, for the Mishnah teaches (*Nedarim* 85a; see also above, 66a): **"If a wife says** to her husband: **'Whatever I produce shall be forbidden to you as a *konam*** [the word *konam* is used in vows as a substitute for the word *korban* — "sacrifice" — in order to avoid using the word *korban* itself],' **he does not have to annul** the vow, for a wife is obligated by law to produce handiwork for her husband, this being one of the duties imposed on a woman by her marriage." [4]**Hence** we see that **since** the wife **is obligated by law to** provide her husband with her handiwork, [5]**it is not in her power to cancel her obligation to him** by means of a vow. [6]**Here too, since** the husband **is obligated** by law **to** maintain his wife, [7]**it should not be in his power to cancel his obligation to her** by means of a vow!

אֶלָּא [8]The Gemara answers: **Rather,** this is how the Mishnah must be understood: **Since** the husband **can** at any point **say to his wife:** [9]**"Use your handiwork for your maintenance,"** meaning: "Keep for yourself the benefits of your handiwork and maintain yourself from your earnings, for I waive my right to your handiwork

CONCEPTS

קוֹנָם ***Konam.*** This is a term for a type of vow and it is explained as a euphemism for the word קָרְבָּן — "sacrifice." The thing which one has forsworn with a *konam* is forbidden to one as though it were intended for sacrifice, though it is not truly sanctified or sacrificed but is merely forbidden to the person who made the vow. Some authorities maintain that a *konam* is more severe than other forms of oaths, as though a real prohibition were placed on the forsworn object.

NOTES

to eat a certain type of fruit, whether the fruit belonged to him or to another person. This leads to a certain difficulty, for there is a general rule that one person cannot take a vow forbidding another person to derive benefit from something that belongs to a third party. The Rishonim explain that this could be a case where the wife took a vow forbidding herself to derive benefit from another person's fruit, and her husband confirmed the vow, making it binding. Alternatively, the husband might have taken a vow forbidding his wife to derive any material benefit from him, or to derive enjoyment from sexual relations with him, if she were to eat a certain type of fruit, so that she cannot now eat of that fruit without being forbidden to derive any benefit from her husband or to cohabit with him (see *Ritva*; *Tosafot*, below, 71a, s.v. בִּשְׁלָמָא).

כָּל כְּמִינֵיהּ דְּמַפְקַע לָהּ לְשִׁיעְבּוּדָהּ **Is it in his power to cancel his obligation to her?** We have learned elsewhere (see 59b) that a *konam* vow imposes something akin to intrinsic sanctity upon the forbidden object, and therefore such a vow can indeed cancel a creditor's lien on that object. Here, however, the husband's vow cannot cancel his wife's entitlement to maintenance. The Sages reinforced the wife's lien on her husband's property, so that it cannot be canceled, in order to ensure that she receives the maintenance upon which her welfare depends (*Tosefot Rash, Ritva;* see also *Tosafot*, above, 59b).

HALAKHAH

a certain type of fruit, we wait thirty days. If after thirty days the vow is still in force, the husband must divorce his wife and pay her her ketubah." (*Rambam, Sefer Nashim, Hilkhot Ishut* 12:24.)

לָאו כָּל כְּמִינָהּ דְּמַפְקַע לֵיהּ לְשִׁיעְבּוּדֵיהּ **It is not in his power to cancel his obligation to her.** "If someone prevents his wife with a vow from deriving any benefit from him, the vow is not binding, for a wife is entitled to maintenance from her husband by virtue of being married to him." (*Shulḥan Arukh, Yoreh De'ah* 235:2.)

TRANSLATION AND COMMENTARY

and thus deprive you of your right to maintenance," [70B] the husband who forbade his wife to derive benefit from him is regarded **as if he** actually **said to her:** [1]**"Use your handiwork for your maintenance."** We interpret his vow forbidding his wife to benefit from him as including a waiver of his right to her handiwork.

וְאִם אִיתָא [2]The Gemara raises an objection: **But if** we accept the solution that has just been proposed, and **we** also **accept what Rav Huna said in the name of Rav,** it is difficult to understand the Mishnah in *Nedarim,* cited above. [3]**For Rav Huna said in the name of Rav: A woman can say to her husband: "I will not** exercise my right to **be maintained** by you, **and I will not do any handiwork** for you." Parallel to the husband's right to substitute her handiwork for his maintenance is the wife's right to make the same arrangement. [4]Hence, when **a woman says** to her husband: **"Whatever I produce is forbidden to you as a *konam*," why** does the Mishnah in *Nedarim* state that the husband **does not** even **need to annul** the vow? [5]**Let us say** that **since** a woman **can** at any point **say** to her husband: **"I will not** exercise my right to **be maintained** by you, **and I will not do any handiwork** for you," the woman who forbids her handiwork to her husband is regarded [6]**as if she** actually **said to him: "I will not** exercise my right to **be maintained** by you, **and I will not do any handiwork** for you"! Therefore her vow should be effective and require annulment, and this contradicts the Mishnah in *Nedarim*!

אֶלָּא [7]**Rather,** answers the Gemara, we must try a different approach. **Do not say** that a husband who forbids his wife from deriving benefit from him is viewed **as if** he said to her: "Use your handiwork for your maintenance." [8]**Rather,** say that our Mishnah is referring to a husband who actually **said to** his wife: **"Use your handiwork for your maintenance."** In such a case, the vow he took forbidding her to derive any benefit from him is effective.

אִי הָכִי [9]The Gemara asks: **If it is true** that the Mishnah is referring to such a case, **why does she need an administrator** to provide for her maintenance? She should be able to maintain herself from her own earnings!

[70B] נַעֲשֶׂה כְּאוֹמֵר לָהּ: [1]"צְאִי מַעֲשֵׂה יָדַיִךְ בִּמְזוֹנוֹתַיִךְ".
[2]וְאִם אִיתָא לְהָא דְּרַב הוּנָא אָמַר רַב, [3]דְּאָמַר רַב הוּנָא אָמַר רַב: יְכוֹלָה אִשָּׁה שֶׁתֹּאמַר לְבַעְלָהּ: "אֵינִי נִיזּוֹנֶת וְאֵינִי עוֹשָׂה", "קוֹנָם שֶׁאֲנִי עוֹשָׂה לְפִיךְ", [4]אַמַּאי אֵינוֹ צָרִיךְ לְהָפֵר? [5]לֵימָא: מִתּוֹךְ שֶׁיְּכוֹלָה לוֹמַר: "אֵינִי נִיזּוֹנֶת וְאֵינִי עוֹשָׂה", [6]נַעֲשָׂה כְּמִי שֶׁאוֹמֶרֶת לוֹ: "אֵינִי נִיזּוֹנֶת וְאֵינִי עוֹשָׂה"! [7]אֶלָּא, לָא תֵּימָא נַעֲשֶׂה, [8]אֶלָּא: בְּאוֹמֵר לָהּ: "צְאִי מַעֲשֵׂה יָדַיִךְ בִּמְזוֹנוֹתַיִךְ".
[9]אִי הָכִי, פַּרְנָס לָמָּה לָהּ?

LITERAL TRANSLATION

[70B] it is as if he says to her: [1]"Use your handiwork for your maintenance."

[2]But if there is [validity] in what Rav Huna said in the name of Rav, [3]for Rav Huna said in the name of Rav: A wife can say to her husband: "I will not be maintained and I will not work," [4][if a wife says:] "What I produce is [forbidden] to you [as] a *konam*," why does he not need to annul [it]? [5]Let us say: Since she can say: "I will not be maintained and I will not work," [6]it is as if she says to him: "I will not be maintained and I will not work"!

[7]Rather, do not say: It is as if, [8]but rather: When he says to her: "Use your handiwork for your maintenance."

[9]If so, why does she need an administrator?

RASHI

נעשה כאומר לה — דאף על גב דלא אמר — הרי הוא כאומר, דודאי אדעתא דהכי אדרה.

NOTES

אִי הָכִי, פַּרְנָס לָמָּה לָהּ If so, why does she need an administrator? *Ritva* infers from here that whenever the husband is exempt from providing his wife with maintenance, he is also exempt from providing her with clothing. Otherwise the Gemara should have answered that the administrator is needed in order to supply the wife with her clothing.

HALAKHAH

"צְאִי מַעֲשֵׂה יָדַיִךְ בִּמְזוֹנוֹתַיִךְ" "Spend your handiwork on your maintenance." "If someone says to his wife: 'Spend your handiwork on your maintenance,' and her handiwork is enough for her major needs but not for her minor ones, the following distinction applies: If her family is accustomed to these minor things, the vow is not binding, for her husband is obligated to provide her with them. But if only the wealthier members of her family are accustomed to these things, and her father is wealthy, and her husband is not, the vow is binding, for her husband is not obligated to provide her with them. If the husband makes the vow, and the wife returns to her father's house, the husband is then obligated to provide her with those minor things that she was accustomed to enjoy before she married. Thus, for thirty days he must provide her with those minor things by way of an administrator." (*Rambam, Sefer Nashim, Hilkhot Ishut* 12:23; *Shulḥan Arukh, Yoreh De'ah* 235:2.)

TRANSLATION AND COMMENTARY

בִּדְלָא סָפְקָה [1]No, the Gemara answers: The Mishnah is referring to a case **where** the woman's earnings **do not suffice** for her maintenance. An administrator must be appointed to provide the balance of her maintenance.

אִי בִּדְלָא סָפְקָה [2]The Gemara objects: **If** the Mishnah is referring to a case **where** the woman's earnings **do not suffice** for her maintenance, [3]then **our** original **difficulty returns,** for if a wife is unable to maintain herself from her own earnings, her husband is obligated to provide for her, even if he has waived his right to her handiwork. How, then, is a husband able to make a vow forbidding his wife to derive any benefit from him?

אֲמַר רַב אַשִׁי [4]**Rav Ashi said:** The Mishnah is dealing with a case **where** the wife's earnings **suffice for the major things** that she absolutely requires, [5]**but they do not suffice for** some of **the minor things** that she would like to have. A husband can cancel by means of a vow his wife's right to receive those minor things, which are regarded as luxuries.

הָנֵי דְּבָרִים קְטַנִּים [6]The Gemara proceeds to clarify Rav Ashi's answer by asking: **How are these minor things to be visualized?** [7]If the wife **is accustomed to** receiving **them** from her husband, then **surely she is accustomed to them,** and consequently her husband is obligated to supply them, and it should not be in his power to annul his wife's right to receive them. [8]Conversely, **if** the wife **is not accustomed to** receiving these minor things from her husband, he is under no obligation to provide them for her. [9]**Why,** then, **must an administrator be appointed** to provide her with things for which she has no claim against her husband?

לָא [10]**No,** the Mishnah's ruling **applies only** if the wife **was accustomed** to receiving these minor things while she was still living **in her father's house.** By right, she could have demanded that her husband provide her with those minor things to which she was accustomed before she married. [11]But **she** was ready to **bear with** her husband and to waive her right to those minor things to which she was entitled. [12]Now, however, **she says to him: "Until now, as long as you did not make a vow forbidding me to benefit from you, I** was ready to **bear with you** and to waive my right to those minor things to which I was accustomed in my father's house. [13]But **now that you have made a vow forbidding me to benefit from you, I am not prepared to bear with you** any longer." Since the wife was not accustomed to receiving those minor things from her husband, he is able to prevent her by means of a vow from receiving them from him. But since she was accustomed to receiving those things while she was still living in her father's house, she is entitled to demand that she be provided with them, and this is why an administrator must be appointed to carry out the task.

LITERAL TRANSLATION

[1]When it does not suffice.

[2]If it is when it does not suffice, [3]our difficulty returns to its place!

[4]Rav Ashi said: When it suffices for major things, [5]but it does not suffice for minor things.

[6][Regarding] these minor things, how do we visualize the case (lit., "how is it like")?

[7]If she was accustomed to them, surely she was accustomed to them. [8]And if she was not accustomed to them, [9]why does she need an administrator?

[10]No, it is necessary when she was accustomed [to them] in her father's house, [11]and she bore with him, [12]for she can say to him: "Until now while you did not forbid me with a vow [to benefit from you], I bore with you. [13]Now that you have forbidden me with a vow, I cannot bear with you."

[1]בִּדְלָא סָפְקָה. [2]אִי בִּדְלָא סָפְקָה, [3]הָדַר קוּשְׁיָין לְדוּכְתֵּיהּ! [4]אֲמַר רַב אַשִׁי: בִּמְסַפֶּקֶת לִדְבָרִים גְּדוֹלִים, [5]וְאֵינָהּ מְסַפֶּקֶת לִדְבָרִים קְטַנִּים. [6]הָנֵי דְּבָרִים קְטַנִּים, הֵיכִי דָּמֵי? [7]אִי דִּרְגִילָה בְּהוּ, הָא רְגִילָה בְּהוּ. [8]וְאִי לָא רְגִילָה בְּהוּ, [9]פַּרְנָס לָמָּה לָהּ? [10]לָא, צְרִיכָא דִּרְגִילָה בְּבֵית נָשָׁא, [11]וְקָא מְגַלְגְּלָא בַּהֲדֵיהּ, [12]דְּאָמְרָה לֵיהּ: "עַד הָאִידָנָא דְּלָא אַדַּרְתַּן גַּלְגֵּילְנָא בַּהֲדָךְ. [13]הָשְׁתָּא דְּאַדַּרְתַּן, לָא מָצֵינָא דְּאִיגַּלְגַּל בַּהֲדָךְ".

RASHI

בדלא ספקה – מזונות למעשה ידיה הקצוב לה במשנת "אף על פי" (כתובות סד,ב). הא רגילה בהו – ומשועבד לה.

TERMINOLOGY

הָדַר קוּשְׁיָין לְדוּכְתֵּיהּ **The question, or difficulty, returned to its place.** Sometimes the Gemara raises an objection, solves it, and then rejects the solution; in such cases the Gemara may use this expression.

NOTES

בִּמְסַפֶּקֶת לִדְבָרִים גְּדוֹלִים **Where it suffices for major things.** *Meiri* explains that the expression "major things" refers to items such as bread and wine, which are regarded as necessities, and the expression "minor things" refers to items such as fruit and legumes, which are considered to be luxuries. *Ritva* explains that the wife's right to these inessential, minor things is not strong enough to cancel her husband's vow.

וְקָא מְגַלְגְּלָא בַּהֲדֵיהּ **And she bore with him.** Our commentary follows the first explanation of *Tosafot,* according to which the Mishnah is referring to the following situation: The wife was entitled to receive from her husband the minor things to which she was accustomed in her father's house, but she was prepared to waive her right to them as

[1]וּמַאי שְׁנָא עַד שְׁלֹשִׁים יוֹם? [2]עַד שְׁלֹשִׁים יוֹם, לָא שָׁמְעֵי בָּהּ אֱינָשֵׁי, [3]וְלָא זִילָא בָּהּ מִילְּתָא. [4]טְפֵי, שָׁמְעֵי בָּהּ אֱינָשֵׁי, [5]וְזִילָא בָּהּ מִילְּתָא.

[6]אִיבָּעֵית אֵימָא: שֶׁהִדִּירָהּ כְּשֶׁהִיא אֲרוּסָה.

[7]אֲרוּסָה מִי אִית לָהּ מְזוֹנֵי?

[8]שֶׁהִגִּיעַ זְמַן וְלֹא נִשְּׂאוּ.

LITERAL TRANSLATION

[1]And what is the difference up to thirty days? [2]Up to thirty days, people do not hear about her, [3]and the matter does not disgrace her. [4]More [than this], people hear about her, [5]and the matter does disgrace her.

[6]If you wish, say: [It is] where he forbade her with a vow while she was betrothed.

[7]Does a betrothed woman have maintenance?

[8][She does] if the time came and they were not married.

RASHI

שהגיע זמן ולא נשאו — דמדאורייתא לא משועבד לה. לפיכך חל הנדר, דאיסור דאורייתא הוא, ומדרבנן חייב לזונה, לפיכך יעמיד פרנס.

TRANSLATION AND COMMENTARY

וּמַאי שְׁנָא [1]The Gemara now proceeds to analyze another aspect of the Mishnah's ruling, and asks: **What is the difference** between a husband making a vow forbidding his wife to derive any benefit from him for **up to thirty days,** when he is not required to divorce her but must appoint an administrator to maintain her, and a husband making a vow forbidding his wife to benefit from him for more than thirty days, when he must grant her a divorce and pay her her ketubah?

עַד שְׁלֹשִׁים יוֹם [2]The Gemara explains: If a husband forbids his wife to derive any benefit for **up to thirty days, people do not** ordinarily **hear about it,** [3]**and** the wife **is not disgraced by** being maintained by an administrator. [4]But if this goes on for **more** than thirty days, **people do hear about it,** [5]**and she is disgraced by the fact** that everybody knows that she is being supported by an administrator. Thus the husband must take steps to have his vow annulled or divorce her.

אִיבָּעֵית אֵימָא [6]The Gemara now offers another solution to its original problem: Since the husband is obligated to maintain his wife, he should not be able to make a vow forbidding her to benefit from him, yet the Mishnah indicates that he can do so. **If you wish,** you can **say** that the Mishnah is referring to a man who **made a vow forbidding** his wife to derive any benefit from him **while she was betrothed** to him but not yet married. According to Jewish law, betrothal precedes marriage. Betrothal creates a legal bond between the bride and the bridegroom which can only be dissolved through divorce or the death of one of the parties; but the monetary rights and obligations, including the woman's right to maintenance from her husband, begin only with marriage. Since a man is not obligated to maintain his betrothed wife, the vow he takes forbidding her to derive any benefit from him can take effect.

אֲרוּסָה [7]The Gemara raises an objection: How can the Mishnah be referring to a case where the husband forbade his betrothed wife to derive any benefit from him? **Is a betrothed woman entitled to maintenance,** so that it is necessary to appoint an administrator to maintain her?

שֶׁהִגִּיעַ זְמַן [8]The Gemara answers: The Mishnah is referring to a case **where the time** that had been set

NOTES

long as her husband did not make a vow forbidding her to derive any benefit from him. Thus the husband's vow was valid, for it was taken when the wife had waived her right to those minor things. But once he had taken the vow, she was no longer willing to waive her right to those minor things, and so he was required to provide them for her by way of an administrator.

Tosafot suggests an alternative explanation, according to which there was no waiver on the part of the wife. The Mishnah is referring to the following situation: The members of the wife's extended family, who were as wealthy as her husband, were not accustomed to enjoying the minor things which she had been accustomed to enjoy in her father's house, for her father, who was a particularly wealthy man, provided them only to her. As long as the husband was maintaining his wife, he was only required to meet the standards of her extended family, and she had to bear with him and do without the minor things to which she had been accustomed in her father's house. But once the husband took the vow forbidding her to derive benefit from him, he was obligated to maintain her by way of an administrator in accordance with the standards of her father's house.

עַד שְׁלֹשִׁים יוֹם Up to thirty days. The Jerusalem Talmud explains the difference between the two cases — up to thirty days, and more than thirty days — slightly differently. By right a wife may refuse to receive her maintenance by way of an administrator, even for only one day, because a married woman is entitled to take her meals together with her husband. But she is willing to bear with her husband and be maintained by an administrator for a period of thirty days in order to give her husband a month to secure a dispensation annulling his vow.

שֶׁהִגִּיעַ זְמַן וְלֹא נִשְּׂאוּ If the time came and they were not married. *Rashi* explains that if the time that had been set for a couple's marriage came but they did not marry, the bridegroom is not obligated by Torah law to provide his bride with maintenance. Thus a vow taken by the bridegroom forbidding his bride to derive any benefit from him can take effect. But since he is required to provide her with maintenance by Rabbinic decree, he must appoint an administrator to maintain her in his place. Many Rishonim

[1]דְּתְנַן: [2]״הִגִּיעַ זְמַן וְלֹא נִשְּׂאוּ, [3]אוֹכְלוֹת מִשֶּׁלּוֹ [4]וְאוֹכְלוֹת בִּתְרוּמָה״.
[5]וּמַאי שְׁנָא עַד שְׁלֹשִׁים יוֹם?
[6]עַד שְׁלֹשִׁים יוֹם, עָבֵיד שָׁלִיחַ שְׁלִיחוּתֵיהּ. [7]טְפֵי, לָא עָבֵיד שָׁלִיחַ שְׁלִיחוּתֵיהּ.

LITERAL TRANSLATION

[1]For we have learned: [2]"[If] the time came and they were not married, [3]they eat of his [food] [4]and they eat terumah."

[5]And what is the difference up to thirty days?

[6]Up to thirty days, an agent performs his agency. [7]More [than this], an agent does not perform his agency.

TRANSLATION AND COMMENTARY

for their marriage **came, but** nevertheless **they were not** yet **married.** [1]**For we have learned** elsewhere in the Mishnah (above, 57a): "A virgin is given twelve months from the time of her betrothal to prepare her trousseau. During that time the bride continues to live in her father's house and the bridegroom is not responsible for her support. [2]But **if the time** set for the marriage **came and they were not married,** [3]**she** is entitled to **eat of** the bridegroom's **food**, for he is responsible for her support from the date on which the wedding was due to take place. Similarly, during the period between betrothal and marriage, a bride is not permitted to eat terumah if she is the daughter of a non-priest and is betrothed to a priest. By Torah law, a woman who is betrothed to a priest is permitted to eat terumah, the portion of produce that is set aside for the priests and is forbidden to non-priests. But the Rabbis decreed that a betrothed woman may not eat terumah until the marriage process has been completed, either because she is still living in her father's house and she may mistakenly give the terumah to other members of her father's household who are forbidden to eat it, or because the husband may find a reason to annul the betrothal and it will then turn out that she herself was forbidden to eat terumah. But if the time set for the marriage came and the marriage did not yet take place, [4]the bride is entitled to **eat terumah.** Since the husband is now responsible for her support, he sets aside a special place for her to eat, and thus there is no concern that her family will eat the terumah. And since the wedding date has already arrived, it is assumed that the bridegroom has completed any investigation concerning his bride and it is unlikely that he will find reason now to annul the betrothal." Thus our Mishnah is referring to a case where the woman is entitled to maintenance, but her entitlement is not strong enough to nullify the vow taken by her husband forbidding her to benefit from him.

וּמַאי שְׁנָא [5]The Gemara asks: According to this interpretation of the Mishnah, **what difference** does it make whether the husband's vow is for more or less than **thirty days?** If the husband forbade his wife to derive benefit from him while she was betrothed to him, the argument presented above — that a woman is not disgraced if she is maintained by an administrator for a period of up to thirty days, but is disgraced if she is maintained by an administrator for a longer period — does not apply, for it is no disgrace for a woman to be maintained by an administrator before she is married.

עַד שְׁלֹשִׁים יוֹם [6]The Gemara answers: **Up to thirty days, an agent** appointed to maintain the woman **performs his agency** faithfully, and therefore she is willing to receive her maintenance from him. [7]But **after** thirty days, **the agent** appointed to maintain the woman **no** longer **performs his agency** scrupulously, and the woman can demand that her husband take steps to secure the annulment of his vow or grant her a divorce.

NOTES

raise the objection that, according to the Gemara's conclusion elsewhere, even after a couple are married, the husband is only obligated to maintain his wife by Rabbinic decree, and so, according to *Rashi's* reasoning, the husband's vow can take effect even after marriage.

Tosafot, Ri Migash, Ramban, and others argue that the Mishnah is referring to a bridegroom who took the vow forbidding his bride to derive any benefit from him while she was betrothed to him, and before the time that had been set for the marriage arrived. At the time of his vow the bridegroom was still not responsible for his bride's maintenance, and so the vow was valid. But once the wedding date arrived, the bridegroom became responsible for his bride's maintenance, and so he had to appoint an administrator to maintain her in his place. Alternatively, suggest *Tosafot* and *Ritva,* the Mishnah is referring to a bridegroom who took the vow after the date that had been set for the marriage. Even though the bride was then entitled to maintenance from the bridegroom, her right was not strong enough to invalidate the vow taken by her husband and so the bridegroom had to appoint an administrator to provide his bride with the maintenance to which she was entitled.

The Jerusalem Talmud asks how it is that the husband's vow forbidding his wife to derive any benefit from him can take effect, when he is required by law to maintain her. It answers that our Mishnah follows the viewpoint that a wife is entitled to maintenance only by Rabbinic decree, and this is why her entitlement to maintenance, even after she is married, is not strong enough to prevent the husband's vow from taking effect.

עַד שְׁלֹשִׁים יוֹם עָבֵיד שָׁלִיחַ שְׁלִיחוּתֵיהּ Up to thirty days, an agent performs his agency. *Ritva* notes that the presumption that an agent will only act faithfully for thirty

TERMINOLOGY

אֶלָּא מְחַוַּורְתָּא כִּדְשַׁנִּינַן מֵעִיקָּרָא Rather it is clear as we answered originally. Sometimes, after proposing two answers to a question, the Talmud rejects the second one and states: "Rather it is clear as we answered originally" (i.e., only the first answer is correct). This expression is used when the first answer was given anonymously. Where, however, the first answer was ascribed to a specific scholar, the expression used is: אֶלָּא מְחַוַּורְתָּא כְּ...' — "Rather it is clear as Rabbi X said."

TRANSLATION AND COMMENTARY

וְאִיבָּעֵית אֵימָא [1]The Gemara offers yet another solution to its original difficulty regarding the husband's authority to make a vow forbidding his wife to derive benefit from him: **And if you wish,** you can **say** that the Mishnah is referring to a case **where** the man **made a vow forbidding his wife** to derive any benefit from him **while she was betrothed** to him, **and** later **they were married.** Since the bridegroom was not responsible for his bride's support during the period of their betrothal, the vow took effect. But once they were married, the husband became obligated to maintain his wife, and thus an administrator had to be appointed to maintain her.

נִישֵּׂאת [2]The Gemara objects: If the woman **married** her husband after he had taken his vow, **surely she** must have **considered** the consequences of being married to a man from whom she could not derive any benefit **and** must have **accepted** that she would receive her maintenance from an administrator! Why, then, can the husband be compelled to grant her a divorce after thirty days and to pay her her ketubah?

דְּאָמְרָה [3]The Gemara answers: The Mishnah is dealing with a case **where** the woman **says:** "When I agreed to the marriage, **I thought that I would be able to accept** an arrangement by which I would not be maintained by my husband but by an administrator. [4]But **now** I see that **I cannot accept** such a condition.

אֵימַר [5]The Gemara rejects this answer: **Granted that we say** that a woman can put forward **such** an argument **with respect to** physical **defects.** We learn elsewhere in this chapter (below, 77a) that, according to Rabban Shimon ben Gamliel, a man with a serious physical defect can be compelled to divorce his wife, even if he already had that defect at the time of his marriage. The Gemara explains that his wife had first thought that she could accept his defect, but she later saw that she was mistaken. [6]But **with respect to maintenance do we say** that a woman can put forward **such** an argument?

אֶלָּא [7]**Rather,** because of the difficulties in this explanation, **it is clear** that the problem must be resolved **as we answered in the beginning:** Either the Mishnah is referring to a case where the husband has waived his right to his wife's earnings, or else the Mishnah is referring to a betrothed couple whose marriage was postponed, and the bridegroom has forbidden his betrothed bride to derive any benefit from him.

עַד שְׁלֹשִׁים יוֹם [8]The Gemara now considers another difficulty posed by the Mishnah's ruling. We learned in the Mishnah: "If someone makes a vow forbidding his wife to derive any material benefit from him for a period of **up to thirty days,** he is not required to divorce her but **must appoint**

[1]וְאִיבָּעֵית אֵימָא: שֶׁהִדִּירָהּ כְּשֶׁהִיא אֲרוּסָה, וְנִישֵּׂאת. [2]נִישֵּׂאת, הָא סָבְרָה וְקִבְּלָה! [3]דְּאָמְרָה: ״כִּסְבוּרָה אֲנִי שֶׁאֲנִי יְכוֹלָה לְקַבֵּל; [4]עַכְשָׁיו אֵין אֲנִי יְכוֹלָה לְקַבֵּל״. [5]אֵימַר דְּאָמְרִינַן הָכִי גַּבֵּי מוּמִין, [6]לְעִנְיַן מְזוֹנֵי מִי אָמְרִינַן הָכִי? [7]אֶלָּא מְחַוַּורְתָּא כִּדְשַׁנִּינַן מֵעִיקָּרָא. [8]״עַד שְׁלֹשִׁים יוֹם יַעֲמִיד

LITERAL TRANSLATION

[1]And if you wish, say: [It is] where he forbade her with a vow while she was betrothed, and she married.

[2][If] she married, surely she considered and accepted [it]!

[3][It is] when she says: "I thought that I could accept [it]; [4]now I cannot accept [it]."

[5]Granted (lit., "say") that we say this regarding defects, [6]do we say this regarding maintenance?

[7]Rather, it is clear as we answered in the beginning.

[8]"Up to thirty days, he must appoint

RASHI

וניסת – דהשתא חייב במזונותיה, והנדר כבר חל עליו. **הא סברה וקבלה** – יודעת היא שנאסר עליו לזונה, וניסת לו. **גבי מומין** – בשלהי פרקין במתניתין (כתובות עז,א). **לענין מזוני מי אמרינן** – סבורה הייתי יודעת היא שאי אפשר לה בלא מזונות.

NOTES

days is restricted to agents who were not directly appointed to their position, but the husband said: "Whoever maintains her will not lose" (see Gemara below). But if a person was directly appointed as an agent, and the principal did not specify the period of time during which the agent was to act on his behalf, we presume that even after thirty days the agent will perform his agency as instructed.

אֵימַר דְּאָמְרִינַן הָכִי גַּבֵּי מוּמִין Granted that we say this regarding defects. Our commentary follows *Rashi*, who argues that the wife ought to have known better than to think she could live without maintenance. However, *Rashba* understands the Gemara's question differently: Regarding defects a woman can claim that though she thought she would be able to accept her husband's defects, she later saw that she was unable to do so, for most women cannot become reconciled to defects. But regarding maintenance we assume that the woman is lying when she says that she can no longer accept receiving maintenance through an administrator, for many women are able to put up with such an arrangement, and she entered the marriage knowing that she would not receive her maintenance directly from her husband.

פַּרְנָס". [1]וּפַרְנָס לָאו שְׁלִיחוּתֵיהּ קָא עָבֵיד? [2]אָמַר רַב הוּנָא: [3]בְּאוֹמֵר: "כָּל הַזָּן אֵינוֹ מַפְסִיד". [4]וְכִי אָמַר הָכִי, לָאו שְׁלִיחוּתֵיהּ קָעָבֵיד? [5]וְהָתְנַן: "מִי שֶׁהָיָה מוּשְׁלָךְ בְּבוֹר וְאָמַר: [6]'כָּל הַשּׁוֹמֵעַ קוֹלוֹ יִכְתּוֹב גֵּט

LITERAL TRANSLATION

an administrator." [1]But does not the administrator perform his agency?

[2]Rav Huna said: [3][It is] when he says: "Whoever maintains [her] will not lose."

[4]But when he says that, does he not perform his agency? [5]But surely we have learned: [6]"[If] someone was cast into a pit and said: 'Whoever hears my (lit., "his") voice should write a bill of divorce

RASHI

ופרנס לאו שליחותיה עביד – בתמיה. נמצא עובר על נדרו!

TRANSLATION AND COMMENTARY

an administrator to maintain his wife in his stead." The Gemara's initial assumption is that the husband must appoint an administrator, instructing him to maintain his wife and obligating himself to cover the administrator's expenses. The Gemara asks: But how can he appoint an administrator to maintain his wife in his stead? [1]When **the administrator** provides the wife with her maintenance, **is he not acting as** the husband's **agent?** Since an agent's act is recognized as the legal act of the principal who appointed him, the administrator's provision of maintenance to the wife should be regarded as a violation of the husband's vow forbidding his wife to derive any benefit from him!

אָמַר רַב הוּנָא [2]**Rav Huna said** in reply: The Mishnah does not mean to say that the husband should explicitly appoint the administrator as his agent, for in such a case the administrator's support of the wife would indeed constitute a violation of the husband's vow. [3]Rather, the Mishnah is referring to a case **where** the husband **proclaims: "Whoever maintains** my wife **will not suffer a loss."** When the husband formulates his instructions in this manner, he does not explicitly appoint anybody as his agent. When the administrator provides the wife with her maintenance, he is regarded as acting on his own initiative.

וְכִי אָמַר הָכִי [4]The Gemara now questions Rav Huna's solution: **But** even **when** the husband formulates his instructions by **saying that** whoever maintains his wife will not suffer a loss, **does not** the administrator **act as** the husband's **agent** when he provides the wife with her maintenance? A person may be treated as an agent acting on behalf of his principal, even if he has not received a specific mandate to serve in that capacity, [5]**for surely we have learned** elsewhere in the Mishnah (*Gittin* 66a): **"If someone was cast into a pit and called out:** [6]**'Whoever hears my voice should write my wife a**

NOTES

לָאו שְׁלִיחוּתֵיהּ קָעָבֵיד **Does he not perform his agency?** It follows from *Rashi* and *Rambam* that if the husband actually appointed an administrator to maintain his wife in his place, and the administrator carried out his instructions, the husband is guilty of violating his vow. The question has been raised: How can the husband be regarded as having violated his vow when there is a general rule that there is no agency for a transgression, so that a principal is not liable for any transgression committed by his agent?

Mishneh LeMelekh explains that the husband would not be in violation of his vow because of the rules of agency, but because of his undertaking to compensate the administrator for his expenses. Since in the end the wife receives her maintenance at her husband's expense, he is regarded as having violated his vow forbidding his wife to derive any benefit from him. *Taz* suggests that the rule that there is no agency for a transgression does not mean that the principal is not regarded as having violated a prohibition if his agent commits a transgression on his behalf, but only that the principal is not liable for punishment (execution or flogging) for that transgression.

כָּל הַשּׁוֹמֵעַ קוֹלוֹ **"Whoever hears my voice."** Even though the man in the pit did not instruct those who heard him to deliver the bill of divorce to his wife, but only to draw it up, those who heard him may indeed write the bill of divorce and deliver it to the wife. We assume that the husband would not have asked that the bill of divorce be written unless he also intended for it to be given to his wife, and so we waive the ordinary requirement that the husband must clearly instruct his agent with respect to the delivery of the bill of divorce. The law here is similar to the law in the case of a critically ill person who asks two people to write his wife a bill of divorce, but does not tell them to give it to her. In such a case they should

HALAKHAH

"כָּל הַזָּן אֵינוֹ מַפְסִיד" **"Whoever maintains her will not lose."** "A husband who has made a vow forbidding his wife to derive any benefit from him and is now obligated to maintain her by way of an administrator must proclaim: 'Whoever maintains my wife will not suffer a loss.' The administrator may provide the wife with her maintenance, and may then recover his expenses from the husband." (*Shulḥan Arukh, Yoreh De'ah* 235:2.)

מִי שֶׁהָיָה מוּשְׁלָךְ בְּבוֹר **If someone was cast into a pit.** "If someone is cast into a pit and says: 'Whoever hears my voice should write my wife a bill of divorce,' and he specifies his and his wife's names and place(s) of residence, those who hear him should write the woman a bill of divorce and give it to her." (*Rambam, Sefer Nashim, Hilkhot Gerushin* 2:13; *Shulḥan Arukh, Even HaEzer* 141:19.)

SAGES

רַבִּי אַמִּי **Rabbi Ammi.** A Palestinian Amora of the third generation. See *Ketubot*, Part II, p.195.

TRANSLATION AND COMMENTARY

bill of divorce,' [1]**those** who hear him **should write** the woman a bill of divorce **and deliver** it to her." The delivery of a bill of divorce must be effected by the husband himself or by an agent appointed by him to act on his behalf. The example from *Gittin* shows that such an appointment need not be directed at a specific person. Similarly, the formulation, "Whoever maintains my wife will not suffer a loss," should be regarded as a valid appointment of an agent, even though it is not directed at a specific person. Thus, the administrator should be regarded as an agent acting on behalf of her husband, and the maintenance provided to her should constitute a violation of the husband's vow forbidding her to derive any benefit from him!

הָכִי הָשְׁתָּא [2]The Gemara rebuts this objection: **Now is this** really **so,** that a comparison can be made between the two formulations? [3]**There,** with respect to the bill of divorce, the husband **said:** "Whoever hears my voice **should write** my wife a bill of divorce and deliver it to her." The husband gave clear instructions that a bill of divorce was to be written and delivered, and therefore the person who fulfills those instructions is regarded as his agent. [4]But **here,** with respect to the wife's maintenance, **did** the husband **say:** "Whoever hears me **should maintain** my wife"? [5]No, he **said: "Whoever maintains** my wife will not suffer a loss." Such a formulation is so general that the administrator who provides the wife with maintenance is regarded as acting on his own initiative, avoiding violation of the husband's vow.

וְהָא אָמַר [6]The Gemara raises an objection: **But** can such a general formulation avoid the problem? **Surely Rabbi Ammi said:** [7]**Regarding a fire** that broke out on Shabbat, **they allowed a person to say** in the presence of a non-Jew: [8]**"Whoever puts out the fire will not lose."** By Rabbinic decree, a Jew may not ask a non-Jew to perform an act on Shabbat that he himself is forbidden to do. He may, however, state in the presence of a non-Jew that whoever puts out the fire will not suffer a loss, for such a declaration is not regarded as an appointment of an agent, and the non-Jew who then puts out the fire is viewed as acting on his own initiative. [9]Now Rabbi Ammi was careful to apply this principle to **a fire** that broke out on Shabbat. [10]**What** kind of case did Rabbi Ammi mean **to exclude?** [11]**Did he not mean to exclude the case** of a husband who makes a vow forbidding his wife to benefit from him? Rabbi Ammi's ruling implies that in such a case the person who answers the husband's call and maintains his wife is regarded as an agent acting on the husband's behalf.

לְאִשְׁתּוֹ׳, [1]הֲרֵי אֵלּוּ יִכְתְּבוּ וְיִתְּנוּ״.
[2]הָכִי הָשְׁתָּא? [3]הָתָם קָאָמַר: ״יִכְתּוֹב״ [4]הָכָא מִי קָאָמַר: ״יָזוּן״? [5]״כָּל הַזָּן״ קָאָמַר.
[6]וְהָא אָמַר רַבִּי אַמִּי: [7]בִּדְלֵיקָה הִתִּירוּ לוֹמַר: [8]״כָּל הַמְכַבֶּה אֵינוֹ מַפְסִיד״! [9]״בִּדְלֵיקָה״ — [10]לְמַעוּטֵי מַאי? [11]לָאו לְמַעוּטֵי כִּי הַאי גַּוְונָא?

LITERAL TRANSLATION

for my (lit., "his") wife,' [1]they should write and deliver [it]."

[2]Now is this so? [3]There he said: "Should write." [4]Here did he say: "Should maintain"? [5]He said: "Whoever maintains."

[6]But surely Rabbi Ammi said: [7]Regarding a fire they allowed [one] to say: [8]"Whoever puts out [the fire] will not lose." [9]"Regarding a fire" — [10]to exclude what? [11]Is it not to exclude such a case?

RASHI

הרי אלו יכתבו ויתנו — אף על גב דלא אמר ליה לסופר ״כתוב״, הכא נמי, אף על גב דלא אמר ליה ״זון״ — שלוחיה הוא. **התם קאמר יכתוב** — לשון צוואה לשומע קולו. **בדליקה התירו לומר** — בשבת, דמתוך שאדם בהול על ממונו, אי לא שרית ליה — אתי לכבויי. **לאו למעוטי כי האי גוונא** — בכל איסורין שבתורה.

NOTES

indeed write the bill of divorce and deliver it to her, for we assume that the husband's intention was that the bill of divorce be given to his wife (see *Gittin* 65b). (*Rivan, Meiri.*)

HALAKHAH

״כָּל הַמְכַבֶּה אֵינוֹ מַפְסִיד״ **"Whoever puts out the fire will not lose."** "If a fire breaks out on Shabbat, a person may say in the presence of a non-Jew: 'Whoever puts out the fire will not lose.' According to some authorities, he may not address the non-Jew directly, saying: 'If you put out the fire, you will not lose.' But *Shiltei Gibborim* allows even such a formulation (see *Mishnah Berurah*)." (*Rambam, Sefer Zemannim, Hilkhot Shabbat* 12:7; *Shulḥan Arukh, Oraḥ Ḥayyim* 334:26.)

TRANSLATION AND COMMENTARY

לָא [1]The Gemara answers: **No,** Rabbi Ammi meant **to exclude the other prohibitions of Shabbat.** A special allowance was made in the case of a fire, because a person becomes very anxious when his property is at sake, and if we do not permit the Jew to ask a non-Jew in an indirect manner to put out the fire, he might put it out himself. However, the Rabbis forbid a Jew from asking a non-Jew to perform other actions for him that are forbidden on Shabbat, even if he conveys his request in an indirect manner, saying: "Whoever does such-and-such will not lose." By contrast, no such decree was enacted regarding someone who makes a vow forbidding somebody else to benefit from him. Such a person may indeed state: "Whoever benefits that other person will not lose."

מְתִיב רַבָּה [2]**Rabbah raised an objection** against Rav Huna's interpretation of our Mishnah from a Baraita, which stated: [3]**"If someone is forbidden by a vow to derive** any material **benefit from another person, and he does not have anything to eat,** and the person who made the vow wishes to support him but is barred from doing so on account of his vow, that person **may approach the shopkeeper from whom he is accustomed to buy,** [4]**and say to him: 'So-and-so is forbidden by a vow to benefit from me, and I do not know what I can do for him.'** [5]The shopkeeper may then **provide** the needy person with whatever he needs, **and** may later **come and collect** the money for what he has provided **from the person** who told him about the poor man's misfortune." [6]It follows from this Baraita that only **such** a roundabout formulation **is permitted.** [7]**But** one is **not** permitted to say: **"Whoever maintains** that other person **will not lose,"** for such a formulation is regarded as appointing an agent. If so, our Mishnah cannot be understood as referring to a case where the husband said: "Whoever maintains my wife will not lose," and this contradicts the explanation given by Rav Huna!

[1]לָא, לְמַעוּטֵי שְׁאָר אִיסּוּרִים דְּשַׁבָּת.
[2]מְתִיב רַבָּה: [3]"הַמּוּדָּר הֲנָאָה מֵחֲבֵירוֹ, וְאֵין לוֹ מַה יֹּאכַל, יֵלֵךְ אֵצֶל חֶנְוָנִי הָרָגִיל אֶצְלוֹ, [4]וְיֹאמַר לוֹ: 'אִישׁ פְּלוֹנִי מוּדָּר הֲנָאָה מִמֶּנִּי, וְאֵינִי יוֹדֵעַ מָה אֶעֱשֶׂה לוֹ'. [5]הוּא נוֹתֵן לוֹ, וּבָא וְנוֹטֵל מִזֶּה". [6]הָכִי הוּא דְּשָׁרֵי, [7]אֲבָל "כָּל הַזָּן אֵינוֹ מַפְסִיד" לָא!

LITERAL TRANSLATION

[1]No, it is to exclude the rest of the prohibitions of Shabbat.

[2]Rabbah raised an objection: [3]"[If] someone is forbidden by a vow to benefit from his fellow, and he does not have anything to eat, [the other person] may go to the shopkeeper to whom he is accustomed [to go], [4]and he may say to him: 'So-and-so is forbidden by a vow to benefit from me, and I do not know what I can do for him.' [5]He gives to him, and he comes and takes from this [man]." [6]It is thus that it is permitted, [7]but [to say] "whoever maintains [her] will not lose" is not!

RASHI

שאר איסורי שבת – דחמירי, ולא התירו כהן לומר "העושה לי מלאכה זו אינו מפסיד" כדי שישמעו נכרים ויעשו. אבל בנדרים לא גזור.

NOTES

לְמַעוּטֵי שְׁאָר אִיסּוּרִים דְּשַׁבָּת **To exclude the rest of the prohibitions of Shabbat.** *Ritva* cites a passage from the Jerusalem Talmud (which does not appear in our texts of that Talmud), according to which Rabbi Ammi specifically mentioned the case of a fire in order to teach us that a person may not make a similar declaration regarding other activities forbidden on Shabbat, even if a dam bursts or heavy rain begins to fall, and there is a threat of significant financial loss. From this it would appear that a special allowance was made in the case of fire, not only because a person becomes overwrought when his property is at stake, but also because there is concern that the fire will put people's lives in danger. Thus the allowance applies only in the case of a fire, and not in the case of some other disaster in which the potential financial loss is the same. Other Rishonim (see *Halakhot Gedolot,* cited by *Rosh, Shabbat* 16:10) maintain that the allowance regarding a fire applies also in the case of a burst dam and in any other case where a person is faced on Shabbat with a sudden disaster threatening a significant financial loss.

Further, according to some Rishonim, Rabbi Ammi meant to exclude only the rest of the Shabbat prohibitions.

HALAKHAH

הַמּוּדָּר הֲנָאָה **If someone is forbidden by a vow to benefit.** "If someone is forbidden by a vow to derive any benefit from another person, and he does not have anything to eat, the person who made the vow may say to a shopkeeper whom he knows: 'So-and-so is forbidden by a vow to benefit from me, and I do not know what I can do for him.' The shopkeeper may then provide that other person with whatever he needs, and may later collect his expenses from the person who made the vow if the latter wishes to reimburse him (but he is not required to reimburse him; *Rema*). And similarly, the person who made the vow may intimate to workers that the person whom he forbade with his vow has work that must be done, and may then compensate them, if he so desires, for their efforts." (*Rambam, Sefer Hafla'ah, Hilkhot Nedarim* 7:12-13; *Shulḥan Arukh, Yoreh De'ah* 221:8.)

[1]״לָא מִיבָּעֲיָא״ קָאָמַר. [2]לָא מִיבָּעֲיָא: ״כָּל הַזָּן אֵינוֹ מַפְסִיד״, [3]דִּלְעָלְמָא קָאָמַר. [4]אֲבָל הַאי, כֵּיוָן דְּרָגִיל אֶצְלוֹ, וְקָאָזֵיל קָאָמַר לֵיהּ, [5]כְּמַאן דְּאָמַר לֵיהּ ״זִיל הַב לֵיהּ אַתְּ״ דָּמֵי. [6]קָא מַשְׁמַע לָן.

[7]גּוּפָא: [8]״הַמּוּדָּר הֲנָאָה מֵחֲבֵירוֹ, וְאֵין לוֹ מַה יֹּאכַל, הוֹלֵךְ אֵצֶל חֶנְוָנִי הָרָגִיל אֶצְלוֹ, [9]וְאוֹמֵר לוֹ: ׳אִישׁ פְּלוֹנִי מוּדָּר הֲנָאָה מִמֶּנִּי, וְאֵינִי יוֹדֵעַ מָה אֶעֱשֶׂה לוֹ׳. [10]הוּא נוֹתֵן לוֹ, וּבָא וְנוֹטֵל מִזֶּה. [11]בֵּיתוֹ לִבְנוֹת, וּגְדֵירוֹ לִגְדּוֹר, וְשָׂדֵהוּ לִקְצוֹר, הוֹלֵךְ אֵצֶל פּוֹעֲלִין הָרְגִילִין אֶצְלוֹ, [12]וְאוֹמֵר לָהֶן:

TRANSLATION AND COMMENTARY

לָא מִיבָּעֲיָא [1]The Gemara answers that the Baraita rules that he may say: "So-and-so is forbidden by a vow to benefit from me, and I do not know what I can do for him," because **it is speaking in the style of "there is no need."** The Baraita intentionally chose to discuss the more problematic case, regarding which one might have thought that a different ruling applies, rather than the more simple case in which "there was no need" to state the law. And the Baraita should be understood thus: [2]**There is no need to teach** the law in a case where the person who took the vow says: **"Whoever maintains** that other person **will not lose," because** it is clear that such a formulation is not regarded as an appointment of an agent, [3]**for he spoke in general** terms **to the** entire **world.** Since he did not direct his words at any specific person, whoever answers his call can certainly not be regarded as his agent. [4]**But** in the case of the Baraita, **since** the person who made the vow **was accustomed to go to the** shopkeeper's **shop, and he went and said to him:** "So-and-so is forbidden by a vow to benefit from me, and I do not know what I can do for him," [5]we might have thought that **he is regarded as if he had said to** the shopkeeper outright: **"You go and give him** whatever he needs." [6]**Hence** the Baraita **teaches us that this is not so.** The person who made the vow is not regarded as having appointed the shopkeeper as his agent, because he did not tell him explicitly to maintain the other person.

גּוּפָא [7]The Gemara now **returns to the Baraita quoted above** and cites it at length: [8]**"If someone is forbidden by a vow to provide** any material **benefit to another person, and that person has nothing to eat,** the one who made the vow **may approach the shopkeeper from whom he is accustomed to buy,** [9]**and say to him: 'So-and-so is forbidden by a vow to benefit from me, and I do not know what I can do for him.'** [10]The shopkeeper may then **provide** the needy person with whatever he needs, **and collect** the money for what he has provided **from the one** who had told him about the poor man's misfortune. [11]**If the house** of the person who was forbidden by a vow to derive material benefit **needs to be built, or his fence needs to be erected, or his field needs to be harvested,** and the one who took the vow wished to help him but is forbidden to do so because of the vow, he **may approach workers who are accustomed to work for him,** [12]**and he may say to them:**

LITERAL TRANSLATION

[1]He was speaking [in the style of] "there is no need." [2]There is no need [to state that he is permitted to say:] "Whoever maintains [her] will not lose," [3]for he spoke (lit., "to the world") in general. [4]But this [man], since he is accustomed [to go] to him, and he went [and] spoke to him, [5]is regarded like one who said to him: "You go [and] give to him." [6][Hence] it tells us [that this is not so].

[7]Returning to the statement quoted above (lit., "the thing itself"): [8]"[If] someone is forbidden by a vow to benefit from his fellow, and he does not have anything to eat, [the other person] may go to the shopkeeper to whom he is accustomed [to go], [9]and he may say to him: 'So-and-so is forbidden by a vow to benefit from me, and I do not know what I can do for him.' [10]He gives to him, and he comes and takes from this [man]. [11][If] his house [needs] to be built, or his fence [needs] to be erected, or his field [needs] to be harvested, he may go to workers who are accustomed [to work] for him, [12]and he may say to them:

RASHI

דלעלמא קאמר – לא דמי לשליחות כלל, דלא ייחד איש לעשותו.
אבל רגיל אצלו – אימא לא כו׳.

NOTES

Because of their great severity a person may not say: "Whoever performs such-and-such a forbidden activity will not lose." But regarding other Torah prohibitions, a formulation similar to "whoever extinguishes the fire will not lose" is permitted. Others argue that the Gemara mentioned "the rest of the prohibitions of Shabbat" only because Rabbi Ammi mentioned the case of fire. But this same ruling applies to all Torah prohibitions. An exception is made in the case of a person who is forbidden by a vow to benefit from another person and who has nothing to eat, and in the case of a woman who is forbidden by a vow to benefit from her husband and who will suffer disgrace if she is not properly maintained (see *Ritva* here, and more fully *Ramban* and *Ritva, Bava Metzia* 69b).

TRANSLATION AND COMMENTARY

'So-and-so is forbidden by a vow to benefit from me, and I do not know what I can do for him.' [1]The workers may then **work for him,** build his house, erect his fence, or harvest his crop, **and** later **they** may **come and collect their wages from** the one who intimated to them that the work was necessary. [2]**If** the one who made the vow and the person who is forbidden by the vow **are traveling** together **on the road, and** the person who is forbidden by the vow **does not have with him anything to eat,** the one who made the vow **may give someone else food as a gift, and the one** who has been forbidden by the vow **may take** the food **and eat** it, **and** the whole arrangement **is permitted,** because the person who is forbidden by the vow does not benefit directly from the one who made the vow. [3]**And if there is nobody else there** with them who can play the role of the middleman, the one who made the vow **may place food on a rock or on a fence,** [4]**and say: 'This food** is **declared ownerless for anybody who wants** to eat **it.'** [5]**And the one** who is forbidden by the vow **may take** the food **and eat** it, **and** the whole arrangement **is permitted,** because the person who is forbidden by the vow does not derive benefit from the one who made the vow, but rather from ownerless property. [6]**But Rabbi Yose forbids** these last two arrangements, whether the person who made the vow gave the food as a gift to a third party or declared it ownerless."

אָמַר רָבָא [7]**Rava said: What is the reasoning of Rabbi Yose?** [8]The Rabbis enacted **a preventive measure on account of** [71A] **the incident** that occurred **in Bet Ḥoron.** The Mishnah (*Nedarim* 48a) reports that in Bet Ḥoron a man once made a vow forbidding his father to derive any benefit from him. Wishing to invite his father to his son's wedding, the man who had made the vow approached an acquaintance and said to him: "The courtyard in which the wedding will take place, as well as the food that will be served there, I give to you as a gift for the limited purpose that my father will be able to participate in my son's wedding feast." The acquaintance replied: "If the courtyard and the food are mine, I wish to dedicate them to the Temple treasury." The man who had made the vow then said: "I gave you the courtyard and the food for the sole purpose of having my father attend my son's wedding." When the matter came before the Sages,

'אִישׁ פְּלוֹנִי מוּדָּר הֲנָאָה מִמֶּנִּי, וְאֵינִי יוֹדֵעַ מָה אֶעֱשֶׂה לוֹ'. [1]הֵן עוֹשִׂין עִמּוֹ, וּבָאִין וְנוֹטְלִים שְׂכָרָן מִזֶּה. [2]הָיוּ מְהַלְּכִין בַּדֶּרֶךְ וְאֵין עִמּוֹ מַה יֹּאכַל, נוֹתֵן לְאַחֵר לְשׁוּם מַתָּנָה, וְהַלָּה נוֹטֵל וְאוֹכֵל, וּמוּתָּר. [3]וְאִם אֵין שָׁם אַחֵר, מַנִּיחַ עַל גַּבֵּי הַסֶּלַע אוֹ עַל גַּבֵּי הַגָּדֵר, [4]וְאוֹמֵר: 'הֲרֵי הֵן מוּפְקָרִין לְכָל מִי שֶׁיַּחְפּוֹץ'. [5]וְהַלָּה נוֹטֵל וְאוֹכֵל, וּמוּתָּר. [6]וְרַבִּי יוֹסֵי אוֹסֵר".

[7]אָמַר רָבָא: מַאי טַעְמָא דְּרַבִּי יוֹסֵי? [8]גְּזֵירָה מִשּׁוּם [71A] מַעֲשֶׂה דְּבֵית חוֹרוֹן.

LITERAL TRANSLATION

'So-and-so is forbidden by a vow to benefit from me, and I do not know what I can do for him.' [1]They work for him, and they come and take their wages from this [man]. [2][If] they were traveling on the road and he did not have with him anything to eat, he may give someone else [food] as a gift, and the other one may take and eat, and it is permitted. [3]And if there is nobody else there, he may place [food] on a rock or on a fence, [4]and he may say: 'These are declared ownerless for anybody who wants [them].' [5]And the other one may take and eat, and it is permitted. [6]But Rabbi Yose forbids [it]."

[7]Rava said: What is the reason of Rabbi Yose? [8][It is] a preventive measure on account of [71A] the incident in Bet Ḥoron.

RASHI

מעשה דבית חורון — בנדרים בפרק "השותפין".

NOTES

מַעֲשֶׂה דְּבֵית חוֹרוֹן The incident in Bet Ḥoron. From the incident that took place in Bet Ḥoron we derive the definition of a gift with respect to vows: A gift that cannot be consecrated by its recipient is not regarded as truly a

HALAKHAH

הָיוּ מְהַלְּכִין בַּדֶּרֶךְ If they were traveling on the road. "If a person who made a vow forbidding another person to derive any benefit from him and that other person are traveling together on the road, and the person who is forbidden by the vow does not have anything to eat, the person who made the vow may give someone else food as a gift, and the recipient of the food may then give it to the person who is forbidden by the vow. (But the person who made the vow may not tell the recipient of the gift that he is giving him the gift so that he may pass it on to the person who is forbidden by the vow; nor may he say anything that proves that this is his intention.) If there is nobody else present, the person who made the vow may place the food on the ground or on a fence and declare it ownerless, and the person who is forbidden by the vow may then take the food and eat it." (*Rambam, Sefer Hafla'ah, Hilkhot Nedarim* 7:14-15; *Shulḥan Arukh, Yoreh De'ah* 221:9.)

TRANSLATION AND COMMENTARY

they said that a gift that cannot be dedicated by its recipient is not regarded as a gift. Thus the father may not benefit from the courtyard and the food that his son gave as a gift to his acquaintance. On account of this incident in Bet Ḥoron the Rabbis decreed that whenever it is clear that a gift is a mere fiction, the gift is not valid. For this reason Rabbi Yose said that if someone forbids another person to benefit from him, he cannot give his property to a third party for the benefit of the person who has been forbidden by the vow, as there is a suspicion that the gift is only a fiction.

[1]״רַבִּי יְהוּדָה אוֹמֵר: בְּיִשְׂרָאֵל, חֹדֶשׁ אֶחָד, וכו׳״. [2]הַיְינוּ תַּנָּא קַמָּא!

[3]אֲמַר אַבַּיֵי: כֹּהֶנֶת אֲתָא לְאַשְׁמוּעִינַן.

[4]רָבָא אֲמַר: חֹדֶשׁ מָלֵא וְחֹדֶשׁ חָסֵר אִיכָּא בֵּינַיְיהוּ.

LITERAL TRANSLATION

[1]"Rabbi Yehudah says: In [the case of] a non-priest, [if his vow was for] one month, etc." [2]This is [the same as] the first Tanna!

[3]Abaye said: He came to teach us about the wife of a priest.

[4]Rava said: There is [a difference] between them [regarding] a full month and a defective month.

RASHI

הײנו תנא קמא — דאיהו נמי שלשים יום קאמר.

רַבִּי יְהוּדָה אוֹמֵר [1]We learned in our Mishnah: **"Rabbi Yehudah says: If** the husband **is a non-priest** and he forbids his wife to derive any benefit from him for a period of **one month,** he may keep her as his wife and must appoint an administrator to maintain her." [2]The Gemara objects: Surely **this is the same as** the ruling of **the** anonymous **first Tanna** of the Mishnah!

אֲמַר אַבַּיֵי [3]**Abaye said:** Rabbi Yehudah's ruling regarding the wife of a non-priest was indeed unnecessary, and is meant only **to teach us about the wife of a priest** — that if her husband forbids her to benefit from him, he may remain married to her but must appoint an administrator to maintain her for a period of two months. Only then must he divorce her.

רָבָא אֲמַר [4]**Rava said: There is a difference between** the anonymous first Tanna of the Mishnah and Rabbi Yehudah **regarding** the matter of **a full month** (a month of thirty days) **and a defective month** (a month of twenty-nine days). The first Tanna said that a husband who makes a vow forbidding his wife to benefit from him may be compelled to divorce her only after thirty days have passed. According to Rabbi Yehudah, the husband may be compelled to divorce his wife after a month has passed. If the month is full, he may be compelled to divorce her after thirty days; and if it is defective, he may be compelled to grant her a divorce after twenty-nine days.

NOTES

gift, for the donor has not fully relinquished it. *Rabbenu Shimshon of Sens* poses a difficulty: A gift given on condition that it must be returned to the donor after a specified time cannot be consecrated by the recipient. Yet such a gift is indeed considered as a gift with respect to certain laws, and it stands to reason that it could be considered a gift regarding vows as well. *Rabbenu Shimshon* distinguishes between the case of a gift given on condition that it be returned, and the case of the gift given in Bet Ḥoron, as follows: A gift given on condition that it be returned must indeed be restored to the donor after a specified time. But while it is in the hands of the recipient it is his to do with as he wishes. But in the incident that occurred in Bet Ḥoron, the donor limited the way the recipient could use his gift, for he gave it to him only to enable the donor's father to participate in his son's wedding.

Rashba explains that, according to the first Tanna, there is no comparison between the incident that occurred in Bet Ḥoron and the case under discussion in the Baraita, for in the latter the donor who made the gift did not state explicitly that he wanted the recipient to hand over the gift to the person who was forbidden to benefit from him, and the recipient was free to consecrate the gift or to do with it as he pleased.

כֹּהֶנֶת אֲתָא לְאַשְׁמוּעִינַן **He came to teach us about the wife of a priest.** *Rashba* notes that Abaye's formulation implies that Rabbi Yehudah does not disagree with the anonymous first Tanna but adds the ruling regarding the wife of a priest, with which the anonymous first Tanna also agrees. This is supported by the Tosefta (7:1), which states that both Rabbi Meir (the anonymous first Tanna is ordinarily identified as Rabbi Meir) and Rabbi Yehudah agree that if a priest forbids his wife to benefit from him, he may keep her as his wife for two months and only afterwards must he divorce her and pay her ketubah. But *Rashba* adds that the Gemara below (71b) implies that the first Tanna makes no distinction between the wife of a priest and the wife of a non-priest.

חֹדֶשׁ מָלֵא וְחֹדֶשׁ חָסֵר **A full month and a defective month.** *Rivan* notes that Rava did not accept Abaye's view because if Rabbi Yehudah only meant to add the ruling regarding the wife of a priest, he should not have restated the ruling regarding the wife of a non-priest. For this reason Rava sought a Halakhic difference between the anonymous first Tanna and Rabbi Yehudah also in the case of the wife of a non-priest.

According to the Jerusalem Talmud (see note above, 70a, s.v וּשְׁנַיִם יוֹצִיא), Rabbi Yehudah maintains that a non-priest cannot be forced to divorce his wife until two complete months have passed and he still has not secured a dispensation nullifying his vow. Accordingly, there would be a difference of a whole month between the anonymous first Tanna and Rabbi Yehudah.

TRANSLATION AND COMMENTARY

אָמַר רַב [1]The Amoraim disagreed as to whether the ruling in our Mishnah invariably applied. **Rav said: This** ruling **applies only when** the husband **specified** the period of time during which his wife would be forbidden to derive benefit from him. [2]**But** if he forbade his wife to derive benefit from him **without specifying** the length of time of the prohibition, he **must divorce** his wife **immediately and pay** her **her ketubah.** [3]**But Shmuel said: Even** if the husband forbids his wife to derive benefit from him **without specifying** the duration of the prohibition, **he is not required to divorce her** immediately. He is given a period of time, [4]**for perhaps he will** go to a Sage and **find a** Halakhic **justification for** nullifying **his vow.**

[5]The Gemara wonders why it was necessary to present the foregoing disagreement: **But surely** Rav and Shmuel have already **disagreed about this** matter **once before!** [6]**For we have learned** in a Mishnah (above, 61b): **"If someone takes** a vow **forbidding** himself to have **sexual relations with his wife,** the Tannaim disagree about how soon he can be compelled to grant her a divorce and to pay her her ketubah. [7]**Bet Shammai say:** The wife must wait **two weeks,** after which her husband must either go to a Sage and request the nullification of his vow, or grant her a divorce and pay her her ketubah. [8]**Bet Hillel** disagree and **say:** After **one week** the husband must take the necessary steps to release himself from the vow or else grant his wife a divorce." [9]**And** regarding this dispute, **Rav said: The dispute** between Bet Shammai and Bet Hillel **is** limited to **when** the husband **specified** a certain period during which he would be forbidden to engage in sexual relations with his wife. [10]**But** if the husband **took a vow** forbidding himself to cohabit with his wife **without specifying** how long he would be forbidden to her, **all agree** — both Bet Shammai and Bet Hillel — **that he must divorce**

[1]אָמַר רַב: לֹא שָׁנוּ אֶלָּא בִּמְפָרֵשׁ, [2]אֲבָל בִּסְתָם, יוֹצִיא לְאַלְתַּר וְיִתֵּן כְּתוּבָּה. [3]וּשְׁמוּאֵל אָמַר: אֲפִילּוּ בִּסְתָם, לֹא יוֹצִיא, [4]שֶׁמָּא יִמְצָא פֶּתַח לְנִדְרוֹ. [5]וְהָא אִיפְלְגוּ בֵּיהּ חֲדָא זִימְנָא! [6]דִּתְנַן: "הַמַּדִּיר אֶת אִשְׁתּוֹ מִתַּשְׁמִישׁ הַמִּטָּה, [7]בֵּית שַׁמַּאי אוֹמְרִים: שְׁתֵּי שַׁבָּתוֹת. [8]וּבֵית הִלֵּל אוֹמְרִים: שַׁבָּת אַחַת". [9]וַאֲמַר רַב: מַחֲלוֹקֶת בִּמְפָרֵשׁ, [10]אֲבָל בִּסְתָם, יוֹצִיא לְאַלְתַּר

LITERAL TRANSLATION

[1]Rav said: They only taught [this] where he specified, [2]but where [he vowed] without specifying, he must divorce [her] immediately and pay [her] ketubah. [3]But Shmuel said: Even where [he vowed] without specifying, he should not divorce [her], [4]in case he will find an opening for his vow.

[5]But surely they disagreed about this once [before]! [6]For we have learned: "[If] someone forbids his wife with a vow to have sexual relations [with him], [7]Bet Shammai say: Two weeks. [8]And Bet Hillel say: One week." [9]And Rav said: The disagreement is where he specified, [10]but where [he vowed] without specifying,

RASHI

במפרש — שפירש שלשים יום הוא דלא כפינן ליה להוציא אלא יעמיד פרנס.

NOTES

לֹא שָׁנוּ אֶלָּא בִּמְפָרֵשׁ **They only taught this where he specified.** The Rishonim offer different explanations of Rav's limitation of the Mishnah's ruling that a husband who makes a vow forbidding his wife to derive any material benefit from him for a period of up to thirty days cannot be compelled to divorce her. *Rashi* maintains that the husband is not required to divorce his wife only if the specified period does not exceed thirty days. But if he specified that she would be forbidden to derive benefit from him for more than thirty days, he must divorce her immediately, as if he had not specified for how long such benefit would be forbidden to her. *Rashba* justifies this position, arguing that if the husband did not specify the length of time his wife would be forbidden to derive any benefit from him, he must divorce her immediately, because we assume that he will not go to a Sage and nullify his vow within thirty days. Thus the same law should apply if the husband specified that his wife would be forbidden to derive benefit from him for more than thirty days.

By contrast, *Ra'ah, Ritva,* and others maintain that, according to Rav, the husband cannot be compelled to divorce his wife immediately if he specified the period of time, even if it exceeds thirty days. He is only required to divorce her immediately if he specified no time limit at all. These Rishonim explain that if the husband did not specify any period of time, the wife thinks that he made the vow because he hates her and will never seek a nullification of his vow, and so she finds it intolerable to continue living with him. But if he specified a time, she assumes that the vow was made in momentary anger, and the husband will go to a Sage for a nullification of his vow as soon as his anger passes.

HALAKHAH

הַמַּדִּיר אֶת אִשְׁתּוֹ **If someone forbids his wife.** "If someone makes a vow forbidding his wife to derive any benefit from him, whether or not he specifies for how long she is forbidden to derive such benefit, we wait thirty days before compelling the man to divorce his wife," following Shmuel against Rav. (*Rambam, Sefer Nashim, Hilkhot Ishut* 12:23; *Shulhan Arukh, Yoreh De'ah* 235:2.)

BACKGROUND

פֶּתַח לְנִדְרוֹ An opening for his vow. The revocation of a vow by a Sage is not an arbitrary decision. It can be made only when he finds a reason to revoke and annul the vow. One of the ways of doing this is by finding an "opening," meaning that the Sage finds that person who made the vow did not foresee or take into account certain consequences or aspects of the vow, and, had he done so, he would not have made it. By means of this kind of "opening," a Sage can annul the entire vow.

וְיִתֵּן כְּתוּבָּה. [1]וּשְׁמוּאֵל אָמַר:
אֲפִילּוּ בִּסְתָם נַמִי, לֹא יוֹצִיא,
[2]שֶׁמָּא יִמְצָא פֶּתַח לְנִדְרוֹ!
[3]צְרִיכָא, דְּאִי אִיתְּמַר בְּהַהִיא,
[4]בְּהַהִיא קָאָמַר רַב, [5]מִשּׁוּם
דְּלָא אֶפְשָׁר בְּפַרְנָס. [6]אֲבָל
בְּהָא, דְּאֶפְשָׁר בְּפַרְנָס, [7]אֵימָא
מוֹדֶה לֵיהּ לִשְׁמוּאֵל. [8]וְאִי
אִתְּמַר בְּהָא, בְּהָא קָאָמַר
שְׁמוּאֵל, [9]מִשּׁוּם דְּאֶפְשָׁר
בְּפַרְנָס. [10]אֲבָל בְּהַהִיא, אֵימָא
מוֹדֶה לֵיהּ לְרַב. [11]צְרִיכָא.
[12]תְּנַן: "הַמַּדִּיר אֶת אִשְׁתּוֹ
שֶׁלֹּא תִּטְעוֹם אֶחָד מִכָּל
הַפֵּירוֹת, יוֹצִיא וְיִתֵּן כְּתוּבָּה.

LITERAL TRANSLATION

[all agree that] he must divorce [her] immediately and pay [her] ketubah. [1]But Shmuel said: Even where [he vowed] without specifying, he should not divorce [her], [2]in case he will find an opening for his vow!

[3]It was necessary, for if it had been stated about this, [4][I might have said that] about this Rav made his statement, [5]because it cannot [be done] through an administrator. [6]But about that, where it can [be done] through an administrator, [7]I might say [that] he agrees with Shmuel. [8]And if it had been stated about that, [I might have said that] about that Shmuel made his statement, [9]because it can [be done] through an administrator. [10]But about this, I might say [that] he agrees with Rav. [11][Therefore both statements were] necessary.

[12]We have learned: "If someone forbids his wife with a vow to taste one of all the fruits, he must divorce [her] and pay [her] ketubah."

TRANSLATION AND COMMENTARY

his wife **immediately and pay** her **her ketubah.** [1]**Shmuel** disagreed and **said: Even** if the husband **took a vow** not to engage in sexual relations with his wife and did **not specify** the length of time, **he is not required to divorce her** immediately. [2]He is given some time **because he may** go to a Sage in order to **find a** Halakhic **justification for nullifying his vow.**

צְרִיכָא [3]To explain why this disagreement appears twice, the Gemara shows that the cases in dispute are not identical: **It was necessary** for the dispute between Rav and Shmuel to be stated in both cases, **for if it had been stated** only **about** the husband who forbade himself to cohabit with his wife, [4]**I might have said that** only **in that** case **did Rav say** that the husband must divorce his wife immediately, if he did not specify the duration of his abstinence, [5]**because** his marital duty **cannot** be fulfilled **through an administrator.** [6]**But in** our Mishnah, where the husband forbids his wife to derive benefit from him, and the things that she cannot afford to buy with her earnings **can be** provided **through an administrator,** [7]**I might have said that** Rav **agrees with Shmuel** that the husband is not required to divorce his wife until a month has passed, even if he did not specify the length of the prohibition. [8]**And if** the dispute **had been stated** only **about** the case raised in our Mishnah, **I might have said that** only **in that** case **did Shmuel say** that the husband is given thirty days before he can be compelled to divorce his wife, [9]**because** her needs **can** be provided **through an administrator.** [10]**But in** the case of a husband who forbids himself to have sexual relations, **I might have said that** Shmuel **agrees with Rav** that the husband must divorce his wife immediately because his conjugal obligation cannot be fulfilled through an administrator. [11]**Thus it was necessary** for the dispute to be stated twice, to teach us that Rav and Shmuel disagree in both cases.

תְּנַן [12]The Gemara now raises an objection against him from what **we learned** in the next clause of our Mishnah: **"If someone makes a vow forbidding his wife to eat a** particular **kind of fruit,** and she is unwilling to continue living with him under such circumstances, **he must grant her a divorce** immediately **and pay** her **her ketubah."** Why is it that in the first case discussed by the Mishnah, concerning the husband who makes a vow forbidding his wife to benefit from him, he is given thirty days before he must grant her a divorce, whereas when by taking a vow he forbids her to eat a particular kind of fruit, he must divorce her

RASHI

משום דאיכא צערא דתרווייהו – לא גרסינן. **יוציא ויתן כתובה** – לאלתר.

NOTES

דְּאִי אִיתְּמַר בְּהַהִיא For if it had been stated about this. A number of Rishonim (see *Tosafot, Ra'ah, Ritva*, and others) cite a different version of this argument (in addition to the version found in the standard text or in place of it), which was rejected by *Rashi*: "And if it had been stated about this, [I might have said that] Shmuel made his statement about this, because there is distress for both of them. But about that, where there is distress only for her, I might say [that] he agrees with Rav." Had the dispute concerned only the husband who forbade himself to cohabit with his wife, I might have said that only in that case did Shmuel say that the husband is given thirty days before he can be compelled to divorce his wife, even if he did not specify the period during which she would be forbidden to him, because in that case both the husband and the wife suffer distress. But in the case of our Mishnah, where only

TRANSLATION AND COMMENTARY

immediately? [1]**There is no problem according to Rav,** who distinguishes between a case where the husband specifies the period of time, and a case where he forbids her for an unspecified period of time. [2]**Here,** in the second clause of the Mishnah, we are dealing with a case **where** the husband forbade his wife to eat a particular kind of fruit **without specifying** the period of time when the prohibition would be in effect. In such a case, he must grant her an immediate divorce and pay her her ketubah. [3]And **here,** in the first clause of the Mishnah, we are dealing with a case **where** the husband **specified** the length of the prohibition. In such a case, the husband is given a period of thirty days before he is required to divorce his wife. [4]**But according to Shmuel,** the Mishnah **is difficult,** for he ruled that the husband is not required to grant his wife an immediate divorce if he does not specify the duration of his vow!

הָכָא בְּמַאי עָסְקִינַן [5]The Gemara answers: **Here we are dealing with** a case **where** it was the wife who **took a vow** forbidding herself to eat a particular kind of fruit **and** her husband **confirmed** the vow **for her.** A husband is empowered to annul his wife's vow on the day he hears of it. But if he explicitly confirms the vow, or if he lets a day pass without annulling it, the vow can no longer be annulled. Now, since she made the vow, there is no reason to think that she will go to a Sage and seek a Halakhic justification for nullifying it. Consequently the husband must divorce her immediately. As for his obligation to pay his wife's ketubah in such circumstances, there is a general principle that anonymous Mishnayot reflect the viewpoint of Rabbi Meir, for when Rabbi Yehudah HaNasi compiled the Mishnah, he relied on the traditions formulated by Rabbi Meir and his school. Thus our Mishnah, which was taught anonymously, reflects the viewpoint of

[1]בִּשְׁלָמָא לְרַב, [2]כָּאן, בִּסְתָם; [3]כָּאן בִּמְפָרֵשׁ. [4]אֶלָּא לִשְׁמוּאֵל, קַשְׁיָא!

[5]הָכָא בְּמַאי עָסְקִינַן? כְּגוֹן שֶׁנָּדְרָה הִיא וְקִיֵּים לָהּ אִיהוּ.

LITERAL TRANSLATION

[1]Granted according to Rav, [2]here [it is] where [he vowed] without specifying; [3]here [it is] where he specified. [4]But according to Shmuel, it is difficult! [5]With what are we dealing here? For example, where she vowed and he confirmed [the vow] for her.

RASHI

שנדרה היא — ומה יש לו עוד להמתין, אי ניחא לה לדידה למישקל כתובתה ומיפק לא תבקש פתח לנדרה, אבל היכא דאדרה איהו כגון מליהנות לו, ימתין שמא ימצא פתח לנדרו.

NOTES

the wife suffers distress, I might have said that Shmuel agrees with Rav that the husband must divorce his wife immediately if he did not limit the period of abstinence. *Tosafot* notes that when the Gemara explains the seemingly unnecessary repetition of a dispute, it often offers two different reasons why each of the positions had to be stated in both cases.

שֶׁנָּדְרָה הִיא When she vowed. Our commentary follows *Rashi,* who explains that if a wife made a vow forbidding herself to eat a particular kind of fruit, and her husband confirmed the vow for her, the husband must grant her an immediate divorce, because she wishes to be granted a divorce and to receive her ketubah and will not seek a dispensation nullifying the vow. Thus there is no reason to wait thirty days.

Other Rishonim (see *Tosafot, Ramban, Ra'ah, Ritva,* and others) raise a number of objections against *Rashi:* First, if the wife is given time, she may indeed reconsider and seek a nullification of her vow. Second, the husband should be given time to seek a nullification of his confirmation. And third, if in a case of a wife's vow, there is no reason to wait, why does the Gemara suggest below (71b): "Let her adorn herself and become forbidden, whether according to Bet Shammai two weeks, or according to Bet Hillel one week"?

Tosafot, Ramban, and others explain that if a man forbids his wife to derive any benefit from him, he is not required to divorce her immediately, because she does not suffer distress. She can receive her maintenance through an administrator. Similarly, if a man forbids himself to engage in sexual relations with his wife, he is not required to grant her an immediate divorce, because one or two weeks of abstinence is not considered distress. A woman often abstains from sexual relations for such periods, such as when she is menstruating or gives birth. But if a wife makes a vow forbidding herself to eat a particular kind of fruit, and her husband confirms the vow for her, he must grant his wife an immediate divorce, because ordinarily she would not be required to suffer the distress of being denied that fruit for even one day.

Ra'avad explains that if a wife makes a vow forbidding herself to eat a particular kind of fruit, and her husband confirms the vow for her, he must divorce her immediately, because she thinks that he must really hate her if he does not annul her vow, and it is distressing to her to continue living with a man who hates her (see below 71b).

וְקִיֵּים לָהּ And he confirmed the vow for her. According to *Rivan, Meiri,* and others, the Mishnah is referring not

HALAKHAH

שֶׁנָּדְרָה הִיא וְקִיֵּים לָהּ אִיהוּ When she vowed and he confirmed the vow for her. "If a wife makes a vow forbidding herself to eat a certain type of fruit, or she makes a Nazirite vow, and her husband confirms or fails to nullify it, he must divorce her immediately and pay her her ketubah, following the anonymous Tanna of the Mishnah and the view that in such a case the husband is regarded as having placed his finger between his wife's teeth (see *Taz* and *Shakh*). According to *Rambam,* if the husband is willing to have his wife live with him while

TRANSLATION AND COMMENTARY

Rabbi Meir. [1]**And Rabbi Meir maintains** that if a wife makes a vow and her husband confirms it, he is regarded as someone who **put his finger between** his wife's **teeth** and caused her to bite him, by not annulling the vow on the day he heard it. Thus, when the husband divorces his wife after she made a vow forbidding herself to eat a particular kind of fruit and he confirmed the oath for her, he must pay her her ketubah, for it is he who is regarded as the party that made the divorce necessary.

וְסָבַר רַבִּי מֵאִיר [2]The Gemara asks: **But does Rabbi Meir** really **maintain** that if a wife makes a vow and her husband confirms it, we regard the husband as having **put his finger between** his wife's **teeth?** [3]**Surely it was taught** otherwise in the following Baraita: **"If a woman vows to forbid herself** to derive benefit from **what** is forbidden **to a Nazirite** [wine and everything else derived from the vine] **and her husband hears** the vow **but does not nullify it for her,** [4]**Rabbi Meir and Rabbi Yehudah say:** The woman is regarded as someone who **put her finger between her** own **teeth,** and caused herself to be bitten; i.e., she is regarded as responsible for the vow. [5]**Therefore, if the husband wishes to nullify** the vow on the day that he hears it, **he is authorized to do so.** [6]**And if he says: 'I do not wish to live** any longer **with a woman who habitually makes vows,'** [7]**she may be divorced without** payment of **her ketubah,** for she made the divorce necessary. [8]**Rabbi Yose**

[1]וְקָסָבַר רַבִּי מֵאִיר: הוּא נוֹתֵן אֶצְבַּע בֵּין שִׁינֶּיהָ.
[2]וְסָבַר רַבִּי מֵאִיר הוּא נוֹתֵן אֶצְבַּע בֵּין שִׁינֶּיהָ? [3]וְהָתַנְיָא: "הָאִשָּׁה שֶׁנָּדְרָה בְּנָזִיר, וְשָׁמַע בַּעְלָהּ וְלֹא הֵפֵר לָהּ, [4]רַבִּי מֵאִיר וְרַבִּי יְהוּדָה אוֹמְרִים: הִיא נָתְנָה אֶצְבַּע בֵּין שִׁינֶּיהָ. [5]לְפִיכָךְ, אִם רָצָה הַבַּעַל לְהָפֵר, יָפֵר. [6]וְאִם אָמַר: 'אִי אֶפְשִׁי בְּאִשָּׁה נַדְרָנִית', [7]תֵּצֵא שֶׁלֹּא בִּכְתוּבָּה. [8]רַבִּי יוֹסֵי

LITERAL TRANSLATION

[1]And Rabbi Meir maintains: He puts a finger between her teeth.

[2]But does Rabbi Meir maintain [that] he puts a finger between her teeth? [3]But surely it was taught: "[If] a woman forbade herself with a vow of a Nazirite, and her husband heard and did not nullify [the vow] for her, [4]Rabbi Meir and Rabbi Yehudah say: She put a finger between her teeth. [5]Therefore, if the husband wishes to nullify [it], he may nullify it. [6]And if he says: 'I do not wish [to live] with a woman who habitually makes vows,' [7]she leaves without a ketubah. [8]Rabbi Yose

RASHI

וקסבר רבי מאיר הוא — שקיים נתן אצבע בין שיניה והשיכה, לפיכך יתן כתובה. וסתם מתניתין רבי מאיר היא. **אם רצה הבעל** — מתחילה להפר יפר. **ואם** — לא רצה וקיים לה ואמר: אי אפשי כו׳.

NOTES

only to a husband who explicitly confirmed the vow taken by his wife but also to a husband who remained silent and allowed a day to pass without annulling his wife's vow. The plain sense of the Gemara below (71b): "But here where she forbade herself with a vow and he was silent," supports this position. But according to *Rashba,* the Mishnah's ruling that the husband must grant his wife an immediate divorce applies only if he explicitly confirmed his wife's vow. Then he is viewed as if he himself had made the vow and is therefore required to divorce his wife and pay her her ketubah. But if the husband was silent and allowed a day to pass without annulling his wife's vow, the husband is not held responsible for it, for he can claim that he was busy and forgot to annul it, and so he is not required to pay her her ketubah. The phrase "and he was silent" alludes to the Biblical term וְהֶחֱרִישׁ לָהּ (Numbers 30:12), which literally means that the husband was silent, but which is also understood to mean that the husband confirmed the vow for his wife.

אִי אֶפְשִׁי בְּאִשָּׁה נַדְרָנִית I do not wish to live with a woman who habitually makes vows. *Rambam* (*Hilkhot Ishut* 12:24) derives from here that if a wife makes a vow forbidding herself to eat a particular kind of fruit or to derive benefit from something forbidden to a Nazirite, and her husband confirms the vow for her, he is not required to divorce her. Only if the husband says that he does not wish to live with a woman who habitually makes vows, must he divorce her and pay her her ketubah. But if he is ready to keep her as his wife despite her vow, he cannot be compelled to divorce her.

Ra'ah, Rivash, and *Ran* (and apparently *Rashi* as well) maintain that if the husband confirms his wife's vow, he is required to divorce her. The expression "I do not wish to live with a woman who habitually makes vows" explains why the husband did not annul his wife's vow. Thus the Baraita teaches that if the husband says that he does not want to live with a woman who habitually makes vows, and therefore he did not annul her vow, he is required to divorce her and pay her her ketubah. As will be explained in the Gemara below, the husband must divorce his wife, because she cannot be compelled to continue living with a man who she thinks hates her.

HALAKHAH

bound by her oath, he is not required to divorce her. But if he wishes to divorce her because he does not want to be married to a woman who habitually makes vows, he must pay her her ketubah (see *Ran* and *Mishneh Lemelekh*)." (*Rambam, Sefer Nashim, Hilkhot Ishut* 12:24; *Shulḥan Arukh, Yoreh De'ah* 235:3.)

TRANSLATION AND COMMENTARY

[1]**and Rabbi Elazar** disagree and **say:** [2]It is the husband who is regarded as having **put his finger between** his wife's **teeth** and caused himself to be bitten. Since he could have invalidated the vow, but he chose not to, he is responsible for it. [3]**Therefore, if the husband wants to nullify** the vow on the day that he hears it, **he is authorized to nullify it.** [4]**And if he says: 'I do not wish to live** any longer **with a woman who habitually makes vows,'** [5]**he must divorce her** immediately **and pay** her **her ketubah,** for he made the divorce necessary." Thus the Baraita states explicitly that, according to Rabbi Meir, if a woman makes a vow and her husband confirms it for her, it is the woman who is regarded as having put her finger between her own teeth!

אֵיפּוּךְ [6]The Gemara answers: To resolve this difficulty we must **reverse** the attributions of the two opinions mentioned in the Baraita, so that it is **Rabbi Meir and Rabbi Yehudah** who **said** that the husband who confirmed his wife's oath is regarded as having **put** his finger between her teeth, [7]and it is **Rabbi Yose and Rabbi Elazar** who **said** that the woman who took the oath is regarded as having **put** her finger between her own teeth. If we reverse the attributions, we can explain that our Mishnah reflects the viewpoint of Rabbi Meir that it is the husband who is regarded as responsible for the vow.

וְסָבַר רַבִּי יוֹסֵי [8]The Gemara now points out that if we reverse the attributions of the two opinions mentioned in the Baraita, we create a new difficulty: **Does Rabbi Yose** really **maintain** that if a wife makes a vow and her husband confirms it for her, we regard the woman as having **put** her finger between her own teeth and caused herself to be bitten? [9]**Surely we have learned** otherwise in our Mishnah: **"Rabbi Yose says: With** respect to a **poor woman,** who is not accustomed to wearing much perfume, **if** her husband makes a vow forbidding her to use a certain perfume, [10]and **he does not limit** the duration of the prohibition, he must divorce her immediately and pay her her ketubah." According to Shmuel, this clause of the Mishnah must be understood as referring to a case where the wife made a vow forbidding herself to use perfume and her husband confirmed it for her. And since Rabbi Yose rules that the wife must be paid her ketubah, it follows that he maintains that it is the man who is regarded as having put his finger between his wife's teeth!

אֵימָא [11]The Gemara answers: **Say** that the Baraita cited above should be slightly emended so that it reads as follows: **Rabbi Meir and Rabbi Yose say** that the husband who confirms his wife's oath is regarded as having **put** his finger between his wife's teeth and must therefore divorce her and pay her her ketubah. [12]**Rabbi Yehudah and Rabbi Elazar** disagree and **say** that the woman who made the vow is viewed as having **put** her finger between her own teeth and may therefore be divorced without payment of her ketubah. Thus there is no contradiction between the viewpoint of Rabbi Yose as recorded in the Baraita, and the viewpoint of that same Tanna as reported in our Mishnah.

[1]וְרַבִּי אֶלְעָזָר אוֹמְרִים: [2]הוּא נוֹתֵן אֶצְבַּע בֵּין שִׁינֶּיהָ. [3]לְפִיכָךְ, אִם רָצָה הַבַּעַל לְהָפֵר, יָפֵר. [4]וְאִם אָמַר: 'אִי אֶפְשִׁי בְּאִשָּׁה נַדְרָנִית', [5]יוֹצִיא וְיִתֵּן כְּתוּבָּה"! [6]אֵיפּוּךְ: "רַבִּי מֵאִיר וְרַבִּי יְהוּדָה אוֹמְרִים: הוּא נוֹתֵן; [7]רַבִּי יוֹסֵי וְרַבִּי אֶלְעָזָר אוֹמְרִים: הִיא נָתְנָה".

[8]וְסָבַר רַבִּי יוֹסֵי הִיא נָתְנָה? [9]וְהָתְנַן: "רַבִּי יוֹסֵי אוֹמֵר: בַּעֲנִיּוֹת, [10]שֶׁלֹּא נָתַן קִצְבָּה"! [11]אֵימָא: "רַבִּי מֵאִיר וְרַבִּי יוֹסֵי אוֹמְרִים: הוּא נוֹתֵן; [12]רַבִּי יְהוּדָה וְרַבִּי אֶלְעָזָר אוֹמְרִים: הִיא נָתְנָה".

LITERAL TRANSLATION

[1]and Rabbi Elazar say: [2]He puts a finger between her teeth. [3]Therefore, if the husband wishes to nullify [it], he may nullify it. [4]And if he says: 'I do not wish [to live] with a woman who habitually makes vows,' [5]he must divorce [her] and pay [her] ketubah"!

[6]Reverse [it]: "Rabbi Meir and Rabbi Yehudah say: He puts; [7]Rabbi Yose and Rabbi Elazar say: She put."

[8]But does Rabbi Yose maintain [that] she put? [9]But surely we have learned: "Rabbi Yose says: In [the case of] poor women, [10][this applies] if he did not set a limit"!

[11]Say: "Rabbi Meir and Rabbi Yose say: He puts; [12]Rabbi Yehudah and Rabbi Elazar say: She put."

RASHI

בעניות שלא נתן קצבה – יוציא ויתן כתובה. אלמא הוא נותן, דהא בנדרה היא וקיים הוא אוקימתא למתניתין.

NOTES

הוּא נוֹתֵן אֶצְבַּע He puts a finger. The Jerusalem Talmud offers a similar explanation of our Mishnah — that it is referring to a wife who made a vow which her husband confirmed for her, and the Mishnah maintains that the husband is regarded as having put his finger between his wife's teeth and caused himself to be bitten. The Jerusalem Talmud adds that our Mishnah can even be understood in accordance with the position that if a wife made a vow and her husband confirmed it for her, she is ordinarily regarded as having put her finger between her own teeth and causing herself to be bitten. For the Mishnah may be referring to a case where the husband angered his wife so that she took

TRANSLATION AND COMMENTARY

וְסָבַר רַבִּי יְהוּדָה [1]The Gemara now argues that this reading of the Baraita leads us to another difficulty: **But does Rabbi Yehudah** really **maintain** that if a wife made a vow and her husband confirmed it for her, we regard her as having **put** her finger between her own teeth? [2]**Surely we have learned** otherwise in our Mishnah: **"Rabbi Yehudah says: If** the husband is **a non-priest** and forbids his wife to eat a certain fruit for a period of **one day, he may keep her** as his wife. But if he forbids her to eat that fruit for two days, he must divorce her and pay her her ketubah." Now, as stated earlier, Shmuel maintains that we are dealing here with a woman who vowed not to eat a particular kind of fruit, and her husband confirmed the vow for her. Since Rabbi Yehudah rules that the woman must be paid her ketubah, it follows that he maintains that the husband who confirmed the vow is regarded as having put his finger between her teeth!

אֵימָא [3]To avoid the foregoing contradiction, the Gemara answers: **Say** that the Baraita cited above should be emended in the following manner: **Rabbi Meir and Rabbi Yehudah and Rabbi Yose** all **say** that the husband who confirmed his wife's oath is regarded as having **put** his finger between his wife's teeth and must therefore pay her her ketubah. [4]**Rabbi Elazar** alone **says** that the woman who made the vow is regarded as having **put** her finger between her own teeth and may therefore be divorced without payment of her ketubah. In this way, Rabbi Yehudah's viewpoint as reported in the Baraita can be reconciled with his viewpoint as recorded in the Mishnah.

וְאִם תִּמְצָא לוֹמַר [5]The Gemara now suggests a different solution to reconcile the Mishnah with the Baraita. **If you wish to say that the Tanna** of the Baraita **taught** the conflicting views of two **pairs** of Tannaim, **say** that the Baraita should be emended to read as follows: [6]**Rabbi Meir and Rabbi Elazar say** that the woman who made the vow that was later confirmed by her husband is regarded as having **put** her finger between her own teeth, [7]and **Rabbi Yehudah and Rabbi Yose say** that the husband who confirmed the vow is regarded as having **put** his finger between his wife's teeth. [8]**And** although generally anonymous Mishnayot reflect the viewpoint of Rabbi Meir, **this anonymous Mishnah** of ours **was not** taught **in accordance with** the viewpoint of **Rabbi Meir.**

וְסָבַר רַבִּי יוֹסֵי [9]The Gemara now argues that another difficulty according to Shmuel's explanation of our Mishnah refers to a wife's vow confirmed by her husband. **Does Rabbi Yose** really **maintain** as stated in the Mishnah that **with** respect to a **poor woman,** [10]**if** her husband made a vow forbidding her to apply a certain perfume, and **he did not limit** the period of time during which she would be forbidden to do so, he must divorce her immediately and pay her her ketubah? According to Shmuel's understanding of the Mishnah, the wife made the vow forbidding herself to use perfume and her husband confirmed the vow. [11]**Hence** it follows that **the husband is authorized to nullify** the vow if he wishes to do so.

[1]וְסָבַר רַבִּי יְהוּדָה הִיא נָתְנָה? [2]וְהָתְנַן: "רַבִּי יְהוּדָה אוֹמֵר: בְּיִשְׂרָאֵל, יוֹם אֶחָד, יְקַיֵּים"! [3]אֵימָא: "רַבִּי מֵאִיר וְרַבִּי יְהוּדָה וְרַבִּי יוֹסֵי אוֹמְרִים: הוּא נוֹתֵן; [4]וְרַבִּי אֶלְעָזָר אוֹמֵר: הִיא נָתְנָה". [5]וְאִם תִּמְצָא לוֹמַר זוּגֵי זוּגֵי קָתָנֵי, אֵימָא: [6]"רַבִּי מֵאִיר וְרַבִּי אֶלְעָזָר אוֹמְרִים: הִיא נָתְנָה; [7]רַבִּי יְהוּדָה וְרַבִּי יוֹסֵי אוֹמְרִים: הוּא נוֹתֵן". [8]וְהָא סְתָמָא דְּלָא כְּרַבִּי מֵאִיר. [9]וְסָבַר רַבִּי יוֹסֵי בַּעֲנִיּוֹת, [10]שֶׁלֹּא נָתַן קִצְבָּה? [11]אַלְמָא בַּעַל מָצֵי מֵיפַר.

LITERAL TRANSLATION

[1]But does Rabbi Yehudah maintain [that] she put? [2]But surely we have learned: "Rabbi Yehudah says: In [the case of] a non-priest, [if his vow was for] one day, he may keep [her]"!

[3]Say: "Rabbi Meir and Rabbi Yehudah and Rabbi Yose say: He puts; [4]and Rabbi Elazar says: She put."

[5]And if you wish to say [that the Tanna] taught pairs, say: [6]"Rabbi Meir and Rabbi Elazar say: She put; [7]Rabbi Yehudah and Rabbi Yose say: He puts." [8]And this anonymous [Mishnah] is not in accordance with Rabbi Meir.

[9]But does Rabbi Yose maintain [that] in [the case of] poor women, [10][this applies] if he did not set a limit? [11]Hence the husband is able to nullify [it].

RASHI

הכי גרסינן: והא תנן רבי יהודה אומר בישראל יום אחד יקיים — גבי "שלא תטעום" דאוקימתא בנדרה היא וקיים הוא, וקאמר רבי יהודה: יום אחד — יקיים, יתר מיכן — יוציא ויתן כתובה. **אלמא בעל מצי מיפר** — נדרי קישוט, מדקנים ליה כתובה על שקיימו.

NOTES

the vow. In such a case all agree that it is the husband who is regarded as having put his finger between his wife's teeth and caused himself to be bitten, and so he is required to divorce her and pay her her ketubah.

TRANSLATION AND COMMENTARY

[1]**But** if this is so, **a contradiction can be raised** between our Mishnah and the following Baraita, which states that a husband is allowed to nullify his wife's vows only if they cause the woman serious discomfort ("Every vow, and every binding oath *to afflict the soul*, her husband may let it stand, or her husband may make it void"; Numbers 30:14), or if they affect the intimate personal relationship between them ("These are the statutes which the Lord commanded Moses *between a man and his wife*"; Numbers 30:17). If the husband nullifies a vow made by his wife that involves self-affliction, the vow is nullified absolutely, even if her husband dies or divorces her. By contrast, if the husband nullifies a vow made by his wife that affects the personal relationship between them, the vow is nullified only as long as she remains married to him, but she is bound by the vow once again if he dies or divorces her and she remarries. [2]**These are the vows that the husband may nullify** absolutely: **Vows that involve self-affliction.** [3]For example, if she made a vow, saying, 'I will forever be forbidden the enjoyment of bathing **if I bathe** today,' or if she took an oath, saying, [4]**'I will not bathe,'** or if she made a vow, saying, [5]'I will forever be forbidden the enjoyment of perfumes **if I adorn myself** with perfumes today,' or if she took an oath, saying, [6]**'I will not adorn myself** with perfumes.' [7]**Rabbi Yose said: Those are not vows involving self-affliction** which the husband may nullify absolutely. **But the following are vows involving self-affliction** which the husband may nullify absolutely: For example, if she made a vow, saying, [8]**'I will not eat meat,' or 'I will not drink wine,' or 'I will not adorn myself** [71B] **with colored clothing.'"** Hence, according to Rabbi Yose, forswearing perfume is not self-affliction, and a husband cannot nullify his wife's vow to that effect. However, if our Mishnah refers to a husband who confirmed his wife's vow forbidding herself to use perfume, this implies that Rabbi Yose agrees that the husband *is* authorized to nullify such a vow!

הָכָא בְּמַאי עָסְקִינַן [9]The Gemara resolves this apparent contradiction: **With what are we dealing here?** [10]**With vows** affecting the intimate personal relationship **between husband and wife.** Although forswearing perfume is not self-affliction, it might affect the intimate personal relationship between the couple. If a wife refrains from using perfumes, her husband may find her repulsive and reject her. Thus the husband is authorized to nullify the vow, and if he fails to do so, he is regarded, according to Rabbi Yose, as someone who put his finger between his wife's teeth and caused himself to be bitten. Therefore he must divorce his wife and pay her her ketubah.

[1]וּרְמִינְהוּ: [2]״אֵלּוּ דְּבָרִים שֶׁהַבַּעַל מֵיפֵר: דְּבָרִים שֶׁיֵּשׁ בָּהֶן עִינּוּי נֶפֶשׁ: [3]׳אִם אֶרְחַץ׳, [4]׳אִם לֹא אֶרְחַץ׳, [5]׳אִם אֶתְקַשֵּׁט׳, [6]׳אִם לֹא אֶתְקַשֵּׁט׳. [7]אָמַר רַבִּי יוֹסֵי: אֵין אֵלּוּ נִדְרֵי עִינּוּי נֶפֶשׁ. וְאֵלּוּ הֵן נִדְרֵי עִינּוּי נֶפֶשׁ: [8]׳שֶׁלֹּא אוֹכַל בָּשָׂר׳, וְ׳שֶׁלֹּא אֶשְׁתֶּה יַיִן׳, וְ׳שֶׁלֹּא אֶתְקַשֵּׁט [71B] בְּבִגְדֵי צִבְעוֹנִין׳״. [9]הָכָא בְּמַאי עָסְקִינַן? [10]בִּדְבָרִים שֶׁבֵּינוֹ לְבֵינָהּ.

LITERAL TRANSLATION

[1]But a contradiction was raised (lit., "cast them together"): [2]"These are the vows [lit., 'things'] that the husband may nullify: Vows that involve self-affliction [lit., "affliction of the soul"]: [3]'If I bathe,' [4]'if I do not bathe,' [5]'if I adorn myself,' [6]'if I do not adorn myself.' [7]Rabbi Yose said: Those are not vows of self-affliction. But these are vows of self-affliction: [8]'That I will not eat meat,' or 'that I will not drink wine,' or 'that I will not adorn myself [71B] in colored clothing.'"

[9]With what are we dealing here? [10]With vows (lit., "things") that are between him and her.

RASHI

אם ארחץ אם לא ארחץ – בנדרים מפרש לה דאמרה: תיאסר הנאת רחיצה עלי אם ארחץ ושבועה שלא ארחץ, וכן אם אתקשט תיאסר הנאת קישוט עלי אם בבשמים אתקשט עד זמן פלוני. **אם לא אתקשט** – שבועה שלא אתקשט. **אין אלו נדרי עינוי נפש** – ואין הבעל מיפר, ד״לענות נפש״ כתיב. **בבגדי צבעונים** – גנאי ובזיון הוא לה ומתגנה עליו. **הכא במאי עסקינן** – קישוט דמתניתין דהכא, **בדברים שבינו לבינה** – סם המשיר את השער.

NOTES

וּרְמִינְהוּ But a contradiction was raised. The Rishonim ask: Why not explain that the Mishnah is referring to a wife who made a vow forbidding herself to adorn herself in colorful clothing, for even Rabbi Yose agrees that such a vow comes under the category of vows involving self-affliction which the husband is authorized to annul? *Rashba* answers that unless it is specified otherwise, the term "adornment" denotes using perfumes (see also *Ritva* and *Rivash*).

HALAKHAH

נִדְרֵי עִינּוּי נֶפֶשׁ Vows involving affliction of the soul. "A husband is authorized to nullify those vows made by his wife that involve self-affliction or affect the intimate personal relationship between the couple. Included under the category of vows involving self-affliction are vows made by a woman that she will not bathe or use perfume, even if she forbids herself from enjoying these things for only a single day, following the anonymous first Tanna.

TRANSLATION AND COMMENTARY

הָנִיחָא [1]The Gemara objects to this solution: **This** explanation of our Mishnah **poses no problem according to the** Amora **who says** that Rabbi Yose maintains that to forswear perfume is not self-affliction. [2]For, as we have seen, it nevertheless falls under the category of **vows** affecting the personal relationship **between husband and wife,** and as such **the husband may nullify** it while she is married to him. [3]**But according to the** Amora **who says** that, according to Rabbi Yose, the forswearing of perfumes is not considered a vow affecting the personal relationship between husband and wife, and **the husband may not nullify** it, [4]**what is there to say?** [5]**For it was stated** that the Amoraim disagree about whether, according to Rabbi Yose, a husband may nullify his wife's forswearing of perfumes, since it belongs to the category of **vows** affecting the personal relationship **between husband and wife.** [6]**Rav Huna said: The husband may nullify** such a vow, [7]but **Rav Adda bar Ahavah said: The husband may not nullify** such a vow, **for,** in popular parlance, [8]**we do not find a fox that died in the dust of its** own **hole,** because a fox grows accustomed to its surroundings. Similarly, a husband can accustom himself to his unadorned wife. Hence the forswearing of adornments does not belong to the category of vows affecting the personal relationship between husband and wife.

[1]הָנִיחָא לְמַאן דְּאָמַר: [2]דְּבָרִים שֶׁבֵּינוֹ לְבֵינָהּ הַבַּעַל מֵיפֵר. [3]אֶלָּא לְמַאן דְּאָמַר: אֵין הַבַּעַל מֵיפֵר, [4]מַאי אִיכָּא לְמֵימַר? [5]דְּאִתְּמַר: דְּבָרִים שֶׁבֵּינוֹ לְבֵינָהּ, [6]רַב הוּנָא אָמַר: הַבַּעַל מֵיפֵר. [7]רַב אַדָּא בַּר אַהֲבָה אָמַר: אֵין הַבַּעַל מֵיפֵר, [8]שֶׁלֹּא מָצִינוּ שׁוּעָל שֶׁמֵּת בַּעֲפַר פִּיר.

LITERAL TRANSLATION

[1]This is well according to the one who says: [2]Vows that are between him and her the husband may nullify. [3]But according to the one who says: The husband may not nullify, [4]what is there to say? [5]For it was stated: [Regarding] vows that are between him and her, [6]Rav Huna said: The husband may nullify [them]. [7]Rav Adda bar Ahavah said: The husband may not nullify [them], [8]for we do not find a fox that died in the dust of [its] hole.

RASHI

בעפר פיר — בעפר חור שהוא גדל שם. כלומר: בדבר שהוא רגיל בו, נקי הוא להשמר — שאינו מזיקו. **פיר** — כמו "פירא דכוורי" (כתובות עט,א) = גומא.

NOTES

הָנִיחָא לְמַאן דְּאָמַר This is well according to the one who says. Most of the Rishonim agree (see *Tosafot, Rabbenu Shimshon, Rashba,* and others) that the Gemara cannot be understood according to its plain sense — that Rav Huna and Rav Adda bar Ahavah disagree about whether or not a husband may nullify the vows made by his wife affecting the intimate personal relationship between them, for all agree that the husband may indeed nullify such vows, as the verse states (Numbers 30:17): "These are the statutes which the Lord commanded Moses, *between a man and his wife.*" Rather, the Amoraim disagree about whether or not, according to Rabbi Yose, a vow made by a wife forbidding adornments to herself belongs to the category of vows that affect the intimate personal relationship between husband and wife. According to this explanation, the Gemara's formulation is imprecise, and it is necessary either to assume that the Gemara is using certain terms in an atypical manner, or to amend the text slightly (see *Sefer HaYashar*).

שֶׁלֹּא מָצִינוּ שׁוּעָל For we do not find a fox. According to *Rashi,* as soon as the Gemara began dealing with the issue of vows affecting the intimate personal relationship between husband and wife, it reinterpreted the Mishnah, understanding that the Mishnah is referring not to "upper adornments" (perfumes and toiletries in general) but rather to "lower adornments" (a depilatory cream for removing the wife's pubic hair). Rav Adda bar Ahavah maintains that a vow forbidding one's wife the use of such a substance is not regarded as a vow affecting the intimate personal relationship between husband and wife, for "we do not find a fox that died in the dust of its hole." Just as a fox does not die in the dust of its own hole, so too will a husband not suffer if his wife refrains from removing her pubic hair. According to *Ra'ah, Ritva,* and others, the Gemara's understanding of adornment as a reference to perfumes and toiletries in general is consistent throughout the passage. Rav Adda bar Ahavah maintains that a vow forbidding one's wife to use perfume is not considered a vow affecting the intimate personal relationship between husband and wife, for "we do not find a fox that died in the dust of its hole." Just as a fox can accustom itself to the dust of its hole, so too can a husband accustom himself to his unadorned wife. The Aḥaronim bring support for this second explanation from the Mishnah's distinction between wealthy women and poor ones, a distinction that is relevant only with respect to "upper adornments."

HALAKHAH

According to some authorities (*Ramban* and others), such vows fall under the category of vows affecting the personal relationship between the couple. *Rambam* appears to say that a vow forbidding bathing falls under the category of vows involving self-affliction, whereas a vow forbidding adornments falls under the category of vows affecting the personal relationship between the couple (see *Kesef Mishneh* and *Leḥem Mishneh*)." (*Rambam, Sefer Hafla'ah, Hilkhot Nedarim* 12:1,4; *Shulḥan Arukh, Yoreh De'ah* 234:55,59.)

[1] אֶלָּא הָכָא בְּמַאי עָסְקִינַן? [2] כְּגוֹן דְּתָלֵינְהוּ לְקִישּׁוּטֶיהָ בְּתַשְׁמִישׁ הַמִּטָּה, [3] דְּאָמְרָה: ״יֵאָסֵר הֲנָאַת תַּשְׁמִישְׁךָ עָלַי אִם אֶתְקַשֵּׁט״, [4] כְּדַאֲמַר רַב כָּהֲנָא. [5] דַּאֲמַר רַב כָּהֲנָא: ״הֲנָאַת תַּשְׁמִישִׁי עָלֶיךָ״, [6] כּוֹפָהּ וּמְשַׁמַּשְׁתּוֹ. [7] ״הֲנָאַת תַּשְׁמִישְׁךָ עָלַי״, יָפֵר, [8] לְפִי שֶׁאֵין מַאֲכִילִין לְאָדָם דָּבָר הָאָסוּר לוֹ.

[9] וְלֹא תִּתְקַשֵּׁט וְלֹא תֵּאָסֵר!

LITERAL TRANSLATION

[1] Rather, with what are we dealing here? [2] For example, where she made sexual relations dependent upon her adornments, [3] if she said: "The pleasure of sexual relations with you shall be forbidden to me if I adorn myself," [4] as Rav Kahana said. [5] For Rav Kahana said: [If a woman says:] "The pleasure of sexual relations with me [shall be forbidden] to you," [6] he can compel her to have sexual relations with him. [7] [But if she says:] "The pleasure of sexual relations with you [shall be forbidden] to me," [8] he must nullify [her vow], because we do not feed a person something that is forbidden to him.

[9] But let her not adorn herself and let her not become forbidden!

TRANSLATION AND COMMENTARY

אֶלָּא [1] The Gemara answers: **Rather, with what are we dealing here** in our Mishnah? [2] **For example, where** the wife made a vow **making** her **sexual relations dependent on her adornments,** [3] **where she said: "The pleasure of sexual relations with you shall be forbidden to me if I adorn myself** with perfume." [4] This interpretation of our Mishnah is in keeping with what **Rav Kahana said,** that a wife's forswearing of sexual relations with her husband requires nullification. [5] **For Rav Kahana said: If a woman says** to her husband: **"The pleasure of sexual relations with me shall be forbidden to you,"** the vow is not binding, [6] and the husband **can compel** his wife **to have sexual relations with him.** [7] **But if** the woman **says: "The pleasure of sexual relations with you shall be forbidden to me,"** the husband **must nullify the vow,** [8] **because we do not feed a person something that is forbidden to him.** Although a wife cannot forbid her husband to enjoy sexual relations with her, she can nevertheless forbid herself to enjoy sexual relations with him, her obligation to cohabit with him notwithstanding. Her vow is binding, and a person cannot be forced to derive pleasure from what he or she has forsworn. When our Mishnah speaks of a vow forbidding a wife to adorn herself with perfumes, it refers to a wife who forswore sexual relations with her husband if she were to adorn herself with perfume. Such a vow affects the personal relationship between husband and wife, and Rabbi Yose agrees that the husband is authorized to nullify it. If he fails to nullify it, he is viewed, according to Rabbi Yose, as someone who put his finger between his wife's teeth and caused himself to be bitten, and he must therefore divorce his wife and pay her her ketubah.

וְלֹא תִּתְקַשֵּׁט [9] The Gemara objects: **But let** the wife **not adorn herself** with perfume **and let her not become forbidden** to engage in sexual relations with her husband! If Rabbi Yose maintains that a vow taken by a wife forbidding herself to use perfume involves neither self-affliction nor the personal relationship between husband and wife, why should the husband be authorized to nullify his wife's vow forbidding herself to engage in sexual relations with him if she adorns herself with perfume? Such a vow would not necessarily prevent sexual relations with her husband!

RASHI

אלא הכא במאי עסקינן דתלינהו לקישוטיה בתשמיש – ומשום הכי מצי מיפר, דדלמא מתקשטת, ומיתסרא הנאת תשמישו עליה. **כופה ומשמשתו** – שאינה יכולה לאסור עצמה עליו. אבל יכולה לאוסרו עליה, שתהא היא מודרת ולא הוא, כגון הנאת תשמישו עליה – דצריך הוא להפר, שלא יאכילנה דבר האסור לה. **ולא תתקשט ולא תאסר** – לרבי יוסי, כיון דאמר אין אלו נדרי עינוי נפש היאך יכול להפר? ואי משום דתלינהו בתשמיש – לא תתקשט ולא תיאסר.

HALAKHAH

דְּתָלֵינְהוּ לְקִישּׁוּטֶיהָ בְּתַשְׁמִישׁ הַמִּטָּה **If she made sexual relations dependent upon her adornments.** "If a wife makes a vow forbidding herself to wear perfume, or if she vows that sexual relations with her husband will be forbidden to her if she so adorns herself, and the husband hears the vow but does not nullify it, he must divorce her and pay her her ketubah." (*Shulhan Arukh, Yoreh De'ah* 235:3; *Even HaEzer* 74:2.)

הֲנָאַת תַּשְׁמִישִׁי עָלֶיךָ **The pleasure of sexual relations with me shall be forbidden to you.** "If a wife says to her husband: 'The pleasure of sexual relations with me shall be forbidden to you,' the vow is not binding, and need not be nullified. But if she says: 'The pleasure of sexual relations with you shall be forbidden to me,' the vow is binding and must be nullified, for we do not feed a person something that is forbidden to him." (*Rambam, Sefer Hafla'ah, Hilkhot Nedarim* 12:9; *Shulhan Arukh, Yoreh De'ah* 234:67.)

TRANSLATION AND COMMENTARY

אִם כֵּן [1]The Gemara answers: **If** the wife refrains from using perfume, people **will call her repulsive.** Since she cannot bear the shame and social rejection, she will be forced to wear perfume, and as a consequence she will be forbidden to engage in sexual relations with her husband.

וְתִתְקַשֵּׁט וְתֵאָסֵר [2]The Gemara now raises an objection: If the Mishnah is indeed referring to a wife who made a vow forbidding herself to engage in sexual relations with her husband if she wore perfume, and her husband confirmed the vow, why must he divorce her immediately and pay her her ketubah? **Let** the wife **adorn herself and become forbidden** to engage in sexual relations with her husband, [3]**whether, according to Bet Shammai,** for **two weeks,** [4]**or, according to Bet Hillel,** for **one week,** and only then will her husband be compelled to grant her a divorce! As we have learned elsewhere in the Mishnah (above, 61b), if a husband forswears sexual relations with his wife, she must wait **two weeks, according to Bet Shammai,** or **one week, according to Bet Hillel,** before he can be compelled to grant her a divorce and pay her her ketubah. Why, then, should the husband be required to divorce his wife immediately if he confirms a vow taken by his wife which results in her being forbidden to engage in sexual relations with him?

הָנֵי מִילֵּי [5]The Gemara explains: The Mishnah's ruling that the husband is given one or two weeks before he is compelled to divorce his wife **applies** only if the husband **made a vow forbidding** himself to engage in sexual relations with his wife. In such a case, she allows her husband some time to seek a dispensation nullifying his vow, [6]**for she thinks** to herself: "My husband **is angry with me,** and this is why he made the vow. [7]**But he will soon calm down** and secure a dispensation nullifying his vow." [8]**But here,** in our Mishnah, the wife **made a vow forbidding** herself to engage in sexual relations with her husband, **and** her husband **was silent,** and thus confirmed the vow. Hence, the husband must grant his wife an immediate divorce, because she cannot bear to continue living with him. [9]**She thinks** to herself: **"Since he remained silent** and did not nullify my vow, **he must hate me,** and he will never seek out a Sage's dispensation nullifying the vow."

[1]אִם כֵּן, קָרוּ לָהּ מְנוּוֶּלֶת. [2]וְתִתְקַשֵּׁט וְתֵאָסֵר, [3]אִי לְבֵית שַׁמַּאי שְׁתֵּי שַׁבָּתוֹת, [4]אִי לְבֵית הִלֵּל שַׁבָּת אַחַת! [5]הָנֵי מִילֵּי הֵיכָא דְּאַדְּרָהּ אִיהוּ, [6]דְּסָבְרָה: ״מִירְתַּח רָתַח עִילָּוַאי, [7]וְהָשְׁתָּא מוֹתִיב דַּעְתֵּיהּ״. [8]אֲבָל הָכָא דְּנָדְרָה אִיהִי וְשָׁתֵיק לָהּ, [9]סָבְרָה: ״מִדְּאִישְׁתַּק, מִיסְנָא הוּא דְּסָנֵי לִי״.

LITERAL TRANSLATION

[1]If so, they will call her repulsive.

[2]But let her adorn herself and let her become forbidden, [3]either according to Bet Shammai [for] two weeks, [4]or according to Bet Hillel [for] one week!

[5]These [rulings] apply (lit., "these words") when he forbade her with a vow, [6]for she thinks: "He is angry with me, [7]and now his mind will be calmed." [8]But here [seeing] that she made a vow and he was silent, [9]she thinks: "Since he was silent, he surely hates me."

RASHI

אם כן קרו לה מנוולת – וכי מבזו – מקשטא, אישתכח דנדר זה אוסרה עליו. לפיכך יכול להפר משום דברים שבינו לבינה. **ותתקשט ותאסר, אי לבית שמאי** – אמאי יוציא לאלתר ויתן כתובה, ותתקשט ותאסר? והות ליה כמדיר את אשתו מתשמיש המטה. ותנן בפרק ״אף על פי״: לבית שמאי שתי שבתות, ולבית הלל שבת אחת! **הני מילי** – שיש לו זמן, שמא ימצא פתח לנדרו – היכא דאדרה איהו. **אבל היכא דנדרה איהי ואישתיק** – ולא היפר אינה יכולה לגור אצלו כלל, ואפילו עד שתאסר על ידי קישוט – דסברה: מיסנא סני לי.

NOTES

קָרוּ לָהּ מְנוּוֶּלֶת **They will call her repulsive.** Our commentary follows *Rashi,* who explains that if the wife refrains from using perfume, people will call her a repulsive woman, and when she is no longer able to bear the shame and the rejection, she will begin to use perfume and become forbidden to her husband. Thus the vow can be regarded as a vow affecting the intimate personal relationship between husband and wife which the husband is authorized to nullify. *Ritva* suggests that since the wife will suffer shame when her neighbors call her a repulsive woman, her husband is authorized to nullify the vow on the grounds that it causes her serious distress.

HALAKHAH

אִי לְבֵית הִלֵּל שַׁבָּת אַחַת **Or according to Bet Hillel for one week.** "If someone makes a vow forbidding himself to cohabit with his wife, we wait seven days, after which he must grant her a divorce and pay her her ketubah, following Bet Hillel. This ruling applies even if the husband is a sailor whose conjugal obligation is only once in six months." (*Rambam, Sefer Nashim, Hilkhot Ishut* 14:6; *Shulḥan Arukh, Even HaEzer* 76:9.)

הֵיכָא דְּאַדְּרָהּ אִיהוּ **Where he forbade her with a vow.** "If someone makes a vow forbidding his wife to wear perfume, and he makes sexual relations with her dependent on her adornments, saying: 'The pleasure of sexual relations with you shall be forbidden to me if you adorn yourself,' she may adorn herself so that sexual relations

TRANSLATION AND COMMENTARY

רַבִּי יוֹסֵי אוֹמֵר [1]We learned in our Mishnah: **"Rabbi Yose says: With** respect to **a poor woman,** who is not accustomed to wearing much perfume, [2]if her husband makes a vow forbidding her to apply a certain perfume, and **he does not limit** the time during which she is forbidden to do so, he must divorce her immediately and pay her her ketubah. But if he forbids her the use of a certain perfume for a limited period of time, he cannot be compelled to divorce her and to pay her her ketubah. Instead, she must wait out that period." [3]The Gemara asks: **What is the definition of** this **limit?** Surely it stands to reason that if a husband prohibits his wife from using a perfume for an extended period of time, he should be regarded as not having set a limit to the period of time!

LITERAL TRANSLATION

[1]"Rabbi Yose says: In [the case of] poor women, [2][this applies] if he did not set a limit." [3]And how much is a limit?

[4]Rav Yehudah said in the name of Shmuel: Twelve months. [5]Rabbah bar Bar Ḥanah said in the name of Rabbi Yoḥanan: Ten years. [6]Rav Ḥisda said in the name of Avimi: [Until] a Festival, for the daughters of Israel adorn themselves on a Festival.

[7]"And in [the case of] rich women, [this applies if he set a limit of] thirty days." [8]What is different [about] thirty days?

---

[1]"רַבִּי יוֹסֵי אוֹמֵר: בַּעֲנִיּוֹת, [2]שֶׁלֹּא נָתַן קִצְבָּה". [3]וְכַמָּה קִצְבָּה?

[4]אָמַר רַב יְהוּדָה אָמַר שְׁמוּאֵל: שְׁנֵים עָשָׂר חֹדֶשׁ. [5]רַבָּה בַּר בַּר חָנָה אָמַר רַבִּי יוֹחָנָן: עֶשֶׂר שָׁנִים. [6]רַב חִסְדָּא אָמַר אֲבִימִי: רֶגֶל, שֶׁכֵּן בְּנוֹת יִשְׂרָאֵל מִתְקַשְׁטוֹת בָּרֶגֶל.

[7]"וּבַעֲשִׁירוֹת, שְׁלֹשִׁים יוֹם". [8]מַאי שְׁנָא שְׁלֹשִׁים יוֹם?

RASHI

וכמה קצבה — כלומר, אם נתן קצבה, עד כמה לא כייפינן ליה להוציא?

אָמַר רַב יְהוּדָה [4]**Rav Yehudah said in the name of Shmuel:** If the husband makes a vow prohibiting his wife from using a certain perfume for a period of **twelve months,** he cannot be compelled to divorce her and pay her her ketubah. Instead, she must bear with him and refrain from using that perfume for twelve months. But if he forbids her its use for longer, he must divorce her immediately and pay her her ketubah. [5]**Rabbah bar Bar Ḥanah said in the name of Rabbi Yoḥanan:** If the husband prohibits his wife from using a certain perfume for up to **ten years,** he cannot be compelled to divorce her, but if he prohibits her from using it for longer than this, he must divorce her immediately and pay her her ketubah. [6]**Rav Ḥisda said in the name of Avimi:** If the husband prohibits his wife from using a certain perfume until **the** next **Festival** (Pesaḥ, Shavuot, or Sukkot), he cannot be compelled to divorce her. But if he prohibits her from using the perfume for a period extending beyond the next Festival, he must grant her an immediate divorce, **for the daughters of Israel** are accustomed to **adorn themselves** with perfume **on** each of the three **Festivals,** and the husband's vow is regarded as being without limit.

וּבַעֲשִׁירוֹת [7]Our Mishnah continues: **"But with** respect to **a rich woman,** if her husband forbids her to apply a certain perfume for **thirty days** or more, he can be compelled to grant her a divorce and to pay her her ketubah. [8]The Gemara asks: **What is different about thirty days?** What is the special significance of a thirty-day prohibition against the wife's use of perfume?

NOTES

שֶׁלֹּא נָתַן קִצְבָּה **If he did not set a limit.** A similar dispute is recorded in the Jerusalem Talmud. The viewpoint cited in the Babylonian Talmud in the name of Rabbi Yoḥanan is cited in the Jerusalem Talmud in the name of Ulla. In the Jerusalem Talmud, Rabbi Yoḥanan is cited as saying: "Except for a Festival." Some of the commentators identify this viewpoint with what is cited in the Babylonian Talmud in the name of Rav Ḥisda. But it can be argued that what is cited in the Jerusalem Talmud is yet another viewpoint — that if the husband makes a vow forbidding his wife to adorn herself, but excludes the Festivals from the period during which the vow will be in effect, he cannot be compelled to divorce her and pay her her ketubah, even if he has not limited the time she will be forbidden to adorn herself.

HALAKHAH

with her husband are now forbidden, and then after seven days her husband must divorce her and pay her her ketubah, following the Sages of the Mishnah (*Rosh*). Some authorities (*Rambam* and others) maintain that if a poor woman's husband makes a vow, forbidding her to adorn herself with perfume, we wait a year, after which the husband must either seek a nullification of his vow or divorce his wife and pay her her ketubah. In the case of a rich woman we wait only thirty days," following Rabbi Yose and Shmuel. (*Rambam, Sefer Nashim, Hilkhot Ishut* 13:8; *Shulḥan Arukh, Even HaEzer* 74:1.)

[1]אָמַר אַבַּיֵי: שֶׁכֵּן אִשָּׁה חֲשׁוּבָה נֶהֱנֵית מֵרֵיחַ קִשּׁוּטֶיהָ שְׁלֹשִׁים יוֹם.

מִשְׁנָה [2]הַמַּדִּיר אֶת אִשְׁתּוֹ שֶׁלֹּא תֵּלֵךְ לְבֵית אָבִיהָ, בִּזְמַן שֶׁהוּא עִמָּהּ בָּעִיר, [3]חוֹדֶשׁ אֶחָד, יְקַיֵּים; [4]שְׁנַיִם, יוֹצִיא וְיִתֵּן כְּתוּבָּה. [5]וּבִזְמַן שֶׁהוּא בְּעִיר אַחֶרֶת, [6]רֶגֶל אֶחָד, יְקַיֵּים; [7]שְׁלֹשָׁה, יוֹצִיא וְיִתֵּן כְּתוּבָּה.

LITERAL TRANSLATION

[1]Abaye said: Because a distinguished woman derives pleasure from the scent of her adornments [for] thirty days.

MISHNAH [2][If] someone prohibits his wife with a vow from going to her father's house, when he [the father] is with her in the town, [3][if the vow was for] one month, he may keep [her]; [4][if it was for] two, he must divorce [her] and pay [her her] ketubah. [5]But when he [the father] is in another town, [6][if the vow was for] one Festival, he may keep [her]; [7][if it was for] three, he must divorce [her] and pay [her] ketubah.

TRANSLATION AND COMMENTARY

אָמַר אַבַּיֵי [1]**Abaye said:** If the husband forbids his wife to adorn herself with perfume for thirty days, he can be compelled to divorce her immediately, **because a distinguished woman derives pleasure from the scent of her adornments for** up to **thirty days** after she applies them. Thus it is only after thirty days have passed that a woman begins to suffer from her husband's vow forbidding her to use perfume.

MISHNAH הַמַּדִּיר אֶת אִשְׁתּוֹ [2]**If someone makes a vow forbidding his wife to go to her father's house,** and the vow is formulated in such a manner that it is able to take effect, **and the wife's father is** living **with her in the** same **town,** so that she is used to visiting him on a regular basis, [3]and if the husband forbids his wife to go to her father's house **for** up to **one month,** he **may keep her** as his wife. [4]But **if** he prohibits her from visiting her father for period of **two months,** and his wife is unwilling to continue living with him without seeing her father, **he must divorce her and pay** her **her ketubah.** [5]**But if the** wife's **father is** living **in another town,** so that she is used to visiting him less frequently, the law is as follows: [6]If the husband prohibits his wife from visiting her father on the next **Festival,** when she would ordinarily pay him a visit, he **may keep her** as his wife. [7]But **if** he forbids her from going to her father's house on the next **three** Festivals, **he must divorce her and pay** her **her ketubah.**

RASHI

נהנית מריח קשוטיה — שנתקשטה לפני הנדר.

משנה כשהן בעיר אחרת — דרך נשים ללכת אצלם ברגלים.

רגל אחד — מצית מוקמא אנפשה, שלשה — לא מצית מוקמא.

ובגמרא פריך: הא שנים — מאי?

NOTES

שֶׁכֵּן אִשָּׁה חֲשׁוּבָה **Because a distinguished woman.** The Geonim explain that even a distinguished woman who never goes without perfume applies it only once in thirty days (see also *Rid,* who has a slightly different reading from that found in the standard text, but explains the passage in the same way). *Melekhet Shlomo* suggests that a distinguished woman does not personally engage in housework, for she has maids who take care of all her household chores, and she is able to remain fresh and clean even if she applies perfume only once a month. But an ordinary woman who does her housework herself must apply perfume more frequently.

הַמַּדִּיר אֶת אִשְׁתּוֹ **If someone forbids his wife with a vow.** The Rishonim ask: How can a man make a vow forbidding his wife to go to her father's house, or to a house of mourning, or to a house of feasting? A person cannot forbid to another person something that is not his!

Most Rishonim explain that the husband took a vow making his wife's sexual relations with him or her benefiting from his property dependent upon her refraining from visiting her father's house or a house of mourning or feasting. Alternatively, we are dealing here with a case where the wife made a vow forbidding to herself all the fruit in the world if she were to visit her father or a house of mourning or feasting (following Shmuel above).

Ri Migash suggests a novel explanation: The vow made by the husband forbidding his wife to visit her father or a house of mourning or feasting is indeed null and void. But since in practice the husband will be able to prevent his wife from visiting her father or fulfilling her ordinary social obligations, he can be required to grant her an immediate divorce and pay her her ketubah.

HALAKHAH

הַמַּדִּיר אֶת אִשְׁתּוֹ שֶׁלֹּא תֵּלֵךְ לְבֵית אָבִיהָ **If someone prohibits his wife with a vow from going to her father's house.** "If someone makes a vow forbidding his wife to go to her father's house by forbidding her to engage in sexual intercourse with him if she visits her father for more than thirty days, if the wife's father lives in the same town, or until after the next Festival, if he lives elsewhere, he may remain married to her for seven days, but then he must divorce her and pay her her ketubah," following the Mishnah. No distinction is made between the wife of a priest and the wife of a non-priest, contrary to the viewpoint of Abaye below (*Maggid Mishneh*). (*Rambam, Sefer Nashim, Hilkhot Ishut* 13:12; *Shulḥan Arukh, Even HaEzer* 74:4; *Yoreh De'ah* 235:6.)

TRANSLATION AND COMMENTARY

הַמַּדִּיר אֶת אִשְׁתּוֹ [1]**If someone takes a vow forbidding his wife to go to a house of mourning** in order to comfort the bereaved, **or to a house of feasting** in order to participate in a wedding celebration, and the husband refuses to take any steps to nullify the vow, [2]**he must divorce** his wife immediately **and pay** her **her ketubah,** [3]**because** by prohibiting his wife from fulfilling these social obligations, **he** is regarded as having **locked doors before her,** and she is not required to accept such limitations. [4]**But if** the husband **claims** that he forbade his wife to go to the house of mourning or to the house of feasting **because of some other** reason (as will be explained in the Gemara), **he is permitted** to make such a vow, and he cannot be compelled to grant his wife a divorce.

אָמַר לָהּ [5]If a wife makes a vow involving self-affliction or affecting the personal relationship between husband and wife, and her husband **says to her:** "I agree to annul your vow **on condition that you tell So-and-so what you told me or what I told you,"** and she is then unable to report the conversation, her husband must divorce her and pay her her ketubah; since he made the nullification of her vow dependent on her fulfilling an impossible condition, he in effect confirmed the vow. [6]Similarly, if the husband tells his wife that he agrees to annul her vow on condition **that she "fill and pour out on the dunghill"** (i.e., thwart the procreative process), **he must divorce her and pay** her **her ketubah.**

GEMARA הָא גוּפָא קַשְׁיָא [7]The Gemara begins by pointing out that the Mishnah **itself is self-contradictory.** [8]First it **says:** "If the wife's father lives in another town and her husband prohibits her from visiting her father on the next **Festival**, when she would ordinarily pay him a visit, the husband **may keep** her as his

[1]הַמַּדִּיר אֶת אִשְׁתּוֹ שֶׁלֹּא תֵּלֵךְ לְבֵית הָאֵבֶל אוֹ לְבֵית הַמִּשְׁתֶּה, [2]יוֹצִיא וְיִתֵּן כְּתוּבָּה, [3]מִפְּנֵי שֶׁנּוֹעֵל בְּפָנֶיהָ. [4]וְאִם הָיָה טוֹעֵן מִשּׁוּם דָּבָר אַחֵר, רַשַּׁאי. [5]אָמַר לָהּ: "עַל מְנָת שֶׁתֹּאמְרִי לִפְלוֹנִי מַה שֶּׁאָמַרְתְּ לִי אוֹ מַה שֶּׁאָמַרְתִּי לָךְ", [6]אוֹ שֶׁתְּהֵא מְמַלְּאָה וּמְעָרָה לָאַשְׁפָּה, יוֹצִיא וְיִתֵּן כְּתוּבָּה.

גמרא [7]הָא גּוּפָא קַשְׁיָא: [8]אָמְרַתְּ: "רֶגֶל אֶחָד, יְקַיֵּים".

LITERAL TRANSLATION

[1][If] someone prohibits his wife with a vow from going to a house of mourning or to a house of feasting, [2]he must divorce [her] and pay [her her] ketubah, [3]because he locks [doors] before her. [4]But if he claimed [that he acted] because of something else, he is permitted.

[5][If] he said to her: "On condition that you tell So-and-so what you told me or what I told you," [6]or [if he told her] that she should fill and pour out on the dunghill, he must divorce [her] and pay [her] ketubah.

GEMARA [7]This itself is difficult: [8]You said: "[If the vow was for] one Festival, he may keep her."

RASHI

שנועל בפניה – בגמרא מפרש. **מחמת דבר אחר** – בגמרא מפרש. **שתאמרי לפלוני** – בגמרא מפרש. **שתהא ממלאה ומערה** – בגמרא מפרש.

NOTES

שֶׁלֹּא תֵּלֵךְ לְבֵית הָאֵבֶל **From going to a house of mourning.** *Ri Migash* asks: Why do the Sages not set a time limit when a husband forbids his wife to go to a house of mourning or to a wedding, as they do when the husband prohibits his wife from visiting her father? He answers: If a man forbade his wife to go to her father's house for up to a month, he need not divorce her, because if she does not visit her father during that month, she can always visit him the next month. But if a man prohibits his wife from going to a house of mourning or to a wedding for even less than a month, he must divorce her immediately, for a death or a wedding may occur at any time, and there is concern that if the wife does not participate in other people's celebrations or bereavements, they will refrain from participating in her future celebrations or bereavements.

רֶגֶל אֶחָד, יְקַיֵּים **If the vow was for one Festival, he may keep her.** The Gemara argues that there is an internal contradiction between what the Mishnah says regarding one Festival and what it says regarding three Festivals, but it does not ask a similar question regarding what the Mishnah says about one month and two. Since the second month follows immediately after the first, the term "two" can be understood to mean the beginning of the second month. If the husband forbids his wife to visit her father for one month, he need not divorce her, but if he forbids her to visit for any longer, he must divorce her immediately.

HALAKHAH

הַמַּדִּיר אֶת אִשְׁתּוֹ שֶׁלֹּא תֵּלֵךְ לְבֵית הָאֵבֶל **If someone prohibits his wife with a vow from going to a house of mourning.** "Someone who makes a vow forbidding his wife to go to a house of mourning or to a wedding by prohibiting her from engaging in sexual intercourse with him if she goes to one of these places, must divorce her and pay her her ketubah after one week. If he claims that he forbade his wife to make these visits on account of the licentious men found there, and it is established that such people were indeed found there, he is believed, and is therefore not required to divorce her. But if it is not so established, he is not believed," following the Mishnah. (*Rambam, Sefer Nashim, Hilkhot Ishut* 13:13; *Shulḥan Arukh, Even HaEzer* 74:6.)

[1]הָא שְׁנַיִם, יוֹצִיא וְיִתֵּן כְּתוּבָּה. [2]אֵימָא סֵיפָא: ״שְׁלֹשָׁה, [3]יוֹצִיא וְיִתֵּן כְּתוּבָּה״. [4]הָא שְׁנַיִם, יְקַיֵּים! [5]אֲמַר אַבַּיֵי: סֵיפָא אֲתָאָן לְכֹהֶנֶת, [6]וְרַבִּי יְהוּדָה הִיא. [7]רַבָּה בַּר עוּלָּא אֲמַר: לָא קַשְׁיָא. [8]כָּאן בִּרְדוּפָה; כָּאן בְּשֶׁאֵינָהּ רְדוּפָה.

LITERAL TRANSLATION

[1]This [implies that if the vow was for] two, he must divorce [her] and pay [her] ketubah. [2]Say the last clause: "[If it was for] three, [3]he must divorce [her] and pay [her] ketubah." [4]But [if the vow was for] two, he may keep [her]!

[5]Abaye said: [In] the last clause we have come to the [case of the] wife of a priest, [6]and it is [according to] Rabbi Yehudah.

[7]Rabbah bar Ulla said: There is no difficulty. [8]Here when she is anxious [to visit]; here when she is not anxious [to visit].

TRANSLATION AND COMMENTARY

wife." [1]**This implies that if** he prohibits her from going to her father's house on the next **two** Festivals, [2]**he must divorce her and pay** her **her ketubah.** [3]But if we **consider the next clause** of the Mishnah, it becomes clear that this inference is problematic, for the next clause says: "But if the husband prohibits his wife from going to her father's house on the next **three** Festivals, **he must divorce her and pay** her **her ketubah."** [4]**This implies that if** he prohibits her from visiting her father on the next **two** Festivals, **he may keep** her as his wife. How can these two contradictory conclusions be reconciled?

אֲמַר אַבַּיֵי [5]**Abaye said:** There is really no contradiction. In the first clause we are dealing with the wife of a non-priest, whereas **in the second clause we are referring to the case of the wife of a priest.** [6]**And** the Mishnah **follows** the viewpoint of **Rabbi Yehudah,** who distinguishes between the wife of a non-priest and the wife of a priest with respect to a vow taken by the husband forbidding his wife to derive any material benefit from him (see above, 70a). A priest is given an extra month to secure a Sage's dispensation nullifying his vow before he is compelled to grant his wife a divorce, because once he divorces her he is forbidden to take her back again as his wife. Thus the meaning of our Mishnah is as follows: If a woman is married to a non-priest and her father lives in another town, and her husband prohibits her from visiting her father on the next Festival, he may keep her as his wife. But if he prohibits her from going to her father on the next two Festivals, he must divorce her and pay her her ketubah. And if the woman is married to a priest and her husband prohibits her from visiting her father on the next two Festivals, he may keep her as his wife. But if he prohibits her from paying her father a visit on the next three Festivals, he must divorce her and pay her her ketubah.

רַבָּה בַּר עוּלָּא [7]The Gemara now offers a second resolution to the apparent contradiction: **Rabbah bar Ulla said: There is no difficulty** in the Mishnah, for the two clauses are dealing with different cases. **Here** in the first clause we are dealing with a wife who **is anxious** to visit her father. If her husband prohibits her from doing so on more than one Festival, she suffers great distress. Consequently, her husband must grant her a divorce and pay her her ketubah. [8]But **here** in the next clause we are dealing with a wife who is **not** particularly **anxious** to visit her father. In such a case, the husband cannot be compelled to divorce his wife unless he prohibits her from visiting her father on the next three Festivals.

RASHI

גמרא סיפא – דקתני ״שלשה יוציא״, הא שנים יקיים – אתאן לכהנת. רדופה – לילך לבית אביה תמיד – שנים יוציא. שאינה רדופה – שנים יקיים. דכתיב – לא גרסינן.

NOTES

סֵיפָא אֲתָאָן לְכֹהֶנֶת **In the last clause we have come to the case of the wife of a priest.** A question may be raised: If the Mishnah follows the viewpoint of Rabbi Yehudah, who distinguishes between the wife of a non-priest and the wife of a priest, why does that distinction not find any expression in the first half of the ruling, with respect to a wife whose father lives in the same town?

Bet Aharon suggests that the Mishnah's ruling that the husband must divorce his wife immediately if he prohibits her with a vow from visiting her father for two months was formulated so that it could be understood in two ways, depending on the husband's status. If he is a non-priest, he must divorce her at the beginning of the second month. But if he is a priest, he is required to divorce her only at the end of the second month.

Ḥever Ben Ḥayyim argues that if the wife's father is living in the same town, even Rabbi Yehudah agrees that we do not distinguish between the wife of a non-priest and the wife of a priest, for the woman suffers particular humiliation and shame if she is forbidden to visit her father who lives so close to her.

כָּאן בִּרְדוּפָה **Here she is anxious to visit.** Our commentary follows *Rashi* and *Rivan,* who explain that an "anxious" woman is one who is eager to visit her father frequently. If a husband prohibits her from visiting her father for more than one Festival, he must grant her an immediate divorce, for he causes her great distress. A woman who is "not anxious" is less concerned about seeing her father. She need not be granted a divorce unless her husband has prohibited her from visiting her father for three Festivals.

According to *Rashi,* there is no connection between Rabbah bar Ulla's remark and Rabbi Yoḥanan's Midrashic

[1]"אָז הָיִיתִי בְעֵינָיו כְּמוֹצֵאת שָׁלוֹם". [2]אָמַר רַבִּי יוֹחָנָן: כְּכַלָּה שֶׁנִּמְצֵאת שְׁלֵמָה בְּבֵית חָמִיהָ, [3]וּרְדוּפָה לֵילֵךְ וּלְהַגִּיד שִׁבְחָהּ בְּבֵית אָבִיהָ.

[4]"וְהָיָה בַיּוֹם הַהוּא, נְאֻם ה׳, תִּקְרְאִי אִישִׁי, וְלֹא תִקְרְאִי לִי עוֹד בַּעְלִי". [5]אָמַר רַבִּי יוֹחָנָן: כְּכַלָּה בְּבֵית חָמִיהָ, [6]וְלֹא כְּכַלָּה בְּבֵית אָבִיהָ.

[7]"הַמַּדִּיר אֶת אִשְׁתּוֹ, וכו׳". [8]בִּשְׁלָמָא לְבֵית הַמִּשְׁתֶּה [72A] אִיכָּא נוֹעֵל בְּפָנֶיהָ. [9]אֶלָּא לְבֵית הָאֵבֶל, [10]מַאי נוֹעֵל בְּפָנֶיהָ אִיכָּא?

LITERAL TRANSLATION

[1]"Then I was in his eyes like one who finds peace." [2]Rabbi Yoḥanan said: Like a bride who is found perfect in her father-in-law's house, [3]and is anxious to go and tell her praise in her father's house.

[4]"And it shall be on that day, says the Lord, that you shall call me Ishi ['my man'], and you shall no more call me Ba'ali ['my husband']." [5]Rabbi Yoḥanan said: Like a bride in her father-in-law's house, [6]and not like a bride in her father's house.

[7]"[If] someone prohibits his wife with a vow, etc." [8]Granted [that with respect] to a house of feasting [72A] there is locking [doors] before her. [9]But with respect to a house of mourning, [10]what locking [doors] before her is there?

TRANSLATION AND COMMENTARY

אָז הָיִיתִי בְּעֵינָיו [1]Having mentioned a wife who was anxious to visit her father, the Gemara now cites a Midrashic exposition of a Biblical verse dealing with the same matter. The verse says (Song of Songs 8:10): **"Then I was in his eyes like one who finds peace."** [2]**Rabbi Yoḥanan said:** The maiden is telling her brothers that she is regarded by her beloved **like a bride who is found perfect in her father-in-law's house,** [3]**and who is anxious to go and tell in her father's house the praise** that was lavished upon her by her husband and his family.

וְהָיָה בַּיּוֹם הַהוּא [4]The Gemara continues with a related Midrashic exposition. The verse says (Hosea 2:18): **"And it shall be on that day, says the Lord, that you shall call me Ishi ['my man'], and you shall no more call me Ba'ali ['my husband']."** [5]**Rabbi Yoḥanan said:** The verse speaks of the day when Israel will be regarded **as a bride** who is living **in her father-in-law's house** following her marriage, and who is already referring to her marriage partner by the intimate term "my man," [6]**and not as a bride** who is still living **in her father's house** and awaiting her marriage, and who still refers to her marriage partner by the less personal term "my husband."

הַמַּדִּיר אֶת אִשְׁתּוֹ [7]We learned in our Mishnah: **"If someone makes a vow forbidding his wife to go** to a house of mourning or to a house of feasting, he must divorce her immediately and pay her her ketubah." [8]**Granted that** if the husband forbade his wife from going to **a house of feasting, he** can be compelled to grant her an immediate divorce, [72A] for he is regarded as having **locked** his wife **in** a prison by preventing her from participating in joyous events. [9]**But** if a husband forbade his wife to go to **a house of mourning,** [10]**why** should he be regarded as having **locked** her **in** a prison? In what way does the wife suffer if her husband prevents her from making a condolence visit?

RASHI

אישי — לשון אישות ונישואין. **בכלה בבית חמיה** — שכבר ניסת; וגם לבה בבעלה, ואינה בושה הימנו. **איכא נועל בפניה** — דלת של שמחה ופיקוח לער.

NOTES

exposition other than that they both refer to an "anxious" woman. *Tosafot* and most other Rishonim follow *Rabbenu Ḥananel*, who explains that an "anxious" woman refers to a newlywed bride who wishes to go to her paternal home and report about the praise lavished upon her in her father-in-law's house. Such a woman must be granted an immediate divorce if her husband prohibits her from visiting her father for more than one Festival. A woman who is "not anxious" is one who has already been married for more than one Festival, who is no longer so concerned about reporting her praise to her father. Such a woman need not be granted a divorce unless her husband has forbidden her to visit her father for three Festivals. These Rishonim read: *"As it is written*: 'Then I was in his eyes, etc.' *And* Rabbi Yoḥanan said, etc." According to this explanation, Rabbi Yoḥanan's exposition was cited by Rabbah bar Ulla in order to explain what he meant by an "anxious" woman.

כְּמוֹצֵאת שָׁלוֹם Like one who finds peace. The word "finds" alludes to marriage, as the verse states (Proverbs 18:22): "He who finds a wife finds a good thing." The word "peace" (שָׁלוֹם) alludes to perfection (שְׁלֵימוּת). Thus the verse refers to a bride who is anxious to report to her father that the woman whom her husband has taken in marriage has been found to be perfect, that her husband has found her free of blemishes (*Rivan*).

נוֹעֵל בְּפָנֶיהָ Locking doors before her. *Rashi* and others explain this expression metaphorically, that a husband who prohibits his wife from visiting a house of feasting or a house of mourning locks the door to happiness during times of celebration and the door to condolence during times of bereavement. *Rambam* understands the expression literally, as locking her in a prison and barring her from fulfilling her ordinary social obligations.

LITERAL TRANSLATION

[1] [A Tanna] taught: "Tomorrow she will die and nobody will eulogize her." [2] And there are [some] who say: "Nobody will treat her with respect." [3] It was taught: "Rabbi Meir used to say: [4] What is [it] that is written: 'It is better to go to a house of mourning than to go to a house of feasting, for that is the end of every man, and the living will lay it to his heart'? [5] What is 'and the living will lay it to his heart'? [6] Matters relating to death. [7] If he eulogizes, they will eulogize him; [8] if he buries, they will bury him; [9] if he lifts up [his voice], they will lift up [their voices]; [10] if he accompanies [the deceased], they will accompany him; [11] if he carries [the deceased], they will carry him."

[12] "But if he claimed [that he acted] because of something else, he is permitted." [13] What is "something else"?

[1] תָּנָא: "לְמָחָר הִיא מֵתָה וְאֵין כָּל בְּרִיָּה סוֹפְדָהּ". [2] וְאִיכָּא דְּאָמְרִי: "אֵין כָּל בְּרִיָּה סוֹפְנָהּ". [3] תַּנְיָא: "הָיָה רַבִּי מֵאִיר אוֹמֵר: [4] מַאי דִּכְתִיב: 'טוֹב לָלֶכֶת אֶל בֵּית אֵבֶל מִלֶּכֶת אֶל בֵּית מִשְׁתֶּה, בַּאֲשֶׁר הוּא סוֹף כָּל הָאָדָם, וְהַחַי יִתֵּן אֶל לִבּוֹ'? [5] מַאי 'וְהַחַי יִתֵּן אֶל לִבּוֹ'? [6] דְּבָרִים שֶׁל מִיתָה. [7] דְּסָפַד, יִסְפְּדוּנֵיהּ; [8] דְּקָבַר, יִקְבְּרוּנֵיהּ; [9] דִּידַל, יִדְלוּנֵיהּ; [10] דִּלְוַאי, יְלַוּוּנֵיהּ; [11] דְּטָעַן, יִטְעֲנוּנֵיהּ". [12] "וְאִם הָיָה טוֹעֵן מִשּׁוּם דָּבָר אַחֵר רַשַּׁאי". [13] מַאי "דָּבָר אַחֵר"?

RASHI

סופנה — קוברה. כשם שלא גמלה חסד — כך לא יגמלו עמה. **דיספד** — יתן אל לבו שאף הוא יספדוהו, ואל ירע לו אם נהג כן. **דידל** — הרים קולו בבכי ובמספד. **דלואי** — ליוה את המטה מבית האבל לקבר.

TRANSLATION AND COMMENTARY

תָּנָא [1] The Gemara answers by citing a Baraita in which **a Tanna taught:** "If someone forbids his wife to go to a house of mourning, he must divorce her immediately and pay her her ketubah, for if she is prevented from visiting mourners, then **in the future when she dies, nobody will** come to **eulogize her.**" [2] **And there are some who report** a slightly different version of the Baraita: "If the wife is prevented from going to a house of mourning, then when she dies, **nobody will treat her with the respect** she deserves." A person who cuts himself off from other people and refrains from participating in their sorrows will not be mourned or respected when he himself passes from the world.

תַּנְיָא [3] The same idea **was taught** in the following Baraita: **"Rabbi Meir said:** [4] **What is** the meaning of **the verse which says** [Ecclesiastes 7:2]: **'It is better to go to a house of mourning than to go to a house of feasting, for that is the end of every man, and the living will lay it to his heart'?** [5] **What is** meant by the words, **'And the living will lay it to his heart'?** When a person visits a house of mourning, [6] he should consider **matters relating to death.** [7] When he dies he will be treated the way he treated others, for **if he eulogizes** the deceased, **others will** one day **eulogize him;** [8] **if he buries** the deceased, **others will** one day **bury him;** [9] **if he lifts up his voice** and laments, **others will** one day **lift up their voices** and lament; [10] if **he accompanies** the deceased to his final resting place, **others will** one day **accompany him** to his final resting place; [11] and **if he carries** the deceased to his grave, **others will** one day **carry him** to his grave."

וְאִם [12] We learned in our Mishnah: **"But if** the husband who made a vow prohibiting his wife from visiting a house of mourning or a house of feasting **claims** that he did so for **some other reason, he is permitted** to make such a vow." [13] The Gemara asks: **What** does the Mishnah mean when it refers to **"some other** reason"?

NOTES

סוֹפְדָהּ Treat her with respect. Our translation follows *Tosafot* (*Moed Katan* 28a, s.v., ספין), who explains the word as meaning "treat her with respect." *Rashi, Arukh,* and others explain that the word means "bury her."

דְּסָפַד יִסְפְּדוּנֵיהּ If he eulogizes, they will eulogize him. Our commentary follows *Rashi,* who explains that the Baraita teaches us that a person should remember that upon his death he will be treated by others the way he treated those who died before him. Consequently a person should participate in other people's funerals so that when he dies other people will participate in his. Thus the Baraita supports what was stated above, that a man who prohibits his wife from visiting a house of mourning must divorce her, because if she is barred from visiting the bereaved, nobody will come to pay respects to her when she dies. Others explain that the Baraita merely reflects on the fact that the grave is the final place of repose of all men. *Ritva* suggests that both ideas are contained in the Baraita and that they complement each other.

דִּידַל If he lifts up his voice. *Rashi* explains the word in the sense of lifting up one's voice in lamentation. Others (*Arukh*) understand the word in the sense of bearing the deceased to his grave.

HALAKHAH

דְּסָפַד יִסְפְּדוּנֵיהּ If he eulogizes, they will eulogize him. "A wife is entitled to leave her house in order to visit her paternal home, or to go to a house of mourning or to a house of feasting in order to offer her condolences or to

[1]אָמַר רַב יְהוּדָה אָמַר שְׁמוּאֵל: [2]מִשּׁוּם בְּנֵי אָדָם פְּרוּצִין שֶׁמְּצוּיִין שָׁם.
[3]אֲמַר רַב אַשִׁי: לָא אֲמָרַן אֶלָּא דְאִיתַּחְזַק, [4]אֲבָל לָא אִיתַּחְזַק, [5]לָא כָּל כְּמִינֵּיהּ.
[6]"וְאִם אָמַר לָהּ: 'עַל מְנָת שֶׁתֹּאמְרִי'". [7]וְתֵימָא!
[8]אָמַר רַב יְהוּדָה אָמַר שְׁמוּאֵל: דְּבָרִים שֶׁל קָלוֹן.
[9]"אוֹ שֶׁתְּהֵא מְמַלְּאָה וּמְעָרָה לָאַשְׁפָּה". [10]וְתִיעֲבֵיד!

LITERAL TRANSLATION

[1]Rav Yehudah said in the name of Shmuel: [2]Because of licentious men who are found there.
[3]Rav Ashi said: We do not say [this] except where it is established, [4]but where it is not established, [5]it is not in his power [to make this claim].
[6]"And if he said to her: 'On condition that you tell.'" [7]But let her tell [him]!
[8]Rav Yehudah said in the name of Shmuel: [It refers to] intimate matters (lit., "things of shame").
[9]"Or [if he told her] that she should fill and pour out on the dunghill." [10]But let her do [it]!

TRANSLATION AND COMMENTARY

אָמַר רַב יְהוּדָה [1]**Rav Yehudah said in the name of Shmuel:** The husband claims that he forbade his wife to visit a house of mourning or a house of feasting [2]**because of the licentious men who are found there.**

אָמַר רַב אַשִׁי [3]**Rav Ashi said: We only say** that this is a valid reason **if it has been established** that licentious people are found there. [4]**But if it has not** already **been established** that licentious people are found in these places, [5]**it is not in** the husband's power to forbid his wife to visit them merely because of his suspicions.

וְאִם אָמַר לָהּ [6]Our Mishnah continues: **"If someone says to** his wife: 'I agree to annul your vow **on condition that you tell** So-and-so what you told me (or what I told you),' he must divorce her and pay her her ketubah." [7]The Gemara objects: **Let** her **report** the conversation and there will be no need for the husband to grant her a divorce!

אָמַר רַב יְהוּדָה [8]**Rav Yehudah said in the name of Shmuel:** The Mishnah **is referring to** a husband who agreed to annul his wife's vow if she reported conversations she had conducted with him relating to **intimate matters,** which she is embarrassed to discuss with anybody else. Since the wife cannot possibly fulfill the condition, her husband is regarded as having confirmed the vow and is thus required to grant her a divorce and to pay her her ketubah.

אוֹ שֶׁתְּהֵא מְמַלְּאָה [9]We learned in our Mishnah: "If a man tells his wife **that she fill** herself with his semen **and pour** it **out on the dunghill,** he must divorce her and pay her her ketubah." [10]The Gemara objects: **Let** the wife **do** whatever her husband asks!

NOTES

דְּבָרִים שֶׁל קָלוֹן **Intimate matters.** Most Rishonim explain that this refers to the intimate matters that a husband and wife discuss regarding sexual relations. *Rambam* explains that it is embarrassing and shameful for a woman to repeat such conversations to a third party. *Rivan* explains that the Mishnah is referring to a husband who orders his wife to report the shameful and demeaning things they have said to each other. In such a case the husband must grant his wife a divorce, for if she does as he says, she will acquire a bad reputation among her neighbors.

שֶׁתְּהֵא מְמַלְּאָה וּמְעָרָה לָאַשְׁפָּה **That she should fill and pour out on the dunghill.** The Jerusalem Talmud explains the Mishnah in the same two ways as the Gemara here. There the Babylonian Sages (whose viewpoint corresponds to that of Shmuel in our Gemara) are reported as having explained that the Mishnah refers to a husband who demanded of his wife that they engage in sexual relations "in the manner of Er and Onan" (see Genesis 38:7-10) and thwart the process of procreation. *Rashba* notes that, according to Shmuel, the words "on the dunghill" should be removed from the Mishnah. *Ritva* explains that the husband asked his wife to practice contraceptive measures, as if she were taking her children and casting them out onto a dunghill. *Meiri* suggests that the husband asked his wife to shake his semen out onto a dunghill, so as not to soil his bed.

HALAKHAH

participate in the celebration, so that other people will come to her when she is in a similar situation." (*Rambam, Sefer Nashim, Hilkhot Ishut* 13:11.)

לָא אֲמָרַן אֶלָּא דְאִיתַּחְזַק **We do not say this except where it is established.** "If a person claims that he made a vow forbidding his wife to visit a house of mourning or a house of feasting because of the licentious men found there, and it is established that such people were indeed found there, he is believed, and can divorce her without paying her her ketubah; but if it is not so established, he is not believed." (*Rambam, Sefer Nashim, Hilkhot Ishut* 13:13; *Shulḥan Arukh, Even HaEzer* 74:6.)

עַל מְנָת שֶׁתֹּאמְרִי **On condition that you tell.** "If a person makes a vow stipulating that his wife must tell another person what he has told her (or what she has told him) regarding the couple's sexual relations, he must divorce her and pay her her ketubah, for she cannot discuss such embarrassing matters with someone else." (*Rambam, Sefer Nashim, Hilkhot Ishut* 14:5; *Shulḥan Arukh, Even HaEzer* 76:12.)

[1]אָמַר רַב יְהוּדָה אָמַר שְׁמוּאֵל: שֶׁתְּמַלֵּא וְנוֹפֶצֶת. [2]בְּמַתְנִיתָא תָּנָא: [3]"שֶׁתְּמַלֵּא עֲשָׂרָה כַּדֵּי מַיִם וּתְעָרֶה לָאַשְׁפָּה". [4]בִּשְׁלָמָא לִשְׁמוּאֵל — [5]מִשּׁוּם הָכִי יוֹצִיא וְיִתֵּן כְּתוּבָּה. [6]אֶלָּא לְמַתְנִיתָא מַאי נָפְקָא לַהּ מִינַּהּ? [7]תִּיעֲבֵיד! [8]אָמַר רַבָּה בַּר בַּר חָנָה אָמַר רַבִּי יוֹחָנָן: [9]מִפְּנֵי שֶׁנִּרְאֵית כְּשׁוֹטָה. [10]אָמַר רַב כָּהֲנָא: הַמַּדִּיר אֶת אִשְׁתּוֹ שֶׁלֹּא תַּשְׁאַל וְשֶׁלֹּא תַּשְׁאִיל נָפָה וּכְבָרָה, [11]רֵיחַיִם וְתַנּוּר,

LITERAL TRANSLATION

[1]Rav Yehudah said in the name of Shmuel: [His request is] that she should fill and shake out [the semen].

[2]It was taught in a Baraita: [3]"[His request is] that she should fill ten jugs of water and pour [them] out on the dunghill."

[4]It is well according to Shmuel — [5]because of this he must divorce [her] and pay [her her] ketubah. [6]But according to the Baraita what is the difference to her? [7]Let her do [it]!

[8]Rabbah bar Bar Ḥanah said in the name of Rabbi Yoḥanan: [9]Because she looks like a madwoman.

[10]Rav Kahana said: [If] someone makes a vow forbidding his wife to borrow or to lend a winnow or a sieve, [11]a mill or an oven,

RASHI

שתהא ממלאה ונופצת — לאחר שתשמש וימלא רחמה שכבת זרע — תרוץ ברגליה ותנפצנו, שלא יקלוט ותתעבר. **ריחיים ותנור** — המטלטלין.

TRANSLATION AND COMMENTARY

אָמַר רַב יְהוּדָה [1]**Rav Yehudah said in the name of Shmuel:** The Mishnah is referring to a husband who demanded that his wife **receive** his semen during sexual intercourse **and** then take steps to ensure that the semen was **shaken out** of her body so that she would not conceive. A wife is not required to accede to this demand. Thus a husband who attaches such a condition to his nullification of his wife's vow can be compelled to grant her a divorce.

בְּמַתְנִיתָא תָּנָא [2]An alternative explanation of our Mishnah **was taught in a Baraita:** [3]"If a man tells his wife that he agrees to annul her vow on condition **that she fill ten jugs of water and** then **pour** them **on the dunghill,** or that she perform some other senseless task, he must divorce her and pay her her ketubah."

בִּשְׁלָמָא לִשְׁמוּאֵל [4]The Gemara continues: **Granted** that **according to Shmuel,** who interpreted our Mishnah as referring to a case where the husband tried to force his wife to practice contraceptive measures, we can understand that [5]**on account of this** condition imposed by the husband on his nullification of his wife's vow **he must divorce her and pay** her **her ketubah.** [6]**But according to the Baraita** which explains that the husband demanded that his wife fill up ten jugs of water and pour them on a dunghill, **what difference** does it make **to** the wife? [7]**Let her do** whatever he asks!

אָמַר [8]**Rabbah bar Bar Ḥanah said in the name of Rabbi Yoḥanan:** The wife can demand a divorce, [9]**because** if she engages in some senseless activity, **she will look like a madwoman,** and no woman is required to subject herself to such humiliation.

אָמַר רַב כָּהֲנָא [10]**Rav Kahana said: If someone makes a vow forbidding his wife to borrow or to lend** out utensils that are commonly lent out, [11]such as **a winnow or a sieve or a** hand **mill or a** portable **oven,**

NOTES

מִשּׁוּם הָכִי יוֹצִיא **Because of this he must divorce her.** The Rishonim cite the opinion of *Rashi* that the husband must divorce his wife if he asks her to "receive his semen and then shake it out," because the wife can claim that she wants children who will attend to her in her old age. *Ra'avad* explains that he must divorce her because he is asking her to violate the prohibition against destroying his seed. The Aḥaronim deal with this matter in their discussion of the permissibility of the various methods of contraception.

HALAKHAH

שֶׁתְּמַלֵּא וְנוֹפֶצֶת **That she should fill and shake out.** "If a person makes a vow stipulating that his wife must adopt measures to prevent conception, he must divorce her and pay her her ketubah," following Shmuel. (*Rambam, Sefer Nashim, Hilkhot Ishut* 14:5; *Tur, Even HaEzer* 76.)

שֶׁתְּמַלֵּא עֲשָׂרָה כַּדֵּי מַיִם **That she should fill ten jugs of water.** "If a person makes a vow stipulating that his wife must perform some senseless task, like filling ten jugs of water and then pouring them out on a dunghill, he must divorce her and pay her her ketubah," following the Baraita. (*Rambam, Sefer Nashim, Hilkhot Ishut* 14:5; *Shulḥan Arukh, Even HaEzer* 76:12.)

הַמַּדִּיר אֶת אִשְׁתּוֹ שֶׁלֹּא תִּשְׁאַל וְשֶׁלֹּא תַּשְׁאִיל **If someone makes a vow forbidding his wife to borrow or to lend.** "If a person makes a vow forbidding his wife to borrow or to lend utensils that are commonly lent to other people, he must divorce her and pay her her ketubah, because he gives her a bad reputation among her neighbors." (*Rambam, Sefer Nashim, Hilkhot Ishut* 13:10; *Shulḥan Arukh, Even HaEzer* 74:3.)

TRANSLATION AND COMMENTARY

[1]**he must divorce her and pay** her **her ketubah,** [2]**for he gives her a bad name among her neighbors.** They will think of her as being either unkind or petty, or haughty.

תַּנְיָא נַמִּי הָכִי [3]The Gemara now supports Rav Kahana's ruling: **The same** thing **was also taught** in a Baraita, which stated: [4]**"If someone makes a vow forbidding his wife to borrow or to lend** out utensils such as **a winnow or a sieve** or [5]a hand **mill or a** portable **oven,** [6]**he must divorce her and pay** her **her ketubah, for he gives her a bad name among her neighbors.** [7]**And similarly, if** a wife **makes a vow forbidding herself to borrow or to lend** out **a winnow or a sieve or a** hand **mill or a** portable **oven,** [8]**or forbidding herself to weave handsome garments for her children,** [9]**she may be divorced without** receiving **her ketubah, for she gives** her husband **a bad name among his neighbors."**

MISHNAH וְאֵלּוּ יוֹצְאוֹת [10]The Mishnayot in this chapter have dealt until now with cases in which the husband can be compelled to divorce his wife and pay her her ketubah. However, sometimes the husband is permitted to divorce his wife without paying her her ketubah: **These** are the women who **may be divorced** from their husbands **without** receiving payment of **their ketubah:** [11]Women **who violate the law of Moses** by misleading their husbands into transgressing a Biblical prohibition, **and** women who violate **Jewish custom** through their immodest and unbecoming behavior. The Mishnah now illustrates these general principles with a number of examples: [12]**Who is** regarded as a woman **who violates**

[1]יוֹצִיא וְיִתֵּן כְּתוּבָּה, [2]שֶׁמַּשִּׂיאָהּ שֵׁם רַע בִּשְׁכֵינוֹתֶיהָ.

[3]תַּנְיָא נַמִּי הָכִי: [4]"הַמַּדִּיר אֶת אִשְׁתּוֹ שֶׁלֹּא תִּשְׁאַל וְשֶׁלֹּא תַּשְׁאִיל נָפָה וּכְבָרָה, [5]רֵיחַיִם וְתַנּוּר, [6]יוֹצִיא וְיִתֵּן כְּתוּבָּה, מִפְּנֵי שֶׁמַּשִּׂיאָהּ שֵׁם רַע בִּשְׁכֵינוֹתֶיהָ. [7]וְכֵן, הִיא שֶׁנָּדְרָה שֶׁלֹּא תִּשְׁאַל וְשֶׁלֹּא תַּשְׁאִיל נָפָה וּכְבָרָה וְרֵיחַיִם וְתַנּוּר, [8]וְשֶׁלֹּא תֶּאֱרוֹג בְּגָדִים נָאִים לְבָנָיו, [9]תֵּצֵא שֶׁלֹּא בִּכְתוּבָּה, מִפְּנֵי שֶׁמַּשִּׂיאָתוֹ שֵׁם רַע בִּשְׁכֵנָיו".

מִשְׁנָה [10]וְאֵלּוּ יוֹצְאוֹת שֶׁלֹּא בִּכְתוּבָּה: [11]הָעוֹבֶרֶת עַל דַּת מֹשֶׁה וִיהוּדִית. [12]וְאֵיזוֹ הִיא דַּת מֹשֶׁה?

LITERAL TRANSLATION

[1]he must divorce [her] and pay [her] ketubah, [2]for he gives her a bad name among her neighbors.

[3]It was also taught thus: [4]"[If] someone makes a vow forbidding his wife to borrow or to lend a winnow or a sieve, [5]a mill or an oven, [6]he must divorce [her] and pay [her] ketubah, for he gives her a bad name among her neighbors. [7]And similarly, [if] she made a vow forbidding herself to borrow or to lend a winnow or a sieve or a mill or an oven, [8]or forbidding herself to weave handsome garments for his children, [9]she goes out without [her] ketubah, for she gives him a bad name among his neighbors."

MISHNAH [10]And these [wives] go out without [their] ketubah: [11]She who violates the law of Moses or Jewish custom. [12]And who is she [who violates] the law of Moses?

RASHI

משנה דת יהודית – שנהגו בנות ישראל, ואף על גב דלא כתיבא.

BACKGROUND

דַּת מֹשֶׁה וִיהוּדִית **Law of Moses and Jewish custom.** The Mishnah distinguishes between transgressions committed by the wife which violate Torah law (דַּת מֹשֶׁה) and those against customs of modesty and morality, which are not explicitly forbidden in the Torah but constitute the kind of behavior that a husband does not expect from his wife, if she behaves like a decent Jewish woman (דַּת יְהוּדִית).

A man's right to divorce his wife does not derive from the severity of the transgression she commits but from her injuring her husband in a way that she is not permitted to do, according either to the Halakhah or to custom.

NOTES

וְאֵלּוּ יוֹצְאוֹת **And these wives go out.** The Rishonim agree that a wife may not be divorced without payment of her ketubah for violating the law of Moses or Jewish custom unless she has received prior warning.

Elsewhere (*Sotah* 25a), the Gemara asks whether the husband of a woman who violates the law of Moses or Jewish custom is required to divorce her, or whether he may maintain her if he so desires. Most Rishonim conclude that the husband is permitted to keep the woman as his wife. *Ra'avad* (cited by *Rosh* and *Rashba*) explains that although the husband is not required to divorce his wife, it is commendable if he does so. *Rambam* adds that even if the husband does not divorce his wife, she is no longer entitled to her ketubah. The Sages enacted the ketubah to make it difficult for a husband to divorce his wife, but they were not concerned about protecting a woman who violates the law of Moses or Jewish custom.

וְאֵיזוֹ הִיא דַּת מֹשֶׁה **And who is she who violates the law of Moses?** The examples provided here teach that the violation of a Biblical commandment does not in itself constitute grounds for divorce without payment of the ketubah. A man may only divorce his wife without payment

HALAKHAH

הָעוֹבֶרֶת עַל דַּת מֹשֶׁה וִיהוּדִית **She who violates the law of Moses or Jewish custom.** "If a wife violates the law of Moses or Jewish custom, she may be divorced without receiving payment of her ketubah, following the Mishnah. A wife who misleads her husband into violating a Biblical prohibition — such as, if she feeds him non-kosher food or engages in sexual relations with him during her menstrual period — belongs to the category of a woman who violates the law of Moses. (This applies only if her testimony regarding the fitness of the food she served or regarding her menstrual state was contradicted by two witnesses. But if she insists that she did not cause her husband to violate a prohibition, and there are no witnesses to contradict her, she is believed; *Rosh,* in the name of the Jerusalem Talmud. *Rambam* and others appear to disagree.) If a wife violates the standards of modesty practiced by most Jewish women,

TRANSLATION AND COMMENTARY

the law of Moses? [1]A woman **who** knowingly **feeds** her husband food **that** is forbidden because it **has not been** properly **tithed,** [2]**or who engages in sexual relations with** her husband **during her menstrual period**, when such relations are forbidden, [3]**or who does not separate *hallah*** from her dough and who then feeds her husband forbidden bread, [4]**or who makes vows but does not fulfill them.**

וְאֵיזוֹהִי [5]**And who is** regarded as a wife **who violates Jewish custom?** [6]A woman **who goes out** to the marketplace **with her head uncovered,** [7]**or who spins in the marketplace** in an immodest manner, [8]**or who talks with everybody.** [9]**Abba Shaul says: Also** included in this category is a woman **who curses** her husband's **parents in his presence.** [10]**Rabbi Tarfon says: Also** included in this category is a woman **who is** overly **loud.** [11]**And who is** regarded as a woman **who is** overly **loud?** [12]One **who talks** so loudly with her husband **inside her house that her neighbors can hear her voice.**

GEMARA מַאֲכִילָתוֹ [13]Our Mishnah stated: "Among those who have violated the law of Moses is a woman **who** knowingly **feeds** her husband food **that** is forbidden because it **has not been** properly **tithed."** [14]The Gemara asks: **How,** precisely, **do we visualize the case?** [15]**If** the husband **knew** that the food had not been properly tithed, **he should have abstained** from eating until the tithes were removed in the proper manner. Otherwise he is equally guilty of misconduct! [16]And **if** the husband **did not know** that it had not been tithed, [17]**how does he know** now that his wife served him untithed produce?

[1]מַאֲכִילָתוֹ שֶׁאֵינוֹ מְעוּשָּׂר, [2]וּמְשַׁמַּשְׁתּוֹ נִדָּה, [3]וְלֹא קוֹצָה לָהּ חַלָּה, [4]וְנוֹדֶרֶת וְאֵינָהּ מְקַיֶּימֶת.

[5]וְאֵיזוֹהִי דַּת יְהוּדִית? [6]יוֹצְאָה וְרֹאשָׁהּ פָּרוּעַ, [7]וְטוֹוָה בַּשּׁוּק, [8]וּמְדַבֶּרֶת עִם כָּל אָדָם. [9]אַבָּא שָׁאוּל אוֹמֵר: אַף הַמְקַלֶּלֶת יוֹלְדָיו בְּפָנָיו. [10]רַבִּי טַרְפוֹן אוֹמֵר: אַף הַקּוֹלָנִית. [11]וְאֵיזוֹהִי קוֹלָנִית? [12]לִכְשֶׁהִיא מְדַבֶּרֶת בְּתוֹךְ בֵּיתָהּ וּשְׁכֵנֶיהָ שׁוֹמְעִין קוֹלָהּ.

גמרא [13]"מַאֲכִילָתוֹ שֶׁאֵינוֹ מְעוּשָּׂר". [14]הֵיכִי דָּמֵי? [15]אִי דְּיָדַע, נִפְרוֹשׁ. [16]אִי דְּלָא יָדַע, [17]מְנָא יָדַע?

LITERAL TRANSLATION

[1][She who] feeds him what is not tithed, [2]or engages in sexual relations with him while she is menstruating, [3]or does not separate *hallah*, [4]or makes vows but does not fulfill [them].

[5]And who is she [who violates] Jewish custom? [6][She who] goes out with her head uncovered, [7]or spins in the marketplace, [8]or talks with everybody. [9]Abba Shaul says: Also she who curses his parents in his presence. [10]Rabbi Tarfon says: Also she who is loud. [11]And who is loud? [12][A woman who] when she talks in her house her neighbors hear her voice.

GEMARA [13]"[She who] feeds him what is not tithed." [14]How do we visualize the case? [15]If he knows, let him abstain. [16]If he does not know, [17]from where does he know?

RASHI

וטווה בשוק – בגמרא מפרש. **במדברת בתוך ביתה** – מפרש בגמרא.

גמרא היכי דמי – דהאכילתו. **אי דידע** – כשאכל. **נפרוש** – ולא יאכל. **מנא ידע** – מי אמר לו אחרי כן, שהוא בא להוציאה.

NOTES

of her ketubah if her violation affects their marital relationship. *Kovetz Shiurim* adds that if the husband himself is a sinner who partakes of forbidden foods, he cannot divorce his wife for having fed him non-kosher food, because her act did not adversely affect their conjugal life.

מַאֲכִילָתוֹ She who feeds him. *Tosafot* and most Rishonim infer from the term "who feeds him" that the husband may divorce his wife without payment of her ketubah only if he actually ate the non-kosher food. But if she merely planned to give him the non-kosher food and he did not actually eat it, he cannot divorce her, for she can always claim that she would have prevented him from actually eating the forbidden food. *Ra'ah* disagrees and says that a husband may divorce his wife for trying to feed him non-kosher food, even if he did not actually eat it. *Meiri* infers from the term "who feeds him" that it is only when the woman misleads her husband into eating forbidden food that he can divorce her without paying her her ketubah, but he cannot divorce her for eating such food herself.

שֶׁאֵינוֹ מְעוּשָּׂר What is not tithed. *Rambam* notes that a husband may divorce his wife without payment of her ketubah not only for feeding him untithed produce, but also for feeding him any other type of forbidden food, and all the more so for feeding him the meat of forbidden animals and reptiles which people regard as an abomination.

מְנָא יָדַע? From where does he know? The Jerusalem Talmud adds: "And in all these cases where there are witnesses." Some Rishonim understand from this that the husband must bring two witnesses who contradict the

HALAKHAH

or curses members of her husband's family in his presence, she belongs to the category of a woman who violates Jewish custom." (*Rambam, Sefer Nashim, Hilkhot Ishut* 24:10-12; *Shulhan Arukh, Even HaEzer* 115:1,4.)

TRANSLATION AND COMMENTARY

לָא [1]The Gemara answers: **No,** the Mishnah's ruling **applies only** in a case **where** the woman **said to** her husband: [2]**"A certain priest tithed the pile** of produce **on my behalf,"** and the husband relied on her word. [3]Later **he went and asked** the priest whether he had tithed the produce for his wife, **and** her story **was found to be a lie.** Since it has been established that the wife caused him to transgress a Biblical injunction, she may be divorced without payment of her ketubah.

וּמְשַׁמַּשְׁתּוֹ נִדָּה [4]Our Mishnah continues: "A woman who **engages in sexual relations with** her husband **during her menstrual period**, also violates the law of Moses." [5]The Gemara asks: **How,** precisely, **do we visualize the case?** [6]**If** the husband **knew** that she was menstruating, **he should have abstained** from sexual contact with her until after she purified herself. If he knowingly engaged in sexual relations while his wife was forbidden to him, surely he cannot divorce her without paying her her ketubah! [7]And **if** the husband **did not know** that she was forbidden to him, [8]**let him rely on her** word that she was indeed permitted to him. [9]**For Rav Ḥinnena bar Kahana said in the name of Shmuel:** [10]**From where** in the Torah **do we derive** the law **that a menstruating woman may count for herself** the seven days that must pass after her period ends before she may undergo ritual immersion and purify herself, and that she is trusted about it? [11]This law is derived from **the verse** that **says** (Leviticus 15:28): **"Then she shall count for herself seven days."** [12]The Hebrew word לָהּ ("to herself") teaches that she may count the seven days **for herself.** Now, if the wife is believed when she says she is permitted to her husband, on what grounds may her husband divorce her without paying her her ketubah?

[1]לָא, צְרִיכָא דְּאָמְרָה לֵיהּ: [2]״פְּלוֹנִי כֹּהֵן תִּיקֵּן לִי אֶת הַכְּרִי״, [3]וְאָזֵיל שַׁיְילֵיהּ, וְאִשְׁתַּכַּח שִׁיקְרָא.

[4]״וּמְשַׁמַּשְׁתּוֹ נִדָּה״. [5]הֵיכִי דָּמֵי? [6]אִי דְּיָדַע בָּהּ, נִפְרוֹשׁ. [7]אִי דְּלָא יָדַע, [8]נִסְמוֹךְ עִילָּוָהּ. [9]דְּאָמַר רַב חִינְנָא בַּר כָּהֲנָא אָמַר שְׁמוּאֵל: [10]מִנַּיִן לְנִדָּה שֶׁסּוֹפֶרֶת לְעַצְמָהּ? [11]שֶׁנֶּאֱמַר: ״וְסָפְרָה לָּהּ שִׁבְעַת יָמִים״. [12]לָהּ לְעַצְמָהּ.

LITERAL TRANSLATION

[1]No, it is necessary where she said to him: [2]"A certain priest prepared the pile for me," [3]and he went [and] asked him, and it was found to be a lie.

[4]"Or engages in sexual relations with him while she is menstruating." [5]How do we visualize the case? [6]If he knows about her, let him abstain. [7]If he does not know, [8]let him rely upon her. [9]For Rav Ḥinnana bar Kahana said in the name of Shmuel: [10]From where [do we derive] that a menstruating woman counts for herself? [11]For it is said: "Then she shall count for herself seven days." [12]*Lah* [means] for herself.

NOTES

wife's claim that a certain priest tithed her produce, or that a certain Sage declared that her blood was ritually pure. But if only the priest or the Sage contradict her claim, she does not forfeit her ketubah, because the testimony of a single witness is insufficient (*Rashba* and others). Others explain that the wife forfeits her ketubah even if her claim is contradicted only by the priest or the Sage, because the wife herself says that she trusted the priest or the Sage and there is good reason to assume that she lied. The Jerusalem Talmud, which says that the Mishnah is referring to a case where there were witnesses, means that the husband must bring witnesses that his wife indeed said that the priest had tithed the produce for her, or that the Sage had declared her blood ritually pure, as well as witnesses that the priest or the Sage denied her claim (*Ra'ah, Ritva*).

The Rishonim ask: Why does the Gemara not suggest that the Mishnah is referring to a wife who confessed that she had misled her husband into violating a Biblical prohibition? *Ra'avad* argues that there is a general rule that a person cannot incriminate himself. Many Rishonim object that this rule does not apply to monetary matters, and that the admission of a party to a monetary dispute is equivalent to the testimony of a hundred witnesses. These Rishonim argue that the Gemara did not suggest this solution because it is uncommon for a person to incriminate himself and confess to a transgression (*Rashba, Ritva*).

פְּלוֹנִי כֹּהֵן **A certain priest.** *Rivan* notes that the same law applies if a wife told her husband that a non-priest tithed the produce for her. The Gemara specifically mentions a priest because it was customary to allow a priest to tithe the one's produce and then take the priestly portion for himself.

HALAKHAH

פְּלוֹנִי כֹּהֵן תִּיקֵּן **A certain priest prepared.** "How does the husband know that his wife has served him untithed produce? The Mishnah refers to the following type of situation: A wife claimed that a certain priest tithed the produce on her behalf, and, after her husband relied on her word and ate the food, he then asked the priest about it, and the priest denied the wife's claim. In such a case, according to *Shulḥan Arukh,* the wife forfeits her ketubah payment only if her husband's claim that she fed him untithed food is supported by the testimony of two witnesses, the priest's denial being insufficient." (*Rambam, Sefer Nashim, Hilkhot Ishut* 24:10-11; *Shulḥan Arukh, Even HaEzer* 115:1,4.)

TRANSLATION AND COMMENTARY

לָא [1]The Gemara answers: **No,** the Mishnah's ruling **applies only** in a case **where** the woman **said to** her husband: [2]**"A certain Sage declared for me that the blood** I saw **was ritually pure** and did not make me forbidden to you," and the husband engaged in sexual relations with her, relying on her word. [3]Later **he went and asked** the Sage, **and** the woman's claim **was found to be a lie.** Since it has been established that the wife lied to her husband and caused him to violate a Biblical prohibition, she may be divorced without payment of her ketubah.

וְאִיבָּעֵית אֵימָא [4]The Gemara now suggests that the Mishnah's ruling may apply to another case: **And if you wish,** you can **say** that the Mishnah's ruling applies to a case **like** the one discussed by **Rav Yehudah.** [5]**For Rav Yehudah said: If** a woman **was established among her neighbors as menstruating,** they having seen her wearing the special garments she ordinarily wears only while menstruating, and the neighbors warned her husband that she was forbidden to him, but he nevertheless engaged in sexual relations with her, [6]**the husband is flogged on account of** his having had sexual relations with **her, because she is** regarded as **a menstruating woman,** even if she claims that she was indeed permitted to her husband. Our Mishnah can thus be understood as referring to a case where a woman concealed from her husband the fact that she was having her period, and after they had engaged in sexual relations her neighbors told the husband that she had previously been established among them as menstruating. Since she misled her husband and caused him to violate a Biblical prohibition, she may be divorced without payment of her ketubah.

וְלֹא [7]We learned in our Mishnah: "A woman who **does not separate *ḥallah*** from her dough, and who then feeds her husband a forbidden loaf of bread, also violates the law of Moses." The Gemara asks: [8]**How,** precisely, **do we visualize the case?** [9]**If** the husband **knew** that *ḥallah* had not been separated, **he should have abstained** from eating the bread. [10]And **if** the husband **did not know** that *ḥallah* had not been separated, [11]**how does he** now **know** that his wife served him bread from which *ḥallah* had not been separated?

LITERAL TRANSLATION

[1]No, it is necessary where she said to him: [2]"A certain Sage declared for me that the blood is ritually pure," [3]and he went [and] asked him, and it was found to be a lie.

[4]And if you wish, say: [It is] in accordance with Rav Yehudah. [5]For Rav Yehudah said: If she was established among her neighbors as menstruating, [6]her husband is flogged on her account because [she is] menstruating.

[7]"Or does not separate *ḥallah*." [8]How do we visualize the case? [9]If he knows, let him abstain. [10]If he does not know, [11]from where does he know?

[1]לָא, צְרִיכָא דְּאָמְרָה לֵיהּ: [2]״פְּלוֹנִי חָכָם טִיהֵר לִי אֶת הַדָּם״, [3]וַאֲזַל שַׁיְילֵיהּ, וְאִשְׁתַּכַּח שִׁיקְרָא.

[4]וְאִיבָּעֵית אֵימָא: כִּדְרַב יְהוּדָה. [5]דְּאָמַר רַב יְהוּדָה: הוּחְזְקָה נִדָּה בִּשְׁכֵינוֹתֶיהָ, [6]בַּעְלָהּ לוֹקֶה עָלֶיהָ מִשּׁוּם נִדָּה.

[7]״וְלֹא קוֹצָה לָהּ חַלָּה״. [8]הֵיכִי דָּמֵי? [9]אִי דְּיָדַע, נִפְרוֹשׁ. [10]אִי דְּלָא יָדַע, [11]מְנָא יָדַע?

RASHI

הוחזקה נדה בשכינותיה – שראוה לובשת בגדי נדות, ולבעלה אמרה: טהורה אני, ושמשה. **בעלה לוקה** – אם התרו בו. וכי האי גוונא משכחת לה למתניתין, דלאחר תשמיש הודיעוהו שכינותיו שהוחזקה נדה.

NOTES

הוּחְזְקָה נִדָּה בִּשְׁכֵינוֹתֶיהָ If she was established among her neighbors as menstruating. *Rashi* explains that a woman may be established among her neighbors as menstruating, if they saw her wearing the special garments that she would ordinarily wear during her period. *Rivan* adds that she may become established among her neighbors as menstruating if those women are familiar with her menstrual pattern and know when she expects to begin her period.

The Gemara did not ask regarding a menstruating woman: "If he does not know, from where does he know?" This is because the husband may have discovered his wife's bloodstained clothing after he had sexual relations with her. Rather, it said: "Let him rely upon her," when she says that her period began after they had already engaged in sexual intercourse (*Tosafot*).

HALAKHAH

הוּחְזְקָה נִדָּה בִּשְׁכֵינוֹתֶיהָ If she was established among her neighbors as menstruating. "If a woman is seen by her neighbors to be wearing the special garments she ordinarily wears while menstruating, she is presumed to be forbidden to her husband. If her husband engages in sexual intercourse with her knowing that she has been established among her neighbors as menstruating, he is liable to lashes. If the wife tells her husband that she is permitted to him, and afterwards it is discovered that she has been established among her neighbors as menstruating, she may be divorced without receiving her ketubah payment." (*Rambam, Sefer Kedushah, Hilkhot Issurei Bi'ah* 1:22; *Shulḥan Arukh, Even HaEzer* 115:2.)

TRANSLATION AND COMMENTARY

לָא [1]The Gemara answers: **No,** the Mishnah's ruling **applies only** in a case **where** the woman **said** to her husband: [2]**"A certain person whose task it was to knead** dough **separated** ***ḥallah*** **from the dough on my behalf,"** and the husband ate the loaf of bread relying on his wife's word, [3]**and** later **he went and asked** the kneader, [4]**and** the wife's story **was found to be a lie.** In such a case, she may be divorced without payment of her ketubah, for she lied to her husband and caused him to transgress a Biblical injunction.

וְנוֹדֶרֶת וְאֵינָהּ מְקַיֶּימֶת [5]Our Mishnah continues: "Concluding the list of women who are regarded as having violated the law of Moses is she who **makes vows but does not fulfill them."** The Gemara now explains why such a woman may be divorced without payment of her ketubah: [6]**For it was said** in a Baraita: "As a punishment **for the transgression of not fulfilling vows** one's **children die** young, [7]**as the verse says** [Ecclesiastes 5:4-5]: 'It is better that you should not vow, than that you should vow and not pay. **Do not let your mouth cause your flesh to sin;** nor say before the angel that it was an error. Why should God be angry at your voice and destroy the work of your hands?' These verses mean: Do not let your mouth utter a vow that will cause your flesh and blood to be held accountable; and do not say before the Temple treasurer that you took the vow in error, and thereby seek to avoid payment. Why should God be angry with you about the vow you made, and destroy the work of your hands? [8]**What is** considered **the** most essential **work of a man's hands?** [9]**You must say** that this refers to a man's **sons and daughters."** Thus, if a woman makes vows but does not fulfill them, her husband is entitled to divorce her without paying her her ketubah, in order to protect his children from early death.

רַב נַחְמָן אֲמַר [10]**Rav Naḥman said: It is from here that we derive** that a person's children die young as a consequence of unfulfilled vows (Jeremiah 2:30): [11]**"In vain have I smitten your children."** [12]**"In vain"** — **in the matter of vows made in vain** — have your children met with early death.

תַּנְיָא [13]**It was taught** in a Baraita: **"Rabbi Meir used to say:** [14]**Anybody who knows that his wife makes vows but** then **fails to fulfill them should make a vow** of his own **forbidding** those same things to **her."**

יַדִּירֶנָּה [15]The Gemara interjects: **Should** the husband really **make a vow** of his own **forbidding** his wife what she has forbidden herself? [16]**How does this remedy her** situation?

אֶלָּא [17]The Gemara explains: **Rather,** Rabbi Meir meant that if someone knows that his wife makes vows but fails to fulfill them, he need not divorce her. [18]Instead **he should make her angry** with him **so that she will repeat** her **vows in his presence,** [19]**and then he can annul** those vows **for her.** A husband can only annul his wife's vows if he knows about them.

[1]לָא, צְרִיכָא דְּאָמְרָה לֵיהּ: [2]"פְּלוֹנִי גַּבָּל תִּיקֵּן לִי אֶת הָעִיסָּה", [3]וְאָזֵיל שַׁיְילֵיהּ, [4]וְאִשְׁתַּכַּח שִׁיקְרָא.
[5]"וְנוֹדֶרֶת וְאֵינָהּ מְקַיֶּימֶת". [6]דְּאָמַר מָר: "בַּעֲוֹן נְדָרִים בָּנִים מֵתִים, [7]שֶׁנֶּאֱמַר: 'אַל תִּתֵּן אֶת פִּיךָ לַחֲטִיא אֶת בְּשָׂרֶךָ, וגו''. [8]וְאֵיזוֹ הֵן מַעֲשֵׂה יָדָיו שֶׁל אָדָם? [9]הֱוֵי אוֹמֵר: בָּנָיו וּבְנוֹתָיו".
[10]רַב נַחְמָן אֲמַר: מֵהָכָא: [11]"לַשָּׁוְא הִכֵּיתִי אֶת בְּנֵיכֶם". [12]"לַשָּׁוְא" — עַל עִסְקֵי שָׁוְא.
[13]תַּנְיָא: "הָיָה רַבִּי מֵאִיר אוֹמֵר: [14]כָּל הַיּוֹדֵעַ בְּאִשְׁתּוֹ שֶׁנּוֹדֶרֶת וְאֵינָהּ מְקַיֶּימֶת יַחֲזוֹר וְיַדִּירֶנָּה". [15]יַדִּירֶנָּה? [16]בְּמַאי מְתַקֵּן לָהּ? [17]אֶלָּא, [18]יַחֲזוֹר וְיַקְנִיטֶנָּה כְּדֵי שֶׁתִּדּוֹר בְּפָנָיו, [19]וְיָפֵר לָהּ.

LITERAL TRANSLATION

[1]No, it is necessary where she said to him: [2]"A certain kneader prepared the dough for me," [3]and he went [and] asked him, [4]and it was found to be a lie.

[5]"Or makes vows but does not fulfill [them]." [6]For the Master said: "For the transgression of [not fulfilling] vows children die, [7]as it is said: 'Do not let your mouth cause your flesh to sin, etc.' [8]And what is the work of a man's hands? [9]You must say: His sons and his daughters."

[10]Rav Naḥman said: [We learn it] from here: [11]"In vain have I smitten your children." [12]"In vain" — in the matter of [vows made] in vain.

[13]It was taught: "Rabbi Meir used to say: [14]Anybody who knows that his wife makes vows but does not fulfill [them] should forbid her again with a vow."

[15]He should forbid her with a vow? [16]In what [way] does he correct her?

[17]Rather, [18]he should make her angry again so that she will make a vow before him [19]and [then] he should annul [it] for her.

RASHI

בנים מתים – בפרק "במה מדליקין" (שבת לב,ב) יליף מ"וחבל את מעשה ידיך". **ידירנה** – משמע, בעצמו: קונס עליך דבר פלוני. **יחזור ויקניטנה** – אין לו להוציאה, אלא כך יתקננה.

BACKGROUND

אֵין אָדָם דָּר עִם נָחָשׁ בִּכְפִיפָה A person cannot dwell in a basket with a serpent. That is, one does not require a person to live in a condition of constant suspicion, like someone confined in a narrow space with a venomous serpent. For a person cannot live in constant apprehension and dread.

אַזְהָרָה Warning. This comes with a negative commandment. The Torah here does not specify the transgression. However, the meaning of the word derives from the act being forbidden to a married woman.

REALIA

כְּפִיפָה Basket. Sometimes called כְּפִיפָה מִצְרִית — "Egyptian basket" — it was woven from palm leaves and used for storing things or for straining drinks. Sometimes these baskets had handles and were hung from animals' necks, so the animals could eat from them. The Gemara's discussion implies that live snakes were sometimes kept in such baskets.

TRANSLATION AND COMMENTARY

אָמְרוּ לוֹ [1]The Baraita continues: "The Sages **said to** Rabbi Meir: The solution you offer is not practical, [2]for **a person cannot dwell in a basket** together **with a serpent.**" A husband can take steps to prevent his wife from violating her vows, but if she habitually makes vows and does not fulfill them, sooner or later she will neglect a vow that her husband has not annulled for her. Thus it is preferable that the husband divorce her.

תַּנְיָא [3]A similar dispute **was taught** in the following Baraita: **"Rabbi Yehudah used to say:** [4]**Anybody who knows that his wife is not** reliable about **separating *hallah*** from her dough **should separate *hallah* again after her.** [5]The Sages **said to** Rabbi Yehudah: This is not a practical solution to the problem, for **a person cannot dwell in a basket** together **with a serpent."** Thus it is preferable that the husband divorce her.

מַאן [6]The Gemara now considers the relationship between the views expressed in the two Baraitot. **The** Tanna **who taught the ruling regarding** the woman who is unreliable about separating *hallah* [7]**would certainly agree** with the solution offered **regarding** the woman who neglects her vows, because the problem of *hallah* arises all the time, whereas the question of vows arises much less frequently. [8]**But the** Tanna **who taught the ruling regarding** the woman who neglects her vows may have offered his solution only with respect to that case, [9]**but regarding** the woman who is unreliable about separating *hallah* he may agree that it is preferable that her husband divorce her, [10]for it is likely that **he will at times happen to eat** what is forbidden to him.

וְאֵיזוֹהִי [11]We learned in our Mishnah: **"And who is** regarded as a wife **who violates Jewish custom** with behavior inappropriate for a daughter of Israel? [12]A woman **who goes out** to the marketplace **with her head uncovered."** The Gemara objects: [13]A wife is forbidden to go out to the marketplace with **an uncovered head**, not only because Jewish women are accustomed to cover their heads when they appear in public, but because such behavior **is forbidden by Torah law,** [14]**as the verse** dealing with a woman suspected of infidelity by her husband **says** (Numbers 5:18): "And the priest shall place the woman before the Lord, **and he shall uncover the woman's head."** [15]**And a Sage of the Academy of Rabbi Yishmael taught:** "**This** verse serves as **a warning**

[1]״אָמְרוּ לוֹ: [2]אֵין אָדָם דָּר עִם נָחָשׁ בִּכְפִיפָה״.
[3]תַּנְיָא: ״הָיָה רַבִּי יְהוּדָה אוֹמֵר: [4]כָּל הַיּוֹדֵעַ בְּאִשְׁתּוֹ שֶׁאֵינָהּ קוֹצָה לוֹ חַלָּה יַחֲזוֹר וְיַפְרִישׁ אַחֲרֶיהָ. [5]אָמְרוּ לוֹ: אֵין אָדָם דָּר עִם נָחָשׁ בִּכְפִיפָה״.
[6]מַאן דְּמַתְנֵי לָהּ אַהָא, [7]כָּל שֶׁכֵּן אַהָךְ. [8]אֲבָל מַאן דְּמַתְנֵי אַהָךְ, [9]אֲבָל הָא, [10]זִימְנִין דְּמִקְרֵי וְאָכֵיל.
[11]״וְאֵיזוֹהִי דַּת יְהוּדִית? [12]יוֹצְאָה וְרֹאשָׁהּ פָּרוּעַ״. [13]רֹאשָׁהּ פָּרוּעַ דְּאוֹרַיְיתָא הִיא, [14]דִּכְתִיב: ״וּפָרַע אֶת רֹאשׁ הָאִשָּׁה״. [15]וְתָנָא דְּבֵי רַבִּי יִשְׁמָעֵאל: ״אַזְהָרָה לִבְנוֹת

LITERAL TRANSLATION

[1]"They said to him: [2]A person cannot dwell in a basket with a serpent."

[3]It was taught: "Rabbi Yehudah used to say: [4]Anybody who knows that his wife does not separate *hallah* for him should separate [*hallah*] again after her. [5]They said to him: A person cannot dwell in a basket with a serpent."

[6]The one who taught [the ruling] about this, [7]all the more so [would he teach] about that. [8]But the one who taught [the ruling] about that, [9]but about this, [10]sometimes he happens to eat.

[11]"And who is she [who violates] Jewish custom? [12][She who] goes out with her head uncovered." [13][But surely] an uncovered head is [forbidden] by Torah law, [14]for it is written: "And he shall uncover the woman's head." [15]And [a Sage] of the Academy of Rabbi Yishmael taught: "[This is] a warning to the daughters

RASHI

בכפיפה – בתוך סל אחד, שכשלא ישמר ישכנו. אף זה יצא לידי שתקלקלנו. **מאן דמתני לה אהא** – דרבי יהודה. דתני תקנתא אחלה – כל שכן אנדרים, דלא שכיחי. **דאורייתא היא** – ואמאי לא קרי לה דת משה? **אזהרה** – מדעבדינן לה הכי לנוולה מדה כנגד מדה, כמו שעשתה להתנאות על בועלה – מכלל דאסור. אי נמי, מדכתיב "ופרע" – מכלל דההוא שעתא לאו פרועה הות, שמע מינה אין דרך בנות ישראל לצאת פרועות ראש. וכן עיקר.

NOTES

וּפָרַע אֶת רֹאשׁ הָאִשָּׁה And he shall uncover the woman's head. *Rashi* explains that since the Torah requires that the head of a woman suspected of adultery by her husband be uncovered, it follows that a married woman must ordinarily appear in public with a head covering. *Ritva* adds that, since the Torah says that the head of a woman suspected of adultery must be uncovered so that she may be disgraced, this implies that a married woman who appears in public without a proper head covering is acting licentiously.

TRANSLATION AND COMMENTARY

to the married **daughters of Israel that they should not go out** into a public place **with their heads uncovered;** for the Torah implies that ordinarily the head of a married woman must remain covered." Why, then, is a wife who goes out to the marketplace with her head uncovered included by our Mishnah in the category of women who violate Jewish custom, and not in the category of women who violate the law of Moses?

דְּאוֹרָיְיתָא [1]The Gemara explains: **By Torah law,** [72B] if a woman covers her head with **her basket,** [2]it **is fine** even if her hair is not entirely covered, and if she goes out like that to the marketplace, her husband cannot divorce her without paying her her ketubah. But **by the custom of Jewish women, even** if her head is covered by **her basket,** she **is still forbidden** to go out to the marketplace without an additional head covering. If she does so, she can be divorced without receiving her ketubah settlement. Thus our Mishnah refers to a woman who leaves for the marketplace with a basket on her head. Such a woman violates only the custom of Jewish women.

אָמַר רַבִּי אַסִּי [3]**Rabbi Assi said in the name of Rabbi Yoḥanan:** If a woman covers her head **with her basket, there is no violation of** the prohibition against going out with **an uncovered head.**

הָוֵי בָּהּ רַבִּי זֵירָא [4]**Rabbi Zera raised** a question about Rabbi Yoḥanan's ruling: **Where** is this woman found? [5]**If you say** that Rabbi Yoḥanan was referring to a woman who goes about **in the marketplace** with her head covered only by her basket, surely that is a problem, for we said above that **this is forbidden by Jewish custom.** [6]**Rather,** Rabbi Yoḥanan must have been referring to a woman who goes about **in a courtyard with** her head covered only by her basket. But this too is problematic. [7]**If this is so, a Jewish woman would not be allowed to live with her husband, for** most women do not maintain a standard of modesty so strict that it requires them to keep their heads completely covered even while in a courtyard!

אָמַר אַבָּיֵי [8]**Abaye said (and there are some who say** that it was **Rav Kahana** who offered this explanation): [9]Rabbi Yoḥanan was referring to a woman going **from** one **courtyard to another by way of an alleyway**

יִשְׂרָאֵל שֶׁלֹּא יֵצְאוּ בְּפֵרוּעַ רֹאשׁ".

[1]דְּאוֹרָיְיתָא, [72B] קַלְתָּהּ שַׁפִּיר דָּמֵי; [2]דָּת יְהוּדִית אֲפִילּוּ קַלְתָּהּ נַמֵּי אָסוּר.

[3]אָמַר רַבִּי אַסִּי אָמַר רַבִּי יוֹחָנָן: קַלְתָּהּ אֵין בָּהּ מִשּׁוּם פֵּרוּעַ רֹאשׁ.

[4]הָוֵי בָּהּ רַבִּי זֵירָא: הֵיכָא? [5]אִילֵימָא בַּשּׁוּק, דָּת יְהוּדִית הִיא. [6]וְאֶלָּא, בְּחָצֵר. [7]אִם כֵּן, לֹא הִנַּחְתָּ בַּת לְאַבְרָהָם אָבִינוּ שֶׁיּוֹשֶׁבֶת תַּחַת בַּעְלָהּ!

[8]אָמַר אַבָּיֵי, וְאִיתֵּימָא רַב כָּהֲנָא: [9]מֵחָצֵר לְחָצֵר, וְדֶרֶךְ מָבוֹי.

LITERAL TRANSLATION

of Israel that they should not go out with an uncovered head."

[1]By Torah law, [72B] her basket is fine; [2]by the custom of Jewish women, even her basket is also forbidden.

[3]Rabbi Assi said in the name of Rabbi Yoḥanan: [With] her basket there is no [violation concerning an] uncovered head.

[4]Rabbi Zera discussed it: Where? [5]If you say in the marketplace, it is [forbidden by] the custom of Jewish women. [6]Rather, in a courtyard. [7]If so, you do not allow the daughter of Abraham our Patriarch to live with her husband!

[8]Abaye said, and there are [some] who say [it was] Rav Kahana: [9]From courtyard to courtyard, and by way of an alleyway.

RASHI

קלתה — סל שיש לו מלמטה בית קבול להולמו בראשו, ובית קיבול מלמעלה לתת בו פלך ופשתן. **הוי** — לשון מקשה. **אם כן** — דבחצר יש בה משום פריעה. **ודרך מבוי** — דלא שכיחי רבים.

LANGUAGE

קַלְתָּהּ **Her basket.** From the Greek κάλαθος, *kalathos,* a basket with a narrow bottom used for carrying wool and women's weaving implements.

A Greek illustration of a woman with a basket of fruit on her head.

NOTES

קַלְתָּהּ **Her basket.** *Rashi* understands that the Gemara refers here to a basket for flax and spinning instruments which has an indentation on the bottom so that it fits on a woman's head. *Rivan* explains that such a basket is an inadequate headcovering for a woman who ventures out to the marketplace, because her hair can still be seen through the holes in the wickerwork.

קַלְתָּהּ שַׁפִּיר דָּמֵי **Her basket is fine.** *Ritva* summarizes the laws regarding a woman's headcovering as follows: A woman who goes out in the public domain with her hair uncovered violates a Biblical prohibition, and even if she goes out with her hair covered by a basket or the like, she is still in violation of Jewish custom. In an alleyway, she must cover her head with some sort of covering, such as a basket. In a courtyard, she may go about without any headcovering at all (so too *Tosafot* and *Rashba*). Some Rishonim (*Shiltei HaGibborim;* see also *Baḥ,* and *Bet Shmuel*) understand from the Jerusalem Talmud that a woman must cover her head in some manner, even in a courtyard. The Rishonim and Aḥaronim disagree about the requirements of the law, but there is general agreement that a pious and modest woman should keep her head covered even in the privacy of her own home (see *Zohar Naso* 126:1).

מֵחָצֵר לְחָצֵר **From courtyard to courtyard.** *Talmidei*

HALAKHAH

מֵחָצֵר לְחָצֵר **From courtyard to courtyard.** "A woman who goes out to the marketplace, or to an open alleyway, or to a courtyard frequented by many people, with her head not properly covered, is regarded as a woman who violates

TRANSLATION AND COMMENTARY

connecting the two. Even though she might pass some strangers on the way, since she does not expose herself to full public view, covering her head with her basket suffices.

וְטוֹוָה בַּשּׁוּק [1]The Mishnah continues: "Also included among those who are regarded as having violated the custom of Jewish women is she who **spins in the marketplace**." [2]The Gemara clarifies its view of this woman's misconduct: **Rav Yehudah said in the name of Shmuel:** The Mishnah refers here to a woman who rolls up her sleeves and **exposes her arms to the people** around her while she spins. [3]**Rav Ḥisda said in the name of Avimi:** We are dealing here with a woman who **spins red wool** and holds it **up to her face** to attract attention to her face.

וּמְדַבֶּרֶת עִם כָּל אָדָם [4]We learned in our Mishnah: "A third woman who is viewed as having violated Jewish custom is she who **talks with everybody.**" [5]The Gemara explains: **Rav Yehudah said in the name of Shmuel:** [6]The Mishnah refers here to a woman who **flirts with** all the **young men** whom she encounters.

אָמַר רַבָּה בַּר בַּר חָנָה [7]The Gemara now offers a concrete example of the immodest behavior referred to in our Mishnah: **Rabbah bar Bar Ḥanah said:** [8]**Once,** as **I was walking behind Rav Ukva, I saw a certain Arab woman who was sitting holding her distaff in** her hand, **and she was spinning red wool** which she held **up to her face.** [9]**When she saw us** approaching, **she tore her distaff loose** from the thread **and cast it aside.** [10]**She said to me: "Young man, give me my distaff."** [11]**Rav Ukva said something about** the woman. [12]The Gemara asks: **What** precisely **did** Rav Ukva **say about** her? Which type of immodest behavior mentioned in the

[1]״וְטוֹוָה בַּשּׁוּק״. [2]אָמַר רַב יְהוּדָה אָמַר שְׁמוּאֵל: בְּמַרְאָה זְרוֹעוֹתֶיהָ לִבְנֵי אָדָם. [3]רַב חִסְדָּא אָמַר אֲבִימִי: בְּטוֹוָה וֶרֶד כְּנֶגֶד פָּנֶיהָ.

[4]״וּמְדַבֶּרֶת עִם כָּל אָדָם״. [5]אָמַר רַב יְהוּדָה אָמַר שְׁמוּאֵל: [6]בִּמְשַׂחֶקֶת עִם בַּחוּרִים.

[7]אָמַר רַבָּה בַּר בַּר חָנָה: [8]זִימְנָא חֲדָא הֲוָה קָאָזֵילְנָא בַּתְרֵיהּ דְּרַב עוּקְבָא. חֲזִיתֵיהּ לְהַהִיא עֲרָבִיָּא דַּהֲוָה יָתְבָה קָא שַׁדְיָא פִּילְכָּהּ, וְטוֹוָה וֶרֶד כְּנֶגֶד פָּנֶיהָ. [9]כֵּיוָן דַּחֲזִיתִינַן, פְּסִיקְתֵיהּ לְפִילְכָּהּ שְׁדִיתֵיהּ. [10]אָמְרָה לִי: ״עוּלֵם, הַב לִי פֶּלֶךְ״! [11]אֲמַר בָּהּ רַב עוּקְבָא מִילְּתָא. [12]מַאי אֲמַר בָּהּ?

LITERAL TRANSLATION

[1]"Or spins in the marketplace." [2]Rav Yehudah said in the name of Shmuel: When she exposes her arms to people. [3]Rav Ḥisda said in the name of Avimi: When she spins red [wool] next to her face.

[4]"Or talks with everybody." [5]Rav Yehudah said in the name of Shmuel: [6]When she flirts with young men.

[7]Rabbah bar Bar Ḥanah said: [8]Once I was walking behind Rav Ukva. I saw a certain Arab woman who was sitting holding her distaff and she was spinning red [wool] next to her face. [9]When she saw us, she tore her distaff loose [and] cast it. [10]She said to me: "Young man, give me a distaff." [11]Rav Ukva said something about her. [12]What did he say about her?

RASHI

בטווה ורד כנגד פניה — טווה בכפה על ירכה, וחוט מתרדד כנגד פניה של מטה. **שדיתיה** — השליכתהו.

LANGUAGE

וֶרֶד Rose. This word is apparently derived from the Middle Persian *vard*, which means "rose." In Talmudic Aramaic (as well as the parallel Greek roots) this word apparently denotes the color "red" in general, and not just rose bushes.

NOTES

Rabbenu Yonah distinguish between the woman's going directly from one courtyard to another by way of an alleyway, and her leaving and spending some time in the alleyway before entering the second courtyard.

The Jerusalem Talmud argues that there are certain courtyards which are treated like alleyways, and certain alleyways which are treated like courtyards. The determining factor is whether the woman is likely to pass strangers along the way.

טוֹוָה וֶרֶד When she spins red wool. *Rashi* appears to read ורד (*sheva* under the ו, and *kamatz* under the ר) — "and goes down." According to *Rashi,* the Mishnah deals with a woman who is spinning wool on her lap, and the thread hangs down across her genital area ("the face below"). *Rabbenu Ḥananel* suggests that the word וֶרֶד be understood as "red wool." The Mishnah thus refers to a woman who is spinning red wool and holding it in such a manner that it casts a red glow on her face and accentuates her beauty. *Rambam* understands the word וֶרֶד to mean "rose." While the woman is spinning wool in the marketplace, she wears a rose or some other red ornament on her face or forehead in an immodest manner. *Talmidei Rabbenu Yonah* suggest that the woman has placed a rose across her lap, drawing attention to her genital area.

HALAKHAH

Jewish custom." (*Rambam, Sefer Nashim, Hilkhot Ishut* 24:12; *Shulḥan Arukh, Even HaEzer* 115:4.)

טוֹוָה בַּשּׁוּק Or spins in the marketplace. "A woman who spins wool in the marketplace with a rose on her forehead or cheek in the manner of a loose woman, or spins wool in the marketplace and exposes her arms to those who pass by (and is accustomed to act in that manner; *Rema* in the name of *Rashba*), is regarded as a woman who violates Jewish custom." (*Rambam, Sefer Nashim, Hilkhot Ishut* 24:12; *Shulḥan Arukh, Even HaEzer* 115:4.)

מְדַבֶּרֶת עִם כָּל אָדָם She talks with everybody. "A woman who flirts with all the young men whom she encounters is

[1]רָבִינָא אֲמַר: ״טוֹוָה בַּשּׁוּק״ אֲמַר בָּהּ. [2]רַבָּנַן אָמְרִי: ״מְדַבֶּרֶת עִם כָּל אָדָם״ אֲמַר בָּהּ.

[3]״אַבָּא שָׁאוּל אוֹמֵר: אַף הַמְקַלֶּלֶת יוֹלְדָיו בְּפָנָיו״. [4]אָמַר רַב יְהוּדָה אָמַר שְׁמוּאֵל: בִּמְקַלֶּלֶת יוֹלִידָיו בִּפְנֵי מוֹלִידָיו. [5]וְסִימָנֵיךְ: ״אֶפְרַיִם וּמְנַשֶּׁה כִּרְאוּבֵן וְשִׁמְעוֹן יִהְיוּ לִי״. [6]אֲמַר רַבָּה: דְּאָמְרָה לֵיהּ: ״נֵיכְלֵיהּ אַרְיָא לְסָבָא״, בְּאַפֵּי בְּרֵיהּ.

[7]״רַבִּי טַרְפוֹן אוֹמֵר: אַף הַקּוֹלָנִית״. [8]מַאי ״קוֹלָנִית״?

LITERAL TRANSLATION

[1]Ravina said: He said about her: "She spins in the marketplace." [2]The Rabbis said: He said about her: "She talks with everybody."

[3]"Abba Shaul says: Also one who curses his parents in his presence." [4]Rav Yehudah said in the name of Shmuel: When she curses his parents in the presence of his children. [5]And your sign is: "Ephraim and Manasseh shall be to me as Reuben and Simeon." [6]Rabbah said: If she said to him: "May a lion eat the grandfather," in the presence of his son.

[7]"Rabbi Tarfon says: Also one who is loud." [8]What is "one who is loud"?

TRANSLATION AND COMMENTARY

the Mishnah did the woman bring to mind? [1]**Ravina said:** Rav Ukva **said about** the woman that she was one "who **spins in the marketplace.**" [2]**The Rabbis** disagreed and **said:** Rav Ukva **said about** the woman that her behavior exemplifies what the Mishnah meant when it spoke of "a woman **who talks with everybody.**"

אַבָּא שָׁאוּל אוֹמֵר [3]Our Mishnah continues: **"Abba Shaul says: Also** included in the category of women who violate the standards of conduct of Jewish women is she **who curses** her husband's **parents in his presence."** [4]The Gemara explains: **Rav Yehudah said in the name of Shmuel:** The Mishnah refers also to a woman who **curses** her husband's **parents in the presence of** her husband's **children.** [5]**And** it may be suggested that the following verse serve as a **mnemonic device** to help remember this ruling (Genesis 48:5): **"Ephraim and Manasseh shall be to me as Reuben and Simeon."** Jacob told Joseph that he viewed his grandsons, Ephraim and Manasseh, as like his sons Reuben and Simeon. Since grandchildren are like children, it is just as bad for a woman to curse her husband's parents in his presence as in the presence of his children. [6]**Rabbah said:** We are dealing here with a woman who, **in the presence of** her husband's **son, said** something like, **"May a lion eat** your **grandfather."**

רַבִּי טַרְפוֹן אוֹמֵר [7]Our Mishnah concludes: **"Rabbi Tarfon says: Also included** in the category of women who violate Jewish custom is she **who is** overly **loud."** [8]**What** does the Mishnah mean when it refers to

RASHI

במקללת יולידיו בפני מולידיו – כלומר, ״בפניו״ דמתניתין לא תימא לפניו ממש, אלא אפילו מקללת אביו של בעל בפני בנו של בעל. **וסימניך אפרים ומנשה וגו׳** – ופסוק זה יהא לך סימן על משנתינו, לזכור על ידו, ד״בפניו״ דמתניתין [לא תימא בפניו ממש, אלא] בפני בנו קאמר, והוי כאילו בפניו. **אפרים ומנשה וגו׳** – בני בניו כבניו. **אמר רבה** – לפרושי מילתיה דרב יהודה, כגון דאמרה: ניכליה אריא לסבא, חמיה. **באפי בריה** – בפני בנו של בעל אומרת כן.

NOTES

יוֹלִידָיו בִּפְנֵי מוֹלִידָיו **His parents in the presence of his children.** Our commentary follows *Rashi* and others. According to them Shmuel argued that, though the Mishnah speaks of a woman who cursed her husband's parents in his presence, the same law applies to a woman who cursed her husband's parents (יוֹלִידָיו) in the presence of her husband's children (מוֹלִידָיו). This is supported by the verse regarding Ephraim and Manasseh, which teaches that grandchildren are treated like children. Rabbah offers the example of a woman who said in the presence of her husband's son: "May a lion eat your grandfather." *Rambam, Ritva,* and others understand that, according to Shmuel, the Mishnah speaks of a woman who cursed her husband's parents (יוֹלִידָיו) in the presence of his (= the parent's) children (מוֹלִידָיו), i.e., her husband. The Gemara cites the end of the verse regarding Ephraim and Manasseh, "And your children [מוֹלַדְתְּךָ] which you will beget after them," to explain that the word מוֹלִידָיו refers to children. Rabbah offers the example of a woman who said: "May a lion eat grandfather," in his (= the grandfather's) son's presence, i.e., in front of her husband. The Jerusalem Talmud has a reading: "Abba Shaul says: Also one who curses his children in the presence of his parents [וְוֹלָדָיו בִּפְנֵי יוֹלְדָיו]."

קוֹלָנִית **One who is loud.** *Rashi* explains that a loud woman

HALAKHAH

seen as a woman who violates Jewish custom." (*Rambam, Sefer Nashim, Hilkhot Ishut* 24:12; *Shulḥan Arukh, Even HaEzer* 115:4.)

מְקַלֶּלֶת יוֹלִידָיו בִּפְנֵי מוֹלִידָיו **She curses his parents in the presence of his children.** "A woman who curses her husband's father in the presence of her husband is considered a woman who violates Jewish custom (following Rabbah, who disagrees with Rav Yehudah; *Rambam,* according to *Kesef Mishneh*). *Rema* adds that the same law applies, according to some authorities (*Rashi*), if she curses her husband's father in his own presence, and according to others (*Ramban*), if she curses her husband to his face." (*Rambam, Sefer Nashim, Hilkhot Ishut* 24:12; *Shulḥan Arukh, Even HaEzer* 115:4.)

הַקּוֹלָנִית **One who is loud.** "A woman who speaks to her husband about their sexual relations in such a loud voice that she can be heard by her neighbors is seen as a woman who violates Jewish custom." (*Rambam, Sefer Nashim,*

TRANSLATION AND COMMENTARY

"a woman **who is overly loud**"? [1]**Rav Yehudah said in the name of Shmuel:** This refers to a woman **who raises her voice about sexual relations.** She quarrels so loudly with her husband about their sexual relations that her neighbors hear everything that she says, and her husband is put to shame.

בְּמַתְנִיתָא תָּנָא [2]**In a Baraita it was taught:** "We are dealing here with a woman **who engages in sexual relations in** a house opening onto a certain **courtyard,** [3]**and** because of the pain, she screams and **her voice is heard** by people **in another courtyard."**

וְנִיתְנְיֵיהּ [4]The Gemara says: If so, **let** the Tanna **teach this regulation among** those governing women who suffer physical **defects** found below **in our Mishnah!** For if a man is entitled to divorce his wife who cries out in pain during sexual intercourse, it is not because of immodest conduct, but rather because she suffers a physical defect which the husband is not required to bear.

אֶלָּא [5]**Rather,** concludes the Gemara, **it is clear** that the Mishnah must be understood **as we answered in the beginning,** as referring to a woman who unabashedly raises her voice and quarrels with her husband about their sexual relations so that all her neighbors can hear.

MISHNAH הַמְקַדֵּשׁ אֶת הָאִשָּׁה [6]The next Mishnah expands the list of women who may be divorced without receiving payment of their ketubah: **If someone betrothed a woman on condition that she was not bound by vows,** [7]**and** it is later discovered that indeed **she was bound by vows, her betrothal is void,** because the

[1]אָמַר רַב יְהוּדָה אָמַר שְׁמוּאֵל: בְּמַשְׁמַעַת קוֹלָהּ עַל עִסְקֵי תַּשְׁמִישׁ.
[2]בְּמַתְנִיתָא תָּנָא: "בִּמְשַׁמֶּשֶׁת בְּחָצֵר זוֹ, [3]וְנִשְׁמַע קוֹלָהּ בְּחָצֵר אַחֶרֶת".
[4]וְנִיתְנְיֵיהּ גַּבֵּי מוּמִין בְּמַתְנִיתִין!
[5]אֶלָּא, מְחַוַּורְתָּא כִּדְשַׁנִּין מֵעִיקָּרָא.
משנה [6]הַמְקַדֵּשׁ אֶת הָאִשָּׁה עַל מְנָת שֶׁאֵין עָלֶיהָ נְדָרִים, [7]וְנִמְצְאוּ עָלֶיהָ נְדָרִים, אֵינָהּ מְקוּדֶּשֶׁת.

LITERAL TRANSLATION

[1]Rav Yehudah said in the name of Shmuel: When she sounds her voice about matters regarding sexual relations.

[2]In a Baraita it was taught: "Where she engages in sexual relations in this courtyard, [3]and her voice is heard in another courtyard."

[4]Let him teach this among the defects in our Mishnah!

[5]Rather, it is clear as we answered in the beginning.

MISHNAH [6][If] someone betroths a woman on condition that there are no vows upon her, [7]and vows were found upon her, she is not betrothed.

RASHI

על עסקי תשמיש — כשמדבר עמה על עסקי עונה, מריבה עמו ומשמעת לשכניו, והוא בוש בדבר. **ונשמע קולה** — שתשמיש קשה לה, וצועקת. **גבי מומין** — בשילהי פירקין.

משנה כנסה סתם — בגמרא מפרש אי קאי ארישא, אהך דקידשה על תנאי, או מילתא באפי נפשה.

NOTES

is one who quarrels with her husband about sexual relations, and raises her voice so that the neighbors hear, and he suffers embarrassment. According to *Rivan*, the Mishnah refers to a woman who refuses to undergo ritual immersion following her period, and her husband has to bring in her friends to persuade her to go, and he suffers embarrassment when the matter becomes public. *Rif* and *Rosh* understand that the Mishnah refers to a woman who demands of her husband that he engage in sexual intercourse with her, and she immodestly raises her voice so that her neighbors overhear the conversation.

HALAKHAH

Hilkhot Ishut 24:12; *Shulḥan Arukh, Even HaEzer* 115:4.)

הַמְקַדֵּשׁ אֶת הָאִשָּׁה עַל מְנָת שֶׁאֵין עָלֶיהָ נְדָרִים **If someone betroths a woman on condition that there are no vows upon her.** "If someone betrothed a woman on condition that she was not bound by vows, and it is later discovered that she was bound by a vow not to eat meat, or not to drink wine, or not to adorn herself with colorful clothing, or that she was bound by a vow affecting the intimate relationship between the couple, the betrothal is not valid. According to some authorities, the woman may not remarry unless she first receives a bill of divorce, lest her vow one day be nullified by a Sage and her betrothal be declared valid. If it is discovered that she is bound by some other vow, the betrothal is valid, even if the man claims that he objects to it. If he betrothed her on condition that she was not bound by any vow, then any vow by which she is bound invalidates the betrothal (following the Jerusalem Talmud)." (*Rambam, Sefer Nashim, Hilkhot Ishut* 7:6; *Shulḥan Arukh, Even HaEzer* 39:1.)

נִמְצְאוּ עָלֶיהָ נְדָרִים **Vows were found upon her.** "If someone married a woman without specifying any conditions, and then discovered that she was bound by a vow of self-affliction — not to eat meat, not to drink wine, or not to adorn herself with colorful clothing — he may divorce her without paying her ketubah." (*Rambam, Sefer Nashim, Hilkhot Ishut* 25:1; *Shulḥan Arukh, Even HaEzer* 117:3.)

[1]כְּנָסָהּ סְתָם, [2]וְנִמְצְאוּ עָלֶיהָ נְדָרִים, [3]תֵּצֵא שֶׁלֹּא בִּכְתוּבָּה. [4]עַל מְנָת שֶׁאֵין בָּהּ מוּמִין, [5]וְנִמְצְאוּ בָּהּ מוּמִין, אֵינָהּ מְקוּדֶּשֶׁת. [6]כְּנָסָהּ סְתָם, וְנִמְצְאוּ בָּהּ מוּמִין, [7]תֵּצֵא שֶׁלֹּא בִּכְתוּבָּה.

[8]כָּל הַמּוּמִין הַפּוֹסְלִין בְּכֹהֲנִים פּוֹסְלִין בְּנָשִׁים.

גמרא [9]וּתְנַן נַמִי גַּבֵּי קִדּוּשִׁין כִּי הַאי גַּוְונָא!

LITERAL TRANSLATION

[1][If] he married her without specifying, [2]and vows were found upon her, [3]she goes out without a ketubah.

[4][If someone betroths a woman] on condition that she has no defects, [5]and defects are found in her, she is not betrothed. [6][If] he marries her without specifying, and defects are found in her, [7]she goes out without a ketubah.

[8]All the defects which disqualify priests disqualify women.

GEMARA [9]And we also learned in *Kiddushin* like this!

RASHI

מומין הפוסלין בכהנים — בבכורות קתני להו.

גמרא כי האי גוונא — משנה זו שנויה בקדושין בפרק "האיש מקדש", ומאי שנא דסתמה רבי תרי זימני?

TRANSLATION AND COMMENTARY

husband's condition was not fulfilled. [1]If the husband **married** his wife **without specifying** any conditions, [2]**and** it is later discovered that the woman **was bound by vows,** the marriage is valid. But since she concealed the vows from her husband, he can claim that he had entered into the marriage under false pretenses, [3]and the woman **may be divorced without** receiving payment of **her ketubah.**

עַל מְנָת [4]Similarly, **if someone betrothed a woman on condition that she had no** physical **defects,** [5]**and** it is later discovered that **she has** such **defects, her betrothal is void,** because the husband's condition has not been fulfilled. [6]If the husband **married** his wife **without specifying** any conditions, **and** it is later discovered that **she has** certain physical **defects,** the marriage is valid. However, since she concealed these defects, and the husband can claim that he entered into the marriage under false pretenses, [7]the woman **may be divorced without** receiving payment of **her ketubah.**

כָּל הַמּוּמִין [8]The Mishnah continues: **All the defects that disqualify priests** from the Temple service **disqualify women.** A woman who has any of these defects may be divorced without receiving payment of her ketubah.

GEMARA וּתְנַן [9]The Gemara notes that **we also learned in** tractate *Kiddushin* (50a) a Mishnah which is word for word **like this** Mishnah. Why was it necessary to teach the very same Mishnah twice?

BACKGROUND

הַמּוּמִין הַפּוֹסְלִין בְּכֹהֲנִים Defects which disqualify priests. Certain types of physical imperfections and deformities render a priest unfit to serve in the Temple, as the verse says (Leviticus 21:17): "Whoever he be of your seed in their generations that has any blemish, let him not approach to offer the bread of his God." The defects which disqualify a priest from serving in the Temple are listed in detail in the seventh chapter of tractate *Bekhorot.*

NOTES

נְדָרִים וּמוּמִים Vows and defects. It may be asked: Why does the Mishnah first teach the law regarding vows and then teach the very same law regarding defects? Let the Mishnah teach the law once regarding both vows and defects! *Melekhet Shlomo* explains that the Mishnah separates the two because the law applies only to three particular vows, as is explained in the Gemara, whereas with respect to defects, the law applies in all cases. It is also possible that the Mishnah does not teach them together because if the woman went to a Sage and her vows were nullified, her betrothal is valid, but if she went to a doctor and her defects were corrected, her betrothal is still void (see Baraita below, 74b).

HALAKHAH

הַמְקַדֵּשׁ עַל מְנָת שֶׁאֵין בָּהּ מוּמִין If someone betroths a woman on condition that she has no defects. "If someone betrothed a woman on condition that she had no physical defects, and it is later discovered that she has a defect of the type that invalidates betrothal, her betrothal is not valid. But if it is found that she has some other type of defect, the betrothal is valid, even if the man claims that he objects." (*Rambam, Sefer Nashim, Hilkhot Ishut* 7:7; *Shulḥan Arukh, Even HaEzer* 39:3.)

כְּנָסָהּ סְתָם, וְנִמְצְאוּ בָּהּ מוּמִין If he married her without specifying, and defects were found in her. "If someone married a woman without specifying any conditions, and then discovered that she had a defect which would disqualify a woman's betrothal, she may be divorced without receiving her ketubah payment." (*Rambam, Sefer Nashim, Hilkhot Ishut* 25:2; *Shulḥan Arukh, Even HaEzer* 117:4.)

כָּל הַמּוּמִין הַפּוֹסְלִין בְּכֹהֲנִים All the defects which disqualify priests. "All the defects which disqualify priests from the Temple service disqualify a woman's betrothal. There are also certain defects which do not disqualify priests from serving in the Temple, but nevertheless disqualify a woman's betrothal." (*Rambam, Sefer Nashim, Hilkhot Ishut* 7:7; *Shulḥan Arukh, Even HaEzer* 39:4)

קִידְּשָׁהּ עַל תְּנַאי וּכְנָסָהּ סְתָם If he betrothed her on condition, and married her without specifying. "If a man attached a certain condition to his wife's betrothal, and then married her or had sexual intercourse with her without specifying any conditions, the woman requires a bill of divorce, even if the condition attached to the betrothal was not fulfilled, for the man might have canceled his condition when he married the woman or had intercourse with her," following Rav. (*Rambam, Sefer Nashim, Hilkhot Ishut* 7:23; *Shulḥan Arukh, Even HaEzer* 38:35.)

[1]הָכָא כְּתוּבּוֹת אִיצְטְרִיכָא לֵיהּ
[2]תָּנָא קִדּוּשִׁין אַטּוּ כְּתוּבּוֹת.
[3]הָתָם קִדּוּשִׁין אִצְטְרִיכָא לֵיהּ,
[4]תָּנָא כְּתוּבּוֹת אַטּוּ קִדּוּשִׁין.
[5]אָמַר רַבִּי יוֹחָנָן מִשּׁוּם רַבִּי
שִׁמְעוֹן בֶּן יְהוֹצָדָק: [6]בְּאֵלּוּ
נְדָרִים אָמְרוּ: שֶׁלֹּא תֹּאכַל בָּשָׂר,
וְשֶׁלֹּא תִּשְׁתֶּה יַיִן, [7]וְשֶׁלֹּא
תִּתְקַשֵּׁט בְּבִגְדֵי צִבְעוֹנִים.
[8]תַּנְיָא נַמִי הָכִי: [9]״בְּאֵלּוּ נְדָרִים
אָמְרוּ — דְּבָרִים שֶׁיֵּשׁ בָּהֶן
עִינּוּי נֶפֶשׁ: [10]שֶׁלֹּא תֹּאכַל בָּשָׂר,
וְשֶׁלֹּא תִּשְׁתֶּה יַיִן, וְשֶׁלֹּא
תִּתְקַשֵּׁט בְּבִגְדֵי צִבְעוֹנִין״.
[11]הָוֵי בָּהּ רַב פַּפָּא: אַהַיָּיא?

LITERAL TRANSLATION

[1]Here he had to [teach] about ketubot, [2][so] he taught about betrothal on account of ketubot. [3]There he had to [teach] about betrothal, [4][so] he taught about ketubot on account of betrothal.

[5]Rabbi Yoḥanan said in the name of Rabbi Shimon ben Yehotzadak: [6]About these vows they spoke: That she would not eat meat, and that she would not drink wine, [7]and that she would not adorn herself in colorful clothing.

[8]It was also taught thus: [9]"About these vows they spoke — matters which involve self-affliction: [10]That she would not eat meat, and that she would not drink wine, and that she would not adorn herself in colorful clothing."

[11]Rav Pappa discussed it: On which?

RASHI

הבא — דמכילתין דהלכה בכתובות קאי, איצטריך ליה למיתנייה משום כתובות, כדקתני סיפא: תצא שלא בכתובה. **תנא קדושין** — רישא דמתניתין "אינה מקודשת". **אטו כתובות** — איידי דנקטה משום כתובות. **שלא תאכל בשר** — דהוי עינוי נפש, ומתגנה עליו.

TRANSLATION AND COMMENTARY

הָכָא כְּתוּבּוֹת [1]The Gemara answers that the two topics are inseparable, but in each Mishnah they receive different emphasis. **Here,** in tractate *Ketubot*, the Tanna **had to teach** us the law regarding the woman's **ketubah** — that if she entered into marriage concealing the fact that she was bound by certain vows or that she had certain defects, she may be divorced without receiving payment of her ketubah. [2]And so the Tanna also **taught** us the law regarding the woman's betrothal — that if her husband had betrothed her on condition that she was free of vows or defects, and it is discovered that she is bound by vows or that she has defects, her betrothal is void **because of** what he taught us regarding **the** woman's **ketubah.** [3]**There**, in tractate *Kiddushin*, the Tanna **had to teach** us the law regarding the woman's **betrothal,** [4]and so **he** also **taught** us the law regarding her **ketubah, because of** what he taught regarding her **betrothal.**

אָמַר רַבִּי יוֹחָנָן [5]The Gemara now clarifies what the Mishnah meant when it spoke of a woman who was bound by vows: **Rabbi Yoḥanan said in the name of Rabbi Shimon ben Yehotzadak:** [6]It was **about these vows** that the Rabbis **spoke:** If the woman took a vow **that she would not eat meat, or that she would not drink wine,** [7]**or that she would not adorn herself in colorful clothing,** each of which involves self-affliction.

תַּנְיָא נַמִי הָכִי [8]**The same thing was also taught** in a Baraita: [9]"It was **about these vows** that the Rabbi **spoke: Vows which involve self-affliction,** [10]such as when the woman took a vow **that she would not eat meat, or that she would not drink wine, or that she would not adorn herself in colorful clothing."**

הָוֵי בָּהּ רַב פַּפָּא [11]**Rav Pappa raised** the following **question**: **To which** clause of the Mishnah was Rabbi

NOTES

הָכָא כְּתוּבּוֹת אִיצְטְרִיכָא לֵיהּ **Here he had to teach ketubot.** The Rishonim ask: If the law regarding the woman's betrothal was taught here because of what the Tanna taught regarding the woman's ketubah, why did the Tanna not first teach the law regarding the ketubah, and then follow with the law regarding betrothal? *Shittah Mekubbetzet* explains that Rabbi Yehudah HaNasi (the compiler of the Mishnah) received our Mishnah in its present form, and included it in both tractate *Kiddushin* and tractate *Ketubot* because of its relevance to both tractates. He taught the Mishnah in both tractates in the form in which he had received it, because he did not want to deviate from the traditional manner in which the Mishnah had been taught, for that would have made it more difficult for the students to commit it to memory.

בְּאֵלּוּ נְדָרִים אָמְרוּ **About these vows they spoke.** *Rif, Rambam, Ra'avad,* and others understand that only if it is discovered that the woman is bound by one of these three vows is her betrothal void. But if it is discovered that she is bound by other vows, even those involving self-affliction, her betrothal remains valid. The same may be inferred from *Rashi,* who explains that the three vows mentioned here involve self-affliction and cause a woman to be found repulsive in her husband's eyes, implying that other vows involving self-affliction are not grounds for voiding the betrothal. *Ra'ah, Ritva* and others maintain that the three vows are mentioned here as examples, and the betrothal is similarly void if it is discovered that the woman is bound by other vows involving self-affliction, or by vows affecting the intimate personal relationship between herself and her husband.

TRANSLATION AND COMMENTARY

Shimon ben Yehotzadak referring? [1]**If you say** that he was referring **to the first clause,** which states that if someone betrothed a woman on condition that she was free of vows, and it was later discovered that she was bound by vows, her betrothal is void, there is a difficulty. [2]**Since** the man stipulated the condition explicitly, demonstrating thereby that **he minds** marrying a woman who is bound by vows, it stands to reason that the betrothal should be void, **even** if she took a vow relating to **other things** which do not involve self-affliction. [3]**Rather,** Rabbi Shimon ben Yehotzadak must have been referring **to the next clause,** which states that if the man married the woman without specifying any conditions, and it was later discovered that she was bound by certain vows, the woman may be divorced without receiving payment of her ketubah. Rabbi Shimon ben Yehotzadak taught that only if the man discovered that his wife was bound by vows involving self-affliction, may he divorce her without paying out her ketubah.

[1]אִילֵימָא אַרֵישָׁא, [2]כֵּיוָן דְּקָא קָפֵיד, אֲפִילּוּ כָּל מִילֵּי נַמִי. [3]אֶלָּא, אַסֵּיפָא.

[4]רַב אַשִׁי אָמַר: לְעוֹלָם אַרֵישָׁא. [5]וּמִידֵי דְּקָפְדֵי בָּהּ אֱינָשֵׁי, [6]הֲוָה קְפֵידֵיהּ קְפֵידָא. [7]מִידֵי דְּלָא קָפְדֵי בָּהּ אֱינָשֵׁי, [8]לָא הָוֵי קְפֵידֵיהּ קְפֵידָא.

[9]אִיתְּמַר: קִידְּשָׁהּ עַל תְּנַאי, [10]וּכְנָסָהּ סְתָם, [11]רַב אָמַר: צְרִיכָה הֵימֶנּוּ גֵּט. [12]וּשְׁמוּאֵל אָמַר: אֵינָהּ צְרִיכָה הֵימֶנּוּ גֵּט. [13]אָמַר אַבַּיֵי: [73A] [14]לָא תֵּימָא טַעְמֵיהּ דְּרַב כֵּיוָן שֶׁכְּנָסָהּ סְתָם,

LITERAL TRANSLATION

[1]If you say on the first clause, [2]since he minds, even all things also. [3]Rather, on the last clause.

[4]Rav Ashi said: In fact, on the first clause. [5]And something about which people mind, [6]his minding is valid (lit., "is a minding"). [7]Something about which people do not mind, [8]his minding is not valid.

[9]It was stated: If he betrothed her on condition, [10]and married her without specifying, [11]Rav said: She requires from him a bill of divorce. [12]And Shmuel said: She does not require from him a bill of divorce.

[13]Abaye said: [73A] [14]Do not say that the reason of Rav is [that] since he married her without stating anything,

RASHI

ארישא — דאתני בהדה. אסיפא — וקסבר: סיפא דמתניתין מילתא באפי נפשה, וקידשה סתם וכנסה סתם קאמר. קידשה על תנאי — שאין עליה נדרים. לא תימא — קסבר רב אחולי לתנאיה, וכתובה בעי למיתב לה אם מגרשה.

רַב אַשִׁי אָמַר [4]**Rav Ashi said: In fact,** it is possible to understand Rabbi Shimon ben Yehotzadak's statement as referring **to the first clause** of the Mishnah, which speaks of someone who betrothed his wife on condition that she be free of vows. [5]**And** it was later discovered that she was bound by a vow pertaining to **something to which** most **people object,** such as a vow involving self-affliction, [6]in which case the man's **objection is valid,** and the betrothal is void. [7]But if it turned out that the woman was bound by a vow pertaining to **something to which** most **people do not object,** then even if this man minded being married to a woman bound by such a vow, [8]**his objection is not valid.**

אִיתְּמַר [9]**It was stated** that the Amoraim disagreed about the following matter: **If** a man **betrothed** a woman **on condition that** she was free of vows, [10]**and** then he **married her without specifying** any conditions, and it was later discovered that she was indeed bound by certain vows, [11]**Rav said:** The betrothal is valid, and so the woman **requires a bill of divorce from** her husband. [12]**And Shmuel said:** Since the condition which had been stipulated by the husband was not fulfilled, the betrothal is void, and so the woman **does not** even **require a bill of divorce from** her husband.

אָמַר אַבַּיֵי [13]**Abaye said:** [73A] [14]**Do not say that Rav reasoned that since** the man **married**

NOTES

לָא הָוֵי קְפֵידֵיהּ קְפֵידָא **His minding is not valid.** Most Rishonim understand from the Jerusalem Talmud that if a man betrothed a woman on condition that she was not bound by vows, and it was later discovered that she was bound by a vow pertaining to something that does not bother most people, his being bothered is not valid, and the betrothal remains intact. But if he betrothed her on condition that she was not bound by any vow, or he specified the vows that bothered him, then even if it was later discovered that she was bound by a vow pertaining to something that does not bother most people, but the vow bothers him, his being bothered is valid, and the betrothal is void. *Ramban* and *Ritva* cite a dissenting view, according to which the husband's being bothered is not valid, even if he stated explicitly that he was betrothing the woman on condition that she was not bound by any vow.

לָא תֵּימָא **Do not say.** Two basic approaches to understanding Abaye's statement are found in the works of the Rishonim.

The Rishonim raise an objection against *Rashi:* Why would we have thought that, where a man married a woman without specifying the condition he had attached earlier to her betrothal, she would be entitled to her ketubah? The Mishnah states explicitly that even if a man

LITERAL TRANSLATION

[1]he waived his condition. [2]Rather, the reason of Rav is: [3]Because a person does not render his act of intercourse one of prostitution.

[1]אַחוּלֵי אַחְלֵיהּ לִתְנָאֵיהּ. [2]אֶלָּא טַעֲמָא דְּרַב: [3]לְפִי שֶׁאֵין אָדָם עוֹשֶׂה בְּעִילָתוֹ בְּעִילַת זְנוּת.

RASHI

אלא טעמא דרב – לענין גט, דקסבר אין אדם עושה בעילתו בעילת זנות, ובעל לשם קידושין, ואפילו ימצא עליה נדרים. אבל לענין ממונא – בתנאיה קאי, שאם ימצא עליה נדרים – תצא בלא כתובה.

TRANSLATION AND COMMENTARY

the woman **without stating** the condition he had earlier attached to the betrothal, [1]**he** must have **waived his condition** and agreed to marry her even if she was bound by vows. If that were Rav's reasoning, then not only would she require a bill of divorce from her husband, but she would even be entitled to payment of her ketubah! [2]**Rather,** say that **Rav reasoned** as follows: [3]There is a Halakhic presumption that **a man does not render sexual intercourse** an act **of prostitution.** Rather, his first act of intercourse is considered a new and unconditional basis of betrothal. Thus, the woman would require a bill of divorce from her husband even if it were found that she had violated the original condition of betrothal. However, she would not be entitled to her ketubah settlement in that case, for we assume he waived his condition only to legitimize their relations. As regards payment of her ketubah, however, his original condition would still stand.

NOTES

married his wife without specifying any conditions, were he later to discover that she was bound by certain vows, he could divorce her without paying her her ketubah. Thus Rav could not construe the act of sexual intercourse as waiving those conditions. To reconcile Rav with the Mishnah, *Tosafot* suggest that perhaps the Mishnah deals with a couple who had not yet engaged in sexual relations, whereas Rav is dealing with a case in which they did so, thereby impelling the man to waive his condition altogether. *Rashba* alternatively proposes that Rav might agree with Resh Lakish (whose view is cited in the Jerusalem Talmud) that if a man betrothed and married a woman without ever specifying that she be free of vows, only later to discover that she was bound by certain vows, she would be entitled to her ketubah settlement. Furthermore, even if Rav were to agree with Rabbi Yoḥanan (whose view is also cited in the Jerusalem Talmud), that in such a case the woman is not entitled to her ketubah settlement, nevertheless if a man betrothed his wife conditionally and then married her without stating anything further, she may be entitled to her ketubah settlement as it can be implied that the husband waived his condition of betrothal.

Ri (cited by *Tosafot*) offers his own interpretation of Abaye's statement. According to this interpretation, the consummation of the marriage has crucial legal significance. Do not say that Rav reasons that, since the man married the woman without repeating his condition of betrothal, it can be assumed — even before they engage in sexual relations — that he must have waived his condition altogether. Rather, Rav's reasoning is based strictly upon the Halakhic presumption regarding a husband's intention when cohabiting with his betrothed — that their relations be considered legitimate and sanctioned. Thus, only after the couple have had sexual relations would the woman require a bill of divorce. *Ri's* position was adopted by *Ra'avad, Ra'ah, Ritva* and *Meiri.*

Rashba raises the following difficulty: If we say that with regard to the woman's ketubah settlement the original condition of betrothal is never waived, then how can her husband have relations with her? For marital relations are considered illicit when there is no concomitant obligation to provide the woman with a ketubah settlement. *Rashba* answers his own question by distinguishing between a case where both parties realize that the obligation to pay the ketubah settlement has been diminished or eliminated, thus undermining the foundations of the marriage and rendering their relations illicit, and our case, where the husband assumes that his betrothed is free of vows. Hence, their sexual relations cannot be considered illicit.

אַחוּלֵי אַחְלֵיהּ לִתְנָאֵיהּ He waived his condition. According to *Tosafot,* the Gemara entertained the possibility that Rav reasoned that, since the man married the woman without restating the condition he had attached to her betrothal, we can assume that he retracted his original condition, and the first betrothal was valid. *Rashba* and others ask: How could the Gemara have thought that a man could nullify his earlier action? Perhaps it may be possible to view a potential act as having already happened (and even then, only with respect to monetary issues); but how is it possible to say that, where one actually did something (i.e., betrothed on condition), we can view it as never having happened? Hence, *Rashba* adopted *Rashi's* understanding of the passage: Since the man married the woman without restating the condition that he had attached to her betrothal, we assume that he waived his condition as of that moment, betrothing her a second time — without condition — through the act of intercourse. *Ra'ah, Ritva* and others disagree with *Rashba* and maintain that a person may indeed nullify an earlier condition of agreement.

Rambam and *Rosh* understand the matter differently. Just as the original condition was established by mere words, so too can it be canceled by mere words. By entering into marriage without restating the original condition of betrothal, the husband demonstrates his wish that it be canceled, so the original betrothal is considered valid, even were it to be discovered that the woman had taken vows. *Ran* utilizes a different argument to arrive at the same conclusion: Even if we were to say like Rashi that the husband betrothed his wife again, and without condition, through the act of intercourse, why should the woman be entitled to a ketubah settlement? In such a case, the act of intercourse would only have accomplished betrothal, not marriage; and a woman who is not married is not entitled to a ketubah. Thus it must be that by entering into marriage unconditionally, one eliminates any previous condition of betrothal. The act of intercourse completes the marriage process and entitles the woman to her ketubah settlement.

אֵין אָדָם עוֹשֶׂה בְּעִילָתוֹ A person does not render his act of intercourse. Shmuel, who disagrees with Rav and says that the woman does not require a bill of divorce, does not

[1]הָא פְּלִיגִי בָּהּ חֲדָא זִימְנָא! [2]דְּאִתְּמַר: [3]קְטַנָּה שֶׁלֹּא מֵיאֲנָה, [4]וְהִגְדִּילָה, עָמְדָה וְנִישֵּׂאת, [5]רַב אָמַר: אֵין צְרִיכָה גֵּט מִשֵּׁנִי.

LITERAL TRANSLATION

[1]Surely, they disagreed about this once [before]! [2]For it was stated: [3][Regarding] a minor [girl] who did not exercise refusal [of marriage], [4]and who [then] reached maturity, [if] she stood and married [another], [5]Rav said: She does not require a bill of divorce from the second [husband].

RASHI

קטנה — יתומה. **שלא מיאנה** — בקטנותה. **והגדילה** — ובא עליה, ואחר כך מיאנה, ועמדה וניסת. **אין צריכה גט משני** — דכי גדלה בא עליה לשם קדושין, דיודע הוא שאין קידושי קטנה כלום. **צריכה גט משני** — דכל הבועל על דעת קדושין הראשונים בועל. ואף על גב דמודה שמואל שאסורה לשני, דמשנה שלמה היא (נדה נב,א) דאין הבת ממאנת משהביאה שתי שערות — גט מיהא בעיא מיניה, דהא דאמרי רבנן גדולה לא ממאנת — מדרבנן הוא. ורב סבר דאורייתא היא, משום דכי בעיל משתגדיל — לשם קדושין בעיל.

TRANSLATION AND COMMENTARY

הָא פְּלִיגִי בָּהּ [1]The Gemara raises an objection: But **surely** Rav and Shmuel already **disagreed about this** matter **once before!**

דְּאִתְּמַר [2]**For it was stated** that Rav and Shmuel disagreed [3]about the case of an orphaned **minor who** was married off by her mother or brothers and **did not exercise "refusal" of marriage** before the age of twelve; [4]**then** after **she reached maturity** and continued cohabiting with her husband, she rejected him, **went and married** another man. According to Torah law, a girl under the age of twelve can be married off by her father, but if he dies she cannot get married while still a minor. Fearing for the welfare of young orphaned girls, the Rabbis decreed that a mother or brothers may marry off a fatherless girl, but only with her consent. Since such a marriage would have no validity according to Torah law, formal divorce proceedings would not be required if the girl should later decide to leave her husband, upon reaching legal majority (the age of twelve). The girl may also terminate the marriage before she reaches majority by performing *me'un,* "refusal" — an outright declaraton that she does not want the marriage. *Me'un* is unlike divorce insofar as it renders the marriage retroactively null and void. [5]**Rav said:** The woman **does not require a bill of divorce from the second husband.** We assume that the first marriage took effect immediately upon her reaching majority, for her sexual relations with her husband create a legal bond of matrimony. Hence the second marriage has no validity whatsoever and a bill of divorce would not be necessary.

NOTES

dispute the Halakhic presumption that people do not engage in relations illicitly when they can enjoy them under the sanction of marriage, for this presumption is derived from an opinion of Bet Hillel in *Gittin* (81a-b) which is accepted as law. We must say, then, that according to Shmuel the husband simply assumed that his wife had taken no vows and that their relations were wholly legitimate.

קְטַנָּה שֶׁלֹּא מֵיאֲנָה וְהִגְדִּילָה **Regarding a minor who did not exercise refusal of marriage and who then reached maturity.** As the Gemara explains elsewhere (*Yevamot* 109b), we are dealing here with a girl who cohabited with her husband after reaching maturity. Thus, the Amoraim disagree whether this first act of adult intercourse is to be considered a new act of betrothal in accordance with Torah law.

The Rishonim object: When the couple cohabited upon the girl's reaching maturity, surely they did not do so in the presence of witnesses! How, then, can their relations be considered the basis for a valid betrothal when the rite of betrothal requires two witnesses? *Ra'ah, Ritva* and others answer that, when a man betroths a woman by means of sexual intercourse, it is not necessary for the witnesses to observe the act itself; simply witnessing the couple retire into seclusion is considered as witnessing the act itself. Here, too, the witnesses who see the couple living together can be considered as witnesses to their having sexual relations, for such relations are assumed to be a normal part of living together as man and wife.

עָמְדָה וְנִישֵּׂאת **If she stood and married.** The Rishonim comment: Elsewhere (*Gittin* 89b) we have learned that, if a married woman accepted betrothal from another man in the presence of her assumed husband, the betrothal is valid — for she would not do so if they were married. Why, then, does Rav maintain here that the girl, who upon reaching majority accepts betrothal from another man with her first husband's knowledge, is assumed to have done so illegitimately? *Ritva* and *Nimukei Yosef* answer: If a woman was once married, we assume that she would not accept betrothal to another unless the first marriage were dissolved;

HALAKHAH

קְטַנָּה שֶׁלֹּא מֵיאֲנָה וְהִגְדִּילָה **Regarding a minor who did not exercise refusal of marriage and who then reached maturity.** "If an orphaned minor was married off by her mother or brothers, and did not declare her refusal to remain married before reaching the age of twelve, as soon as her husband cohabits with her after she reaches that age, her marriage is considered valid by Torah law. Thus, if she accepted betrothal from another man, she does not require a bill of divorce from him. If, however, her first husband did not cohabit with her since her reaching maturity, her marriage to him remains valid by Rabbinic decree alone. Thus, if she accepted betrothal from another man, she would require a bill of divorce from both husbands." (*Rambam, Sefer Nashim, Hilkhot Gerushin* 11:6; *Shulḥan Arukh, Even HaEzer* 155:20-21.)

TRANSLATION AND COMMENTARY

[1]**And Shmuel said:** The woman **requires a bill of divorce from the second husband,** because her first marriage was valid only by Rabbinic enactment. Consequently, the second marriage was valid according to Torah law. Shmuel assumes that when her first husband had sexual intercourse with her after she reached majority, his intention was to rely upon the prior marital bond and not to view their first act of adult relations as a new basis for betrothal and marriage. Consequently, the woman's first marriage never assumed validity by Torah law, and the second marriage was valid. As a result, she requires a bill of divorce when forced to separate from her second husband. In both cases Rav assumed that the act of sexual intercourse created a new matrimonial bond, and Shmuel disagreed. Why, then, did both cases have to be presented?

צְרִיכָא [2]The Gemara answers: **It was necessary** to state the dispute in both cases, **for had it been stated in** the second case alone, regarding the orphaned minor who had been married off by her mother or brothers, [3]**you might have said that** only **in this case did Rav say what he said,** [4]**since** the issue was **not** one of **a condition** being attached to the initial betrothal, but rather whether the marriage would have any validity by Torah law. [5]**But in the** case **of** the husband who attached **a condition** to his wife's betrothal and then married her without specifying any conditions, [6]**you might have said that** Rav **agrees with Shmuel.** In that case the husband would have had no reason to view their relations as the basis of a new betrothal, since he assumed the condition to have been fulfilled. If it turned out later that the condition had not been fulfilled, the woman would not require a bill of divorce from her husband as she was never his legal wife. The marriage itself, between two consenting adults, was in principle valid according to Torah Law, unlike a marriage between a man and a minor orphan girl. [7]**And had the** dispute **been stated** only **in** the case of a man who had attached a condition to his wife's betrothal, and then married her without specifying any conditions, [8]**you might have said that** only **in that** case **did Shmuel say what he said,** having assumed that the husband relied upon his original betrothal. [9]**But in** the case of the orphaned minor married off by her mother or brothers, **you might have said that** Shmuel **agrees with Rav** that when the husband first cohabited with her upon her reaching maturity, he did so with the intention of betrothing her anew so that the marriage would assume validity by Torah law. [10]Thus **it was necessary** for the dispute to have been stated twice, so that we may see that Rav and Shmuel do in fact disagree in both cases.

תְּנַן [11]The Gemara now raises an objection against the view of Shmuel: **We have learned** in our Mishnah: **"If a man married** a woman **without stating anything** in the way of conditions, **and** it was later discovered that she **was bound by vows,** the marriage is valid. But since she concealed her vows from her husband, he can claim false pretenses, [12]and the woman **may be divorced without** receiving payment of **her ketubah** settlement." [13]Now, although the Mishnah implies that the woman **is not entitled to her ketubah** settlement, [14]**nevertheless a** proper **bill of divorce would be required** as the marriage was valid.

[1]וּשְׁמוּאֵל אָמַר: צְרִיכָה גֵּט מִשֵּׁנִי!

[2]צְרִיכָא, דְּאִי אִתְּמַר בְּהַהִיא — [3]בְּהַהִיא קָאָמַר רַב, [4]מִשּׁוּם דְּלֵיכָּא תְּנָאָה. [5]אֲבָל בְּהָא, דְּאִיכָּא תְּנָאָה, [6]אֵימָא מוֹדֵי לֵיהּ לִשְׁמוּאֵל. [7]וְאִי אִתְּמַר בְּהָא — [8]בְּהָא קָאָמַר שְׁמוּאֵל, [9]אֲבָל בְּהַךְ — אֵימָא מוֹדֵי לֵיהּ לְרַב, [10]צְרִיכָא.

[11]תְּנַן: "כְּנָסָהּ סְתָם, וְנִמְצְאוּ עָלֶיהָ נְדָרִים, [12]תֵּצֵא שֶׁלֹּא בִּכְתוּבָּה". [13]כְּתוּבָּה הוּא דְּלָא בָּעֲיָא, הָא גִּיטָּא — [14]בָּעֲיָא!

LITERAL TRANSLATION

[1]And Shmuel said: She requires a bill of divorce from the second [husband]!

[2]It was necessary, for had it been stated in this [case alone, [3]you might have said that] in this [case] Rav said [what he did], [4]because there is no condition. [5]But in that [case], where there is a condition, [6]say [that] he agrees with Shmuel. [7]And had it been stated in that [case, [8]you might have said that] in that [case] Shmuel said [what he did], [9]but in this [case], say that he agrees with Rav. [10]It was necessary.

[11]We have learned: "[If] he married her without stating anything, and there were found to be vows upon her, [12]she goes out without a ketubah." [13]A ketubah is what she does not require, but a bill of divorce — [14]she does require!

RASHI

דליכא תנאה — והכל יודעין שאין במעשה קטנה כלום, וגמר ובעל לשם קדושין. **דאיכא תנאה** — וסבר הוא שתקיים תנאה, דהואיל ומינסבא ליה — אין עליה נדר, ולא מסיק אדעתיה לבעול לשם קידושין, דאינו חפץ באשה נדרנית. **בהא קאמר שמואל** — דכיון דאתני — אתנאי סמיך, דאינו חפץ בנדרנית.

NOTES

however, in the case of a girl whose first marriage was arranged while she was still a minor, she might accept betrothal to another without realizing that the first marriage was indeed valid.

TRANSLATION AND COMMENTARY

[1]**Does not** the second clause of the Mishnah refer back to the first, so that we are referring here to the case of a man **who betrothed** a woman **on condition** that she was free of vows, [2]**and who then married her without specifying** any conditions, only later to discover that she was indeed bound by certain vows? If so, the fact that the marriage is considered valid — to the point of her requiring a bill of divorce — indicates that her husband specifically intended that their sexual relations constitute a new betrothal. Regarding payment of her ketubah settlement, however, the husband's original condition still stands. [3]Thus the Mishnah supports the position of Rav and serves as **a refutation of Shmuel!**

[73B] לָא [4]The Gemara answers: **No,** the second clause of the Mishnah refers to a case **where** a man **betrothed** a woman **without stating** any conditions and then **married her without stating anything** as well. In such a case, if it were discovered that the woman was bound by certain vows, she would require a bill of divorce — as the marriage was valid — but she would not receive payment of her ketubah settlement. The case in dispute between Rav and Shmuel, however, is not the subject of this clause at all.

אֲבָל [5]The Gemara now questions this interpretation: **But** if this is the case referred to in the Mishnah, would it not follow that **if** the man **betrothed** the woman **on condition** that she was free of vows, **and** then **married her without stating anything** further (only to discover later that she indeed was bound by certain vows), [6]the marriage would be void and **she would not even require a bill of divorce?** Following the logic of this interpretation of the second clause of the Mishnah, we find that the first clause should have been formulated differently: [7]**Rather than teach: "If one betroths a woman on condition that no vows are upon her,** [8]**and** then **vows were** indeed **found upon her, she is not** considered **betrothed,"** [9]**let** the Tanna of the Mishnah **teach** the case with the more far-reaching implications: **"If one** betroths a woman on condition that there are no vows upon her, and then **marries her without stating anything** further, should **vows** indeed be **found upon her, she is not** considered **betrothed."** [10]Once such a case is established, it would follow **all the more** that even if he did not marry her subsequent to that betrothal, and vows were discovered upon her, she should not be considered betrothed!

הָכִי נַמִי קָאָמַר [11]The Gemara answers: **So indeed did it state** in the Mishnah, meaning that this is actually how the Mishnah should be understood: [12]**"If one betroths a woman on condition that no**

[1]מַאי לָאו — קִידְּשָׁהּ עַל תְּנַאי. [2]וּכְנָסָהּ סְתָם? [3]תְּיוּבְתָּא דִּשְׁמוּאֵל!

[73B] [4]לָא, קִידְּשָׁהּ סְתָם וּכְנָסָהּ סְתָם.

[5]אֲבָל קִידְּשָׁהּ עַל תְּנַאי וּכְנָסָהּ סְתָם, [6]הָכִי נַמִי דְּלָא בָּעֲיָא גִּיטָּא? [7]אַדְּתָנֵי: ״הַמְקַדֵּשׁ אֶת הָאִשָּׁה עַל מְנָת שֶׁאֵין עָלֶיהָ נְדָרִים, [8]וְנִמְצְאוּ עָלֶיהָ נְדָרִים, אֵינָהּ מְקוּדֶּשֶׁת״, [9]לִיתְנֵי: ״כְּנָסָהּ סְתָם וְנִמְצְאוּ עָלֶיהָ נְדָרִים, אֵינָהּ מְקוּדֶּשֶׁת״, [10]וְכָל שֶׁכֵּן הָא!

[11]הָכִי נַמִי קָאָמַר: [12]הַמְקַדֵּשׁ אֶת הָאִשָּׁה עַל מְנָת שֶׁאֵין עָלֶיהָ

LITERAL TRANSLATION

[1]Is it not that he betrothed her on condition, [2]and married her without stating anything? [3]A refutation of Shmuel!

[73B] [4]No, he betrothed her without stating anything and married her without stating anything.

[5]But [if] he betrothed her on condition and married her without stating anything, [6]so too does she not require a bill of divorce? [7]Rather than teach: "[If] one betroths a woman on condition that no vows are upon her, [8]and vows were found upon her, she is not betrothed," [9]let it teach: "[If] he married her without stating anything, and vows were found upon her, she is not betrothed," [10]and all the more so this!

[11]So too did it state: [12][If] one betroths a woman on condition that no vows are upon her,

RASHI

מאי לאו קידשה כו׳ — וסיפא ארישא קאי. וקאמר: כתובה הוא דלא בעיא, דלענין ממונא לא אחיל תנאי. אבל גיטא — בעיא, דלשם קדושין בעל. דאי משתכח עלה נדרים — לא תהא בעילתו זנות, כרב. **לא קידשה סתם כו׳** — ומילתא באפי נפשה היא. ולקמיה פריך: מאי שנא גט ומאי שנא כתובה? **ליתני כנסה סתם** — בגוה ליכלליה, וליתני הכי: המקדש על מנת שאין עליה נדרים וכנסה סתם כו׳. **וכל שכן** — בלא כנסה. אבל השתא משמע דדווקא בשלא כנסה קאמר. **הכי נמי קאמר** — דהאי ״ונמצאו עליה״ דקתני — לאחר שניסת קאמר.

NOTES

הָכִי נַמִי קָאָמַר **So too did it state.** *Rashba* and others note that the Gemara does not wish to imply that certain words were omitted from the Mishnah. Rather, it understands the Mishnah as setting down two basic principles: If a man betrothed a woman on condition, and later discovered that she violated the condition, the betrothal is void regardless of whether the violation was discovered prior to the marriage or only afterwards. However, if he betrothed her

TRANSLATION AND COMMENTARY

vows are upon her, and then **marries her without stating anything** further, [1]**should vows** indeed be **found upon her, she is not** considered **betrothed.** [2]**But if he betrothed her without stating** any condition **and** then **married her without stating anything** as well — only later to discover that she indeed was bound by certain vows — then the marriage is valid and she requires a bill of divorce; however, [3]**when she goes out,** she does so **without payment of her ketubah.**"

כְּתוּבָּה [4]We have tentatively established that Shmuel's interpretation of the Mishnah is as follows: If no condition was explicitly stated, and after the marriage it was discovered that the woman was bound by certain vows, **it is a ketubah** settlement **which she does not require, but a bill of divorce she would require.** [5]The Gemara asks: **What is the difference with regard to a ketubah** settlement, **that** the woman **is not entitled to one,** while she does require a bill of divorce? [6]She is not entitled to her ketubah settlement **because** her husband **can say: "I do not wish to live with a woman who tends to take vows."** Had he known she was a habitual taker of vows, he would not have married her. Thus the marriage was based on false pretenses. [7]However, **if this is so,** the woman **should not require a bill of divorce either,** as this implicit condition of betrothal was never met and the marriage was entered into erroneously!

אָמַר רַבָּה [8]**Rabbah said:** In truth, **she requires a bill of divorce** in this case **by Rabbinic decree** only. In terms of Torah law, the presumption that no man wishes to be married to a woman who is bound by vows is sufficient to render the marriage invalid even without a bill of divorce. However, the Rabbis decreed that since an explicit condition was not attached to the marriage, the woman would still require a proper bill of divorce. [9]**And similarly, Rav Ḥisda said:** In such a case, the woman **requires a bill of divorce by Rabbinic decree** alone.

רָבָא אָמַר [10]**Rava stated** another possible way of understanding why a bill of divorce is necessary while payment of the ketubah settlement is not: [11]**The Tanna** of our Mishnah **was in doubt** as to whether an implicit understanding is attached to all marriages that the woman has taken no vows.

LITERAL TRANSLATION

and marries her without stating anything, [1]and vows are found upon her, she is not betrothed. [2][If] he betrothed her without stating anything and married her without stating anything, [3]she goes out without a ketubah settlement. [4]It is a ketubah which she does not require, but a bill of divorce she would require. [5]What is the difference [with regard to] a ketubah settlement that she does not require? [6]For he can say: "I do not wish [to live] with a woman who tends to take vows." [7]If so, a bill of divorce she should also not require! [8]Rabbah said: She requires a bill of divorce by Rabbinic decree (lit., "by their words"). [9]And similarly, Rav Ḥisda said: She requires a bill of divorce by Rabbinic decree. [10]Rava said: [11]The Tanna was in doubt.

נְדָרִים, וּכְנָסָהּ סְתָם [1]וְנִמְצְאוּ עָלֶיהָ נְדָרִים אֵינָהּ מְקוּדֶּשֶׁת. [2]קִידְּשָׁהּ סְתָם וּכְנָסָהּ סְתָם, [3]תֵּצֵא שֶׁלֹּא בִּכְתוּבָּה. [4]כְּתוּבָּה הוּא דְּלָא בָּעֲיָא, הָא גִּיטָּא בָּעֲיָא. [5]וּמַאי שְׁנָא כְּתוּבָּה דְּלָא בָּעֲיָא? [6]דְּאָמַר: "אִי אֶפְשִׁי בְּאִשָּׁה נַדְרָנִית". [7]אִי הָכִי, גֵּט נַמִי לָא תִּיבָּעֵי! [8]אָמַר רַבָּה: צְרִיכָה גֵּט מִדִּבְרֵיהֶם. [9]וְכֵן אָמַר רַב חִסְדָּא: צְרִיכָה גֵּט מִדִּבְרֵיהֶם. [10]רָבָא אָמַר: [11]תַּנָּא סַפּוֹקֵי

RASHI

דאמר אי אפשי כו' — ואף על גב דלא אתני — כמאן דאתני דמי. גט נמי לא תיבעי — דהא שמואל לית ליה אין אדם עושה בעילתו זנות, כדאשמועינן גבי קטנה.

NOTES

without stating any conditions, she requires a bill of divorce but is not entitled to receive her ketubah settlement.

צְרִיכָה גֵּט מִדִּבְרֵיהֶם **She requires a bill of divorce by Rabbinic decree.** The Rabbis were concerned that, since the condition was never explicitly stated at the time of the betrothal, people may not understand the reason for rendering the betrothal null and void, and may come to assume that a married woman can end her marriage without receiving a proper bill of divorce. However, if the condition was explicitly stated at the time of the betrothal, the woman does not require a bill of divorce — even by Rabbinic decree — for people will realize that the betrothal

was never valid since the condition attached to it had not been met (*Rivan*).

סַפּוֹקֵי מְסַפְּקָא לֵיהּ **The Tanna was in doubt.** The Rishonim explain the Tanna's doubt in differing ways. *Rashi* understands the Tanna of our Mishnah as being in doubt as to whether it can be presumed that no man is willing to marry a woman who tends to take vows. Others suggest that the Tanna was in doubt as to whether there is a Halakhic presumption that no one wishes to engage in marital relations if the legitimacy of the marriage is in question. Our commentary, however, follows the opinion of *Re'ah*, *Rashba*, *Ritva* and others who understand the Tanna

מְסַפְּקָא לֵיהּ; [1]גַּבֵּי מָמוֹנָא, לְקוּלָּא, [2]גַּבֵּי אִיסּוּרָא, לְחוּמְרָא. [3]אָמַר רַבָּה: מַחֲלוֹקֶת בְּטָעוּת שְׁתֵּי נָשִׁים. [4]אֲבָל בְּטָעוּת אִשָּׁה אַחַת, [5]דִּבְרֵי הַכֹּל אֵין צְרִיכָה הֵימֶנּוּ גֵּט.

LITERAL TRANSLATION

[1]Regarding monetary matters, for leniency; [2]as regards prohibitions, for stringency.

[3]Rabbah said: The dispute is in [the case of] a mistake involving two women. [4]But in [the case of] a mistake involving one woman, [5]all agree [that] she does not require a bill of divorce from him.

TRANSLATION AND COMMENTARY

[1]Therefore, **regarding monetary matters,** such as payment of the woman's ketubah settlement, the Tanna favored **leniency** toward the husband. [2]**As regards matters of prohibition**, however, the issue of permitting the woman to marry another man, the Tanna favored **stringency** by requiring her to receive a bill of divorce so as to ensure that she is definitely not married and thus permissible to other men.

אָמַר רַבָּה [3]The Gemara now seeks to limit the disagreement between Rav and Shmuel: **Rabbah said: The dispute is limited** to **a mistake involving two** different **women.** If a man conditionally betroths one woman and then marries another without specifying any conditions at all, should the second woman be discovered to have taken vows, Rav maintains that she requires a bill of divorce, as her marriage took place without any conditions. We do not assume that the conditions stipulated regarding the first wife necessarily apply to the second. Shmuel, on the other hand, would disagree. Thus the second woman would also require a bill of divorce should she be discovered to have taken vows. [4]**But in** the case of **a mistake involving** only **one woman,** whom a man betrothed on condition that she was free of vows and then married without stating anything further, only to discover later that she was indeed bound by certain vows, [5]**all** — both Rav and Shmuel — **agree that** the woman **does not require a bill of divorce from** her husband, since he must have certainly had his original condition in mind when he concluded the marriage.

RASHI

ספוקי מספקא ליה – על סתם אדם, אם אפשי באשה נדרנית אם לאו. **גבי ממונא לקולא** – דהמוציא מחבירו עליו הראיה. וכיון דמספקא לן – לא גבית. **מחלוקת** – דרב ושמואל. **בטעות שתי נשים** – קידש לאחת על תנאי, ואשה אחרת כנס סתם אחריה, ונמצאו עליה נדרים. והיינו טעותא; רב סבר: כיון דלא אתני בהדה דהך, אף על פי שכבר גילה דעתו שאי אפשי בנדרנית – צריכה הימנו גט, דלמא לגבה דהך חביבה עליה, ולא קפיד. ושמואל אמר: כיון דגלי דעתיה – גלי. **אבל בטעות אשה אחת** – קידשה על תנאי וכנסה סתם – אפילו רב מודה דדעתיה אתנאיה.

NOTES

as being in doubt as to whether the absence of vows, when not specified at the time of betrothal or marriage, is implicitly assumed to be a condition or considered irrelevant.

גַּבֵּי מָמוֹנָא, לְקוּלָּא **Regarding monetary matters, for leniency.** *Mordekhai* proves from this passage that, whenever the Gemara ends a discussion concerning a monetary issue without a definitive resolution, we rule in favor of the lenient opinion. Even though there is no real leniency or stringency in rulings regarding monetary matters, for a leniency toward one party is stringency for the other, we nevertheless invoke the rule that money (or any other object) is presumed to belong to its immediate possessor unless proved otherwise.

טָעוּת שְׁתֵּי נָשִׁים **A mistake involving two women.** The Rishonim are divided in their opinions as to how we understand this expression (as well as its accompanying one: "a mistake involving one woman"). Our commentary follows the opinion of *Rashi*, who understands "a mistake involving two women" as referring to a man who betrothed one woman on condition that she was free of vows, and then betrothed, as well as married, another woman without attaching any condition whatsoever. Subsequently, should the second woman be discovered to have taken vows, Rav and Shmuel disagree as to whether we can assume that the man implicitly intended the condition to apply to her as well.

Rif and *Meiri* understand the case somewhat similarly in that they agree it involves a man who betrothed one woman after imposing a condition and then another without; however, they are of the opinion that it is the first woman whose marriage was then concluded without the restating of any condition. In this view, Rav and Shmuel disagree as to whether the man's failure to repeat his condition upon betrothing the second woman, or upon marrying the first, indicates that the condition is no longer important to him. *Rif* cites an alternative opinion (which he rejects), according to which the case is seen as that of a man who, after betrothing two women, one on condition and the other not, forgot who was who and proceeded to marry the one whose betrothal was conditional without making sure.

The opinion of *Ri Migash* (also followed by *Ramban* and his school) is that "a mistake involving two women" refers to a man who betrothed two women, both on condition that they were free of vows, and then married them both without specifying the condition again. Rav maintains that, since he married twice without restating the condition, this proves that the omission was intentional. Shmuel disagrees and says that, even in such a case, we must assume that he married both women while relying upon the condition that he had attached to their betrothals.

According to *Rav Natronai Gaon* (see also *Rashi*, who cites this explanation in the name of his teachers), "a mistake involving two women" refers to a man who betrothed a woman on condition that she was free of vows and then later entered into marriage without restating his condition,

[1]אֲמַר לֵיהּ אַבַּיֵי: וְהָא מַתְנִיתִין דְּטָעוּת אִשָּׁה אַחַת הִיא, [2]וְקָמוֹתְבִינַן תְּיוּבְתָּא מִינֵּיהּ! [3]אֶלָּא, אִי אִתְּמַר הָכִי אִתְּמַר: [4]אֲמַר רַבָּה: מַחֲלוֹקֶת בְּטָעוּת אִשָּׁה אַחַת כְּעֵין שְׁתֵּי נָשִׁים. [5]אֲבָל בְּטָעוּת אִשָּׁה אַחַת גְּרֵידָתָא, [6]דִּבְרֵי הַכֹּל אֵינָהּ צְרִיכָה הֵימֶנּוּ גֵּט.

LITERAL TRANSLATION

[1]Abaye said to him: But surely our Mishnah is [dealing with] a mistake involving one woman, [2]and we raised an objection from it!

[3]Rather, if something was said, it was said thus: [4]Rabbah said: The dispute is in [the case of] a mistake involving one woman which is like [that of] two women. [5]But in [the case of] a mistake involving only one woman, [6]all agree [that] she does not require a bill of divorce from him.

TRANSLATION AND COMMENTARY

אֲמַר לֵיהּ אַבַּיֵי [1]**Abaye said to** Rabbah: **But surely our Mishnah is dealing with** a case of **a mistake involving** only **one woman,** [2]**and** nevertheless **we raised an objection from it** against the viewpoint of Shmuel — thus indicating that he and Rav must have disagreed about such a case as well!

אֶלָּא [3]The Gemara now reformulates Rabbah's position: **Rather, if something was said** about the dispute between Rav and Shmuel, **it was this that was said:** [4]**Rabbah said: The dispute** between Rav and Shmuel **is** limited to the case of **a mistake involving one woman which is like that of two women,** when a man betroths a woman on condition that she is free of vows and then divorces her, only to betroth her a second time, with no conditions, then concluding the marriage. If after this second marriage it is discovered that the woman has certain vows upon her, Rav maintains that the woman would require a bill of divorce. Although her husband attached a condition to her first betrothal, there is no reason to assume that he intended to apply that condition upon marrying her the second time. Thus she is like another woman. Shmuel, however, disagrees, maintaining that the condition that her husband attached to the first betrothal proves that he is indeed opposed to marrying a woman with vows under any circumstances, even if he did not explicitly reiterate that condition. [5]**But in** the case of **a mistake involving only one woman,** if a man betroths a woman on condition that she is free of vows and then marries her without stating anything further, only to discover afterwards that she was in fact bound by certain vows, [6]**all agree** — both Rav and Shmuel — **that she does not require a bill of divorce from him,** for surely he had his condition in mind when he concluded the marriage with her.

RASHI

והא מתניתין דטעות אשה אחת היא — למאי דסלקא דעתין דסיפא ארישא קאי טעות אשה אחת היא, וקא מותבינן מינה לעיל. אלמא — איכא דסבירא ליה דטעות דאשה אחת נמי צריכה גט. ואף על גב דאנן הוא דאותבינן, ולאו רב איירי בה — קושיא היא לרבה, דהאי "דברי הכל" דקאמר — סברא דידיה היא, ולאו מרב ושמואל שמעה, שהרי לא היה בדורם. אלא דקסבר: ליכא למאן דאמר בכי האי גוונא דלאו דעתיה אתנאיה. והא קא חזינן דכל בני מדרשא דאותבוה סלקא דעתין למימר הכי. **מחלוקת בטעות אשה אחת כעין שתי נשים** — קידשה על תנאי, וגירשה מן האירוסין, וחזר וכנסה סתם. בההיא אמר רב צריכה גט — דכי אשה אחרת דמי, ולשם קדושין בעל, וליכא למימר אתנאיה קמא סמיך. ושמואל סבר: הא גלי לה דעתיה מעיקרא, דאם היא נדרנית — אי אפשי בה. ועל תנאי כך חזר וקידשה. **אבל בטעות אשה אחת גרידתא** — שכנסה על ידי קדושין הראשונים דברי הכל כו'. וכי אותבינן לעיל ממתניתין הכי אותבינן: מאי לאו קידשה על תנאי וכנסה סתם, משגירשה. דבלא גירשה ליכא למאן דאמר. והיכא דגירשה מיהא קתני: כתובה לא בעיא, הא גיטא — בעיא. ואני שמעתי: טעות אשה אחת כעין שתי נשים — כגון שקדש רחל על תנאי, ואחר כך נתכוין לכנוס לאה, וכנסה סתם, ונמצאת רחל. וקשיא לי: נהי נמי דנתכוין לבעול לשם קידושין — הא לאו לרחל איכוין, ואמאי צריכה גט?

NOTES

only to discover that another woman had been substituted in her place. Rav maintains that, should the woman be discovered to have taken vows, she would require a bill of divorce — as she was married without condition. Shmuel, on the other hand, maintains that she would not require a bill of divorce, because her husband married her while relying upon the condition that had been attached to the other woman's betrothal.

אִשָּׁה אַחַת כְּעֵין שְׁתֵּי נָשִׁים **A mistake involving one woman which is like that of two women.** Here, too, the Rishonim propose various ways of understanding the case under discussion. Our commentary follows *Rashi,* who explains the Gemara as referring to a man who betrothed a woman on condition that she was free of vows and then divorced her, only to betroth and marry her again later — but this time without stating any conditions. Should it then be discovered that the woman took vows, Rav and Shmuel disagree as to whether the husband intended his original condition to be applied to the second marriage as well.

Rif explains the case as referring to a man who betrothed a woman on condition that she was free of vows, and then waited a certain period of time before proceeding to marry her without condition. Rav and Shmuel argue as to whether we should assume that the husband waived his condition as a result of the time that had passed between the betrothal and the marriage. However, in the case of a mistake involving only one woman, whom the man married immediately after the conditional betrothal, all agree that the condition still holds.

According to *Ra'ah,* the case refers to a man who betrothed a woman on condition that she was free of vows, and then divorced her, only to betroth her a second time

[1]אִיתִיבֵיהּ אַבַּיֵי: [2]"קִידְּשָׁהּ בְּטָעוּת, וּפָחוֹת מִשָּׁוֶה פְּרוּטָה, [3]וְכֵן קָטָן שֶׁקִּידֵּשׁ, [4]אַף עַל פִּי שֶׁשָּׁלַח סִבְלוֹנוֹת לְאַחַר מִיכָּן, [5]אֵינָהּ מְקוּדֶּשֶׁת, שֶׁמֵּחֲמַת קִדּוּשִׁין הָרִאשׁוֹנִים שָׁלַח. [6]וְאִם בָּעֲלוּ, קָנוּ. [7]רַבִּי שִׁמְעוֹן בֶּן יְהוּדָה מִשּׁוּם רַבִּי יִשְׁמָעֵאל אָמַר: אִם בָּעֲלוּ, לֹא קָנוּ". [8]וְהָא הָכָא דְּטָעוּת אִשָּׁה אַחַת הִיא, [9]וּפְלִיגִי! [10]מַאי לָאו טָעוּת נְדָרִים?

LITERAL TRANSLATION

[1]Abaye raised an objection against him: [2]"[If a man] betrothed [a woman] by mistake, or [with] less than the value of a perutah, [3]and similarly, [if] a minor betrothed [a woman], [4]even if he sent gifts subsequently, [5]she is not betrothed, for as a result of the first betrothal he sent [the gifts]. [6]But if they had intercourse, they acquired [them]. [7]Rabbi Shimon ben Yehudah said in the name of Rabbi Yishmael: If they had intercourse, they did not acquire [them]." [8]And surely here it is a mistake involving one woman, [9]and they disagree! [10]Is it not a mistake involving vows?

TRANSLATION AND COMMENTARY

אִיתִיבֵיהּ אַבַּיֵי [1]**Abaye raised an objection against** this second version of Rabbah's position from a Baraita which stated: [2]**"If one betrothed a woman by mistake, or** if he betrothed her **with less than the value of a perutah,** the minimum value by which betrothal may be effected, [3]**and similarly, if a minor** whose actions have no legal validity in Torah law **betrothed a woman,** [4]**even if subsequently** (in the case of the minor, after he reached majority) the bridegroom **sent** his bride **gifts,** [5]**she is** still **not betrothed, for** we assume that the gifts were **sent** simply **as a result of the first** invalid **betrothal** and not of the second betrothal. [6]**But if** any of these men subsequently **had intercourse** with their brides (in the case of the minor, after she reached maturity), then **they** would have **acquired them** as their wives, for we assume that the act of sexual intercourse indicates a specific intention that the betrothal be legitimate. [7]**Rabbi Shimon ben Yehudah said in the name of Rabbi Yishmael:** Even **if** these men subsequently **had intercourse** with their brides, **they would not have acquired them** as wives — for we assume that they engaged in sexual intercourse on the basis of the original, invalid betrothal." [8]**And surely here,** in this Baraita, we are dealing with the case of **a mistake involving only one woman,** for it refers to a man who took a woman through faulty betrothal and then had sexual relations with her, [9]**and** nevertheless the Tannaim **disagree** about the validity of the betrothal! [10]**Is not** the mistake referred to in this Baraita **a mistake involving vows?** In this case the betrothal is invalid, and we find that the Tannaim of the Baraita argue as to whether the man acquires his wife through intercourse, despite the invalid betrothal. This refutes the position of Rabbah just stated, that in such a case all would agree that the marriage is invalid and that the woman does not require a bill of divorce.

RASHI

קידשה בטעות — קא סלקא דעתך טעות נדרים, כדמפרש ואזיל. **קטן** — אין קדושיו כלום, דלאו בר קיחה הוא — "כי יקח איש" כתיב. **אף על פי ששלח סבלונות** — אכולה קאי. **סבלונות** — מגדנות שהחתן שולח לארוסתו. **אינה מקודשת** — ואף על פי ששלח משהגדיל. ולא אמרינן ניהוי סבלונות קידושין לפי שמחמת קידושין הראשונים שלח, לשם סבלונות, ולא לשם קידושין. **מאי לאו טעות נדרים** — שהתנה עמה על מנת שאין עליה נדרים, והטעתו — שהיו עליה נדרים. וכן למומין, ולכל תנאי שיתנה. וקאמר תנא קמא: אם בעלו קנו. אלמא איכא למאן דאמר אפילו בתנאי לא בעיל איניש אדעתא דתנאה, דמסיק אדעתיה דלמא לא מיקיים, והויא בעילת זנות.

NOTES

on condition that she was free of vows and conclude the marriage without restating his condition.

Rabbenu Zeraḥyah HaLevi and others explain the Gemara as referring to the case of a man who betrothed a woman on condition that she was free of vows and then married her, and engaged in intercourse, without restating his condition. Should the woman be found to have taken vows, Shmuel maintains that she does not require a bill of divorce, as the marriage was presumably entered into on the same condition as had been attached to the betrothal. Rav differs and maintains that she does require a bill of divorce, for the fact that he both married her and engaged in sexual relations without restating his condition strengthens the assumption that he must have intended to waive the original condition.

According to *Rabbenu Natronai Gaon,* the case is one of a man who betrothed one woman with a condition and another without, only then mistakenly to marry the first woman without referring to his original condition. *Rif, Ramban* and their disciples discuss these matters at great length, analyzing each of the positions for points of weakness with respect to the issues involved and the wording of the Talmudic passage.

HALAKHAH

קִידְּשָׁהּ בְּפָחוֹת מִשָּׁוֶה פְּרוּטָה **If one betrothed a woman with less than the value of a perutah.** "If a man betrothed a woman with less than the value of a perutah, the betrothal is invalid even if he should later send her a gift worth more than a perutah. Similarly, betrothal performed by a minor is invalid even if, after reaching maturity, he should send

TRANSLATION AND COMMENTARY

לָא [1]Abaye reads the Baraita as referring to two separate instances, a mistake regarding the conditions of betrothal and a betrothal effected with less than a perutah. The Gemara disagrees: **No, the** mistake spoken of in the Baraita **is a mistake** involving a man who betroths a woman with money that is worth **less than a perutah,** and the Tannaim argue as to whether the subsequent act of intercourse constitutes a new betrothal. However, in the case of a man attaching a condition to betrothal which the woman secretly violates, all would agree that the subsequent act of intercourse was initiated upon the mistaken premise that the original betrothal was valid.

פָּחוֹת מִשָּׁוֶה פְּרוּטָה [2]The Gemara immediately questions this interpretation of the Baraita: The case of a mistake involving betrothal with **less than the value of a perutah is taught explicitly** in the very next clause of the Baraita: [3]**"If a man betrothed a woman by mistake, or** betrothed her **with less than the value of a perutah,** she is not betrothed." How can the first clause regarding an erroneous betrothal be referring to the same case as that explicitly stated right after?

פֵּרוּשֵׁי קָא מְפָרֵשׁ [4]The Gemara answers: The second clause of the Baraita **is explaining** what was meant by the first: **"If one betrothed a woman by mistake...."** [5]**How** is that **so? For example, "if he betrothed her with less than the value of a perutah."**

בְּמַאי קָא מִיפַּלְגִי [6]The Gemara now inquires into the theoretical basis of the Tannaitic dispute regarding the case of one who betroths a woman with less than the value of a perutah: **About what do** the Tannaim **disagree?** [7]The Gemara explains: **One Sage** — the first Tanna of the Baraita — **maintained: A man** surely **knows that betrothal is not valid** when effected **with less than the value of a perutah,** [8]**and so we assume** that **he decided** in his mind to **engage in intercourse with the** express **intention of** effecting a valid **betrothal.** [9]Whereas **the other Sage** — Rabbi Shimon ben Yehudah — **maintained: A man does not know that betrothal is invalid** when effected **with less than the value of a perutah,** [10]**and so we assume that, when he engaged in intercourse, it was with the original betrothal in mind that he did so.**

LITERAL TRANSLATION

[1]No, [it is] a mistake of less than the value of a perutah.

[2]Less than the value of a perutah is taught explicitly: [3]"[If] one betrothed [a woman] by mistake, or [with] less than the value of a perutah"!

[4]It is explaining: [If] one betrothed [a woman] by mistake. [5]How so? For example, if he betrothed her with less than the value of a perutah.

[6]About what do they disagree? [7][One] Sage maintained: A man knows that betrothal is not valid with less than the value of a perutah, [8]and [so] he concluded and engaged in intercourse for the sake of betrothal. [9]And [the other] Sage maintained: A man does not know that betrothal is invalid with less than the value of a perutah, [10]and [so] when he engaged in intercourse, it was with the original betrothal in mind that he did so.

[1]לָא, טָעוּת פָּחוֹת מִשָּׁוֶה פְּרוּטָה.

[2]פָּחוֹת מִשָּׁוֶה פְּרוּטָה בְּהֶדְיָא קָתָנֵי לָהּ: [3]"קִידְּשָׁהּ בְּטָעוּת, וּפָחוֹת מִשָּׁוֶה פְּרוּטָה"!

[4]פֵּרוּשֵׁי קָא מְפָרֵשׁ: קִידְּשָׁהּ בְּטָעוּת. [5]כֵּיצַד? כְּגוֹן, שֶׁקִּידְּשָׁהּ בְּפָחוֹת מִשָּׁוֶה פְּרוּטָה. [6]בְּמַאי קָא מִיפַּלְגִי? [7]מָר סָבַר: אָדָם יוֹדֵעַ שֶׁאֵין קִדּוּשִׁין תּוֹפְסִין בְּפָחוֹת מִשָּׁוֶה פְּרוּטָה, [8]וְגָמַר וּבָעַל לְשֵׁם קִדּוּשִׁין. [9]וּמָר סָבַר: אֵין אָדָם יוֹדֵעַ שֶׁאֵין קִדּוּשִׁין תּוֹפְסִין בְּפָחוֹת מִשָּׁוֶה פְּרוּטָה, [10]וְכִי קָא בַּעַל, אַדַּעְתָּא דְּקִדּוּשִׁין הָרִאשׁוֹנִים בָּעַל.

RASHI

לא טעות פחות משוה פרוטה — דטעה בקדושין, דסבר שמקדשין בכך. ועלה קאמר: אם בעלו קנו — דאדם יודע שאין קדושין בפחות משוה פרוטה, וגמר ובעל לשם קדושין. אבל בטעות תנאי — לא מסיק אדעתיה לבעול לשם קדושין, שסמוך עליה; אם לא שתנאה קיים — לא היתה ניסת לי לחופה. במאי קמיפלגי — לדידך דאמרת דלאו בתנאה פליגי במאי פליגי, גבי פחות משוה פרוטה, מאי טעמא דרבי שמעון? בכולהו גרסינן: והא הכא דטעות אשה אחת היא.

NOTES

אָדָם יוֹדֵעַ שֶׁאֵין קִדּוּשִׁין **A man knows that betrothal, etc.** The Rishonim ask: If everyone knows that betrothal is invalid when effected with less than the value of a perutah, then why did he betroth her with that amount to begin with? Furthermore, since we can just as well assume that everyone knows that a violated condition of betrothal

HALAKHAH

his betrothed a gift worth at least a perutah. In both cases, it is assumed that the bridegroom sent the gifts as a follow-up to the initial betrothal, rather than as a basis for re-betrothing the woman." (*Rambam, Sefer Nashim, Hilkhot Ishut* 4:20; *Shulḥan Arukh, Even HaEzer* 31:9.)

[1]אֵיתִיבֵיהּ: ״׳הֲרֵינִי בּוֹעֲלֵיךְ עַל מְנָת שֶׁיִּרְצֶה אַבָּא,׳ [2]אַף עַל פִּי שֶׁלֹּא רָצָה הָאָב, מְקוּדֶּשֶׁת. [3]רַבִּי שִׁמְעוֹן בֶּן יְהוּדָה אוֹמֵר מִשּׁוּם רַבִּי שִׁמְעוֹן: רָצָה הָאָב, מְקוּדֶּשֶׁת; [4]לֹא רָצָה הָאָב, אֵינָהּ מְקוּדֶּשֶׁת״. [5]וְהָא הָכָא דְּכִי טָעוּת אִשָּׁה אַחַת דָּמֵי, [6]וּפְלִיגִי!

[7]הָתָם בְּהָא קָמִיפַּלְגִי: [8]מָר סָבַר: ״עַל מְנָת שֶׁיִּרְצֶה הָאָב״

LITERAL TRANSLATION

[1]He raised an objection against him: "[If a man said:] 'Behold I will have sexual intercourse with you on condition that [my] father will consent,' [2]even if the father did not consent, she is betrothed. [3]Rabbi Shimon ben Yehudah said in the name of Rabbi Shimon: [If] the father consented, she is betrothed; [4][if] the father did not consent, she is not betrothed." [5]And surely here it is like a mistake involving one woman, [6]and they disagree!

[7]There they argue about this: [8][One] Sage maintained: "On condition that the father will consent" —

TRANSLATION AND COMMENTARY

אֵיתִיבֵיהּ [1]Abaye **raised** another **objection against** Rabbah from another Baraita which stated: **"If a man said** to a woman in the presence of two witnesses: **'Behold I** hereby intend to **have sexual intercourse with you** for the sake of betrothal but **on condition that my father will consent** to the marriage,' [2]then **even if the father did not consent** to the marriage, **she is** considered **betrothed** upon their having relations. [3]**Rabbi Shimon ben Yehudah said in the name of Rabbi Shimon: If the father consented** to the marriage, then **she is** considered **betrothed;** [4]but **if the father did not consent, she is not** considered **betrothed."** [5]**And surely** the case **here,** in this Baraita, **is like** that of **a mistake involving one woman,** [6]**but** nevertheless the Tannaim **disagree** about the validity of the betrothal: The first Tanna maintains that even if the condition was not met, we assume that the man engages in intercourse with the specific intention that it be the basis of a valid betrothal, while the second Tanna assumed that the groom was relying upon the initial conditional betrothal. Thus, the Baraita contradicts the position of Rabbah, who held that in the case of a mistake involving only one woman, all agree that the bridegroom relies on his original condition, even upon initiating sexual relations.

הָתָם בְּהָא קָמִיפַּלְגִי [7]The Gemara rebuts this objection against Rabbah as well: **There,** in the Baraita, the Tannaim **argue about** an entirely different matter: [8]**One Sage** — the first Tanna of the Baraita — **maintained:** When the bridegroom stipulated that he was betrothing the woman **on condition that his father would consent**

RASHI

והא הכא דכי טעות אשה אחת דמי — דזו שהטעתו היא שהתנת עמו, ולא גרשה בינתיים, ואיכא למאן דאמר מקודשת **וטעמא מאי** — לפי שאין אדם עושה בעילתו זנות, וגמר ובעל בלא שום תנאי.

NOTES

renders the betrothal invalid, why do we not contend that if the man insists on proceeding with the marriage, he does so with the intention that the betrothal be effected anew regardless of the condition? *Ra'ah* and *Ritva* explain the matter as follows: In truth, we cannot assume that everyone necessarily knows that a betrothal effected with less than the value of a perutah is invalid. Nevertheless, assuming that a man is interested in the betrothal taking effect, we presume that he did know that the betrothal was invalid because less than a perutah was paid to the bride. Thus, when first engaging in intercourse with his bride, he intended that the act constitute a betrothal. However, in the case of a condition attached to betrothal, it is assumed that one is particular that the condition be met and so relies upon the woman's acceptance of it throughout the process of marriage.

HALAKHAH

עַל מְנָת שֶׁיִּרְצֶה הָאָב **On condition that my father will consent.** "If someone betroths a woman on condition that his father will consent to the marriage, and the father does in fact consent, then the betrothal is valid. If, however, the father does not consent, or remains silent, or dies before hearing about the betrothal, then the betrothal is not valid. If a man betroths a woman on condition that his father will not object to the marriage, and the father indeed objects, then the betrothal is not valid. If the father does not raise any objections, or dies before hearing about the betrothal, then the betrothal is valid (according to *Rambam,* unequivocally; whereas other authorities view the betrothal as only questionably valid). According to some authorities, betrothal on condition of paternal consent is considered the same as betrothal on condition of one's father not objecting (*Ra'avad*). Others maintain that it is considered the same as betrothal on condition that one's father will remain silent. (*Tur* in the name of *Rosh, Maggid Mishneh* in the name of *Ramban.*) In actual practice, it is proper to follow the stringencies of each position (*Bet Shmuel*). The law follows the view of Rabbi Shimon ben Yehudah, which forms the anonymous basis of the Mishnah in *Kiddushin.*" (*Rambam, Sefer Nashim, Hilkhot Ishut* 7:1; *Shulḥan Arukh, Even HaEzer* 38:8.)

עַל מְנָת שֶׁיִּרְצֶה הָאָב **Regarding a minor whose father married her off.** "If a minor was married off by her father and then divorced, only later to remarry the same man who then dies without children before the girl reaches maturity, she may not enter into levirate marriage with her late husband's brother. According to *Rambam,* she does not

— [1]עַל מְנָת שֶׁיִּשְׁתּוֹק הָאָב, [2]וְהָא שָׁתֵיק לֵיהּ. [3]וּמָר סָבַר: [4]עַל מְנָת שֶׁיֹּאמַר אַבָּא "הֵין", [5]וְהָא לָא אֲמַר אַבָּא "הֵין".
[6]אֵיתִיבֵיהּ: [7]"מוֹדִים חֲכָמִים לְרַבִּי אֱלִיעֶזֶר בִּקְטַנָּה שֶׁהִשִּׂיאָהּ אָבִיהָ וְנִתְגָּרְשָׁה, [8]וְהִיא יְתוֹמָה בְּחַיֵּי הָאָב, וְהֶחֱזִירָהּ — [9]שֶׁחוֹלֶצֶת וְלֹא מִתְיַבֶּמֶת, [10]מִפְּנֵי שֶׁגֵּירוּשֶׁיהָ גֵּירוּשִׁין גְּמוּרִין, [11]וְאֵין חֲזָרָתָהּ חֲזָרָה גְּמוּרָה.

LITERAL TRANSLATION

[1]on condition that father will remain silent, [2]and he did remain silent. [3]And [the other] Sage maintained: [4]On condition that father will say "Yes," [5]and behold the father did not say "Yes."

[6]He raised an objection against him: [7]"The Sages agree with Rabbi Eliezer regarding a minor whose father married her off and who was [then] divorced, [8][thus] becoming an orphan in her father's lifetime, and if he [then] remarried her — [9]she undergoes *ḥalitzah* and not levirate marriage, [10]because her divorce was a complete divorce, [11]and her remarriage was not a complete remarriage.

TRANSLATION AND COMMENTARY

to the marriage, [1]he meant that he was betrothing her **on condition that his father would remain silent** and not raise any objections; [2]**and** indeed **he did remain silent**. Thus the condition attached to the betrothal was met, and the betrothal is valid. [3]**The other Sage** — Rabbi Shimon ben Yehudah — **maintained** otherwise: [4]The bridegroom stipulated that he was betrothing the woman on condition that his father consented, and he meant **on condition that his father would say: "Yes,** I agree to the marriage" — [5]**and behold, his father,** while not raising any objections, still **did not say, "Yes,** I agree to the marriage." Consequently, the condition of the betrothal was not met, and the marriage becomes invalid.

אֵיתִיבֵיהּ [6]Abaye **raised** yet another **objection against** Rabbah's viewpoint — this time from a Baraita relating to a Mishnah in *Yevamot* (108b-109a) which states: "If someone divorced his wife and later remarried her, and then died without offspring, his widow is permitted to her late husband's brother in levirate marriage. Rabbi Eliezer disagrees and says that she is forbidden to enter into levirate marriage, because of a Rabbinic decree which was enacted on account of the case of 'an orphan during her father's lifetime,' which will be explained below. Similarly, if a man divorced an orphan girl who had been given to him in marriage by her mother or brothers while she was still a minor (the marriage being valid only by Rabbinic enactment), and later remarried her, and then died without offspring, the widowed girl is permitted to her late husband's brother. Rabbi Eliezer disagrees with this ruling as well, arguing that the Rabbis forbade her to enter into levirate marriage because of the same decree that was enacted on account of the case of 'an orphan during her father's lifetime.' But if a man divorced an orphan girl who had been given to him in marriage by her father (the marriage being valid by Torah law) — so that she is now 'an orphan during her father's lifetime' (meaning that her father no longer has authority over her), should her ex-husband remarry her and then die childless, all while she is still a minor, then all agree — both the first Tanna and Rabbi Eliezer — that the widowed girl is forbidden to her late husband's brother (as the remarriage was only Rabbinic in nature)." Regarding this Mishnah, the Baraita states: [7]**"The Sages** [the first Tanna of the Mishnah] **agree with Rabbi Eliezer regarding** the law of **a minor** girl **whose father married her off and who was** then **divorced** while still a minor — [8]thus assuming the status of **an orphan in her father's lifetime** — that should the same man **remarry her** as a minor and then die childless, [9]**she undergoes *ḥalitzah* and** may **not** enter into **levirate marriage** with her late husband's brother; [10]**for** while **her divorce was completely valid** by Torah law, rendering her forbidden to the *levir* as his brother's ex-spouse, [11]**her** subsequent **remarriage was not completely valid**, since it involved a minor who was not married off by her father. Thus by Torah law she is still regarded as an ex-spouse and not as a widow permitted to the *levir*.

RASHI

מודים חכמים לרבי אליעזר — ביבמות תנן: המגרש את האשה והחזירה, ומת — מותרת ליבם, ורבי אליעזר אוסר. והתם מפרש טעמא דרבי אליעזר, דגזר משום יתומה בחיי האב. והיא המפורשת כאן, שהודו לו חכמים בה. **ונתגרשה** — וקבל אביה גיטה. **והיא יתומה בחיי האב** — אף בחיי אביה היא כיתומה, לפי שיצאה מרשותו מנשואין הראשונים, ושוב אין לו זכות בה לקבל קידושיה. **והחזירה** — בקטנותה. ומעשה קטנה אינו כלום. **שגירושיה גירושין גמורים** — ונאסרה עליו איסור כרת, משמת גרושת אחיו, שהתורה אמרה "ערות אחיך וגו'". **ואין חזרתה גמורה** — לחזור ולהיות אשת אחיו במקום מצוה, להתייבם.

HALAKHAH

require *ḥalitzah* either. According to *Tur* and *Rosh,* she requires *ḥalitzah*, although it does not release her husband's other wives from the levirate duty." (*Rambam, Sefer Nashim, Hilkhot Yibum VaḤalitzah* 7:13; *Shulḥan Arukh, Even HaEzer* 173:16.)

¹בַּמֶּה דְּבָרִים אֲמוּרִים? ²שֶׁגֵּירְשָׁהּ כְּשֶׁהִיא קְטַנָּה, וְהֶחֱזִירָהּ כְּשֶׁהִיא קְטַנָּה. ³אֲבָל גֵּירְשָׁהּ כְּשֶׁהִיא קְטַנָּה וְהֶחֱזִירָהּ כְּשֶׁהִיא גְּדוֹלָה, ⁴אוֹ שֶׁהֶחֱזִירָהּ כְּשֶׁהִיא קְטַנָּה וְגָדְלָה אֶצְלוֹ, וּמֵת — ⁵אוֹ חוֹלֶצֶת אוֹ מִתְיַבֶּמֶת. [74A] ⁶מִשּׁוּם רַבִּי אֱלִיעֶזֶר אָמְרוּ: ⁷חוֹלֶצֶת וְלֹא מִתְיַיבֶּמֶת״. ⁸וְהָא הָכָא, דִּכְטָעוּת אִשָּׁה אַחַת דָּמֵי, ⁹וּפְלִיגִי!

¹⁰הָתָם נַמִי בְּהָא קָמִיפַּלְגִי: ¹¹מָר סָבַר: אָדָם יוֹדֵעַ שֶׁאֵין קִידּוּשֵׁי קְטַנָּה כְּלוּם, ¹²וְגָמַר וּבָעַל לְשֵׁם קִידּוּשִׁין. ¹³וּמָר סָבַר: אֵין אָדָם יוֹדֵעַ שֶׁאֵין קִידּוּשֵׁי קְטַנָּה כְּלוּם,

LITERAL TRANSLATION

[1]In what [circumstances] are these things said? [2]If he divorced her when she was a minor, and remarried her when she was a minor. [3]But if he divorced her when she was a minor and remarried her when she was an adult, [4]or if he remarried her when she was a minor and she reached maturity with him, and he died — [5]either she undergoes *ḥalitzah* or she enters into levirate marriage. [74A] [6]In the name of Rabbi Eliezer they said: [7]She undergoes *ḥalitzah* but cannot enter into levirate marriage." [8]And surely here it is like [the case of] a mistake involving one woman, [9]and they disagree!

[10]There, too, it is about this that they disagree: [11][One] Sage maintains: A man knows that the betrothal of a minor amounts to nothing, [12]and [so] he decided and engaged in intercourse for the sake of betrothal. [13]And [the other] Sage maintains: A man does not know that the betrothal of a minor amounts to nothing,

TRANSLATION AND COMMENTARY

[1]**In what circumstances are these words** forbidding her to her brother-in-law **stated?** [2]**If her husband divorced her while she was a minor, and** then **remarried her while she was** still **a minor,** thus rendering her remarriage valid by Rabbinic law alone. [3]**But if** her husband **divorced her while she was a minor and** then **remarried her when she was** already **an adult,** [4]**or remarried her while she was** still **a minor and** then **died** childless, but only **died** after **she reached maturity with him,** [5]then **either she undergoes *ḥalitzah* or enters into levirate marriage** with her late husband's brother like any other widow who is governed by the laws of levirate marriage and *ḥalitzah*. For in either case, the remarriage takes effect according to Torah law. [74A] [6]**In the name of Rabbi Eliezer it was said:** Even in such a case, when the marriage was still in effect after she reached majority, [7]**she undergoes *ḥalitzah* but cannot enter into levirate marriage** with her late husband's brother." [8]**And surely here it is like** the case of **a mistake involving** only **one woman,** [9]**but** nevertheless the Tannaim **disagree!** Ostensibly, they disagree about whether, when she reaches majority, her husband intends to betroth her anew with the commencement of adult sexual relations, or continues to rely upon the Rabbinically recognized betrothal that took place when she was a minor. The Sages, who maintain the former position, are of the opinion that the second marriage is now valid even according to Torah law. Thus, when her husband dies, she can either undergo *ḥalitzah* or enter into levirate marriage. If this interpretation is correct, then this Baraita refutes the viewpoint of Rabbah, who stated that if a man has relations with a woman subsequent to an imperfect betrothal, all agree that she does not require a bill of divorce.

הָתָם נַמִי [10]The Gemara defends Rabbah: **There too,** in the case of the married girl who reached majority, **it is about this that** the Tannaim **disagree:** [11]**The** Sages of the Baraita **maintained: A person** surely **knows that the betrothal of a minor amounts to nothing** in terms of Torah law. Thus we assume that as soon as she reached majority, [12]her husband decided to **engage in** his first act of adult **intercourse** with the specific intention of it being **for the sake of** effecting a **betrothal** valid by Torah law. Hence, if he died without offspring, she became permitted to her brother-in-law in levirate marriage. [13]**And** Rabbi Eliezer **maintained: A person does not** necessarily **know that the betrothal of**

RASHI

משום רבי אליעזר אמרו חולצת ולא מתייבמת — אף בשהחזירה כשהיא גדולה פליג. ואף במגרש גדולה והחזירה. וטעמיה — משום דגזור בה משום יתומה בחיי האב. **והא הכא** — גבי "החזירה כשהיא קטנה וגדלה אצלו". **דטעות אשה אחת היא** — טעות קידושי קטנה. **ופליגי** — דקאמרי רבנן: מתייבמת. אלמא: כי בעל משגדלה — לשם קדושין בעל. וקא סלקא דעתך — הוא הדין לטעות נדרים. הכי גרסינן: התם היינו טעמא אדם יודע שאין קדושי קטנה כלום, אבל קדשה על תנאי ובעל, דעתיה אתנאה. ולא גרסינן: בהא קמיפלגי. דהא רבי אליעזר במגרש את הגדולה נמי אמר דכי החזירה אסורה לייבם, דטעמא לאו משום קדושי טעות הוא. ומאן דגריס לה, מפרש דהאי "משום רבי אליעזר אמרו" דברייתא — א"החזירה כשהיא קטנה וגדלה אצלו" הוא דפליג. ולית ליה לתנא דברייתא אליבא דרבי אליעזר הא דתנא דמתניתין דיבמות (קט,א), דאמר דבמגרש גדולה והחזירה — נמי אסר רבי אליעזר.

NOTES

חוֹלֶצֶת וְלֹא מִתְיַיבֶּמֶת **She undergoes *ḥalitzah* but does not enter into levirate marriage.** *Rashi* understands Rabbi Eliezer

[1] וְכִי קָא בָּעַל, אַדַּעְתָּא דְּקִידּוּשִׁין הָרִאשׁוֹנִים קָא בָּעַל. [2] אִתְּמַר נַמִי, אָמַר רַב אַחָא בַּר יַעֲקֹב אָמַר רַבִּי יוֹחָנָן: [3] ״הַמְקַדֵּשׁ עַל תְּנַאי וּבָעַל, [דִּבְרֵי הַכֹּל] אֵינָהּ צְרִיכָה הֵימֶנּוּ גֵּט״. [4] אֵיתִיבֵיהּ רַב אַחָא בְּרֵיהּ דְּרַב אִיקָא בַּר אַחְתֵּיהּ: [5] ״חֲלִיצָה מוּטְעֵת כְּשֵׁירָה״. [6] אֵיזוֹ הִיא חֲלִיצָה מוּטְעֵת? [7] אָמַר רֵישׁ לָקִישׁ: כָּל שֶׁאוֹמֵר לוֹ: ״חֲלוֹץ לָהּ וּבְכָךְ אַתָּה כּוֹנְסָהּ״.

LITERAL TRANSLATION

[1] and [so] when he engaged in intercourse, it was with the first betrothal in mind that he did so.

[2] It was also stated: Rav Aḥa bar Ya'akov said in the name of Rabbi Yoḥanan: [3] [If] one betrothed [a woman] on condition and [then] engaged in intercourse, all agree [that] she would not require a bill of divorce from him.

[4] Rav Aḥa the son of Rav Ika, [who was] his [Rav Aḥa bar Ya'akov's] nephew, raised an objection against him: [5] "A mistaken *ḥalitzah* is valid." [6] Which is a mistaken *ḥalitzah*? [7] Resh Lakish said: Whenever one says to him: "Perform *ḥalitzah* and thus you will marry her."

RASHI

אתמר נמי — כרבה, דאמר בטעות אשה אחת גרידתא אין צריכה הימנו גט.

TRANSLATION AND COMMENTARY

a minor amounts to nothing according to Torah law. [1] Thus we assume that **when he engaged in intercourse** subsequent to his wife's reaching majority, **he did so with the first betrothal in mind.** Hence, if he died without offspring, she remains forbidden to her brother-in-law as the second marriage was only valid by Rabbinic enactment. Thus by law she was still his brother's ex-wife from the very first marriage. However, in the case of a man who betrothed a woman on condition and then had relations with her, only to discover that she deceived him by having violated the condition, all might agree that she does not require a bill of divorce as the husband cohabited with her while under the impression that the earlier betrothal was indeed valid.

אִתְּמַר נַמִי [2] An early Amoraic tradition supports Rabbah's statement: **It was also stated** that **Rav Aḥa bar Ya'akov said in the name of Rabbi Yoḥanan:** [3] If a man **betrothed a woman on condition, and** then **engaged in intercourse** without cancelling the condition, **all agree that** the woman **would not require a bill of divorce from** her husband if it is discovered that the condition was not met.

אֵיתִיבֵיהּ [4] **Rav Aḥa the son of Rav Ika, who was** also Rav Aḥa bar Ya'akov's **nephew, raised an objection against** Rav Aḥa bar Ya'akov: We have learned in a Baraita: [5] **"A mistaken *ḥalitzah* is** nevertheless **valid."** The question was raised: [6] **Which is** the case of **a mistaken *ḥalitzah*** that is nevertheless valid? [7] **Resh Lakish said: Whenever one** misleads the brother-in-law and **says to him: "Perform** the ***ḥalitzah*** ceremony with your late brother's wife **and in that way you will marry her."** In fact, the result of performing *ḥalitzah* is precisely the opposite, and if the brother-in-law wished to marry his brother's widow, he should have refused to perform the *ḥalitzah* ceremony. Nevertheless, although the brother-in-law was misled, the *ḥalitzah* is valid and the

NOTES

as disagreeing with the Sages of the Baraita even if the husband first divorced the girl after she reached majority and only then remarried her. Though by Torah law such a woman could enter into levirate marriage, nevertheless Rabbi Eliezer was of the opinion that the Rabbis decreed she may not enter into such a marriage lest her case be confused with that of a girl whose ex-husband remarried her while she was still a minor. Many Rishonim reject *Rashi's* explanation on the basis that it implies that the Rabbis enacted one preventive measure (forced *ḥalitzah* for the divorced minor whose ex-husband remarried her after reaching maturity) so as to avoid violation of another (forced *ḥalitzah* for the girl who was both divorced and remarried while still a minor but whose husband died only after she reached majority). Moreover, *Rashi's* explanation necessitates emending the Talmudic text in a way that does not significantly improve the clarity of the passage. Consequently, many of the Rishonim propose a different understanding of Rabbi Eliezer: The prohibition against entering into levirate marriage for a girl who was both divorced and remarried while still a minor, and whose husband died only after she reached maturity, is actually Biblical in nature — as we assume that the husband continued relying upon the earlier marriage even after she reached majority; thus, she

HALAKHAH

חֲלִיצָה מוּטְעֵת A mistaken *ḥalitzah*. "Both the *levir* and his brother's widow must have in mind that the *ḥalitzah* will release the woman from the levirate tie. If the *levir* intended to free the woman with the *ḥalitzah*, but the woman did not intend to be released thereby, or vice versa, then the *ḥalitzah* would not be valid — although it disqualifies her from entering into levirate marriage with either that brother or any other brother of her late husband," in accordance with Rabbi Yoḥanan. (*Rambam, Sefer Nashim, Hilkhot Yibbum VaḤalitzah* 4:16; *Shulḥan Arukh, Even HaEzer* 169:44.)

TRANSLATION AND COMMENTARY

woman is permissible to other men. [1]**Rabbi Yoḥanan** disagreed with Resh Lakish and **said:** [2]**I teach** the following principle regarding *ḥalitzah*: **Regardless of whether** the *levir* **intended** to free his brother's widow while **she did not intend** to be released, [3]**or she** was the one who **intended to** be released while **he** (the *levir*) **did not intend** to free her, [4]the ***ḥalitzah* is invalid until both** the *levir* and the widow **have the same intention** of effecting a release from the levirate tie. [5]**And** yet **you say that** the ***ḥalitzah* is valid** even if the *levir* thought that he was thereby acquiring the woman as his wife! [6]**Rather, Rabbi Yoḥanan said** that the Baraita means to teach that **when one misleads** the *levir* **by saying to him:** [7]**"Perform** the ***ḥalitzah* on condition that** your brother's widow will **give you two hundred zuz,"** and then after the ceremony the woman refuses to hand over the money, admitting to having deceived him, the *ḥalitzah* is still valid. [8]**Hence, since** the *levir* **performed the act** of *ḥalitzah* without explicitly stating the condition at the time, [9]**surely he must have waived the condition.** [10]**Here too,** in the case stated by Rav Aḥa bar Ya'akov, it would stand to reason that **since** the husband **engaged in intercourse** without restating the condition he had earlier attached to the betrothal, [11]**surely he must have waived his condition.** Thus, Rav Aḥa bar Ya'akov's statement in the name of Rabbi Yoḥanan is contradicted by another statement attributed directly to Rabbi Yoḥanan!

אֲמַר לֵיהּ [12]Rav Aḥa bar Ya'akov **said to** Rav Aḥa the son of Rav Ika: **Student, have you** indeed **spoken rightly?** A conditional *ḥalitzah* is valid according to Rabbi Yoḥanan, even if the condition is not met, not because we assume the condition to have been waived but, rather, because it never took effect from the outset. [13]**From where do we learn** the laws that govern **any condition?**

[1]אָמַר רַבִּי יוֹחָנָן: [2]אֲנִי שׁוֹנֶה: בֵּין שֶׁנִּתְכַּוֵּין הוּא וְלֹא נִתְכַּוְּונָה הִיא, [3]בֵּין שֶׁנִּתְכַּוְּונָה הִיא וְלֹא נִתְכַּוֵּין הוּא, [4]חֲלִיצָתָהּ פְּסוּלָה עַד שֶׁיִּתְכַּוְּונוּ שְׁנֵיהֶם — [5]וְאַתְּ אָמְרַתְּ חֲלִיצָתָהּ כְּשֵׁרָה? [6]אֶלָּא אָמַר רַבִּי יוֹחָנָן: כָּל שֶׁאוֹמֵר לוֹ [7]"חֲלוֹץ לָהּ עַל מְנָת שֶׁתִּתֵּן לְךָ מָאתַיִם זוּז". [8]אַלְמָא, כֵּיוָן דַּעֲבַד מַעֲשֶׂה, [9]אַחוּלֵי אַחְלֵיהּ לִתְנָאֵיהּ. [10]הָכָא נַמִי, כֵּיוָן דְּבָעַל, [11]אַחוּלֵי אַחְלֵיהּ לִתְנָאֵיהּ?

[12]אֲמַר לֵיהּ: בַּר בֵּי רַב, שַׁפִּיר קָא אָמְרַתְּ? [13]מִכְּדִי כָּל תְּנַאי מֵהֵיכָא גָּמְרִינַן?

LITERAL TRANSLATION

[1]Rabbi Yoḥanan said: [2]I teach: [Regardless of] whether he intended and she did not intend, [3]or she intended and he did not intend, [4]her *ḥalitzah* is invalid until they both intend — [5]and you say her *ḥalitzah* is valid? [6]Rather, Rabbi Yoḥanan said: Whenever one says to him: [7]"Perform *ḥalitzah* on condition that she give you two hundred zuz." [8]Hence, since he performed an action, [9]surely he waived his condition. [10]Here too, since he engaged in intercourse, [11]surely he waived his condition!

[12]He said to him: Student (lit., "son of the Academy"), have you spoken rightly? [13]Now from where do we deduce [regarding] every condition?

RASHI

שנתכוין הוא — לחליצה. על מנת שתתן כו׳ — ואף על גב דלא יהבה — כשרה. שפיר קאמרת — בתמיה. דטעמא דהכא — לאו משום דאחליה לתנאיה הוא, אלא משום דמעיקרא לאו תנאה הוא. כל תנאי מהיכן גמרינן מתנאי בני גד ובני ראובן — ד"אם יעברו...ונתתם" "ואם לא יעברו...ונאחזו בתוככם" (במדבר לב).

NOTES

was never married by Torah law. Consequently, the prohibition against levirate marriage in this case can serve as the basis for enacting a preventive measure prohibiting it in the case of a divorced minor whose ex-husband only remarried her after she reached majority. (*Ramban, Ra'ah,* and *Rashba.*) *Ritva* suggests that perhaps Rabbi Eliezer would agree with the Sages about a divorced minor whose ex-husband remarried her after she reached majority, and only differ in the case where he remarried her while she was still a minor and then died after she reached maturity.

שַׁפִּיר קָא אָמְרַתְּ Have you spoken rightly? *Shittah Mekubbetzet* explains Rav Aḥa bar Ya'akov's query as directed against his nephew's understanding of Rav Yoḥanan's position in the Baraita concerning *ḥalitzah*. How could

HALAKHAH

חֲלוֹץ לָהּ עַל מְנָת שֶׁתִּתֵּן לְךָ Perform *ḥalitzah* on condition that she give you. "Where a *levir* is misled into believing that he could perform *ḥalitzah* on condition that his brother's widow will give him two hundred zuz, the *ḥalitzah* is valid even if the condition is never fulfilled. This is true even where the *levir* stipulates the condition in dual fashion, saying, 'If you give me the money, you are released; if not, you remain forbidden to remarry,' as dictated by the laws of setting conditions. (*Rosh.*) Although the *ḥalitzah* is valid, if the woman willingly accepted the obligation to pay, she must do so, as the *levir* deserves no less than anyone else who is retained in her service for a wage. If, however, the woman had good reason not to be joined to this particular *levir*, and he refused to release her

[1] מִתְּנַאי בְּנֵי גָד וּבְנֵי רְאוּבֵן, [2] תְּנָאָה דְּאֶפְשָׁר לְקַיּוּמֵיהּ עַל יְדֵי שָׁלִיחַ, [3] כִּי הָתָם — הָוֵי תְּנָאֵיהּ תְּנָאָה, [4] דְּלָא אֶפְשָׁר לְקַיּוּמֵיהּ עַל יְדֵי שָׁלִיחַ [5] כִּי הָתָם — לָא הָוֵי תְּנָאָה.
[6] וְהָא בִּיאָה, דְּלָא אֶפְשָׁר לְקַיּוּמֵיהּ עַל יְדֵי שָׁלִיחַ כִּי הָתָם, [7] וְקָא הָוֵי תְּנָאָה!

LITERAL TRANSLATION

[1] From the condition of the sons of Gad and the sons of Reuben, [2] a condition that can be fulfilled by an agent, [3] like there — his condition as a condition, [4] [one] that cannot be fulfilled by an agent [5] like there — it is not a condition.
[6] But surely the act of intercourse, which cannot be performed by way of an agent like there, [7] and yet it is [subject to] a condition!

RASHI

דאפשר לקיומיה — למעשה של תנאי, דהיינו "ונתתם". **על ידי שליח** — כי התם, שהרי משה צוה ליהושע לתת להם את הארץ, שהיה שלוחו של משה ונתנה להם. **אבל חליצה** — אי אפשר לקיימה על ידי שליח — אין יכול לומר לשלוחו: אם תתן לך פלונית מאתים זוז — חלוץ לה. **הלכך** — לאו תנאה הוא לבטל החליצה. **והא ביאה** — הבועל לשם קידושין. **וקא הוי תנאיה תנאה** — כדאמרינן לעיל: הריני בועליך על מנת כו'.

TRANSLATION AND COMMENTARY

[1] **From the condition** that Moses stipulated **with the tribes of Gad and Reuben** in response to their request, prior to entering the Land of Israel, that certain lands on the eastern side of the Jordan River be allocated to them as their share. Moses agreed to their request, but on condition that they first cross the Jordan with the other ten tribes and assist them in conquering the Land of Israel. This agreement was adopted in Jewish law as the formal model for all other such agreements incorporating intrinsic conditions. [2] **Hence, only a** conditional agreement **which is capable of being fulfilled by an agent,** [3] **like** the case of Moses, who was forced to entrust his successor Joshua with the responsibility of allocating the land after its conquest, is considered an agreement whose **condition is valid.** [4] But **a conditional** agreement **which is not capable of being fulfilled by an agent,** as with the tribes of Gad and Reuben, [5] is considered an agreement whose **condition is not valid.** Since one cannot perform *ḥalitzah* by proxy, any condition attached to the *ḥalitzah* would thus be considered invalid. Hence, a "mistaken *ḥalitzah,*" which had a condition attached to it that is never met, is nevertheless effective, since the condition never had any validity. In the case of betrothal, however, since it is a rite that can be executed by **an agent**, any condition attached to it would have validity and could thus prevent the marriage if it were not met.

וְהָא בִּיאָה [6] The Gemara raises an objection: **But surely** betrothal effected through **intercourse cannot be performed by an agent as** it was **there,** in the case of the condition established with the tribes of Gad and Reuben. [7] **And yet** we have seen, above, that betrothal effected by way of intercourse **is subject to** the attachment of **a condition** that must be met in order for the betrothal to take effect!

NOTES

ḥalitzah, performed with the understanding that one would not allow any condition to stand in its way, be called a "mistaken *ḥalitzah*"? Rather, as Rav Aḥa points out, Rav Yoḥanan understands the idea of a condition as being totally inapplicable to a situation of *ḥalitzah.*

עַל יְדֵי שָׁלִיחַ כִּי הָתָם By proxy like there. Most Rishonim understand the role of the proxy as relevant to Moses' side of the agreement, as we see from Joshua and the elders who represented Moses in the conquest of the land and its subsequent distribution among the various tribes. *Meiri,* however, understands the role of the proxy as relevant to the condition accepted by the tribes of Gad and Reuben in joining in the campaign to conquer the land on the other side of the Jordan, for this was not necessarily fulfilled by the same individuals who entered into the agreement with Moses.

תְּנָאֵיהּ תְּנָאָה, דְּלָא אֶפְשָׁר לְקַיּוּמֵיהּ עַל יְדֵי שָׁלִיחַ A condition which cannot be fulfilled by a proxy. *Tosafot* comment that one cannot view the conditional agreement between Moses and the tribes of Gad and Reuben as an absolute model, for according to all opinions, one cannot derive all the laws of conditions as though they were exactly similar to those between Moses and the tribes of Gad and Reuben. Rather, there must be sufficient reason for applying the model. *Tosafot* explain this reason as follows: Any action that can be performed by proxy is fully within the control of the party represented by proxy. Therefore that party can also stipulate conditions. But if one cannot do it by proxy it means that basically one has only limited power over this act, and therefore cannot attach binding conditions. *Pnei Yehoshua* (whose position is similar to that of *Ritva*, *Meiri* and others) explains the matter slightly differently: If any action cannot be performed by proxy, it means that the action itself is the main thing, and the verbal authorization given by the concerned party is not significant. Since the action itself is the main thing, a person cannot annul the action verbally by stipulating a condition.

HALAKHAH

through *ḥalitzah* unless she paid him money in return, then, even if she were to accept his condition and he performed *ḥalitzah,* she would not be required to pay him the money." (*Rambam, Sefer Nashim, Hilkhot Yibbum VaḤalitzah* 4:24; *Shulḥan Arukh, Even HaEzer* 169:50-51.)

[1]הָתָם מִשּׁוּם דְּאִיתְקוּשׁ הֲוָיוֹת לַהֲדָדֵי.
[2]אָמַר רַב עוּלָּא בַּר אַבָּא אָמַר עוּלָּא אָמַר רַבִּי אֶלְעָזָר: [3]הַמְקַדֵּשׁ בְּמִלְוֶה וּבָעַל, [4]עַל תְּנַאי וּבָעַל, [5]בְּפָחוֹת מִשָּׁוֶה פְּרוּטָה וּבָעַל — [6]דִּבְרֵי הַכֹּל צְרִיכָה הֵימֶנּוּ גֵּט.

LITERAL TRANSLATION

[1]There, because [the various] ways of becoming [betrothed] are equated one to the other.
[2]Rav Ulla bar Aba said in the name of Ulla who said in the name of Rabbi Elazar: [3][Where] one betroths [a woman] with a loan and [then] has intercourse, [4][or] on condition and [then] has intercourse, [5][or] with less than the value of a perutah and [then] has intercourse — [6]all agree [that] she requires a bill of divorce from him.

TRANSLATION AND COMMENTARY

הָתָם [1]The Gemara answers: Although, as a general rule, a condition is only valid if attached to an agreement which can be fulfilled by way of an agent, **there**, in the case of betrothal through intercourse, this rule is suspended **because** of the Scriptural inference (Deuteronomy 24:2) that teaches us **that the various ways of becoming betrothed** — through money, a marital contract, or intercourse — **are equated one to the other.** Hence, just as a condition can be attached to betrothal effected by money or a contract, formalities that can be carried out by an agent as well, so too can a condition be attached to betrothal effected through intercourse, though such a betrothal cannot be executed by an agent.

אָמַר [2]The Gemara continues with another Amoraic opinion in contradiction to that of Rabbah: **Rav Ulla bar Aba said in the name of Ulla who said in the name of Rabbi Elazar:** [3]**If a man betroths a woman with a loan**, by designating money that she already owes him as betrothal money for her to retain (which is not a valid way of betrothal), **and** then **has intercourse** with her; [4]**or** if he betroths her with a stipulated **condition** which he learns later she did not meet, **and** then **has intercourse** with her; [5]**or** if he betroths her **with less than the value of a perutah, and** then **has intercourse** with her — [6]**all agree** that even though each of these circumstances renders the betrothal invalid, the woman still **requires a bill of divorce from** her husband since they engaged in intercourse, and we assume that they must have done it with the intention to effect betrothal, should earlier means prove insufficient.

RASHI

דאיתקוש הויות — "והיתה לאיש אחר" (דברים כד) כל הויות קידושין במשמע: כסף ושטר וביאה; כי היכי דמהני תנאי בקידושי כסף ושטר, דאפשר לקיומיה על ידי שליח — מהני נמי בביאה. **במלוה** — שמחל לה מלוה שחייבת לו. ואמרינן בקידושין (ו,ב) דאינה מקודשת; דמשום דמשעה שלוותה ניתנה להוצאה, וברשותה קיימא, והשתא לאו מידי יהיב לה. **צריכה הימנו גט** — ואפילו הטעתו בתנאי — דאין אדם עושה בעילתו זנות.

NOTES

דְּאִיתְקוּשׁ הֲוָיוֹת לַהֲדָדֵי The ways of becoming betrothed are equated one to the other. *Pnei Yehoshua* points out that the equation referred to in the Gemara between the ways of effecting betrothal is not a strict *hekesh* (Scriptural equation) insofar as nowhere in Scripture are these methods explicitly referred to in the same verse. Rather, the Gemara means that all the methods used to effect betrothal are essentially one, commonly subsumed within the same general expression (Deuteronomy 24:2): "...and becometh another man's wife...." It is pointed out that betrothal by intercourse emulates the other methods of betrothal in their ability to sustain a condition (rather than those methods emulating betrothal by intercourse in its inability to do so) because the other methods comprise a majority and thus set the tone for the character of betrothal as a whole.

הַמְקַדֵּשׁ עַל תְּנַאי וּבָעַל Where a man betroths a woman on condition and then has intercourse. The Jerusalem Talmud cites the same ruling in the name of Rabbi Yoḥanan: If a man attaches a condition to his betrothal and then marries without restating his condition, the betrothal is valid and his wife will require a bill of divorce. It is further stated there that even Resh Lakish, who disputes this ruling, might possibly agree that if the marriage was effected through intercourse, the woman would definitely require a bill of divorce.

דִּבְרֵי הַכֹּל צְרִיכָה הֵימֶנּוּ גֵּט All agree that she would require a bill of divorce. There are many variant readings attached to this line in the Talmud, the central problem being the

HALAKHAH

הַמְקַדֵּשׁ בְּמִלְוֶה וּבָעַל If a man betroths a woman with a loan and then has intercourse. "If one betrothed a woman with a loan and then had intercourse with her (it being sufficient for witnesses to simply see the couple entering into seclusion together), she would require a bill of divorce by reason of doubt that perhaps he intended the intercourse to be a new basis of betrothal," in accordance with the words of Rabbi Elazar. (*Rambam, Sefer Nashim, Hilkhot Ishut* 7:23; *Shulḥan Arukh, Even HaEzer* 28:16.)

הַמְקַדֵּשׁ עַל תְּנַאי וּבָעַל If a man betroths a woman on condition and then has intercourse. "If a man betrothed a woman after imposing a condition which, it turns out, was never met, and then married her or engaged in sexual relations without restating this condition, she would require a bill of divorce by reason of doubt that perhaps he may have intended the intercourse to be a new basis of betrothal. If afterwards she accepted an offer of betrothal from another man, she would require a bill of divorce from both husbands by reason of the same uncertainty [*Rema*]." (*Rambam, Sefer Nashim, Hilkhot Ishut* 7:23; *Shulḥan Arukh, Even HaEzer* 38:35.)

הַמְקַדֵּשׁ בְּפָחוֹת מִשָּׁוֶה פְּרוּטָה וּבָעַל If a man betroths a woman with less than the value of a perutah. "If a man betrothed a woman with less than the value of a perutah

TRANSLATION AND COMMENTARY

אָמַר [1]**Rav Yosef bar Abba said in the name of Rabbi Menaḥem, who said in the name of Rabbi Ammi:** [2]**If a man betroths a woman with less than the value of a perutah and** then **has intercourse** with her, [3]**the woman would require a bill of divorce from** him. Why does Rabbi Ammi distinguish between betrothing with a loan, an unmet condition, and betrothal with less than a perutah? [4]**In the case** of betrothal effected with less than the value of a perutah, it is assumed that **a man does not make a mistake** and knows full well that such a betrothal is invalid. Thus he would certainly wish to invest the subsequent act of intercourse with the specific intention of effecting betrothal. [5]**However, in these other cases,** it is possible that **he** indeed **would make a mistake** and assume the original betrothal to be valid — in the case of the loan, through sheer ignorance of the law; and in the case of the condition, by assuming that his wife indeed met it. Hence, the subsequent act of intercourse was not intended to serve as the basis for a new betrothal. There would have been no marriage and thus no need for a bill of divorce. Rabbi Ammi's position thus supports that of Rabbah.

אָמַר [6]The Gemara now adduces additional support for the position of Rabbi Elazar against that of Rabbah: **Rav Kahana said in the name of Ulla:** [7]**If a man betroths a woman after making a condition** which later proves to have gone unmet, **and** then **has intercourse** with her, [8]**the woman** is considered to have been betrothed through intercourse and will thus **require a bill of divorce from** him.

זֶה הָיָה מַעֲשֶׂה [9]**This actually occurred** once. When the matter came before the Sages, [10]they **did not have the power to release the woman without a bill of divorce.** Because they were unable to decide whether the betrothal was valid, they had to take the stringent position and require her to receive a bill of divorce.

[1]אָמַר רַב יוֹסֵף בַּר אַבָּא אָמַר רַבִּי מְנַחֵם אָמַר רַבִּי אַמִי: [2]הַמְקַדֵּשׁ בְּפָחוֹת מִשָּׁוֶה פְּרוּטָה וּבָעַל, [3]צְרִיכָה הֵימֶנּוּ גֵּט. [4]בְּהָא הוּא דְּלָא טָעֵי; [5]אֲבָל בְּהָנָךְ, טָעֵי.

[6]אָמַר רַב כָּהֲנָא מִשְּׁמֵיהּ דְּעוּלָּא: [7]הַמְקַדֵּשׁ עַל תְּנַאי וּבָעַל, [8]צְרִיכָה הֵימֶנּוּ גֵּט.

[9]זֶה הָיָה מַעֲשֶׂה, [10]וְלֹא הָיָה כֹּחַ בַּחֲכָמִים לְהוֹצִיאָהּ בְּלֹא גֵּט.

LITERAL TRANSLATION

[1]Rav Yosef bar Abba said in the name of Rabbi Menaḥem who said in the name of Rabbi Ammi: [2][If] a man who betroths [a woman] with less than the value of a perutah and [then] has intercourse, [3]she requires a bill of divorce from him. [4][It is] in this [case] that he does not make a mistake; [5]but in these [other cases], he would make a mistake.

[6]Rav Kahana said in the name of Ulla: [7][If] a man who betroths [a woman] on condition and [then] has intercourse, [8]she requires a bill of divorce from him.

[9]This was an actual occurrence, [10]and the Sages did not have the power to release her without a bill of divorce.

RASHI

רבי אמי – פליג אדרבי אלעזר ואמר: המקדש בפחות משוה פרוטה ובעל – הוא דצריכה גט, אבל המקדש במלוה או על תנאי, ובעל – אינה צריכה הימנו גט. מאי טעמא – בהא הוא דלא טעי, להיות סבור שפחות משוה פרוטה יהיו קידושין, הילכך גמר ובעל לשם קידושין. אבל בהנך טעי – כסבור: יודעת היא שאין עליה נדרים, לכך היא נשאת. וכי בעיל אדעתא דקידושי קמאי בעיל, ולא לשם קידושין. במלוה לאו הכל בקיאין בהלכות קידושין.

NOTES

words "all agree," since the Gemara has already identified a dispute among Tannaim regarding the very cases mentioned. The *Ra'ah* therefore suggests that the words "all agree" be omitted entirely. Others prefer to read the line as: "All agree that she would *not* require a bill of divorce." *Rashba*, realizing that this does not eliminate the core problem, chooses to read the line simply as: "She would not require a bill of divorce." *Rash* avoids the problem altogether by pointing out that the words "all agree" are not meant to refer to all Talmudic Sages, but just to the Amoraim Rav and Shmuel, who are in agreement on the matter (see also *Tosafot* and *Rosh*).

בְּהָא הוּא דְּלָא טָעֵי **It is in this case that he does not make a mistake.** Our commentary follows the opinion of *Rashi*, who understands Rabbi Ammi as exclusively singling out the man who betroths a woman with less than the value of a perutah as being aware of the flaw in his betrothal and determined to re-effect it through his subsequent act of intercourse. *Ritva* and others, on the other hand, understand Rabbi Ammi as referring to any and all cases of deficient betrothal, including that of betrothal by loan. However, Rabbi Ammi would assume that a man indeed made a mistake in presuming his betrothal valid in the case of betrothal effected with a condition, when he takes it for granted that his condition will be met and thus relies upon the initial betrothal.

HALAKHAH

and they then engaged in intercourse (with witnesses to their seclusion), she would definitely require a bill of divorce, as in this case it is certain that he was aware of the problem with the initial betrothal and thus intended the act of intercourse to constitute a new betrothal." (*Rambam, Sefer Nashim, Hilkhot Ishut* 7:23; *Shulḥan Arukh, Even HaEzer* 31:9; *Rema* 28:16.)

[1]לְאַפּוּקֵי מֵהַאי תַּנָּא, [2]דְּאָמַר רַב יְהוּדָה אָמַר שְׁמוּאֵל מִשּׁוּם רַבִּי יִשְׁמָעֵאל: [3]"וְהִיא לֹא נִתְפָּשָׂה" — אֲסוּרָה. [4]הָא נִתְפְּשָׂה, מוּתֶּרֶת. [5]וְיֵשׁ לְךָ אַחֶרֶת, שֶׁאַף עַל פִּי שֶׁלֹּא נִתְפְּשָׂה מוּתֶּרֶת, [6]וְאֵיזוֹ זוֹ? [7]שֶׁקִּידּוּשֶׁיהָ קִידּוּשֵׁי טָעוּת, [8]שֶׁאֲפִילּוּ בְּנָהּ מוּרְכָּב עַל כְּתֵיפָהּ, [74B] מְמָאֶנֶת וְהוֹלֶכֶת לָהּ".

[9]תָּנוּ רַבָּנַן: "הָלְכָה אֵצֶל חָכָם

LITERAL TRANSLATION

[1][This is] to exclude [the opinion] of this Tanna, [2]for Rav Yehudah said in the name of Shmuel who said in the name of Rabbi Yishmael: [3]"And she was not forcibly seized" — she is forbidden. [4]But, if she was [forcibly] seized, she is permitted. [5]And you have another one who, even though she was not [forcibly] seized, is permitted. [6]And which is this? [7][She] whose betrothal was a betrothal in error, [8]where even if her son is mounted upon her shoulder, [74B] may refuse and walk away.

[9]Our Rabbis taught: "[If] she went to a Sage

RASHI

הלכה — אחר קידושין אצל חכם.

TRANSLATION AND COMMENTARY

לְאַפּוּקֵי מֵהַאי תַּנָּא [1]This anecdote is adduced in order **to negate** the viewpoint of **the Tanna** who maintained that in such a case the woman's betrothal would definitely be invalid, [2]**for Rav Yehudah said in the name of Shmuel, who said in the name of Rabbi Yishmael:** The Torah (Numbers 5:13) teaches us that if a married woman is suspected of having intercourse with a man who is not her husband, [3]and it was determined that **"she was not forcibly seized," she is forbidden** to her husband until her fidelity can be established. [4]**This** implies that **if she was** indeed **forcibly seized** and raped by the man **she is permitted** to her husband. Now, from the emphasis in the verse on 'she (הִיא)' having "not been forcibly seized" and thus forbidden to her husband, [5]it would appear that **there is another woman who, even though "she was not forcibly seized"** and willingly engaged in relations, **is** nevertheless **permitted** to her husband. [6]**And which** woman **is this?** [7]**She whose betrothal was a betrothal of error.** [8]Even if such a woman has continued to live with her husband, and **even if her child** from him **is** now **mounted upon her shoulder,** [74B] **she may** at any time **refuse** the marriage **and walk away** from her husband without a bill of divorce, as the betrothal, being a faulty one, never took effect. In such a case, if the woman engaged in sexual relations with another man while ostensibly married, she would be permitted to remain with her presumed husband, if their marriage was correctly contracted.

Thus, according to Rabbi Yishmael, betrothal based upon a condition that was never met annuls the marriage, even if the couple had commenced having marital relations.

תָּנוּ רַבָּנַן [9]**Our Rabbis taught** in a Baraita: **"If** a man betrothed a woman on condition that she was free of vows, but she was not, and **she** then **went to a Sage who released her from her vow, she is betrothed.**

NOTES

מְמָאֶנֶת וְהוֹלֶכֶת **She may refuse and walk away.** The term מְמָאֶנֶת usually refers to a girl's right to "refuse marriage." If a girl was orphaned by the death of her father and agreed to be married off by her mother or brothers while still a minor, she may refuse to remain married upon reaching majority. In the context of a betrothal which proves to have been made in error, the Rishonim question whether we are dealing with the ordinary form of "refusal." A related issue which they discuss is whether Rabbi Yishmael's ruling also applies to a woman who was betrothed as a minor and wishes to exercise her right of "refusal" even after reaching majority. *Tosafot* and others insist that Rabbi Yishmael did indeed intend his ruling to apply to such a case (unlike *Rivan*, who dissents). However, they assume at the same time that Shmuel, who is quoting Rabbi Yishmael, agrees with his ruling only regarding the case of a woman betrothed on the basis of an unmet condition. Consequently, the term מְמָאֶנֶת can be understood either as a formal declaration that the husband has discovered that the condition was unmet and thus the marriage is invalid, or simply as an expression indicating the woman's right to leave the marriage whenever she so wishes, without requiring a bill of divorce.

הָלְכָה אֵצֶל חָכָם וְהִתִּירָהּ **If she went to a Sage and he released her from her vow.** This implies that if the woman did not ask a Sage to dissolve her vow, then her betrothal would not be valid. The Rishonim ask: Why are we not concerned that if she is permitted to marry another man, she might subsequently ask to be released from her vow, thereby rendering her first betrothal retroactively valid and her children from the second marriage illegitimate? This question is discussed in the Jerusalem Talmud, where it is resolved that either the woman should be allowed to remarry with no more than a warning that she must not

HALAKHAH

הָלְכָה אֵצֶל חָכָם וְהִתִּירָהּ **If she went to a Sage and he released her from her vow.** "If a man betrothed a woman on condition that she was free of vows, only to discover that his presumption was mistaken, should the woman go to a Sage who releases her from her vow, the betrothal is valid. However, this is only so if the Sage dissolves the vow before it comes to the husband's attention. If the husband becomes aware of the vow before his bride can have it dissolved, the betrothal is invalid. There are those (*Rosh* and others) who say that if the woman came from a

וְהִתִּירָהּ, מְקוּדֶּשֶׁת. [1]אֵצֶל רוֹפֵא וְרִיפֵּא אוֹתָהּ, אֵינָהּ מְקוּדֶּשֶׁת". [2]מַה בֵּין חָכָם לְרוֹפֵא? [3]חָכָם עוֹקֵר אֶת הַנֶּדֶר מֵעִיקָּרוֹ, [4]וְרוֹפֵא אֵינוֹ מְרַפֵּא אֶלָּא מִכָּאן וּלְהַבָּא.

[5]וְהָתַנְיָא: [6]"אֵצֶל חָכָם וְהִתִּירָהּ, [7]אֵצֶל רוֹפֵא וְרִיפֵּא אוֹתָהּ, אֵינָהּ מְקוּדֶּשֶׁת"!

LITERAL TRANSLATION

and he released her [from her vow], she is betrothed. [1][If she went] to a doctor and he cured her, she is not betrothed." [2]What is [the difference] between a Sage and a doctor? [3]A Sage uproots the vow from its root, [4]while a doctor only cures from now on.

[5]But surely it was taught: [6]"[If she went] to a Sage and he released her [from her vow, [7]or] to a doctor and he cured her, she is not betrothed"!

TRANSLATION AND COMMENTARY

Her husband cannot have the betrothal annulled on the grounds that she was bound by vows, since she has been released from all vows retroactively. [1]However, **if** he betrothed her on condition that she had no physical defects, only to discover later that she indeed did have a defect, if **she went to a doctor who remedied her** defect, **she is** still **not** considered **betrothed."** [2]The Gemara asks: **What is the difference between a Sage** who dissolves a vow **and a doctor who** remedies a physical defect? [3]The Gemara explains: When releasing someone from a vow that he regrets having taken, a **Sage uproots the vow completely**, as if it had never been made. Thus, the condition attached to the betrothal is retroactively fulfilled. [4]However, when **a doctor** remedies an objective physical defect, he **only cures** it **from** that point on. The defect still existed at the time of the betrothal, thereby violating the condition upon which it was based and rendering it invalid.

וְהָתַנְיָא [5]The Gemara now quotes a contradictory Baraita: **But surely it was taught** elsewhere in a Baraita: "If a man betrothed a woman on condition that she was free of vows, only later to discover otherwise, [6]if subsequently she went **to a Sage and he released her from her vow,** or if he betrothed her on condition that she had no physical defects, only to discover that she indeed had, [7]**or** if subsequently she went **to a doctor and he cured her** of her defect — in both cases, **she is not** considered **betrothed"!**

RASHI

והתירה — מן הנדרים. **אצל רופא וריפא אותה** — מן המומין. **עוקר הנדר מעיקרו** — שהרי פותח לה בחרטה: אדעתא דהכי מי קא נדרת? והיא אומרת לו: לא. וחכם אומר לה: הרי הוא בא לך לידי כך — הילכך לאו נדר הוא, ומותר לך. נמצא כמי שלא היה עליה בשעת קידושין. **מכאן ולהבא** — אבל עד עכשיו היו עליה. נמצא שבשעת תנאי הקידושין הטעתו. הכי גרסינן: **והתניא אצל חכם והתירה אצל רופא וריפא אותה אינה מקודשת** — וקשיא חכם אחכם.

NOTES

ask to be released from her earlier vow, or she should be allowed to remarry only after first accepting a bill of divorce from her first husband as insurance against any future complications. *Ritva* sees the Babylonian Talmud as dismissing this concern altogether, since it is assumed that the court, in allowing her to remarry after the vow is discovered, permanently invalidates the first betrothal. In actual practice, however, the Rishonim agree that the concern cited in the Jerusalem Talmud should be addressed, by requiring the woman to obtain a bill of divorce before remarrying.

אֵצֶל רוֹפֵא וְרִיפֵּא אוֹתָהּ If she went to a doctor and he cured her. *Shittah Mekubbetzet* cites a different reading of the second Baraita: "[If she went] to a Sage and he released her [from her vow], she is not betrothed; [if she went] to a doctor and he cured her [of her defect], she is betrothed." According to this reading, it can be said that the Baraitot argue on two points. According to the first Baraita, which follows the view of Rabbi Meir, a man is prepared to have his wife shame herself in court, but he is not prepared to have her humiliate herself before a doctor by receiving treatment for her defect. According to the second Baraita, which follows the view of Rabbi Elazar, the opposite is true: A man is prepared to have his wife humiliate herself before a doctor but not before a court.

חָכָם עוֹקֵר The Sage uproots. In tractate *Nedarim*, a basic distinction is made between the nullification of a woman's vow by her husband and its dissolution by a Sage: The Sage can cause a vow to be dissolved retroactively, while the husband's nullification only takes effect from that moment onward. Insofar as the cure of a defect is concerned, a woman's having had it at the time of her betrothal cannot be reversed by the doctor's subsequent remedy. *Tosafot* view a cured defect as differing from a dissolved vow in another respect: The thought of her once having had a defect continues to affect her husband's attitude toward her, thus weakening the basis of their betrothal; whereas the thought of her once having been bound by a vow would not affect their relationship.

HALAKHAH

distinguished family, the validity of the betrothal remains in doubt even if the vow was dissolved before the husband became aware of it; this, in light of Rava's position below (75a)." (*Rambam, Sefer Nashim, Hilkhot Ishut* 7:8; *Shulḥan Arukh, Even HaEzer* 39:2.)

אֵצֶל רוֹפֵא וְרִיפֵּא אוֹתָהּ If she went to a doctor and he cured her. "If a man betrothed a woman on condition that she was free of physical defects, only to discover that she indeed had a defect, should she go to a doctor and be cured, the betrothal remains invalid," in accordance with the second Baraita cited in the Gemara. (*Rambam, Sefer Nashim, Hilkhot Ishut* 7:9; *Shulḥan Arukh, Even HaEzer* 39:6.)

[1]אֲמַר רָבָא: לָא קַשְׁיָא; [2]הָא רַבִּי מֵאִיר, [3]הָא רַבִּי אֶלְעָזָר. [4]הָא רַבִּי מֵאִיר, דְּאָמַר: [5]אָדָם רוֹצֶה שֶׁתִּתְבַּזֶּה אִשְׁתּוֹ בְּבֵית דִּין. [6]הָא רַבִּי אֶלְעָזָר, דְּאָמַר: אֵין אָדָם רוֹצֶה שֶׁתִּתְבַּזֶּה אִשְׁתּוֹ בְּבֵית דִּין. [7]מַאי הִיא? [8]דִּתְנַן: "הַמּוֹצִיא אֶת אִשְׁתּוֹ מִשּׁוּם נֶדֶר, לֹא יַחֲזִיר; [9]מִשּׁוּם שֵׁם רַע, לֹא יַחֲזִיר. [10]רַבִּי יְהוּדָה אוֹמֵר: כָּל נֶדֶר שֶׁיָּדְעוּ בּוֹ רַבִּים, לֹא יַחֲזִיר;

LITERAL TRANSLATION

[1]Rava said: It is not difficult. [2]This [according to] Rabbi Meir; [3]this [according to] Rabbi Elazar.

[4]This [according to] Rabbi Meir, who said: [5]A man is willing to have his wife humiliate herself in court. [6]This [according to] Rabbi Elazar, who said: A man is unwilling to have his wife humiliate herself in court.

[7]What is it? [8]As we have learned: "[If a man] divorces his wife because of a vow, he may not remarry [her]; [9]because of a libel, he may not remarry [her].

[10]Rabbi Yehudah says: [In the case of] any vow which many knew of, he may not remarry [her];

TRANSLATION AND COMMENTARY

אֲמַר רָבָא [1]**Rava said : This is** really **not difficult** as each Baraita reflects the opinion of a different Tanna. [2]**The first Baraita**, which retroactively validates the betrothal of a woman who is released from her vow, agrees with the view of **Rabbi Meir.** [3]**The second Baraita,** which maintains that in such a case the betrothal remains invalid, agrees with the view of **Rabbi Elazar.**

הָא רַבִּי מֵאִיר [4]The Gemara explains: **The first** Baraita is in accordance with the view of **Rabbi Meir, who said:** [5]**A man is willing to have his wife humiliate herself in court** by pleading publicly before a Sage for the purpose of releasing her from her vow and reinstating the betrothal. [6]**The second Baraita** is in accordance with the view of **Rabbi Elazar, who said: A man is unwilling to have his wife humiliate herself in court**, even for the purpose of securing a release from her vow. Consequently, even if she does appear in court and nullify her vow, her betrothal would still be invalid, because we assume that her husband would have opposed the public humiliation of her appearance in court.

מַאי הִיא [7]**What** issue **is it** in regard to which Rabbi Meir and Rabbi Elazar originally disagreed? [8]**We have learned** in the Mishnah (*Gittin* 45b): **"If a man divorces his wife because of a vow** which she took but wishes to retract, **he may not remarry her.** [9]Similarly, if a man divorces his wife **on account of a libel** of adultery leveled against her, and then regrets having done so, wishing to take her back, **he may not remarry her.** Even though a man normally retains the right, by Torah law, to remarry his ex-wife (provided she has been married to no one else since their divorce), in these instances the Sages forbade him to do so.

רַבִּי יְהוּדָה אוֹמֵר [10]**Rabbi Yehudah says:** The reason for the decree is to restrain women from frivolously taking vows that cannot be nullified. Thus, only when a man has divorced his wife because of **a vow which** at least ten people **knew of**, thereby rendering it immune to nullification, **may he not remarry her.**

RASHI

הא — דקתני "מקודשת" — רבי מאיר היא. **דאמר אדם רוצה** — אינו מקפיד אם תלך אצל חכם. **אין אדם רוצה כו'** — הילכך, אדעתא דהכי לא קידשה. **משום נדר** — שהיתה נדרנית. **לא יחזיר** — מפרש במסכת גיטין תרי טעמי; איכא למאן דאמר: משום קלקולא; שאם אתה אומר יחזיר — שמא תלך ותנשא, ונמצא שם רע שאינו שם רע, או נדר נעקר על ידי חכם, ומקלקלה זה, ואומר: אילו הייתי יודע שכן הוא — אפילו נותנין לי מאה מנה לא הייתי מגרשיך. לפיכך אומרים לו: הוי יודע שהמוציא את אשתו משום שם רע או משום נדר — לא יחזיר, ואם חביבה היא עליך — לא תמהר להוציאה. ואי אתי תו לקלקל — לא מהימן, שהרי יודע שנאסרה עליו, ולא חש לבדוק את הדבר. ואיכא למאן דאמר: כדי שלא יהו בנות ישראל פרוצות בעריות ובנדרים. **כל נדר שידעו בו רבים** — שנדרתו בפני עשרה. **לא יחזיר** — קסבר: טעמא משום שלא יהו פרוצות בנדרים הוא, וכי נדרה בפני רבים, וזהו נדר שאין לו הפרה, כדאמרינן בגיטין, פרצה יותר מדאי — קנסוה.

NOTES

אָדָם רוֹצֶה שֶׁתִּתְבַּזֶּה אִשְׁתּוֹ **A man is willing to have his wife humiliate herself.** *Ritva* attempts to prove from here that a person who made a vow is not allowed to address the court by proxy or written correspondence but rather must appear in person, because if one could do this the wife would not need to go to court. According to *Rash,* who maintains that one can communicate in writing with the Sages of the court, it becomes necessary to say that a man's sensitivity extends to any public airing of his wife's private concerns.

כָּל נֶדֶר שֶׁיָּדְעוּ בּוֹ רַבִּים **Any vow of which many knew.** Our commentary follows the opinion of *Rashi* and others who understand Rabbi Yehudah as basing his distinction upon the second reason cited in *Gittin* (46a) for the

HALAKHAH

הַמּוֹצִיא אֶת אִשְׁתּוֹ מִשּׁוּם שֵׁם רַע **If a man divorces his wife on account of a libel.** "If a man divorced his wife because of a libel leveled against her, or because of her having frivolously taken vows, he may never remarry her, in accordance with the first Tanna of the Mishnah. According to some (*Rosh*), this applies only if the husband explicitly

BACKGROUND

לֹא יַחֲזִיר **He may not remarry her.** The Gemara in *Gittin* (46a) offers two possible reasons for the decree: (1) Should the husband retain the right to remarry his ex-wife in these cases, the divorced woman might marry another man and have children from him, only to discover later that her first husband has learned that the libel was untrue or that her earlier vow had been nullified and wishes to invalidate their divorce. Any such invalidation would obviously render her second marriage, as well as the children produced through it, illegitimate. Thus, the Rabbis decreed that in such cases the husband must be warned to investigate the matter thoroughly, for if he should decide to divorce his wife, he will forfeit the option of remarrying her or calling the divorce into question. (2) An alternative reason for the decree forbidding a man to remarry his ex-wife in these cases is the Rabbis' desire to dissuade women from engaging in morally questionable behavior or frivolously taking vows, lest their husbands divorce them as a result and be forbidden to remarry them.

TRANSLATION AND COMMENTARY

[1] However, if he divorced her because of **a vow which many did not know of**, and thus *was* subject to nullification, **he may** indeed **remarry her** afterwards. [2] **Rabbi Meir says:** The reason for the decree is fear of what might happen should the woman marry another man, have children, and then find her divorce invalidated. Thus, it is only if a man divorced his wife because of **a vow which requires the investigation of a Sage** before it can be nullified (i.e., any vow other than those involving self-affliction or affecting the intimacy between man and wife — these being subject to her husband's approval) that **he may not remarry her.** For he might claim that, had he known his wife's vow could be dissolved by a Sage, he would never have divorced her. [3] However, if he divorced her because of **a vow which does not require the investigation of a Sage** in order to be nullified, **he may** indeed **remarry her.** He could not possibly claim that, had he known the vow could be nullified, he would not have divorced her, since he himself could have nullified the vow while they were still married. [4] **Rabbi Elazar says: Whether it is a case of a vow which requires** the investigation of a Sage in order to be nullified, [5] **or a case of a vow which does not require** the investigation of a Sage, the husband **may not remarry** his wife. Explaining his position, [6] **Rabbi Elazar said:** In the case of a man who divorced his wife because of a vow which he himself was authorized to nullify, we fear that he may later claim that he did not know he was entitled to do so and thus attempt to invalidate the divorce. Thus the Rabbis made it clear that he could not remarry his ex-wife if he divorced her for taking a vow of any kind. [7] However, **they only forbade** him from remarrying his ex-wife in the case of **a vow which requires the investigation** of a Sage **because of** the case of **a vow which does not require such investigation,** and not because of concern lest he later claim that, had he known her vow could be dissolved by a Sage, he would never have divorced her."

[1] לֹא יָדְעוּ בּוֹ רַבִּים, יַחֲזִיר. [2] רַבִּי מֵאִיר אוֹמֵר: כָּל נֶדֶר שֶׁצָּרִיךְ חֲקִירַת חָכָם, לֹא יַחֲזִיר; [3] וְשֶׁאֵינוֹ צָרִיךְ חֲקִירַת חָכָם, יַחֲזִיר. [4] רַבִּי אֶלְעָזָר אוֹמֵר: אֶחָד צָרִיךְ [5] וְאֶחָד אֵינוֹ צָרִיךְ, לֹא יַחֲזִיר. [6] אָמַר רַבִּי אֶלְעָזָר: [7] לֹא אָסְרוּ צָרִיךְ אֶלָּא מִפְּנֵי שֶׁאֵינוֹ צָרִיךְ.

LITERAL TRANSLATION

[1] [in a case] which many did not know of, he may remarry [her]. [2] Rabbi Meir says: [In the case of] any vow that requires the investigation of a Sage, he may not remarry [her]; [3] [in a case] which does not require the investigation of a Sage, he may remarry [her]. [4] Rabbi Elazar says: [Whether a vow] requires [investigation by a Sage] [5] or does not require [it], he may not remarry [her]. [6] Rabbi Elazar said: [7] They only forbade [in the case of a vow] requiring [investigation] because of [a vow] not requiring [investigation]."

RASHI

שלא ידעו בו רבים — דיש לו הפרה — לא קנסוה. והכי אמר התם, דרבי יהודה לא חייש בנדר לקלקולא. **רבי מאיר אומר כל נדר שצריך חקירת חכם** — שאין הבעל יכול להפר — שאינו מדברים שבינו לבינה, ולא עינוי נפש, **לא יחזיר** — קסבר טעמא משום קלקולא. הלכך, בהאי איכא קלקולא, דאומר: אילו הייתי יודע דחכם יכול להתירו — לא הייתי מגרשיך, דרוצה הייתי שתתבזה בבית דין ויתירו לך. **ושאינו צריך חקירת חכם** — נדר שהבעל יכול להפר. **יחזיר** — דבהאי לא מצי לקלקלה, שהיה לו להפר ולא הפר. **לא אסרו צריך** — חקירת חכם. **אלא מפני שאינו צריך** — שהצריך חקירת חכם אין בו קלקול, דלאו כל כמיניה לומר "אילו הייתי יודע", לפי שאין אדם רוצה שתתבזה אשתו בבית דין. אלא מפני מה אסרוהו — מפני שאינו צריך, דיכול הוא לכחש ולומר: לא הייתי יודע שאני יכול להפר. וגזרו האי אטו האי.

NOTES

Rabbinic decree preventing a man from remarrying his ex-wife, if he divorced her because of a vow: In order to deter women from frivolously taking vows that are not subject to nullification. Thus, it applied only in the case of a vow taken before a large group of people, which cannot be nullified, showing a greater degree of brazenness on her part. *Meiri*, however, explains Rabbi Yehudah's distinction as based on the first reason cited in *Gittin*: The fear is that, after she is married to another man and has children, her husband might attempt to claim that, had he known the vow was voidable, he would never have divorced her. Thus, only if the vow was taken in public can the husband definitively identify it as the reason for his having initially divorced his wife; however, if the vow was not a matter of public knowledge, we can always say to the husband that it is not at all clear that he divorced his wife because of her vow.

HALAKHAH

informed his wife that it was for that reason that he was divorcing her, adding that otherwise he would not have done so. But if he did not add this second clause, he may remarry her. Others (including *Ramban* and *Rashba*) maintain that even if he left out this additional clause, as long as he specified the reason he was divorcing her, he may not remarry her. A third opinion (that of *Rambam*) maintains that he may not remarry her even if he did not explicitly inform her of the reason." (*Rambam, Sefer Nashim, Hilkhot Gerushin* 10:12; *Shulḥan Arukh, Even HaEzer* 10:3.)

[1]מַאי טַעֲמָא דְּרַבִּי יְהוּדָה? [2]דִּכְתִיב [75A] [3]״וְלֹא הִכּוּם בְּנֵי יִשְׂרָאֵל כִּי נִשְׁבְּעוּ לָהֶם נְשִׂיאֵי הָעֵדָה״.
[4]וְכַמָּה ״רַבִּים״?
[5]רַב נַחְמָן בַּר יִצְחָק אָמַר: שְׁלֹשָׁה. ״יָמִים״ — שְׁנַיִם. ״רַבִּים״ — שְׁלֹשָׁה.
[6]רַבִּי יִצְחָק אָמַר: עֲשָׂרָה. [7]״עֵדָה״ כְּתִיב בְּהוּ.
[8]״רַבִּי מֵאִיר אוֹמֵר: כָּל נֶדֶר שֶׁצָּרִיךְ חֲקִירַת חָכָם, לֹא יַחֲזִיר. [9]רַבִּי אֶלְעָזָר אוֹמֵר: לֹא אָסְרוּ צָרִיךְ אֶלָּא מִפְּנֵי שֶׁאֵינוֹ צָרִיךְ״. [10]בְּמַאי קָמִיפַּלְגִי? [11]רַבִּי מֵאִיר סָבַר: אָדָם רוֹצֶה שֶׁתִּתְבַּזֶּה

LITERAL TRANSLATION

[1]What is the reason of Rabbi Yehudah? [2]For it is written: [75A] [3]"And the Children of Israel did not smite them, because the princes of the congegration had sworn to them."

[4]And how many is "many"? [5]Rav Naḥman bar Yitzḥak said: Three. "Days" — two. "Many" — three.

[6]Rabbi Yitzḥak said: Ten. [7]"Congregation" is written regarding them.

[8]"Rabbi Meir says: [In the case of] any vow which requires the investigation of a Sage, he may not remarry [her]. [9]Said Rabbi Elazar: They only forbade [in the case of a vow which] requires [investigation] because of [the case of a vow] which does not require [investigation]." [10]About what do they disagree? [11]Rabbi Meir maintains: A man is willing to have his wife humiliated

TRANSLATION AND COMMENTARY

מַאי טַעֲמָא [1]The Gemara first clarifies the position of Rabbi Yehudah: **What is Rabbi Yehudah's reason?** What is the Biblical source for his position that a vow known to many people cannot be nullified? [2]**For the verse** (Joshua 9:18) **says:** [75A] [3]**"And the Children of Israel did not smite them, because the princes of the congregation had sworn to them."** The Gibeonites, a Canaanite people, tricked Joshua into concluding a covenant of peace by misrepresenting themselves as foreigners from a distant land. Nevertheless, the Israelites were bound to the covenant by virtue of its having been based upon an oath. Thus, we see that an oath taken in public cannot be nullified, even if made in error.

וְכַמָּה רַבִּים [4]But **how many** people must know about the vow to make it public?

רַב נַחְמָן בַּר יִצְחָק [5]**Rav Naḥman bar Yitzḥak said:** The term "many" implies **three**, as is evident from the Rabbis' interpretation elsewhere of a verse (Leviticus 15:25) that contains the expression "many days" — the word **"days"** implies at least **two**. Use of the word **"many"** raises the minimum to **three**. Thus, a vow is regarded as known to "many" once it has become known to at least three people.

רַבִּי יִצְחָק אָמַר [6]**Rabbi Yitzḥak said:** The term "many," as applied to public knowledge of a vow, implies at least **ten** people, as is evident from the above verse in Joshua from which we learn that a public vow cannot be nullified. [7]The word **"congregation" is written** there **regarding** the princes who undertook the oath, and, as is known from another verse (Numbers 14:35), the term "congregation" indicates an assembly of ten.

רַבִּי מֵאִיר אוֹמֵר [8]The Gemara now considers the positions of Rabbi Meir and Rabbi Elazar in the Mishnah: **"Rabbi Meir says:** If a man divorced his wife because of **a vow which requires investigation by a Sage** before it can be nullified, **he may not remarry her.** However, if the vow does not require investigation by a Sage in order to be nullified, he may later remarry her. [9]**Rabbi Elazar said:** The Rabbis **forbade** the husband from remarrying his ex-wife if he divorced her as the result of a vow which **requires the investigation** of a Sage **only because of** the prohibition that applies if he divorced her because of a vow **which does not require such investigation."** [10]Now, **about what** principle is it that Rabbi Meir and Rabbi Elazar **disagree?** The Gemara explains: Both Rabbi Meir and Rabbi Elazar agree that the Rabbis were concerned lest the husband later attempt to void the divorce by claiming that, had he known the vow could be nullified, he would never have divorced her. [11]However, **Rabbi Meir maintained** that this concern arises only with regard to a vow which requires nullification by a Sage, since **a man is willing to have his wife humiliate herself in court**

RASHI

מאי טעמא דרבי יהודה — דאמר: נדר שהודר ברבים אין לו הפרה. **ולא הכום בני ישראל** — בגבעונים כתיב.

NOTES

וְכַמָּה ״רַבִּים״? And how many is "many"? *Shittah Mekubbetzet* suggests that this question is relevant to the opinion of Rabbi Yehudah, who prohibits remarrying a woman whom one divorced for taking a vow in public. One could understand the criteria for "many" as depending upon the rationale behind this opinion.

HALAKHAH

וְכַמָּה ״רַבִּים״? How many is "many"? "Regarding the issue of vows, 'many' is defined as three," in accordance with the opinion of Rav Naḥman bar Yitzḥak. (*Shulḥan Arukh, Yoreh De'ah* 228:21.)

TRANSLATION AND COMMENTARY

for the sake of gaining release from her vows. But if he divorced his wife because of a vow which he could have nullified himself without the intervention of a Sage, he cannot claim that the divorce was due to her vow since he could have nullified it himself. [1]**Rabbi Elazar**, on the other hand, **maintained:** If a man divorced his wife because of a vow which could only be nullified by a Sage, there is no concern that he might later claim that, had he known it was possible, he would have preferred having her go to the Sage rather than divorcing her — [2]for **a man is not willing to have his wife humiliate herself in court.** However, if he divorced her because of a vow which he himself could have nullified, he might later claim that, had he known he was authorized to do so, he would have nullified the vow rather than divorce her.

רָבָא אָמַר [3]The Gemara now returns to the contradiction between the two Baraitot dealing with a woman who accepted betrothal under false pretenses and then went to have her vows nullified by a Sage. **Rava said:** Even were one to assume that a man is prepared to have his wife humiliate herself in court to gain release from her vows, **here** — in the Baraita which invalidates the betrothal even after she appears in court — **we are dealing with** the case of **an important woman** from a distinguished family. In such a case, the husband would prefer not to revalidate the betrothal. [4]**For he can say:** "I prefer not taking the risk of divorcing her for taking vows in the future, as **it is not agreeable to me that,** as a result of such a divorce, **I should become forbidden to her relatives**, her mother and sisters, who are also distinguished women." However, in the case of an ordinary woman, the husband would not entertain such concerns and thus would willingly agree to reinstate the betrothal as soon as the woman has her original vow dissolved by a Sage, although he may wish to divorce her in the future, should she prove to be a habitual vow-taker.

אִי הָכִי [5]The Gemara raises an objection against this resolution of the contradictory Baraitot: **If** it is **so,** then a difficulty arises with regard to **the last clause** of the Baraita, **which teaches:** [6]**"But** if a man betrothed a woman on condition that he was free of vows or physical defects, and it turned out not to be so, and **he went to a Sage who released him** from his vow, [7]or **to a doctor who cured him,** then **she is** considered **betrothed."** If Rava's understanding of the Baraita is correct, [8]then **let** the Baraita **teach** in the last clause, too, that **the woman is not betrothed.** [9]**And let us say: "Here,** in this continuation of the Baraita, **we are dealing with** the case of **an important man** from a distinguished family, [10]**when** it is assumed that the bride **would say:** 'I prefer not to reinstate the betrothal, even should he secure release from his vow, to avoid divorcing him in the future, should he prove to be a habitual vow-taker, as **it is not agreeable to me that,** as a result of the divorce, **I should become forbidden to his relatives** who are also distinguished men!'"

אִשְׁתּוֹ בְּבֵית דִּין. [1]רַבִּי אֶלְעָזָר סָבַר: [2]אֵין אָדָם רוֹצֶה שֶׁתִּתְבַּזֶּה אִשְׁתּוֹ בְּבֵית דִּין.
[3]רָבָא אֲמַר: הָכָא בְּאִשָּׁה חֲשׁוּבָה עָסְקִינַן, [4]דְּאָמַר: "לָא נִיחָא לִי דְּאִיתַּסַּר בִּקְרוֹבוֹתֶיהָ".
[5]אִי הָכִי, סֵיפָא דְּקָתָנֵי: [6]"אֲבָל הוּא שֶׁהָלַךְ אֵצֶל חָכָם וְהִתִּירוֹ, [7]אֵצֶל רוֹפֵא וְרִיפֵּא אוֹתוֹ, מְקוּדֶּשֶׁת". [8]לִיתְנֵי "אֵינָהּ מְקוּדֶּשֶׁת", [9]וְלֵימָא: "הָכָא בְּאָדָם חָשׁוּב עָסְקִינַן [10]דְּאָמְרָה: 'לָא נִיחָא לִי דְּאִיתַּסַּר בִּקְרִיבֵיהּ'"!

LITERAL TRANSLATION

in court. [1]Rabbi Elazar maintains: [2]A man is not willing to have his wife humiliated in court.

[3]Rava said: Here we are dealing with an important woman, [4]when he said: "It is not agreeable to me to become forbidden to her relatives."

[5]If so, the last clause which teaches: [6]"But [if it is] he who went to a Sage and [the Sage] released him [from his vow, [7]or] to a doctor and [the doctor] cured him, she is betrothed." [8]Let it teach: "She is not betrothed," [9]and let us say: "Here we are dealing with an important man, [10]when she said: 'It is not agreeable to me to become forbidden to his relatives!'"

RASHI

רבא אמר — הא דקתני: אבל חכם והתירה — אינה מקודשת. **באשה חשובה** — בת גדולים. דאפילו למאן דאמר רוצה אדם שתתבזה אשתו בבית דין — הכא אמר: אי אפשי באשה נדרנית. וגט — נמי לא ניחא לי למיתבא לה — דאתסר באמה ואחותה, ולא ניחא לי דליהוו קדושין. **אבל הוא** — אם אמר לה: על מנת שאין עלי מומין ונדרים.

NOTES

אִשָּׁה חֲשׁוּבָה **A distinguished woman.** Rabbah explains the contradiction between the two Baraitot as reflecting a Tannaitic dispute between Rabbi Meir and Rabbi Elazar. If so, the law is in accordance with the first Baraita, which follows Rabbi Meir. Thus, if a man betrothed a woman on condition that she was free of vows, and at the time of the betrothal she was indeed bound by a certain vow, but she went to a Sage who released her from the vow, the betrothal is valid, even if the woman came from a distinguished family.

But Rava maintains that the two Baraitot deal with different cases. If the woman came from an ordinary family,

TRANSLATION AND COMMENTARY

איהי [1]The Gemara answers: The Baraita would never have drawn such an equation between the case of a man and that of a woman, because a woman **is agreeable to** living with practically **anyone, as** is evident from **that** statement **by Resh Lakish.** [2]**For Resh Lakish said:** There is a popular adage among women: **It is better to sit two together,** regardless of your mate's faults or imperfections, **than to sit** alone and bereft of companionship **like a widow.** [3]The Gemara continues with a number of similar statements. **Abaye said:** There is a proverb: **Even** a woman **whose husband is as small** and lowly **as an ant** is still proud to **place her chair among the noblewomen,** for having a husband makes her feel their equal. [4]**Rav Pappa said: Even** a woman **whose husband is a wool-beater,** a fairly wretched occupation, is proud to **call him to the doorsill** so as to **sit down** with him in full view of all. [5]**Rav Ashi said:** Women are accustomed to say: Even a woman **whose husband is repulsive** is so happy to be married that she **does not** even **request lentils for the pot.** [6]**It was taught** by a certain Tanna: **"And** as for **all of** these women, it can be assumed that **they** freely **commit adultery and** then **attribute** the paternity of **their offspring to their husbands."**

כָּל מוּמִין [7]We learned in the last clause of our Mishnah: **"All the defects that disqualify** priests from executing the Temple service disqualifies women if a condition was made regarding physical imperfections." [8]**A Tanna taught** the following Baraita: "The Rabbis **added** these defects **to** those which render a woman unfit for betrothal even though they would not disqualify a priest from executing his Temple duties: Unusually heavy **perspiration, or a wart, or fetid breath."**

[1]אִיהִי בְּכָל דְּהוּ נִיחָא לָהּ, כִּדְרֵישׁ לָקִישׁ. [2]דַּאֲמַר רֵישׁ לָקִישׁ: טַב לְמֵיתַב טַן דּוּ מִלְּמֵיתַב אַרְמְלוּ. [3]אַבַּיֵי אֲמַר: דְּשׁוּמְשְׁמָנָא גַּבְרָא, כּוּרְסֵיה בֵּי חֲרָאתָא רָמֵי לָהּ. [4]רַב פַּפָּא אֲמַר: דְּנַפְסָא גַּבְרָא תִּיקְרְיֵיהּ בְּסִיפֵּי בָּבָא, וְתֵיתִיב. [5]רַב אַשִׁי אֲמַר: דְּקַלְסָא גַּבְרָא לָא בָּעֵי טַלְפְּחֵי לְקִידְרָא. [6]תָּנָא: ״וְכוּלָּן מְזַנּוֹת וְתוֹלוֹת בְּבַעֲלֵיהֶן״.

[7]״כָּל מוּמִין שֶׁפּוֹסְלִין וכו׳״. [8]תָּנָא: הוֹסִיפוּ עֲלֵיהֶן: ״זֵיעָה, וְשׁוּמָא, וְרֵיחַ הַפֶּה״.

LITERAL TRANSLATION

[1]She is agreeable to anyone, as that of Resh Lakish. [2]For Resh Lakish said: It is better to sit two together than to sit like a widow. [3]Abaye said: [Even one] whose husband is like an ant places her chair among the noblewomen. [4]Rav Pappa said: [Even one] whose husband is a wool-beater calls him to the doorsill, and sits down [with him]. [5]Rav Ashi said: [She] whose husband is repulsive does not request [even] lentils for the pot. [6]It was taught [by a Tanna]: "And all of them commit adultery and attribute [the offspring] to their husbands."

[7]"All the defects that disqualify, etc." [8][A Tanna] taught: "They added to them: Perspiration, and a wart, and odor of the mouth."

RASHI

טן דו — גוף שנים. משל הדיוט הוא שהנשים אומרות: טוב לשבת עם גוף שנים משבת אלמנה. **דשומשמנא גברא** — משל הדיוט הוא מי — שבעלה קטן כנמלה. **כורסיה בי חראתא רמיא** — כסאה בין השרות, בנות חורין, מושיבה. כלומר: גם לי בעל כמוכם. **נפסא** — מנפס צמר. ואומנות מאוסה היא. **תיקרייה בסיפי בבא ותיתיב** — אינה בושה לקרותו על מפתן הבית לישב שם אצלו בפני הכל. **קולסא** — ממשפחת דופי. **טלפחי** — עדשים, שהוא מאכל קל, ואין חסרון כיס כל כך, אינה שואלת הימנו, אך יקרא שמו עליה. **וכולן מזנות ותולות בבעליהן** — כל אלו שבעליהן שפלים ומראות להם חבה — אינו אלא שמזנות תחתיהן, וכשמתעברות הן תולות את העובר בבעל [ונוח להן באנשים כל שהן, לפי שמזנות תחתיהן]. **הוסיפו עליהם** — בנשים, שאין בכהנים. **זיעה** — זועה תמיד. **שומא** = *וורוא״ה.

BACKGROUND

שׁוּמְשְׁמָנָא Ant. *Arukh* and others read שושמנא, and still others read שומשנא. Both of these words have parallels in Aramaic and Arabic, which also mean "ant" (or some particular type of ant).

LANGUAGE

טַן דּוּ Two bodies. The etymology of this expression is unclear. Some suggest that טן דו comes from the Persian *tan do* — "with two people, together" — although this is questionable.

נַפְסָא Wool-beater. Various explanations of the meaning and etymology of this word have been suggested: Some argue that the Aramaic נפסא = the Hebrew נפץ, and thus our word means "carder, wool-beater." Alternatively, נַפְסָא might be derived from the Latin *napus,* a type of radish (נפוס in Rabbinic Hebrew), while Rabbenu Ḥananel apparently derives our word from the Greek νήπιος, *nepios,* which means "childish, foolish."

קַלְסָא Contemptible. From the Greek καυλός, *kaolus,* which means "stalk" (especially cabbage stalks), hence "cabbage-head." Alternatively, this term may refer to someone who guards cabbage patches; such a person clearly has no ability to do anything worthwhile (*Arukh*).

LANGUAGE (RASHI)

וורוא״ה* From the Old French *verrue,* meaning "wart."

NOTES

the betrothal is valid, and if she came from a distinguished family, the betrothal is void. *Rosh* notes that the Geonim disagree about whether the law is in accordance with Rabbah or Rava. There is a general rule that the law follows the master where he differs with his disciple, and Rabbah was Rava's teacher. But there is also a second rule that, with respect to differences of opinion which arose from the days of Rava onwards, the law is in accordance with the later opinion, which in this case is that of Rava. Thus, in all cases the woman requires a bill of divorce, following Rabbah that in all cases the betrothal is valid. According to some authorities (see *Rosh, Rashba*), the validity of the betrothal in the case of a woman from a distinguished family is in doubt, because the law might be in accordance with Rava. If such a woman accepted betrothal from a second man, she would therefore require a bill of divorce from him as well.

בֵּי חֲרָאתָא רָמֵי She places her chair among the noblewomen. The Geonim interpret these words with a slight variation, suggesting that the noblewomen themselves make place for the woman's chair because they recognize any married woman as their equal.

הוֹסִיפוּ עֲלֵיהֶן They added to them. The Jerusalem Talmud notes that the additional defects identified in this Baraita

HALAKHAH

הוֹסִיפוּ עֲלֵיהֶן They added to them. "All defects which disqualify priests from the Temple service also constitute defects with regard to a woman's betrothal. In addition, certain defects render a woman unfit for betrothal but do

BACKGROUND

מְזוֹהָם A foul-smelling person. The Gemara refers to a person who smells bad because of an organic disorder (such as a kidney ailment), and not because of excessive perspiration or inattention to personal hygiene. Thus, this sort of foul odor is a permanent condition (unlike perspiration), and generally cannot be treated.

[1] וְהָנֵי בְּכָהֲנֵי לָא פָּסְלֵי? [2] וְהָתְנַן: "הַזָּקֵן וְהַחוֹלֶה וְהַמְזוֹהָם". [3] וּתְנַן: מוּמִין אֵלּוּ, [4] בֵּין קְבוּעִין בֵּין עוֹבְרִין, פְּסוּלִין בְּאָדָם"!

[5] אָמַר רַבִּי יוֹסֵי בְּרַבִּי חֲנִינָא: לָא קַשְׁיָא: [6] כָּאן, בְּזֵיעָה עוֹבֶרֶת; [7] כָּאן, בְּזֵיעָה שֶׁאֵינָהּ עוֹבֶרֶת.

[8] רַב אַשִׁי אֲמַר: זֵיעָה אַמְזוֹהָם קָא רָמֵית? [9] הָתָם גַּבֵּי כֹּהֲנִים,

LITERAL TRANSLATION

[1] And these do not disqualify priests? [2] But surely we have learned: "[An animal which is] old, or ill or putrid." [3] And we have learned: "These defects, [4] be they lasting or passing, [also] disqualify a man"!

[5] Said Rabbi Yose, the son of Rabbi Ḥanina: It is not difficult: [6] Here, [it is talking about] perspiration that is removable; [7] here, [it is talking about] perspiration that is not removable.

[8] Rav Ashi said: Are you raising [a contradiction from the case of] perspiration to (lit., "onto") [that of] one who is putrid? [9] There, with respect to priests,

TRANSLATION AND COMMENTARY

וְהָנֵי [1] The Gemara asks: **And** is it true that **these** defects **do not disqualify priests** from the Temple service? [2] **But surely we have learned** elsewhere in the Mishnah (*Bekhorot* 41a): "These are [the animals with defects] which are not to be slaughtered in the Temple: **One which is old, or ill or putrid."** [3] **And we have** also **learned** in a subsequent Mishnah (*Bekhorot* 43a): **"These defects** [that disqualify animals from slaughter], [4] **be they lasting or passing,** also **disqualify a man** from serving as a priest in the Temple"! How, then, can the Baraita state that perspiration and mouth odor are defects in a woman which are not relevant to a priest, when we have just seen that the Mishnah identifies one who is "putrid" as being unfit to serve in the Temple?

אָמַר [5] **Rabbi Yose, the son of Rabbi Ḥanina, said: It is not difficult,** for the two Tannaitic sources refer to dissimilar defects: [6] **Here,** in the Baraita which implies that heavy perspiration does not disqualify a priest from serving in the Temple, **it is talking about perspiration that is removable** by washing. [7] **There,** in the Mishnah which implies that heavy perspiration does disqualify a priest from the Temple service, **it is talking about perspiration that is not removable** by washing.

רַב אַשִׁי אֲמַר [8] **Rav Ashi** objects to this line of argument, because perspiration and foul odor are not the same. He **said: Are you raising** a contradiction from the ruling regarding a priest who suffers from excessive **perspiration to** the ruling regarding one who is **putrid?** A priest who is putrid cannot rid himself of his foul odor, and thus is disqualified from serving in the Temple, whereas heavy perspiration and mouth odor are defects which can be rectified! Should you ask why they are nevertheless considered defects with respect to betrothal, the answer is this: [9] **There, as regards priests, it is possible** for them **to**

RASHI

הזקן והחולה והמזוהם — לגבי מומי בהמה תנן. וקא סלקא דעתך: זיעה וריח הפה דאדם בכלל מזוהם. **זיעה אמזוהם קא רמית** — לאו רומיא היא; מזוהם — גופו מסריח, ובאדם נמי פוסל. אבל זיעה דאדם — אינה פוסלת בכהנים, כדקתני: "הוסיפו עליהם".

NOTES

include only those which one might think would disqualify a priest as well; other defects, which are exclusively relevant to women, such as baldness or facial hair, are not enumerated in the Baraita although they too would invalidate her betrothal. For the same reason, *Rivan* points out that the Baraita does not make mention of a woman who cannot help screaming out in pain when she engages in sexual intercourse, for this is obviously a defect unique to women.

זֵיעָה עוֹבֶרֶת Perspiration that passes. According to *Rivan*, a person who suffers from "perspiration that passes" is someone who does not always suffer from unusually heavy

HALAKHAH

not disqualify priests from serving in the Temple. These include chronic perspiration, warts, severe halitosis (according to some, nose odor as well; *Rema*), and other imperfections enumerated here in the Gemara. As far as those defects which are not mentioned in the Gemara, specifically those of a serious nature such as leprosy or chronic incontinence, *Bet Yosef* maintains that they be treated as *bona fide* faults invalidating betrothal, whereas *Darkhei Moshe* remains in doubt. *Taz* rules, as a result of the doubt, that while the woman is entitled to her ketubah settlement, her husband can nevertheless divorce her against her will — even though (since the *ḥerem* of Rabbenu Gershom) consent is normally required." (*Rambam, Sefer Nashim, Hilkhot Ishut* 7:7; *Shulḥan Arukh, Even HaEzer* 39:4.)

הַזָּקֵן וְהַחוֹלֶה וְהַמְזוֹהָם A priest who is old, or ill or putrid. "A priest who is so old that he trembles while standing, or so ill that he shakes from his ailment, suffers from a defect disqualifying him from service in the Temple. A priest who reeks from excessive perspiration, yet who can rid himself of his odor through proper hygiene, is permitted to serve in the Temple. So, too, must a priest who suffers from bad breath freshen his mouth with some form of palliative before he is allowed to serve in the Temple. If, however, he should attempt to serve while still emitting a putrid smell, his service would be as unacceptable as that of any other priest possessed of a bodily defect," in accordance with our Mishnah and the opinion of Rav Ashi. (*Rambam, Sefer Avodah, Hilkhot Bi'at Mikdash* 7:12-13.)

בֵּין קְבוּעִין בֵּין עוֹבְרִין Be they lasting or passing. "A priest who has a defect, be it lasting or passing, may not enter

אֶפְשָׁר לְעַבְרָה בְּקִיוּהָא דְּחַמְרָא. [1]וּמֵרִיחַ הַפֶּה נַמִּי, [2]אֶפְשָׁר דְּנָקַט פִּילְפְּלָא בְּפוּמֵיהּ וְעָבֵיד עֲבוֹדָה.
[3]אֲבָל גַּבֵּי אִשָּׁה לָא אֶפְשָׁר.
[4]הַאי שׁוּמָא, הֵיכִי דָּמְיָא? [5]אִי דְּאִית בָּהּ שֵׂעָר [6]הָכָא וְהָכָא פָּסְלָה. [7]אִי דְּלָא אִית בָּהּ שֵׂעָר: [8]אִי שׁוּמָא גְּדוֹלָה הִיא, הָכָא וְהָכָא פָּסְלָה; [9]אִי שׁוּמָא קְטַנָּה הִיא, הָכָא וְהָכָא לָא פָּסְלָה. [10]דְּתַנְיָא: "שׁוּמָא שֶׁיֵּשׁ בָּהּ שֵׂעָר הֲרֵי זֶה מוּם. [11]אֵין בָּהּ שֵׂעָר: גְּדוֹלָה, הֲרֵי זֶה מוּם; [12]קְטַנָּה, אֵין זֶה מוּם. [13]וְאֵיזוֹהִי גְּדוֹלָה? [14]פֵּירַשׁ רַבָּן שִׁמְעוֹן בֶּן גַּמְלִיאֵל: עַד כְּאִיסָּר הָאִיטַלְקִי"!
[15]אָמַר רַבִּי יוֹסֵי בְּרַבִּי חֲנִינָא: בְּעוֹמֶדֶת עַל פַּדַּחְתָּהּ.

LITERAL TRANSLATION

it is possible to remove it with wine vinegar. [1]And mouth odor as well, [2]it is possible that he take a pepper in his mouth and perform the service.
[3]But as regards a woman, it is not possible.
[4]That wart, what is it like? [5]If it has in it a hair, [6][both] here and here it disqualifies. [7]If it does not have in it a hair: [8]If it is a large wart, [both] here and here it disqualifies; [9]if it is a small wart, [both] here and here it does not disqualify. [10]For it was taught: "A wart which has in it a hair, this is a defect. [11][One which] does not have in it a hair: [If it is] large, this is a defect; [12][if it is] small, this is not a defect. [13]And which [one] is [considered a] large [wart]? [14]Explained Rabban Shimon ben Gamliel: [One the size of] an Italian isar"!
[15]Rabbi Yose, the son of Rabbi Ḥanina, said: [The Baraita is talking] about one situated upon her forehead.

TRANSLATION AND COMMENTARY

remove the foul odor of perspiration while performing the Temple service, by cleansing themselves **with wine vinegar.** [1]**And mouth odor** is **also** treatable, [2]as **it is possible** for the priest who suffers from it **to take a pepper in his mouth** in order to neutralize the smell, **and** then proceed to **perform the service.**

אֲבָל [3]**But as regards a woman, it is not possible** to rid herself of these flaws, because the remedies proposed are merely temporary.

הַאי שׁוּמָא [4]It was taught in the Baraita that a wart on a woman disqualifies her betrothal. The Gemara asks: **That wart, what** exactly **is it like?** [5]**If it has a hair** growing **in it,** [6]both **here** in the case of a woman's betrothal **and there** with regard to the priestly service, the wart would be considered a defect which **disqualifies.** [7]And even **if it does not have a hair** growing **in it:** [8]**If it is a large wart,** both **here and there** the wart would be considered a defect which **disqualifies;** [9]and **if it is a small wart,** then both **here and there** the wart **does not disqualify** at all. [10]**For it was taught** in a Baraita dealing with those defects which disqualify a priest from the Temple service: **"A wart which has a hair** growing **in it,** is regarded as **a** disqualifying **defect;** [11]whereas **one which does not have a hair** growing **in it** — **if it is large, it is** regarded as **a** disqualifying **defect,** [12]and **if it is small, it is not** regarded as **a** disqualifying **defect.** [13]**And which** size wart **is considered** sufficiently **large** to disqualify the priest even if hair is not growing from it? [14]**Explained Rabban Shimon ben Gamliel:** One which is at least the size of **an Italian isar** [a small Roman coin]."

אָמַר [15]**Rabbi Yose, the son of Rabbi Ḥanina, said:** Our Baraita, which speaks of a wart that renders a woman unfit for betrothal while not disqualifying the priestly service, is talking **about** a wart **situated upon** the woman's **forehead.**

RASHI

דאפשר לעברה בקיוהא דחמרא — ביין קהה, *אייגר"א בלע"ז, עד שיעבוד עבודתו. **וריח הפה נמי כו'** — אבל גבי אשה, שהוא מדבר עמה כל שעה, לא אפשר. **בעומדת על פדחתה** — ולעולם בשאין בה שער, וקטנה. **פדחתה** = מצחה.

LANGUAGE (RASHI)

אייגר"א* From the Old French *aigre,* meaning "vinegar."

NOTES

perspiration, but only from time to time. *Meiri* explains that "perspiration that passes" is heavy perspiration which can be attributed to a particular cause, such as strenuous work or heavy clothing. Our commentary follows *Tosafot* and *Ritva,* who explain that "perspiration that passes" refers to perspiration that can easily be removed with water or a cloth.

HALAKHAH

into the area of the Temple Courtyard which lies beyond the outer altar or perform the Temple service. If he should do either, he is liable to be flogged." (*Rambam, Sefer Avodah, Hilkhot Bi'at Mikdash* 6:1.)

שׁוּמָא Wart. "A wart with a hair growing from it constitutes a defect in a woman regardless of where it is found. A wart found upon the forehead constitutes a defect even when small and hairless, if it is high enough on the woman's forehead that it is only occasionally visible, while at other times it is concealed by the woman's head covering. For if the wart is always visible, the betrothal cannot be invalidated as we assume the bridegroom surely saw it and was at peace with it." (*Rambam, Sefer Nashim, Hilkhot Ishut* 7:7; *Shulḥan Arukh, Even HaEzer* 39:4.)

LITERAL TRANSLATION

[1] [Upon] her forehead? [2] He saw [it] and he accepted (lit., "was at peace with") [it]!

[3] Rav Pappa said: [The Baraita is talking] about one situated underneath the covering on her head, [4] which at times is visible and at times is not visible.

[5] Rav Ḥisda said: This matter I heard from a great man. [6] And who is he? [7] Rabbi Shela: [If] a dog bit her, and the site [of the wound] became a scar, [8] this is a defect.

[9] Rav Ḥisda said: A husky voice in a woman, this is a defect, [10] as it is said: "For your voice is sweet, and your appearance is comely."

[11] Rabbi Natan Bira'ah taught: "Between a woman's breasts, [the space of] a handbreadth."

[12] Rav Aḥa, the son of Rava, thought to say before Rav Ashi: "A handbreadth" — to advantage. [13] Rav Ashi said to him: It is with regard to defects that it was taught.

[14] And how much? [15] Said Abaye: Three fingers.

[1] פַּדַּחְתָּהּ? [2] רָאָה וְנִיפַּיֵּיס הוּא! [3] אָמַר רַב פַּפָּא: בְּעוֹמֶדֶת לָהּ תַּחַת כִּפָּה שֶׁל רֹאשָׁהּ, [4] וְזִימְנִין דְּמִתְחַזְיָא, וְזִימְנִין דְּלָא מִתְחַזְיָא.

[5] אָמַר רַב חִסְדָּא: הָא מִילְּתָא מִגַּבְרָא רַבָּה שְׁמִיעַ לִי. [6] וּמַנּוּ? [7] רַבִּי שֵׁילָא: נְשָׁכָהּ כֶּלֶב וְנַעֲשָׂה מְקוֹמוֹ צַלֶּקֶת, [8] הֲרֵי זֶה מוּם. [9] אָמַר רַב חִסְדָּא: קוֹל עָבֶה בְּאִשָּׁה הֲרֵי זֶה מוּם, [10] שֶׁנֶּאֱמַר: "כִּי קוֹלֵךְ עָרֵב וּמַרְאֵיךְ נָאוֶה". [11] תָּנֵי רַבִּי נָתָן בִּירָאָה: בֵּין דַּדֵּי אִשָּׁה טֶפַח. [12] סָבַר רַב אַחָא בְּרֵיהּ דְּרָבָא קַמֵּיהּ דְּרַב אַשִׁי לְמֵימַר: טֶפַח — לְמַעַלְיוּתָא. [13] אָמַר לֵיהּ רַב אַשִׁי: גַּבֵּי מוּמִין תַּנְיָא. [14] וְכַמָּה? [15] אָמַר אַבַּיֵי: שָׁלֹשׁ אֶצְבָּעוֹת.

RASHI

ונעשה מקומו צלקת — שנשאר שם רושם משחייתה המכה. **צלקת** — *פינדרור״א. ודוגמתה בשחיטת חולין (קכד,א) גבי תנור כלי חרס, דצלקיה מצלק. **למעליותא** — והכי קאמר: נוי הוא לאשה שיהו דדיה מובדלים טפח. **גבי מומין תניא** — הך מתניתין גבי מומין תניא, דקא חשיב זיעה ושומא וריח הפה ושאר מומין, וטפח בין שני דדי אשה. **וכמה** — נוי לה. **וכמה** — יהו גסין (אחת) משל חברותיה ויהא מום.

LANGUAGE (RASHI)

פינדרור״א* From the Old French *fenderure,* meaning "furrow."

TRANSLATION AND COMMENTARY

פַּדַּחְתָּהּ [1] The Gemara asks: Can the Baraita really be referring to a wart **on** the woman's **forehead?** [2] But surely we can assume that her groom **saw it** before he betrothed her, **and,** if so, **he** surely **accepted it!** How, then, can he later seek to disqualify the betrothal on its account?

אָמַר רַב פַּפָּא [3] **Rav Pappa said:** The Baraita is really talking **about** a small hairless wart **situated on** the woman's forehead, **underneath the covering** she wears **on her head,** [4] **which at times is visible and at times is not.** The husband thus may never have seen it, so he may indeed use it as grounds for disqualifying the betrothal.

אָמַר רַב חִסְדָּא [5] The Gemara continues its discussion of physical defects which disqualify a woman's betrothal. **Rav Ḥisda said: The following matter I heard from a great man.** [6] **And who is** that great man? [7] **Rabbi Shela.** And this is what he said: **If a dog bit** a woman so severely that **the site** of the wound **became** permanently **scarred** after healing, [8] **this is** regarded as **a defect** which disqualifies a woman's betrothal.

אָמַר רַב חִסְדָּא [9] **Rav Ḥisda said: A husky voice in a woman is** regarded as **a defect** which disqualifies her betrothal, [10] **as it is said** (Song of Songs 2:14): **"For your voice is sweet, and your appearance is comely."**

תָּנֵי רַבִּי נָתָן בִּירָאָה [11] **Rabbi Natan Bira'ah taught** the following Baraita: **"Between a woman's breasts,** the space of **a handbreadth."** When this Baraita came up for discussion among the Amoraim, it was not immediately clear to them whether a handbreadth separating a woman's breasts is regarded as a defect or as a desirable feature. [12] **Rav Aḥa, the son of Rava, thought to say before Rav Ashi:** The space of **"a handbreadth"** between a woman's breasts **is to be considered an advantage**, since it renders her more attractive. [13] **Rav Ashi said to him: It was with regard to** identifying **defects that this** Baraita **was taught**, thus indicating that such a space is undesirable.

וְכַמָּה [14] The Gemara asks: **And how much**, then, is considered to be the ideal space between a woman's breasts? [15] **Abaye said:** A width of **three fingers.**

HALAKHAH

צַלֶּקֶת **Scar.** "If a scar forms at the site of a dog bite, it is regarded as a defect that can invalidate a woman's betrothal," as stated by Rabbi Shela. (*Rambam, Sefer Nashim, Hilkhot Ishut* 7:7; *Shulḥan Arukh, Even HaEzer* 39:4.)

קוֹל עָבֶה **A husky voice.** "A husky voice in a woman is considered to be a defect," as maintained by Rav Ḥisda. (*Rambam, Sefer Nashim, Hilkhot Ishut* 7:7; *Shulḥan Arukh, Even HaEzer* 39:4.)

דַּדֵּי אִשָּׁה **A woman's breasts.** "If a woman's breasts are a handbreadth larger than those of most other women, or are separated by the space of a handbreadth, they constitute a defect which is capable of invalidating her betrothal," in accordance with Rabbi Natan as explained in the Gemara. (*Rambam, Sefer Nashim, Hilkhot Ishut* 7:7; *Shulḥan Arukh, Even HaEzer* 39:4.)

TRANSLATION AND COMMENTARY

תַּנְיָא [1]**It was taught** in a Baraita: **"Rabbi Natan says:** [2]**Any woman whose breasts are** significantly **larger than those of** most **other women is** considered to have **a defect** which may disqualify her betrothal."

וְכַמָּה [3]The Gemara asks: **And how much** larger than the average breast must a woman's breasts be to be considered a defect? [4]**Rabbi Meyasha, the grandson of Rabbi Yehoshua ben Levi, said in the name of Rabbi Yehoshua ben Levi: A handbreadth** larger.

וּמִי אִיכָּא [5]The Gemara asks in astonishment: **And are there** really **such** women whose breasts are that large? [6]The Gemara answers: **Yes, as Rabbah bar Bar Ḥanah said:** [7]**I** once **saw an Arab woman who flipped her breasts behind her** back **and nursed her child.**

וּלְצִיּוֹן [8]Having just cited a statement by Rabbi Yehoshua ben Levi's grandson, the Gemara proceeds to cite another statement made by the same Sage: The verse reads (Psalms 87:5): **"And of Zion it shall be said, This man and that man shall be born in her; and He shall establish her as supreme."** [9]**Rabbi Meyasha, the grandson of Rabbi Yehoshua ben Levi, said:** [10]The reference in the verse to two men of Zion is meant to imply that **both he who was born in** Zion **and he who** was born outside, yet who **anticipates seeing her** once again in all her glory, are considered to be her "children."

אֲמַר אַבַּיֵי [11]The Gemara now cites a discussion between Abaye and Rava regarding the caliber of those Sages living in Eretz Israel as compared to their counterparts in Babylonia. **Abaye said: One of them** from Eretz Israel **is worth two of us** Babylonians insofar as sharpness of intelligence is concerned. [12]**Rava**

[1]תַּנְיָא: "רַבִּי נָתָן אוֹמֵר: [2]כָּל אִשָּׁה שֶׁדַּדֶּיהָ גַּסִּין מִשֶּׁל חַבְרוֹתֶיהָ, הֲרֵי זֶה מוּם".
[3]וְכַמָּה? [4]אָמַר רַבִּי מְיָישָׁא בַּר בְּרֵיהּ דְּרַבִּי יְהוֹשֻׁעַ בֶּן לֵוִי מִשְּׁמֵיהּ דְּרַבִּי יְהוֹשֻׁעַ בֶּן לֵוִי: טֶפַח.
[5]וּמִי אִיכָּא כִּי הַאי גַּוְונָא? [6]אִין, דַּאֲמַר רַבָּה בַּר בַּר חָנָה: [7]אֲנִי רָאִיתִי עֲרָבִיָּא אַחַת, שֶׁהִפְשִׁילָה דַּדֶּיהָ לַאֲחוֹרֶיהָ, וְהֵנִיקָה אֶת בְּנָהּ.
[8]"וּלְצִיּוֹן יֵאָמַר אִישׁ וְאִישׁ יֻלַּד בָּהּ וְהוּא יְכוֹנְנֶהָ עֶלְיוֹן". [9]אָמַר רַבִּי מְיָישָׁא בַּר בְּרֵיהּ דְּרַבִּי יְהוֹשֻׁעַ בֶּן לֵוִי: [10]אֶחָד הַנּוֹלָד בָּהּ וְאֶחָד הַמְצַפֶּה לִרְאוֹתָהּ.
[11]אֲמַר אַבַּיֵי: וְחַד מִינַּיְיהוּ עָדִיף כִּתְרֵי מִינַּן. [12]אֲמַר רָבָא: וְחַד

LITERAL TRANSLATION

[1]It was taught: "Rabbi Natan says: [2]Any woman whose breasts are larger than those of her fellow women, this is a defect."

[3]And how much? [4]Rabbi Meyasha, the grandson of Rabbi Yehoshua ben Levi, said in the name of Rabbi Yehoshua ben Levi: A handbreadth.

[5]And is there such a case? [6]Yes, for Rabbah, the son of Bar Ḥanah, said: [7]I saw an Arab woman who flipped her breasts behind her and nursed her child.

[8]"And of Zion it shall be said, This man and that man shall be born in her; and He shall establish her as supreme." [9]Rabbi Meyasha, the grandson of Rabbi Yehoshua ben Levi, said: [10]Both he who was born in her and he who anticipates seeing her.

[11]Abaye said: And one of them is worth two of us. [12]Rava said: And one

RASHI

ולציון יאמר — משום דאיירי בה רבי מיישא נקיט לה. "ולציון יאמר איש ואיש יולד בה". לעתיד לבא, כשיתקיים מקרא שכתוב: "והביאו את כל אחיכם מנחה לה' וגו'" כל מקום שימצאו שם ישראל יאמרו העמים: זהו מבני ציון, זה יולד בה — נביאנו שם. **ולציון** — כמו "וישאלו אנשי המקום לאשתו" (בראשית כו) — על אשתו. **אחד הנולד בה כו'** — "איש" "איש" יתירא קא דריש: אחד הנולד בה, ואחד המצפה לראותה יקרא מבניה, ויביאוהו אצלה. **והוא יכוננה עליון** — הקדוש ברוך הוא יכוננה להיות עליון, למעלה על כל העולם. **וחד מינייהו** — מבני ארץ ישראל. **עדיף** — פקחים וחריפים.

REALIA

דַּדֵּי אִשָּׁה A woman's breasts. The space between a woman's breasts depends on their size, and the determination of a certain space as beautiful depends, of course, on time and place. A space of three fingers is normal, and a handbreadth is found only between breasts that are smaller than average. There are also considerable differences in the length of breasts between one woman and another; and even today breasts that are a handbreadth larger than average are regarded as an aesthetic and medical flaw, and are sometimes surgically corrected. Extremely long breasts, such as were seen by Rabbah bar Bar Ḥannah, are rare but have been attested to.

NOTES

אֶחָד הַנּוֹלָד בָּהּ Both he who was born in her. *Maharsha* explains that, normally, a place-name is identified with those who were either born there or at least lived there for a significant period of time. Jerusalem is different, however, for its name is attached to any person who merely anticipates its being restored to its former glory. *Shittah Mekubbetzet* explains the connection between this Scriptural interpretation and the following statement of Abaye in terms of the distinction with regard to the greater cleverness and erudition of those who live there, as opposed to those who merely anticipate the restoration of Zion from afar.

וְחַד מִינַּיְיהוּ עָדִיף One of them is worth two of us. *Rashi* understands the advantage of a Torah scholar in Eretz Israel over his counterpart in Babylonia as one of superior intelligence. *Rivan* adds that he is also his superior in erudition. *Ritva* explains that there are two reasons why a Torah scholar living in Eretz Israel is worth two scholars in Babylonia: First, the climate of Eretz Israel makes a person wise. And second, his Torah achievements are greater by virtue of the merit earned by fulfilling the obligation to live in Eretz Israel.

וְחַד מִינַּן And one of us. *Ritva* explains that a Babylonian scholar who moves to Eretz Israel is worth two scholars who are native to that land, for he brings with him the merit of leaving the impurity of the lands of the Gentiles and entering the country in which the Divine Presence

מִינַּן, ¹כִּי סָלֵיק לְהָתָם — עָדִיף כְּתְרֵי מִינַּיְיהוּ. ²דְּהָא רַבִּי יִרְמְיָה, דְּכִי הֲוָה הָכָא, ³לָא הֲוָה יָדַע מַאי קָאָמְרִי רַבָּנַן; ⁴כִּי סָלֵיק לְהָתָם, קָרֵי לַן בַּבְלָאֵי טִפְּשָׁאֵי.

מִשְׁנָה ⁵הָיוּ בָּהּ מוּמִין וְעוֹדָהּ בְּבֵית אָבִיהָ, ⁶הָאָב צָרִיךְ לְהָבִיא רְאָיָה שֶׁמִּשֶּׁנִּתְאַרְסָה הָיוּ בָּהּ מוּמִין הַלָּלוּ, ⁷וְנִסְתַּחֲפָה שָׂדֵהוּ. ⁸נִכְנְסָה לִרְשׁוּת הַבַּעַל, ⁹הַבַּעַל צָרִיךְ לְהָבִיא רְאָיָה שֶׁעַד שֶׁלֹּא נִתְאָרְסָה הָיוּ בָּהּ מוּמִין אֵלּוּ,

TRANSLATION AND COMMENTARY

said: It must, however, be added that **one of us** from Babylonia, ¹**when he goes up there** to Eretz Israel, **is worth two of them.** ²**For behold Rabbi Yirmiyah who, when he was** living **here** in Babylonia, ³**did not understand what the Rabbis were saying,** ⁴yet **when he went up there** to Eretz Israel, he quickly became so advanced in his studies that **he would call us "the stupid Babylonians."**

MISHNAH הָיוּ בָּהּ מוּמִין ⁵The next Mishnah concerns a woman in whom certain physical defects were discovered subsequent to her betrothal. In a case **where** physical **defects were** found **in** a betrothed woman **while she was still** living **in her father's house,** before the marriage was concluded, and the father insists that the unwilling bridegroom must pay the ketubah settlement before abandoning the bride, ⁶then **the father needs to bring proof that it was** only **after she had been betrothed that these defects were** formed **in her,** ⁷**and that it was** a simple matter of the bridegroom's misfortune, not unlike **a case of his field having been flooded.** ⁸However, if the defects were first discovered only after **she** had already married and **entered into her husband's domain,** ⁹then it is **the husband** who **needs to bring proof that these defects were** already present

LITERAL TRANSLATION

of us, ¹when he goes up there, is worth two of them. ²For behold Rabbi Yirmiyah who, when he was here, ³did not understand what the Rabbis were saying; ⁴[yet] when he went up there, he called us "the stupid Babylonians."

MISHNAH ⁵[Where] defects were [found] in her while she was still in her father's house, ⁶the father must bring proof that it was only after she had been betrothed that these defects were [formed] in her, ⁷and that [it was like a case of] his field having been flooded. ⁸[However, if] she [had already] entered into the husband's domain, ⁹the husband must bring proof that [even] before she was betrothed these defects were in her,

RASHI

משנה האב צריך להביא ראיה — אם בא לתבוע כתובה מן האירוסין מזה שממאן לקחתה. נכנסה לרשות הבעל — ניסת והוא בא להוציאה בלא כתובה על מומין שבה. הבעל צריך להביא ראיה — עדים וכולה מפרש בגמרא.

SAGES

רַבִּי יִרְמְיָה **Rabbi Yirmiyah.** A fourth-generation Amora from Eretz Israel. Rabbi Yirmiyah was born in Babylonia and studied there in his youth, although he did not attain distinction as a Torah scholar there. Later, he immigrated to Eretz Israel, where he studied with the leading scholars of his generation, Rabbi Zera and Rabbi Abbahu, who were Rabbi Yoḥanan's disciples.

Rabbi Yirmiyah was known for his sharp questions, some of which were considered so provocative that he was expelled for a while from the yeshivah.

He occasionally referred to the Babylonian scholars as בַּבְלָאֵי טִפְּשָׁאֵי, "stupid Babylonians," although the Babylonian Sages apparently accepted his criticism submissively.

Rabbi Yirmiyah became one of the leading scholars in Eretz Israel, and his teachings are cited frequently in both the Babylonian Talmud and the Jerusalem Talmud. In the Babylonian Talmud, his teachings are not always explicitly attributed to him, and are often introduced by the term אָמְרִי בְּמַעַרְבָא — "they say in the West" (=Eretz Israel; see *Sanhedrin* 17a).

NOTES

dwells. Moreover, a person who leaves his country of birth and engages in Torah study in Eretz Israel, can devote himself more fully to his studies. *Rivash* suggests that the Babylonian method of Torah study is superior to that of Eretz Israel, and so when a Babylonian scholar moves to Eretz Israel and is inspired by the special climate there, his achievements quickly surpass those of scholars born in that country.

קָרֵי לַן בַּבְלָאֵי טִפְּשָׁאֵי **He called us stupid Babylonians.** *Ritva* explains the anecdote as proving Rabbi Yirmiyah's superiority over the native scholars of Eretz Israel by virtue of the fact that he perceived and referred to his former colleagues as "stupid Babylonians," whereas scholars native to Eretz Israel apparently did not. *Maharam Shiff* explains that the purpose of the anecdote is not to prove Rabbi Yirmiyah's superiority over native Israeli scholars, but rather to illustrate that if Rabbi Yirmiyah, who was an undistinguished scholar in Babylon, could advance to the level of a scholar native to Eretz Israel by transplanting himself there, then surely one who was an accomplished scholar in Babylonia could hope to advance beyond that level should he follow the same example.

הַבַּעַל צָרִיךְ לְהָבִיא רְאָיָה **The husband needs to bring proof.** *Rashi* notes that the husband must bring proof in the form

HALAKHAH

הָיוּ בָּהּ מוּמִין **When defects were found in her.** "When a defect is discovered in a woman subsequent to her betrothal, the following distinction is applied with regard to her entitlement to a ketubah settlement: If the defect was discovered after the woman had married and entered her husband's domain, then the husband must prove that the defect was there before he betrothed her, should he wish to invalidate the betrothal without paying the ketubah settlement; if the defect was discovered before the marriage was concluded, while the girl was still living in her father's house, then the father must prove that she acquired the defect only after the betrothal, if he wishes to obtain the ketubah settlement for her. *Rema* notes that, at least according to some authorities (*Maggid Mishneh* in the name of *Rashba*), the husband must support his claim in such a case as long as the father declares with certainty that the defect first appeared only after she was betrothed. Others (*Rabbenu Yeruḥam*) add that if the designated time for concluding the marriage had arrived, the woman was automatically considered as having entered her husband's domain with respect to responsibility for proving when her defect(s) arose, even though the marriage had not yet actually taken place." (*Rambam, Sefer Nashim, Hilkhot Ishut* 25:4; *Shulḥan Arukh, Even HaEzer* 117:8.)

TRANSLATION AND COMMENTARY

betrothed, [1]**and that his acquisition was made in error** under false pretenses, should he wish to divorce the woman without paying the ketubah settlement. [2]**These are the words of Rabbi Meir.** [3]**And the Sages ask: In what** case **are the words** of Rabbi Meir stated, allowing the man to claim that his betrothal was made in error? They reply: [4]In the case of **defects** which appear on parts of the body **that are** ordinarily **hidden** from view. Thus one might assume that the groom was indeed unaware of the existence of the defects at the time of betrothal. [75B] [5]**But when defects are** discovered on a part of the wife's body which is ordinarily **exposed,** the husband **cannot claim** betrothal under false pretenses. [6]**And if there is a** public **bathhouse in that town,** where all the women come to bathe, then **even if defects are** on a part of her body which is ordinarily **hidden** from sight, [7]the husband **cannot claim** a mistaken betrothal, **for he** can **examine her** prior to betrothal **through his** female **relatives,** who undress with her at the bathhouse and would report any imperfections.

GEMARA טַעֲמָא [8]The Mishnah teaches that if a betrothed woman is found to have certain defects while still living in her father's house, and her husband wishes to cancel the betrothal because of them, her father must bring proof that she only acquired them after the betrothal, in order to secure her rights to the ketubah settlement. The Gemara infers from this that **the reason** the husband must honor his commitment to pay her ketubah settlement **is that the father brings proof** to the effect that his daughter only acquired her defects after the betrothal. [9]**But** it follows that if **the father does not bring proof,** then

[1]וְהָיָה מִקָּחוֹ מִקַּח טָעוּת, [2]דִּבְרֵי רַבִּי מֵאִיר. [3]וַחֲכָמִים אוֹמְרִים: בַּמֶּה דְּבָרִים אֲמוּרִים? [4]בְּמוּמִין שֶׁבְּסֵתֶר, [75B] [5]אֲבָל בְּמוּמִין שֶׁבְּגָלוּי, אֵינוֹ יָכוֹל לִטְעוֹן. [6]וְאִם יֵשׁ מֶרְחָץ בְּאוֹתָהּ הָעִיר, אַף מוּמִין שֶׁבְּסֵתֶר [7]אֵינוֹ יָכוֹל לִטְעוֹן, מִפְּנֵי שֶׁהוּא בּוֹדְקָהּ בִּקְרוֹבוֹתָיו.

גמרא [8]טַעֲמָא דְּמַיְיתֵי הָאָב רְאָיָה. [9]הָא לָא מַיְיתֵי הָאָב

LITERAL TRANSLATION

[1]and [that] his acquisition was an acquisition of error. [2][These are] the words of Rabbi Meir. [3]And the Sages say: In what [case] are the words stated? [4][In the case of] defects that are hidden [from view]. [75B] [5]But when defects are exposed he cannot claim. [6]And if there is a bathhouse in that town even hidden defects [7]he cannot claim, for he examines her through his female relatives.

GEMARA [8]The reason is that the father brings proof. [9]But if the father does not bring

RASHI

במה דברים אמורים – שהבעל יכול לטעון על המומין. **אין יכול לטעון** – דידע ונתפייס.

NOTES

of witnesses. It is explained that this is necessary as a result of the fact that the husband is attempting to undo both the Halachic presumption of the woman's initial fitness for marriage as well as his own prior commitment to marry her. Moreover, his claim is at best an estimated one, while the girl and her father insist otherwise with stated certainty.

בּוֹדְקָהּ בִּקְרוֹבוֹתָיו **He examines her through his relatives.** *Rambam* concludes from here that if a man does not have female relatives who could examine his bride for him before their betrothal, he is believed should he later claim that he betrothed her under false pretenses, since he discovered a defect on a part of her body ordinarily hidden from view. Moreover, where it is customary that unmarried women never leave the house to go to market, the husband can claim a mistaken betrothal even if the defect was found on a part of her body which is ordinarily visible. According to the Geonim, not having female relatives to examine his bride in the bathhouse is insufficient basis for supporting the husband's claim, for he could have examined her just

HALAKHAH

אֲבָל בְּמוּמִין שֶׁבְּגָלוּי **But when defects are exposed.** "If there is a public bathhouse in the town, a man cannot claim that he did not know about his wife's defects at the time of their marriage, even if they are on a part of her body which is ordinarily covered, since we assume that he had her examined by his female relatives and then agreed to marry her in spite of the defects they found. However, if there is no public bathhouse in the town, or if the husband has no female relatives in the area, he can make such a claim as long as the defects he discovers after marrying her are on a part of her body which is ordinarily covered. *Rema* adds that, according to some (*Tur* in the name of Geonim), the lack of female relatives in the town is not sufficient basis for the husband to claim that he knew nothing of her defects when he married her, since he could have had her examined by the wives of his acquaintances as well. As regards the discovery of defects which are on an ordinarily exposed part of her body, the man can make no claim whatsoever unless he lives in a place where unmarried women refrain from frequenting the marketplace or only visit the bathhouse secretly after dark, in which case he could not be expected to know of her defects — be they normally hidden or exposed." (*Rambam, Sefer Nashim, Hilkhot Ishut* 25:2; *Shulḥan Arukh, Even HaEzer* 117:5-6; *Rema,* 39:4.)

לָא מַיְיתֵי הָאָב רְאָיָה **If the father does not bring proof.** "When a woman is discovered to have a defect which perforce existed prior to her betrothal, such as one which

TRANSLATION AND COMMENTARY

the husband is believed when he claims, without proof, that the woman possessed these defects before her betrothal — thereby rendering it null and void by virtue of its having taken place under false pretenses. [1]**Who,** then, is the author of our Mishnah? [2]Surely **it is Rabbi Yehoshua who said,** elsewhere in the Mishnah (*Ketubot* 12b), that if a groom discovers that his bride is not a virgin, and she claims that she was raped after her betrothal (thus retaining rights to her ketubah settlement), while her husband insists she had already lost her virginity previously (which would cancel her rights to the ketubah settlement), [3]we follow the words: **"Not from the** words of **her mouth do we live."** Rather, she must bring proof to verify her claim should she wish to retain the rights to her ketubah settlement. Two legal principles are at odds with each other here: The principle that the burden of proof lies upon the litigant who seeks to receive payment, and the principle that a bride is presumed to be a virgin. According to Rabbi Yehoshua, the husband's possession of those assets designated for paying out her ketubah outweighs the presumption of her virginity at the time of betrothal, a presumption which would have forced him to honor his financial commitment. Similarly in our Mishnah, it appears that the husband's right to his assets overpowers the presumption of his wife's freedom from defect at the time of her betrothal, thus forcing her father to prove his claim should he wish to obtain payment of her ketubah settlement.

אֵימָא סֵיפָא [4]The Gemara points out a difficulty with attributing the Mishnah to Rabbi Yehoshuah: **State the last clause** in this section of our Mishnah: "If the defects were not discovered until **she** left her father's house and **entered into her husband's domain** through marriage, [5]then it is **the husband** who **needs to bring proof** that these defects were present in her before she was betrothed, and that his acquisition was made in error under false pretenses, should he wish to divorce the woman without paying the ketubah settlement." [6]One can infer that **the reason** the woman may be divorced without receiving her ketubah settlement **is that the husband brings proof** that her defects existed before the betrothal. [7]**But** it follows that **if the husband does not bring such proof,** [8]**the father is believed** without proof when he says that she only acquired her defects after the betrothal. [9]**We have** thus **come to** approximate in this clause of our Mishnah the position

רְאָיָה, הַבַּעַל מְהֵימַן. [1]מַנִּי? [2]רַבִּי יְהוֹשֻׁעַ הִיא, דְּאָמַר: [3]"לֹא מִפִּיהָ אָנוּ חַיִּין". [4]אֵימָא סֵיפָא: [5]"נִכְנְסָה לִרְשׁוּת הַבַּעַל, הַבַּעַל צָרִיךְ לְהָבִיא רְאָיָה". [6]טַעֲמָא דְּמַיְיתֵי הַבַּעַל רְאָיָה. [7]הָא לָא מַיְיתֵי הַבַּעַל רְאָיָה, [8]הָאָב מְהֵימַן. [9]אֲתָאן

LITERAL TRANSLATION

proof, the husband is believed. [1]Who [is it]? [2]It is Rabbi Yehoshua, who said: [3]"Not from her mouth do we live."

[4]State the last clause: "If she entered the husband's domain, [5]the husband must bring proof." [6]The reason is that the husband brings proof. [7]But if the husband does not bring proof, [8]the father is believed. [9]We have [thus] come

RASHI

גמרא הבעל מהימן – דאמר: הואיל וספק הוא אם הטעתו ואם לאו – העמד ממון על חזקתו. **מני רבי יהושע היא דאמר** – בפרק קמא היא אומרת: משארסתני נאנסתי, והוא אומר: עד שלא ארסתיך – לא מפיה אנו חיין, שתהא נאמנת, אלא העמד ממון על חזקתו. ולא אזלינן בתר חזקה דגופא, לומר: הואיל וספק בידינו על שעת אירוסין מה היא – העמד הגוף על חזקתו של קודם לכן, והרי נולדה בתולה. והכא נמי: לא אמרינן העמד הגוף על חזקתו, ובלא מומין נולדה.

NOTES

as well through the wives of his acquaintances. Similarly, *Meiri* argues that the custom whereby unmarried women refrain from going to market is insufficient to support the claim that the man betrothed his wife in error, should he later discover a defect on a part of her body which is ordinarily visible, for such defects still become common knowledge through her friends, from whom she cannot hide them.

מַנִּי רַבִּי יְהוֹשֻׁעַ הִיא **Who is it? It is Rabbi Yehoshua.** Our commentary follows *Rashi* and others who understand that the main issue here is the relative strength of the conflicting presumptions mentioned, particularly that regarding the constancy of a body's native state versus that regarding ownership of an asset which is retained in one's private possession. What appears not to be considered is the relative certainty with which the respective claims are made. *Ramban* and his students also take into consideration the fact that the woman and her father can advance their claim with utter certainty while the husband can at best base his claim on likelihood. This issue appears quite relevant in earlier Talmudic discussions (see 12b) of how to resolve conflicting clauses in the Mishnah. The Rishonim and the Aḥaronim consider at great length the question of whether degree of certainty is a relevant factor in our own discussion.

HALAKHAH

is congenital, the father must bring proof that her husband knew about it before he agreed to marry her should he wish to prevent the husband from divorcing her without paying the ketubah settlement." (*Rambam, Sefer Nashim, Hilkhot Ishut* 25:4; *Shulḥan Arukh, Even HaEzer* 117:7.)

[1]לְרַבָּן גַּמְלִיאֵל, דְּאָמַר: ״נֶאֱמֶנֶת״! [2]אָמַר רַבִּי אֶלְעָזָר: תַּבְרָא, [3]מִי שֶׁשָּׁנָה זוֹ לֹא שָׁנָה זוֹ. [4]אֲמַר רָבָא: לָא תֵּימָא רַבִּי יְהוֹשֻׁעַ לָא אָזֵיל בָּתַר חֲזָקָה דְּגוּפָא כְּלָל. [5]אֶלָּא, כִּי לָא אָזֵיל רַבִּי יְהוֹשֻׁעַ בָּתַר חֲזָקָה דְּגוּפָא, [6]הֵיכָא דְּאִיכָּא חֲזָקָה דְּמָמוֹנָא. [7]אֲבָל הֵיכָא דְּלֵיכָּא חֲזָקָה דְּמָמוֹנָא, [8]אָזֵיל רַבִּי יְהוֹשֻׁעַ בָּתַר חֲזָקָה דְּגוּפָא. [9]דְּתַנְיָא: ״אִם בַּהֶרֶת קוֹדֶם

LITERAL TRANSLATION

to Rabban Gamliel, [1]who said: "She is believed"! [2]Rabbi Elazar said: [It is] a contradiction, [3]he who taught this, did not teach this.

[4]Rava said: Do not say [that] Rabbi Yehoshua does not go after any presumption [regarding] the body whatsoever. [5]Rather, when Rabbi Yehoshua does not go after a presumption [regarding] the body, [6][it is] where there is monetary possession. [7]But where there is not monetary possession, [8]Rabbi Yehoshua goes after a presumption [regarding] the body.

[9]For it was taught: "If a bright spot precedes

RASHI

אתאן לרבן גמליאל דאמר — דהתם: היא נאמנת, דחזקה דגופא עדיפא. **תברא** — קשיא רישא לסיפא.

מי ששנה זו לא שנה זו — רישא לרבי יהושע, והוא הדין לנכנסה לרשות הבעל. וסיפא לרבן גמליאל והוא הדין לעודה בבית אביה, שאין לנו טעם לחלק בין עודה בבית אביה לנכנסה לחופה. **לא תימא רבי יהושע לא אזיל בתר חזקה דגופא כלל** — אפילו במקום שאין חזקת ממון עומדת נגדה להכחישה. **היכא דאיכא חזקה דממונא** — עומדת לנגדה כי הכא.

TRANSLATION AND COMMENTARY

of **Rabban Gamliel** and Rabbi Eliezer, [1]**who** argued with Rabbi Yehoshuah in the Mishnah cited above and **said:** "The woman **is believed** when she claims that she was raped after the betrothal, and therefore she is still entitled to her ketubah settlement." These Tannaim maintain that the presumption of virginity persists until the husband can prove that she was not a virgin, even though such a presumption makes him liable to pay the ketubah settlement. Similarly in our case, the Tanna maintains that presumption of the girl's freedom from physical defect persists until the husband can prove that she suffered from a blemish. Thus, the first clause of the Mishnah appears to agree with the view of Rabbi Yehoshua, who favors the husband's claim to his assets over any presumption regarding the woman's physical state, while the second appears to agree with the view of Rabban Gamliel and Rabbi Eliezer, who maintain just the opposite!

אָמַר רַבִּי אֶלְעָזָר [2]**Rabbi Elazar said:** Indeed, there is an irreconcilable **contradiction** between the two clauses in our Mishnah. [3]Thus, we are forced to conclude that the Tanna **who taught** the first clause **did not teach** the second.

אֲמַר רָבָא [4]In order to reconcile the two clauses in our Mishnah, the Gemara must show that the first one does not reflect the ruling of Rabbi Yehoshua. Hence it now examines the position of Rabbi Yehoshua, and shows that an entirely different legal principle is at issue: The presumption regarding constancy of a person's physical state. **Rava Said: Do not say that Rabbi Yehoshua**'s refusal to believe the woman's claim that she was still a virgin at the time of her betrothal indicates that he **does not accept any presumption whatsoever regarding the** constancy of a **body**'s native state. [5]**Rather, when does Rabbi Yehoshua reject a presumption regarding the** constancy of a **body**'s native state? [6]It is only **in opposition to** a claim of **monetary possession,** as in the case of a woman who is found not to be a virgin. Rabbi Yehoshua favors the husband's claim to his money over the presumption that the woman was still a virgin when she was betrothed. Similarly in our Mishnah, the author of the first clause favored the husband's claim to the money in his possession over the presumption (so long as it cannot be proven otherwise) of his wife's freedom from physical defect. [7]**But when there is not** an opposing claim of **monetary possession,** [8]**Rabbi Yehoshua** agrees that one **accepts the presumption regarding** the constancy of **a body**'s native state.

דְּתַנְיָא [9]This can be proven from a Baraita dealing with the laws of *tzara'at*, a condition that renders

NOTES

תַּבְרָא **A contradiction.** *Rashi* understands this word in its literal sense, as a "break" or contradiction within a single Mishnah or Baraita that can only be resolved by attributing the opposing clauses to separate Tannaitic sources. According to *Rabbenu Ḥananel* (cited by *Tosafot*), the word תַּבְרָא is used here as a term of oath-taking meant to emphasize the certainty with which the two opposing clauses are seen as being irreconcilably in contradiction. The connection between the simple meaning of תַּבְרָא and an oath can be understood in light of the Gemara in *Moed Katan* (17b) which describes an oath as a "house-breaker" insofar as its intentioned violation can wreak great damage upon one's self and one's household.

אִם בַּהֶרֶת קוֹדֶם **If a bright spot precedes.** Normally, when

HALAKHAH

אִם בַּהֶרֶת קוֹדֶם **If a bright spot precedes.** "White hair growing from a bright lesion on the skin is not a sure indication

TRANSLATION AND COMMENTARY

one ritually impure. **For it was taught** in the Mishnah of *Negaim* (4:11): **"If** the appearance of **a bright spot** on the skin, minimally the size of a bean, **precedes** the appearance on the same spot of at least two **white hairs,** the afflicted one **is** immediately declared by the priest to be **ritually impure.** [1]But **if** the appearance of two **white hairs precedes** the appearance in the same place of **a bright spot,** then **he is** still considered to be **ritually pure.** [2]**In case of doubt,** the individual **is** declared to be **ritually impure.** [3]**And Rabbi Yehoshua says: It became dim."** [4]The Gemara asks: **What** did Rabbi Yehoshua mean when he said: **"It became dim"?** [5]**Rabbah said:** The expression **"it became dim"** means that in a case of doubt we treat the spot as if it has receded, and the afflicted individual **is** still considered to be **ritually pure.** Rabbi Yehoshua's reasoning is based on the presumption that in cases of doubt we should view the body as retaining its native state of health. Thus it is clear that when no opposing claim of monetary possession exists, Rabbi Yehoshua agrees that one presumes constancy of the body's native state.

לְשֵׂעָר לָבָן, טָמֵא. [1]אִם שֵׂעָר לָבָן קוֹדֶם לְבַהֶרֶת, טָהוֹר. [2]סָפֵק, טָמֵא. [3]וְרַבִּי יְהוֹשֻׁעַ אוֹמֵר: כֵּהָה". [4]מַאי "כֵּהָה"? [5]אָמַר רַבָּה: "כֵּהָה" טָהוֹר.

LITERAL TRANSLATION

white hair, [he is ritually] impure. [1]If white hair precedes a bright spot, [he is] ritually pure. [2][When there is] doubt, [he is] ritually impure. [3]And Rabbi Yehoshua says: It became dim." [4]What is [meant by] "it became dim"? [5]Rabbah said: "It became dim" [means] he is ritually pure.

RASHI

טמא — דהכי כתיב קרא (ויקרא יג) "שער לבן בבהרת". **רבי יהושע אומר כהה** — כדמפרש רבה. **כהה טהור** — הרי הוא ככהה הנגע ממראהו, שהוא טהור. ומשם רבי משה הדרשן שמעתי: ורבי יהושע קיהה. מאי קיהה? אמר רבה: קיהה — וטיהר. כלומר, קיהה בדבר, ונחלק עליהם וטיהר. [כאדם שנקהו שיניו על אדם שאין משגיח לדבריו]. וכן מצאתי בתורת כהנים: ורבי יהושע קיהה טיהר. אלמא, העמד הגוף על חזקתו ולא תטמאנו מספק.

NOTES

a bright white spot is found on a person's body, the priest places the individual in isolation for seven days and then reexamines the spot to see if it has spread. However, if he discerns from the start at least two white hairs growing from the affected patch of skin, he can immediately declare the person ritually impure. The Baraita here teaches that this is only so if one can determine that the hairs turned white after the spot had already appeared. *Rashi* understands this law as being derived from the verse (Leviticus 13:25) that states: "If the hair in the bright spot be turned white" — implying that the spot preceded the hairs' turning white. *Rivan* derives the law from a related verse (Leviticus 13:3): "And when the hair in the plague is turned white." Finally, *Rambam* deduces the law from yet a third verse (Leviticus 13:10), which is more explicit: "And it [the swelling] turned the hair white" — affirming that it is the lesion itself that causes the hair to turn white.

וְרַבִּי יְהוֹשֻׁעַ אוֹמֵר: כֵּהָה And Rabbi Yehoshua says: It became dim. Our translation and commentary follows *Rashi's* initial reading: וְרַבִּי יְהוֹשֻׁעַ אוֹמֵר כֵּהָה — "And Rabbi Yehoshua says: It became dim." Rabbah then clarifies this: Rabbi Yehoshua's remark was meant to say that, in case of doubt, we view the spot as having become dimmer than true *tzara'at*, so that the person is declared ritually pure. *Rashi*, however, cites an alternative reading of Rabbi Yehoshua in the name of *Rabbi Moshe HaDarshan*: וְרַבִּי יְהוֹשֻׁעַ קֵהָה — "And Rabbi Yehoshua blunted [his teeth]," a Rabbinic expression which implies taking a tough and unyielding stance on some issue. According to this reading, Rabbah states that Rabbi Yehoshua was unrelenting in his disagreement with the Sages and insisted upon declaring the afflicted person ritually pure in the case of doubt (see also *Arukh*). *Ritva* suggests that the initial reading, כֵּהָה, also be interpreted as referring to a form of rebuke or disagreement, as evident from the following verse in Samuel I (3:13): "And he did not rebuke [כֵּהָה] them."

כֵּהָה טָהוֹר It became dim means he is ritually pure. Elsewhere in the Talmud (*Nazir* 65b) it is explained that this ruling, regarding a situation of doubt, derives from the verse (Leviticus 13:59) that sums up the laws of *tzara'at* by infected garments: "This is the Torah of the plague of *tzara'at* in a garment . . . to pronounce it ritually pure or to pronounce it ritually impure" — indicating that preference should be given to a pronouncement of purity over one of impurity when the law is in doubt. *Rabbenu Tam* (cited by *Tosafot* and in *Sefer HaYashar*) and others maintain that the disagreement in the Baraita regarding doubt is only relevant when the afflicted individual was previously declared ritually impure in the case of some earlier skin eruption. However, when doubt arises with regard to someone who has otherwise been unafflicted, even the Sages would agree that he remain ritually pure on the basis of presuming constancy with regard to his native state of ritual purity.

The Rishonim ask further: If Rabbi Yehoshua's ruling here

HALAKHAH

of *tzara'at* unless the skin erupted before the hair whitened. Where the hair turned white first, the afflicted patch of skin is regarded as one without hair altogether and is thus cause for isolation for seven days before the priest renders his diagnosis. When there is doubt as to whether the eruption preceded the whitening of hair, or vice versa, the afflicted person is declared ritually impure. According to *Rambam*, this state of ritual impurity is imposed despite continued doubt as to his true status (even according to the first Tanna of the Baraita; *Kesef Mishneh*), and does not reflect some underlying certainty as to the order in which these signs are assumed to appear." (*Rambam, Sefer Taharah, Hilkhot Tum'at Tzara'at* 2:6,9.)

TRANSLATION AND COMMENTARY

רָבָא אָמַר [1]The Gemara now suggests an alternative to Rabbi Elazar's "splitting" of the Mishnah, whereby the apparent contradiction between its first two clauses can be reconciled: **Rava said:** In truth, the entire Mishnah is taught in accordance with the view of Rabban Gamliel and Rabbi Eliezer mentioned above — that the presumption regarding the constancy of a body's native state is maintained against a claim of monetary possession. [2]In **the first clause** of our Mishnah we apply a general principle which implies that, since it was **here** in the father's house that the woman's defects **were** first **found,** [3]it is reasonable to believe that it was **here** in the father's house that **they** first **came into being**, even before the betrothal. Thus the woman's father must bring proof to support his claim that she acquired these defects only after the betrothal. [4]In **the second clause** of the Mishnah the same principle applies **as well:** [5]Since it was **here** in the husband's domain that the defects **were** first **found,** [6]it is reasonable to believe that it was **here** in the husband's domain that **they came into being.** Thus the husband must bring proof that she acquired her defects before their betrothal, if he wishes to divorce her without paying her ketubah settlement.

אֵיתִיבֵיהּ אַבַּיֵי [7]**Abaye raised an objection against** Rava's resolution of the contradiction in our Mishnah from the Mishnah itself: [8]"If the defects were first discovered only after **she** had left her father's house and **entered into her husband's domain** through marriage, then **the husband must bring proof that before she was betrothed these defects were** already found **in her,** [9]**and that his acquisition was one of error**, made under false pretenses, should he wish to divorce the woman without having to pay the ketubah settlement." [10]This clause of the Mishnah indicates that if the husband can prove that his wife had already possessed a defect **before she was betrothed,** we say **yes,** he is exempt from paying the ketubah settlement. [11]However, if he can only prove that she possessed a defect **after she was betrothed** yet while still in her father's house, then **no,** he is not exempt from paying her ketubah settlement. [12]But if one were to apply Rava's principle, **why** would this be so? The husband's discovery of his wife's defects after she leaves her father's house indicates that she possessed them while she was still in her father's house. [13]If so, **one** should **say** that, since it was **here** in the father's house that the defects **were found,** [14]it is reasonable to believe that it was **here** in the father's house that **they came into being** before the betrothal! By this logic, the girl's father must bring proof in either

[1]רָבָא אָמַר: [2]רֵישָׁא — כָּאן נִמְצְאוּ, [3]וְכָאן הָיוּ. [4]סֵיפָא נַמִי — [5]כָּאן נִמְצְאוּ, [6]וְכָאן הָיוּ.

[7]אֵיתִיבֵיהּ אַבַּיֵי: [8]״נִכְנְסָה לִרְשׁוּת הַבַּעַל, הַבַּעַל צָרִיךְ לְהָבִיא רְאָיָה שֶׁעַד שֶׁלֹּא תִּתְאָרֵס הָיוּ בָּהּ מוּמִין אֵלּוּ, [9]וְהָיָה מִקָּחוֹ מִקַּח טָעוּת״. [10]עַד שֶׁלֹּא תִּתְאָרֵס, אִין; [11]מִשֶּׁתִּתְאָרֵס, לָא. [12]וְאַמַּאי? [13]לֵימָא: כָּאן נִמְצְאוּ, [14]וְכָאן הָיוּ!

LITERAL TRANSLATION

[1]Rava said: [2][As regards] the first clause — here they were found, [3]and here they came into being. [4][As regards] the last clause as well — [5]here they were found, [6]and here they came into being.

[7]Abaye raised an objection against him: [8]"[When] she entered the husband's domain, the husband must bring proof that before she was betrothed she [already] had these defects, [9]and that his acquisition was an acquisition of error." [10]Before she was not yet betrothed, yes; [11]after she was betrothed, no. [12]And why? [13]Let one say: Here they were found, [14]and here they came into being!

RASHI

רבא אמר רישא כאן נמצאו כאן היו — רבא מהדר לאוקמא כולה כרבן גמליאל, דאוקמינן הלכתא כוותיה בפרק קמא. לעולם חזקה דגופא עדיף, ורישא טעמא משום דכיון דבבית אביה נמצאו המומין — איתרע חזקתיה דאב, דאיכא למימר: כאן היו קודם אירוסין. ובפרק קמא נמי פלוגתייהו בנכנסה לרשות הבעל היא, וקא אמר רבן גמליאל דלא הורעה חזקת אביה בכך. **משנתארסה לא** — אם הביא הבעל ראיה שראו בה מומין הללו משנתארסה, והיא עודה בבית אביה, לאו ראיה היא. ואי טעמא משום כאן נמצאו כאן היו — הרי בבית אביה נמצאו. אלא על כרחך רישא וסיפא פליגי, ואפילו באו לדין בעודה בבית אביה — אית ליה לתנא דסיפא דהיא נאמנת.

NOTES

is based — as the Gemara in *Nazir* indicates — on the wording of the verse, how then can Rava suggest that we generalize this presumption to *all* cases where there is no issue of monetary possession? *Tosafot* suggests that Rabbi Yehoshua does derive the principle of presuming that the body maintains a consistent state of purity and health from this verse. *Ra'avad* (cited by *Rashba* and others) suggests that the verse serves only supportively as a textual allusion to this presumption rather than as a formal Biblical source. Thus, were Rabbi Yehoshua not convinced of the presumption's viability, he would never have read it into the verse.

כָּאן נִמְצְאוּ, וְכָאן הָיוּ **Here they were found, and here they came into being.** This Halakhic principle is primarily put forth with regard to situations of ritual impurity (see *Niddah* 4a), where it implies that when one finds an impure object in a particular place, one is to assume that it originated there and thus does not affect the purity of any other locale. In our case, this principle is generalized so as to

¹אֲמַר לֵיהּ: מִשֶּׁנִּתְאָרְסָה, ²מִשּׁוּם דְּאִיכָּא לְמֵימַר: חֲזָקָה אֵין אָדָם שׁוֹתֶה בְּכוֹס אֶלָּא אִם כֵּן בּוֹדְקוֹ. ³וְהַאי, רָאָה וְנִיפַּיֵּיס הוּא.

⁴אִי הָכִי, עַד שֶׁלֹּא תִּתְאָרֵס נַמִי!

⁵אֶלָּא, אָמְרִינַן חֲזָקָה אֵין אָדָם מִיפַּיֵּיס בְּמוּמִין. ⁶הָכָא נַמִי, ⁷חֲזָקָה אֵין אָדָם מִיפַּיֵּיס בְּמוּמִין!

⁸אֶלָּא, מִשֶּׁנִּתְאָרְסָה, מִשּׁוּם דְּאִיכָּא תַּרְתֵּי: ⁹חֲזָקָה הַעֲמֵד הַגּוּף עַל חֶזְקָתוֹ; ¹⁰וַחֲזָקָה אֵין אָדָם שׁוֹתֶה בְּכוֹס אֶלָּא אִם כֵּן

LITERAL TRANSLATION

[1]He said to him: After she was betrothed, [2]because there is to say: The presumption [exists] that a person does not drink from a cup unless he examines it. [3]And this one — he saw and was reconciled.

[4]If so, while she was not yet betrothed also!

[5]Rather, we say a presumption [exists] that a person is not reconciled to defects. [6]Here too, [7]a presumption [exists] that a person is not reconciled to defects!

[8]Rather, after she was betrothed, because there are two: [9][There is] a presumption, leave (lit., "stand") the body in its presumptive state; [10]and the presumption [that] a person does not drink from a cup unless he examines it,

TRANSLATION AND COMMENTARY

case, showing that, as Rabbi Elazar originally maintained, the two clauses disagree with each other and thus derive from separate Tannaitic sources.

אֲמַר לֵיהּ [1]Rava **said to** Abaye: When a husband can only prove that his wife possessed a defect **after she was betrothed,** yet while she was still living in her father's house, he may not divorce her without paying the ketubah settlement, [2]**because there is** reason **to say** that **a presumption** exists which overrides the principle of "here they were found, here they came into being." The presumption **is that a person does not drink from a cup unless he examines it** first. In other words, we presume that the husband examined the girl for possible defects before betrothing her. Thus, even if she possessed defects before betrothal, [3]**this** man surely **saw** them **and was reconciled.**

אִי הָכִי [4]But **if** it is **so,** that we make such a presumption, then even if the husband can prove that she possessed these defects **while not yet betrothed,** we should **also** say that he knew of them and agreed to marry her anyway!

אֶלָּא [5]**Rather, we say** a **presumption** exists **that a person is not** ordinarily **reconciled in regard to** marrying a woman with **defects**, and thus is believed when he says that he betrothed her without knowing about them. [6]But if that is the case, then **here, too,** if the husband can only prove that she had defects some time after she was betrothed, yet while still in her father's house, [7]we should adopt the **presumption that a person is not** ordinarily **reconciled to** marrying a woman with **defects** and, hence, should be believed when he claims to have been unaware of them at the time of betrothal.

אֶלָּא [8]**Rather,** the distinction between the two cases must be understood as follows: When the husband can only prove that his wife possessed defects some time **after she was betrothed,** yet while still in her father's house, we support her claim to the ketubah settlement, [9]**because two** presumptions are in her favor: First, **the presumption** that in cases of doubt a **person should be left in his presumptive state.** Since there is a doubt as to whether the woman acquired her defects before or after her betrothal, she is presumed to be free of defects until it can be proven otherwise; [10]**and** second, **the presumption that a person does not drink from a cup before examining it** — thus implying that had the woman indeed acquired her defects before

RASHI

אמר ליה — לעולם רישא משום כאן נמצאו כאן היו הוא, ומשנתארסה, משום דאיכא תרתי. והיכא שהביא עדים שראו בה מומין הללו משנתארסה בבית אביה — משום הכי לאו ראיה היא, דאיכא תרתי ליפות כחה: חדא — העמד הגוף על חזקתו, ולא היו בה בשעת אירוסין, שהכל הולך אחר אותה שעה. ואם תאמר הורעה החזקה — הואיל וכאן נמצאו — חזקה אין אדם שותה בכוס אלא אם כן בודקו. ואפילו כאן היו קודם קדושין זה שהכניסה לחופה, וזו היא שתיית הכוס, בידוע שבדקה ונודע לו, וראה ונפייס.

NOTES

imply that any phenomenon one encounters (such as a woman's defect) is assumed to be exclusively local in nature and to have endured in that place over time. *Rashba* maintains that this principle is not to be viewed as a Halakhic presumption (חֲזָקָה), whereby one would have to take into consideration opposing presumptions, but rather as a decisive axiom that neutralizes all other logical contentions (see *Kovetz Shiurim* for a thorough discussion of the opinions of the Aḥaronim regarding this principle).

HALAKHAH

חֲזָקָה אֵין אָדָם שׁוֹתֶה בְּכוֹס A presumption exists that a person does not drink from a cup. "If a man had intercourse with his wife, and then after a few days claimed to have discovered at the time that she suffered from a defect — we do not accept his claim even where the defect is on a part of her body that is normally concealed, since

TRANSLATION AND COMMENTARY

she was betrothed, [1]surely **this** man **saw** them **and was reconciled** to them since he married her anyway. [2]Now **what did you say** to challenge the woman's right to her ketubah settlement? [3]That there exists **the presumption that a person is not** ordinarily **reconciled to** marrying a woman with **defects,** and thus should be believed when he claims to have married her under false pretenses. [4]But **it is** [76A] **one** presumption **in place of two** opposing presumptions, [5]**and we do not say** that **one** presumption should be sustained **in place of two** opposing presumptions. Thus, the husband may not divorce his wife without paying her ketubah settlement. But in the case where the husband can prove that his wife had defects [6]**"before she was betrothed"** there is only one presumption in the woman's favor. How so? [7]That the woman **should be left in the presumptive state** of being free of defects it is impossible to say, for proof was brought that defects existed prior to her betrothal. [8]**What,** then, **is there** left to say in the woman's favor? [9]Only **the presumption that a person does not drink from a cup** before **examining** it, [10]leaving reason to assume that **this** man **saw** the woman's defects before he married her and **was** reconciled to them. [11]**On the contrary!** [12]An opposing **presumption** exists **that a man is not** ordinarily reconciled **to** marrying a woman with **defects.** Consequently we should assume that he did not know about them. Thus the two presumptions cancel each other out and we are left with the principle that when neither party in a civil suit can prove his claim, [13]we **leave the money** in question in the possession of **its presumptive owner,** the party in whose possession it is currently found, in this case, the husband. Thus, he can divorce her without having to pay her ketubah settlement.

בּוֹדְקוֹ. [1]וְהַאי — רָאָה וְנִיפַּיֵּיס הוּא. [2]מַאי אָמְרַתְּ? [3]חֲזָקָה אֵין אָדָם מִיפַּיֵּיס בְּמוּמִין. [4]הָוֵי [76A] חֲדָא בִּמְקוֹם תַּרְתֵּי, [5]וַחֲדָא בִּמְקוֹם תַּרְתֵּי לָא אָמְרִינַן. [6]"עַד שֶׁלֹּא תִּתְאָרֵס" — [7]הַעֲמֵד הַגּוּף עַל חֶזְקָתוֹ לָא אִיכָּא לְמֵימַר. [8]מַאי אִיכָּא? [9]חֲזָקָה דְּאֵין אָדָם שׁוֹתֶה בְּכוֹס אֶלָּא אִם כֵּן בּוֹדְקוֹ, [10]וְהַאי רָאָה וְנִיפַּיֵּיס הוּא. [11]אַדְּרַבָּה, [12]חֲזָקָה אֵין אָדָם מִיפַּיֵּיס בְּמוּמִין. [13]וְהַעֲמֵד מָמוֹן עַל חֶזְקָתוֹ.

LITERAL TRANSLATION

[1]and this one — he saw and was reconciled. [2]What did you say? [3]The presumption that a person is not reconciled to defects. [4]It is [76A] one in place of two, [5]and one in place of two we do not say. [6]"Until she was betrothed" — [7]leave the body in its presumptive state it is not possible to say. [8]What is there? [9]The presumption that a person does not drink from a cup unless he examines it, [10]and this one saw and he was reconciled. [11]On the contrary, [12]a presumption [exists] that a person is not reconciled to defects. [13]And leave the money in its presumptive state.

RASHI

חדא במקום תרתי — דהעמד ממון על חזקתו לא אמרינן, דניהוו נמי הכא תרתי — דבמקום חזקה דגופא חזקה דממונא לאו כלום היא. **עד שלא תתארס** — אבל היכא שהביא עדים שראו בה עד שלא תתארס. **העמד הגוף על חזקתו ליכא למימר** — להודיע שלא היו בה בשעת קדושין — דהא קיימי עדים. **והעמד ממון על חזקתו** — כי ליכא חזקה דגופא.

NOTES

חֲדָא בִּמְקוֹם תַּרְתֵּי One in place of two. The Rishomin ask: Why is it that the presumption that money should remain with its possessor in the absence of proof of a claim against him is not counted as a second presumption in the husband's favor? *Rashi* suggests that this presumption is outweighed by the presumption of constancy with regard to a person's native physical state. *Ritva* agrees that presumption of ownership remains irrelevant to our case but for a different reason: The husband's claim is one of likelihood, that her defect probably existed before the betrothal, and we do not invoke a presumption in order to support what is at best a claim based upon likelihood when there is an established financial obligation on the husband's part, the ketubah, which opposes it.

The Rishonim raise a second question: Why is it that the principle of "here they [the betrothed woman's defects] were found [while still in her father's house], here they came into being [even before she was betrothed]," is also not counted in the husband's favor? *Tosafot* and many other Rishonim answer: The standing presumption in the husband's favor — that he would not have agreed to marry the woman had he known of her defects — in effect already assumes the relevant conclusion derived from this principle, that the defect originated prior to the betrothal. Since only the combination of both the presumption and the principle allows him to support his claim, the two are considered as one unit of reasoning in his favor. In the woman's case, however, the two presumptions invoked in her favor each represent an independent reason for validating her claim to the ketubah.

HALAKHAH

we presume that 'a person does not drink from a cup before carefully examining it.' *Rema* adds (in the name of *Maharik*) that if a man has been married for at least thirty days, he cannot make any claim that presumes he has not engaged in intercourse with his wife over that entire period," as is evident from the Gemara in various places. (*Rambam, Sefer Nashim, Hilkhot Ishut* 25:6; *Shulḥan Arukh, Even HaEzer* 117:10.)

¹רַב אַשִׁי אֲמַר: ²רֵישָׁא — ״מָנֶה לְאַבָּא בְּיָדְךָ״. ³וְסֵיפָא ״מָנֶה לִי בְּיָדְךָ״.

⁴אֵיתִיבֵיהּ רַב אַחָא בְּרֵיהּ דְּרַב אָוְיָא לְרַב אַשִׁי: ⁵״מוֹדֶה רַבִּי מֵאִיר בְּמוּמִין הָרְאוּיִין לָבֹא

LITERAL TRANSLATION

[1] Rav Ashi said: [2] The first clause — "A maneh of father's is in your possession." [3] And the last clause — "A maneh of mine is in your possession."

[4] Rav Aḥa, the son of Rav Avya, raised an objection against Rav Ashi: [5] "Rabbi Meir agrees about defects which are likely [lit., 'suited'] to [have] come

TRANSLATION AND COMMENTARY

רַב אַשִׁי אֲמַר [1] The Gemara now offers another resolution of the apparent contradiction between the first two clauses of the Mishnah: **Rav Ashi said:** In truth, the entire Mishnah agrees with the view of Rabban Gamliel and Rabbi Eliezer. We presume that the bride was without defects until the time they were discovered, unless it can be proven otherwise, even if this presumption challenges the presumed status of money found in another's possession. [2] Nevertheless, in **the first clause** of our Mishnah, where a defect is discovered in a betrothed maiden (one younger than twelve-and-a-half) while still in her father's house and under his guardianship, her claim to the ketubah settlement amounts to saying: **"A maneh of** my **father's is in your possession," since** all payments she receives legally go directly to him. Since the girl herself is not party to the suit, any legal presumption pertaining exclusively to her has no weight in deciding the status of the contested money. Hence her father must prove that she contracted her defect only after she was betrothed, should he wish to obtain payment of her ketubah settlement. [3] **And in the last clause** of our Mishnah, where the defect is discovered only after the girl has entered her husband's domain through marriage, thereby divesting her father of any financial interest in her assets, her claim to the ketubah settlement now becomes equivalent to her saying: **"A maneh of mine is in your possession."** Consequently, we honor the presumption that she was free of defects at the time of her betrothal, and unless her husband can prove otherwise, we support her claim to the ketubah.

אֵיתִיבֵיהּ [4] **Rav Aḥa, the son of Rav Avya, raised an objection against Rav Ashi**'s understanding of the Mishnah from a Baraita concerning a defect discovered in a woman after she has entered her husband's domain through marriage: [5] **"Rabbi Meir agrees in regard to defects which are likely to** have **come with**

RASHI

רב אשי אמר כו׳ — מהדר נמי לאוקמה כולה כרבן גמליאל — דחזקה דגופא עדיפא. ורישא, להכי לא מהניא חזקה דגופא — לפי שאין הטענה שלה אלא של אביה, שכתובת אירוסין לאב והוה ליה ״מנה לאבא בידך״. וגבי אב לא אמרינן בגוף שלה דתיהני חזקתה. מודה רבי מאיר גרסי׳ בתוספתא. אף על גב דאמר: נכנסה לרשות הבעל — על הבעל להביא ראיה, מודה הוא במומין הראויין לבא עמה כו׳. וקא סלקא דעתך בכל מומין שיש לספק ולומר שמבית אביה באו.

NOTES

מָנֶה לְאַבָּא בְּיָדְךָ **A maneh of father's is in your possession.** Our commentary follows the opinion of *Rashi* (which is also adopted by *Tosafot, Meiri* and *Rid*), according to whom Rav Ashi seeks to reconcile the entire Mishnah with the view of Rabban Gamliel, who advocates the presumption of constancy with regard to one's bodily integrity unless the contrary can be proven. Since this presumption only appears to be given weight in the second clause of the Mishnah, Rav Ashi must explain why it does not operate in the first as well, where the betrothed girl is divorced while still in her father's domain. This he does by pointing out that, since it is the father who stands to profit from the ketubah settlement in that situation, any presumption that deals exclusively with the girl is perforce irrelevant. Many Rishonim (see *Ra'ah, Rashba, Ritva* and others) argue against *Rashi*'s approach, insisting that the presumption of a woman's being free from defect until proven otherwise should remain relevant regardless of whether the girl or her father stands to profit from the ketubah as a result. According to these Rishonim, the father cannot rely upon this presumption in claiming the ketubah settlement, because, even according to Rabban Gamliel, it can only be invoked as a valid support to a claim that is put forth with certainty — whereas the father cannot state with absolute assuredness that his daughter did not possess this hidden defect before her betrothal. In the second clause of the Mishnah, where the girl claims the ketubah settlement for herself, the presumption is invoked in support of her claim since she is obviously stating with certainty that her defect first appeared after the betrothal.

מוֹדֶה רַבִּי מֵאִיר **Rabbi Meir agrees.** *Tosafot*'s reading of the Baraita differs somewhat from *Rashi*'s in that it states: "Rabbi Meir *admits to the Sages,* in regard to defects which are likely to have come with her from her father's house, that it is [incumbent] upon the father to bring proof...." The inference is that, in general, the Sages are more favorably disposed toward the husband than Rabbi Meir. *Tosafot* points out the difficulty with this inference, since the Mishnah actually demonstrates the opposite: Rabbi Meir's view is generally more favorable to the husband than that of the Sages, for Rabbi Meir allows the husband to plead betrothal under false pretenses if defects are discovered on a part of her body which is ordinarily visible, whereas the Sages limit him to defects which would ordinarily be hidden from view. Consequently, *Tosafot* favors *Rabbenu Ḥananel*'s reading of the Baraita: "The Sages admit to Rabbi Meir etc...." *Rashi*'s reading, which suggests a somewhat ambiguous "Rabbi Meir agrees," also poses a certain difficulty as it does not make clear with whom Rabbi Meir agrees. *Rabbenu Shimshon* and *Rashba* explain away this difficulty by pointing out that the expression "one agrees" does not necessarily have to imply that one agrees with a disputant, but can sometimes be used as a qualification of a previously held position.

עִמָּהּ מִבֵּית אָבִיהָ, [1]שֶׁעַל הָאָב לְהָבִיא רְאָיָה״. [2]וְאַמַּאי? [3]״מָנֶה לִי בְּיָדְךָ הוּא״!
[4]הָכָא בְּמַאי עָסְקִינַן? [5]בְּיַתֶּירֶת.
[6]יַתֶּירֶת — [7]מַאי רְאָיָה מָיְיתִ?
[8]רְאָיָה דְּרָאָה וְנִיפַּיֵּיס הוּא.
[9]אֲמַר רַב יְהוּדָה אָמַר שְׁמוּאֵל: [10]הַמַּחֲלִיף פָּרָה בַּחֲמוֹר, [11]וּמָשַׁךְ בַּעַל הַחֲמוֹר אֶת הַפָּרָה,

LITERAL TRANSLATION

with her from her father's house, [1]that it is [incumbent] upon the father to bring proof." [2]And why? [3][It is a case of:] "A maneh of mine is in your possession"!

[4]Here with what are we dealing? [5]With a woman with an additional [part of the body]. [6]A woman with an additional [part of the body] — [7]what proof does he bring? [8]Proof that he saw and he was reconciled.

[9]Rav Yehudah said in the name of Shmuel: [10][If] one exchanges a cow for an ass, [11]and the owner of the ass pulled the cow,

TRANSLATION AND COMMENTARY

her from her father's house, [1]**that it is** incumbent **upon the father to bring proof** that they arose only after she had already been betrothed," if he wants his daughter to collect her ketubah settlement. [2]**Why**, according to Rav Ashi, should Rabbi Meir agree even in such a case? [3]Since this **is** a case of the woman claiming **"a maneh of mine is in your possession,"** the presumption that she was free of defects at the time of her betrothal should automatically validate her claim to the ketubah settlement, unless her husband can disprove it.

הָכָא בְּמַאי עָסְקִינַן [4]The Gemara counters Rav Aḥa's objection: **Here,** in the Baraita, **with what case are we dealing?** [5]That of **a woman with an additional part of the body,** such as an extra toe or finger. In such a case, there can be no presumption that she was free of defect at the time of her betrothal since the defect is clearly congenital.

יַתֶּירֶת [6]Now one may ask: If the Baraita is referring to **a woman with an additional part of the body,** [7]**what proof can** the father conceivably **bring** to support his daughter's claim to the ketubah settlement? [8]It must be that he brings **proof that** the husband **saw** the defect before he married the girl **and was reconciled** to it.

אֲמַר רַב יְהוּדָה [9]The Gemara now introduces an Amoraic statement regarding an entirely different topic: **Rav Yehudah said in the name of Shmuel:** [10]**Where one exchanges a cow for an ass,** using the mode of acquisition known as *ḥalifin* ("barter" or "exchange"), whereby one party's taking possession of his animal effects acquisition for both, [11]**and the owner of the ass pulled the cow** — a recognized method of acquisition

RASHI

שעל האב להביא ראיה — ואף על פי שנכנסה לרשות הבעל. **מנה לי בידך הוא** — ונימא: העמד הגוף על חזקתו. **ביתירת** — אצבע יתירה, דליכא למימר לאחר אירוסין נולד. **ומשך בעל החמור את הפרה** — והחמור היה בבית בעליו. ותנן בקדושין (כח,א): כל הנעשה דמים באחר, כיון שזכה זה, שמשך אחד מהם — נתחייב חברו באונסי חליפין, בכל מקום שהן.

NOTES

בְּיַתֶּירֶת **About a woman with an additional part of the body.** *Ramban* explains that the Gemara's clarification of the Baraita refers to a woman with an extra toe, a deformity that would ordinarily be hidden from view — thus strengthening the husband's claim. If the additional part were a finger, we would have to assume that the husband knew about it at the time of betrothal, since it would ordinarily be exposed; thus the burden of proof would fall upon him to show that he did not know about the defect when he betrothed her and, therefore, he should not have to pay her ketubah settlement in the event of divorce.

הַמַּחֲלִיף פָּרָה בַּחֲמוֹר **If one exchanges a cow for an ass.** The commentators find it difficult to explain why the owner of the ass must bear the burden of proof that his animal was still alive when he pulled the cow into his possession. His claim to the cow appears to be supported by two valid presumptions (so long as there is no proof to the contrary): (1) The presumption of ownership accruing to the one who has physical possession, and (2) the presumption that living things (in this case, the ass) retain their physical integrity over time. Why, then, is it not the original owner of the cow who must bear the burden of proof? One answer suggested by *Tosafot,* and adopted by other Rishonim as well, is that the owner of the ass cannot state with absolute certainty that his animal was indeed alive at the exact moment he executed his acquisition of the cow. Therefore the presumptions referred to above are irrelevant. Hence we presume that the cow still belongs to its original owner. Thus, as the one who wishes to change the cow's presumed status, the owner of the ass must bring proof that his acquisition was valid. Another approach to understanding Shmuel's law raised by *Tosafot* (though in the end

HALAKHAH

בְּמוּמִין הָרְאוּיִין לָבֹא עִמָּהּ מִבֵּית אָבִיהָ **With her from her father's house.** "Where a certain defect is discovered in a married woman which appears to be congenital or of early onset, the father must bring proof — should he wish to ensure that his daughter receive her ketubah settlement — that the husband knew about the defect and accepted it before he married her." (*Rambam, Sefer Nashim, Hilkhot Ishut* 25:4; *Shulḥan Arukh, Even HaEzer* 117:7.)

הַמַּחֲלִיף פָּרָה בַּחֲמוֹר **If one exchanges a cow for an ass.** "If a cow is exchanged for an ass, and the owner of the

[1] וְלֹא הִסְפִּיק בַּעַל הַפָּרָה לִמְשׁוֹךְ אֶת הַחֲמוֹר עַד שֶׁמֵּת הַחֲמוֹר — [2] עַל בַּעַל הַחֲמוֹר לְהָבִיא רְאָיָה שֶׁהָיָה חֲמוֹרוֹ קַיָּים בִּשְׁעַת מְשִׁיכַת פָּרָה.
[3] וְתַנָּא תּוּנָא כַּלָּה.
[4] הֵי כַּלָּה? [5] אִילֵימָא [76B] כַּלָּה בְּבֵית אָבִיהָ. [6] מִי דָּמֵי?

LITERAL TRANSLATION

[1] and the owner of the cow could not manage to pull the ass before the ass died — [2] it is [incumbent] upon the owner of the ass to bring proof that his ass was alive at the time of pulling in the cow.

[3] And our Tanna taught [regarding] a bride.

[4] Which [teaching regarding a] bride? [5] If one were to say [76B] a bride in her father's house, [6] is it similar?

TRANSLATION AND COMMENTARY

known as *meshikhah* the "pulling" of an object; [1] **and the owner of the cow did not pull the ass before it died,** [2] **it is** incumbent **upon the owner of the ass to bring proof that his ass was alive at the time the cow was pulled,** should he wish to legitimize the exchange and retain possession of the cow. Otherwise, the cow reverts to its original owner, and the death of the ass is considered as his loss alone.

וְתַנָּא תּוּנָא כַּלָּה [3] Shmuel added: **The Tanna of our Mishnah taught** a law regarding **a bride** with a defect which serves as the basis of his ruling.

הֵי כַּלָּה [4] The Gemara asks: **Which** teaching in our Mishnah, regarding a **bride** and her defects, can be brought as a basis for Shmuel's ruling? [5] **If one were to say** [76B] that support for Shmuel's statement can be brought from the first clause of our Mishnah which deals with the case in which the woman's defects were discovered while, as a bride, she was still living **in her father's house.** In that case, a doubt arose as to whether the woman acquired her defects before or after her betrothal, and in Shmuel's case, a doubt arose as to whether the ass died before or after the cow was acquired. Just as there the father must prove that his daughter was free of defects at the time of her betrothal, and in the absence of such proof, the bridegroom may divorce his wife without paying her ketubah settlement, so too here in the case of barter, the owner of the ass must prove that his animal was alive when he drew the cow into his possession, and in the absence of such proof, the cow must be returned to its original owner. [6] But **are** the two cases really **similar?**

RASHI

עד שמת החמור – זה אומר: עד שלא משכת את פרתי מת חמורך, ולך מת. וזה אומר: משמשכתי מת, וכבר קנוי הוא לך. **ותנא תונא כלה** – תנא דמתניתין דאיירי במומי כלה מסייע ליה. **הי כלה** – הי מילתא דמתניתין מסייעתא? **אילימא כלה בבית אביה** – רישא דמתניתין, שבאו לדין בעודה ארוסה, דקתני: האב צריך להביא ראיה. וסבירא ליה לשמואל כרבי אלעזר דמוקי לה בתרי תנאי, ואפילו נכנסה לחופה אית ליה לתנא דרישא שהאב צריך להביא ראיה, ואף על פי שלא נולד ספק ברשותו. אלמא: אינו גובה ממון מספק. והאי נמי – לא יחזיק בפרת חבירו מספק, ואף על גב שהספק ברשות חבירו נולד, שהרי כבר נעשית משיכה.

NOTES

rejected) involves applying a principle similar to the one we find in matters of ritual impurity (see *Niddah* 4a): Where we find an object in a particular state, we assume that it has maintained that state for as long as it has been in that place. Thus, by finding the ass dead in the domain of its original owner, we must assume that it was dead all along unless its owner can prove otherwise. *Rabbenu Tam* (*Sefer HaYashar,* 1) invokes a similar principle, one we are already familar with, in order to explain Shmuel's position: "Here they were found, and here they came into being." Rav Yehudah is seen as interpreting Shmuel's use of this principle to imply that if the ass is found dead in a particular physical domain (in this case, its original owner's), we must assume that it died while still belonging to that domain. (Accordingly, this rule would only apply if the ass was found dead on its owner's property; were it found dead somewhere else, the burden of proof might indeed devolve upon the owner of the cow.) Rami bar Yeḥezkel (see p. 66b), who ruled in the opposite way, would be seen by *Rabbenu Tam* as interpreting Shmuel's use of the principle in the following way: Since the ass was found dead while in the presumed legal domain of its new owner, having been acquired through the *meshikhah* performed upon the cow that had been his, we must assume that it died while in his possession as well. Thus, the burden of proof falls upon him should he wish to invalidate the acquisition and retrieve his cow. (See *Ramban* and others who raise objections against *Rabbenu Tam*'s explanation.) *Rabbenu Zeraḥyah HaLevi* and *Ra'avad* maintain that the burden of proof always falls upon the party whose ownership is the subject of doubt. Thus, since the initial owner of the ass is the only one whose ownership was at every point certain, he must prove that the ass was still alive at the time of *meshikhah* should he wish to keep the cow.

כַּלָּה בְּבֵית אָבִיהָ **A bride in her father's house.** According to *Rashi,* the Gemara assumes Rabbi Elazar's understanding

HALAKHAH

ass pulls the cow into his possession, should the owner of the cow not manage to pull the ass into his possession before it dies, the owner of the ass must prove that it was alive when he took the cow into his possession. This is because the burden of proof always falls upon the party in whose domain the object in question is found when the doubt comes into being (in accordance with Shmuel). *Rema* notes that, according to some authorities (*Tur* in the name of *Rosh*), the burden of proof falls upon the former owner of the cow, as he is presumed to have acquired the ass at the moment that *meshikhah* was performed on the cow. Thus the ass was in his domain when the doubt came into being (this, in accordance with Rami bar Yeḥezkel)." (*Rambam, Sefer Kinyan, Hilkhot Mekhirah* 20:14; *Shulḥan Arukh, Ḥoshen Mishpat* 224:1.)

TRANSLATION AND COMMENTARY

[1] **There,** in the Mishnah, **the father must bring proof** to support his claim, for he wishes to **collect** his daughter's ketubah settlement from her husband. The burden of proof falls upon the father because the husband is presumed to have rightful ownership of the money in his possession, and the father wishes to challenge that presumption. [2] But **here** Shmuel ruled that **the owner of the ass must bring proof** to support his claim, so that he might **retain** the cow that he had already drawn into his possession. In such a case, it might have been argued that the party who drew the cow into his possession should be recognized as its rightful owner unless proved otherwise.

אָמַר רַבִּי אַבָּא [3] **Rabbi Abba said:** Support for Shmuel's statement can be brought from the second clause of our Mishnah, where the woman's defects were discovered after **the bride** was married and living **in her father-in-law's house.** Just as there the husband must prove his claim that his wife already had her defects at the time of her betrothal, and only if he provides such proof may he retain his wife's ketubah settlement, so too here, in the case of barter, the owner of the ass must prove that his animal was alive when he acquired the cow. Otherwise he will have to surrender it.

[1] הָתָם, מַיְיתֵי אָב רְאָיָה וּמַפֵּיק; [2] הָכָא מַיְיתֵי בַּעַל הַחֲמוֹר רְאָיָה וּמוֹקִים! [3] אָמַר רַבִּי אַבָּא: כַּלָּה בְּבֵית חָמִיהָ.

LITERAL TRANSLATION

[1] There, the father brings proof and collects; [2] here, the owner of the ass brings proof and retains! [3] Rabbi Abba said: A bride in her father-in-law's house.

RASHI

מי דמי התם – דין הוא שצריך להביא ראיה, שהרי הוא המוציא מחברו, הלכך מייתי ראיה ומפיק ממונא. ומשם אתה בא ללמוד את זה שמוחזק בפרה זו ועומד, ואת אומר: נייתי ראיה ונוקים ממון שבידו? **כלה בבית חמיה** – סיפא דמתניתין, דקתני על הבעל להביא ראיה, דרבן גמליאל אמרה. ופליג נמי ברישא, אפילו נמצאו בבית אביה, דלא נולד ספק ברשותו – נמי על הבעל להביא ראיה להפקיע כח כתובתה. וראיה זו לא להוציא היא אלא להחזיק, וצריך להביאה. ואף זה – כל שכן שיביא ראיה להחזיק, שהרי בשל אחרים בא להחזיק.

NOTES

of the Mishnah (see above, p. 75b), that there is an irreconcilable contradiction between Rabbi Yehoshua and Rabban Gamliel. Rabbi Yehoshua ruled that if the woman's defects were discovered while she was still in her father's house, her father must prove his claim that she acquired those defects only after she was betrothed, and he must also bring such proof even if the defects were not discovered until his daughter had entered into her husband's possession in marriage. Contrary to this position, Rabban Gamliel ruled that if the woman's defects were not discovered until she had entered into marriage, the husband must prove his claim that she had acquired those defects before her betrothal, and the husband must bring such proof even if the defects were discovered while the woman was still in her father's house. Thus, when the Gemara suggests that support for Shmuel can be brought from the Mishnah's ruling regarding a bride who was still living in her father's house, it refers to Rabbi Yehoshua's position. Just as, according to Rabbi Yehoshua, the father must prove that his daughter acquired her defects only after her betrothal, even though the doubt arose while she was already in her husband's possession, so too here in the case of *ḥalifin* ("barter" or "exchange"), the owner of the ass must prove his claim that his animal was alive when he acquired the cow, even though the doubt arose while the ass was already in the other party's possession. Conversely, when the Gemara suggests that support for Shmuel can be brought from the Mishnah's ruling regarding a bride who was already living in her father-in-law's house, it means that support can be brought from Rabban Gamliel. Just as, according to Rabban Gamliel, the husband must prove that the woman had acquired her defects before her betrothal, even though the doubt arose while she was still living in her father's house, so, too, in the case of *ḥalifin,* must the owner of the ass prove his claim that his animal was alive when he acquired the cow, even though the doubt arose while the ass was already in the other party's possession. When Rav Naḥman concludes that support for Shmuel can be brought from the Mishnah's ruling regarding a bride who was still living in her father's house, he, too, meant that support can be brought from Rabbi Yehoshua. *Rashi* argues that the Gemara cannot be understood according to Rava or Rav Ashi, for they maintain that the burden of proof falls upon the party in whose possession the bride was at the time that the doubt arose — the father, if she was still living in his house; and the husband, if she had already entered into marriage. By contrast, Shmuel maintains that the burden of proof falls upon the owner of the ass, even though the ass was not in his possession when the doubt arose. *Tosafot* and most Rishonim raise various objections against *Rashi*'s interpretation of the Gemara.

As was explained in the previous note, *Rabbenu Tam* understands that Shmuel's ruling is based on the principle: Here they were found, and here they came into being. Since the ass was found dead in the house of its original owner, it is assumed to have died while it was still in his possession. Thus, the owner of the ass must prove that his ass was alive when he drew the cow into his possession. Otherwise the cow must be returned to its original owner. According to *Rabbenu Tam,* just as the father must prove his claim if his daughter's defects were discovered while she was still living in his house, and just as the husband must prove his claim if his wife's defects were discovered only after she entered his house in marriage, so, too, must the owner of the ass prove his claim, for otherwise we assume that the ass died while it was in his possession.

Rabbenu Zeraḥyah HaLevi (see previous note) understands that, according to Shmuel, the burden of proof always falls upon the party whose property is the subject of the doubt.

LITERAL TRANSLATION

[1]But still it is not similar. [2]There, the husband brings proof [3]and weakens the presumption of the father; [4]here, the owner of the ass brings proof [5]and confirms the presumption in his hand!

[6]Rav Naḥman bar Yitzḥak said: A bride in her father's house, [7]and for the [bride's] betrothal [money].

[1]וְאַכַּתִּי לָא דָּמֵי. [2]הָתָם, בַּעַל מַיְיתֵי רְאָיָה [3]וּמֵרַע לֵיהּ לְחַזְקֵיהּ דְּאָב; [4]הָכָא, בַּעַל הַחֲמוֹר מַיְיתֵי רְאָיָה [5]וּמוֹקִים חַזְקֵיהּ בִּידֵיהּ!

[6]אֲמַר רַב נַחְמָן בַּר יִצְחָק: כַּלָּה בְּבֵית אָבִיהָ, [7]וּלְקִדּוּשִׁין.

TRANSLATION AND COMMENTARY

וְאַכַּתִּי [1]**But still** the two cases **are not similar,** since the former weakens a presumption and the latter confirms one. [2]**There,** in the Mishnah, **the husband must bring proof to** support his claim, because we presume that his wife had no defects until the moment when it can be proven that she did have them, and this presumption supports the father's claim that his daughter is entitled to receive her ketubah settlement, [3]**and** so the husband must bring proof in order to **weaken** that **presumption** which supports **the father.** The presumption that she remained free of defects is stronger than the presumption that the husband has rightful ownership of the money in his possession. [4]But **here** Shmuel ruled that **the owner of the ass must bring proof** to support his claim, even though his claim is supported by the presumption that a previously known state of affairs persists until the contrary can be proved. For just as a woman is presumed to have remained free of defects until the moment it can be proved that she had the defects, so too is the ass presumed to have been alive until the moment it can be proved that it was dead. If the owner of the ass must bring proof to support his claim, [5]it can only be to further **confirm the presumption** that the ass was alive when he acquired the cow.

אֲמַר [6]**Rav Naḥman bar Yitzḥak said:** In fact, support for Shmuel's statement can be brought from the first clause of our Mishnah, which deals with defects that were discovered while **the bride** was still living **in her father's house.** As for the objection raised earlier, that in the case of the Mishnah the father must bring proof in order to collect his daughter's ketubah settlement from her husband, whereas in Shmuel's case the owner of the ass must bring proof in order to retain the cow he had already drawn into his possession, there is really no difficulty, for the father must bring proof not only to collect his daughter's ketubah settlement, [7]but also to retain **for** himself his daughter's **betrothal money.** For if the father cannot prove that his daughter was free of defects at the time of her betrothal, the husband can claim that the betrothal was made in error, and demand a refund of the money he gave the bride's father in order to effect her betrothal. Just as the Mishnah rules that the father must prove his claim that his daughter was free of defects at the time of her betrothal, so that he may retain the betrothal money, so too, argues Shmuel, must the owner of the ass prove his claim that his animal was alive when he drew the cow into his possession, so that he

RASHI

ואכתי לא דמי התם — דין הוא שיצטרך לראיה, משום דחזקת הגוף מייפה כח האב, ויש לומר: העמידנו על חזקתו. הלכך בעל מייתי ראיה שעד שלא תתארס היו בה, ומרע לה להאי חזקה. הכי גרסינן: **הכא בעל החמור מייתי ראיה ואוקי חזקה בידיה** — אף חזקת הגוף מייפה את כחו, שכשתאמר העמד את החמור בשעת משיכה על חזקתו הקודמת — בחזקת חי תעמידנו, וברשות בעל הפרה מת. ולמה אתה מצריכו ראיה? **אמר רב נחמן בר יצחק כלה בבית אביה ולקדושין** — רישא דמתניתין סייעתיה, דמטיל הבאת ראיה על האב אף על פי שחזקת גוף אצלו. וכרבי אלעזר דאמר: רבי יהושע היא, ובסיפא נמי פליג [להטיל ראיה על אב], ואף על פי שלא נולד ספק ברשותו. ודקשיא לך: ההיא ראיה להוציא היא — הראיה צריכה לו אף לעכב לו הקדושין שבידו, שאם לא יביא ראיה — יחזירם, וזו — להחזיק היא בידו.

NOTES

כַּלָּה בְּבֵית אָבִיהָ וּלְקִדּוּשִׁין **A bride in her father's house, and for the betrothal money.** *Rashi* explains that the father must bring proof that his daughter acquired her defect(s) only after her betrothal, not only so that she may collect her ketubah settlement, but also so that he may retain the money which he had received from his son-in-law to effect his daughter's betrothal. *Ramban* asks: How does Rav Naḥman know that the father must prove his claim in order to retain his daughter's betrothal money? Perhaps he only has to bring proof in order to collect her ketubah settlement! And if Rav Naḥman came to that conclusion through his own reasoning, how can he say that our Mishnah supports Shmuel's ruling? *Ramban* explains that the Mishnah deals with a case where the husband did not write the woman a ketubah, for the ketubah is usually not written at the time of betrothal, but rather at the time of marriage. Thus, the monetary claim can only relate to the betrothal money. *Rashba* points out that, according to *Rashi*, Rav Naḥman brings support for Shmuel's ruling from the case where the woman's defects were not discovered until she entered into her husband's possession in marriage, and in that case the woman is certainly entitled to a ketubah settlement. Rather, the Mishnah implies that the father must bring proof not only to collect his daughter's ketubah settlement, but also to retain her betrothal money, for if the husband must bring proof to collect the betrothal money, the Mishnah should not have said that the burden of proof falls upon the father, for the burden of proof falls also upon the husband.

TRANSLATION AND COMMENTARY

may retain the cow. Rav Naḥman bar Yitzḥak added: [1]**And do not say** that that which was just said — that if the father wishes to keep the betrothal money, he must prove that she was free of defects at the time of her betrothal — is only true **according to the** authority **who said:** [2]**The betrothal money is not given by** the bridegroom to his bride with the intention **that it should be lost** if for some reason the betrothal does not lead to marriage. According to this authority, we well understand that the father must prove that his daughter was free of defects at the time of her betrothal, so that he may retain the betrothal money. [3]But **rather,** this is true **even according to the** authority **who said:** [4]**The betrothal money is given** by the bridegroom to his bride with the knowledge **that it will be lost** to him if for some reason the betrothal does not lead to marriage. [5]Even that authority agrees that **this** only **applies to a betrothal** whose validity was **certain.** [6]**But** if **the betrothal** was nullified because it had been made **in error,** the bridegroom claiming that he betrothed his wife under false pretenses, the law is different. [7]If the father **can bring proof** that his daughter was free of defects at the time of her betrothal, he may **indeed** keep the betrothal money. [8]But **if** he is **not able** to bring such proof, he may **not** keep it. The Gemara here has drawn a parallel between two situations of doubt: (1) When did the bride acquire her defects? And: (2) When did the ass die? By shifting the discussion in the first case from the ketubah settlement to the betrothal money, the Gemara has made possession in both cases depend on the resolution of doubt. Both the Mishnah and Shmuel argue that those whose possession is in doubt (the bride's father and the ass's owner) must prove the validity of their claims.

מֵיתִיבֵי [9]**An objection was raised** against Shmuel's position from a Baraita, which stated: [10]If **a needle was found** stuck **in the thick wall of the second stomach** of a ritually slaughtered animal, [11]but it only protruded **from one side** of the organ's wall, the animal **is kosher,** for the organ was not wholly perforated by the needle. [12]If, however, the needle protruded **from both sides** of the organ's wall, the animal **is not kosher,** for the complete perforation to the cavity of the second stomach is included among the defects and injuries that will cause an animal to die within the next twelve months and therefore render it trefah and forbidden to be eaten. [13]**If a drop of** dry **blood was found on** the tip of the needle,

[1]וְלָא תֵּימָא אַלִּיבָּא דְּמַאן דְּאָמַר: [2]קִדּוּשִׁין לָאו לְטִיבּוּעִין נִיתְּנוּ. [3]אֶלָּא אֲפִילּוּ לְמַאן דְּאָמַר: [4]קִדּוּשִׁין לְטִיבּוּעִין נִיתְּנוּ [5]הָנֵי מִילֵּי קִידּוּשֵׁי וַדַּאי. [6]אֲבָל קִידּוּשֵׁי טָעוּת, [7]אִי מַיְיתֵי רְאָיָה אִין; [8]אִי לָא, לָא.
[9]מֵיתִיבֵי: [10]״מַחַט שֶׁנִּמְצֵאת בְּעוֹבִי בֵּית הַכּוֹסוֹת, [11]מִצַּד אֶחָד, כְּשֵׁרָה; [12]מִשְּׁנֵי צְדָדִין טְרֵפָה. [13]נִמְצָא עָלֶיהָ קוֹרֶט דָּם,

LITERAL TRANSLATION

[1]And do not say according to the one who said: [2]The betrothal [money] is not given to be sunk. [3]But rather even according to the one who said: [4]The betrothal [money] is given to be sunk — [5]this applies (lit., "these words") to a betrothal [which is] certain. [6]But a betrothal in error, [7]if he brings proof, yes; [8]if not, no.

[9]They raised an objection: [10]"A needle which was found in the thick wall of the second stomach, [11]from one side, it is kosher; [12]from both sides, it is not kosher. [13][If] a drop of blood was found on it,

RASHI

ולא תימא — הא דאמינא שהראיה צריכה אף לעכב לו הקדושין שבידו. **אליבא דמאן דאמר קדושין לאו לטיבועין ניתנו** — שאם קדושין לאו לטיבועין ניתנו, שאם מת החתן — הקדושין חוזרין. הלכך הכא, כי הוו קדושין ספק — אין כחה יפה בהן, וצריכה להביא ראיה. והך פלוגתא בבבא בתרא. ואי קשיא: היכי מוקמינן סוגיא דשמעתא דשמואל כרבי אלעזר, ומדרבי יהושע מייתי סייעתא, הא שמואל הלכה כרבן גמליאל אמר בפרק קמא (כתובות יב,ב)! — אין הכי נמי, ומסקנא מוקמינן דלא אמר שמואל הכי. ואם תאמר: מי מזקיקני להעמיד סוגיא זו בלשון זה? נוקמה כרבא ורב אשי! אי אפשר לומר, דקשיא לרבא ורב אשי מתניתין דווקא קתני; רישא על האב וסיפא על הבעל שהספק נולד ברשותן. ואילו שמואל — על מי שלא נולד הספק ברשותו הצריך לבקש ראיה. **בעובי בית הכוסות** — מקום יש בראש הכרס סמוך להמסס קרוי בית הכוסות, שהוא כעין כוס, ויש בו סביב שפתו עובי שני כפלים כפולים ודבוקים, ובלעז *לדובלי״ן. ונמצא מחט תחובה באותו עובי, ומתוך עוביו אפשר לה שלא נקבתה כולו. **מצד אחד** — אין המחט נראה אלא מבפנים. **כשרה** — שאין זה נקב.

LANGUAGE (RASHI)

לדובלי״ן* From the Old French *doblon* meaning the thick wall of the second stomach of an animal that chews its cud.

HALAKHAH

קִדּוּשִׁין לְטִיבּוּעִין נִיתְּנוּ **The betrothal money is given for being sunk.** "If someone betrothed a woman, whether he retracted or she retracted, whether he died or she died or he divorced her, the betrothal money need not be returned, even if the bridegroom paid a thousand dinars. This only applies to a betrothal whose validity was certain; but if the betrothal was nullified because it had been made in error, the betrothal money must be returned to the bridegroom." (*Rambam, Sefer Kinyan, Hilkhot Zekhiyah U'Matanah* 6:18-19; *Shulḥan Arukh, Even HaEzer* 50:1.)

מַחַט שֶׁנִּמְצֵאת בְּעוֹבִי בֵּית הַכּוֹסוֹת **A needle which was found in the thick wall of the second stomach.** "If a needle was found stuck in the thick wall of the second stomach of a ritually slaughtered animal, but the needle did not wholly perforate the organ, the animal is kosher. But if the needle perforated the organ, and a drop of blood was found

LITERAL TRANSLATION

[1]we know that it was from before the slaughter. [2][If] a drop of blood was not found on it, [3]we know that it was from after the slaughter. [4][If] the surface of the wound was covered with a scab, [5]we know that it was from three days before the slaughter. [6][If] the surface of the wound was not covered with a scab, [7]the one who [seeks to] remove from his fellow, upon him is the [burden] of proof." [8]And if the butcher gave the money, [9]he must bring proof [in order to] collect. [10]But why? [11]The owner of the animal should have to bring proof [12][in order to] retain!
[13]If the butcher did not give the money.

[1]בְּיָדוּעַ שֶׁהוּא לִפְנֵי שְׁחִיטָה.
[2]לֹא נִמְצָא עָלֶיהָ קוֹרֶט דָּם,
[3]בְּיָדוּעַ שֶׁהוּא לְאַחַר שְׁחִיטָה.
[4]הוּגְלַד פִּי הַמַּכָּה, [5]בְּיָדוּעַ
שֶׁשְּׁלֹשָׁה יָמִים קוֹדֶם שְׁחִיטָה.
[6]לֹא הוּגְלַד פִּי הַמַּכָּה, [7]הַמּוֹצִיא
מֵחֲבֵירוֹ עָלָיו הָרְאָיָה״. [8]וְאִי
יָהֵיב טַבָּח דָּמֵי, [9]בָּעֵי לְאִיתּוּיֵי
רְאָיָה וּמַפֵּיק. [10]וְאַמַּאי? [11]בַּעַל
בְּהֵמָה לַיְיתֵי רְאָיָה [12]וְנוֹקִים!
[13]בִּדְלָא יָהֵיב טַבָּחָא דָּמֵי.

TRANSLATION AND COMMENTARY

[1]**we know** that the perforation **was** made **before** the animal **was slaughtered,** and so the animal is forbidden as trefah. [2]But **if a drop of blood was not found on** the tip of the needle, [3]**we know that** the organ **was** perforated only **after** the animal **was slaughtered,** and so the animal remains fit to be eaten. [4]**If the surface of the wound** caused by the needle **was covered with a scab,** [5]**we know that** the needle perforated the organ at least **three days before** the animal **was slaughtered, allowing** the wound to begin to heal and form a scab. Thus, if the butcher purchased the animal from its previous owner less than three days prior to the animal's slaughter, it was a purchase made in error, for the animal was already then trefah, and so the butcher may demand a refund of his purchase money. [6]But **if the surface of the wound** caused by the needle **was not** yet **covered with a scab,** it cannot be determined with certainty when the animal suffered the wound that rendered it trefah. [7]In cases of doubt, it **is on the one who seeks to take** money **away from his fellow to provide** the **proof.** A defendant is presumed to have rightful ownership of the money in his possession unless the plaintiff can prove his claim. [8]Now, it follows from the Baraita that **if the butcher** already **paid** for the animal, so that he is the plaintiff demanding a refund, [9]it is **he** who **must bring proof, and** only then may he **collect** the purchase money from the person who sold him the animal. [10]**But** according to Shmuel, **why** is this so? If, as Shmuel says, the owner of the ass must bring proof that his ass was alive at the time he drew the cow into his possession, and only then may he retain possession of the cow, [11]so too **the** previous **owner of the animal should have to bring proof** that his animal was only rendered trefah after it had already been sold to the butcher, [12]**and** only then should he be permitted to **retain** for himself the purchase money he received from the butcher!

בִּדְלָא [13]The Gemara answers: When the Baraita stated that the burden of proof falls upon the plaintiff, it was referring to a case **where the butcher had not** yet **paid** for the animal, but purchased it on credit. If the previous owner of the animal wishes to receive the money which the butcher has agreed to pay for the animal, he must prove that his animal was not trefah at the time of the sale, otherwise the butcher is not required to pay for the animal, for we accept his claim that his purchase was made in error.

RASHI

שהוא לפני שחיטה — וטריפה. **שהוא לאחר שחיטה** — וכשירה. **שלשה ימים קודם שחיטה** — ואם לקחה טבח זה בתוך שלשה ימים — מקח טעות הוא, ויחזיר לו בעליה הדמים — שמכר לו טריפה. **לא הוגלד פי המכה** — זה אומר: עד שלא לקחתי ניקב, וזה אומר: משמכרתי. **המוציא מחבירו כו׳** — ואי יהיב הטבח דמי — נמצא הוא המוציא, ועליו הראיה. ואי לא אשכח ראיה — יחזיק זה במעותיו מספק, והרי בבהמתו נמצא ריעותא, דומיא דחמור דשמואל. **ואמאי** — אי כשמואל — לייתי בעל בהמה ראיה להעמיד המעות בידו, דומיא דבעל החמור. **דלא יהיב טבח דמי** — הא דקתני המוציא מחבירו — בבעל בהמה קאמר, וכגון דאיהו קא תבע.

HALAKHAH

there, the animal is forbidden as trefah, for it is clear that the needle perforated the organ before the animal was slaughtered. However, if no blood is found, the animal is kosher, for it is clear that the organ was perforated only after the animal was slaughtered. If the surface of the wound was covered with a scab, we know that the animal became trefah at least three days before it was slaughtered. If the wound was not covered by a scab, it cannot be determined when the animal became trefah. In such a case the butcher must prove that the animal was already trefah at the time of purchase, and if he is unable to do so he must pay the animal's previous owner for the animal he purchased." (*Rambam, Sefer Kinyan, Hilkhot Mekhirah* 20:15; *Sefer Kedushah, Hilkhot Shekhitah* 6:12; *Shulḥan Arukh, Yoreh De'ah* 48:8; *Ḥoshen Mishpat* 224:2.)

[1] מַאי פָּסְקָא?
[2] אֶלָּא, כִּי אֲתָא רָמִי בַּר יְחֶזְקֵאל, אֲמַר: [3] לָא תְּצַיְּיתִינְהוּ לְהָנֵי כְּלָלֵי דְּכָיֵיל יְהוּדָה אָחִי מִשְּׁמֵיהּ דִּשְׁמוּאֵל. [4] הָכִי אֲמַר שְׁמוּאֵל: [5] כָּל שֶׁנּוֹלַד סָפֵק בִּרְשׁוּתוֹ,

LITERAL TRANSLATION

[1] Why the unqualified ruling?
[2] Rather, when Rami bar Yeḥezkel came, he said: [3] Do not obey those rules which Yehudah, my brother, ruled in the name of Shmuel. [4] Thus said Shmuel: [5] He in whose possession the doubt came into being,

RASHI

מאי פסקא – בתמיה: מאי קאמרת? אי סבירא ליה לתנא דלעולם ראיה על בעל בהמה היא – בין הוא המוציא ובין הוא המעמיד, היאך הוא שונה "המוציא מחבירו" בבעל בהמה, וקורהו לבעל בהמה לעולם "המוציא מחבירו"? וכי פסק התנא דבר קבוע שלעולם מוכרים בהמות באמנה, והוא המוציא?! **יהודה אחי** – רב יהודה ורמי שניהם בני (רב) יחזקאל הוו. **כל שנולד ספק ברשותו** – על בעל הפרה להביא ראיה שמת החמור קודם משיכה, הואיל וספק ברשותו נולד – שלא נמצא החמור מת עד לאחר משיכת פרה.

TRANSLATION AND COMMENTARY

מַאי פָּסְקָא [1] However, if the Baraita applies only under particular circumstances, **why** does it make **an unqualified ruling?** Why does the Baraita invoke the sweeping rule that the burden of proof falls upon the party seeking to take money away from his fellow, implying that the burden of proof always falls upon the plaintiff?

אֶלָּא [2] **Rather, when Rami bar Yeḥezkel came** to Babylonia from Eretz Israel, **he said:** [3] **Do not accept** as authoritative **those rules which Yehudah, my brother, stated in the name of Shmuel,** for some of the traditions he reported in Shmuel's name are misquotations. [4] As for the matter under discussion, **Shmuel** did not formulate his ruling as was reported by my brother, but **said as follows:** If someone exchanged a cow for an ass using *ḥalifin,* and the owner of the ass drew the cow into his possession, but the owner of the cow did not manage to draw the ass into his possession before the ass died, and the original owner of the cow claimed that the ass died before his cow was drawn into the other party's possession, so that the whole transaction was null and void, but the owner of the ass claimed that the transaction was valid because his animal died only after he drew the cow into his possession, [5] in such a case it is **he whose possession the doubt came into being**

NOTES

מַאי פָּסְקָא? What is this rule? Sometimes the Talmud interprets a Mishnah (or a Biblical verse) as applying only under particular circumstances, though these are not specified in the text itself. This may be done to rebut an objection or to reconcile contradictory sources. In such cases, the Talmud may ask: "Why the unqualified, categorical statement?" In other words: How can you interpret the Mishnah (or Biblical verse) as applying only under limited conditions, if this is not explicitly stated in the text? As the Gemara explains, below, sometimes there is a good reason for establishing a Mishnah as referring to a particular case. But here it is problematic to say that people always sell their animals on credit, so that the Mishnah can invoke the rule that the burden of proof falls upon the plaintiff, when it means that the burden of proof falls upon the original owner of the animal.

כָּל שֶׁנּוֹלַד סָפֵק בִּרְשׁוּתוֹ He in whose possession the doubt came into being. Our commentary follows *Rashi, Rabbenu Tam, Rosh* and others, who understand that Rami bar Yeḥezkel disagrees with his brother Rav Yehudah and says that the burden of proof falls on the party in whose possession the doubt came into being, which in Shmuel's case is the owner of the cow, for the ass was found to be dead only after the cow had already been drawn into the other party's possession, at which time the original owner of the cow automatically acquired the ass. As was explained in an earlier note (p. 76a, s.v., המחליף את הפרה), *Rabbenu Tam* explains that both Rav Yehudah and Rami bar Yeḥezkel understood that Shmuel's ruling is based on the principle: Here they were found, and here they came into being. According to Rav Yehudah, the ass is assumed to have died while it was owned by the person in whose physical possession it was found to be dead, and so the burden of proof falls upon the owner of the ass. According to Rami bar Yeḥezkel, the ass is assumed to have died while it was owned by the person in whose *legal* possession it was found to be dead, and so the burden of proof falls upon owner of the cow.

Rabbenu Zeraḥyah HaLevi, Ra'avad and others understand that Rami bar Yeḥezkel agrees with Rav Yehudah about Shmuel's opinion, that the burden of proof falls upon the owner of the ass. The two disagree only about Shmuel's rationale. According to Rav Yehudah, the burden of proof falls upon the party whose property is the subject of the doubt. The ass was certainly at some point in the possession of its first owner, and so it is he who must prove that it was still alive when he drew the cow into his possession. According to Rami bar Yeḥezkel, the burden of proof falls upon the party in whose physical possession the animal was found to be dead. Since the ass was discovered to be dead while it was still in its first owner's house, he must prove that the animal was still alive when the cow was drawn into his possession. *Ra'ah, Rashba* and others note that *Rif* (and apparently *Rambam* as well) must have understood the Gemara in a similar fashion, for he records Rav Yehudah's version of Shmuel's position as law.

HALAKHAH

כָּל שֶׁנּוֹלַד סָפֵק בִּרְשׁוּתוֹ He in whose possession the doubt came into being. "In cases of doubt, the burden of proof falls upon the person in whose domain the doubt came into being," following Rami bar Yeḥezkel. (*Rambam, Sefer Kinyan, Hilkhot Mekhirah* 20:14; *Shulḥan Arukh, Ḥoshen Mishpat* 224:1.)

TRANSLATION AND COMMENTARY

upon whom falls the burden of proof. The original owner of the cow must prove that the ass died before his cow was drawn into the other party's possession. The doubt regarding the time of the ass's death arose while it was in his possession, for the ass was only found to be dead after the cow had already been drawn into the other party's possession.

וְתַנָּא תּוּנָא כַּלָּה [1]Shmuel added: **The Tanna of our Mishnah** who **taught** a law regarding the defects discovered in **a bride** supports this ruling. For our Mishnah teaches that if a betrothed woman's defects were discovered while she was still living in her father's house, the father must prove that she acquired those defects only after she had already been betrothed. And if her defects were only discovered after she had already entered into her husband's possession in marriage, the husband must bring proof to his claim that she possessed those defects before the betrothal. Thus we see from the Mishnah that the burden of proof falls upon the party in whose possession the doubt came into being, as argued by Shmuel in the new version of his teaching.

מֵיתִיבֵי [2]**An objection was raised** against this version of Shmuel's statement from the Baraita, which stated: If **a needle was found** stuck **in the thick wall of the second stomach** of a ritually slaughtered animal, the burden of proof as to when the animal had become trefah falls upon the party who seeks to take money

LITERAL TRANSLATION

upon him is [the burden of] proof.

[1]And our Tanna taught a bride.

[2]They raised an objection: "A needle which was found in the thick wall of the second stomach, etc."

עָלָיו הָרְאָיָה.

[1]וְתַנָּא תּוּנָא כַּלָּה.

[2]מֵיתִיבֵי: ״מַחַט שֶׁנִּמְצֵאת בְּעוֹבִי בֵּית הַכּוֹסוֹת כו׳״.

RASHI

ותנא תונא כלה – וסבירא ליה לשמואל דכולה מתניתין חד תנא הוא, וכדתרצה רבא לעיל. ורישא וסיפא סייעתא, שמי שנמצא, הסימפון ברשותו – עליו להביא ראיה: עודה בבית אביה – על האב להביא ראיה, נכנסה לחופה שהיא ברשות הבעל – על הבעל להביא ראיה. ואפילו הוא דר בבית חמיו – ברשותו היא.

NOTES

עָלָיו הָרְאָיָה **Upon him is the burden of proof.** *Tosafot* and others raise an objection: Elsewhere (*Bava Metzia* 100a), the Mishnah states that if someone exchanged a cow for an ass, and the owner of the cow drew the ass into his possession, thereby simultaneously transferring ownership of the cow to the other person, and at approximately the same time the cow gave birth, but it is not known whether it gave birth before the former owner of the cow drew the ass into his possession, in which case the calf belongs to him, or whether the cow gave birth after the transaction was completed, in which case the calf belongs to the cow's new owner, the two parties must divide the value of the calf between them. Regarding this Mishnah the Gemara asks: Why should the two parties divide the calf between them? Let us see in whose possession the calf is now found, and let the other party be considered the one who is seeking to take property away from someone else, so that he must prove his claim! *Tosafot* asks: Why, according to the Gemara in *Bava Metzia*, should the burden of proof fall upon the original owner of the ass, if the calf was in the possession of the original owner of the cow? Just as in our case we assume that the ass died after it had been acquired by the former owner of the cow, so that the burden of proof falls upon him if he claims otherwise, so too in the case of the calf we should assume that the calf was born after the cow had been acquired by the former owner of the ass, so that the burden of proof should fall upon the former owner of the cow if he claims otherwise! *Tosafot* distinguishes between a doubt which is לטיבותא (lit., "advantageous") and a doubt which is לגריעותא (lit., "disadvantageous"). *Rivash* (cited by *Shittah Mekubbetzet* and *Maharam Schiff*) understands that *Tosafot* means that here, if the doubt is לגריעותא, it might lead to a nullification of the transaction (for if the ass died before the act of acquisition was completed, the exchange is void). Thus the burden of proof falls upon the party in whose possession the doubt arose. But if the doubt is לטיבותא, it will not lead to a nullification of the transaction (for there is no dispute about the validity of the exchange, but only about who is entitled to the calf). Hence we do not consider in whose possession the doubt arose, but only who has present possession of the calf. *Shittah Mekubbetzet* explains that *Tosafot* means that in cases of doubt we do not actively (לטיבותא) remove property from one party and award it to another, and the former owner of the ass must prove that he is entitled to the calf; and if he is unable to do so, the calf remains with the former owner of the cow, who has present possession of the animal. But we passively (לגריעותא) allow the present situation to continue, and so it falls upon the former owner of the cow to prove that the ass died before the act of acquisition that had been performed on his cow was completed; and if he is unable to do so, the former owner of the ass keeps the cow, and the former owner of the cow keeps the dead ass.

וְתַנָּא תּוּנָא כַּלָּה **And our Tanna taught a bride.** The Rishonim explain this statement in various ways, according to their understanding of the entire passage (see above, note s.v. כל שנולד). Our commentary follows *Rashi,* who understands that Rami bar Yeḥezkel supports Shmuel's ruling both with the first clause of the Mishnah dealing with the bride whose defects were discovered while she was still living in her father's house, as well as with the second clause dealing with the bride whose defects were only discovered after she had already entered into her husband's possession in marriage. According to *Tosafot,* only the second clause supports Shmuel's ruling. According to *Ra'a'vad* and *Rabbenu Zeraḥyah HaLevi,* support for Shmuel's ruling is brought from the first clause.

TRANSLATION AND COMMENTARY

away from his fellow. [1]Now, it follows from the Baraita that **if the butcher did not yet pay** for the animal which he purchased, so that the animal's original owner is the plaintiff demanding the purchase money, [2]it is **the** original **owner of the animal** who **must bring proof** to his claim that the animal only became trefah after it had already been sold to the butcher, [3]**and only** then may he **collect** the purchase money from him. [4]**But** according to Rami bar Yeḥezkel's version of Shmuel's position, **why** is this so? If the burden of proof falls upon the party in whose possession the doubt came into being, the butcher should have to bring proof that the animal became trefah before he bought it, [5]for **the doubt came into being** while the animal **was in the butcher's possession,** and if he is unable to provide such proof, he should be required to pay for the animal.

דְּיָהֵיב טַבָּח דְּמֵי [6]The Gemara answers: When the Baraita stated that the burden of proof falls upon the plaintiff, it was referring to the case **where the butcher had** already **paid** for the animal. If the butcher wishes to receive a refund, he must prove that the animal was already trefah at the time of the purchase. If the butcher is unable to provide such proof, the animal's previous owner is not required to refund the money, for we accept his claim that the sale was valid.

וּמַאי פָּסְקָא [7]The Gemara asks: But if the Baraita applies only under particular circumstances, **why** does it make **an unqualified ruling?** Why does the Baraita invoke the principle that the burden of proof falls upon the party seeking to take money away from his fellow, implying that the burden of proof always falls upon the plaintiff?

סְתָמָא דְּמִילְּתָא [8]The Gemara answers: **The general way of things is that as long as the person** buying the animal **does not give the seller** the purchase **money,** [9]**the person** selling the animal **does not give** the purchaser **the animal**. Thus the butcher would ordinarily have paid for the animal before he slaughtered it. And so in the case where a doubt arose as to whether the animal had been trefah at the time of the sale, ordinarily the plaintiff would be the butcher seeking a refund of the purchase money, and not the animal's previous owner seeking payment for his animal. Thus, it is appropriate for the Baraita to refer to the butcher as the party who wishes to take money away from his fellow.

וַחֲכָמִים אוֹמְרִים [10]We learn in the next clause of the Mishnah: **And the Sages say: When does this apply** that the husband can claim that he had betrothed his wife in error, and so can divorce her without paying her ketubah settlement? [11]When it is discovered that she has **defects on a part** of her body **which is** ordinarily **covered,** in which case the husband can claim that he did not know of them, and had he been aware of them, he would never have betrothed the woman. But if it is discovered that the woman has defects on a part of her body which is ordinarily visible, the husband cannot claim that he betrothed her in error, for surely he knew of the defects at the time of the betrothal, and he agreed to betroth her despite her imperfections. [12]**Rav Naḥman said:** [77A] [13]**And an epileptic is** treated **like** one who suffers from **"defects that are hidden** from view." Thus, a man who discovers that he married an epileptic under false pretenses can divorce her without having to pay her ketubah settlement.

[1]וְאִי דְּלָא יָהֵיב טַבָּח דְּמֵי [2]בַּעַל בְּהֵמָה בָּעֵי לְאִיתוּיֵי רְאָיָה [3]וּמַפֵּיק. [4]וְאַמַּאי? [5]סְפֵיקָא בִּרְשׁוּת טַבָּח אִיתְיְילִיד! [6]דְּיָהֵיב טַבָּח דְּמֵי. [7]וּמַאי פָּסְקָא? [8]סְתָמָא דְּמִילְּתָא כַּמָּה דְּלָא יָהֵיב אִינִישׁ זוּזֵי [9]לָא יָהֵיב אִינִישׁ חֵיוָתָא. [10]״וַחֲכָמִים אוֹמְרִים: בַּמֶּה דְּבָרִים אֲמוּרִים? [11]בְּמוּמִין שֶׁבְּסֵתֶר״. [12]אָמַר רַב נַחְמָן: [77A] [13]וְנִכְפֶּה כְּ״מוּמִין שֶׁבְּסֵתֶר״ דָּמֵי.

LITERAL TRANSLATION

[1]And if the butcher did not give the money, [2]the owner of the animal must bring proof [3][in order to] collect. [4]But why? [5]The doubt came into being in the possession of the butcher!

[6]If the butcher gave the money.

[7]Why the unqualified ruling?

[8]The general [way of] things [is that] as long as the person does not give the money, [9]the [other] person does not give the animal.

[10]"And the Sages say: In what [case] are these things said? [11]Regarding defects that are in a covered [place]." [12]Rav Naḥman said: [77A] [13]And an epileptic is like "defects that are hidden."

RASHI

ספיקא ברשות טבח אתייליד — שלא נמצא הטרפות עד שבאת לידו. **דיהיב טבח דמי** — ואפילו לא יהיב — נמי הראיה עליו היא. אלא מסתמא, תנא לטבח — "המוציא מחבירו" קרי ליה. **נכפה** — חולי שממנו נופל לארץ ויש לו זמן לבא. **כמומין שבסתר דמי** — לפי שנזהרת ביום זמנה מלבאת בין הבריות.

BACKGROUND

נִכְפֶּה An epileptic. Epileptic fits are usually sudden (although they may occasionally be brought on by external stimuli, such as being singed). Sometimes the crisis occurs at specific times; thus, some people have attacks only while they are sleeping, and some women only have epileptic fits when they menstruate.

HALAKHAH

וְנִכְפֶּה כְּמוּמִין שֶׁבְּסֵתֶר דָּמֵי **An epileptic is like one with a defect which is hidden.** "Where a woman suffers epileptic

TRANSLATION AND COMMENTARY

וְהָנֵי מִילֵּי [1]The Gemara notes: **These words** apply only **if** the epileptic fit always occurs at **a set time**, thus enabling the woman and her family to avoid publicly exposing the fact of her disease. [2]**But if** the epileptic fit **does not occur at a set time**, [3]the woman **is** treated **like** one who suffers from **"defects that are** ordinarily **exposed** to view," for the woman or her family could not have concealed her condition, and the husband cannot claim that he did not know about her condition at the time of betrothal.

MISHNAH הָאִישׁ [4]In the case of **a man in whom** certain **defects arose** after he was married, and whose wife demanded a divorce — **we do not compel him to divorce** her. [5]**Rabban Shimon ben Gamliel said: In what case were these things said?** [6]**In** the case of **minor defects,** which his wife is expected to tolerate. [7]**But in** the case of **major defects**, **we do** indeed **compel him to divorce** her and pay her ketubah settlement.

GEMARA רַב יְהוּדָה תָּנֵי [8]The Gemara notes two different versions of the opening language in our Mishnah: **Rav Yehudah taught the** Mishnah as cited above: "A man in whom certain defects **arose** after he was married." [9]**Ḥiyya bar Rav taught** the Mishnah differently: "A man in whom certain defects **existed** before he was married."

[1]וְהָנֵי מִילֵּי דִּקְבִיעַ לֵיהּ זְמַן, [2]אֲבָל לָא קְבִיעַ לֵיהּ, [3]כְּ״מוּמִין שֶׁבְּגָלוּי״ דָּמֵי.

מִשְׁנָה [4]הָאִישׁ שֶׁנּוֹלְדוּ בּוֹ מוּמִין, אֵין כּוֹפִין אוֹתוֹ לְהוֹצִיא. [5]אָמַר רַבָּן שִׁמְעוֹן בֶּן גַּמְלִיאֵל: בַּמֶּה דְּבָרִים אֲמוּרִים? [6]בְּמוּמִין הַקְּטַנִּים. [7]אֲבָל בְּמוּמִין הַגְּדוֹלִים, כּוֹפִין אוֹתוֹ לְהוֹצִיא.

גְּמָרָא [8]רַב יְהוּדָה תָּנֵי: ״נוֹלְדוּ״. [9]חִיָּיא בַּר רַב תָּנֵי: ״הָיוּ״.

LITERAL TRANSLATION

[1]And these words [apply] if it has a set time, [2]but if it has no set [time], [3]it is like "defects that are visible."

MISHNAH [4]A man in whom defects arose (lit., "were born") we do not compel him to divorce [his wife]. [5]Rabban Shimon ben Gamliel said: In what [case] are these things said? [6]In [the case of] minor defects. [7]But in [the case of] major defects, we compel him to divorce [her].

GEMARA [8]Rav Yehudah taught: "They arose." [9]Ḥiyya bar Rav taught: "They existed."

RASHI

משנה מומין גדולים – מפרש בגמרא.

גמרא נולדו – משנשאה.

NOTES

אֵין כּוֹפִין אוֹתוֹ לְהוֹצִיא **We do not compel him to divorce his wife.** *Nemukei Yosef* reasons that, while we cannot compel a man with defects to divorce his wife and pay her ketubah settlement, should the woman be willing to forfeit the ketubah settlement, we do indeed honor her request for a divorce because of the general rule stated elsewhere, that a woman who finds her husband physically repulsive cannot be forced to remain married to him.

אֲבָל בְּמוּמִין הַגְּדוֹלִים כּוֹפִין **But with respect to major defects we compel him to divorce his wife.** The Rishonim (see *Tosafot* and *Rash*) comment: We have already seen that if a woman acquired a defect after she was betrothed, she can claim before her husband that it is no different from the case where "his field became flooded." It is simply his misfortune that she acquired the defect, and she should not be penalized by losing entitlement to her ketubah settlement as a result (see above, p. 75a). Why, then, do we not say that in the reverse case — when the husband acquired the defect after they were married — it is similar to the *woman's* field being flooded, and therefore her husband should not be penalized by compelling him to divorce his wife and pay the ketubah settlement? *Shittah Mekubbetzet* explains that the comparison to a field which is flooded is only made when the one who wishes to end the marriage is indeed seeking to penalize the other party. When the husband contracts the defect, his wife is not seeking to penalize him by demanding her ketubah settlement since it is hers by right, in the event of divorce, therefore we do not declare it a case of her misfortune (like a flooded field), and her husband can be compelled to divorce her with full payment of her ketubah settlement.

HALAKHAH

fits at predictable intervals, her condition is regarded as a 'defect which is hidden from view.' But if the fits occur unpredictably, the condition is regarded as a 'defect which is exposed.'" (*Rambam, Sefer Nashim, Hilkhot Ishut* 25:2; *Shulḥan Arukh, Even HaEzer* 39:4 [*Rema*], 117:5, 154:5 [*Rema*].)

הָאִישׁ שֶׁנּוֹלְדוּ בּוֹ מוּמִין **A man in whom defects arose.** "A man who acquired defects after he was married, even to the extent of losing an arm, a leg or the use of an eye, cannot be compelled to divorce his wife, in accordance with the view of the Sages in our Mishnah and Rava's ruling in the Gemara. *Rema* notes that, according to some authorities (*Rosh* and *Tur*), this only applies to one who lost a single arm, leg, or eye; but if a man lost both arms or legs, or the use of both eyes, he can indeed be compelled to divorce his wife." (*Rambam, Sefer Nashim, Hilkhot Ishut* 25:11; *Shulḥan Arukh, Even HaEzer* 154:4.)

[1]מַאן דְּאָמַר ״נוֹלְדוּ״, [2]כָּל שֶׁכֵּן הָיוּ, [3]דְּקָסָבְרָה וְקִיבְּלָה. [4]מַאן דְּאָמַר ״הָיוּ״, [5]אֲבָל נוֹלְדוּ, לָא.
[6]תְּנַן: ״אָמַר רַבָּן שִׁמְעוֹן בֶּן גַּמְלִיאֵל: [7]בַּמֶּה דְּבָרִים אֲמוּרִים? [8]בְּמוּמִין קְטַנִּים. [9]אֲבָל בְּמוּמִין גְּדוֹלִים, כּוֹפִין אוֹתוֹ לְהוֹצִיא״. [10]בִּשְׁלָמָא לְמַאן דְּאָמַר ״נוֹלְדוּ״, [11]הַיְינוּ דְּשָׁאנֵי בֵּין גְּדוֹלִים לִקְטַנִּים. [12]אֶלָּא לְמַאן דְּאָמַר ״הָיוּ״, [13]מַה לִּי גְּדוֹלִים מַה לִּי קְטַנִּים? [14]הָא סָבְרָה וְקִיבְּלָה!
[15]כִּסְבוּרָה הִיא שֶׁיְּכוֹלָה לְקַבֵּל, [16]וְעַכְשָׁיו אֵין יְכוֹלָה לְקַבֵּל.
[17]וְאֵלּוּ הֵן מוּמִין גְּדוֹלִים? [18]פֵּירַשׁ רַבָּן שִׁמְעוֹן בֶּן גַּמְלִיאֵל:

LITERAL TRANSLATION

[1]The one who said "they arose," [2]all the more so [if] they existed, [3]for she considered and accepted [them]. [4]The one who said "they existed," [5]but [if] they arose, not.

[6]We have learned: "Rabban Shimon ben Gamliel said: [7]In what [case] are these things said? [8]In [the case of] minor defects. [9]But in [the case of] major defects, we compel him to divorce [his wife]." [10]It is well according to the one who said "they arose," [11]that is why there is a difference between major [defects] and minor [defects]. [12]But according to the one who said "they existed," [13]what is it to me [if they were] major [defects] or minor [defects]? [14]Behold she considered and accepted [them]!

[15]She thought that she would be able to accept [them], [16]but now she is not able to accept [them].

[17]And which are major defects? [18]Rabban Shimon ben Gamliel explained:

TRANSLATION AND COMMENTARY

מַאן דְּאָמַר [1]The Gemara now clarifies the two versions of the Mishnah: **The** Amora **who said** that the Mishnah, in refusing to compel a divorce, was referring to a man in whom certain defects **"arose"** only after marriage, [2]would agree **all the more** that he not be compelled to divorce his wife if those defects **existed** before they were married, [3]**for** surely in such a case the woman must have **considered** the defects **and accepted** them when she agreed to marry him. [4]But **the** Amora **who said** that the Mishnah was speaking of a man in whom certain defects **"existed"** before marriage, would maintain that only in such a case do we refrain from compelling him to grant his wife a divorce, since she knew of the defects and accepted them. [5]**But** where the defects **arose** only after they were married, she did **not** agree to accept them, and thus he would be compelled to divorce her.

תְּנַן [6]The Gemara now considers these two versions of the Mishnah's opening statement in light of what **we learned** in the second half of the Mishnah: [7]**"Rabban Shimon ben Gamliel said:** [8]**In what case are these things said,** that a man with defects need not be compelled to divorce his wife? [9]**In** the case of **minor defects,** which his wife is expected to tolerate. **But in** the case of **major defects, we do** indeed **compel him to divorce** her and pay her her ketubah." [10]The Gemara comments: **It is well according to the one who said** that the Mishnah is speaking of a man in whom certain defects **"arose"** after he was married. [11]**That is why there is a difference between major** defects, which we cannot expect her to live with once discovered, **and minor** defects, which are tolerable. [12]**But according to the one who said** that the Mishnah is speaking of a man in whom certain defects **"existed"** prior to his marriage, [13]**what is** the difference **to me** if the defects were **major or minor?** [14]In both cases the woman **considered** the defects **and accepted** them.

כִּסְבוּרָה הִיא [15]The Gemara answers: In the event of major defects, the woman can always claim that **she thought she would be able to accept** the defects, [16]**but now** that she is married, she sees that **she cannot accept them.**

וְאֵלּוּ הֵן [17]**And which are** the **major defects?** [18]**Rabban Shimon ben Gamliel explained: For example, if** the

NOTES

כִּסְבוּרָה הִיא שֶׁיְּכוֹלָה **She thought that she would be able to accept them.** This argument appears to contradict the position of the Sages in the next Mishnah, who maintain that a woman who knew about her husband's defect before she married must accept him as he is and cannot demand a divorce. Indeed, the Jerusalem Talmud concludes that Rabban Shimon ben Gamliel is in agreement with the view of Rabbi Meir in the next Mishnah, allowing the woman to rescind her initial commitment to accept the man's defects. *Rashba* and *Ritva* suggest that only if the husband expressly stipulated before marrying her that she accept his defects, as in the case of the next Mishnah, do we say that she cannot later withdraw her commitment. However, if no explicit stipulation was made, even the Sages would agree that she can withdraw her initial agreement to tolerate his defects. Others maintain otherwise, insisting that the Sages would never allow the woman to make such a claim once it is established that she knew of the defects prior to the marriage. (*Rambam,* according to *Maggid Mishneh; Ramah.*)

כְּגוֹן, נִיסְמֵית עֵינוֹ, נִקְטְעָה יָדוֹ, וְנִשְׁבְּרָה רַגְלוֹ.

[1] אִתְּמַר: רַבִּי אַבָּא בַּר יַעֲקֹב אָמַר רַבִּי יוֹחָנָן: [2] הֲלָכָה כְּרַבָּן שִׁמְעוֹן בֶּן גַּמְלִיאֵל. [3] רָבָא אָמַר רַב נַחְמָן: הֲלָכָה כְּדִבְרֵי חֲכָמִים.

[4] וּמִי אָמַר רַבִּי יוֹחָנָן הָכִי? [5] וְהָא אָמַר רַבָּה בַּר בַּר חָנָה אָמַר רַבִּי יוֹחָנָן: [6] בְּכָל מָקוֹם שֶׁשָּׁנָה רַבָּן שִׁמְעוֹן בֶּן גַּמְלִיאֵל בְּמִשְׁנָתֵנוּ, [7] הֲלָכָה כְּמוֹתוֹ, [8] חוּץ מֵעָרֵב וְצַיְדָן וּרְאָיָה אַחֲרוֹנָה!

[9] אֲמוֹרָאֵי נִינְהוּ, וְאַלִּיבָּא דְּרַבִּי יוֹחָנָן.

משנה [10] וְאֵלּוּ שֶׁכּוֹפִין אוֹתוֹ

LITERAL TRANSLATION

For example, where his eye was blinded, his hand was cut off, or his leg was broken.

[1] It was stated: Rabbi Abba bar Ya'akov said in the name of Rabbi Yohanan: [2] The law is in accordance with Rabban Shimon ben Gamliel. [3] Rava said in the name of Rav Nahman: The law is in accordance with the words of the Sages.

[4] And did Rabbi Yoḥanan say thus? [5] But surely Rabbah bar Bar Hanah said in the name of Rabbi Yoḥanan: [6] Wherever Rabban Shimon ben Gamliel taught [something] in our Mishnah, [7] the law is in accordance with him, [8] except for [the cases of] a guarantor, Tzaidan, and the latter [ruling about] proof!

[9] They are Amoraim [in dispute], and according to Rabbi Yoḥanan.

MISHNAH [10] And these are [defects] for which we compel [a man]

TRANSLATION AND COMMENTARY

man's **eye was blinded,** or **his hand was cut off, or his leg was broken.** In each of these cases, the man can be compelled to divorce his wife with full payment of her ketubah settlement.

אִתְּמַר [1] **It was stated** with regard to a dispute among Amoraim: **Rabbi Abba bar Ya'akov said in the name of Rabbi Yohanan:** [2] **The law is in accordance with Rabban Shimon ben Gamliel,** who drew a distinction between major and minor defects. [3] **Rava said in the name of Rav Naḥman: The law is in accordance with the words of the Sages** in the anonymous first clause of the Mishnah, who teach that a man cannot be compelled to divorce his wife, whatever defect he suffers from.

וּמִי אָמַר [4] The Gemara now asks: **And did Rabbi Yoḥanan** indeed **say** that in this specific instance the law is in agreement with Rabban Shimon ben Gamliel, as if we wouldn't know that otherwise? [5] **But surely** this is known already from **Rabbah bar Bar Ḥanah,** who **said in the name of Rabbi Yoḥanan:** [6] **Wherever Rabban Shimon ben Gamliel taught** something **in our Mishnah,** [7] **the law is** decided **in accordance with him,** even if the Sages disagree, [8] **except for** the cases of **a guarantor,** the divorce in **Tzaidan, and the latter** ruling concerning matters of **proof!** Since our Mishnah does not concern one of these three cases, why does Rabbi Yoḥanan reiterate that the law is in agreement with Rabban Shimon ben Gamliel?

אֲמוֹרָאֵי נִינְהוּ [9] The Gemara answers: Rabbi Abba bar Ya'akov and Rabbah bar Bar Ḥanah **are Amoraim** in dispute with each other as to when exactly, **according to Rabbi Yoḥanan,** Rabban Shimon ben Gamliel's opinion is favored over that of the Sages. Rabbah bar Bar Ḥanah maintained that Rabbi Yoḥanan issued a general ruling declaring that, with three specific exceptions, the law is always in accordance with the opinion of Rabban Shimon ben Gamliel; whereas according to Rabbi Abba bar Ya'akov, Rabbi Yoḥanan never issued any such general ruling, preferring to decide the law on the basis of each individual case.

MISHNAH וְאֵלּוּ [10] The next Mishnah lists those defects appearing in a man which all agree serve as grounds for compelling him to divorce his wife with full payment of her ketubah. **And these are** defects

RASHI

ומי אמר רבי יוחנן הכי – דהלכה כרבן שמעון בהא לחודא, והא בכל מקום ששנה קאמר! **ערב וצידן וראיה אחרונה** – ערב ב"גט פשוט", צידן ב"מי שאחזו קורדיקוס", ראיה אחרונה בסנהדרין בפרק "זה בורר", ובשתי ראיות נחלק, הלכה כמותו בראשונה ולא באחרונה: אמרו לו הבא ראיה, אמר אין לי ראיה כו'.

NOTES

אָמַר רַבִּי יוֹחָנָן הֲלָכָה כְּרַבָּן שִׁמְעוֹן בֶּן גַּמְלִיאֵל **Rabbi Yoḥanan said: The law is in accordance with Rabban Shimon ben Gamliel.** *Ritva* cites a variant reading according to which Rabbi Abba ben Yaakov stated in Rabbi Yoḥanan's name that the law is *not* in accordance with Rabban Shimon ben Gamliel. According to this reading, the Gemara's objection, based on the general ruling attributed to Rabbi Yoḥanan, is not directed against Rabbi Abba's statement in the sense of its being redundant, but rather in the sense of its being contradictory to the general rule.

וְאֵלּוּ שֶׁכּוֹפִין **And these are the defects for which we compel.** According to most Rishonim, the defects described in our Mishnah necessitate compelling the husband not only to divorce his wife but also to pay her ketubah settlement. *Rabbenu Gershom* maintains, however, that we indeed compel him to divorce his wife, but he cannot be forced to pay the ketubah settlement (see *Ritva* for a full discussion of the two positions).

לְהוֹצִיא: [1]מוּכֵּה שְׁחִין, וּבַעַל פּוֹלִיפּוּס; וְהַמְקַמֵּץ, וְהַמְצָרֵף נְחוֹשֶׁת, וְהַבּוּרְסִי. [2]בֵּין שֶׁהָיוּ עַד שֶׁלֹּא נִישְּׂאוּ, וּבֵין מִשֶּׁנִּישְּׂאוּ נוֹלְדוּ.

[3]וְעַל כּוּלָּן אָמַר רַבִּי מֵאִיר: [4]אַף עַל פִּי שֶׁהִתְנָה עִמָּהּ, [5]יְכוֹלָה הִיא שֶׁתֹּאמַר: ״סְבוּרָה הָיִיתִי שֶׁאֲנִי יְכוֹלָה לְקַבֵּל, [6]וְעַכְשָׁיו אֵינִי יְכוֹלָה לְקַבֵּל״. [7]וַחֲכָמִים אוֹמְרִים: מְקַבֶּלֶת הִיא עַל כָּרְחָהּ, [8]חוּץ מִמּוּכֵּה שְׁחִין, [9]מִפְּנֵי שֶׁמְּמַקַּתּוֹ.

[10]מַעֲשֶׂה בְּצִידוֹן בְּבוּרְסִי אֶחָד שֶׁמֵּת, וְהָיָה לוֹ אָח בּוּרְסִי. [11]אָמְרוּ חֲכָמִים: יְכוֹלָה הִיא שֶׁתֹּאמַר: [12]״לְאָחִיךָ הָיִיתִי יְכוֹלָה לְקַבֵּל, [13]וּלְךָ אֵינִי יְכוֹלָה לְקַבֵּל״.

LITERAL TRANSLATION

to divorce [his wife]: [1]One who is afflicted with skin sores and one who has a *polypus*; and the gatherer, and the copper smelter, and the tanner. [2][Regardless of] whether they existed before they were married or arose [only] after they were married.

[3]And about all of them Rabbi Meir said: [4]Even if he stipulated with her, [5]she can say: "I thought that I would be able to accept [it], [6]but now I am not able to accept [it]." [7]And the Sages say: She must accept [them] against her will, [8]except for one who is afflicted with skin sores, [9]because it causes [his flesh to] decay.

[10][There was] an incident in Sidon regarding a certain tanner who died and who had a brother who was [also] a tanner. [11]The Sages said: She can say: [12]"Your brother I was able to accept, [13]but you I am not able to accept."

TRANSLATION AND COMMENTARY

for which we compel a man **to divorce** his wife: [1]**One who is afflicted with skin sores, and one who has a polyp;** as well as **the gatherer, and the copper smelter, and the tanner** — on account of the offensive stench associated with their occupations. Any man with these defects can be compelled to divorce his wife, [2]regardless of **whether they existed before they were married or arose** only **after they were married.**

וְעַל כּוּלָּן [3]And about all of these categories, **Rabbi Meir said:** [4]**Even if** the husband **made it clear** to his wife before marriage that she would have to accept his defects, [5]**she can** later **say:** "Before I was married **I thought that I would be able to accept** your defect or occupation, [6]**but now** that I am married I realize that **I am not able to accept it."** [7]**The Sages** disagree and **say:** If the woman knew of these problems before she married her husband, **she must accept** them even **against her will,** [8]**except** in the case of **a man who is afflicted with skin sores,** when we compel him to divorce her, [9]**because she causes** his flesh to **decay** even further by engaging in sexual relations with him.

מַעֲשֶׂה [10]The Mishnah concludes with the following anecdote: There was **an incident in Sidon involving a certain tanner who died** childless, **and who had a brother who was also a tanner** who wished to enter into levirate marriage with his deceased brother's widow. [11]Ruling on the case, **the Sages said:** The widow **can say:** [12]**"Your brother I was able to accept** in spite of his repugnant occupation, [13]**but you I am not able to accept** under the same conditions." Thus, the brother must release her from the levirate tie with *ḥalitzah* and pay her her ketubah.

RASHI

משנה בעל פוליפוס – מפרש בגמרא. **המקמץ והמצרף נחשת** – מפרש בגמרא וכולן מפני שאומנות מסרחת היא. **שממקתו** – לשון ״המק בשרו״ (זכריה יד).

LANGUAGE

פּוֹלִיפּוּס Polypus. From the Greek πολύπους, *polypus,* meaning "morbid excrescence of the nose."

מְקַמֵּץ One who gathers. This word, which is related to קומץ — "collect, gather" — means "one who gathers."

בּוּרְסִי Tanner. From the Greek βυρσεύς, *burseus,* meaning "tanner."

BACKGROUND

בַּעַל פּוֹלִיפּוּס Someone with a *polypus*. Nowadays, polyps (which are generally benign) are defined as growths found on mucous membranes. However, our Mishnah might be referring to a chronic inflammation of the nasal canals (or the tonsils), which causes the nose (or the mouth) to have a foul smell.

הַמְקַמֵּץ One who gathers. Different views are cited in the Tosefta as to whether this refers to a "small tanner," a tanner who handles small quantities of material and therefore does all the tanning himself, or to someone who collects dog excrement.

Up to the previous century, leather was softened by putting dog excrement into the water in which it was soaked; since the fermenting agents and the enzymes in the dog feces helped to tan the leather.

הַמְצָרֵף נְחוֹשֶׁת One who smelts copper. Solid copper blocks are relatively rare, since most copper is found in the form of copper sulfide ore. This ore must be smelted to separate the copper from the sulfur, and some of the chemicals discharged in the course of the smelting process emit a foul odor. People who smelt copper on a regular basis absorb this smell, and so does their clothing.

HALAKHAH

וְאֵלּוּ שֶׁכּוֹפִין אוֹתוֹ לְהוֹצִיא And these are defects for which they compel him to divorce his wife. "If a man acquired certain defects, such as odor of the mouth or the nose, or became employed as a gatherer of dog excrement, a tanner, or a copper miner, he can be compelled to divorce his wife and pay her ketubah settlement. However, should the woman wish to remain with him, she can choose to do so. *Rema* adds that if the woman knew about the defect before she married, she cannot demand a divorce from her husband," in accordance with the Sages of our Mishnah and against Rabbi Meir. (*Rambam, Sefer Nashim, Hilkhot Ishut* 25:11; *Shulḥan Arukh, Even HaEzer* 154:1.)

מוּכֵּה שְׁחִין A man who is afflicted with skin sores. "If a man acquires certain skin diseases, he can be compelled to divorce his wife even against her will, since sexual relations between them constitute a danger to his health," in accordance with the Mishnah. (*Rambam, Sefer Nashim, Hilkhot Ishut* 25:12; *Shulḥan Arukh, Even HaEzer* 154:1.)

הָיָה לוֹ אָח בּוּרְסִי Who had a brother who was a tanner. "If a woman chose to remain with her husband despite one of those defects for which divorce can be compelled, and then he dies childless, she can refuse to enter into a levirate marriage with his brother should he suffer from the same defect as her dead husband. She can say: 'I was willing to accept your brother with this defect; but in your case, I am not willing.' In such a case, the man must release the woman from the levirate tie with *ḥalitzah* and pay her her ketubah." (*Rambam, Sefer Nashim, Hilkhot Ishut* 25:13; *Shulḥan Arukh, Even HaEzer* 154:2; 165:4.)

TRANSLATION AND COMMENTARY

GEMARA מַאי בַּעַל פּוֹלִיפּוֹס [1]The Gemara asks: **What** does the Mishnah mean when it refers to **"one who has a polyp"?**

אָמַר רַב יְהוּדָה [2]**Rav Yehudah said in the name of Shmuel**: This refers to one who has a sinus polyp which causes **odor of the nose.** [3]**In a Baraita it was taught** that such polyps cause **odor of the mouth."**

רַב אַסִי [4]**Rav Assi taught the reverse**, that it was Shmuel who identified a person afflicted with a polyp as one who suffers from bad breath, and that it was the Baraita that said the term refers to one who has odor of the nose. [5]**And he suggested a mnemonic device** to make it easier to remember Shmuel's position. [6]**Shmuel did not sever his mouth from the entire chapter,** since he knew it so well that it was always at the tip of his tongue. When one bears in mind this statement about Shmuel, one also remembers that it was Shmuel who identified a person afflicted with a polyp as one who suffers from odor of the mouth, and not of the nose.

וְהַמְקַמֵּץ [7]The Gemara continues to explore the language of the Mishnah: **"And the gatherer."** [8]**What is** meant by **a gatherer?** [9]**Rav Yehudah said: This is** referring to **one who collects the excrement of dogs** which is later to be used in the tanning process.

מֵיתִיבֵי [10]Some Sages **raised an objection** against Rav Yehudah from a Baraita which states: **"A gatherer — this is a tanner"!**

וּלְטַעֲמִיךְ [11]The Gemara counters this: **According to your reasoning,** that a gatherer is actually a tanner, **our Mishnah should be difficult for you,** for it states: [12]**"The gatherer, and the copper smelter, and the tanner,"** implying that the gatherer and the tanner are engaged in different occupations!

בִּשְׁלָמָא [13]The Gemara rebuts this counterargument: **Granted** that **our Mishnah is not difficult** in light of the Baraita, [14]for we can say that **here** in the Mishnah the tanner who is listed separately from the gatherer is **a major tanner,** [15]whereas the tanner identified **here** in the Baraita with the gatherer is **a minor tanner.** [16]**But according to Rav Yehudah,** who identifies the gatherer as one who collects dog excrement, **it is difficult** in light of the Baraita that equates a gatherer with a tanner!

גמרא [1]מַאי "בַּעַל פּוֹלִיפּוֹס"? [2]אָמַר רַב יְהוּדָה אָמַר שְׁמוּאֵל: רֵיחַ הַחוֹטֶם. [3]בְּמַתְנִיתָא תָּנָא: רֵיחַ הַפֶּה.

[4]רַב אַסִי מַתְנֵי אִיפְּכָא, [5]וּמַנַּח בָּהּ סִימָנָא: [6]שְׁמוּאֵל לָא פָּסֵיק פּוּמֵיהּ מִכּוּלֵּיהּ פִּירְקִין.

[7]"וְהַמְקַמֵּץ". [8]מַאי מְקַמֵּץ? [9]אָמַר רַב יְהוּדָה: זֶה הַמְקַבֵּץ צוֹאַת כְּלָבִים.

[10]מֵיתִיבֵי: מְקַמֵּץ — זֶה בּוּרְסִי! [11]וּלְטַעֲמִיךְ, תִּיקְשֵׁי לָךְ מַתְנִיתִין: [12]"הַמְקַמֵּץ וְהַמְצָרֵף נְחוֹשֶׁת וְהַבּוּרְסִי"! [13]בִּשְׁלָמָא מַתְנִיתִין לָא קַשְׁיָא — [14]כָּאן בְּבוּרְסִי גָּדוֹל, [15]כָּאן בְּבוּרְסִי קָטָן. [16]אֶלָּא לְרַב יְהוּדָה קַשְׁיָא!

LITERAL TRANSLATION

GEMARA [1]What is "one who has a *polypus*"? [2]Rav Yehudah said in the name of Shmuel: [One who has] odor of the nose. [3]In a Baraita it was taught: "[One who has] odor of the mouth."

[4]Rav Assi taught the reverse, [5]and laid down a sign: [6]Shmuel's mouth never ceased from our entire chapter.

[7]"And the gatherer." [8]What is a gatherer? [9]Rav Yehudah said: This is one who collects the excrement of dogs.

[10]They raised an objection: "A gatherer — this is a tanner"! [11]And according to your reasoning, our Mishnah should be difficult for you: [12]"The gatherer, and the copper smelter, and the tanner." [13]Granted our Mishnah is not difficult — [14]here a major tanner, [15]here a minor tanner. [16]But according to Rav Yehudah, it is difficult.

RASHI

גמרא לא פסק פומיה — סימנא דשמואל ריח הפה אמר. **לא פסק פומיה מכולי פירקין** — תמיד היה שגור בפיו. **תיקשי לך מתניתין** — דקא חשיב להו בתרין. **מקמץ צואת כלבים** — לא ידעתי מה צורך בה. אבל באשכנז ראיתי ששורין בהם הבגדים לפני כובסן יום או יומים.

NOTES

שְׁמוּאֵל לָא פָּסֵיק פּוּמֵיהּ **Shmuel's mouth did not cease.** *Rashi* explains that this statement reflects Shmuel's deep knowledge of our chapter, whose laws he would constantly recite over and over. According to *Maharam* of *Rotenburg* the statement means that Shmuel issued halakhic opinions relating to almost every Mishnah found in our chapter. *Rivan* apparently believes that this statement was intended only as a mnemonic device, yet was composed to dignify Shmuel at the same time.

בּוּרְסִי גָּדוֹל וְקָטָן **A major and a minor tanner.** *Rashi* implies that the major tanner is one who maintains and processes a larger stock of skins than the minor tanner, who cannot afford the investment. The former would therefore be expected to smell worse due to the number of skins that he processes. *Ritva* suggests, however, that the major tanner is less susceptible to offensive odors since he can afford to hire others to tan the skins, whereas the minor tanner must do the work himself.

[1] תַּנָּאֵי הִיא. [2] דְּתַנְיָא: ״מְקַמֵּץ — זֶה בּוּרְסִי. [3] וְיֵשׁ אוֹמְרִים: זֶה הַמְקַמֵּץ צוֹאַת כְּלָבִים״. [4] ״וְהַמְצָרֵף נְחוֹשֶׁת וְהַבּוּרְסִי״. [5] מַאי מְצָרֵף נְחוֹשֶׁת? [6] רַב אַשִׁי אֲמַר: חַשְׁלֵי דוּדֵי. [7] רַבָּה בַּר בַּר חָנָה אֲמַר: זֶה הַמְחַתֵּךְ נְחוֹשֶׁת מֵעִיקָּרוֹ. [8] תַּנְיָא כְּוָותֵיהּ דְּרַבָּה בַּר בַּר חָנָה: ״אֵיזֶהוּ מְצָרֵף? [9] זֶה הַמְחַתֵּךְ נְחוֹשֶׁת מֵעִיקָּרוֹ״. [10] אָמַר רַב: הָאוֹמֵר: [11] ״אֵינִי זָן וְאֵינִי מְפַרְנֵס״, יוֹצִיא וְיִתֵּן כְּתוּבָּה. [12] אֲזַל רַבִּי אֶלְעָזָר. אֲמָרָהּ לִשְׁמַעֲתָא קַמֵּיהּ דִּשְׁמוּאֵל. [13] אֲמַר: ״אַכְסוּהּ שַׂעֲרֵי לְאֶלְעָזָר, [14] עַד שֶׁכּוֹפִין אוֹתוֹ לְהוֹצִיא, יִכְפּוּהוּ לָזוּן״!

LITERAL TRANSLATION

[1] It is [a dispute between] Tannaim. [2] For it was taught: "A gatherer — this is a tanner. [3] And some say: This is one who gathers the excrement of dogs."

[4] "And the copper smelter, and the tanner." [5] What is a copper smelter? [6] Rav Ashi said: Kettlesmiths. [7] Rabbah bar Bar Ḥanah said: This is one who extracts copper from its source. [8] It was taught in accordance with Rabbah bar Bar Ḥanah: "Who is a smelter? [9] This is one who extracts copper from its source."

[10] Rav said: One who says: [11] "I will not sustain and I will not provide," he must divorce and give the ketubah. [12] Rabbi Elazar went [and] stated the teaching before Shmuel. He said: "Give Elazar barley to chew. [13] Before they compel him to divorce, [14] let them compel him to sustain her!"

TRANSLATION AND COMMENTARY

תַּנָּאֵי הִיא [1] The Gemara answers: There is really no difficulty, for the proper identification of a gatherer **is** a matter of dispute between **Tannaim.** [2] **For it was taught** in yet another Baraita: **"A gatherer — this is a tanner.** [3] **And some** authorities **say:** A gatherer **is one who gathers** together **the excrement of dogs."** Thus one can persuasively argue that the Baraita cited earlier follows the first Tanna of this Baraita, while Rav Yehudah follows the opinion of the other dissenting Sages.

וְהַמְצָרֵף נְחוֹשֶׁת [4] Among those listed in our Mishnah as having repugnant vocations are: **"The copper smelter and the tanner."** [5] The Gemara asks: **What is** meant by **a copper smelter?** [6] **Rav Ashi said: Kettlesmiths,** whose work with copper leaves an awful odor. [7] **Rabbah bar Bar Ḥanah said: This** refers to **one who refines copper from its source** in the ground. [8] A Baraita **was taught in accordance with Rabbah bar Bar Ḥanah: "Which one is a smelter?** [9] **One who refines copper from its source."**

אָמַר רַב [10] Since our Mishnah mentioned cases where the husband can be compelled to divorce his wife, the Gemara discusses another case where the same regulation applies. **Rav said: If someone says:** [11] **"I will not maintain** my wife **and I will not provide for her support," he must divorce** her immediately **and pay her** her **ketubah.** [12] **Rabbi Elazar went** to the Academy **and reported** Rav's **teaching before Shmuel.** [13] After hearing Rav's ruling, Shmuel **said: "Feed Elazar barley** as if he were an animal, for what he said is nonsense. If a man refuses to support his wife, then **instead of compelling him to divorce her,** [14] **let** the court **compel him to maintain her!"**

RASHI

חשלי דודי – מחשלין ומרדדין נחשת, ועושין ממנו יורות, ומסריח הוא. **מעיקרו** – ממקום מוצאו מן הארץ. **אכסוהו שערי** – האכילוהו שעורים כבהמה. כל הנאכל שלא כדרכו קרי ליה כוסס.

NOTES

יוֹצִיא וְיִתֵּן כְּתוּבָּה He must divorce and give the ketubah. The Rishonim disagree about the meaning of this expression. According to *Ra'avad* and *Rosh,* the term יוֹצִיא ("He must divorce") implies that he can be compelled by the courts to do so. *Ramban* and his disciples treat this issue at length, and conclude that the term יוֹצִיא does not always mean the same thing. In some places it means that the courts can force the husband to divorce his wife, whereas elsewhere it means that he is expected to grant his wife a divorce but cannot be compelled to do so. *Rashba* maintains that when this term is used without explicit reference to force, it implies that the husband is forbidden to divorce and can only be coerced in relation to paying the ketubah settlement accompanying the divorce, but not to grant the actual divorce itself.

HALAKHAH

אֵינִי זָן וְאֵינִי מְפַרְנֵס I will not sustain and I will not provide. "If a man refuses to support his wife, he can be compelled to do so by the courts. If they are unable to collect from him, because he has no assets and is unwilling to work, they can compel him to divorce his wife, should she so desire, and pay her ketubah settlement; this is in accordance with the opinion of Shmuel adopted in the Gemara. *Bet Shmuel* adds that since some authorities rule in accordance with the opinion of Rav (that the husband can immediately be compelled to divorce his wife if he refuses to sustain her), the woman is not considered a 'rebellious wife' who forfeits her rights to a ketubah settlement should she refuse to live with him in the interim." (*Rambam, Sefer Nashim, Hilkhot Ishut* 12:4; *Shulḥan Arukh, Even HaEzer* 154:3.)

[1]וְרַב? [2]אֵין אָדָם דָּר עִם נָחָשׁ בִּכְפִיפָה.
[3]כִּי סָלֵיק רַבִּי זֵירָא, אַשְׁכַּחֵיהּ לְרַבִּי בִּנְיָמִין בַּר יֶפֶת, [4]דְּיָתֵיב וְקָאָמַר לָהּ מִשְּׁמֵיהּ דְּרַבִּי יוֹחָנָן. [5]אֲמַר לֵיהּ: עַל דָּא אַכְסוּהּ שַׂעֲרִין לְאֶלְעָזָר בְּבָבֶל.
[6]אָמַר רַב יְהוּדָה אָמַר רַב אַסִי: [7]אֵין מְעַשִּׂין אֶלָּא לִפְסוּלוֹת. [8]כִּי אָמְרִיתָהּ קַמֵּיהּ דִּשְׁמוּאֵל אָמַר: [9]כְּגוֹן אַלְמָנָה לְכֹהֵן גָּדוֹל, [10]וּגְרוּשָׁה וַחֲלוּצָה לְכֹהֵן הֶדְיוֹט, [11]מַמְזֶרֶת וּנְתִינָה לְיִשְׂרָאֵל, [12]בַּת יִשְׂרָאֵל לְנָתִין וּלְמַמְזֵר. [13]אֲבָל נָשָׂא אִשָּׁה וְשָׁהָה עִמָּהּ עֶשֶׂר שָׁנִים וְלֹא

LITERAL TRANSLATION

[1]And Rav? [2]A person cannot dwell in a basket with a serpent.

[3]When Rabbi Zera went up, he found Rabbi Binyamin bar Yefet, [4]who was sitting and stating it in the name of Rabbi Yoḥanan. [5]He said to him: For this they gave Elazar barley to chew in Babylonia.

[6]Rav Yehudah said in the name of Rav Assi: [7]We do not force except in regard to disqualified women. [8]When I stated it before Shmuel, he said: [9]For example, a widow to a High Priest, [10]or [either] a divorcee or a *ḥalutzah* to an ordinary priest, [11][either] a *mamzeret* or a *netinah* to an Israelite, [12][or] the daughter of an Israelite to a *natin* or a *mamzer*. [13]But [if] he married a woman and stayed with her ten years and she did not

TRANSLATION AND COMMENTARY

[1]The Gemara asks: **And** how would **Rav** respond to Shmuel's criticism? [2]**A person cannot** be forced to **dwell in a basket** together **with a serpent.** Thus a woman cannot be expected to live with a man who only provides for her when the courts compel him to do so.

כִּי סָלֵיק [3]It was related that **when Rabbi Zera emigrated** from Babylonia to Eretz Israel, **he found Rabbi Binyamin bar Yefet,** [4]**who was sitting** in the Academy **and saying** the ruling, which in Babylonia had been attributed to Rav, **in the name of Rabbi Yoḥanan.** [5]Rabbi Zera **said to** Rabbi Binyamin bar Yefet: Be careful what you say, for it was **for** repeating **this ruling** that **they fed Elazar barley in Bablylonia.**

אָמַר רַב יְהוּדָה [6]The Gemara continues its discussion of the circumstances in which a man may be compelled to divorce his wife: **Rav Yehudah said in the name of Rav Assi:** [7]The courts **do not force** men to divorce their wives **unless** they are married to women who are **disqualified** by law from marrying them. [8]**When I stated** this ruling **before Shmuel, he said:** [9]We are talking about marriages between **a widow and a High Priest,** [10]**a divorcee or a *ḥalutzah*** (a woman released from the levirate tie) **and an ordinary priest,** [11]**a *mamzeret*** (one born from either an incestuous or an adulterous relationship) **or a *netinah*** (a descendant of the Gibeonites whose conversion to Judaism during the days of Joshua was called into question) **and an** ordinary **Israelite,** [12]or **the daughter of an** ordinary **Israelite and a *natin*** or a ***mamzer.*** Although in each of these cases the marriage takes effect, because they are forbidden to marry by Torah law, the couple must immediately divorce. [13]**But** if a man **married a woman and stayed with her** for **ten years,** and **she did not bear**

RASHI

וקאמר לה – להא מילתא דרב. **משמיה דרבי יוחנן** – דאיהו נמי כרב סבירא ליה. **אין מעשין** – אין כופין להוציא.

NOTES

אַכְסוּהּ שַׂעֲרֵי Give him barley to chew. The word אַכְסוּהּ is derived from the root כסס, "to chew," thereby denoting the way an animal eats (chewing the barley whole), as opposed to a person who eats it ground and cooked. *Rivan* cites a different reading: אבסוה, from the root אבס, "to fatten with feed," implying that Elazar was to be fattened with barley as if he were an animal.

כְּגוֹן אַלְמָנָה לְכֹהֵן גָּדוֹל For example, a widow to a High Priest. The Jerusalem Talmud (11:7) asks: What about relationships that involve "secondary" prohibitions, which were deemed incestuous by Rabbinic decree alone? It answers that Shmuel's intention was not to imply that relationships forbidden only Rabbinically need not be severed, but rather to exclude those relationships which are not prohibited but yet are problematic — such as a childless marriage.

אֲבָל נָשָׂא אִשָּׁה But if he married a woman. *Rashi* explains that a man who was married for at least ten years without children is not Biblically required to divorce his wife, because by Torah law he can marry another woman with whom he can fulfill his obligation to procreate. The Rabbis, however, decreed that he must divorce her, for they were concerned that otherwise he would not marry another woman. Rav Assi and Rav Taḥlifa bar Avimi nevertheless

HALAKHAH

אֵין מְעַשִּׂין אֶלָּא לִפְסוּלוֹת They only force divorce in regard to disqualified women. "A priest is forbidden by Torah law to marry a divorcee, a *zonah* or a *ḥalalah.* If he married one of them regardless, he is obligated to divorce her and can be compelled to do so by the courts." (*Rambam, Sefer Kedushah, Hilkhot Issurei Bi'ah* 17:7; *Shulḥan Arukh, Even HaEzer* 6:1.)

יָלְדָה, [1]אֵין כּוֹפִין אוֹתוֹ. [2]וְרַב תַּחֲלִיפָא בַּר אֲבִימִי אָמַר שְׁמוּאֵל: אֲפִילּוּ נָשָׂא אִשָּׁה וְשָׁהָה עִמָּהּ עֶשֶׂר שָׁנִים וְלֹא יָלְדָה, [3]כּוֹפִין אוֹתוֹ.
[4]תְּנַן: "אֵלּוּ שֶׁכּוֹפִין אוֹתוֹ לְהוֹצִיא: [5]מוּכֵּה שְׁחִין, וּבַעַל פּוֹלִיפּוֹס". [6]בִּשְׁלָמָא לְרַב אַסִי, דְּרַבָּנַן, קָתָנֵי; [7]דְּאוֹרַיְיתָא, לָא קָתָנֵי. [8]אֶלָּא לְרַב תַּחֲלִיפָא בַּר אֲבִימִי, [9]לִיתְנֵי: נָשָׂא אִשָּׁה וְשָׁהָה עִמָּהּ עֶשֶׂר שָׁנִים וְלֹא יָלְדָה — [10]כּוֹפִין אוֹתוֹ!
[11]אֲמַר רַב נַחְמָן: לָא קַשְׁיָא;

LITERAL TRANSLATION

bear any children, [1]we do not compel him. [2]And Rav Taḥlifa bar Avimi said in the name of Shmuel: Even [if] he married a woman and stayed with her ten years and she did not bear any children, [3]we compel him.

[4]We have learned: "These are [defects] for which we compel [a man] to divorce [his wife]: [5]One who is afflicted with skin sores and one who has a *polypus*." [6]Granted [that according] to Rav Assi [obligations] that are Rabbinic, it taught; [7]that are from the Torah, it did not teach. [8]But according to Rav Taḥlifa bar Avimi, [9]let it teach: [If] he married a woman and stayed with her ten years and she did not bear any children, [10]we compel him!

[11]Rav Naḥman said: It is not difficult;

TRANSLATION AND COMMENTARY

him **any children,** [1]**we do not compel him** to divorce her, although by remaining married to her, he neglects his Biblical obligation to procreate. [2]**And Rav Taḥlifa bar Avimi said in the name of Shmuel: Even** in the case of a man who **married a woman and stayed with her** for **ten years,** if **she did not bear** him **any children,** [3]**we compel him** to divorce so that he can remarry and fulfill his Biblical obligation to procreate.

תְּנַן [4]The Gemara now considers these rulings in light of our Mishnah, where **we have learned: "These are** defects **for which we compel** a man **to divorce** his wife: [5]**One who is afflicted with skin sores, and one who has a polyp."** Conspicuously missing from the list in our Mishnah are all those cases just cited. [6]**Granted that this agrees with the position of Rav Assi,** who spoke only of men who were married in contravention of Torah law — he can claim that only divorce-obligations **that are Rabbinic** in nature were **taught** in the Mishnah; [7]whereas those **that are** derived **from the Torah,** such as the ones he referred to in his ruling, the Mishnah **did not teach.** [8]**But** if the law was **according to Rav Taḥlifa bar Avimi,** who extended Rav Assi's prescription of force to include even one who had no Torah obligation to divorce (he who was married to a barren woman), [9]our Mishnah **ought to have taught** that if a man **married a woman and stayed with her** for **ten years,** and **she did not bear** him **any children,** [10]**we compel him** to divorce her, as in all the other instances listed in the Mishnah.

אֲמַר רַב נַחְמָן [11]**Rav Naḥman said: It is** really **not difficult,** even according to Rav Taḥlifa bar Avimi.

RASHI

אין כופין — דלא כפינן אפריה ורביה. **ואלו שכופין** — הני אין, אפריה ורביה — לא. **בשלמא לרב אסי** — לא תקשי הא דלא חשיב פסולות במתניתין, דאיכא לשנויי. **דרבנן קתני** — הנך דאיסורא דידהו לא כתיבא באורייתא. **ליתני נשא אשה ושהה כו'** — דמדאורייתא לא מיחייב לאפוקה, דאפשר ליקח לו אשה אחרת אעלה. אבל מדרבנן קאמר, דכל כמה דאיתא להא גביה לא נסיב אחריתי.

NOTES

disagree as to whether or not the Rabbis also decreed that the courts must compel a childless couple to divorce.

Birkat Avraham explains Rav Assi's position — that the courts cannot force divorce upon a childless couple — in terms of the uncertainty as to whether the man's second marriage will prove more fruitful than the first and produce the number of children needed to fulfill one's Biblical duty of procreation (generally accepted as one boy and one girl).

These words are based on the Halakhic conclusion that the commandment to be fruitful and multiply applies only to men. Therefore the discussion here applies only to men. However, if a woman maintains that she wishes to give birth because she does not want to be alone, without support, and her husband is sterile, this is a reason for the court to order her husband to divorce her.

HALAKHAH

נָשָׂא אִשָּׁה וְשָׁהָה עִמָּהּ עֶשֶׂר שָׁנִים If he married a woman and stayed with her for ten years. "If a man married a woman and lived with her for ten years, and she did not bear him any children, he can be compelled to divorce her and pay the ketubah settlement (or, in places where it is permitted, take another wife), in accordance with Rav Taḥlifa. *Rema* writes in the name of some authorities (*Rivash*) that this only applies if the man had no children at all. If he did have children, but not the requisite number to fulfill his obligation to procreate, he cannot be compelled to divorce his wife. Today the custom is to never compel divorce for reasons of childlessness." (*Rambam, Sefer Nashim, Hilkhot Ishut* 15:7; *Shulḥan Arukh, Even HaEzer* 154:10.)

TRANSLATION AND COMMENTARY

[1]In **this** case, where the man is married to a barren woman, it is only **with words**, through argument and persuasion, that we can compel him to divorce his wife. [2]However, in **these** cases listed in our Mishnah, we can compel the man to divorce his wife even **with whips**, if need be.

מַתְקִיף לָהּ [3]**Rabbi Abba strongly objected to** this solution of Rav Tahlifa's difficulty: It is wrong to assume that the court is ever limited to the use of mere words to compel someone to divorce, for the verse (Proverbs 29:19) teaches us that [4]**"with words, a servant will not be corrected."** [5]**Rather, Rabbi Abba said:** Both in **this** case, of a man married to a barren woman, as well as in **these** cases of our Mishnah, the husband can be compelled **with whips** to divorce his wife. [77B] Nevertheless, the Mishnah still chose not to include the case of a man who is Rabbinically required to divorce his barren wife because of the following legal difference: [6]**There,** in our Mishnah, **when** the woman **says:** [7]"Although I am entitled to a divorce, I still wish **to be with him," we let her** remain married; [8]whereas **here,** in the case of a man married to a barren woman, **even though she says:** [9]**"**I still wish **to be with him," we do not let her** remain married.

וַהֲרֵי מוּכֵּה שְׁחִין [10]The Gemara raises an objection: **Yet behold** the case in our Mishnah of **a man who is afflicted with skin sores, for even though** his wife **said:** [11]**"**I still wish **to be with him," we do not let her** — [12]**for we have learned** in the very same Mishnah, that according to the Sages, a woman who knew of her husband's defect prior to marrying him must accept him as he is, **"except for a man who is afflicted with skin sores,** in which case they are compelled to divorce **since** sexual intercourse with her **causes** his flesh to **decay** even further." The law here is ostensibly the same as that which we apply in the case of a man who is required to divorce a barren woman. [13]Nevertheless the Mishnah **teaches it,** while not mentioning the latter case at all!

[1]הָא, בְּמִילֵּי; [2]הָא, בְּשׁוֹטֵי.
[3]מַתְקִיף לָהּ רַבִּי אַבָּא:
[4]"בִּדְבָרִים לֹא יִוָּסֶר עָבֶד".
[5]אֶלָּא אֲמַר רַבִּי אַבָּא: הָא וְהָא בְּשׁוֹטֵי. [77B] [6]הָתָם, כִּי אָמְרָה:
[7]"הָוֵינָא בַּהֲדֵיהּ", שָׁבְקִינַן לָהּ.
[8]הָכָא, אַף עַל גַּב דְּאָמְרָה:
[9]"הָוֵינָא בַּהֲדֵיהּ", לָא שָׁבְקִינַן לָהּ.
[10]וַהֲרֵי מוּכֵּה שְׁחִין, דְּאַף עַל גַּב דְּאָמְרָה: [11]"הָוֵינָא בַּהֲדֵיהּ", לָא שָׁבְקִינַן לָהּ, [12]דִּתְנַן: "חוּץ מִמּוּכֵּה שְׁחִין, מִפְּנֵי שֶׁמְּמַקְתּוֹ".
[13]וְקָתָנֵי!

LITERAL TRANSLATION

[1]This, with words; [2]this, with whips.
[3]Rabbi Abba strongly objected to it: [4]"With words, a servant will not be corrected."
[5]Rather, Rabbi Abba said: This and this with whips.
[77B] [6]There, when she says: [7]"I shall be with him," we let her. [8]Here, even though she says: [9]"I shall be with him," we do not let her.
[10]Yet behold [the case of] one who is afflicted with skin sores, for even though she said: [11]"I shall be with him," we do not let her, [12]for we have learned: "Except for one who is afflicted with skin sores, because she causes [his flesh to] decay."
[13]And it taught [it]!

RASHI

הא במילי — אפריה ורביה במילי מייסרינן, בשוטי לא רדינן ליה. אבל הנך — בשוטי נמי רדינן ליה — שאי אפשר לה לקבל. **התם** — גבי מתניתין. **כי אמרה** — מקבלנא ליה והוינא בהדיה — שבקינן לה.

HALAKHAH

בְּשׁוֹטֵי **With whips.** "Wherever the Sages say that a man can be compelled to divorce his wife, the implication is that it can be done even through use of a whip. Some authorities maintain that a whip can only be used when it states explicitly that he is forced to divorce by the courts (כּוֹפִין לְהוֹצִיא); when it merely states that he is obligated to divorce (יוֹצִיא), but makes no mention of coercion, a whip cannot be used. The court may use only words of admonishment condemning him as a 'transgressor.' *Rema* writes (in the name of *Rosh*) that since it is a matter of dispute as to when a whip can be used, it is preferable not to compel a man to divorce his wife with a whip, so that it not be regarded as a 'coerced divorce,' which is invalid. If, however, a man is married to a woman who is forbidden to him by law, all agree that he can be compelled to divorce her by means of a whip. Use of excommunication (חֵרֶם) is equivalent to use of a whip (*Mordekhai*), and thus should not be employed in place of it. However, the Sages are at liberty to employ lesser measures of persuasion, such as decreeing that no one may conduct business with him (*Sha'arei Dura, Maharik*) or circumcise his sons or bury them until he gives his wife a divorce (*Binyamin Ze'ev*). In situations of doubt as to whether compulsion is in order, a man cannot be compelled to divorce; but he can be coerced to pay his wife's ketubah settlement and dowry, if he does agree to divorce her." (*Rambam, Sefer Nashim, Hilkhot Ishut* 15:7; *Shulhan Arukh, Even HaEzer* 154:21.)

TRANSLATION AND COMMENTARY

הָתָם [1]The Gemara now explains the difference between the two cases: **There,** in the case of a woman who is married to a man with skin sores, **when she says:** [2]**"**Rather than have to divorce my husband for fear that sexual contact might endanger him, **I shall live with him with witnesses** to prevent intimacy,**" we let her** remain with him. [3]Whereas **here,** in the case of a woman who has been married for ten years without bearing children, **even though she says:** [4]**"I shall live with him with witnesses," we do not let her** remain married, because her husband must fulfill his obligation to procreate. And for that reason we obligate the husband to divorce her and require him to fulfill the commandment with another wife.

תַּנְיָא [5]**It was taught** in a Baraita: **"Rabbi Yose said:** [6]**A certain elder of the people of Jerusalem told me** that **there are twenty-four** different varieties of **skin sores,** [7]**and** regarding **all of** those who suffer from **them, the Sages said: Sexual intercourse aggravates them,** [8]**and** for **those who have** ***ra'atan*** (a particularly severe skin disorder) — sexual contact **is the worst of all** aggravating factors."

מִמַּאי הָוֵי [9]The Gemara asks: **From what is** the disease of *ra'atan* acquired? [10]The answer is **taught** in a Baraita: **"If a man lets blood and** then **has intercourse** soon afterwards, **he will have sickly children.** [11]**If both** husband and wife **let blood and** then **have intercourse** soon afterwards, [12]**he will have children who have** ***ra'atan*****."**

אָמַר רַב פַּפָּא [13]**Rav Pappa said: We did not say** that engaging in intercourse after letting blood produces ailing children, **except if the man did not eat anything** before having relations. [14]**But if he ate something, we have no** problem **with it** since eating eliminates the adverse effects.

LITERAL TRANSLATION

[1]There, when she says: [2]"I shall live with him with witnesses," we let her. [3]Here, even though she says: [4]"I shall live with him with witnesses," we do not let her.

[5]It was taught: "Rabbi Yose said: [6]A certain elder of the people of Jerusalem related to me: There are twenty-four [varieties of] skin sores [7]and [regarding] all of them the Sages said: Sexual intercourse aggravates them, [8]and [for] those who have *ra'atan*, it is worst of all."

[9]From what is it? [10]As it was taught: "[If] one let blood and [then] had intercourse, he will have sickly children. [11][If] both of them let [blood] and had intercourse, [12]he will have children who have *ra'atan*."

[13]Rav Pappa said: We did not say [this] other than when he did not taste anything. [14]But [if] he tasted something, we have no [problem] with it.

[1]הָתָם, כִּי אָמְרָה: [2]״דָּיֵירְנָא בַּהֲדֵיהּ בְּסָהֲדֵי״, שָׁבְקִינַן לָהּ. [3]הָכָא, אַף עַל גַּב דְּאָמְרָה: [4]״דָּיֵירְנָא בַּהֲדֵיהּ בְּסָהֲדֵי״, לָא שָׁבְקִינַן לָהּ.

[5]תַּנְיָא: ״אָמַר רַבִּי יוֹסֵי: [6]שָׂח לִי זָקֵן אֶחָד מֵאַנְשֵׁי יְרוּשָׁלַיִם: עֶשְׂרִים וְאַרְבָּעָה מוּכֵּי שְׁחִין הֵן, [7]וְכוּלָּן אָמְרוּ חֲכָמִים: תַּשְׁמִישׁ קָשֶׁה לָהֶן, [8]וּבַעֲלֵי רָאתָן, קָשֶׁה מִכּוּלָּן״.

[9]מִמַּאי הָוֵי? [10]דְּתַנְיָא: ״הִקִּיז דָּם וְשִׁימֵּשׁ, הָוְיָין לוֹ בָּנִים וִיתָיְקִין. [11]הִקִּיזוּ שְׁנֵיהֶם, וְשִׁימְּשׁוּ, [12]הָוְיָין לוֹ בָּנִים בַּעֲלֵי רָאתָן״.

[13]אֲמַר רַב פַּפָּא: לָא אֲמָרָן אֶלָּא דְּלָא טָעֵים מִידֵי. [14]אֲבָל טָעֵים מִידֵי, לֵית לָן בָּהּ.

RASHI

בעלי ראתן – סרכן יש לו במוחו. ויתיקין = חלשים.

REALIA

רָאתָן ***Ra'atan.*** This illness is mentioned in several places in the Talmud and the Midrash, although it has not been identified conclusively (various attempts to identify it have been made). In all probability, though, *ra'atan* is a type of leprosy (Hansen's disease).

This illness is characterized by profuse secretion of nasal mucus and by the hardening of the skin in many places, which may cause the victim to lose his sense of touch there, or in the entire affected limb. Later stages of this leprosy are marked by serious damage to the skin, and eventually by the necrosis of the external organs. The disease is contagious, but only after close and prolonged contact with the victim; however, since it is so severe (and, indeed, incurable), people have been very careful to avoid contact with lepers, and even with flies that could have come into contact with lepers' excreta or things they touched.

In light of the above, it is very difficult to understand what connection there is between *ra'atan* and a parasite in the brain. Perhaps there was some connection with other diseases caused by parasites. Certain types of parasites (such as dog ascarids) wander from place to place in the body, and cause serious injury to the victim.

LANGUAGE

וִיתָיְקִין **Sickly.** The etymology and meaning of this word are unclear. *Rabbi Benyamin Musafiya* derives it from the Greek φθιαικός, *phthisikos,* "consumptive," while others derive the word from ἑκτικός, *hektikos,* which also means "consumptive" (*inter alia*).

NOTES

שָׂח לִי זָקֵן אֶחָד **A certain elder related to me.** A similar story is reported in the Jerusalem Talmud, where the elder is described as a resident of Sepphoris who himself suffered from skin sores.

HALAKHAH

דָּיֵירְנָא בַּהֲדֵיהּ בְּסָהֲדֵי **I shall live with him with witnesses.** "If a man has a defect for which he could theoretically be compelled to divorce his wife, and yet the woman wishes to remain with him, they need not separate. However, if he suffers from skin sores, they can be forced to divorce even against their will, as sexual contact aggravates his condition. If they are prepared, however, to live in the company of witnesses who will prevent them from secluding themselves, then they may remain together. If a man is married to a woman who cannot bear him children (or, what's worse, if the marital relationship is one that is forbidden), the couple are compelled to divorce, even if they are prepared to live in the company of witnesses." (*Rambam, Sefer Nashim, Hilkhot Ishut* 25:12; *Shulḥan Arukh, Even HaEzer* 154:1,10.)

LITERAL TRANSLATION

[1]What are his symptoms?[2]His eyes tear, and his nostrils drip, and drool comes out from his mouth, and flies land on him.

[3]And what is his remedy? [4]Abaye said: Pila, and ladanum, [5]the shavings of a nut tree and the scrapings of a hide, [6]and a *kelil malka*, and the calyx of a red date-palm. [7]And he boils them together, and he brings him into a house of marble. [8]And if there is no house of marble, he brings him into a house [which is] seven-and-a-half bricks [thick]. [9]And he pours three hundred cups over his head until his skull is softened, [10]and he splits through to his brain, [11]and he brings four myrtle leaves, and lifts up each leg and places one, [12]and he takes it with tongs, and burns it, [13]for if not, it will return upon him.

[14]Rabbi Yoḥanan proclaimed: Take caution from the flies of those who have *ra'atan*. [15]Rabbi Zera would not sit in [the path of] his breeze.

[1]מַאי סִימָנֵיהּ? [2]דָּלְפָן עֵינֵיהּ, וְדָיְיבֵי נְחִירֵיהּ, וְאַתְיָא לֵיהּ רִירָא מִפּוּמֵיהּ, וּרְמוּ דִּידְבֵי עִילָּוֵיהּ.

[3]וּמַאי אָסוּתֵיהּ? [4]אָמַר אַבָּיֵי: פִּילָא, וְלוֹדָנָא, [5]גִּירְדָא דֶאֱגוֹזָא, וְגִירְדָא דְאַשְׁפָּא, [6]וּכְלִיל מַלְכָּא, וּמַתְחַלָא דְדִיקְלָא סוּמְקָא. [7]וְשָׁלֵיק לְהוּ בַּהֲדֵי הֲדָדֵי, וּמְעַיֵּיל לֵיהּ לְבֵיתָא דְשִׁישָׁא. [8]וְאִי לָא אִיכָּא בֵּיתָא דְשִׁישָׁא, מְעַיֵּיל לֵיהּ לְבֵיתָא דְּשַׁב לִבְנֵי וְאָרִיחָא. [9]וְנָטֵיל לֵיהּ תְּלָת מְאָה כָּסֵי עַל רֵישֵׁיהּ עַד דְּרַפְיָא אַרְעִיתָא דְמוֹחֵיהּ, [10]וְקָרַע לְמוֹחֵיהּ, [11]וּמַיְיתֵי אַרְבַּע טַרְפֵּי דְּאָסָא, וּמַדְלֵי כָּל חַד כַּרְעָא וּמוֹתִיב חַד, [12]וְשָׁקֵיל בִּצְבָתָא, וְקָלֵי לֵיהּ, [13]דְּאִי לָא, הָדַר עִילָּוֵיהּ.

[14]מַכְרִיז רַבִּי יוֹחָנָן: הִזָּהֲרוּ מִזְּבוּבֵי שֶׁל בַּעֲלֵי רָאתָן. [15]רַבִּי זֵירָא לָא הֲוָה יָתֵיב בְּזִיקֵיהּ.

TRANSLATION AND COMMENTARY

מַאי סִימָנֵיהּ [1]The Gemara proceeds to explore the situation of one who is afflicted with *ra'atan*: **What are the symptoms of *ra'atan*?** [2]**His eyes tear, and his nostrils drip, and drool comes out of his mouth, and flies land on him.**

וּמַאי אָסוּתֵיהּ [3]**And what is his remedy?** [4]**Abaye said: Pila** and **ladanum** (types of herbs), [5]**the** bark **shavings of a nut** tree **and the scrapings of a hide,** [6]**and** ***kelil malka*** (a variety of rose), **and the calyx of a red date-palm.** One collects all these **and** then **boils them together.** [7]The person administering the remedy then **brings** the one suffering from *ra'atan* **into a house** made of **marble,** ensuring that it is perfectly insulated, [8]**and if there is no house of marble** available for this purpose, **he brings him into a house which** has walls that are at least **seven-and-a-half bricks** thick. [9]**He** then **pours three hundred cups** of the mixture **over** the afflicted one's **head until his skull is softened** and ready for surgery. [10]**He** then **splits through** the skull **to** reveal the man's **brain** and the parasite that is clinging to it. [11]**He** then **brings four myrtle leaves, lifts up each leg** of the parasite individually, **and places one** myrtle leaf under each leg to prevent it from attaching itself to the brain. [12]**He** then **takes** the parasite **with** a pair of **tongs and burns it** immediately, [13]**for if** the parasite is **not** destroyed, **it will return upon him.**

מַכְרִיז רַבִּי יוֹחָנָן [14]To avoid contracting the disease, **Rabbi Yoḥanan** was accustomed to **proclaim: Take caution from the flies** that hover over **those who have *ra'atan*,** for they can easily transmit the disease. [15]**Rabbi Zera would not sit in** the path of **a breeze**

RASHI

ורמו דידבי עליה — זבובין כרוכין אחריו. **פילא** — עשב שקורין *פוליו"ן. **ולודנא** = **אליישינ"א. **גירדא דאגוזא** — קליפי עץ האגוז. **גירדא דאשפא** — מה שגוררין מן העור. **כליל מלכא** = חבצלת. **מתחלא דדיקלא סומקא** — שומר שיש להם לתמרים בקטנותן, כעין שיש לאגוזים קטנים. **לביתא דשישא** — של שיש. כלומר, מקום שאין רוח שולט שם. **שב לבני ואריחא** — שכותלן עב, שבעה לבנים זה אצל זה ואריח, שהוא חצי לבינה. והלבינה שלשה טפחים. **ונטיל ליה** — ושופך לו מאותן מים. **עד דרפיא ארעיתא דמוחיה** — גולגלתו מתרככת, ונוחה ליקרע בסכין. **טרפי** = עלין. **ומדלי כל חד כרעא** — מגביה רגלו של שרץ, ומושיב העלה תחת רגלו. שאם לא יעשה כן, לכשיחזיק בגופו ליטלו — ינעוץ צפרניו במוחו, ויקוץ את הקרום. **בצבתא** = ***טנליי"ש. **דאי לא** — אם לא ישרפנו — יחזור עליו. **הזהרו מזבובי בעלי ראתן** — זבובים השוכנים עליו, קשות להביא אותו חולי על איש אחר. **בזיקיה** — במקום שהנשב רוח אחת על שניהם.

LANGUAGE

פִּילָא Pila. This word is apparently derived from the Greek φύλλον, *phyllon*, meaning "plant" or "dog's mercury" (*Mercurialis*). Some suggest that pila means "laurel leaves."

לוֹדָנָא Ladanum. From the Greek λάδανον, *ladanon* (=Latin *ladanum*), a type of resin derived from the rock-rose. Some commentators suggest that the *lot* mentioned in Genesis 43:11 is ladanum.

LANGUAGE (RASHI)

פוליו"ן* (read: פּוּלְיוֹ״ל) From the Old French *poliol*, meaning "a type of mint."

אליישינ"א** From the Old French *aloisne*, meaning "a type of wormwood."

טנליי"ש*** From the Old French *tenailles*, meaning "tongs."

REALIA

כְּלִיל מַלְכָּא *Kelil malka.*

According to *Assaf HaRofeh*, *kelil malka* is wormwood (*Artemisia;* certain species of this plant are found in Israel). These plants grow in plains and sandy areas, and have small flowers. An ethereal type of oil is derived from certain types of wormwood, and this oil was often used for medicinal purposes in ancient times.

לוֹדָנָא Ladanum. This is apparently the resin from a type of Cistus plant

NOTES

גִּירְדָא דֶאֱגוֹזָא The bark shavings of a nut tree. Our translation follows the reading of *Rashi* and most other commentators: דֶּאֱגוֹזָא. According to *Arukh*, however, the Gemara reads גִּירְדָא דְּאַזוּגָא — "slivers of glass."

גִּירְדָא דְאַשְׁפָּא The scrapings of a hide. A variant reading with the same implication appears in some texts as גִּירְדָא דְאוּשְׁכָּפָא — "the skin scrapings of a shoemaker," produced in the process of tanning leather.

בֵּיתָא דְשִׁישָׁא A marble house. Our passage, like others in the Talmud, suggests that this was a special building used for performing surgery, possibly because it was clean and well sealed, so germs could be kept out.

TRANSLATION AND COMMENTARY

which had first passed over a person suffering from *ra'atan*. [1]**Rabbi Elazar would not enter into the tent** or any other living quarter occupied by a person with *ra'atan*. [2]**Rabbi Ammi and Rabbi Assi would not eat from eggs of that** particular **alley** or compound where the one with *ra'atan* lived, for fear of contamination..

רַבִּי יְהוֹשֻׁעַ בֶּן לֵוִי [3]Unlike them, **Rabbi Yehoshua ben Levi would associate with** those who suffered from *ra'atan* **and engage in Torah** study with them, [4]**saying:** The verse in Proverbs (5:19) describes the Torah as **"a loving deer and a graceful gazelle,"** the latter expression — יַעֲלַת חֵן — having the additional connotation in Hebrew of "arousing grace." [5]**If** the Torah **bestows grace upon those who learn it,** [6]**will it not protect** them from danger as well?

כִּי הֲוָה שְׁכִיב [7]It was related that **when** Rabbi Yehoshua ben Levi **was dying,** the heavenly hosts **said to the Angel of Death:** [8]**"Go, and carry out his will."** [9]The Angel of Death immediately **went and appeared before him.** [10]Rabbi Yehoshua ben Levi **said to** him: **"Show me my place** in the Garden of Eden." [11]The angel **said to him: "Very well.** I shall do as you please." [12]Rabbi Yehoshua ben Levi then **said to him: "Give me your knife, lest you frighten me** with it **along the way."** [13]The angel complied and **gave it to him.**

כִּי מְטָא לְהָתָם [14]**When he arrived** at the gate to the Garden of Eden, the Angel of Death **lifted him and showed him** his place. [15]Rabbi Yehoshua ben Levi **jumped** over the gate **and fell on** the other

[1]רַבִּי אֶלְעָזָר לָא עָיֵיל בְּאָהֳלֵיהּ. [2]רַבִּי אַמִי וְרַבִּי אַסִי לָא הָווּ אָכְלֵי מִבֵּיעֵי דְּהַהִיא מְבוֹאָה.

[3]רַבִּי יְהוֹשֻׁעַ בֶּן לֵוִי מִיכְרַךְ בְּהוּ וְעָסֵיק בַּתּוֹרָה, [4]אָמַר: "אַיֶּלֶת אֲהָבִים וְיַעֲלַת חֵן". [5]אִם חֵן מַעֲלָה עַל לוֹמְדֶיהָ, [6]אַגּוּנֵי לָא מַגְנָא?

[7]כִּי הֲוָה שְׁכִיב, אָמְרוּ לֵיהּ לְמַלְאַךְ הַמָּוֶת: [8]"זִיל, עֲבֵיד לֵיהּ רְעוּתֵיהּ". [9]אֲזַל אִיתְחֲזִי לֵיהּ. [10]אֲמַר לֵיהּ: "אַחֲוֵי לִי דּוּכְתַּאי"! [11]אֲמַר לֵיהּ: "לְחַיֵּי". [12]אֲמַר לֵיהּ: "הַב לִי סַכִּינָךְ דִּלְמָא מְבַעֲתַתְּ לִי בְּאוֹרְחָא". [13]יָהֲבָהּ נִיהֲלֵיהּ.

[14]כִּי מְטָא לְהָתָם, דַּלְיֵיהּ, קָא מַחֲוֵי לֵיהּ. [15]שְׁוַור נָפַל לְהַהוּא

LITERAL TRANSLATION

[1]Rabbi Elazar would not enter into his tent. [2]Rabbi Ammi and Rabbi Assi would not eat from eggs of that alley.

[3]Rabbi Yehoshua ben Levi would associate with them and engage in Torah, [4]saying: "A loving deer and a graceful gazelle." [5]If it bestows grace upon those who learn it, [6]will it not protect [them]?

[7]When he was dying, they said to the Angel of Death: [8]"Go, do for him his will." [9]He went [and] appeared to him. [10]He said to him: "Show me my place!" [11]He said to him: "Very well." [12]He said to him: "Give me your knife, lest you frighten me along the way." [13]He gave it to him.

[14]When he arrived there, he lifted him, [and] showed him. [15]He jumped [and] fell on that

RASHI

מיכרך בהו — נדבק אצלם בשעה שעוסק בתורה, ומושיבן אצלו, ומובטח הוא שתגין התורה עליו ולא יוזק. **כי הוה שכיב** — כשהגיע זמנו ליפטר. **אחוי לי דוכתאי** — הוליכני לגן עדן, והראני מקומי. **שוור** = קפץ. **איתשיל אשבועתא** — אם נשבע בשבועה מעולם, ונשאל עליה להתירה.

(rockrose, a green bush with plain, wrinkled leaves found throughout Israel).

The rockrose's flowers are large and white or red (depending on the exact species). The fruit, which grows in the plant's uniquely shaped capsules, ripens at the end of summer. Its resin was frequently used for medicinal purposes in ancient times, and even today it is used in cosmetics.

NOTES

לָא הָווּ אָכְלֵי מִבֵּיעֵי **They would not eat eggs.** *Rivan* and *Talmidei Rabbenu Yonah* explain that Rabbi Ammi and Rabbi Assi would abstain from eating any food that came from the immediate vicinity of a person with *ra'atan*. The Gemara specifically mentions eggs in order to show the extent of their caution. They shunned even eggs, which are enclosed in shells and thus unlikely to be contaminated; so they avoided foods which were not protected by any outer covering even more.

מִיכְרַךְ בְּהוּ וְעָסֵיק בַּתּוֹרָה **He would associate with them and engage in Torah.** *Rashi, Rivan* and others interpret this to mean that Rabbi Yehoshua ben Levi, when engaged in Torah study, would seek the company of those suffering from *ra'atan*, confident that the merit of his learning would protect him from the danger of contracting the disease. *Ritva* adds to this that Rabbi Yehoshua would remain in the company of the afflicted even after completing his study, as the power of his Torah continued to provide protection (in accordance with *Sotah* 21a). *Ahavat Eitan* suggests that Rabbi Yehoshua was actually engaged in *teaching* Torah to those suffering from *ra'atan*, rather than pursuing his own study; only in such a case was he permitted to expose himself to such imminent danger, since he was performing a mitzvah which had communal benefit.

אִם חֵן מַעֲלָה **If it bestows grace upon those who learn it.** *Maharam Shiff* explains: If the Torah has the power to "arouse grace" and make an unattractive person more comely, then surely it must protect those who already possess grace — the saintly and the learned — from losing it to a disease as ravaging as *ra'atan*.

אַחֲוֵי לִי דּוּכְתַּאי **Show me my place.** The Angel of Death assumed that Rabbi Yehoshua ben Levi was interested in seeing his destined place in the Garden of Eden to lessen his anxiety and fear of death, as is recorded regarding other righteous men who were shown their place in the World to Come in order to console them as they approached death.

שְׁוַור נָפַל לְהַהוּא גִּיסָא **He jumped and fell on that side.** Rabbi Yehoshua ben Levi is listed in *Avot* of Rabbi Natan

LANGUAGE

תַּכְטְקֵי Stool. From the Persian *taxta,* meaning "chair."

LANGUAGE (RASHI)

פליסטי״ל* (read: פלדישטו״ל) From the Old French *faldestol,* meaning "folding chair."

TRANSLATION AND COMMENTARY

side. [1]The angel **seized him by the corner of his cloak,** intending to put him to death before allowing him to assume his place in Eden. [2]Rabbi Yehoshua ben Levi resisted the angel's pull and **said to him: "By an oath, I will not come** back to you." [3]**The Holy One, blessed be He, said: "If** Rabbi Yehoshua ben Levi ever **asked** a Sage **for release from a vow** and had it granted, [4]then **let him** return now to the angel, as the vow he just made can be similarly absolved. [5]But **if he never** asked for such absolution, **let him not return** to the angel's grip." Since Rabbi Yehoshua ben Levi had never sought absolution from a vow, he was allowed to remain in the Garden of Eden without first consigning himself to the Angel of Death. [6]The angel then **said to him: "Give me** back **my knife."** [7]Wanting to spare others from death, Rabbi Yehoshua ben Levi **would not give it to him.** [8]**A heavenly voice issued forth and said to him:** [9]**"Give** it back **to** the angel, **as it is needed for the creatures."**

מַכְרִיז אֵלִיָּהוּ קַמֵּיהּ [10]As Rabbi Yehoshua ben Levi proceeded to his place in Eden, **Elijah** the Prophet **proclaimed before him: "Clear a place for the son of Levi! Clear a place for the son of Levi!"** [11]Rabbi Yehoshua **entered** the Garden of Eden **and found Rabbi Shimon ben Yoḥai, who was sitting on thirteen stools of gold.** [12]Seeing him approaching, Rabbi Shimon ben Yoḥai **said to him: "Are you the son of Levi?"** [13]Rabbi Yehoshua **replied: "Yes,** I am." Rabbi Shimon ben Yoḥai then asked: [14]**"Was a rainbow** ever **seen in your day?"** [15]Rabbi Yehoshua ben Levi **replied: "Yes."** [16]Rabbi Shimon ben Yoḥai concluded: **"If so,** then **you are not** truly **the son of Levi.** He was perfectly righteous, and therefore a rainbow would not have appeared in his time." (The rainbow is a sign that the world will never again be destroyed as at the time of the great flood. We are taught that in those generations that are blessed with men of great saintliness, the appearance of a rainbow is unnecesary, because the righteous deeds of these men protect the world.) [17]The Gemara notes: **And** what Rabbi Yehoshua answered Rabbi Shimon **was not** really **so, for** in fact **there was no** rainbow **at all** in his day. [18]**Rather,** Rabbi Yehoshua concealed the truth, **thinking** to himself: **"I shall not take** the **credit for myself."**

גִּיסָא. [1]נַקְטֵיהּ בְּקַרְנָא דִּגְלִימֵיהּ. [2]אֲמַר לֵיהּ: ״בִּשְׁבוּעֲתָא, דְּלָא אָתֵינָא״. [3]אֲמַר קוּדְשָׁא בְּרִיךְ הוּא: ״אִי אִיתַּשֵּׁיל אַשְׁבוּעֲתָא, [4]נִיהְדַר. [5]אִי לָא, לָא נִיהֲדַר״. [6]אֲמַר לֵיהּ: ״הַב לִי סַכִּינָאי״! [7]לָא הֲוָה קָא יָהֵיב לֵיהּ. [8]נָפְקָא בַּת קָלָא וְאָמְרָה לֵיהּ: [9]״הַב נִיהֲלֵיהּ, דְּמִיתְבְּעָא לִבְרִיָּיתָא״. [10]מַכְרִיז אֵלִיָּהוּ קַמֵּיהּ: ״פַּנּוּ מָקוֹם לְבַר לִיוָאי, פַּנּוּ מָקוֹם לְבַר לִיוָאי״! [11]אֲזַל אַשְׁכַּחֵיהּ לְרַבִּי שִׁמְעוֹן בֶּן יוֹחַאי דַּהֲוָה יָתֵיב עַל תְּלָת עֲשַׂר תַּכְטְקֵי פִּיזָא. [12]אֲמַר לֵיהּ: ״אַתְּ הוּא בַּר לִיוָאי״? [13]אֲמַר לֵיהּ: ״הֵן״. [14]״נִרְאֲתָה קֶשֶׁת בְּיָמֶיךָ״? [15]אֲמַר לֵיהּ: ״הֵן״. [16]״אִם כֵּן, אִי אַתָּה בַּר לִיוָאי״. [17]וְלָא הִיא, דְּלָא הֲוַאי מִידֵי. [18]אֶלָּא סָבַר: ״לָא אַחֲזִיק טִיבוּתָא לְנַפְשַׁאי״.

LITERAL TRANSLATION

side. [1]He seized him by the corner of his cloak. [2]He said to him: "By an oath, I will not come." [3]The Holy One, blessed be He, said: "If he [ever] asked [for release] from a vow, [4]let him return. [5]If not, let him not return." [6]He said to him: "Give me my knife!" [7]He would not give it to him. [8]A heavenly voice arose and said to him: [9]"Give [it] to him, as it is needed for the creatures."

[10]Elijah proclaimed before him: "Clear a place for the son of Levi! Clear a place for the son of Levi!" [11]He went [and] found Rabbi Shimon ben Yoḥai who was sitting on thirteen stools of gold. [12]He said to him: "Are you the son of Levi?" [13]He said to him: "Yes." [14]"Was a rainbow seen in your day?" [15]He said to him: "Yes." [16]"If so, you are not the son of Levi." [17]And it is not so, for there was not at all. [18]Rather he thought: "I shall not take credit for myself."

RASHI

תכטקי = *פליסטי״ל. **אם כן לית את בר ליואי** — אין אתה ראוי לכרוז זה שאני שומע. שהקשת אינו אלא אות ברית שלא יחרב העולם, ואם יש צדיק גמור בדור — אין צריך אות. **לא הואי מידי** — לא נראה הקשת בימיו.

NOTES

as one of ten people who entered the Garden of Eden while still alive. *Terumat HaDeshen* and others discuss what it actually means to enter the next world while still alive. It would appear from the sources that these people did not retain their physicality, but rather took leave of their bodies through a painless spiritual ascent referred to as "death by divine kiss," thus avoiding the fearsome grip of the Angel of Death.

נִרְאֲתָה קֶשֶׁת בְּיָמֶיךָ Was a rainbow seen in your day? It may be argued: Surely, a rainbow is formed by the sun's rays refracting through rain or mist. *Shelah* (in the name of *Rema*) suggests that perhaps it always rained at night. As the Gemara explains elsewhere, night rain constitutes a special sign of blessing since it falls when people are normally indoors and allows them to carry on their daytime activities undisturbed.

לָא אַחֲזִיק טִיבוּתָא לְנַפְשַׁאי I shall not give credit to myself. The question has been asked: How could Rabbi Yehoshua

TRANSLATION AND COMMENTARY

רַבִּי חֲנִינָא בַּר פַּפָּא [1]It was further related that **Rabbi Ḥanina bar Pappa was a good friend** of the Angel of Death, who often visited him. [2]**When** Rabbi Ḥanina **was dying,** the heavenly hosts **said to the Angel of Death:** [3]**"Go, do for him his will."** [4]And so the angel immediately **went to him and appeared to him.** [5]Rabbi Ḥanina bar Pappa **said to him: "Leave me** alone for **thirty days until I** have a chance to **review my learning,** and then I will be ready, [6]**for** I am told **they say** in the next world that **"fortunate is he who comes here with his learning in his hand."** [7]The Angel of Death complied with his request and **left him** alone to review his studies. [8]**After thirty days,** the angel **went** once again **and appeared to him.** [9]Rabbi Ḥanina bar Pappa **said to him: "Show me my place** in the Garden of Eden." [10]The angel **said to him: "Very well."** [11]Rabbi Ḥanina then **said to him: "Give me your knife** and let me hold it on the journey, [12]**lest you frighten me** with it **along the way."** [13]The angel **said to him: "As your friend** Rabbi Yehoshua ben Levi did to me, **you wish to do to me** as well?" [14]Rabbi Ḥanina **said to him: "Bring a Torah scroll and see: Is there anything that is written in it that I did not fulfill?** Surely I am no less deserving than my friend Rabbi Yehoshua ben Levi of entering the Garden of Eden alive!" [15]Questioning Rabbi Ḥanina's claim, the angel **said to him: "Did you** ever **associate with those who have** *ra'atan* **and engage in Torah** study, as did Rabbi Yehoshua ben Levi?" The Gemara notes: [16]**And even though** Rabbi Ḥanina bar Pappa was not Rabbi Yehoshua ben Levi's equal, nevertheless **when he died,** [17]**a pillar of fire interposed itself between him and the** rest of the **world.** [18]**And we have learned** elsewhere **that a pillar of fire does not interpose itself** in this manner **other than for one in a generation or for two in a generation.**

קְרֵב לְגַבֵּיהּ [19]The pillar of fire made it impossible to bury Rabbi Ḥanina. **Rabbi Alexandri approached**

[1]רַבִּי חֲנִינָא בַּר פַּפָּא שׁוֹשְׁבִינֵיהּ הֲוָה. [2]כִּי הֲוָה קָא נַיְחָא נַפְשֵׁיהּ, אָמְרוּ לֵיהּ לְמַלְאַךְ הַמָּוֶת: [3]"זִיל, עֲבִיד לֵיהּ רְעוּתֵיהּ". [4]אֲזַל לְגַבֵּיהּ וְאִיתְחֲזֵי לֵיהּ. [5]אֲמַר לֵיהּ: "שְׁבַקִי תְּלָתִין יוֹם עַד דְּנִהֲדַר תַּלְמוּדַאי, [6]דְּאָמְרִי: 'אַשְׁרֵי מִי שֶׁבָּא לְכָאן וְתַלְמוּדוֹ בְּיָדוֹ'". [7]שְׁבַקֵיהּ. [8]לְבָתַר תְּלָתִין יוֹמִין אֲזַל אִיתְחֲזִי לֵיהּ. [9]אֲמַר לֵיהּ: "אַחֲוֵי לִי דּוּכְתַּאי". [10]אֲמַר לֵיהּ: "לְחַיֵּי". [11]אֲמַר לֵיהּ: "הַב לִי סַכִּינָךְ, [12]דִּלְמָא מְבַעֲתַתְּ לִי בְּאוֹרְחָא". [13]אֲמַר לֵיהּ: "כְּחַבְרָךְ בָּעֵית לְמֶיעֱבַד לִי"? [14]אֲמַר לֵיהּ: "אַיְיתֵי סֵפֶר תּוֹרָה וַחֲזִי: מִי אִיכָּא מִידֵי דִּכְתִיב בֵּיהּ דְּלָא קַיַּימְתֵּיהּ"? [15]אֲמַר לֵיהּ: מִי אִיכַּרְכַתְּ בְּבַעֲלֵי רָאתָן וְאִיעַסְקַתְּ בַּתּוֹרָה"? [16]וַאֲפִילּוּ הָכִי, כִּי נָח נַפְשֵׁיהּ, [17]אַפְסֵיק לֵיהּ עַמּוּדָא דְּנוּרָא בֵּין דִּידֵיהּ לְעָלְמָא. [18]וּגְמִירִי, דְּלָא מַפְסִיק עַמּוּדָא דְּנוּרָא אֶלָּא לְחַד בְּדָרָא אוֹ לִתְרֵין בְּדָרָא.
[19]קְרֵב לְגַבֵּיהּ רַבִּי אֲלֶכְּסַנְדְּרִי,

LITERAL TRANSLATION

[1]Rabbi Ḥanina bar Pappa was his good friend. [2]When he was dying, they said to the Angel of Death: [3]"Go, do for him his will." [4]He went to him and appeared to him. [5]He said to him: "Leave me [for] thirty days until I review my learning, [6]for they say: 'Fortunate is he who comes here with his learning in his hand.'" [7]He left him. [8]After thirty days he went [and] appeared to him. [9]He said to him: "Show me my place." [10]He said to him: "Very well." [11]He said to him: "Give me your knife, [12]lest you frighten me along the way." [13]He said to him: "As your friend [did] you wish to do to me?" [14]He said to him: "Bring a Torah scroll and see: Is there anything that is written in it that I did not fulfill?" [15]He said to him: "Did you [ever] associate with those who have *ra'atan* and engage in Torah?" [16]And even so, when he died, [17]a pillar of fire interposed itself between him and the world. [18]And we have learned that a pillar of fire does not interpose itself other than for one in a generation or for two in a generation.

[19]Rabbi Alexandri approached him,

RASHI

שושביניה — אוהבו, ורגיל אצלו מלאך המות. **מי איכרכת בבעלי ראתן ועסקת בתורה** — כדהוה עביד איהו, שהיה מסכן בנפשו לכבד את התורה.

NOTES

ben Levi have resorted to falsehood, even for reasons of modesty? *Ahavat Tzion* suggests that a rainbow was indeed seen in his lifetime — that is, during his youth and prior to his attaining greatness. Consequently, his answer was not a lie, although it was somewhat deceptive, since the purpose of Rabbi Shimon's question was to determine whether he had ever achieved the kind of greatness that caused rainbows to disappear. *Ḥever ben Ḥayyim* explains that Rabbi Yehoshua meant that, were it a matter of his own merit, a rainbow would have been seen in his day; the fact that no rainbow was seen indicated to him that it was due to someone else's merit.

TRANSLATION AND COMMENTARY

him, **and said:** [1]**"Act for the sake of the Sages' honor** and remove the pillar." [2]But **he did not pay heed.** Rabbi Alexandri approached him again and said: "If you are not ready to act for the sake of the Sages' honor, [3]then at least **act for the sake of your father's honor!"** [4]Rabbi Ḥanina still **did not pay heed.** Finally, Rabbi Alexandri implored him: [5]"If for no other reason, **act for the sake of your own honor!"** [6]This time the pillar of fire **removed itself,** so Rabbi Ḥanina could be properly buried.

אָמַר אַבָּיֵי [7]**Abaye said:** The pillar of fire surrounded Rabbi Ḥanina in order **to exclude from** his company **anyone who did not fulfill** the Torah as fully as he did, which includes **even** one who fulfilled the entire Torah except for **one letter.**

אֲמַר לֵיהּ [8]**Rav Adda bar Matana said to** Abaye: The pillar of fire appeared in order **to exclude** from Rabbi Ḥanina's presence someone like **Master, who does not have a** proper **railing for his roof** (as required by Deuteronomy 22:8 to protect people from falling). [9]Yet the Gemara notes: **It is not so,** for **there certainly was** a railing around Abaye's roof, [10]**but at that** particular **hour** when Rav Adda bar Matana reproached Abaye, **the wind had knocked it down.**

אָמַר רַבִּי חֲנִינָא [11]**Rabbi Ḥanina said: Why are there no people with** ***ra'atan*** found **in Babylonia?** [12]**Because** Babylonians **eat beet greens and drink beer of izma.** [13]**Rabbi Yoḥanan said: Why are there no lepers** found **in Babylonia?** [14]**Because** Babylonians **eat beet greens, and drink beer, and bathe in the waters of the Euphrates** — all of which strengthen the body's resistance to disease.

LITERAL TRANSLATION

[and] said: [1]"Act for the sake of the Sages' honor!" [2]He did not pay heed. [3]"Act for the sake of your father's honor!" [4]He did not pay heed. [5]"Act for the sake of your own honor!" [6]It removed itself.

[7]Abaye said: To exclude from anyone who did not fulfill even one letter.

[8]Rav Adda bar Matana said to him: To exclude Master who does not have a railing for his roof. [9]And it is not so; there certainly was, [10]but at that hour the wind had knocked it down.

[11]Rabbi Ḥanina said: Why are there no people with *ra'atan* in Babylonia? [12]Because they eat beets and drink beer of izma. [13]Rabbi Yoḥanan said: Why are there no lepers in Babylonia? [14]Because they eat beets, and drink beer, and bathe in the waters of the Euphrates.

אָמַר: [1]"עֲשֵׂה בִּשְׁבִיל כְּבוֹד חֲכָמִים"! [2]לָא אַשְׁגַּח. [3]"עֲשֵׂה בִּשְׁבִיל כְּבוֹד אָבִיךָ"! [4]לָא אַשְׁגַּח. [5]"עֲשֵׂה בִּשְׁבִיל כְּבוֹד עַצְמְךָ"! [6]אִיסְתַּלֵּק.

[7]אָמַר אַבָּיֵי: לְאַפּוּקֵי מִמַּאן דְּלָא קַיֵּים אֲפִילּוּ אוֹת אַחַת.

[8]אֲמַר לֵיהּ רַב אַדָּא בַּר מַתָּנָא: לְאַפּוּקֵי מָר, דְּלָא אִית לֵיהּ מַעֲקֶה לְאִיגָּרֵיהּ. [9]וְלָא הִיא; מִיהֲוָה הֲוָה, [10]וְהַהִיא שַׁעְתָּא הוּא דְּשַׁדְיֵיהּ זִיקָא.

[11]אָמַר רַבִּי חֲנִינָא: מִפְּנֵי מָה אֵין בַּעֲלֵי רָאתָן בְּבָבֶל? [12]מִפְּנֵי שֶׁאוֹכְלִין תְּרָדִין, וְשׁוֹתִין שֵׁכָר שֶׁל הִיזְמֵי. [13]אָמַר רַבִּי יוֹחָנָן: מִפְּנֵי מָה אֵין מְצוֹרָעִין בְּבָבֶל? [14]מִפְּנֵי שֶׁאוֹכְלִין תְּרָדִין, וְשׁוֹתִין שֵׁכָר, וְרוֹחֲצִין בְּמֵי פְּרָת.

הדרן עלך המדיר את אשתו

RASHI

בשביל כבוד עצמך — שיקרנו אליך, ויספדו, ויתעסקו בך. **אמר אביי לאפוקי ממאן דלא קיים** — עמוד זה בא להוציא מעליו מי שלא קיים את כל התורה, כמו שמקיים הוא. **של היזמי** — שמטילין בו כשות שגדל בהיזמי.

הדרן עלך המדיר

NOTES

אֲפִילּוּ אוֹת אַחַת **Even one letter.** *Maharsha* explains that there are certain Torah obligations which are not stated explicitly in the Biblical text, but are alluded to by way of a superfluous letter. The pillar of fire came to exclude from Rabbi Ḥanina's company even those who were not scrupulous about observing such obligations.

Conclusion to Chapter Seven

Regarding vows, it was concluded that if an explicit condition was attached to the marriage agreement that the husband or wife be free of vows, and the condition was not fulfilled, the marriage is void. After clarifying how it is at all possible for the husband to take a vow forbidding his wife to enjoy something which he is obligated to provide her, the Gemara concludes that if the husband took a vow which forces his wife to abstain from something which she is legally entitled to enjoy, the woman may demand a divorce with payment of her ketubah. The time given the husband to grant his wife a divorce depends on the nature of his vow. The greater the imposition that he imposed upon his wife, the sooner the courts intervene and compel the husband to divorce her.

A woman's unfit conduct stands in opposition to the basic marriage agreement (expressed in the formula recited at the time of betrothal, "in accordance with the law of Moses and Israel"). Thus, a woman's breach of a basic standard of modesty or her violation of a prohibition which directly affects the couple's marital relationship is a valid cause for divorce without payment of her ketubah.

Regarding physical defects, the Gemara concluded that with respect to a woman, an unattractive blemish (as defined in the Gemara) provides her husband with grounds for divorce. But with respect to a man, divorce can only be imposed upon him if he suffers from a "major defect" (as defined in the Gemara). The Gemara distinguished between defects found on those parts of the body which are ordinarily revealed, about which the husband cannot put forward the claim that he had entered into the marriage in error, and defects found on those parts of the body which are ordinarily covered, about which the husband can argue that he discovered the defect only after he was married. The Gemara's extended clarification of this matter led to a more general discussion of the question of which party the burden of proof falls upon when something might have happened to cancel the validity of a transaction. The Gemara concluded that the burden of proof falls upon the party who possessed the disputed object when the doubt came into being.

Introduction to Chapter Eight

הָאִשָּׁה שֶׁנָּפְלוּ

This chapter deals primarily with the laws governing a woman's usufruct property. The property that a woman brings into her marriage from her father's home and which is not included in her ketubah as her dowry, as well as the property that the woman inherits or receives as a gift after her marriage is known as *nikhsei melog*, or usufruct property. The woman retains ownership of the property throughout the period of her marriage, but her husband is permitted to use the property and enjoy the right of usufruct. Thus, the husband is entitled to all the benefits deriving from the property in a manner that leaves the principal intact.

This divided ownership of usufruct property — the principal belonging to the woman, the usufruct belonging to the husband — gives rise to a series of questions regarding the right of each of the parties to sell the property or give it away as a gift. The law varies in different cases, depending on whether the woman is only betrothed to her husband or already married to him, or whether she is bound to her deceased husband's brother by the levirate tie.

Another question which arises is how to preserve the woman's property in such a manner that the principal will remain intact for her, while at the same time the usufruct can be enjoyed by her husband. It is necessary in this connection to put forward clear criteria by which to distinguish between principal, which must remain in the woman's possession, and usufruct, to which the husband is entitled. This is particularly difficult in cases where the woman's property will not replenish itself if the husband enjoys the usufruct, so that the husband's enjoyment of the usufruct will lead to a gradual depletion of the woman's principal.

Another issue which comes under discussion is what to do when the marriage ends in divorce. A particular problem arises in the case where the woman's property yielded produce, but it was still attached to the ground at the time of her divorce. Is such produce regarded as principal, which belongs to the woman, or usufruct, which goes to the husband? Another problem arises in the case where the husband invested his own money in his wife's property, expecting to enjoy the usufruct, but then divorced her before he was able to recoup his investment or even enjoy any usufruct at all. Is the husband entitled to any compensation for his expenses, or not?

These and related issues constitute the subject matter of our chapter.

הָאִשָּׁה

[1]שֶׁנָּפְלוּ לָהּ נְכָסִים עַד שֶׁלֹּא תִּתְאָרֵס — [2]מוֹדִים בֵּית שַׁמַּאי וּבֵית הִלֵּל שֶׁמּוֹכֶרֶת וְנוֹתֶנֶת, [3]וְקַיָּים.
[4]נָפְלוּ לָהּ מִשֶּׁנִּתְאָרְסָה, [5]בֵּית שַׁמַּאי אוֹמְרִים: תִּמְכּוֹר. [6]וּבֵית הִלֵּל אוֹמְרִים: לֹא תִּמְכּוֹר. [7]אֵלּוּ וָאֵלּוּ מוֹדִים, שֶׁאִם מָכְרָה וְנָתְנָה, [8]קַיָּים.
[9]אָמַר רַבִּי יְהוּדָה: אָמְרוּ חֲכָמִים לִפְנֵי רַבָּן גַּמְלִיאֵל: [10]הוֹאִיל וְזָכָה בְּאִשָּׁה, [11]לֹא יִזְכֶּה בַּנְּכָסִים? [12]אָמַר לָהֶם: עַל הַחֲדָשִׁים אָנוּ בּוֹשִׁים,

LITERAL TRANSLATION

MISHNAH [1]A woman to whom property fell before she was betrothed — [2]Bet Shammai and Bet Hillel agree that she may sell [the property] or give it away, [3]and it is valid.

[4][If the property] fell to her after she was betrothed, [5]Bet Shammai say: She may sell. [6]And Bet Hillel say: She may not sell. [7]These and these agree that if she sold [property] or gave [it] away, [8]it is valid. [9]Rabbi Yehudah said: The Sages said before Rabban Gamliel: [10]Since he acquired the woman, [11]does he not acquire the property? [12]He said to them: Regarding the new [property] we are confounded,

TRANSLATION AND COMMENTARY

MISHNAH הָאִשָּׁה [1]In the case of **a woman who acquired property** either as an inheritance or as a gift **before she was betrothed,** and who then became betrothed — [2]**Bet Shammai and Bet Hillel agree that while** she is betrothed **she may sell the property or give it** as a gift, [3]**and** her action **is valid.**

נָפְלוּ לָהּ מִשֶּׁנִּתְאָרְסָה [4]If she **acquired** the property **after she was betrothed,** [5]**Bet Shammai say: She may sell** it or give it away before she is married. [6]**And Bet Hillel say: She may no** longer **sell** the property or give it away. [7]Nevertheless, Bet Shammai **and** Bet Hillel both **agree that if she did sell** the property **or give it away** during her betrothal, [8]her action **is valid.**

אָמַר רַבִּי יְהוּדָה [9]**Rabbi Yehudah said: The Sages said before Rabban Gamliel:** [10]**Since** the man legally **acquired the woman** as his wife through betrothal and she is now forbidden to all other men, [11]**would he not** also **acquire** any **property** which fell to her once betrothed? [12]Rabban Gamliel **answered: Regarding new property** which came into her possession after marriage, **we are perplexed**

RASHI

משנה האשה. עד שלא תתארס — ונתארסה. **בית שמאי אומרים תמכור** — בעודה ארוסה. אבל משנשאת — לא, כדתני לקמן: עד שלא ניסת וניסת וכו׳. **הואיל וזכה באשה** — שהיא ארוסתו. **לא יזכה בנכסים** — בגמרא מפרש אהי מינייהו קיימי — אלכתחלה דבית שמאי או אדיעבד דבית הלל. **על החדשים** — שנפלו לה משנשאת. **אנו בושים** — מה ראו חכמים לומר: אם מכרה ונתנה הבעל מוציא מיד הלקוחות, כדתנן לקמן במתניתין.

NOTES

וְקַיָּים **And it is valid.** The words "and it is valid" appear to be superfluous, for surely if the woman is permitted to sell the property or give it away, the transaction must be valid. *Hafla'ah* explains that if the Mishnah had not said that the transfer is valid, we might have thought that the property remains in the possession of its recipient only until she marries, at which point it reverts to the husband. Therefore, the Mishnah states that the sale or the gift is absolutely valid and remains in effect even after the woman is married.

תִּמְכּוֹר...לֹא תִּמְכּוֹר **She may sell...she may not sell.** The Mishnah states that Bet Shammai and Bet Hillel disagree about whether a woman who acquired property after her betrothal may sell it before her marriage, without explicitly mentioning their positions in regard to donating the property. Immediately afterward, however, the Mishnah explicitly equates a sale and a gift, terming them both valid after the fact. Consequently, it is suggested that a distinction can be drawn between a sale and a gift: Since the wife receives money for what she sells, and her husband can benefit from that money after the marriage, Bet Shammai permit her to sell it. A gift, on the other hand, is against the husband's financial interest, and thus Bet Shammai might agree with Bet Hillel that she is not allowed to give the property away. After the fact, however, all would agree that any action she took with respect to her property is valid. According to this interpretation of Bet Shammai, we understand better why the Mishnah reads "these *and these* agree (that once done, the transfer is valid)" as opposed to "Bet Hillel agree etc.": Both Bet Hillel and Bet Shammai agree about the initial prohibition against her giving the property away, and they also agree that after the fact her transfer is valid. (*Shevet Sofer.*)

עַל הַחֲדָשִׁים אָנוּ בּוֹשִׁים **Regarding the new property we are perplexed.** The Rishonim offer various explanations for Rabban Gamliel's statement that we are perplexed as to

HALAKHAH

נָפְלוּ לָהּ מִשֶּׁנִּתְאָרְסָה **If the property fell to her after she was betrothed.** "A betrothed woman may not sell property which she inherited after she was betrothed. Nevertheless, if she either sold or gave the property away during her betrothal, the transfer is valid." (*Rambam, Sefer Nashim, Hilkhot Ishut* 22:8; *Shulḥan Arukh, Even HaEzer* 90:11.)

TRANSLATION AND COMMENTARY

as to why she should not have the right to sell it, since it is hers. ¹**And you** wish to **burden us with** the issue of **the old** property as well, by suggesting that she cannot sell it or donate it before her marriage?!

נָפְלוּ לָהּ מִשֶּׁנִּשֵּׂאת ²**If the property** came into her possession **after she was married,** ³Bet Shammai **and** Bet Hillel both **agree that** she may not transfer it, ⁴**and if she** indeed **sold** it or **gave it away,** ⁵**the husband may remove it from the possession of the buyer** or the recipient.

עַד שֶׁלֹּא נִשֵּׂאת ⁶**If the property became hers before she was married, and** then **she married,** ⁷**Rabban Gamliel says: If she sold** it or **gave it away** as a gift after she was married, her action **is valid.**

אָמַר ⁸**Rabbi Ḥanina ben Akavyah said: The Sages said before Rabban Gamliel:** ⁹**Since** the man legally **acquired the woman** as his wife through marriage, **would he not** also **acquire the property** that she inherited or received as a gift before she was married? ¹⁰Rabban Gamliel **said to the** Sages: **Regarding new property** which she acquired after her marriage, **we are perplexed** as to why she should not have the right to sell or donate it. ¹¹**And you** wish to **burden us** with the need to justify limiting her rights in respect of **the old** property as well!

חוֹלֵק בֵּין נְכָסִים לִנְכָסִים ¹²**Rabbi Shimon distinguishes between** one form of **property and** another form of **property:** ¹³**Property which is known to the husband, she may not sell** or give away after the marriage, ¹⁴**and if she sold** the property **or gave it away, the transfer is void.** ¹⁵**Nor may she sell** property **which is not known to the husband,** ¹⁶**but if she sold** it **or gave it away,** her action **is valid.**

LITERAL TRANSLATION

¹and you roll the old upon us?!

²[If the property] fell to her after she was married, ³these and these agree, ⁴that if she sold [it] or gave [it] away, ⁵the husband may remove [it] from the hand of the buyers.

⁶[If she acquired the property] before she was married, and she married, ⁷Rabban Gamliel says: If she sold [it] or gave [it] away, it is valid.

⁸Rabbi Ḥanina ben Akavyah said: They said before Rabban Gamliel: ⁹Since he acquired the woman, does he not acquire the property? ¹⁰He said to them: Regarding the new [property] we are confounded, ¹¹and you roll the old upon us?!

¹²Rabbi Shimon distinguishes between property and property. ¹³Property which is known to the husband she may not sell, ¹⁴and if she sold [it] or gave [it] away, it is void. ¹⁵[That] which is not known to the husband she may not sell, ¹⁶but if she sold [it] or gave [it] away, it is valid.

¹אֶלָּא שֶׁאַתֶּם מְגַלְגְּלִין עָלֵינוּ אֶת הַיְּשָׁנִים?!
²נָפְלוּ לָהּ מִשֶּׁנִּשֵּׂאת, ³אֵלּוּ וָאֵלּוּ מוֹדִים, ⁴שֶׁאִם מָכְרָה וְנָתְנָה, ⁵שֶׁהַבַּעַל מוֹצִיא מִיַּד הַלָּקוֹחוֹת. ⁶עַד שֶׁלֹּא נִשֵּׂאת, וְנִשֵּׂאת, ⁷רַבָּן גַּמְלִיאֵל אוֹמֵר: אִם מָכְרָה וְנָתְנָה, קַיָּם. ⁸אָמַר רַבִּי חֲנִינָא בֶּן עֲקַבְיָא: אָמְרוּ לִפְנֵי רַבָּן גַּמְלִיאֵל: ⁹הוֹאִיל וְזָכָה בָּאִשָּׁה, לֹא יִזְכֶּה בִּנְכָסִים? ¹⁰אָמַר לָהֶם: עַל הַחֲדָשִׁים אָנוּ בּוֹשִׁים, ¹¹אֶלָּא שֶׁאַתֶּם מְגַלְגְּלִין עָלֵינוּ הַיְּשָׁנִים?! ¹²חוֹלֵק בֵּין נְכָסִים לִנְכָסִים. ¹³נְכָסִים הַיְדוּעִין לַבַּעַל לֹא תִמְכּוֹר, ¹⁴וְאִם מָכְרָה וְנָתְנָה, בָּטֵל. ¹⁵שֶׁאֵינָן יְדוּעִין לַבַּעַל לֹא תִמְכּוֹר, ¹⁶וְאִם מָכְרָה וְנָתְנָה, קַיָּם.

RASHI

עד שלא נשאת — כגון משנתארסה, או קודם לכך. ואחר כך נשאת. הכי גרסינן: רבן גמליאל אומר: אם מכרה ונתנה קיים. הואיל וזכה באשה — שנשאה. על החדשים — שנפלו לה משניסת.

NOTES

why a woman may not dispose of property which she received after her marriage. According to some, the Rabbis perceived an inequity in granting her husband rights of usufruct in her property simply because of the obligation he takes upon himself to redeem her from captivity, a highly unlikely eventuality. Others suggest that the Rabbis find it difficult to understand why the husband can forcibly retake the actual land itself should his wife transfer it to a third party, when he himself has only rights of usufruct. This is especially puzzling because the proceeds become available to the husband if she sells the property! (Shittah Mekubbetzet, Ayelet Ahavim.)

רַבָּן גַּמְלִיאֵל אוֹמֵר אִם מָכְרָה וְנָתְנָה **Rabban Gamliel says: If she sold it or gave it away.** According to an alternative reading, Rabban Gamliel said מוֹכֶרֶת וְנוֹתֶנֶת וְקַיָּים — "she may sell (the property) or give it away (from the outset), and it is valid." (See Rashi, Tosafot and other Rishonim.) However, the reading of the Jerusalem Talmud supports our own version here in the Babylonian Talmud. Ramban notes that in instances like this the Jerusalem Talmud's reading should be regarded as more authentic, for the text of the Babylonian Talmud was occasionally amended by its transcribers when they felt logic dictated doing so.

HALAKHAH

נְכָסִים הַיְדוּעִין לַבַּעַל...וְשֶׁאֵינָן יְדוּעִין לַבַּעַל **Property which is known to the husband...and that which is not known to the husband.** "If a married woman sold property in which her husband had rights of usufruct, the transaction

גמרא [1]מַאי שְׁנָא רֵישָׁא דְּלָא פְּלִיגִי, [2]וּמַאי שְׁנָא סֵיפָא דִּפְלִיגִי?

[3]אָמְרִי דְּבֵי רַבִּי יַנַּאי: רֵישָׁא — בִּזְכוּתָהּ נָפְלוּ, [4]סֵיפָא — בִּזְכוּתוֹ נָפְלוּ.

[5]אִם בִּזְכוּתוֹ נָפְלוּ, [6]כִּי מָכְרָה וְנָתְנָה, אַמַּאי קַיָּים?

[7]אֶלָּא רֵישָׁא, וַדַּאי [8]בִּזְכוּתָהּ נָפְלוּ. [9]סֵיפָא — [10]אֵימַר בִּזְכוּתָהּ, אֵימַר בִּזְכוּתוֹ.

LITERAL TRANSLATION

GEMARA [1]What is different [about] the first clause, that they do not disagree, [2]and what is different [about] the last clause, that they do disagree?

[3][The Sages] of Rabbi Yannai's School said: The first clause — into her right [of ownership] it fell. [4]The last clause — into his right [of ownership] it fell.

[5]If into his right [of ownership] it fell, [6]when she sold [it] or gave [it] away, why is it valid?

[7]Rather, the first clause — [8]it is certain that into her right [of ownership] it fell. [9]The last clause — [10]say into her right [of ownership], say into his right [of ownership].

TRANSLATION AND COMMENTARY

GEMARA מַאי שְׁנָא רֵישָׁא [1]The Gemara opens with a question regarding the first two rulings in the Mishnah: **What is the difference** between the case discussed in **the first clause** of the Mishnah (regarding property which a woman acquired before she was betrothed), **about which** Bet Shammai and Bet Hillel **do not disagree,** both maintaining that she may sell it or give it away after she is betrothed; [2]**and** the case discussed in **the next clause** of the Mishnah (regarding property which a woman acquired after she was betrothed), **about which** Bet Shammai and Bet Hillel **do disagree.** What difference does it make whether she acquired the property before or after her betrothal?

אָמְרִי [3]The Gemara answers: **The Sages of Rabbi Yannai's School said:** With regard to the case discussed in **the first clause** of the Mishnah, the property came **into her ownership.** Since she was not betrothed, no one else had any rights to her or her property. Consequently, Bet Hillel and Bet Shammai both agree that she may do as she wishes with this property, even after she becomes betrothed. [4]However, **in the next clause** of the Mishnah, the property came into her possession only after she was already betrothed, so it fell **into his ownership** too. Consequently, Bet Hillel argue that the woman may not sell the property or give it away while betrothed.

אִם בִּזְכוּתוֹ נָפְלוּ [5]The Gemara asks: **If** Bet Hillel maintain that the property **fell into** her husband's **ownership,** [6]then **why, when she sold** it **or gave it away,** do they agree that the transfer **is valid?**

אֶלָּא רֵישָׁא [7]**Rather, in the first clause** of the Mishnah, [8]**it is certain that** the property **fell into** the unattached woman's **ownership** and belongs entirely to her. Hence, Bet Hillel agree with Bet Shammai that she may do with the property as she wishes, even after she becomes betrothed. [9]However, in **the next clause** of the Mishnah, it is not clear into whose ownership the property fell, since betrothal is a transitional state — [10]you might **say** that it fell **into** the woman's **ownership** since she is not yet married, but you might also **say** that it fell **into** the husband's **ownership** since he has certain rights to her person by virtue of betrothal.

RASHI

הידועים לבעל — בגמרא מפרש.

גמרא מאי שנא רישא דלא פליגי — הרי נתארסה, ומשום דנפלו לה קודם לכן הורע כחו?! **בזכותה נפלו** — עדיין לא היה זכאי בשלה, ולא בה, אלא היא עצמה. **בזכותו** — כבר זכה בה ובנכסיה. **אימר בזכותו כו׳** — דאירוסין עושה ספק נישואין — שמא תבא לידי נישואין שמא לא תבא.

NOTES

מַאי שְׁנָא רֵישָׁא? **What is different about the first clause?** The Gemara's question is as follows: According to Bet Hillel, who support the bridegroom's right to freeze the woman's property during their betrothal, why should that right be limited to property which she received only after becoming betrothed? *Shittah Mekubbetzet* proceeds to sharpen the Gemara's question. If anything, Bet Hillel should have made the opposite distinction: In the first case, the woman acquired the property before she was betrothed, so one might say that it is even more logical to give the husband rights over it, since he may have agreed to betroth her partially because of those assets; and in the second case, the woman acquired the property only after her betrothal, so we might say that there is more reason to strengthen her hand, since that property played no role in influencing her husband to betroth her. Moreover, his actual rights of usufruct only begin after marriage and thus should not dictate his rights while betrothed.

אֵימַר בִּזְכוּתָהּ, אֵימַר בִּזְכוּתוֹ **Say into her ownership, say into his ownership.** The Gemara explains that, according

HALAKHAH

is void and he may reclaim the property from its buyer. This ruling applies only to property which the husband knew was in his wife's possession. Property which was unknown to the husband may not be sold either; however if it is sold, the transaction is valid and the husband may not reclaim it," following the opinion of Rabbi Shimon. (*Rambam, Sefer Nashim, Hilkhot Ishut* 22:8; *Shulḥan Arukh, Even HaEzer* 90:11.)

TRANSLATION AND COMMENTARY

Because of the doubt about the matter, Bet Hillel rule: [1]**From the start**, the woman **should not sell** the property or give it away during her betrothal, lest that indeed be a privilege designated for her bridegroom. [2]However, **if she did sell** the property **or give it away,** the transfer **is valid,** since she might have the right to dispose of it.

אָמַר רַבִּי יְהוּדָה [3]We learned in the Mishnah: **"Rabbi Yehudah said:** The Sages **said before Rabban Gamliel:** Since the man legally acquired the woman as his wife through betrothal, would he not also acquire any property which came into her possession once betrothed?" [4]**It was asked of** the Sages as they were discussing our Mishnah: [5]Regarding the question just cited by **Rabbi Yehudah** as having been posed before Rabban Gamliel, did it refer to Bet Shammai's position (that **from the start**, the woman may dispose of any property that she acquires during her betrothal), thereby implying that there is no problem with Bet Hillel's agreeing that her action is valid after the fact, [6]**or** perhaps the question was also asked in reference **to** Bet Hillel's position (that, **after the fact**, the transfer may be declared void and the husband may reclaim the property from the buyer or the recipient of her gift)?

LITERAL TRANSLATION

[1]From the start, she may not sell. [2]If she sold [it] or gave [it] away, it is valid.

[3]"Rabbi Yehudah said: They said before Rabban Gamliel." [4]It was asked of them: [5]Rabbi Yehudah — on [the case] from the start [6]or on [the case] after the fact?

[1]לְכַתְּחִלָּה, לֹא תִּמְכּוֹר. [2]אִם מָכְרָה וְנָתְנָה, קַיָּים.

[3]״אָמַר רַבִּי יְהוּדָה: אָמְרוּ לִפְנֵי רַבָּן גַּמְלִיאֵל״. [4]אִיבַּעְיָא לְהוּ: [5]רַבִּי יְהוּדָה אַלְּכַתְּחִלָּה [6]אוֹ אַדִּיעֲבַד?

RASHI

איבעיא להו — הנך רבנן דאמרו לו. **אלכתחלה** — פליגי, ואמרי: אמאי מוכרת לכתחלה לבית שמאי, הואיל וזכה באשה שאירסה — לא יזכה בנכסיה? אבל אדיעבד — מודו בית הלל. או דלמא אדיעבד נמי פליגי, ובעי למימר: מכרה בטל.

NOTES

to Bet Hillel, there is doubt as to whether property acquired by a woman during her betrothal is subject to her ownership or her bridegroom's. *Rashi* explains the doubt as follows: Perhaps the betrothal will lead to marriage, in which case her husband will benefit from this property; but perhaps they will not marry, in which case the property will remain fully in the woman's control. *Tosafot* ask: Since the betrothed woman's claim to ownership, based upon physical possession, is a certain one, while the man's is only doubtful, why should we not apply the rule favoring the certain claim and allow the woman to dispose of the property as she pleases? The Gemara in fact uses this very argument to explain why a widow, in line for levirate marriage (see below, 80b, and *Yevamot* 38a), may sell property which she inherits while waiting for the brother of her deceased husband to marry her. *Tosafot* themselves answer: When a woman is waiting for her brother-in-law to acquit himself of his levirate duty, it is impossible to predict whether he will exercise his right to marry her or choose instead to perform *ḥalitzah*, thereby releasing her altogether. Therefore her claim to the property is regarded as certain, while his is merely doubtful, and we affirm her right to dispose of the property as she wishes. In our case, however, the woman inherited property during her betrothal, and betrothals ordinarily lead to marriage. Thus, she may not dispose of the property despite the presumption that she is its rightful owner. *Nemukei Yosef* emphasizes that we still cannot consider such property as the bridegroom's privilege, for if "we are perplexed regarding new property" that she received after marriage, how much more so will we be perplexed when there is some doubt as to whether the marriage will take place.

Tosafot Yom Tov remains uncomfortable with *Tosafot*'s answer: Even if we accept the distinction between a betrothed woman and one who is eligible for levirate marriage, doubt still remains even in the case of the betrothed woman as to whether her bridegroom will conclude the marriage; thus, the woman's claim to her property should be strengthened! He answers that in our case the woman would in fact be permitted to sell the property; however, the potential buyer is not allowed to purchase it from her, since he himself cannot rely upon her presumption of rightful ownership. Therefore we do not approve of her initiating the transaction, but if they did conclude the transaction, it is valid.

Ra'avad explains the Gemara's doubt in an entirely different manner: The doubt here is not as to whether the betrothal will lead to marriage, but rather as to whether the bridegroom has rights to his wife's property while they are only betrothed and not yet married. On the one hand we can say that he has no such rights, since he does not enjoy usufruct from her property until after they are married. On the other hand, we might say that the high likelihood that they will marry grants him certain rights in her property even now. The Jerusalem Talmud's statement to the effect that property acquired after betrothal is considered to have fallen "into both her ownership and his" seems to support *Ra'avad's* interpretation.

אַלְּכַתְּחִלָּה אוֹ אַדִּיעֲבַד **From the start or after the fact.** The Rishonim explain the Gemara's question in various ways, relying upon variant readings of the text found in the Mishnah and the Gemara. The discussion is complicated by the fact that the Rishonim had a manuscript of *Rashi's* explaining the passage differently from the way Rashi appears in our standard edition of the Talmud (and even this manuscript appeared in different versions).

According to *Rashi* in our standard edition of the Talmud (which is the second explanation cited by *Tosafot*, as well as that adopted by *Rif*), the Gemara assumes that the question posed by the Sages before Rabban Gamliel was directed at the clause in the Mishnah discussing property which a woman inherited after she was betrothed. The Gemara seeks to know whether the question was aimed solely at Bet Shammai's position — that from the very start the woman may dispose of the property — or perhaps it was even aimed at Bet Hillel who maintain that if the

TRANSLATION AND COMMENTARY

תָּא שְׁמַע [78B] [1]The Gemara answers: **Come and hear** a solution to this problem, **for it was taught** in a Baraita: [2]**"Rabbi Yehudah said:** The Sages **said before Rabban Gamliel:** [3]**Since this** woman, who already entered into marriage, **is** considered to be **a wife, and this** woman, who was only betrothed, **is** also considered to be **a wife,** [4]it should follow that, **just as** we say about the married woman that if she sold or gave away property which she inherited or received as a gift after she was already married, **her sale** or gift **is void,** [5]**so too** we should say about the betrothed woman that, if she sold or gave away property which she inherited or received by way of a gift after she was already betrothed, **her sale** or gift **is void!** [6]Rabban Gamliel **said to** the Sages: **Regarding** the law that was taught about **the** woman's **new property,** i.e., the property she inherited or received as a gift after she was already married, **we fail to understand** why the transaction is not valid if she sold it or gave it away. [7]**And you** wish to extend the law and **cast upon us the old** property as well, i.e., the property the woman inherited or received as a gift after she was betrothed, and argue that if the woman sold or gave away such property during the period of her betrothal, the transaction should not be valid?!"

[78B] [1]תָּא שְׁמַע, דְּתַנְיָא: [2]"אָמַר רַבִּי יְהוּדָה: אָמְרוּ לִפְנֵי רַבָּן גַּמְלִיאֵל: [3]הוֹאִיל וְזוֹ אִשְׁתּוֹ וְזוֹ אִשְׁתּוֹ — [4]זוֹ מִכְרָהּ בָּטֵל, [5]אַף זוֹ מִכְרָהּ בָּטֵל! [6]אָמַר לָהֶן: עַל הַחֲדָשִׁים אָנוּ בּוֹשִׁים. [7]אֶלָּא שֶׁאַתֶּם מְגַלְגְּלִים עָלֵינוּ אֶת הַיְּשָׁנִים"?! [8]שְׁמַע מִינָּהּ: דִּיעֲבַד קָאָמַר.

[9]שְׁמַע מִינָּהּ.

[10]תַּנְיָא: [11]"אָמַר רַבִּי חֲנִינָא בֶּן עֲקַבְיָא: [12]לֹא כָּךְ הֱשִׁיבָן רַבָּן גַּמְלִיאֵל לַחֲכָמִים, [13]אֶלָּא כָּךְ הֱשִׁיבָן: לֹא, אִם אֲמַרְתֶּם

LITERAL TRANSLATION

[78B] [1]Come [and] hear, for it was taught: [2]"Rabbi Yehudah said: They said before Rabban Gamliel: [3]Since this is his wife and that is his wife — [4][just as] this, her sale is void, [5]so too that, her sale is void! [6]He said to them: Regarding the new [property] we are confounded. [7]And you roll upon us the old?!" [8]Infer from this: He spoke about after the fact.

[9]Infer from this.

[10]It is taught: [11]"Rabbi Ḥanina ben Akavya said: [12]Not so did Rabban Gamliel respond to the Sages, [13]but rather like this he responded to them: No, if you said [it]

RASHI

תא שמע אמר רבי יהודה כו׳ הואיל וזו אשתו — נשואה. **וזו אשתו** — ארוסה. מה נשואה נפלו לה משנשאת — מכרה בטל, כדקתני במתניתין: הבעל מוציא כו׳. **אף זו** — שנפלו לה כשהיא ארוסה — יהא מכרה בטל, ואפילו כשהיא עודה ארוסה. **אמר להם על החדשים** — שאתם אומרים עליהם: מה זו מכרה בטל — **אנו בושים** — על מה שאמרנו בטל, אלא שאתם אומרים לי עליהם מה זו מכרה בטל כו׳. ולא גרסינן אמר להם אף זו לא תמכור. וכן מצאתי בתוספתא. **שמע מינה** — מדקאמרי ליה: אף זו מכרה בטל — שמע מינה דיעבד נמי קשיא להו. **לא כך השיבן** — בעוד שדנו לפניו במוכרת בעודה ארוסה. לא כך הוצרך להשיבם: על החדשים אנו בושים — שהרי תשובה נכחת יש כאן, שיש להפריש בין ארוסה לנשואה, וכן השיבן עליה: לא אם אמרתם כו׳.

[8]**Infer from this** Baraita that the Sages did indeed **ask about** the law that applies **after the fact** even according to Bet Hillel, that if a betrothed woman sold or gave away the property she inherited or received by way of a gift after she was betrothed, the transaction is valid. In this Baraita, the Sages argued explicitly that in such a case the transaction should be void.

שְׁמַע מִינָּהּ [9]The Gemara confirms that its conclusion is correct: Indeed it may be **inferred from this** Baraita that the Sages challenged the ruling that if a betrothed woman sold or gave away property acquired after her betrothal, the transaction is valid after the fact.

תַּנְיָא [10]The Gemara continues: In a related Baraita **it was taught:** [11]**"Rabbi Ḥanina ben Akavya said:** [12]**Rabban Gamliel did not** originally **respond to the Sages in this manner.** [13]**But rather** Rabban Gamliel **refuted** the Sages'

NOTES

woman transferred the property, the transfer is valid, but only after the fact.

According to the other version of *Rashi* (which accords with the first explanation in *Tosafot*), the Sages' question is directed at the first clause in the Mishnah discussing property which a woman inherited before she was betrothed. Both Bet Shammai and Bet Hillel agree that she may sell such property or give it away during the period of her betrothal. The Gemara now wishes to know whether the Sages' objection to this ruling was aimed solely at the initial permission given the woman to dispose of her property, but that after the fact they would agree that her actions are valid, or perhaps they even objected to validating her actions after the fact.

Rabbenu Tam dismisses the first explanation of the Gemara because it assumes that our entire discussion revolves around the view of Bet Shammai which is ultimately rejected. Neither does he accept the second explanation because it necessitates revising the Baraita which the Gemara later cites to answer the question. Instead, he proposes that the Gemara's question be understood as follows: Did the Sages object to the ruling found in the first clause of the Mishnah, that a woman may dispose of property that she received before she was betrothed even after her betrothal, or did they object to Bet Hillel's ruling in the second clause of the Mishnah which validates, after the fact, actions taken by the woman in respect to property which she acquired even after having become betrothed? *Rabbenu Tam*'s explanation is accepted by *Rabbenu Zeraḥyah Halevi, Rashba,* and *Ritva.*

TRANSLATION AND COMMENTARY

objection **in the following way: No, if you said about a married woman** — [1]**whose husband is entitled to what she finds and to her handiwork, and** is authorized **to nullify her vows** — that if she sold the property she inherited after she was married, the transaction is void, [2]does it follow that **you should also say about a betrothed woman** — [3]**whose husband is not entitled to what she finds or to her handiwork, nor** authorized **to nullify her vows** — that if she sold the property she inherited after she was betrothed, the transaction is void? The law governing property sold or given away by a married woman teaches us nothing about the law that should be applied to property sold or given away by a betrothed woman. [4]The Sages **said to** Rabban Gamliel: **Master,** we accept what you said with respect to property which the betrothed woman **sold before she was married**, that the transaction is indeed valid. [5]But **what is the law if** the woman **was married, and then sold property** which she had acquired during her betrothal? [6]Rabban Gamliel **said to** the Sages: **Even this married woman may sell or give away** the property she acquired during her betrothal, **and** the transaction **is valid.** [7]The Sages **said to** Rabban Gamliel: **Since** the husband **acquired the woman** as his wife when he married her, **does he not** also **acquire the property** that she acquired before she was married? [8]Rabban Gamliel **said to them: Regarding** the law that was taught about **the** married woman's **new property, we are perplexed.** [9]**And you wish** to extend the law and **roll upon us her old** property as well and argue that if the woman sold or gave away such property only after she was married, the transaction should not be valid?"

וְהָאֲנַן תְּנַן [10]The Gemara now points out a contradiction between the Baraita just cited and our Mishnah: According to the Baraita, Rabban Gamliel maintains that a woman who acquired property during her betrothal may sell it or give it away after she is married, and the transaction is valid. **But surely we have learned** otherwise in our Mishnah: [11]**"If** a woman **inherited property** or received it by way of a gift **before she was married, and** then **she was married,** [12]**Rabban Gamliel says: If she sold** the property

בִּנְשׂוּאָה — [1]שֶׁכֵּן בַּעְלָהּ זַכַּאי בִּמְצִיאָתָהּ וּבְמַעֲשֵׂה יָדֶיהָ וּבַהֲפָרַת נְדָרֶיהָ, [2]תֹּאמְרוּ בַּאֲרוּסָה [3]שֶׁאֵין בַּעְלָהּ זַכַּאי לֹא בִּמְצִיאָתָהּ וְלֹא בְּמַעֲשֵׂה יָדֶיהָ וְלֹא בַּהֲפָרַת נְדָרֶיהָ! [4]אָמְרוּ לוֹ: רַבִּי, מָכְרָה לָהּ עַד שֶׁלֹּא נִשֵּׂאת. [5]נִשֵּׂאת וְאַחַר כָּךְ מָכְרָה, מַהוּ? [6]אָמַר לְהוּ: אַף זוֹ מוֹכֶרֶת וְנוֹתֶנֶת, וְקַיָּים. [7]אָמְרוּ לוֹ: הוֹאִיל וְזָכָה בָּאִשָּׁה, לֹא יִזְכֶּה בַּנְּכָסִים?! [8]אָמַר לָהֶם: עַל הַחֲדָשִׁים אָנוּ בּוֹשִׁין. [9]אֶלָּא שֶׁאַתֶּם מְגַלְגְּלִין עָלֵינוּ אֶת הַיְּשָׁנִים״?

[10]וְהָאֲנַן תְּנַן: [11]״עַד שֶׁלֹּא נִשֵּׂאת וְנִשֵּׂאת, [12]רַבָּן גַּמְלִיאֵל אוֹמֵר:

LITERAL TRANSLATION

of a married woman — [1]whose husband is entitled to what she finds, and her handiwork, and the nullification of her vows, [2]should you say [it] of a betrothed woman [3]whose husband is not entitled to her finds, or her handiwork, or the nullification of her vows? [4]They said to him: Master, [we accept what you said if] she sold for herself before she was married. [5][But if] she was married and afterwards she sold [property], what [is the law]? [6]He said to them: This one too may sell [property] and give [it] away, and it is valid. [7]They said to him: Since he acquired the woman, does he not acquire the property? [8]He said to them: Regarding the new [property] we are confounded. [9]And you roll upon us the old?"

[10]But surely we have learned: [11]"[If the property came to her] before she was married, and she married, [12]Rabban Gamliel says:

RASHI

ולא בהפרת נדריה — לבדו, אלא אם כן אביה עמו. דתנן: אביה ובעלה מפירין נדריה. **אמרו לו רבי מכרה עד שלא ניסת** — נראין דבריך במוכרת בעודה ארוסה. **ניסת ואחר כך מכרה** — נכסים שנפלו לה קודם נישואין מהו? **אמר להן אף זו מוכרת וקיים אמרו לו הואיל וזכה באשה** — למציאתה ולמעשה ידיה והפרת נדריה, לא יזכה בנכסים שתיקנו לאכול פירותיהן בחייה? והיאך מכרה קיים! הכי גרסינן: — **והא אנן תנן עד שלא נשאת ונשאת רבן גמליאל אומר אם מכרה ונתנה קיים! אמר רב זביד: תני מוכרת ונותנת וקיים. ורב פפא אמר לא קשיא כו׳** — מתניתין [דקתני: אם מכרה] רבי יהודה היא, דאיהו מסיק ואמר לה, [דסבירא ליה אליבא דרבן גמליאל אפילו בעודה ארוסה לא תמכור לכתחילה, וכל שכן בנשאת קודם מכירה.] ואף על גב דאיירי רבי חנינא בסיפא — לאו דמודה לרבי יהודה דרבן גמליאל אם מכרה אית ליה, אלא מוכרת לכתחילה. ומאי דלא פריש רבי חנינא במתניתין פריש בברייתא. הכי גרסינן: ורבי חנינא בן עקביא דאמר כמאן, כבית שמאי? — בתמיה, דהא בית הלל

NOTES

שֶׁכֵּן בַּעְלָהּ זַכַּאי בִּמְצִיאָתָהּ **Whose husband is entitled to what she finds.** *Maharam Shiff* points out that it would have been more appropriate for Rabban Gamliel to have answered that a betrothed woman cannot be compared to a married woman, for the husband of a married woman is entitled to the usufruct of her property, and so it stands to reason that if she sold her property, the sale is void. But in the case of a betrothed woman, the husband is not entitled to the usufruct of her property, and so if she sold her property, the transaction is valid.

אִם מָכְרָה וְנָתְנָה, קַיָּים״!
[1]אָמַר רַב זְבִיד: [2]תְּנֵי: מוֹכֶרֶת וְנוֹתֶנֶת, וְקַיָּים.
[3]רַב פַּפָּא אָמַר: לָא קַשְׁיָא. [4]הָא, רַבִּי יְהוּדָה אַלִּיבָּא דְּרַבָּן גַּמְלִיאֵל; [5]הָא, רַבִּי חֲנִינָא בֶּן עֲקַבְיָא אַלִּיבָּא דְּרַבָּן גַּמְלִיאֵל.
[6]וְרַבִּי חֲנִינָא בֶּן עֲקַבְיָא כְּבֵית שַׁמַּאי?
[7]הָכִי קָאָמַר: לֹא נֶחְלְקוּ בֵּית שַׁמַּאי וּבֵית הִלֵּל עַל דָּבָר זֶה.

LITERAL TRANSLATION

if she sold [it] or gave [it] away, it is valid!" [1]Rabbi Zevid said: Teach: [2]She may sell [the property] or give [it] away, and it is valid.

[3]Rav Pappa said: It is not difficult. [4]This, Rabbi Yehudah according to Rabban Gamliel; [5]that, Rabbi Ḥanina ben Akavya according to Rabban Gamliel.

[6]But is Rabbi Ḥanina ben Akavya like Bet Shammai?

[7]He said thus: Bet Shammai and Bet Hillel did not disagree about this matter.

TRANSLATION AND COMMENTARY

the property **or gave it away** after she was married, the transaction **is valid."** Whereas in the Baraita Rabban Gamliel states that the woman has the right to dispose of her property, the Mishnah implies that although the transaction is valid after the fact, if the woman asks the court whether she is permitted to sell the property or give it away, she will be told that she should not do so!

אָמַר רַב זְבִיד [1]**Rabbi Zevid said** that the text of the Mishnah should be corrected: **Teach** it as follows: If a woman inherited property or received it by way of a gift before she was married, Rabban Gamliel says: [2]**After her marriage she may sell the property or give it away, and** the transaction **is valid.** Thus, the Mishnah's ruling conforms to that which is found in the Baraita.

רַב פַּפָּא אָמַר [3]**Rav Pappa said:** The text of the Mishnah is correct as is, but still **there is no difficulty,** for the Mishnah and the Baraita reflect two different viewpoints. [4]The Mishnah's ruling reflects the view of **Rabbi Yehudah's understanding of Rabban Gamliel,** which is that a woman may not sell property acquired during her betrothal, either before or after her marriage, but such a transaction is valid after the fact. [5]And the Baraita's ruling reflects **Rabbi Ḥanina ben Akavya's understanding of Rabban Gamliel,** which is that a woman may sell property acquired during her betrothal whenever she wishes.

וְרַבִּי חֲנִינָא בֶּן עֲקַבְיָא [6]The Gemara asks: **But** according to these two solutions of the contradiction between the Baraita and the Mishnah, does it turn out that **Rabbi Ḥanina ben Akavya follows** the view of **Bet Shammai?** Bet Shammai and Bet Hillel disagree about a woman who inherited property after she was betrothed. According to Bet Shammai she may dispose of it while betrothed, and according to Bet Hillel she may not do so. According to both Rav Zevid and Rav Pappa, Rabbi Ḥanina ben Akavya agrees with Bet Shammai against Bet Hillel. Since the law follows Bet Hillel against Bet Shammai, it is preferable not to suggest that Rabbi Ḥanina ben Akavya follows the view of Bet Shammai.

הָכִי קָאָמַר [7]The Gemara answers: **This** is what Rabbi Ḥanina ben Akavya **said: Bet Shammai and Bet Hillel did not disagree about the matter** of property which the woman received during her betrothal, for they both agree that the woman may dispose of it both before and after her marriage.

RASHI

אפילו במוכרת באירוסין אמרי לכתחילה לא. ואם בא לוקח לבית דין לימלך – אמרינן ליה: לא תיזבון, כל שכן משנישאת.
לא נחלקו – אלא לכתחילה תמכור.

NOTES

תְּנֵי: מוֹכֶרֶת וְנוֹתֶנֶת **Teach: She may sell the property or give it away.** *Tosafot* ask: Why did Rav Zevid revise the text of the Mishnah to have it agree with the Baraita? He should have revised the text of the Baraita to make it conform with the Mishnah. In that way Rabban Gamliel would be in agreement with Bet Hillel, and not Bet Shammai. *Ra'avad* answers that had Rav Zevid revised the Baraita, Rabbi Ḥanina ben Akavya's position would be identical with Rabbi Yehudah's, and the sources imply that there is a difference between them. *Shittah Mekubbetzet* suggests that nothing in the Mishnah forces us to accept one reading rather than the other. But Rabbi Ḥanina ben Akavya's argument in the Baraita can only be understood if we assume that its reading, "She may sell it or give it away, and it is valid," is precise. Thus, Rav Zevid changed the text of the Mishnah to make it conform to the Baraita, and not the other way around. *Maharam Shiff* argues that Rav Zevid revised the Baraita to make it read מוֹכֶרֶת וְנוֹתֶנֶת קַיָּים (a reading found in old and reliable texts), and not וְקַיָּים. According to this reading, Rabban Gamliel did not say that the woman may sell the property or give it away from the start, but rather that if she disposed of it, the transaction is valid, and so Rav Zevid indeed revised the Baraita to have it agree with the Mishnah. *Tosafot* cite the position of *Rabbenu Ḥananel,* who read in the Mishnah: "She may sell or give away from the start," and in the Baraita he reads: "If she sold the property or gave it away, it is valid." Rav Zevid preferred to emend the Mishnah in accordance with the Baraita, to place Rabban Gamliel in agreement with the position of Bet Hillel. Similarly, the Jerusalem Talmud notes that the Mishnah originally read: "She may sell the property or give it away, and it is valid," and Rabbi Ḥiyya taught a Baraita which read: "She may not sell it or give it away, but if she sold it or gave it away, it is valid." The Mishnah in the Jerusalem Talmud appears to have been revised in accordance with Rabbi Ḥiyya's Baraita.

וְרַבִּי חֲנִינָא בֶּן עֲקַבְיָא כְּבֵית שַׁמַּאי? **But is Rabbi Ḥanina ben Akavya like Bet Shammai?** *Rashba* notes that while the Gemara asks this question after presenting Rav Pappa's solution of the contradiction between the Baraita and the

TRANSLATION AND COMMENTARY

רַב וּשְׁמוּאֵל דְּאָמְרִי תַּרְוַיְיהוּ [1]**Rav and Shmuel both said: Whether** a woman **inherited property before she was betrothed,** [2]**or inherited the property after she was betrothed, and** then **married,** and subsequently disposed of the property, the transaction is void, [3]and **the husband may recover** the property **from the recipient.**

כְּמַאן [4]The Gemara asks: **In accordance with which Tanna** did Rav and Shmuel issue their ruling? [5]Their ruling is **not in accordance with** the view of the Sages cited by **Rabbi Yehudah, nor** is it **in accordance with** the view of the Sages cited by **Rabbi Ḥanina ben Akavya,** for according to both Rabbi Yehudah and Rabbi Ḥanina ben Akavya, the Sages agree that if a woman inherited property before she was betrothed, and then disposed of it after she was married, the transaction is valid!

אִינְהוּ [6]The Gemara answers: Rav and Shmuel **ruled in accordance with** the view of **our Rabbis,** [7]**for it was taught** in another Baraita: **"Our Rabbis reconsidered** the matter **and decided:** [8]**Whether** a woman **inherited property before she was betrothed** [9]**or inherited the property after she was** already **betrothed, and then married,** and subsequently disposed of the property, the transaction is void, [10]and **the husband may recover** the property **from the recipient."**

מִשֶּׁנִּיסֵּת [11]We have learned in our Mishnah: **"If** the woman **inherited property** or received it as a gift **after after she was married, both** Bet Shammai and Bet Hillel **agree** that she may not dispose of it, and that if she does so, her husband may recover it from the recipient." [12]The Gemara asks: **Shall we say that we have learned** in the Mishnah **the enactment** that was passed by the Sanhedrin when it was sitting in **Usha?** This enactment concerned a special category of property known as usufruct property, which a woman brings into her marriage but which is not recorded in her ketubah, so that the husband bears no

[1]רַב וּשְׁמוּאֵל דְּאָמְרִי תַּרְוַיְיהוּ: בֵּין שֶׁנָּפְלוּ לָהּ נְכָסִים עַד שֶׁלֹּא נִתְאָרְסָה, [2]בֵּין שֶׁנָּפְלוּ לָהּ נְכָסִים מִשֶּׁנִּתְאָרְסָה וְנִיסֵּת [3]הַבַּעַל מוֹצִיא מִיַּד הַלָּקוֹחוֹת. [4]כְּמַאן? [5]דְּלָא כְּרַבִּי יְהוּדָה וְלָא כְּרַבִּי חֲנִינָא בֶּן עֲקַבְיָא! [6]אִינְהוּ דְּאָמְרִי כְּרַבּוֹתֵינוּ, [7]דְּתַנְיָא: רַבּוֹתֵינוּ חָזְרוּ וְנִמְנוּ: [8]בֵּין שֶׁנָּפְלוּ לָהּ עַד שֶׁלֹּא תִּתְאָרֵס, [9]וּבֵין שֶׁנָּפְלוּ לָהּ מִשֶּׁנִּתְאָרְסָה וְנִיסֵּת, [10]הַבַּעַל מוֹצִיא מִיַּד הַלָּקוֹחוֹת". [11]"מִשֶּׁנִּיסֵּת, אֵלּוּ וָאֵלּוּ מוֹדִים". [12]לֵימָא תָּנֵינָא לְתַקָּנַת אוּשָׁא?

LITERAL TRANSLATION

[1]Rav and Shmuel both said: Whether the property fell to her [as an inheritance] before she was betrothed, [2]or the property fell to her after she was betrothed and [then] married, [3]the husband may extricate [it] from the hand of the buyers.

[4]In accordance with whom? [5]Not in accordance with Rabbi Yehudah, and not in accordance with Rabbi Ḥanina ben Akavya!

[6]They said in accordance with our Rabbis, [7]for it was taught: "Our Rabbis reconsidered and decided: [8]Whether [the property] fell to her before she was betrothed, [9]or it fell to her after she was betrothed and [then] married, [10]the husband may extricate [it] from the hand of the buyers."

[11]"[If the property fell to her] after she was married, these and those agree." [12]Shall we say [that] we have learned the enactment of Usha?

RASHI

וניסת – ולאחר כך מכרה.

NOTES

Mishnah, the same objection can be raised against Rav Zevid, for according to him Rabbi Ḥanina ben Akavya follows the view of Bet Shmuel. *Shittah Mekubbetzet* adds that, according to *Rabbenu Ḥananel*'s understanding of Rav Zevid (see previous note), the Gemara's question only applies to Rav Pappa.

דְּאָמְרִי כְּרַבּוֹתֵינוּ **They said in accordance with our Rabbis.** The Rishonim ask: Why did Rav and Shmuel repeat the ruling that had already been issued by our Rabbis of the Baraita? They should simply have stated that the law is in accordance with the view of our Rabbis! *Ritva* answers that Rav and Shmuel restated the ruling because the Baraita was not well known in the Academy. *Shittah Mekubbetzet* suggests that when Rav and Shmuel issued their ruling, they did not issue it in their own name, but rather in the name of our Rabbis.

HALAKHAH

תַּקָּנַת אוּשָׁא **The enactment of Usha.** "If a woman sells usufruct property after her marriage, even though she acquired the property before she was betrothed, her husband may recover the usufruct of that property from the buyer during her lifetime, but not the property itself. If the woman predeceases her husband, he may recover the property from the buyer without paying compensation. According to some authorities (*Tur* and *Rosh*), the husband may remove the property itself from the buyer even during his wife's lifetime. If the purchase money is available (or money which can be assumed to be the buyer's purchase money is found in the woman's possession; *Tur,* in the name of *Rosh*), it must be returned to the buyer when the husband repossesses the property." (*Rambam, Sefer Nashim, Hilkhot Ishut* 22:7; *Shulḥan Arukh, Even HaEzer* 90:9.)

[1]דְּאָמַר רַבִּי יוֹסֵי בְּרַבִּי חֲנִינָא: בְּאוּשָׁא הִתְקִינוּ: [2]הָאִשָּׁה שֶׁמָּכְרָה בְּנִכְסֵי מְלוֹג בְּחַיֵּי בַעְלָהּ וּמֵתָה, [3]הַבַּעַל מוֹצִיא מִיַּד הַלָּקוֹחוֹת!

[4]מַתְנִיתִין — [5]בְּחַיֶּיהָ וּלְפֵירוֹת. [6]תַּקָּנַת אוּשָׁא — בְּגוּפָהּ שֶׁל קַרְקַע, [7]וּלְאַחַר מִיתָה.

[8]״רַבִּי שִׁמְעוֹן חוֹלֵק בֵּין נְכָסִים״. [9]אֵלּוּ הֵן יְדוּעִין וְאֵלּוּ הֵן שֶׁאֵינָן יְדוּעִין?

LITERAL TRANSLATION

[1]For Rabbi Yose the son of Rabbi Ḥanina said: In Usha they enacted: [2]A woman who sold part of her usufruct property in her husband's lifetime and died, [3]the husband may extricate [it] from the hand of the buyers!

[4]Our Mishnah — [5]during her lifetime and for the usufruct. [6]The enactment of Usha — for the land itself, [7]and after death.

[8]"Rabbi Shimon distinguishes between property [and property]." [9]Which is that which is known and which is that which is not known?

RASHI

מתניתין בחייה — קאמר, הבעל מוציא כדי לאכול פירות בחייה, ולאחר מותה יחזיר הקרקע ללוקח. ואפילו מתה בחייו לא ירשנה הבעל. ואתו באושא ותקון, דאפילו גופה של קרקע יורש הבעל. **רבי שמעון חולק בו׳** — יש נכסים שמכרה קיים, ויש נכסים שמכרה בטל.

TRANSLATION AND COMMENTARY

responsibility for returning its full value should the marriage be dissolved. [1]**For Rabbi Yose the son of Rabbi Ḥanina said: In Usha the Sages enacted:** [2]If **a woman sold part of her usufruct property in her husband's lifetime and** she subsequently **died,** [3]**the husband may recover it from the buyers** without even returning their purchase money! At first glance the Mishnah seems to be teaching the regulation that was enacted in Usha, but this presents a difficulty, for the decrees of Usha were not included in the Mishnah, since they were accepted only in the Amoraic period.

מַתְנִיתִין [4]Hence there must be a distinction between the law taught in our Mishnah and the Ushan enactment: **Our Mishnah** teaches that if a woman sold usufruct property, [5]her husband may recover the property from the buyer **during her lifetime in order** to enjoy **the usufruct** of that property. Property which a woman brings into her marriage and is not recorded in her ketubah belongs to her even after she is married, but her husband is entitled to the usufruct, and if she predeceases him, he inherits it along with the rest of her estate. Now, since the woman retains possession of the property, she may sell it. However, our Mishnah teaches that as long as the marriage lasts, the sale has no practical effect, because the woman cannot sell her husband's right to the usufruct. Therefore the husband may recover the property from the buyer for the purpose of enjoying the usufruct during his wife's lifetime. Nevertheless, the sale is valid, and if the woman dies before her husband, he will not inherit the property. Upon the woman's death, the buyer gains full title to it. [6]But **an enactment** was passed **in Usha regarding the land itself,** that if a woman sold it during her husband's lifetime, [7]**after** her **death** the husband may recover it from the buyer. According to that enactment a husband who inherits his wife's property is considered to have bought it at the time of their marriage. Thus, after his wife's death, he is the first buyer of the property and can reclaim it from the person who purchased it from his late wife while she was married.

רַבִּי שִׁמְעוֹן [8]We have learned in our Mishnah: **"Rabbi Shimon distinguishes between different** types of **property.** Property which is known to the husband, she may not sell, and if she sold it or gave it away, the transaction is void. Property which is not known to the husband she may not sell, but if she sold it or gave it away, the transaction is valid." [9]The Gemara asks: **What** is the property **that is known** to the husband, **and what is** the property **that is not known** to him?

NOTES

רַבִּי שִׁמְעוֹן חוֹלֵק בֵּין נְכָסִים **Rabbi Shimon distinguishes between property and property.** *Ra'ah* and others maintain that Rabbi Shimon refers to the last case of the Mishnah, in which the woman inherited property before she was married. In such a case, Rabbi Shimon distinguishes between property that is known to the husband and property that is unknown to him. But regarding the earlier case of the Mishnah, in which the woman inherited the property after her marriage, even Rabbi Shimon agrees that there is no difference between the different types of property, and the husband may repossess any property which was sold by his wife. *Rabbenu Yehonatan* and others argue that Rabbi Shimon refers to the earlier case of the Mishnah, in which the woman inherited the property after her marriage. The first Tanna maintains that in all cases the sale is void. Rabbi Shimon argues that this ruling is limited to the sale of property known to the husband, but if she sold property unknown to him, the sale is valid. However, regarding the case discussed later in the Mishnah, in which the woman inherited the property before her marriage, Rabbi Shimon does not distinguish between the different types of property. Some understand that, according to *Rashi* and *Rivan,* Rabbi Shimon distinguishes between the two types of property regardless of whether the woman inherited it before or after she was married.

[1]אָמַר רַבִּי יוֹסֵי בְּרַבִּי חֲנִינָא: [2]יְדוּעִין — מְקַרְקְעֵי. [3]שֶׁאֵינָן יְדוּעִין — מִטַּלְטְלִין.
[4]וְרַבִּי יוֹחָנָן אָמַר: אֵלּוּ וְאֵלּוּ יְדוּעִין הֵן. [5]וְאֵלּוּ הֵן שֶׁאֵינָן יְדוּעִין — [6]כָּל שֶׁיּוֹשֶׁבֶת כָּאן, וְנָפְלוּ לָהּ נְכָסִים בִּמְדִינַת הַיָּם.
[7]תַּנְיָא נַמִי הָכִי: [8]״אֵלּוּ הֵן שֶׁאֵינָן יְדוּעִין — כָּל שֶׁיּוֹשֶׁבֶת כָּאן וְנָפְלוּ לָהּ נְכָסִים בִּמְדִינַת הַיָּם.

LITERAL TRANSLATION

[1]Rabbi Yose the son of Rabbi Ḥanina said: [2]That which is known — land. [3]That which is not known — movable goods.

[4]And Rabbi Yoḥanan said: These and those are known. [5]And these are the ones that are not known — [6]whenever she lives here, and property fell to her in a country overseas.

[7]It was also taught thus: [8]"These are the ones that are not known — whenever she lives here and property fell to her in a country overseas."

TRANSLATION AND COMMENTARY

אָמַר [1]**Rabbi Yose the son of Rabbi Ḥanina said:** [2]When Rabbi Shimon spoke of property **which is known** to the husband, he was referring to **land,** which cannot be concealed. [3]And when he spoke of property **which is not known** to the husband, he was referring to **movable goods,** which can be kept hidden. If a married woman sold or gave away land, the transaction is void, for the husband can claim that he married her on the understanding that he would inherit the property upon her death. But if she sold movable goods, the transaction is valid, for the husband cannot claim that he had such expectations about property which can easily be concealed from him.

וְרַבִּי יוֹחָנָן אָמַר [4]**Rabbi Yoḥanan** disagreed and **said: Both** land and movable goods can fall into the category of property **which is known** to the husband, for even regarding movable goods, the husband can claim that he married his wife on the understanding that he would inherit such property upon her death. [5]**And these are the types** of property **that are** regarded as **not known** to the husband — [6]**whatever** property **she inherits** or receives as a gift **overseas while living here.** The husband cannot argue that he had expected to inherit such property after his wife's death.

תַּנְיָא נַמִי הָכִי [7]The Gemara notes: **The same** thing **was also taught** in a Baraita, which stated: [8]**"This is** the property **which is not known** to the husband — **whenever the** woman **lives here, and she inherited property** or received it as a gift **overseas."**

RASHI

ידועין מקרקעי — ועל מנת אותן נכסים נשאה — לפיכך מכרה בטל, שהיה מצפה שתפול לה אותה ירושה.

NOTES

יְדוּעִין **That which is known.** *Rashi* and others explain that the sale of property which was known to the husband is void, because the husband can claim that he married his wife with the expectation of inheriting the property upon her death. *Ramah* (cited by *Rosh*) offers a different explanation of Rabbi Shimon's distinction. As the Gemara explains, our Mishnah teaches that if a woman sold usufruct property, her husband may recover it from the buyer during her lifetime in order to enjoy the usufruct. And as is explained elsewhere (*Ketubot* 47a), the Rabbis entitled the husband to the usufruct of his wife's property, in exchange for which he is obligated to pay his wife's ransom should she be taken captive. The Rabbis were concerned that if they did not entitle the husband to the usufruct of his wife's property, he would not pay her ransom, arguing that she should ransom herself with the usufruct. Now this argument is only relevant if the husband knows about his wife's property, otherwise he would be willing to ransom her with his own money. Thus, argued Rabbi Shimon, if the woman sold property which was known to her husband, the sale is void, and the husband may repossess it. But if she sold property which was not known to her husband, the sale is valid.

מְקַרְקְעֵי **Land.** According to *Tosefot Rid,* land is always regarded as property which is known to the husband, even if he did not actually know that his wife had inherited the property, for by its very nature land cannot be concealed. The husband can always claim that he married his wife with the expectation of benefiting from her real-estate holdings. By contrast, movable goods are always considered property which is not known to the husband, for movable goods can be hidden, and so the husband relinquishes his rights to them from the outset.

בִּמְדִינַת הַיָּם **In a country overseas.** The Rishonim disagree about whether Rabbi Yoḥanan specifically meant property overseas (so *Rosh* understands according to *Rashi*), or whether "overseas" is a general expression for any property which the woman inherited unbeknownst to her husband. (*Ri Migash, Ra'ah, Rashba, Ritva,* and others.) Many Rishonim note that the sale of such property is only valid if it was executed before the husband became aware that his wife had inherited the property.

HALAKHAH

שֶׁאֵינָן יְדוּעִין **That which is not known.** "If a married woman sells usufruct property, her husband may recover the usufruct from the buyer during her lifetime, provided that the property is known to the husband at the time of the sale. But if the husband does not know about the property, for example if it is in another country, the woman's sale of her usufruct property is valid," following Rabbi Yoḥanan, against Rabbi Yose the son of Ḥanina. (*Rambam, Sefer Nashim, Hilkhot Ishut* 22:8; *Shulḥan Arukh, Even HaEzer* 90:11.)

[1] הַהִיא אִיתְּתָא דְּבָעֲיָא דְּתַבְרְחִינְהוּ לְנִכְסָהּ מִגַּבְרָהּ, [2] כְּתַבְתִּינְהוּ לִבְרַתָּהּ. [3] אִינְסִיבָה וְאִיגַּרְשָׁה. [79A] [4] אֲתַאי לְקַמֵּיהּ דְּרַב נַחְמָן. [5] קְרָעֵיהּ רַב נַחְמָן לִשְׁטָרָא. [6] אֲזַל רַב עָנָן לְקַמֵּיהּ דְּמָר עוּקְבָא, אֲמַר לֵיהּ: [7] "חֲזִי, מָר, נַחְמָן חַקְלָאָה הֵיכִי מְקָרַע שְׁטָרֵי דְּאֱינָשֵׁי"! [8] אֲמַר לֵיהּ: "אֵימָא לִי, אִיזִי, [9] גּוּפָא דְּעוּבְדָא הֵיכִי הֲוָה"? [10] אֲמַר לֵיהּ: "הָכִי וְהָכִי הֲוָה". [11] אֲמַר לֵיהּ: "שְׁטַר מַבְרַחַת קָא אָמְרַתְּ? [12] הָכִי אֲמַר

LITERAL TRANSLATION

[1] A certain woman who wanted to withhold her property from her husband [2] wrote [the property] over to her daughter. [3] She was married and [later] she was divorced. [79A] [4] She came before Rav Naḥman. [5] Rav Naḥman tore up the deed. [6] Rav Anan went before Mar Ukva, [and] said to him: [7] "See, Master, how Naḥman the peasant tears up people's deeds!" [8] He said to him: "Tell me, my friend, [9] how was the incident itself?" [10] He said to him: "It was such-and-such." [11] He said to him: "Do you say a deed of feigned transfer? [12] Thus said

TRANSLATION AND COMMENTARY

הַהִיא אִיתְּתָא [1] The Gemara now relates a story about **a certain woman** who had been widowed or divorced, and now wished to marry again. The woman **wanted to withhold her property from her** prospective **husband.** [2] In order to accomplish this before the second marriage, **she wrote the property over** as a gift **to her daughter** from her first marriage. [3] After having disposed of her assets, the woman **was married** but soon **was divorced** from her second husband. The woman then asked her daughter to return her property, arguing that she had never intended that the daughter acquire the property as an absolute gift, but only that she gain formal title to the property so that it would be kept from her husband. But the daughter refused, claiming that the deed in her possession proved that the assets had been transferred to her unconditionally. [79A] [4] **The mother came** with her daughter **before Rav Naḥman** for a ruling. [5] After **Rav Naḥman** heard both sides, he **tore up the deed,** accepting the mother's argument that there had been no actual transfer of ownership. [6] When **Rav Anan** heard about Rav Naḥman's action, he **went before Mar Ukva** the Exilarch, **and said to him:** [7] **"See, Master, how that peasant Naḥman tears up people's** valid **deeds!"** [8] Mar Ukva **said to him: "Tell me, my friend,** [9] **what was the incident itself** to which you refer?" [10] Rav Anan **said to Mar** Ukva: **"Such-and-such was** the incident." [11] After hearing the facts of the case, Mar Ukva **said to** Rav Anan: **"Did you say** that the case involved **a deed of feigned transfer,** to prevent the woman's husband from acquiring the right to inherit the property? [12] But

RASHI

דבעיא דתברחינהו לנכסה – אלמנה היתה, ובאת להנשא, והיתה מקדמת ונותנן לבתה כדי להבריח זכות בעלה מהם, שלא יזכה בהם. והודיעה לעדים שאין מתנה זו מתנה אלא להבריח, ולא שתזכה בהם הבת אם תתאלמן היא או תתגרש. **אתאי לקמיה דרב נחמן** – לתבוע את בתה להחזיר לה הנכסים, והבת הוציאה שטר מתנתה, וקרעיה רב נחמן. **חקלאה** – אינו בקי בדינין. ומר עוקבא אב בית דין הוה.

NOTES

דְּבָעֲיָא דְּתַבְרְחִינְהוּ Who wanted to withhold. According to *Rashi,* the woman who wrote over her property as a gift to her daughter informed the witnesses to the transaction that she was doing so in order to withhold the property from her prospective husband. Most Rishonim disagree with *Rashi,* arguing that if indeed the woman informed witnesses of her intentions, Rav Anan would not have objected to Rav Naḥman's ruling on the matter. Furthermore, the Gemara elsewhere (*Bava Batra* 151a) says that all agree that a deed of feigned transfer is void, if the person disposing of his assets made his intentions clear. Most agree with *Ri Migash* that the deed is void not only if the woman notified witnesses that she had no intention of actually disposing of her assets, but even if she only announced that she was giving away her property on account of her impending marriage. The deed is void in any event, even if the woman did not say anything at all, for we assume that she gave the property to her daughter only in order to withhold it from her husband. Despite the general principle that "matters of the heart have no legal validity," this is not considered a matter which is in this specific woman's heart, but rather a matter which would be in anyone's heart, for we assume that no sane person gives away all of his property during his lifetime. *Ramban* compares this to the gift of a person on his deathbed. The gift of a dying person is valid even if a formal act of acquisition is not performed. But the gift is invalidated if the patient recovers, for we assume that he would never have given away his property had he known he would get well.

HALAKHAH

שְׁטַר מַבְרַחַת A deed of feigned transfer. "If before she entered into marriage a woman transferred all her property to someone other than her future husband (whether or not the recipient was her relative), then even though the gift will become invalid if the woman is divorced or widowed, her husband does not enjoy the usufruct of the property during her lifetime, nor does he inherit the property upon her death, for the gift was made before the marriage, following Shmuel and Rav Naḥman. If the woman predeceases her husband, the recipient acquires absolute possession of the property." (*Rambam, Sefer Nashim, Hilkhot Ishut* 22:9; *Sefer Kinyan, Hilkhot Zekhiyah U'Mattanah* 6:12; *Shulḥan Arukh, Even HaEzer* 90:7.)

TRANSLATION AND COMMENTARY

surely **Rav Ḥanilai bar Idi** said **in the name of Shmuel** as follows: [1]**'I am an authorized judge,** and I am ready to state unequivocally: [2]**When** it is clear that **a deed of feigned transfer has come into my hand,** and the ostensible beneficiary tries to claim title to the property by virtue of that deed,' I **tear up** the deed. Thus Rav Naḥman acted properly."

אָמַר לֵיהּ רָבָא [3]When **Rava** saw that Rav Naḥman tore up the daughter's deed, he **said to him:** Shmuel's ruling that a deed of feigned transfer is to be torn up should not have been applied in this case. [4]**What is the reason** that Shmuel would invalidate a deed of feigned transfer? [5]**Because** we assume that **a person does not forsake himself and give** his property away **to others.** In most instances, the donor clearly does not intend to effect the gift. [6]However, **this assumption applies** only with respect to gifts to **people outside** the donor's family. [7]**But** regarding a gift to **a daughter, it** is reasonable to assume that the mother did in fact intend to **give** the property away. Thus, you should not have torn up the deed.

אֲפִילּוּ הָכִי [8]Rav Naḥman defended his ruling and said: **Even** regarding a woman's gift to **her daughter,** [9]we assume that her **own welfare is more important to her** than that of her daughter. Clearly the deed of gift was only a subterfuge to keep the property away from the woman's husband.

מֵיתִיבֵי [10]**An objection was raised** against Shmuel from a Baraita which stated: "If **a woman wishes to withhold her property from her** prospective **husband,** [11]**what should she do?** [12]**She should write** over the property in **a deed of trust to a third person,** trusting that he will not not try to keep it for himself. [13]This is **the position of Rabban Shimon ben Gamliel.** [14]**And the Sages say:** This would be imprudent, for **if** the donee **wants, he can laugh at** the woman and keep the property, [15]**unless she writes her** property over to the other

רַב חֲנִילָאי בַּר אִידִי אָמַר שְׁמוּאֵל: [1]'מוֹרֶה הוֹרָאָה אֲנִי. [2]אִם יָבֹא שְׁטַר מַבְרַחַת לְיָדִי, אֶקְרָעֶנּוּ'". [3]אֲמַר לֵיהּ רָבָא לְרַב נַחְמָן: [4]טַעֲמָא מַאי? [5]דְּלָא שָׁבֵיק אִינִישׁ נַפְשֵׁיהּ וְיָהֵיב לְאַחֲרִינֵי. [6]הָנֵי מִילֵּי לְאַחֲרִינֵי. [7]אֲבָל לִבְרַתָּהּ, יָהֵיבָא! [8]אֲפִילּוּ הָכִי, [9]בִּמְקוֹם בְּרַתָּהּ נַפְשָׁהּ עֲדִיפָא לָהּ. [10]מֵיתִיבֵי: "הָרוֹצָה שֶׁתַּבְרִיחַ נְכָסֶיהָ מִבַּעְלָהּ, [11]כֵּיצַד הִיא עוֹשָׂה? [12]כּוֹתֶבֶת שְׁטַר פַּסִּים לַאֲחֵרִים; [13]דִּבְרֵי רַבָּן שִׁמְעוֹן בֶּן גַּמְלִיאֵל. [14]וַחֲכָמִים אוֹמְרִים: רָצָה, מְצַחֵק בָּהּ, [15]עַד שֶׁתִּכְתּוֹב

LITERAL TRANSLATION

Rav Ḥanilai bar Idi in the name of Shmuel: [1]'I am an authorized judge. [2]If a deed of feigned transfer comes into my hand, I tear it up.'"

[3]Rava said to Rav Naḥman: [4]What is the reason? [5]Because a person does not forsake himself and give to others. [6]This applies (lit., "these words") to outsiders. [7]But to her daughter, she gives!

[8]Even so, [9]in the place of her daughter her own [welfare] is more important to her.

[10]They raised an objection: "A woman who wishes to withhold her property from her husband, [11]how should she act? [12]She should write a deed of trust to others; [13][these are] the words of Rabban Shimon ben Gamliel. [14]And the Sages say: [If] he wants, he can laugh at her, [15]unless she writes

RASHI

מורה הוראה אני — נטלתי רשות מריש גלותא, כדאמרינן בפרק קמא דסנהדרין (ה,א) דמהני רשותא. ולא יהבי רשותא אלא לבקי בדבר. **אם יבא שטר מברחת לידי** — שירצה המקבל מתנה להחזיק בנכסים על פיו, שלא להחזירם לנותן — אקרענו. ולקמיה פריך: הואיל ולאו שטרא הוא — היאך הועיל להבריח? **אמר ליה** — רבא לרב נחמן, כשקרע אותו שטר: היכי סמכת בהא אדשמואל וקרעת ליה? **טעמא מאי** — אמר שמואל אקרענו. **דלא שביק איניש נפשיה כו'** — ולא גמר להקנותו אלא בעוד שהוא דואג מאחרים שלא יחזיקו בהם. **הני מילי** — בנותנתן לאיש נכרי, איכא למימר דלא גמרה ואקניא. **אבל לברתה יהבה לה** — מתנה חלוטה. **שטר פסים** — שטר פיוסים. שמפייסתו לקבל מתנה זו להפקיע זכות בעלה קודם נישואין, ולא שיזכה מקבל זה בהם. **אם רצה** — המקבל הזה. **מצחק בה** — ומחזיק בהן עולמית. **עד שתכתוב** — בשטר זה: מהיום נתונים לך ולכשארצה. יש כאן הברחה מבעלה, שאם בא לזכות — תאמר: אני רוצה (במתנה, ונמצא קיימת למפרע. ואם זה שנכתב שטר יבוא להחזיק — תאמר: איני רוצה).

NOTES

מוֹרֶה הוֹרָאָה אֲנִי I am an authorized judge. According to *Rashi* and *Rivan,* Shmuel meant to emphasize that he spoke with authority, for he had been empowered by the exilarch to act as a judge. *Ritva* cites an alternative reading (apparently a Gaonic tradition): מִירֵאֵי הוֹרָאָה אֲנִי — "I am from among those who hesitate to issue rulings." Ordinarily, Shmuel was very careful about deciding on matters of law, but he had no doubt about his position that a deed of feigned transfer has no legal validity, and that the deed should be destroyed.

כּוֹתֶבֶת שְׁטַר פַּסִּים She should write a deed of trust. The Aḥaronim ask: How can we advise a woman to write over

HALAKHAH

עַד שֶׁתִּכְתּוֹב לוֹ: 'מֵהַיּוֹם וְלִכְשֶׁאֶרְצֶה' Unless she writes him: 'From today and when I shall want.' "If the woman transferred only a part of her property, the gift remains valid even if the woman is divorced or widowed, following

TRANSLATION AND COMMENTARY

person using the following formula: [1]'My property shall be given over to you **from today and when I shall want** the gift to be valid.' [2]The Baraita implies that, according to the Sages, **the reason** that the recipient cannot claim the woman's property **is that she wrote him** that it would be given to him from a particular day and when she would want the gift to be valid; and if she should die before validating the gift, her husband inherits it. [3]**But** from this it follows that **if** the woman **did not write** the deed **in this manner,** [4]**the recipient** of the gift indeed **acquires the** property! Thus, we see that a deed attesting to a transfer of property is valid, even if it is evident that the transaction was fictitious; and this position is against Shmuel's ruling!

לוֹ: [1]'מֵהַיּוֹם וְלִכְשֶׁאֶרְצֶה'". [2]טַעֲמָא דְּכָתְבָה לֵיהּ הָכִי. [3]הָא לָא כָּתְבָה לֵיהּ הָכִי, [4]קָנַנְהִי לוֹקֵחַ!

[5]אָמַר רַבִּי זֵירָא: לָא קַשְׁיָא. [6]הָא, בְּכוּלָּהּ. [7]הָא, בְּמִקְצָתָהּ.

[8]וְאִי לָא קָנַנְהִי לוֹקֵחַ, [9]נִיקְנִינְהוּ בַּעַל!

LITERAL TRANSLATION

him: [1]'From today and when I shall want.'" [2]The reason is that she wrote him thus. [3]But if she did not write him thus, [4]the recipient acquired it!

[5]Rabbi Zera said: It is not difficult. [6]This, regarding all of it. [7]This, regarding part of it.

[8]But if the recipient did not acquire it, [9]let the husband acquire it!

RASHI

קננהי לוקח — תיובתא דשמואל. **הא בכולה** — כי אמר שמואל: לא קני — בכותבת לו כל נכסיה. דכיון דלא שיירה מידי לנפשה אם תתגרש — אנן סהדי דלא גמרה ומקניא. והא דקתני: רצה מלאחק בה — בכותבת מקצתן. **ואי לא קננהי לוקח לקנינהו בעל** — לשמואל, בכותבת כולן, דאמר: לא קני. כיון דלא קני — מאי הבריחה איכא? ליקנינהו בעל ויאכל פירות, וירשנה אם תמות תחתיו.

אָמַר רַבִּי זֵירָא [5]**Rabbi Zera said: There is no difficulty.** [6]Shmuel was referring to the disposition of **all** the woman's property. This could never have been meant as an absolute gift, for surely no one forgoes all his property. [7]However, the Baraita was referring to the disposition of only **part of** her property. In such a case, the gift is valid.

וְאִי לָא [8]The Gemara asks: **But if the** ostensible **recipient** of all the woman's property **does not acquire title** to it, how does that fictitious document keep the property from the woman's husband? [9]By right **her husband should** enjoy the usufruct while his wife is alive, and he should inherit it.

NOTES

her property in a deed of trust to a third person, when the Gemara states elsewhere (*Ketubot* 19a) that it is forbidden for a person even to retain such a document in his house? *Rashba* explains that we are not dealing here with an actual deed of trust, but that this deed is similar to a deed of trust because it has no legal validity.

מֵהַיּוֹם וְלִכְשֶׁאֶרְצֶה **From today and when I shall want.** The Rishonim disagree about this passage. Our commentary follows *Rashi* and others, who understand that when the woman formulates her gift in this manner, it only takes effect if the woman later expresses her desire that it should do so. According to this approach, the woman merely lays the groundwork for her gift to take effect retroactively, in case her husband claims the property. But if the ostensible recipient claims the property, the woman can state explicitly that she does not want the gift to be valid. Thus, if the woman predeceases her husband, he inherits the property, for the gift to the third party never took effect (*Ra'ah*). However, the ostensible recipient would keep the usufruct of the property that he enjoyed during the woman's lifetime, either because it is regarded as property which was not known to the husband so that he did not acquire it, or because the husband is presumed to have relinquished his right to it (see *Ra'ah, Rosh*). *Rabbenu Ḥananel*, who had a slightly different reading ("From today and as long as I shall want"), understood the passage differently: The woman gives away her property with the provision that if she wishes to cancel the gift, she may do so. According to this approach, the gift is valid right away, so the husband does not inherit the property if she predeceases him. *Rambam* agrees with this ruling that the husband does not inherit the property, even though he maintains that the gift is only valid if the woman later says that she wants it to take effect. (See also *Rashba* and *Ran*.)

וְאִי לָא קָנַנְהִי לוֹקֵחַ **But if the buyer did not acquire it.** Our commentary follows *Rashi* and others who explain that the Gemara is asking about the interpretation of Shmuel's position, namely that a deed attesting to the donation of all of a person's property is invalid. If the gift is invalid, then the property should remain in the woman's possession, and her husband should enjoy the usufruct during her lifetime and inherit the property upon her passing. How, then, does the deed of feigned transfer help the woman withhold her property from her husband? Alternatively, the Gemara's question can be understood as an objection against Shmuel. If indeed the gift is invalid, then it follows that the husband should acquire rights to the property. But since it is clear that the woman did not want her husband to acquire such rights, but intended to withhold the property from him, we should say that the gift to the other person is valid, against Shmuel's ruling (*Rabbenu Shimshon*, cited by *Rosh*).

HALAKHAH

Rabbi Zera. If she wrote over part or all of her property using the formulation, 'From today and when I shall want,' the gift is not effective until she says that she wants it to be so, and the husband does not enjoy the usufruct of the property, nor does he inherit the property if she predeceases him." (*Rambam, Sefer Nashim, Hilkhot Ishut* 22:9; *Sefer Kinyan, Hilkhot Zekhiyah U'Mattanah* 6:12; *Shulḥan Arukh, Even HaEzer* 90:7.)

[1]אֲמַר אַבַּיֵי: עֲשָׂאוּם כִּנְכָסִים שֶׁאֵין יְדוּעִין לַבַּעַל, [2]וְאַלִּיבָּא דְּרַבִּי שִׁמְעוֹן.

משנה [3]נָפְלוּ לָהּ כְּסָפִים, [4]יִלָּקַח בָּהֶן קַרְקַע, [5]וְהוּא אוֹכֵל פֵּירוֹת.

[6]פֵּירוֹת הַתְּלוּשִׁין מִן הַקַּרְקַע [7]יִלָּקַח בָּהֶן קַרְקַע, [8]וְהוּא אוֹכֵל פֵּירוֹת.

[9][פֵּירוֹת] הַמְחוּבָּרִים בַּקַּרְקַע — [10]אָמַר רַבִּי מֵאִיר: [11]שָׁמִין אוֹתָהּ כַּמָּה הִיא יָפָה בְּפֵירוֹת

LITERAL TRANSLATION

[1]Abaye said: They made it like property which is not known to the husband, [2]and in accordance with Rabbi Shimon.

MISHNAH [3][If] money fell to her [as an inheritance], [4]land must be bought with it, [5]and he eats the fruit.

[6]Produce which is detached from the ground, [7]land must be [8]bought with it, and he eats the fruit.

[9][Produce] which is attached to the ground — [10]Rabbi Meir said: [11]We assess how much it is worth with the produce

TRANSLATION AND COMMENTARY

אֲמַר אַבַּיֵי [1]**Abaye said:** The Sages **treated** the property included in a deed of feigned transfer **like property which is not known to the husband,** [2]**and in accordance with** the view of **Rabbi Shimon** that if the woman sold or gave away such property after she was married, the transaction is valid. The husband cannot argue that he had expected to inherit the property after his wife's death. Similarly, if a man's wife made a written disposition of her property in favor of another person, the husband does not enjoy the usufruct during her lifetime, nor does he inherit the property.

MISHNAH נָפְלוּ לָהּ כְּסָפִים [3]If a woman **inherited money** or received money as a gift, [4]**land must be bought with** the money, so that her principal will remain intact, [5]**and** the husband **enjoys the usufruct.**

פֵּירוֹת [6]Similarly, if a woman inherited or received as a gift **produce which was** already **detached from the ground,** the produce must be sold, [7]**land must be bought with** the proceeds of the sale, [8]**and** the husband **enjoys the usufruct.**

פֵּירוֹת [9]If a woman inherited or received as a gift **produce which was** still **attached to the ground,** in other words, land together with the produce growing on it, the Tannaim disagree about whether the produce is to be regarded as principal, which remains in the woman's possession, or usufruct, which belongs to the husband. [10]**Rabbi Meir said:** The produce growing on the woman's property when she acquired it is principal over which the woman retains ownership. In order to determine the value of that produce, [11]**we assess how**

RASHI

כנכסים שאינן ידועין — שהרי על מנת שאינן שלה נשאה, דסבור שהמתנה גמורה.

משנה והוא אוכל פירות — והקרן קיימת לה. שלא תיקנו לו חכמים תחת פירקונה אלא פירות.

NOTES

וְאַלִּיבָּא דְּרַבִּי שִׁמְעוֹן And in accordance with Rabbi Shimon. Most Rishonim infer from this passage that the law is in accordance with Rabbi Shimon's position in the Mishnah, even though it is the view of a single authority against the majority opinion. *Rid* understands Abaye's answer differently: The Sages treated the property involved in a deed of feigned transfer like property which is not known to the husband and according to Rabbi Shimon. Just as Rabbi Shimon maintains that if a woman sold such property, the sale is valid, because the husband did not have it in mind when he married, so, too, do the Sages maintain that if a woman donated all her property to someone other than her husband, he does not acquire any rights to the property, because he abandoned hope of receiving it. Further, according to *Rid*, while indeed we rule that a deed of feigned transfer has no legal validity, we do not do so in accordance with the view of Rabbi Shimon. *Tosafot* reject this explanation of Abaye's position, arguing that the Gemara's formulation, "And in accordance with Rabbi Shimon," implies that those who maintain that a deed of feigned transfer is invalid must agree with Rabbi Shimon. If *Rid*'s position were correct, *Tosafot* argue, the Gemara should have read: "In accordance with Rabbi Shimon," without the conjunction "and."

נָפְלוּ לָהּ כְּסָפִים If money fell to her. *Melekhet Shelomo* asks: Since the law relating to money and the law relating to detached produce are one and the same, why did the Mishnah teach the two laws in separate clauses? He answers that Rabbi Yehudah HaNasi received two separate traditions regarding money and detached produce, and while he combined the two into a single Mishnah, he did not tamper with their original formulation. Alternatively, the first clause regarding money was taught separately in order to teach that even if the woman acquired money as compensation for a bodily injury she suffered, the money is regarded as principal, so that it must be invested in land, the usufruct of which may be enjoyed by the husband during the woman's lifetime, in accordance with the view of Rabbi Yehudah ben Betera (*Ketubot* 65b).

HALAKHAH

נָפְלוּ לָהּ כְּסָפִים If money fell to her. "The husband is entitled to the fruit of his wife's usufruct property. If the woman has property which does not produce fruit (movable goods or money), the property must be sold, whether she brought it with her into the marriage, or received it later. Land is bought with the proceeds of the sale, and the husband enjoys the usufruct." (*Rambam, Sefer Nashim, Hilkhot Ishut* 22:21; *Shulḥan Arukh, Even HaEzer* 85:13.)

וְכַמָּה הִיא יָפָה בְּלֹא פֵּירוֹת, [1]וּמוֹתָר — [2]יִלָּקַח בָּהֶן קַרְקַע וְהוּא אוֹכֵל פֵּירוֹת. [3]וַחֲכָמִים אוֹמְרִים: הַמְחוּבָּרִים לַקַּרְקַע שֶׁלּוֹ. [4]וְהַתְּלוּשִׁין מִן הַקַּרְקַע שֶׁלָּהּ, [5]וְיִלָּקַח בָּהֶן קַרְקַע, [6]וְהוּא אוֹכֵל פֵּירוֹת.

[7]רַבִּי שִׁמְעוֹן אוֹמֵר: מָקוֹם שֶׁיִּפָּה כֹּחוֹ בִּכְנִיסָתָהּ, [8]הוּרַע כֹּחוֹ בִּיצִיאָתָהּ. [9]מָקוֹם שֶׁהוּרַע כֹּחוֹ בִּכְנִיסָתָהּ, [10]יָפֶה כֹּחוֹ בִּיצִיאָתָהּ. [11]כֵּיצַד? [12]פֵּירוֹת הַמְחוּבָּרִים לַקַּרְקַע — [13]בִּכְנִיסָתָהּ שֶׁלּוֹ, [14]וּבִיצִיאָתָהּ שֶׁלָּהּ, [15]וְהַתְּלוּשִׁין מִן הַקַּרְקַע — בִּכְנִיסָתָהּ שֶׁלָּהּ, [16]וּבִיצִיאָתָהּ שֶׁלּוֹ.

גמרא [17]פְּשִׁיטָא: [18]אַרְעָא

LITERAL TRANSLATION

and how much it is worth without the produce, [1]and the difference — [2]land must be bought with it, and he eats the fruit. [3]And the Sages say: That which is attached to the ground is his. [4]And that which is detached from the ground is hers, [5]and land must be bought with it, [6]and he eats the fruit.

[7]Rabbi Shimon says: Where his power was strengthened when she comes in, [8]his power was weakened when she leaves. [9]Where his power was weakened when she comes in, [10]his power was strengthened when she leaves. [11]How so? [12]Produce which is attached to the ground — [13]when she comes in [it] is his, [14]and when she leaves [it] is hers. [15]And that which is detached from the ground — when she come in [it] is hers, [16]and when she leaves [it] is his.

GEMARA [17]It is obvious: [18]Land

TRANSLATION AND COMMENTARY

much the land **is worth together with the produce and how much** the land **is worth without the produce.** [1]**The difference** reflects the present value of the produce, which belongs to the woman. [2]She must be paid that amount, **land must be bought with** the money, **and** her husband **enjoys the usufruct** of the property. [3]**The Sages disagree** and **say:** The produce **that was** still **attached to the ground** when the property was acquired by the woman **belongs to her husband.** [4]**But** even the Sages agree that produce **which had been detached from the ground** when it was acquired **belongs to the woman,** and is regarded as principal. [5]It must be sold, **land must be bought** with the proceeds of the sale, [6]**and** the husband **enjoys the usufruct** of the property.

רַבִּי שִׁמְעוֹן אוֹמֵר [7]The Mishnah continues: **Rabbi Shimon says:** Regarding the produce to **which** the Sages **strengthened** the husband's **power if** it was acquired by his wife **while she was married** to him, [8]they **weakened his power at the time of divorce.** And the reverse is also true: [9]Regarding the produce to **which** the Sages **weakened** the husband's **power** if it was acquired by his wife **while she was married** to him, [10]they **strengthened his power at the time of divorce.** [11]**How so?** [12]Regarding **produce which is** still **attached to the ground** — [13]if it was inherited by a woman **while she was married**, the produce **belongs to her husband,** following the Sages above, who maintain that such produce is treated like usufruct. [14]And if the woman had such produce in her possession **when she was divorced**, it **belongs to her.** [15]**And** regarding the produce **that was** already **detached from the ground** — if it was inherited by a woman **while she was married**, it **belongs to her.** [16]**And** if she had such produce in her possession **when she was divorced**, the produce **belongs to her husband.**

GEMARA פְּשִׁיטָא [17]We learned in the Mishnah that if a married woman receives property which does not bear fruit, it is converted into land which will allow the woman's principal to be preserved and at the same time allow her husband to enjoy the usufruct. Land includes all types of real estate. The Gemara discusses disagreement between husband and wife about what type of property to buy: **It is obvious** that if one of them [18]wishes to buy agricultural **land, and** the other wishes to buy houses,

RASHI

שמין אותה כו׳ — דקסבר: מה שגדל ברשותו הוו פירות, ומה שלא גדל ברשותו — הוי קרן. לפיכך, מה שדמי הקרקע יקרים עכשיו בשביל תבואה זו — צריך ליתן לה דמים, ויקנו מהן קרקע, ויאכל הוא פירותיה. **וחכמים אומרים** — אף אלו שלא גדלו ברשותו. תורת פירות נתנו בהן, הואיל והקרקע קיימת לה. **ביציאתה** — אם בא לגרשה. **פירות המחוברין לקרקע בכניסה שלו** — כלומר: בשעת נפילתן שלו, כרבנן. ובגמרא פריך: היינו תנא קמא. [**ביציאתה שלה** — המגרש את אשתו והיו בנכסים פירות מחוברין — נוטלת קרקעותיה עם פירות שבהן. **בכניסתה שלה** — וילקח בהן קרקע, והוא אוכל פירות]. **וביציאתה שלו** — דמה שקדם ותלש בעודה תחתיו — זכה בהן מדין פירות נכסי מלוג.

גמרא פשיטא לי ארעא ובתי ארעא — נפלו לה כספים, ובאו ליקח לה קרקע. זה אומר: קרקע בת זריעה אני רוצה, וזאת אומרת: בתים אני רוצה ליקח, או איפוך.

HALAKHAH

פֵּירוֹת הַמְחוּבָּרִים **Produce which is attached.** "If a married woman inherits produce which is still attached to the ground, the produce belongs to her husband, even if it is already fit to be harvested. If she inherits produce which has been detached from the ground, the produce belongs to her. In which case, the produce must be sold, land is bought with the proceeds, and the husband enjoys the usufruct." (*Rambam, Sefer Nashim, Hilkhot Ishut* 22:24; *Shulḥan Arukh, Even HaEzer* 85:15.)

וּבָתֵּי, [1]אַרְעָא; [2]בָּתֵּי וְדִיקְלֵי, [3]בָּתֵּי; [4]דִּיקְלֵי וְאִילָנֵי, [5]דִּיקְלֵי; [6]אִילָנֵי וְגוּפְנֵי, [7]אִילָנֵי. [8]אַבָּא, [9]זַרְדְּתָא, [10]וּפֵירָא דְּכַוְורֵי — [11]אָמְרִי לָהּ: פֵּירָא. [12]וְאָמְרִי לָהּ: קַרְנָא. [13]כְּלָלָא דְּמִילְּתָא: [14]גִּזְעוֹ מַחֲלִיף,

LITERAL TRANSLATION

or houses, [1]land; [2]houses or palms, [3]houses; [4]palms or [other] trees, [5]palms; [6]trees or grapevines, [7]trees. [8]A forest, [9]sorb bushes, [10]and a fishpond — [11]there are some who say: Fruit. [12]And there are some who say: Principal. [13]The rule of the matter: [14][If] its stump sends forth new shoots,

RASHI

ארעא — זבינן מינייהו. ששכרה מרובה, ואינה מרקבת. ושניהם מעכבים; הבעל יכול לומר: דבר שפירותיו מרובים אני חפץ. וכן אם בא הוא ליקח בית — יכולה היא לומר: איני רוצה בדבר שהוא כלה והולך והקרן מתמעט. **בתי** — שכרן מרובה מדיקלי, שהן עשויין ליבש. **דיקלי** = תמרים. **אילני** — שאר אילנות. **אבא** = יער, לחתוך עצים. **זרדתא** — אילנות של עוזרדין. ולא היו פריין חשוב להן, וקוצצין אותן לעצים. **ופירא דבוורי** = חפירה של דגים, שקורין *ויוויי״ר. **אמרי לה פירא** — אם נפלו לה בירושה, קציצת העצים ודגים שבחפירה — הוא פריין, והקרקע הוא קרן. **ואמרי לה** — כולהו הוו קרנא, הואיל והעצים והדגים כלים. והכל ימכר מיד, וילקח בהן קרקע, והוא אוכל פירות. אילן אין גזעו מחליף.

TRANSLATION AND COMMENTARY

[1]they buy **land.** Land is beneficial to both parties, because it produces greater benefits and does not depreciate through wear or deterioration. [2]Similarly, if one spouse wishes to buy **houses and** the other wishes to buy date **palms,** [3]they buy **houses,** for houses generate more income and retain their value longer than date palms. [4]So, too, if one of the parties wishes to buy date **palms, and** the other wishes to buy fruit **trees** of another type, [5]they buy date **palms,** for date palms survive longer than other fruit trees. [6]And finally, if one of the parties wishes to buy fruit **trees, and** the other wishes to buy **grapevines,** [7]they buy fruit **trees,** for trees survive longer than grapevines.

אַבָּא [8]Further, if a married woman received **a forest** of trees which do not bear fruit but can be cut down for their wood, [9]or **sorb bushes which** bear low-quality fruit, and are therefore exploited primarily through their wood, [10]**or a fishpond,** the Sages disagree about the law. [11]**Some say** that the wood and the fish are regarded as **usufruct,** which belongs to the husband, and the land on which the trees stand or the pond in which the fish swim is regarded as principal, which is retained by the woman. [12]**And others say** that since the wood and the fish will be totally depleted, they too are regarded as **principal,** which must be preserved for the woman. [13]**The rule regarding the matter** can be summed up as follows: [14]Any tree whose **stump will send forth new shoots,** may be cut down by the

NOTES

פְּשִׁיטָא: אַרְעָא וּבָתֵּי It is obvious: Land or houses. *Rivan* deletes the phrase, "it is obvious," arguing that this expression is used to introduce a question, first indicating what issues have obvious answers, and then setting out those which must be resolved. Here, however, the expression, "it is obvious," does not lead up to a question.

אַבָּא, זַרְדְּתָא, וּפֵירָא דְּכַוְורֵי A forest, sorb bushes, and a fishpond. *Rashi* understands that we are dealing here with three different things — a forest, sorb bushes, and a fishpond. But the Geonim and *Rabbenu Ḥananel* understand that אַבָּא זַרְדְּתָא is one entity: The Geonim explain the term as referring to a timber forest, while according to *Rabbenu Ḥananel* the expression refers to aged willows.

Our commentary follows *Rashi*, who understands that there is no connection between this and the previous discussion. Here the Gemara discusses whether these three different things — a forest, sorb bushes, and a fishpond — are regarded as usufruct, so that if they are inherited by a woman, they may be enjoyed by her husband, while the land is the principal and retained by the woman. Or perhaps these things are regarded as principal, and so they must be sold, and land must be purchased with the proceeds of the sale.

Rabbenu Tam explains that this passage is a continuation of the previous discussion. If a woman inherited money, which must be invested in land so that the husband may enjoy the usufruct, while she retains the principal, may the money be invested in a forest, a fishpond or the like? The opinions differ as to whether these things are treated as principal or as fruit.

Meiri understands that the connection between this passage and the previous one is even more direct. If a woman inherited money, and she and her husband disagree about what type of property to buy, one party wishing to buy a timber or reed forest, and the other party wishing to buy a fishpond, they buy a forest. The expression אָמְרִי לָהּ...וְאָמְרִי לָהּ is not used here in its usual sense to indicate a difference of opinion. Here the expression means that we say that some of them (i.e., the forest) are principal, and some of them (i.e., the fishpond) are usufruct.

כְּלָלָא דְּמִילְּתָא The rule of the matter. Our commentary follows the reading and explanation of *Rashi,* according to

HALAKHAH

אַרְעָא וּבָתֵּי Land or houses. "If a married woman has property which does not bear fruit, and it has to be sold in order to purchase fruit-producing property, property which produces the highest yield at the lowest cost must be bought, whether that fulfills the husband's wishes or those of his wife. They only buy property which will replenish itself after the husband enjoys the usufruct to which he is entitled." (*Rambam, Sefer Nashim, Hilkhot Ishut* 22:33; *Shulḥan Arukh, Even HaEzer* 85:13.)

LANGUAGE

אַבָּא Forest. This word (cf. Syriac אבא) is apparently related to the word אבים — "green plants" — in Song of Songs (6:11).

BACKGROUND

זַרְדְּתָא Sorb bushes. The fruit that grows on sorb bushes is of little value (although its thin branches are used for fuel). Various attempts to identify this plant have been made; *Rashi* claims that this is the hawthorn shrub (*Crataegus azarolus*), while the *Arukh* maintains that this is a jujube (a type of Ziziphus).

LANGUAGE (RASHI)

ויוויי״ר* From the Old French *vivier,* meaning "fishpond."

TRANSLATION AND COMMENTARY

husband. [1]The wood **is considered** as **usufruct,** since the stump will grow new shoots, and the woman's principal will be preserved. [2]But a tree whose **stump will not send forth new shoots,** may not be cut down by the husband, [3]for the tree **is considered** as **principal,** which must be preserved for the woman. It must be sold, and land must be bought with the proceeds, the usufruct of which belongs to the husband.

אָמַר רַבִּי זֵירָא [4]**Rabbi Zera said in the name of Rabbi Oshaya, who said in the name of Rabbi Yannai,** [5]**and there are some who say that Rabbi Abba said in the name of Rabbi Oshaya, who said in the name of Rabbi Yannai:** [6]If **someone stole** [79B] [7]**the offspring of an animal of usufruct property,** owned by a woman at the time of her marriage or acquired thereafter, [8]he **must make the double payment to the wife.** The thief must restore the principal to the owner — the article itself, or when the article is unavailable, its value — and he must make an additional payment equal to the value of the article. Rabbi Yannai's ruling seems to assume that the offspring of an animal of usufruct property is not considered usufruct which belongs to the husband. For if it were usufruct, the double payment would have to be made to the husband. Thus, since it is not usufruct, it must be principal.

כְּמַאן [9]The Gemara asks: **In accordance with which** Tannaitic opinion was Rabbi Yannai's ruling issued? [10]It could **not** have been issued **in accordance with** the view of **the Rabbis, nor** could it have been issued **in accordance with** the view of **Hananyah,** who disagrees with the Rabbis! About what do these Tannaim disagree? [11]**As it was taught** in the following Baraita: **"The offspring of an animal of usufruct property** belongs **to the husband.** [12]However, **the child of a** non-Jewish **maidservant of usufruct property** belongs **to the wife.** This is the opinion of the Rabbis. [13]**Hananyah ben Ahi Yoshiyah** disagrees and **says:** [14]The Sages **treated the**

[1]פֵּירָא. [2]אֵין גִּזְעוֹ מַחֲלִיף, [3]קַרְנָא.

[4]אָמַר רַבִּי זֵירָא אָמַר רַבִּי אוֹשַׁעְיָא אָמַר רַבִּי יַנַּאי, [5]וְאָמְרִי לַהּ אָמַר רַבִּי אַבָּא אָמַר רַבִּי אוֹשַׁעְיָא אָמַר רַבִּי יַנַּאי: [6]הַגּוֹנֵב [79B] [7]וְלַד בֶּהֱמַת מְלוֹג, [8]מְשַׁלֵּם תַּשְׁלוּמֵי כֶפֶל לָאִשָּׁה.

[9]כְּמַאן? [10]לֹא כְּרַבָּנַן וְלֹא כַּחֲנַנְיָה! [11]דְּתַנְיָא: ״וְלַד בֶּהֱמַת מְלוֹג — לַבַּעַל. [12]וְלַד שִׁפְחַת מְלוֹג — לָאִשָּׁה. [13]וַחֲנַנְיָה בֶּן אֲחִי יֹאשִׁיָּה אָמַר: [14]עָשׂוּ וְלַד

LITERAL TRANSLATION

[1]it is fruit. [2][If] its stump does not send forth new shoots, [3]it is principal.

[4]Rabbi Zera said in the name of Rabbi Oshaya who said in the name of Rabbi Yannai, [5]and there are some who say that Rabbi Abba said in the name of Rabbi Oshaya who said in the name of Rabbi Yannai: [6]Someone who steals [79B] [7]the offspring of an animal of usufruct property, [8]must make the double payment to the wife.

[9]In accordance with whom? [10]Not in accordance with the Rabbis and not in accordance with Hananyah! [11]As it was taught: "The offspring of an animal of usufruct property — to the husband. [12]The child of a maidservant of usufruct property — to the wife. [13]And Hananyah ben Ahi Yoshiyah said: [14]They made the child

RASHI

ולד בהמת מלוג — שנפלה לה בהמה בירושה, וילדה. **תשלומי כפל לאשה** — ולא לבעל. קא סלקא דעתך דקסבר אין הוולדות פירי אלא קרן, וילקח בהן קרקע, דחיישינן שמא תמות האם ויכלה הקרן. **וולד שפחת מלוג לאשה** — לקמן מפרש טעמא.

NOTES

which the rules are as follows: The fruit of plants that will send forth new shoots is considered usufruct, which belongs to the husband. And the fruit of plants that will not send forth new shoots is considered principal, which may not be cut down by the husband but must be preserved for the woman. *Rabbenu Hananel* had the opposite reading: "The rule of the matter: [If] its stump sends forth new shoots, it is principal. [If] its stump does not send forth new shoots, it is fruit." According to this the rules are as follows: Plants that send forth new shoots are considered principal and need not be sold to purchase land. And plants that do not send forth new shoots are considered fruit, which must be sold if inherited by a woman, and land must be purchased with the proceeds. According to this view, a forest and a fishpond are fruit.

HALAKHAH

הַגּוֹנֵב וְלַד בֶּהֱמַת מְלוֹג **Someone who steals the offspring of an animal of usufruct property.** "If someone stole the offspring of an animal of usufruct property, and he was apprehended, he must make the double payment to the woman, for the double payment is not considered usufruct to which the husband is entitled." (*Rambam, Sefer Nashim, Hilkhot Ishut* 22:28; *Tur, Even HaEzer* 85.)

וְלַד בֶּהֱמַת מְלוֹג לַבַּעַל **The offspring of an animal of usufruct property — to the husband.** "The offspring of an animal of usufruct property and the child of a maidservant of usufruct property belong to the husband," following Hananyah. (*Rambam, Sefer Nashim, Hilkhot Ishut* 22:25; *Shulhan Arukh, Even HaEzer* 85:16.)

TRANSLATION AND COMMENTARY

child of a maidservant of usufruct property like the offspring of an animal of usufruct property, so that both belong to the husband." Although the Rabbis (the anonymous first Tanna of the Baraita) and Ḥananyah disagree about the offspring of a maidservant of usufruct property, they do agree that the offspring of an animal of usufruct property belongs to the husband. Why, then, does a thief who stole the offspring of an animal of usufruct property make the double payment to the wife and not to her husband?

אֲפִילּוּ תֵּימָא [1]The Gemara answers: **You may even say** that Rabbi Yannai issued his ruling in accordance with **all** the Tannaim — both the Rabbis and Ḥananyah — for it is possible to distinguish between the one who has title to the offspring of the animal of usufruct property and the one who is entitled to receive the double payment that must be paid if the offspring is stolen. [2]**The Rabbis enacted in favor of** the husband, giving him the right to benefit from all the **fruit** of his wife's property, and the offspring of an animal of her usufruct property falls into that category. [3]But **the Rabbis did not enact** that the husband is entitled to enjoy **the fruit of the fruit** of his wife's property. The mother animal is the usufruct property that remains in the wife's possession. The offspring is the usufruct of that property which, according to all the Tannaim, belongs to the husband. However, the double compensation paid by the thief who stole the offspring is the usufruct of the usufruct that — according to Rabbi Yannai — belongs to the wife.

בִּשְׁלָמָא [4]The Gemara now points out a difficulty with regard to the position of the Rabbis: **We can understand** the law **according to Ḥananyah**, who equates the offspring of an animal of usufruct property with the child of a maidservant of usufruct property. In both cases **we are not concerned** lest the mother **die** and the woman's principal be totally depleted. The mother is preserved for the wife, and the offspring belong to her husband. [5]**But according to the Rabbis** who distinguish between the offspring of an animal of usufruct property and the child of a maidservant of usufruct property, the following difficulty arises: **If they are concerned** lest the mother **die** and the woman's principal be totally depleted, and therefore they argue that the child of the maidservant should be preserved for the wife as her principal, [6]then **even the offspring of an animal of usufruct property should not** belong to the husband, lest the mother animal die and the

שִׁפְחַת מְלוֹג כְּוָלָד בֶּהֱמַת מְלוֹג״!

[1]אֲפִילּוּ תֵּימָא דִּבְרֵי הַכֹּל. [2]פֵּירָא תַּקִּינוּ לֵיהּ רַבָּנַן. [3]פֵּירָא דְפֵירָא לָא תַּקִּינוּ לֵיהּ רַבָּנַן. [4]בִּשְׁלָמָא לַחֲנַנְיָה, הַיְינוּ דְּלָא חָיְישִׁינַן לְמִיתָה. [5]אֶלָּא רַבָּנַן — אִי חָיְישֵׁי לְמִיתָה — [6]אֲפִילּוּ וְלַד בֶּהֱמַת מְלוֹג נַמִי

LITERAL TRANSLATION

of a maidservant of usufruct property like the offspring of an animal of usufruct property."

[1]You may even say [that it is in accordance with] the words of all. [2]Fruit the Rabbis enacted for him. [3]The fruit of fruit the Rabbis did not enact for him.

[4]Granted according to Ḥananyah, it is because we are not apprehensive about death. [5]But [according to] the Rabbis — if they are not apprehensive about death, [6]even the offspring of an animal of usufruct property should also

RASHI

פירא — גוף הוולד. **פירא דפירא** — כפל הבא עליו.

NOTES

פֵּירָא דְפֵירָא לָא תַּקִּינוּ **The fruit of fruit they did not enact.** The Rishonim comment: Elsewhere (*Ketubot* 83a), the Mishnah states explicitly that the husband is entitled not only to the usufruct of his wife's property, but also to the usufruct of the usufruct. *Tosafot* distinguish between the natural fruit of property and subsidiary benefits relating to property. Thus, the fruit that grew on land which had been purchased with the fruit of a wife's usufruct property falls under the category of usufruct of usufruct, which belongs to the husband. But the double compensation paid by a thief who stole the offspring of an animal of a wife's usufruct property belongs to the wife. *Rashba, Ritva* and others distinguish between common usufruct, the natural fruit of property, and uncommon usufruct, such as double compensation. These Rishonim all agree with *Rivan* that the wife is entitled not only to the double compensation paid by a thief who stole the offspring of an animal of her usufruct property, but also to the double compensation paid by a thief who stole the usufruct animal itself, for the Rabbis never entitled the husband to that type of usufruct. *Rif* insists on the husband's right to enjoy the usufruct. Thus, if he sold the usufruct of his wife's property and purchased land with the proceeds, he is entitled to the usufruct of that property. Otherwise it would turn out that he enjoyed neither the usufruct of his wife's property nor the usufruct of the usufruct. But if the husband received the offspring of an animal of his wife's usufruct property, he is not entitled to the double compensation paid by the thief who stole it. According to *Rif,* it follows that the double compensation paid by a thief who stole the usufruct animal itself would indeed belong to the husband.

דְּלָא חָיְישִׁינַן לְמִיתָה **Because we are not concerned with death.** *Rashba* asks: How can Ḥananyah argue that we do not consider the possibility that the mother will die? While we do find authorities who say elsewhere that we do not consider the possibility of death, they refer to limited periods. It is possible to argue that we are not concerned that within a specific time a certain person or animal will die. But with respect to an unlimited period of time, all agree that we must take into consideration the possibility

לָא, [1]וְאִי לָא חָיְישֵׁי לְמִיתָה, [2]אֲפִילּוּ וְלַד שִׁפְחַת מְלוֹג נַמִי! [3]לְעוֹלָם חָיְישֵׁי לְמִיתָה. [4]וְשָׁאנֵי בְּהֵמָה, [5]דְּאִיכָּא עוֹרָהּ.

[6]אָמַר רַב הוּנָא בַּר חִיָּיא אָמַר שְׁמוּאֵל: הֲלָכָה כַּחֲנַנְיָה.

[7]אֲמַר רָבָא אֲמַר רַב נַחְמָן: אַף עַל גַּב דַּאֲמַר שְׁמוּאֵל הֲלָכָה כַּחֲנַנְיָה, [8]מוֹדֶה חֲנַנְיָה שֶׁאִם נִתְגָּרְשָׁה, נוֹתֶנֶת דָּמִים וְנוֹטַלְתָּן, [9]מִפְּנֵי שֶׁבַח בֵּית אָבִיהָ.

[10]אָמַר רָבָא אָמַר רַב נַחְמָן: הִכְנִיסָה לוֹ עֵז לַחֲלָבָהּ,

LITERAL TRANSLATION

not [be his], [1]and if they are not apprehensive about death, [2]even the child of a maidservant of usufruct property should also [be his]!

[3]In fact, they are apprehensive about death. [4]But an animal is different, [5]for there is its hide.

[6]Rav Huna bar Ḥiyya said in the name of Shmuel: The law is in accordance with Ḥananyah.

[7]Rava said in the name of Rav Naḥman: Even though Shmuel said [that] the law is in accordance with Ḥananyah, [8]Ḥananyah admits that if she is divorced, she gives money and takes them, [9]for [they are of] the pride (lit., "praise") of her father's house.

[10]Rava said in the name of Rav Naḥman: [If] she brought in to him a goat for its milk,

TRANSLATION AND COMMENTARY

wife be left without any principal. [1]**And if they are not concerned** lest the mother **die** and the wife be left without any principal, and therefore they argue that the offspring of the animal is treated as usufruct which belongs to the husband, [2]then **the offspring of a maidservant of usufruct property should also be his,** for the maidservant should be treated as the principal that will be preserved for the wife, and her child should be treated as usufruct which belongs to the husband!

לְעוֹלָם חָיְישֵׁי לְמִיתָה [3]The Gemara answers: **In fact,** the Rabbis **are concerned** lest the mother **die** and the wife's principal be depleted. [4]**But** they argue that **an animal is different** from a maidservant, **for** if the maidservant dies, the wife's principal is lost, and so the Rabbis declared that the maidservant's children should remain in the wife's possession to preserve her principal. But if the animal dies, the woman's principal is not totally depleted, [5]for **there is** still the animal's **hide that** remains, and this is worth something.

אָמַר [6]The Gemara now cites a practical ruling on the matter: **Rav Huna bar Ḥiyya said in the name of Shmuel: The law is in accordance with** the view of **Ḥananyah,** that the child of a maidservant of usufruct property belongs to the husband.

אֲמַר רָבָא [7]The Gemara now adds a qualification to this ruling: **Rava said in the name of Rav Naḥman: Even though Shmuel said that the law is in accordance with** the view of [8]**Ḥananyah,** that the child of a maidservant of usufruct property belongs to the husband, **Ḥananyah agrees that when** a woman **is divorced, she may pay** her husband **money and take** her maidservant's children with her, [9]**for** her maidservants and their children **are the pride of her father's house, and** it would put her family to shame if they remained in someone else's possession. Even though the husband had already acquired the children by virtue of his right to the usufruct of his wife's property, she can compel her husband to accept payment for the offspring, and then take them with her when she returns to her paternal home.

אָמַר רָבָא [10]**Rava said in the name of Rav Naḥman: If** a woman, as part of her dowry, **brought** her husband

RASHI

דאיכא עורה – ואין הקרן כלה כולו. **שאם נתגרשה** – והבעל זכה בולדות, שהן כפירות תלושין. **נותנת** – לו האשה דמים, ונוטלת בני שפחתה. **עז לחלבה** – לאכול חלבה.

NOTES

of death! *Rashba* answers that here, too, we are dealing with a limited period. Ḥananyah's position here is that we are not concerned that the animal (or the maidservant) will die during the wife's lifetime while she is still married. For if she dies before the animal (or the maidservant) or before her husband, it no longer makes any difference if the animal (or the maidservant) dies, for it (or she) already belongs to the husband. *Halakhot Gedolot* explains that Ḥananyah agrees that if the mother dies, one of its offspring takes its place as the principal that is preserved for the wife, but the rest belong to the husband, and therefore the possibility of the mother's death is no reason for concern.

עֵז לַחֲלָבָהּ **A goat for its milk.** Our commentary follows *Rashi* and others who explain that the husband may enjoy

HALAKHAH

נוֹתֶנֶת דָּמִים וְנוֹטַלְתָּן **She gives money and takes them.** "The offspring of an animal or the child of a maidservant of usufruct property belongs to the husband. If a man divorces his wife, she may pay him and take her maidservant's children with her, for the maidservant and her children are part of the pride of her father's house," following Shmuel. This is the view of *Rashi* and *Rambam,* but according to *Tur,* an animal of usufruct property and its offspring are also part of the pride of the woman's paternal home (*Bet Shmuel*). (*Rambam, Sefer Nashim, Hilkhot Ishut* 22:25; *Shulḥan Arukh, Even HaEzer* 85:16.)

עֵז לַחֲלָבָהּ **A goat for its milk.** "If a woman has property which produces fruit, but does not restore itself, the property need not be sold, even though the principal will

TRANSLATION AND COMMENTARY

a goat for its supply of **milk,** which he might benefit from, [1]**or a ewe for its wool, or a chicken for its eggs, or a date palm for its fruit,** [2]the husband **may continue to enjoy** the usufruct of his wife's property **until the principal is consumed.** Even after the livestock and the tree die, some of the principal will be preserved for the woman — i.e., the hide, the feathers, and the wood. Thus, the milk, the wool, the eggs, and the fruit are usufruct, which belongs to the husband.

אָמַר רַב נַחְמָן [3]**Rav Naḥman said:** If a woman **brought a cloak for** her husband as part of her usufruct property, [4]wearing the garment **is** considered "enjoyment of its **fruit.**" [5]Thus, the husband **may continue to cover himself with** the cloak, **until it is worn out.** The rags to which the cloak will become reduced can be preserved for the woman as her principal.

כְּמַאן [6]The Gemara asks: **In accordance with which** Tannaitic opinion was Rav Naḥman's ruling issued? The Gemara answers: [7]**It** is **in accordance with** the view of **this Tanna,** i.e., the Sages who disagree with Rabbi Meir. [8]**For it was taught** in a Baraita: "If a woman brought into her marriage or acquired thereafter a **salt** pond **or** a **sand** pit, the husband may mine the salt or the sand, [9]for **they are** regarded as **usufruct.** This kind of property need not be sold to purchase agricultural land, for the salt and the sand will never be totally consumed. [10]But if the woman brought her husband **a sulfur quarry** or **an alum mine,** the Tannaim disagree about the status of the sulfur and the alum. [11]**Rabbi Meir says:** They are **principal,** for they can be depleted.

LITERAL TRANSLATION

[1]or a ewe for its wool, or a chicken for its egg, or a date palm for its fruit, [2]he may continue to eat [the fruit] until the principal is consumed.

[3]Rav Naḥman said: [If] she brought in to him a cloak, [4]it is fruit, [5][and] he may continue to cover himself in it until it is worn out.

[6]In accordance with whom? [7]In accordance with this Tanna. [8]For it was taught: "Salt and sand — [9]it is fruit. [10]A sulfur quarry, an alum mine, [11]Rabbi Meir says: Principal.

[1]וְרָחֵל לְגִיזָּתָהּ, וְתַרְנְגוֹלֶת לְבֵיצָתָהּ, וְדֶקֶל לְפֵירוֹתָיו, [2]אוֹכֵל וְהוֹלֵךְ עַד שֶׁתִּכְלֶה הַקֶּרֶן.

[3]אֲמַר רַב נַחְמָן: עַיְילָא לֵיהּ גְּלִימָא, [4]פֵּירָא הָוֵי, [5]מְכַסֵּי בֵּיהּ וְאָזֵיל עַד דְּכַלְיָא.

[6]כְּמַאן? [7]כִּי הַאי תַּנָּא. [8]דְּתַנְיָא: ״הַמֶּלַח וְהַחוֹל — [9]הֲרֵי זֶה פֵּירוֹת. [10]פִּיר שֶׁל גָּפְרִית, מַחְפּוֹרֶת שֶׁל צָרִיף, [11]רַבִּי מֵאִיר אוֹמֵר: קֶרֶן.

RASHI

לגיזותיה — הן עיקר שלה, להכי נקט להו. והוא הדין דשקיל חלב וולדות. **אוכל והולך** — דגבי בהמה איכא עורה, וגבי תרנגולת איכא נוצה, וגבי דקל כשייבש — איכא עציו. אבל הני כולהו — פירות נינהו, שמתחדשין תמיד, ודרך הנאתם היא. **עיילא ליה גלימא** — טלית בנכסי מלוג, אף על פי שלא שמאתו (בכתובה) בנכסי צאן ברזל, וצריך להיות קרן שמור לה. **פירא הוי** — כסויו שמכסה הימנו — הן פירותיו. **ומיכסי ואזיל ביה עד דבלי** — והשחקין יהיו לה לקרן. **כמאן** — אמרה רב נחמן להא דשיראי פורתא הוי ליה קרנא. **כי האי תנא** — רבנן דפליגי אדרבי מאיר. **המלח והחול** — נפלה לה ירושה על שפת הים חריצין עשויין, שמי הים נכנסים בהן והחמה מייבשתן ועושין מלח, והן ״משרפות מים״ האמורין במקרא (יהושע יא), ומתרגמינן ״חריצי ימא״. **והחול** — מקום שנוטלין חול לבנין. **הרי זה פירות** — ולא אמרינן: ימכר אותו מקום וילקח בהן קרקע בר זריעה — לפי שאין פריו כלה לעולם, ובהא מודה רבי מאיר. **פיר גפרית** — גומא שחופרין הימנה גפרית. וכן מחפורת של צריף = *אלו״ס בלע״ז שצובעין בהן בגדים ומשי, וחופרים אותו בקרקע, וסופו לכלות ולהגיע ליסוד קרקע בעלמא. **רבי מאיר אומר קרן** — וימכר וילקח בדמיו קרקע, לפי שפריו כלה.

REALIA

פִּיר שֶׁל גָּפְרִית **Sulfur quarries.** This element is found in many places throughout the world, particularly in volcanic areas, sometimes mixed with dirt. Sulfur quarries are holes dug deep in the earth from which the sulfur can be taken out.

צָרִיף **Alum.** This is a double sulfate of aluminum and potassium. This compound is frequently present in alunite, a crystalline mineral found in the cracks of volcanic rocks throughout the world.

Alum is used in the leather industry, and for dyeing; today it is often used for manufacturing paper, and it also has certain medicinal uses.

LANGUAGE (RASHI)

אלו״ם* From the Old French *alum,* meaning "alum."

NOTES

the goat's milk, the ewe's wool, or the chicken's eggs until the goat, the ewe, or the chicken dies, because in each of these cases at least some portion of the principal will be preserved for the woman. *Rif* (and afterwards *Ramban* and his school) understands that Rav Naḥman is dealing with cases where the woman did not own the principal of the goat, the ewe, or the chicken, but only the right to enjoy the milk, the wool, or the eggs. In such cases, the husband is permitted to take the milk, the wool, or the eggs, even though there will be nothing left for the woman, for those things are defined as usufruct to which the husband is entitled.

הַמֶּלַח וְהַחוֹל **Salt and sand.** *Rashi* explains that we are dealing with a constant renewal of the supply of salt or sand, as when salt is obtained from ponds of sea water, or sand from the beach. Thus the husband may take the salt or the sand, for his wife's principal will never be totally consumed. But, according to Rabbi Meir, the husband may not mine the woman's sulfur or alum. *Rid* offers a different explanation: The husband may take the salt or the sand, because salt and sand are usually taken from a very large pond or pit, and so the husband's consumption of the principal is negligible. But he may not take the sulfur or the alum, which cannot be found so easily.

HALAKHAH

be depleted. Similarly, if the woman brought into the marriage a garment or household item, the husband may wear or use it until it is entirely worn out, and if he divorces his wife, he need not compensate her for the wear or ruin of her property," following *Rif* and *Rambam,* against *Rashi* and *Rosh.* (*Rambam, Sefer Nashim, Hilkhot Ishut* 22:34; *Shulḥan Arukh, Even HaEzer* 85:13.)

TRANSLATION AND COMMENTARY

[1]**The Sages** disagree and **say:** The sulfur and the alum are treated like **usufruct,** which belongs to the husband. There is no need to sell the quarry or the mine, and replace it with agricultural land, for even if stripped clean, the quarry or the mine itself will be preserved for the woman as her principal." Rav Naḥman, who ruled that the husband may wear out the cloak brought into the marriage by his wife, follows the view of the Sages, who ruled that the husband may deplete his wife's sulfur quarry or alum mine. In both cases, the benefit derived from the woman's property is regarded as usufruct to which the husband is entitled, for a portion of the principal — albeit an insignificant portion — will be preserved for the wife.

רַבִּי שִׁמְעוֹן אוֹמֵר [2]We learned in the concluding portion of the Mishnah: **"Rabbi Shimon says:** Regarding the produce to **which** the Sages **strengthened** the husband's **power** if it was acquired by his wife after their marriage, they weakened his power at the time of divorce. And regarding the produce to which the Sages weakened the husband's claim if it was acquired by his wife after their marriage, they strengthened his power at the time of divorce." [3]The Gemara asks: Surely the viewpoint of **Rabbi Shimon** in our Mishnah **is the same as** the viewpoint of **the first Tanna,** the Sages, with whom Rabbi Meir disagrees? For the Sages stated in the first part of the Mishnah that produce which was still attached to the ground when the property was acquired by his wife, belongs to the husband, and produce which was already detached from the ground at that time, belongs to the wife, and Rabbi Shimon expressed the identical view.

אֲמַר רָבָא [4]**Rava explained:** There is a practical difference **between** the view of Rabbi Shimon and that of the Sages regarding the produce **that was attached** to the ground **at the time of** the woman's **divorce.** Rabbi Shimon maintains that if the woman had such produce in her possession when she was being divorced from her husband, the produce belongs to her, and she leaves the marriage together with her land and the produce growing on it. The Sages, whose opinion on the matter is not explicitly recorded in the Mishnah, disagree and say that the produce belongs to the husband, for it grew on his wife's property while he was entitled to the usufruct.

[1]וַחֲכָמִים אוֹמְרִים: פֵּירוֹת״. [2]״רַבִּי שִׁמְעוֹן אוֹמֵר: מָקוֹם שֶׁיִּפָּה כֹּחוֹ״. [3]רַבִּי שִׁמְעוֹן הַיְינוּ תַּנָּא קַמָּא! [4]אֲמַר רָבָא: מְחוּבָּרִין בִּשְׁעַת יְצִיאָה אִיכָּא בֵּינַיְיהוּ.

LITERAL TRANSLATION

[1]And the Sages say: Fruit."

[2]"Rabbi Shimon says: Where his power was strengthened." [3]Rabbi Shimon is the same as the first Tanna!

[4]Rava said: That which is attached at the time of leaving is between them.

RASHI

וחכמים אומרים פירות – ומקום הגומא יהיה לה לקרן, ומזה יאכל הבעל עד שיכלה – שזה פריו ודרך הנאתו. והוא הדין לגלימא. ולא דמו לכספים ופירות התלושין שנאכלין מבלי שיור, וכל פרוטה ופרוטה הואיל ואינן עושים פרי – הויא קרן לעצמה. **היינו תנא קמא** – חכמים. **מחוברים בשעת יציאה** – דלא איירו בהו, רבנן לית להו הא דאמר רבי שמעון: ביציאתה שלה. דקסברי: מה שגדל ברשותו – שלו. ותלוש בשעת יציאה למימר דפליגי עליה ונימרו: שלה. דכיון דתלשן – הכל מודים שזכה בהן.

NOTES

מְחוּבָּרִין בִּשְׁעַת יְצִיאָה **That which is attached at the time of leaving.** In the Jerusalem Talmud, Rabbi Yirmiyah argues that Rabbi Meir in our Mishnah follows his own opinion stated elsewhere that produce which is still attached to the ground is regarded as having been detached from the ground, and so land must be bought with the value of the attached produce, the usufruct of which belongs to the husband. Rabbi Yose rejects this argument, arguing that Rabbi Meir's ruling applies only to produce which is about to be harvested, whereas in our Mishnah he refers even to produce which is not yet ready to be harvested, for he maintains that the produce growing on the property when the wife acquired it is regarded as principal and belongs to her.

According to *Ritva,* the principle that attached produce which is ready to be harvested is regarded as detached produce applies in our Mishnah as well. Thus, regarding produce which was still attached to the ground, but ready to be harvested — if it was inherited by a woman while she was married, the produce belongs to her, just as it would belong to her if it were already harvested, and if she had such produce in her possession while divorced, the produce belongs to her husband. *Rabbenu Yonah* and *Rosh* disagree, arguing that the law is just the opposite, for the Rabbis enacted that produce which is harvested while a couple are married belongs to the husband, but produce which was not harvested while they were married, even if it was ready then to be harvested, belongs to the woman.

אִיכָּא בֵּינַיְיהוּ **Is between them.** According to the standard reading, the anonymous first Tanna and Rabbi Shimon disagree about produce which was attached to the ground

HALAKHAH

מָקוֹם שֶׁיִּפָּה כֹּחוֹ **Where his right was strengthened.** "If at the time of a woman's divorce produce was growing on her usufruct property, she receives the property together with the produce growing there, even if the produce is fit for harvest. If the husband harvested the produce before the divorce, the produce belongs to him, even if the

TRANSLATION AND COMMENTARY

MISHNAH נָפְלוּ לָהּ עֲבָדִים [1]As we learned in the previous Mishnah, a married woman who acquired property retains ownership of it, and her husband enjoys the right of usufruct. Unproductive property must be converted into productive property, so that the husband will be able to derive benefit from it. Therefore, **if** a woman **inherited old manservants or maidservants** who are incapable of heavy work, they **must be sold,** [2]**land must be bought with** the proceeds of the sale, **and** the husband **enjoys the usufruct,** while the land itself remains his wife's property. [3]**Rabban Shimon ben Gamliel** disagrees and **says:** The woman **need not sell** the servants, [4]**for they are** part **of the pride of her father's house,** and it would put her family to shame if they were sold to another person.

נָפְלוּ לָהּ זֵיתִים [5]Similarly, **if** a woman **inherited old olive trees or old grapevines** which are unproductive, the old trees **must be sold** for wood, [6]**land must be bought with** the proceeds, **and** the husband **enjoys the usufruct.** [7]**Rabbi Yehudah** disagrees and **says:** The woman **need not sell** the trees, [8]**for they are** part **of the pride of her father's house,** and her family would be disgraced if they were sold.

משנה [1]נָפְלוּ לָהּ עֲבָדִים וּשְׁפָחוֹת זְקֵנִים, יִמָּכְרוּ [2]וְיִלָּקַח מֵהֶן קַרְקַע, וְהוּא אוֹכֵל פֵּירוֹת. [3]רַבָּן שִׁמְעוֹן בֶּן גַּמְלִיאֵל אוֹמֵר: לֹא תִּמְכּוֹר, [4]מִפְּנֵי שֶׁהֵן שֶׁבַח בֵּית אָבִיהָ.

[5]נָפְלוּ לָהּ זֵיתִים וּגְפָנִים זְקֵנִים, יִמָּכְרוּ, [6]וְיִלָּקַח בָּהֶן קַרְקַע, וְהוּא אוֹכֵל פֵּירוֹת. [7]רַבִּי יְהוּדָה אוֹמֵר: לֹא תִּמְכּוֹר, [8]מִפְּנֵי שֶׁהֵן שֶׁבַח בֵּית אָבִיהָ.

LITERAL TRANSLATION

MISHNAH [1][If] old manservants and maidservants fell to her [as an inheritance], they must be sold [2]and land must be bought with them, and he eats the fruit. [3]Rabban Shimon ben Gamliel says: She need not sell [them], [4]because they are [of] the pride of her father's house.

[5][If] old olive trees or vines fell to her [as an inheritance], they must be sold, [6]and land must bought with them, and he eats the fruit. [7]Rabbi Yehudah says: She need not sell [them], [8]because they are [of] the pride of her father's house.

RASHI

משנה לא תמכור – יכולה היא לעכב.

NOTES

at the time of the divorce. Most Rishonim rule in accordance with the view of Rabbi Shimon, even though his is the minority opinion. (*Ra'avad,* cited by *Rosh,* brings several proofs that the law follows the view of Rabbi Shimon.) *Halakhot Gedolot* had a slightly different reading of the passage: "That which is attached at the time of leaving he comes to teach us." According to this reading, Rabbi Shimon does not disagree with the anonymous first Tanna, but clarifies what was left untaught by him. The first Tanna did not say which spouse is entitled to the produce that is attached to the wife's usufruct property at the time of their divorce, and Rabbi Shimon teaches that this produce belongs to the wife. Thus, the law is in accordance with Rabbi Shimon's position. *Rid* and others disagree and rule in accordance with the view of the anonymous first Tanna.

נָפְלוּ לָהּ עֲבָדִים וּשְׁפָחוֹת זְקֵנִים **If old manservants and maidservants fell to her as an inheritance.** The Jerusalem Talmud cites a Baraita which teaches that the Tannaim disagree about servants who do not produce enough to cover their upkeep. If they produce that minimum, all agree that the wife need not sell them, for they are the pride of her paternal home. (The law recognizes this distinction; see Halakhah.) *Ritva* asks: If the servants do not produce enough to justify their upkeep, who will buy them? He explains that the Mishnah refers to servants who are too old and feeble to do hard physical labor but are still able to attend to their master's personal needs. Thus, they are not fit for people of modest means, but they can be sold to wealthy people.

יִמָּכְרוּ **They must be sold.** *Rosh* explains that the Mishnah's ruling that the servants must be sold applies when the husband wants the servants to be sold, so that he can enjoy the usufruct of the land that will be bought with the proceeds of the sale. In such a case, the wife cannot object to the sale and say that she wants to keep the servants. But if the husband objects to the sale, his wife cannot compel him to sell the servants and buy land with the money, so that her principal will stay intact. Other authorities disagree and say that when the law dictates that the wife's usufruct property must be sold, neither she nor her husband may object to the sale of the property.

HALAKHAH

produce was not fit for harvest," following Rabbi Shimon. (*Rambam, Sefer Nashim, Hilkhot Ishut* 22:24; *Shulḥan Arukh, Even HaEzer* 88:6.)

נָפְלוּ לָהּ עֲבָדִים וּשְׁפָחוֹת זְקֵנִים **If old manservants and maidservants fell to her as an inheritance.** "If a married woman inherited old servants, they need not be sold, for they are the pride of her father's house," following Rabban Shimon ben Gamliel, whose views in the Mishnah are always accepted as law. (*Rambam, Sefer Nashim, Hilkhot Ishut* 22:23; *Shulḥan Arukh, Even HaEzer* 85:14.)

נָפְלוּ לָהּ זֵיתִים **If old olive trees fell to her.** "If a married woman inherits olive trees or grapevines without also inheriting the land on which they grow, and they produce enough fruit to defray the cost of caring for them, they need not be sold, because they are the pride of the woman's paternal home. But if they do not produce enough fruit to defray the cost of caring for them, they must be sold for their wood, land must be bought with the proceeds of the sale, and the husband enjoys the usufruct," following the view of the anonymous first Tanna (*Maggid Mishneh*), and the explanation of Rav Kahana. (*Rambam, Sefer Nashim, Hilkhot Ishut* 22:23; *Shulḥan Arukh, Even HaEzer* 85:14.)

TRANSLATION AND COMMENTARY

GEMARA אָמַר רַב כָּהֲנָא [1]**Rav Kahana said in the name of Rav: The dispute** between the Sages and Rabbi Yehudah regarding old olive trees and grapevines **is** limited to **inherited** trees which stand **in her** own **field.** Only in such a case does Rabbi Yehudah say that the woman can object to the sale, for it would put her family to shame if the land were sold to another person. [2]**But** if the trees or the vines stand **in a field which is not hers,** meaning that she inherited only the trees but not the land on which they stand, there is no disagreement among the Tannaim. [3]**All** — i.e., both the Sages and Rabbi Yehudah — **agree that** the woman **must sell** the trees, and buy land with the proceeds, [4]**because when** the trees cease to give fruit, **the principal will be depleted.**

מַתְקִיף לָהּ [5]**Rav Yosef strongly objected to this** understanding of the dispute: [6]**Surely menservants and maidservants are similar to** olive trees and grapevines that stand in **a field which is not hers,** for after the servants die, the woman's principal will be entirely depleted. [7]**And nevertheless** we see that the Tannaim — the Sages and Rabban Shimon ben Gamliel — **disagree** about whether she can object to the sale of her old servants! According to Rabban Shimon ben Gamliel, as long they are alive they contribute to her family's honor. The same argument can be made with respect to olive trees and grapevines. So it stands to reason that Rabbi Yehudah maintains that a wife is not required to sell her old trees, even if she inherited them without inheriting the land on which they stand, in contradiction to Rav!

אֶלָּא אִי אִיתְּמַר [8]The Gemara now suggests a different version of Rav's limitation of the dispute between the Sages and Rabbi Yehudah: **Rather, if** something **was said** by Rav on the matter, **it was said as follows:** [9]**Rav Kahana said in the name of Rav: The dispute** between the Sages and Rabbi Yehudah regarding old olive trees and grapevines **is** limited to trees standing **in a field which is not hers.** Only in such a case do the Sages say that the wife cannot object to the sale, for after the trees wither, her principal will be totally depleted. [10]**But** if the wife inherited old olive trees or grapevines which were standing **in her** own **field,** there is no disagreement among the Tannaim. [11]In such a case, **all** — i.e., both the Sages and Rabbi Yehudah — **agree that** the wife **need not sell** the trees, [12]**for** the trees and the land on which they stand **are** part **of the pride of her father's house,** and her family would suffer disgrace if they were sold.

MISHNAH הַמּוֹצִיא [13]Since the husband is entitled to the usufruct of his wife's property, he is obligated to defray the expenses of maintaining it. If the usufruct is insufficient, and the husband **spent** his own

גמרא [1]אָמַר רַב כָּהֲנָא אָמַר רַב: מַחֲלוֹקֶת שֶׁנָּפְלוּ בְּשָׂדֶה שֶׁלָּהּ. [2]אֲבָל בְּשָׂדֶה שֶׁאֵינָהּ שֶׁלָּהּ, [3]דִּבְרֵי הַכֹּל תִּמְכּוֹר, [4]מִשּׁוּם דְּקָא כַּלְיָא קַרְנָא. [5]מַתְקִיף לָהּ רַב יוֹסֵף: [6]הֲרֵי עֲבָדִים וּשְׁפָחוֹת, דְּכִי שָׂדֶה שֶׁאֵינָהּ שֶׁלָּהּ דָּמֵי, [7]וּפְלִיגִי! [8]אֶלָּא, אִי אִיתְּמַר, הָכִי אִיתְּמַר: אָמַר רַב כָּהֲנָא אָמַר רַב: [9]מַחֲלוֹקֶת בְּשָׂדֶה שֶׁאֵינָהּ שֶׁלָּהּ. [10]אֲבָל בְּשָׂדֶה שֶׁלָּהּ, [11]דִּבְרֵי הַכֹּל לֹא תִּמְכּוֹר, [12]מִפְּנֵי שֶׁבַח בֵּית אָבִיהָ.

משנה [13]הַמּוֹצִיא הוֹצָאוֹת

LITERAL TRANSLATION

GEMARA [1]Rav Kahana said in the name of Rav: The dispute [is about] when they fell [as an inheritance] in her field. [2]But in a field that is not hers, [3]all agree that she must sell [them], [4]because the principal is consumed.

[5]Rav Yosef strongly objected to this: [6]Surely menservants and maidservants are like a field which is not hers, [7]and they disagree!

[8]Rather, if it was said, it was said as follows: Rav Kahana said in the name of Rav: [9]The dispute is in a field that is not hers. [10]But in her field, [11]all agree that she need not sell [them], [12]because they are [of] the pride of her father's house.

MISHNAH [13][If] someone put out expenses

RASHI

גמרא מחלוקת – דזיתים וגפנים – **בשדה שלה.** שנפל לה הקרקע עם האילנות – דכי יבשי זיתים הוי לה קרקע לקרן. **אבל בשדה שאינה שלה** – כגון שהיו לאביה זיתים שקנה בלא קרקע, על מנת שיהיו בקרקע המוכר, והלוקח יאכל פירות עד שיבשו. **דברי הכל תמכור** – וילקח בהן קרקע, ואין אחד מהן יכול לעכב במכירתן, שאין כאן שבח בית אב היכא דכליא קרנא. **והא עבדים ושפחות כו׳** – דכי מייתי – כליא קרנא לגמרי, ופליגי. דכל זמן דהן קיימין הויא לה ולבית אביה לשם ולתפארת.

NOTES

בְּשָׂדֶה שֶׁאֵינָהּ שֶׁלָּהּ **In a field which is not hers.** According to the Jerusalem Talmud, the Babylonian scholars maintain that the Tannaim disagree about the case where the wife inherits old olive trees or grapevines but not the land on which they grow. But if she inherits the trees or vines together with the land, all agree that the trees and vines need not be sold. The scholars of Eretz Israel disagree and say that the Tannaim disagree about both cases.

HALAKHAH

הַמּוֹצִיא הוֹצָאוֹת עַל נִכְסֵי אִשְׁתּוֹ **If someone put out expenses on his wife's property.** "If a man spent his own money maintaining or improving his wife's usufruct property and then divorced her, whether he spent little and consumed a

TRANSLATION AND COMMENTARY

money on his wife's usufruct property, and then decided to divorce her, he is generally not entitled to any compensation for his expenses. He is assumed to have waived any claim for reimbursement, since he invested the money expecting to enjoy increased benefit. [1]**Whether he spent a great deal and consumed little, or spent little and consumed a great deal,** [2]**what he spent** is considered **spent, and what he consumed** is considered **consumed.** [3]**If, however,** the husband **spent** his own money on his wife's usufruct property, **and did not benefit from** any usufruct at all, [4]**he may take an oath concerning how much** money **he spent, and collect** that sum from his wife.

GEMARA וְכַמָּה קִימְעָא [5]Regarding the husband's out-of-pocket expenses, **how much is a little?**

אָמַר רַבִּי אַסִי [6]**Rabbi Assi said:** Even if the husband ate only **one dry fig,** he is not entitled to any compensation for his expenses. [7]**This** ruling applies only **if he consumed** the fig **in a dignified manner,** in the ordinary way that a person enjoys his own fruit. [80A] [8]**Rabbi Abba said that they said in the School of Rav: Even** if the husband ate only **pressed dates,** he is not entitled to compensation for his expenses.

עַל נִכְסֵי אִשְׁתּוֹ, [1]הוֹצִיא הַרְבֵּה וְאָכַל קִימְעָא, קִימְעָא וְאָכַל הַרְבֵּה, [2]מַה שֶּׁהוֹצִיא הוֹצִיא, וּמַה שֶּׁאָכַל אָכַל. [3]הוֹצִיא וְלֹא אָכַל [4]יִשָּׁבַע כַּמָּה הוֹצִיא, וְיִטּוֹל.

גמרא [5]וְכַמָּה קִימְעָא? [6]אָמַר רַבִּי אַסִי: אֲפִילּוּ גְּרוֹגֶרֶת אַחַת. [7]וְהוּא שֶׁאֲכָלָהּ דֶּרֶךְ כָּבוֹד. [8]אֲמַר [80A] רַבִּי אַבָּא אָמְרִי בֵּי רַב: אֲפִילּוּ שִׁיגְרָא דְּתַמְרֵי.

LITERAL TRANSLATION

on his wife's property, [1][whether] he spent much and consumed little, [or spent] little and consumed much, [2]what he spent he spent, and what he consumed he consumed. [3]If he spent and did not consume [at all], [4]he may swear how much he spent, and take.

GEMARA [5]And how much is a little?

[6]Rabbi Assi said: Even one dry fig. [7]And that is where he consumed it in a dignified manner. [80A] [8]Rabbi Abba said that they said in the School of Rav: Even pressed dates.

LANGUAGE (RASHI)

טרויות* Some commentators take this as a French word (which should apparently read טרוי״א), from the Old French *troje,* meaning "package," or "bundle."

RASHI

משנה מה שהוציא הוציא — אם גירשה.

גמרא רבי אבא אמר אפילו שיגרא דתמרי — תמרים נידוכין יחד, כדרך שדורסין תאנים יחד, ליטראות ליטראות, אף אלו כן, ומיקרי "שיגרא". ואני שמעתי: שיגרא — *טרויות כמין אשכול תמרים, וקשיא לי: מאי אפילו דרבי אבא? הא גרוגרות גריעי מתמרים, כדתנן: אכל גרוגרות ושילם תמרים — תבא עליו ברכה. ואי הוה גרסינן להא דרבי אבא ברישא, מקמי דרבי אסי — לא הוה קשיא לי מידי. יש ספרים משובשים וכתוב בהן: וכמה הרבה — אמר רבי אבא כו'. וגירסת שוטים היא זו; כמה הרבה למאי הלכתא איבעיא להו, ומאי נפקא לן מינה? כל כמה דהוי יותר על גרוגרת אחת — הוי הרבה, עד לעולם.

NOTES

יִשָּׁבַע כַּמָּה הוֹצִיא **He may swear how much he spent.** *Rabbenu Ḥananel* (cited by *Tosafot* and others) asks: Why is the case discussed in our Mishnah not included in the Mishnah (*Shevuot* 44b) that lists those cases when the plaintiff takes an oath to confirm his claim and is then allowed to collect the sum he claims? He answers that our case was not included in that Mishnah, because that Mishnah deals with cases where the plaintiff's claim is contradicted by the claim of the defendant. Here, however, the husband claims with certainty that he spent a certain amount, and his wife cannot contradict him, for she does not know how much he spent.

דֶּרֶךְ כָּבוֹד **In a dignified manner.** *Talmidei Rabbenu Yonah* explain that this measure applies only when the husband consumed the fig in a dignified manner at his table in his own house, and not in the public domain in front of everyone. Others explain (in the name of the Geonim) that this measure applies only when the fruit was brought to the husband in a basket, and not when he himself picked it.

שִׁיגְרָא דְּתַמְרֵי **A cluster of dates.** The Rishonim offer various explanations of the terms *shigra* and *huvtza. Rashi* reports a tradition that a *shigra* is a cluster of dates and that a *huvtza* is a pressed mash of dates (so, too, does *Arukh*). *Rashi* objects that, according to this explanation, it is difficult to understand Rabbi Abba's formulation, *"even* a *shigra,"* for it follows from the Gemara elsewhere (*Pesaḥim* 32a) that dates are more valuable than dry figs, and so if the husband is not entitled to compensation for his expenses if he ate only a dry fig, then surely he is not entitled to compensation if he ate as much as a cluster of dates. *Rabbenu Tam* answers that single dates are better

HALAKHAH

great deal, or spent a great deal and consumed little, what he spent is considered spent, and what he consumed is considered consumed. No accounting is made." (*Rambam, Sefer Nashim, Hilkhot Ishut* 23:8; *Shulḥan Arukh, Even HaEzer* 88:7.)

אָכַל קִימְעָא **He consumed little.** "How much is a little? Even if he ate only one dried fig in a dignified manner, i.e., in the way that a person eats fruit in his own house," following Rabbi Assi. (*Rambam, Sefer Nashim, Hilkhot Ishut* 23:8; *Shulḥan Arukh, Even HaEzer* 88:7.)

¹בָּעֵי רַב בֵּיבָי: חוּבְצָא דְּתַמְרֵי, מַאי?
²תֵּיקוּ.
³לֹא אֲכָלָהּ דֶּרֶךְ כָּבוֹד, מַאי?
⁴אֲמַר עוּלָּא: פְּלִיגִי בָּהּ תְּרֵי אֲמוֹרָאֵי בְּמַעַרְבָא. ⁵חַד אֲמַר: בְּכְאִיסָּר. ⁶וְחַד אֲמַר: בִּכְדִינָר.
⁷אָמְרִי דַּיָּינֵי דְּפוּמְבְּדִיתָא: ⁸עֲבַד רַב יְהוּדָה עוּבְדָא בַּחֲבִילֵי זְמוֹרוֹת.

LITERAL TRANSLATION

[1] Rav Bevai asked: [Regarding] a mash of dates, what [is the law]?

[2] Let it stand.

[3] If] he did not eat it in a dignified manner, what [is the law]?

[4] Ulla said: Two Amoraim in Eretz Israel (lit., "the West") disagreed about it. [5] One said: In the amount of an isar. [6] And one said: In the amount of a dinar.

[7] The judges of Pumbedita said: [8] Rav Yehudah performed an act with a bundle of branches.

TRANSLATION AND COMMENTARY

בָּעֵי רַב בֵּיבָי [1] **Rav Bevai asked:** If the husband ate **a mash of dates, what** is the law? Is he viewed as having consumed the dates in a dignified manner, so that he is not entitled to reimbursement for his expenses, or not?

תֵּיקוּ [2] The Gemara offers no solution to the problem posed by Rav Bevai, and concludes: The problem raised here **remains unresolved.**

לֹא אֲכָלָהּ דֶּרֶךְ כָּבוֹד [3] The Gemara asks: **If** the husband ate a little usufruct, but **did not eat it in a dignified manner, what** is the law?

אֲמַר עוּלָּא [4] **Ulla said: Two Amoraim** living **in Eretz Israel disagreed about** this matter. [5] **One** of the Sages **said:** If the husband consumed fruit **in the amount of an isar** (a small coin having the value of four barleycorns of silver, or about ninety-six milligrams of silver), he is viewed as having consumed some of the usufruct of his wife's property, even if he consumed the fruit in a haphazard manner. [6] **And the other** Sage **said:** Only fruit **in the amount of a dinar** (a coin worth twenty-four isars) is viewed as usufruct of his wife's property.

אָמְרִי דַּיָּינֵי דְּפוּמְבְּדִיתָא [7] **The judges of Pumbedita** (identified elsewhere as the court of Rav Pappa bar Shmuel) **said:** [8] **Rav Yehudah issued a ruling** about a husband who took **a bundle of branches from** his wife's usufruct property and used it to feed to his animals. That benefit is viewed as consumption of usufruct, so he is not entitled to compensation for his expenses with respect to the property.

RASHI

חובצא דתמרי – לאחר שעשו בהן שכר, ונשאר הפסולת. אי נמי, נידוכין הרבה כדי לעשות מהן שכר. **לא אכלה דרך כבוד מאי** – בכמה הויא אכילה. **בבאיסר** – שוה איסר. **דייני דפומבדיתא** – רב פפא בר שמואל, בפרק קמא דסנהדרין (יז,ב). **עבד רב יהודה עובדא** – דחשבה אכילה בחבילי זמורות, שהן מאכל לפילין, והאכיל מהן הבעל לבהמתו, וגירש את אשתו, ואמר רב יהודה: מה שאכל אכל.

SAGES

דַּיָּינֵי דְּפוּמְבְּדִיתָא The judges of Pumbedita. Elsewhere (*Sanhedrin* 17a) the Gemara explains that the expression "judges of Pumbedita" refers to Rav Pappa bar Shmuel, a fourth-generation Babylonian Amora, who had studied with Rav Ḥisda and Rav Sheshet.

His relations and disputes with Rava are mentioned in several places in the Talmud.

NOTES

than dry figs, but a cluster of dates are not as good because there are so many packed together. *Rabbenu Ḥayyim* (cited by *Rosh*) answers that a *kav* of dates is better than a *kav* of dry figs, for the dates outnumber the figs. But single dates are less significant than single dry figs, for they are smaller.

Rivan suggests that a *shigra* is a cluster of dates which did not fully ripen, and they are less significant than dry figs. Similar to this is *Re'ah's* suggestion that a *shigra* refers to unripe dates which fell from the tree.

Rashi himself argues that a *shigra* of dates refers to pressed dates, and a *huvtza* of dates refers to the residue of dates that were used for the production of beer. According to the Geonim, the term *shigra* refers to the palm matting in which the dates are packed, and the term *huvtza* refers to pressed dates. The Jerusalem Talmud's formulation, "if a person ate a baleful of dates," supports the position of the Geonim.

עֲבַד רַב יְהוּדָה עוּבְדָא בַּחֲבִילֵי זְמוֹרוֹת Rav Yehuda performed an act with a bundle of branches. The Rishonim understand Rav Yehudah's ruling and the relationship between it and the Gemara's previous discussion in various ways. According to *Rashi*, Rav Yehudah ruled that if a person fed an animal the usufruct of his wife's property, he is viewed as if he himself had consumed the usufruct, and so he is not entitled to compensation for investing in his wife's property. *Rivan* explains that, according to Rav Yehudah, an animal's consumption of usufruct is not regarded as consumption, and so the husband who fed his animal branches of his wife's usufruct property is still entitled to compensation for his expenses with respect to that property, unless he derived benefit worth an isar or a dinar. The Gemara notes that Rav Yehuda follows his own opinion that if a person fed his animals the shoots of a tree while the produce of that tree was *orlah*, he did not establish proof of ownership, for the animal's consumption of the shoots is not regarded as consumption (see next note).

HALAKHAH

לֹא אֲכָלָהּ דֶּרֶךְ כָּבוֹד If he did not eat it in a dignified manner. "If the husband invested his own money in his wife'e usufruct property, and consumed fruit worth a dinar, even if he consumed it in an undignified manner, and even if he took only a bundle of branches, what he spent he spent and what he consumed he consumed," following the Amora who required the larger measure, and Rav Yehudah. (*Rambam, Sefer Nashim, Hilkhot Ishut* 23:8; *Shulḥan Arukh, Even HaEzer* 88:7.)

TRANSLATION AND COMMENTARY

רַב יְהוּדָה לְטַעֲמֵיהּ [1]The Gemara notes: **Rav Yehudah's** ruling **is in accordance with his own opinion** stated elsewhere regarding proof of ownership. Possession of land known to have belonged to another person does not prove that the possessor has legal title to the property. He must prove that the property entered into his possession in a legal manner. If, however, he held unchallenged possession for three consecutive years, without protest on the part of the previous owner, the possessor's claim that he bought the property or received it as a gift, and that he later lost the deed attesting to the transaction, is accepted. In order to establish title to the property, the possessor must prove that he used the property for three years in the way that such property is normally used. In the case of a field, he must prove that he enjoyed the produce of the field for that time. [2]Regarding proof of ownership, **Rav Yehudah said:** If the possessor can prove that **he derived benefit** from a field whose fruit was ***orlah*** (fruit which grew on a tree during the first three years after it was planted), [3]**Sabbatical produce** (produce which grew during the Sabbatical year), **or *kilayim*** (produce which grew in a vineyard in which food crops had also been planted), he has established **proof of ownership.** This ruling shows that Rav Yehudah was referring to a case where the possessor can prove that he derived benefit from the branches of the trees growing in the field and not from the fruit, because produce which is *orlah* or *kilayim* is forbidden to be consumed, and Sabbatical produce is ownerless. Hence the original owner of the property would have had no reason to lodge an objection against the person who now claims ownership, for taking the produce. But if the possessor derived benefit from the branches, which are not included in the prohibition of *orlah* and *kilayim,* and which do not become ownerless during the Sabbatical year, the failure of the original owner to object serves as proof that the possessor has legal title. Just as Rav Yehudah maintains that the benefit received by the possessor of property from branches can serve as proof of ownership, so too does he maintain that the benefit derived by the husband from the branches of trees growing on his wife's property is considered consumption of usufruct, making him ineligible to receive compensation for his expenses in maintaining that property.

[1]רַב יְהוּדָה לְטַעֲמֵיהּ. [2]דְּאָמַר רַב יְהוּדָה: אֲכָלָהּ עָרְלָה, [3]שְׁבִיעִית וְכִלְאַיִם, הֲרֵי זוֹ חֲזָקָה.

LITERAL TRANSLATION

[1]Rav Yehudah [according] to his [own] opinion. [2]For Rav Yehudah said: [If] he ate from it *orlah,* [3]Sabbatical produce, or *kilayim,* it is proof of ownership.

RASHI

אכלה – לוקח שני ערלה, שאין הנאתן אלא בזמורות, שהפרי אסור בהנאה. או שביעית, שהוא הפקר. או שזרעה כלאים, והזמורות לא נאסרו. **הרי זו חזקה** – עולין לו למנין שלש שנים, אי אחת מהשלש שנית אחת מאלו. הרי זו חזקה גרסינן הכא ובבבא בתרא.

NOTES

אֲכָלָהּ עָרְלָה, שְׁבִיעִית, וְכִלְאַיִם If he ate from it *orlah,* Sabbatical produce, or *kilayim.* Our commentary follows *Rashi, Tosafot, Ra'avad, Meiri* and others who understand that Rav Yehudah is dealing with benefit from branches, which are not included in the prohibition of *orlah* or *kilayim*, and which do not become ownerless during the Sabbatical Year. (See *Tosafot* who constructs a case where the prohibition of *kilayim* applies only to the fruit and not to the branches.) Just as Rav Yehudah maintains that the benefit derived from branches is considered consumption of usufruct, which can serve as proof of ownership, so too does he maintain that the benefit derived from branches of usufruct property is considered consumption of usufruct, making the husband ineligible to receive compensation for his expenses with respect to that property. Understanding the passage in an entirely different manner, the Geonim, *Rambam* and *Ramban* explain that Rav Yehudah deals with benefit from the *orlah* or *kilayim* produce that was indeed forbidden for consumption. Even though the possessor of the field consumed produce which was forbidden to him, since he derived benefit from the produce, his consumption can serve as proof of ownership. Following this opinion, Rav Yehudah ruled that however the husband consumed the usufruct of his wife's property, whether he himself or an animal ate the produce, he can no longer collect compensation for his investment.

The Rishonim point out that in a parallel passage in *Bava Batra* 36a, Rav Yehudah's ruling reads as follows: "[If] he ate from it *orlah,* Sabbatical produce, or *kilayim,* it is *not* proof of ownership." *Rabbenu Shimshon* (cited by *Tosafot*) explains that there Rav Yehudah refers to a case where the possessor ate the fruit itself. Produce which is *orlah* or *kilayim* is forbidden for consumption, and Sabbatical produce is ownerless. Thus the original owner of the property would have had no reason to raise objections against the person who now claims ownership for taking the produce, and the possessor's deriving benefit from such produce cannot be considered as proof of ownership. Many Rishonim accept the reading of *Rabbenu Ḥananel* and *Rabbenu Gershom,* according to which the Gemara in *Bava Batra* agrees with our Gemara that if a person ate from a field *orlah*, Sabbatical produce, or *kilayim*, it is proof of ownership. *Rivan* prefers the reading found in *Bava Batra*, and revises the reading in our passage accordingly. Thus,

HALAKHAH

אֲכָלָהּ עָרְלָה, שְׁבִיעִית, וְכִלְאַיִם If he ate from it *orlah,* Sabbatical produce, or *kilayim.* "If somebody consumed the produce of a field for three years, and the produce was *orlah*, Sabbatical produce, or *kilayim*, then he even though he derived benefit from that which was forbidden to him, he established proof of ownership. According to some authorities (*Tur, Rosh* and *Ra'avad*), proof of ownership is only established if the possessor consumed branches or the like

TRANSLATION AND COMMENTARY

אָמַר רַב יַעֲקֹב [1]Rav Ya'akov said in the name of Rav Ḥisda: [2]If someone spent money on property belonging to his wife, who had been orphaned with the death of her father and then married off by her mother or brothers while she was still a minor, and he incurred the expenses before she chose to dissolve the marriage prior to reaching the age of twelve, [3]he is treated like someone who spends money on the property of another person who is not his wife. Thus, he is entitled to receive a share in any improvement in the field's value as a result of his investment, as if he were a tenant-farmer.

מַאי טַעֲמָא [4]The Gemara asks: What is the reason that a man whose young wife dissolved their marriage by performing *mi'un* is treated like a tenant-farmer who is entitled to receive a share in any improvement in the field's value as a result of his investment? The Gemara explains: When a man marries an adult woman, he does not assume that he will divorce her. He is ready to invest money in her property, for he knows he will enjoy the usufruct. But the husband of a minor can never be sure that he will retain his wife's property in his possession long enough to make it worthwhile for him to improve it. To remove the temptation to misuse the property by overfarming it and avoiding long-term investment, [5]the Rabbis instituted an enactment that the husband be treated like a tenant-farmer and receive a share in any improvement in the field's value as a result of his investment, [6]so that he should not damage the property. The husband no longer has any reason to refrain from investing in the property, for if the girl does not terminate the marriage, he will enjoy the usufruct, and if indeed she does end the marriage, he will receive compensation for his expenses.

[1]אֲמַר רַב יַעֲקֹב אֲמַר רַב חִסְדָּא: [2]הַמּוֹצִיא הוֹצָאוֹת עַל נִכְסֵי אִשְׁתּוֹ קְטַנָּה [3]כְּמוֹצִיא עַל נִכְסֵי אַחֵר דָּמֵי.
[4]מַאי טַעֲמָא? [5]עָבְדוּ בָּהּ רַבָּנַן תַּקַּנְתָּא [6]כִּי הֵיכִי דְּלָא נִיפְסְדִינְהוּ.

LITERAL TRANSLATION

[1]Rav Ya'akov said in the name of Rav Ḥisda: [2]Someone who incurs expenses on the property of his wife who is a minor [3]is like one who spends [money] on the property of a stranger.

[4]That is the reason? [5]The Rabbis instituted an enactment [6]so that he not damage it.

RASHI

אשתו קטנה — יתומה שהשיאתה אמה ואחיה יכולה למאן. **שמוציא על נכסי אחר** — ואם מיאנה בו — שמין לו שבח שהשביח, ונוטל כמשפט אריסי המדינה. **עבדו ליה רבנן הך תקנתא** — דשמין לו כאריס. **כי היכי דלא ליפסדינהו** — שלא יכסיף ויקלקל הקרקעות, ויאכל ולא ישביח, שדואג שמא תמאן. וכיון דשיימינן ליה כאריס — תו לא מפסיד להו. מימר אמר: שמא לא תמאן, ואם תמאן — הרי אטול שבחי לפי עמלי.

BACKGROUND

הוֹצָאוֹת עַל נִכְסֵי אִשְׁתּוֹ קְטַנָּה Expenses on the property of his wife who is a minor. By Torah law, a father is authorized to arrange the marriage of his minor daughter; but if he is no longer alive, she cannot marry while a minor. The Sages, however, enacted that she may contract a marriage, either by herself, or, with her consent, through her mother or brothers. The girl may terminate such a marriage before the age of twelve by performing *mi'un,* or "refusal," i.e., declaring that she does not want the marriage to continue. When a girl performs *mi'un,* the marriage is nullified retroactively, so she does not require a bill of divorce. Once the marriage is dissolved, the property that the girl had brought into the marriage is returned to her. Now, if an adult woman is divorced, her property reverts to her in its condition at the time of the divorce, and the husband is not entitled to compensation for his investment in the property. But if a young girl dissolved her marriage by performing *mi'un,* the husband is treated as if he had been a tenant-farmer on her property. Thus, we appraise how much the husband spent, how much he consumed, and how much the field improved, and we award him his share as if he were a tenant-farmer.

NOTES

he argues that Rav Yehudah ruled that feeding branches to an animal is not regarded as consumption of usufruct, which bars the husband from collecting compensation for his investment in his wife's usufruct property, just as the animal's eating of branches is not regarded as consumption of usufruct, which can serve as proof of ownership. *Rabbenu Tam* argues that there is no reason to revise the text in *Bava Batra,* for parallel Talmudic passages often contradict each other, sometimes attributing particular positions to different authorities, and sometimes setting out the positions themselves differently. Both versions are valid, and they reflect the different traditions that were received by the Amoraim.

הַמּוֹצִיא הוֹצָאוֹת עַל נִכְסֵי אִשְׁתּוֹ קְטַנָּה Someone who incurs expenses on his wife's property while she is a minor. According to most Rishonim, the husband is regarded as someone who entered another person's property and cultivated it with the owner's permission. Therefore he is compensated as if he were a tenant-farmer. *Rashba* and others note that this enactment was instituted for the husband's benefit, but he may choose to be treated as an ordinary husband. Thus, if he has spent little and already consumed a lot, he may invoke the Mishnah's ruling that what was spent was spent and what was consumed was consumed. According to *Rivan,* the husband is similar to someone who entered another person's property and cultivated it without permission, and so he has the lower hand. Thus, we assess his expenses and the improvement to the property, and award him the lower of the two assessments.

HALAKHAH

which are not included in the various prohibitions." (*Rambam, Sefer Mishpatim, Hilkhot To'en VeNit'an* 12:12; *Shulḥan Arukh, Ḥoshen Mishpat* 141:11.)

הַמּוֹצִיא הוֹצָאוֹת עַל נִכְסֵי אִשְׁתּוֹ קְטַנָּה Someone who puts out expenses on his wife's property while she is a minor. "If someone spent money on property belonging to his wife who had been orphaned with the death of her father and then married off by her mother or brothers while she was still a minor, and the girl then declared her refusal to remain married to her husband, we assess how much usufruct he consumed, how much he spent on the property, and how much the property increased in value, and we compensate the husband as if he were a tenant-farmer. Since he cultivated the field with his wife's permission, he may collect his expenses according to the increase in value of the property. If he spent only a little and consumed a great deal, what he consumed he consumed." (*Rambam, Sefer Nashim, Hilkhot Ishut* 23:10; *Shulḥan Arukh, Even HaEzer* 88:10.)

[1] הַהִיא אִיתְּתָא דִּנְפְלוּ לָהּ אַרְבַּע מְאָה זוּזֵי בֵּי חוֹזָאֵי. [2] אָזֵיל גַּבְרָא אַפֵּיק שִׁית מְאָה, [3] אַיְיתֵי אַרְבַּע מְאָה. [4] בַּהֲדֵי דְּקָאָתֵי, אִיצְטְרִיךְ לֵיהּ חַד זוּזָא [5] וְשָׁקַל מִנַּיְיהוּ.

[6] אֲתָא לְקַמֵּיהּ דְּרַבִּי אַמִּי. [7] אֲמַר לֵיהּ: [8] מַה שֶּׁהוֹצִיא הוֹצִיא, [9] וּמַה שֶּׁאָכַל אָכַל. [10] אָמְרוּ לֵיהּ רַבָּנַן לְרַבִּי אַמִּי: [11] הָנֵי מִילֵּי הֵיכָא דְּקָאָכֵיל פֵּירָא. [12] הָא קַרְנָא קָאָכֵיל, [13] וְהוֹצָאָה הִיא! [14] אִם כֵּן הֲוָה לֵיהּ: [15] "הוֹצִיא וְלֹא אָכַל, [16] יִשָּׁבַע כַּמָּה הוֹצִיא, וְיִטּוֹל".

[17] "יִשָּׁבַע כַּמָּה הוֹצִיא וְיִטּוֹל".

LITERAL TRANSLATION

[1] [There was] a certain woman to whom fell [as an inheritance] four hundred zuz in Bei Ḥozai. [2] [Her] husband went [and] spent six hundred, [3] [and] brought four hundred. [4] While he was coming, he needed one zuz [5] and he took from them.

[6] He came before Rabbi Ammi. [7] He said to him: [8] What he spent he spent, [9] and what he consumed he consumed. [10] The Rabbis said to Rabbi Ammi: [11] This applies (lit., "these things") where he consumed fruit. [12] This one consumed principal, [13] and it is an expense! [14] If so this is: [15] "If he spent and did not consume [at all], [16] he may swear how much he spent, and take."

[17] "He may swear how much he spent, and take."

TRANSLATION AND COMMENTARY

הַהִיא אִיתְּתָא [1] The following anecdote illustrates the Mishnah's ruling: **There was a certain woman who inherited four hundred zuz,** but the money was in **Bei Ḥozai,** a distant region in central Babylonia. [2] **Her husband went** there to receive the money on her behalf. He spent **six hundred** zuz of his own money on travel expenses, [3] **and brought** back **the four hundred** zuz belonging to his wife. [4] **On his way back, he needed one zuz** for his personal needs, [5] **and he took** a zuz **from** his wife's money.

אֲתָא לְקַמֵּיהּ [6] When the husband later decided to divorce his wife, **he came before Rabbi Ammi** and asked him whether he was entitled to compensation for the expenses he had incurred while collecting his wife's inheritance. [7] Rabbi Ammi **said to him:** You derived a small benefit from her property, and so we invoke the Mishnah's ruling: "Regardless of the amount, [8] **what he spent** is **spent,** [9] **and what he consumed** is **consumed."** Thus, you are not entitled to reimbursement. [10] Upon hearing this ruling, **the Rabbis said to Rabbi Ammi:** [11] But surely the Mishnah's ruling **applies** only **when** the husband **consumed usufruct** of his wife's property! [12] But in **this** case, the husband **consumed** a small portion of his wife's **principal.** [13] Thus, he incurred six hundred zuz of **expenses,** without enjoying any usufruct whatsoever! [14] Rabbi Ammi said: **If so, this** case **is** governed by the ruling recorded at the end of the Mishnah: [15] **"If** the husband **spent** his own money on his wife's usufruct property, **and did not consume** any usufruct at all, [16] **he may swear** that **he spent** a certain amount **and collect** that sum from his wife."

יִשָּׁבַע [17] We have learned in our Mishnah: "If the husband spent his own money on his wife's usufruct property, and did not consume any usufruct at all, **he may swear** that **he spent** a certain amount, **and collect**

BACKGROUND

בֵּי חוֹזָאֵי Bei Ḥozai. Now called Huzistan, it was one of the larger provinces of the Persian kingdom, extending from the Elamite mountains to the Persian Gulf. This district was an important agricultural and commercial center, but it was very far from the main Jewish settlements in Babylonia. Since the journey there was arduous, and transportation in that direction was hard to come by, it could take a whole year to get to Bei Ḥozai and back, and such trips were therefore very expensive.

RASHI

חוזאי — שם מקום, והיה רחוק הימנה, והיה מפיק עליה שית מאה בהולכת הדרך משלו.

NOTES

אַפֵּיק שִׁית מְאָה He spent six hundred. The Rishonim claim: The Gemara below teaches that if the husband's expenses were greater than the improvement to his wife's usufruct property, he is only entitled to collect the amount of the improvement. In this case, however, there was no improvement at all, so the husband should not be entitled to collect anything! *Talmidei Rabbenu Yonah* respond that the wife would have had to pay to send an agent to collect her inheritance. Thus the money that the husband saved for her by going to Bei Ḥozai to receive her inheritance, is regarded as improvement to the property which he can collect. *Meiri* suggests that the ruling that the husband can only collect his expenses in the amount of the improvement is limited to when the husband acted on his own. But if he spent money on his wife's property at her request, he can collect his expenses, even if they are greater than the improvement. Thus, according to one opinion cited by *Meiri,* the husband can collect the six hundred zuz he spent in order to receive his wife's inheritance on her behalf.

HALAKHAH

דִּנְפְלוּ לָהּ אַרְבַּע מְאָה זוּזֵי בֵּי חוֹזָאֵי To whom fell as an inheritance four hundred zuz in Bei Ḥozai. "If a woman inherited property which was at a great distance from where she lived, and her husband went to receive the property on her behalf, incurring expenses and consuming some of the property on the way, and then he divorced her, he is not regarded as having derived benefit from the usufruct, for it was the woman's principal that he consumed. Thus, the husband may take an oath stating the amount of money he spent and then collect that sum up to the amount of the increase in value he effected by bringing the property to the woman from the place where it had first been found," following Rabbi Assi and Rava. (*Rambam, Sefer Nashim, Hilkhot Ishut* 23:9; *Shulḥan Arukh, Even HaEzer* 88:7-8)

TRANSLATION AND COMMENTARY

that sum from his wife." [1]**Rabbi Assi said: This** ruling **applies** only **where** the husband's investment brought about **an improvement** in his wife's usufruct property and an increase in value **corresponding to the** husband's **expenses.**

לְמַאי הִלְכְתָא [2]The Gemara asks: **Regarding what** was this **law** stated? Rabbi Assi's ruling can be taken as a leniency or a stringency with respect to requiring the husband to take an oath. If the husband may swear and collect his expenses only when his investment in his wife's property increases in value corresponding to his expenses, this may be construed as a leniency for the husband. For if his investment results in an improvement of his wife's property which is greater than his expenses, perhaps he may collect the sum he invested even without an oath. Conversely, if the husband's investment brings an improvement in his wife's property that is worth less than his investment, perhaps he may not collect his full expenses even with an oath, but only a sum corresponding to the value of the improvement of the property — and this would be construed as a stringency.

אָמַר אַבַּיֵי [3]**Abaye said:** Rabbi Assi meant to be lenient to the husband by ruling **that if the improvement** to the woman's usufruct property **is greater than his expenses,** [4]**he may collect his expenses** from his wife even **without an oath.**

אֲמַר לֵיהּ רָבָא [5]**Rava responded:** If this is **so,** then the husband **will deceive** his wife and collect more than is due. He will claim that he spent a sum only slightly smaller than the improvement in his wife's property, and thus he will be able to collect that sum without taking an oath or bringing any other proof to corroborate his claim!

אֶלָּא אָמַר רָבָא [6]**Rather, Rava said:** Rabbi Assi meant to issue a stringent ruling for the husband, **that if his expenses exceeded the improvement** to his wife's usufruct property, [7]**he is entitled to** collect no more than **the amount of the improvement,** [8]**and** in any case he may only collect his expenses after taking **an oath.**

אִיבַּעֲיָא לְהוּ [9]**The following problem arose** in discussion among the Sages: [10]**If the husband brought in tenant-farmers** to cultivate his wife's usufruct property **in his place,** [11]**what** is the law? Tenant-farmers farm the land in return for a certain proportion of the crop (usually one-half, one-third, or one-quarter), and if tenant-farmers improve the land, they must be compensated. The Sages wish to know whether, in the case of a divorce, the tenant-farmers are entitled to a share in the improvement in the field's value

[1]אָמַר רַבִּי אַסִי: וְהוּא, שֶׁיֵּשׁ שֶׁבַח כְּנֶגֶד הוֹצָאָה.
[2]לְמַאי הִלְכְתָא?
[3]אָמַר אַבַּיֵי: שֶׁאִם הָיָה שֶׁבַח יָתֵר עַל הוֹצָאָה, [4]נוֹטֵל אֶת הַהוֹצָאָה בְּלֹא שְׁבוּעָה.
[5]אֲמַר לֵיהּ רָבָא: אִם כֵּן, אָתֵי לְאִיעֲרוּמֵי!
[6]אֶלָּא אָמַר רָבָא: שֶׁאִם הָיְתָה הוֹצָאָה יְתֵירָה עַל הַשֶּׁבַח, [7]אֵין לוֹ אֶלָּא הוֹצָאָה שִׁיעוּר שֶׁבַח, [8]וּבִשְׁבוּעָה.
[9]אִיבַּעֲיָא לְהוּ: [10]בַּעַל שֶׁהוֹרִיד אֲרִיסִין תַּחְתָּיו, [11]מַהוּ?

LITERAL TRANSLATION

[1]Rabbi Assi said: And this is when there is improvement corresponding to the expenses.

[2]For which law?

[3]Abaye said: That if the improvement was greater than the expenses, [4]he takes the expenses without an oath.

[5]Rava said to him: If so, he will come to deceive!

[6]Rather, Rava said: That if the expenses were greater than the improvement, [7]he only has the expenses in the amount of the improvement, [8]and with an oath.

[9]It was asked of them: [10][If] the husband brought in tenant-farmers in his place, [11]what [is the law]?

RASHI

שהיה שבח כנגד יציאה – הוא דאמרינן: ישבע ויטול. **למאי הלכתא** – קאמר והוא שהיה שבח כנגד יציאה – לאקולי עליה, דאי איכא שבח טפי – לא בעי שבועה או לאחמורי עליה, ולמימר: דאי יציאה יתירה – לא שקיל אלא כשיעור שבח, ואפילו בשבועה, לא אמרינן ישבע כמה הוציא ויטול. **אתי לאיערומי** – ואמר: בציר משבחא פורתא – דלישקול בלא שבועה, ואף על גב דלא אפיק כולי האי. **אלא אמר רבא** – הא דרבי (יוסי) (אסי) לאחמורי עליה אתא ולומר שאם יציאה יתירה על שבח שהשביחה – לא אמרינן יטול כל מה שהוציא, אלא מן היציאה יחזירו לו שיעור השבח. **ובשבועה** – שישביעוהו שכך הוציא. **שהוריד אריסין** – בנכסי אשתו, ליטול מחצה או שליש ועמד וגרשה משאכל קימעא. **מהו** – שיטלו האריסין כפי שבחם.

HALAKHAH

וְהוּא, שֶׁיֵּשׁ שֶׁבַח כְּנֶגֶד הוֹצָאָה And this is when there is improvement corresponding to the expenses. "If someone spent money on his wife's usufruct property, and his expenses were greater than the improvement that his investment produced, he may take an oath stating the amount of money he spent and collect that sum up to the amount of the improvement to the property," following Rabbi Assi and Rava. (*Rambam, Sefer Nashim, Hilkhot Ishut* 23:9; *Shulḥan Arukh, Even HaEzer* 88:7-8.)

בַּעַל שֶׁהוֹרִיד אֲרִיסִין תַּחְתָּיו If the husband brought in tenant-farmers in his place. "If the husband brought in tenant-farmers to cultivate his wife's usufruct property, and then divorced her, and the husband was himself a farmer, the tenant-farmers cannot collect their usual share, but instead

TRANSLATION AND COMMENTARY

resulting from their investment. Do we say that since the husband, and not his wife, made the arrangements, [1]the tenant-farmers **came in having the husband's** rights **in mind?** [2]**Now, since the husband can be removed** from the property without receiving compensation for his expenses, [3]perhaps **they,** too, **can be removed** from the property without receiving any such compensation. [4]**Or perhaps** we say that the tenant-farmers **came in having the** benefit of the **land in mind,** [5]**and as long as the land is there** to be worked, **it is there for tenant-farmers,** for had the husband not brought them in as tenant-farmers, his wife would surely have done so! Thus, they cannot be removed from the property without receiving a share of the increase in the field's value that resulted from their investment.

מַתְקִיף לָהּ [6]**Rava bar Rav Ḥanan strongly objected to** the question itself: [7]**How is this** case **different from** the case discussed elsewhere (*Bava Metzia* 101a), about which the following ruling was issued: "**If someone entered another person's field and planted** trees there **without** the owner's **permission,** [8]**we assess** the planter's expenses in planting the trees and what his work added to the value of the field, [9]and the planter **is at a disadvantage"?** In other words, he receives the lower of the two assessments. While he cannot receive more than his investment, the tenant-farmers brought in by the husband should not be in a worse position. How can it even be suggested that a tenant-farmer who was brought in by the husband to farm his wife's property in his place can be removed from his position without receiving any compensation whatsoever?

הָתָם [10]The Gemara responds that the two cases are not similar. For **there,** if someone entered another person's field and planted trees without the owner's permission, **there was no other person who would have exerted himself** cultivating the field. [11]But **here,** if the husband brought in tenant-farmers to cultivate his wife's usufruct property in his place, **there is the husband who would have exerted himself** and farmed the property had the tenant-farmers not been brought in. Since the wife would not have been required to reimburse her husband for his expenses, she should also not be required to compensate the tenant-farmers for their expenses when she removes them from her property.

LITERAL TRANSLATION

[1]They came in having the husband in mind, [2][so that when] the husband is removed, [3]they are removed. [4]Or perhaps they came in having the land in mind, [5]and while the land stands, it stands for tenant-farmers?

[6]Rava bar Rav Ḥanan strongly objected to this: [7]How is this different from: [If] someone entered his fellow's field and planted it without permission, [8]we assess for him, [9]and he is at a disadvantage (lit., "his hand is lower")?

[10]There, there is no [other] person who will exert himself. [11]Here, there is the husband who will exert himself.

[1]אַדַּעְתָּא דְּבַעַל נְחִית, [2]אִיסְתַּלֵּיק לֵיהּ בַּעַל, [3]אִיסְתַּלֵּיקוּ לְהוּ. [4]אוֹ דִּלְמָא אַדַּעְתָּא דְּאַרְעָא נְחִית, [5]וְאַרְעָא כִּי קַיְימָא, לַאֲרִיסֵי קַיְימָא? [6]מַתְקִיף לָהּ רָבָא בַּר רַב חָנָן: [7]מַאי שְׁנָא: מֵהַיּוֹרֵד לְתוֹךְ שְׂדֵה חֲבֵירוֹ וּנְטָעָהּ שֶׁלֹּא בִּרְשׁוּת, [8]שָׁמִין לוֹ, [9]וְיָדוֹ עַל הַתַּחְתּוֹנָה? [10]הָתָם, לֵיכָּא אִינִישׁ דְּטָרַח. [11]הָכָא, אִיכָּא בַּעַל דְּטָרַח.

RASHI

אדעתא דבעל נחית — הוא הכניסם, ולא היא. **וכי איסתלק ליה בעל** — איסתלקו אינהו, ולא שקלי מידי; כי דיניה, דמה שהוציא — הוציא, ומה שאכל — אכל. **לאריסי קיימא** — אם לא הורידם הבעל — היתה היא מורידה לתוכה אריסין. **שמין לו וידו על התחתונה** — ליטול היציאה כשיעור שבח, כדאמר בבבא מציעא ב"השואל", והכא אמר: בעי לסלוקי בלא כלום. **ליבא למאן דטרח** — ראה זה שלא היה איש משביחן, וירד להן, ומה הפסידן? הלכך יציאה שיעור שבח מיהת יהיב ליה. **הכא איכא בעל** — שיטריח בהן. ואמרה להו: אי לא נחתיתו אתון — איהו עביד, ולא הוה שקיל השתא מידי.

NOTES

הַיּוֹרֵד לְתוֹךְ שְׂדֵה חֲבֵירוֹ **If someone entered his fellow's field.** Basing himself on the Gemara's conclusion regarding the case of the husband who brought in tenant-farmers to cultivate his wife's usufruct property, *Ra'avad* inferred that if someone planted another person's field without the owner's permission, a distinction is made between an

HALAKHAH

we assess their expenses and the value of their improvements to the land, and award them the lower of the two assessments. If the husband was not himself a farmer, the tenant-farmers can collect their usual share from the woman. *Rema* notes that, according to some authorities (*Tur, Rosh*), this law applies only if the tenant-farmers knew that the property belonged to the woman. But if they did not know this, they may collect their usual share from the husband (*Helkat Meḥokek*), even if the husband was a farmer." (*Rambam, Sefer Nezikin, Hilkhot Gezelah* 10:12; *Shulḥan Arukh, Even HaEzer* 88:12.)

הַיּוֹרֵד לְתוֹךְ שְׂדֵה חֲבֵירוֹ וּנְטָעָהּ שֶׁלֹּא בִּרְשׁוּת **If someone entered his fellow's field and planted it without permission.** "If someone entered another person's field and planted it without the owner's permission, and it was a field which was ordinarily planted, we assess how much a

TRANSLATION AND COMMENTARY

מַאי הָוֵי עֲלָהּ [1] The Gemara now asks: **What is the decision regarding** the matter? How should the law in the case be decided?

אָמַר [2] **Rav Huna the son of Rav Yehoshua said:** [3] **We consider** the circumstances in each individual case: **If the husband was himself a tenant-farmer** who could have cultivated his wife's property on his own, [4] we say that since **the husband can be removed** from the property without receiving any compensation for his expenses, [5] the tenant-farmers **can** also **be removed** from the property without receiving any compensation. For in such a case it can be argued that, had the husband not brought in the tenant-farmers, he would have farmed his wife's property. Since the woman would not have been required to reimburse her husband for his expenses, she should also not be required to compensate his tenant-farmers. [6] But **if the husband was not** himself **a** professional **farmer,** [7] we say that the woman's **land was standing for the tenant-farmers.** Had the husband not brought in the tenant-farmers, his wife would surely have had to do so. In such a case, the woman cannot remove the tenant-farmers from her property without giving them a share in the improvement of the field's value that resulted from their investment.

אִיבַּעְיָא לְהוּ [8] Another **problem arose** in discussion among the Sages: **If the husband sold** his wife's usufruct **land for its fruit,** meaning that he sold his right to derive benefit from his wife's usufruct property, **what** is the law? Is the sale valid or not? [9] The Gemara now explains the two sides of the question: **Do we say** that **he sold that which** he **acquired from** his wife upon their marriage, i.e., his right to the usufruct of her property? Since the husband has the right to benefit from his wife's usufruct property, he should also be authorized to sell that right to another person. [10] **Or perhaps** we say that the husband's right to the fruit of his wife's property is not absolute, for **when the Rabbis enacted** that the **usufruct** of the wife's property **belongs to the husband,** [80B] **it was for** the purpose of adding to **the comfort of their home.** To make it easier for a husband to support his household, the Rabbis ordained that he is entitled to receive the fruit of his wife's property. [11] **But** they did **not** rule that he may **sell** his right to the usufruct of his wife's property solely for his personal advantage!

[1] מַאי הָוֵי עֲלָהּ?
[2] אָמַר רַב הוּנָא בְּרֵיהּ דְּרַב יְהוֹשֻׁעַ: [3] חָזֵינַן: אִי בַּעַל אָרִיס הוּא, [4] אִיסְתַּלַּק לֵיהּ בַּעַל [5] אִסְתַּלְּקוּ לְהוּ. [6] אִי בַּעַל לָאו אָרִיס הוּא, [7] אַרְעָא לַאֲרִיסֵי קַיְימָא.
[8] אִיבַּעְיָא לְהוּ: בַּעַל שֶׁמָּכַר קַרְקַע לְפֵירוֹת, מַהוּ? [9] מִי אָמְרִינַן: מַאי דְּקָנֵי לָהּ אַקְנֵי? [10] אוֹ דִלְמָא, כִּי תַּקִּינוּ לֵיהּ רַבָּנַן פֵּירוֹת לַבַּעַל, [80B] מִשּׁוּם רֶוַח בֵּיתָא. [11] אֲבָל לְזַבּוּנֵי — לָא!

LITERAL TRANSLATION

[1] What was there about it?

[2] Rav Huna the son of Rav Yehoshua said: [3] We see: If the husband is a farmer, [4] [when] the husband is removed, [5] they are removed. [6] If the husband is not a farmer, [7] the land stands for tenant-farmers.

[8] It was asked of them: [If] the husband sold land for [its] fruit, what [is the law]? [9] Do we say: That which he acquired, he sold? [10] Or perhaps: When the Rabbis enacted fruit for the husband, [80B] [it was] for the comfort of the home. [11] But to sell — no!

RASHI

אי בעל זה אריס הוא — וידע נטיע אריסות; שאם לא ירדו אלו, היה הוא עצמו עובדה. **אסתלקו להו — דאמרה** להו: קא מפסידתו לי, דאי לא נחתיתו — הוה איהו נחית ועביד, ולא הוה שקיל השתא מידי. **שמכר קרקע לפירות — מכר לאחרים קרקע** מלוג, שיעשה הלוקח ויאכל פירות. **משום רווח ביתא — שיכניס** הפירות לביתו ויהא מזון הבית מצוי, וייטיב לה.

NOTES

owner who was a farmer and who could have cultivated the field himself, in which case the planter is only compensated for his out-of-pocket expenses, but not for his labor, and an owner who was not a farmer, in which case the planter is compensated for his labor as well.

אִי בַּעַל אָרִיס הוּא If the husband is a farmer. *Ra'ah* notes that although the Gemara says that the wife can remove the tenant-farmers from her property without compensating them for their expenses, they can collect their expenses from the husband who hired them. *Ritva* distinguishes between the case where the husband hired them saying that he would be responsible for their wages, and the case where he hired them without specifying who would pay them.

מִשּׁוּם רֶוַח בֵּיתָא For the comfort of the home. Our commentary follows *Rashi, Ra'avad* and most Rishonim who understand that Rava sanctioned the husband's action, because his first wife's maidservant still added to the

HALAKHAH

person would be willing to pay to have such a field planted, and the planter may collect that sum from the owner of the field. If it was a field which was not ordinarily planted, we assess the planter's expenses and the improvement to the field, and award the planter the lower of the two assessments." (*Rambam, Sefer Nezikin, Hilkhot Gezelah* 10:4; *Shulḥan Arukh, Ḥoshen Mishpat* 375:1.)

[1]יְהוּדָה מָר בַּר מָרֵימָר מִשְּׁמֵיהּ דְּרָבָא אָמַר: [2]מַה שֶּׁעָשָׂה עָשׂוּי. [3]רַב פַּפָּא אָמַר מִשְּׁמֵיהּ דְּרָבָא: לֹא עָשָׂה וְלֹא כְלוּם. [4]אָמַר רַב פַּפָּא: הָא דִּיהוּדָה מָר בַּר מָרֵימָר לָאו בְּפֵירוּשׁ אִתְּמַר, [5]אֶלָּא מִכְּלָלָא אִתְּמַר. [6]דְּהַהִיא אִיתְּתָא דְּעַיְּילָה לֵיהּ לְגַבְרָא תַּרְתֵּי אַמְהָתָא. [7]אֲזַל גַּבְרָא נְסֵיב אִיתְּתָא אַחֲרִיתֵי, [8]עַיֵּיל לַהּ חֲדָא מִנַּיְיהוּ. [9]אֲתַאי לְקַמֵּיהּ דְּרָבָא, צְוַוחָה, [10]לָא אַשְׁגַּח בַּהּ. [11]מַאן דַּחֲזָא סָבַר מִשּׁוּם דְּסָבַר: [12]מַה שֶּׁעָשָׂה עָשׂוּי. [13]וְלָא הִיא. [14]מִשּׁוּם רֶוַוח בֵּיתָא, [15]וְהָא קָא רָוַוח. [16]וְהִלְכְתָא: בַּעַל שֶׁמָּכַר קַרְקַע לְפֵירוֹת, [17]לֹא עָשָׂה וְלֹא כְלוּם.

LITERAL TRANSLATION

[1]Yehudah Mar the son of Maremar said in the name of Rava: [2]What he did is done. [3]Rav Pappa said in the name of Rava: He did not do anything.

[4]Rav Pappa said: This [ruling] of Yehudah Mar the son of Maremar was not said explicitly, [5]but was said by implication. [6]For [there was] a certain woman who brought in for her husband two maidservants. [7]The husband went [and] married another woman, [8][and] gave her one of them. [9]She came before Rava [and] cried out, [10][but] he did not pay attention to her. [11]He who saw thought that he maintains: [12]What he did was done. [13]But it is not so. [14][The reason is] for the comfort of the home, [15]and there was comfort [of the home].

[16]And the law is: [If] the husband sold land for its fruit, [17]he did not do anything.

TRANSLATION AND COMMENTARY

יְהוּדָה מָר בַּר מָרֵימָר [1]Some actions which are not permitted from the outset are nonetheless valid after the fact, and the Amoraim disagree as to whether the husband's sale of usufruct from his wife's property belongs in this category. **Yehudah Mar the son of Maremar said in the name of Rava:** [2]**What he did is done,** and the sale is valid. [3]**Rav Pappa said in the name of Rava: He did not accomplish anything,** for the sale is void.

אֲמַר רַב פַּפָּא [4]**Rav Pappa said: The ruling** cited by **Yehudah Mar the son of Maremar** in the name of Rava **was not stated explicitly** by Rava, [5]**but** instead **was deduced by implication** from the following ruling: [6]**There was a certain woman who brought in two** non-Jewish **maidservants for her husband** as part of her usufruct property. [7]**The husband took another woman as his** second **wife** [8]**and gave her one of the** two maidservants as her personal attendant. By doing so, he in effect transferred the benefit he personally derived from his first wife's slave from himself to his second wife. [9]The first wife **came before Rava and cried out** against this injustice. [10]**But** Rava **did not pay** any **attention to her** complaint. [11]**The person who witnessed** this **thought that Rava maintains** that if the husband sold or gave away his right to the usufruct of his wife's property, [12]**what was done was done,** and the transaction is valid. [13]**But it is not so.** [14]For Rava maintains that the husband may enjoy the usufruct from his wife's property only to increase **the comfort of their home.** Thus the husband may not sell or give away his right to the usufruct. [15]Here, however, the maidservant **added to the comfort** of the home.

וְהִלְכְתָא [16]The Gemara arrives at the following conclusion: **And the final law is: If the husband sold** his wife's usufruct **land for its fruit,** [17]**he did not accomplish anything,** for the sale is void.

RASHI

לאו בפירוש איתמר — לא שמעה מרבא בהדיא. **תרתי אמהתא** — שפחות מלוג היו, ולא שמאתם לו בכתובתה. **עייל לה חדא מנייהו** — לצרת לשניה. **אתאי** — קמייתא לקמיה דרבא. **מה שעשה עשוי** — ואפילו נתנה לאחרת לשימושה. **ולא היא** — לעולם משום רווח ביתא אית ליה לרבא תקנת פירות. **והא קא רווח** — ביתא, שאף עתה היא עושה לצרכי הבית.

NOTES

comfort of the home, even when she served the second wife. For the second wife is no worse than a guest who would be served by the maidservant.

Rif understands the Gemara entirely differently. Rava sanctioned the husband's action because his first wife still had the other maidservant to attend to her needs. According to *Rif,* it follows that not only could the husband give the maidservant to his second wife, but he could also sell her or give her away.

HALAKHAH

דְּעַיְּילָה לֵיהּ לְגַבְרָא תַּרְתֵּי אַמְהָתָא **She brought in for her husband two maidservants.** "A husband can compel his wife to allow some of the servants which she brought into the marriage (whether as *melog* property or as *tzon barzel* property) to serve him in a house where he lives with another wife. But he may not take those servants with him to another town without his wife's consent. *Rema* writes that the husband cannot compel the servants to serve his other wife in her house" (*Bet Yosef;* see *Helkat Meḥokek*). (*Rambam, Sefer Nashim, Hilkhot Ishut* 22:35; *Shulḥan Arukh, Even HaEzer* 85:19.)

בַּעַל שֶׁמָּכַר קַרְקַע לְפֵירוֹת **If the husband sold land for its fruit.** "A husband may not sell his wife's usufruct property for its fruit, if the buyer pays the husband in advance for

TRANSLATION AND COMMENTARY

מַאי טַעֲמָא [1]The Gemara asks for a clarification of this ruling: **What is the reason** why the sale is void? [2]**Abaye said:** The Rabbis **were concerned** that the property **might suffer damage** as a result of the buyer's negligence. Since he did not acquire the land itself, but only the fruit, he can never be sure that the property will remain in his possession long enough to justify investment in its improvement, for at any time the husband might divorce his wife, and the land will revert to her. But the husband has an incentive to improve the land. For he does not expect to divorce his wife, and he will inherit the property if she predeceases him. [3]**Rava said:** The sale is void because the husband may use the usufruct of his wife's property only to add to **the comfort of their home.** A husband may not sell his right to the usufruct solely for his personal advantage.

מַאי בֵּינַיְיהוּ [4]The Gemara asks: **What is the** practical **difference between these** two explanations?

אִיכָּא בֵּינַיְיהוּ [5]The Gemara answers: **There is** a difference **between** the two explanations if the wife's **land is close to the town where** the couple live. If the Rabbis rendered void the husband's sale of the right to the usufruct of his wife's property to preserve it from damage, here the sale should be valid, for the husband can keep an eye on the field. But if the husband may not use the usufruct solely for his personal advantage, the sale of usufruct rights to a field close to the town where the couple live should be void. [6]**Alternatively,** there is a difference between the two explanations if **the husband** sells the right to the usufruct of his wife's property, but remains on the land as **a tenant-farmer** who actually works the land. Here, too, there is no concern that the field will suffer damage, but the sale of the usufruct adds nothing to the comfort of the home. [7]**Alternatively,** there is a difference between the two explanations if the husband takes the **money** that he received for the usufruct **and does business with it.** In such a case, there is indeed concern that the buyer will damage the property. But the sale contributes to the comfort of the home, for the husband has invested the proceeds in a business, the profits of which he will be able to use to support his household.

[1]מַאי טַעֲמָא? [2]אַבַּיֵי אֲמַר: חָיְישִׁינַן שֶׁמָּא תַּכְסִיף. [3]רָבָא אֲמַר: מִשּׁוּם רֶוַוח בֵּיתָא. [4]מַאי בֵּינַיְיהוּ? [5]אִיכָּא בֵּינַיְיהוּ אַרְעָא דְּמִקָּרַב לְמָתָא. [6]אִי נַמִי בַּעַל אָרִיס הוּא. [7]אִי נַמִי זוּזֵי וְקָא עָבֵיד בְּהוּ עִיסְקָא.

LITERAL TRANSLATION

[1]What is the reason? [2]Abaye said: We are concerned that perhaps it will depreciate. [3]Rava said: [The reason is] for the comfort of the home. [4]What is [the difference] between them? [5]There is between them land that is close to the town. [6]Or also [if] the husband is a tenant-farmer. [7]Or also money and he does business with it.

RASHI

שמא תכסיף – השדה, שלא יחוש הלוקח לזבלה ולטייבה, דקא סבר: למחר נפקא מנאי, שאין הגוף שלי. אבל בעל מצפה שמא תמות היא בחייו, ויירש את גוף הקרקע ומשבח לה. **דמקרב למתא** – דחזיא ליה כל שעתא אי מכסיף לה. **אי נמי בעל אריס הוא** – כלומר, שנותן ללוקח פירות מזומנים. **אי נמי זוזי וקא עביד בהו עיסקא** – שהבעל עושה סחורה במעות שקיבל מן הלוקח, ומשתכר בהן ואיכא רווח ביתא.

NOTES

אַרְעָא דְּמִקָּרַב לְמָתָא **Land that is close to the town.** Our commentary follows *Rashi* and most Rishonim who understand that if the woman's property is close to the town where the couple live, the husband can make sure that the person who buys the usufruct takes proper care of the property. Therefore a ruling on this case determines whether the issue at stake is potential damage to the wife's property or exclusive use of the usufruct for the benefit of the household.

Rav Hai Gaon suggests that there is a practical difference between the explanations of Rava and Abaye if the property is situated far away. If the Rabbis were concerned that the property might suffer damage as a result of the sale, here there is such a concern and the sale should be void. But if the husband was only given the usufruct to add to the comfort of the house, the sale should be valid. Since the woman's property is far from town, it is costly for the husband to market the produce, and so when the husband sells the usufruct to another person, he adds to the prosperity of the house.

בַּעַל אָרִיס הוּא **If the husband is a tenant-farmer.** Most Rishonim understand that in this instance the husband sold the right to the usufruct of his wife's property, but remained on the land as a tenant-farmer who actually worked the land. There is no concern that the field will suffer damage, for he will maintain it. But there is a decrease of comfort in the home, for the husband will receive only a portion of the produce like any other tenant-farmer, and not the entire crop as he would have had if he did not sell the usufruct. *Talmidei Rabbenu Yonah* suggest that in this instance the husband sold the right to the usufruct of his wife's property, and then went to work as a tenant-farmer in some other field. There is concern that his wife's field will suffer damage, for the buyer may not care for it properly. But there is an increase in the comfort of the house, for the husband is now earning an income.

HALAKHAH

many years' harvest, unless he plans to invest the proceeds of the sale in a profitable business (following the Gemara's conclusion and Rava's explanation). But he may sell each year's crop at the end of the harvest." (*Rambam, Sefer Nashim, Hilkhot Ishut* 22:20; *Shulḥan Arukh, Even HaEzer* 85:17.)

TRANSLATION AND COMMENTARY

MISHNAH שׁוֹמֶרֶת יָבָם [1]A man whose brother died without children is obliged by Torah law to marry his deceased brother's widow or release her from the levirate tie by performing *ḥalitzah* (see Deuteronomy 25:5-10). As long as neither levirate marriage nor *ḥalitzah* has taken place, the woman is tied to her brother-in-law by the levirate bond and is forbidden to marry another man. Now, if a man died without children, and his widow **was waiting** for her brother-in-law to take her in **levirate marriage** or to perform *ḥalitzah,* and she **inherited property** or received it as a gift, [2]**Bet Shammai and Bet Hillel** both **agree** [3]**that she may sell the property or give it away** as she pleases, **and** the transaction **is valid.**

מֵתָה [4]Our Mishnah now considers what is to be done with the property that belongs to a widow who **died** while she was waiting for her brother-in-law to take her as his wife or to perform *ḥalitzah:* **What should be done with her ketubah** settlement? The basic sum guaranteed to a wife is two hundred dinarim in the case of a woman who was a virgin at the time of marriage and a hundred dinarim in the case of a woman who was not, as well as any increment that the husband may add on his own, in addition to the dowry that is recorded in the ketubah, which is the woman's *nikhsei tzon barzel.* [5]**And** what becomes of **the property that comes** with the woman at the time of her marriage **and goes with her** in the condition it's in when she is widowed or divorced, her usufruct property? [6]**Bet Shammai say:**

משנה [1]שׁוֹמֶרֶת יָבָם שֶׁנָּפְלוּ לָהּ נְכָסִים — [2]מוֹדִים בֵּית שַׁמַּאי וּבֵית הִלֵּל [3]שֶׁמּוֹכֶרֶת וְנוֹתֶנֶת, וְקַיָּים. [4]מֵתָה, מַה יַּעֲשׂוּ בִּכְתוּבָּתָהּ [5]וּבִנְכָסִים הַנִּכְנָסִין וְהַיּוֹצְאִין עִמָּהּ? [6]בֵּית שַׁמַּאי אוֹמְרִים:

LITERAL TRANSLATION

MISHNAH [1]A widow waiting for levirate marriage to whom property fell — [2]Bet Shammai and Bet Hillel agree [3]that she may sell [the property] or give it away, and it is valid.

[4][If] she died, what shall they do with her ketubah settlement [5]and the property that comes in and goes out with her? [6]Bet Shammai say:

RASHI

משנה שנפלו לה נכסים — כשהיא שומרת יבם. **בכתובתה** — בנדוניא שהכניסה לו, ושמאתן לו בכתובתה, וקיבל עליו אחריותן ורשאי להוציאם. **ובנכסים הנכנסים והיוצאים עמה** — הן נכסי מלוג, שאין שמין אותם עליו, ואינו רשאי להוציאן. אלא משנכנסה לרשותו — נכנסין עמה, וכשהיא יוצאה — יוצאין עמה. **בית שמאי אומרים כו'** — ביבמות פרק "החולץ" קא מפרש: מאי שנא רישא כשהיא קיימת דלא פליגי, שאין לו כח בהם — ומאי שנא סיפא כשמתה, אמרו בית שמאי יחלוקו יורשי הבעל בהם. ומפרש נמי, דדוקא נקט יחלוקו יורשי הבעל עם יורשי האב בנכסי מלוג, אבל יורשי האב לא יחלוקו בכתובת הבעל. ואף על גב דנקט רישא מה יעשו בכתובתה — תניא ושבקה.

BACKGROUND

נִכְסֵי מְלוֹג וְנִכְסֵי צֹאן בַּרְזֶל **Usufruct property and *tzon barzel* property.** A married woman's property is divided into two categories, *nikhsei melog* (usufruct property) and *nikhsei tzon barzel.* Usufruct property is any property brought into the marriage from the wife's father's home but not specifically recorded in her ketubah deed, as well as what she inherits or receives as a gift after her marriage. This property remains hers, but the husband is entitled to its fruits. The husband bears no responsibility with respect to the principal, both its loss and its gain being only hers. If he dies or divorces his wife, the property is returned to her as it stands. If the wife dies before the husband, he inherits the property along with the rest of her estate. By contrast, *tzon barzel* property is brought into the marriage and recorded in the ketubah deed. This property is given over to the husband's ownership, and any profit or loss accruing from his use of it belongs to him. However, he bears full responsibility for the value of the property, and if he dies or divorces his wife, the value of the property as fixed in the ketubah must be restored to the woman.

NOTES

שׁוֹמֶרֶת יָבָם שֶׁנָּפְלוּ לָהּ נְכָסִים **A widow waiting for levirate marriage to whom property fell.** Earlier in the chapter (p.78a), Bet Shammai and Bet Hillel disagree on whether a woman who inherited property while she was betrothed is permitted to sell it or give it away during her betrothal. Here, however, even Bet Hillel agree that the widow may sell or give away the property she inherited while waiting for her brother-in-law to take her as his wife. This is because the levirate tie is not as strong as the bond created through betrothal, since betrothal is expected to end in marriage, whereas the levirate tie may lead either to levirate marriage or to *ḥalitzah.*

Elsewhere (*Yevamot* 38a-b), the Gemara discusses at length why in the first clause of our Mishnah Bet Shammai agree with Bet Hillel that the widow's usufruct property is considered to be in her full possession, so that she may sell it or give it away, while in the next clause of the Mishnah Bet Shammai rule that if the widow dies, her husband's heirs are entitled to half of the property, indicating that it was not in her full possession.

HALAKHAH

שׁוֹמֶרֶת יָבָם שֶׁנָּפְלוּ לָהּ נְכָסִים **A widow who was waiting for her brother-in-law to whom property fell.** "If a widow inherited property while waiting for levirate marriage, she may the sell it or give it away, and the transaction is valid, for the brother-in-law has no right to the property until he marries her. The law applies whether the woman was widowed while married or betrothed." (*Rambam, Sefer Nashim, Hilkhot Ishut* 22:10; *Shulḥan Arukh, Even HaEzer* 160:5.)

מֵתָה, מַה יַּעֲשׂוּ בִּכְתוּבָּתָהּ וּבִנְכָסִים הַנִּכְנָסִין וְהַיּוֹצְאִין עִמָּהּ? **If she died, what shall they do with her ketubah settlement and the property that comes in and goes out with her?** "If a widow dies while waiting for her brother-in-law to take her in levirate marriage, her heirs succeed to her *melog* property and half of her *tzon barzel* property (and any property which she may have received from her brother-in-law as a gift; *Rema*). Her husband's heirs succeed to her whole ketubah settlement, and half of the *tzon barzel* property, following Bet Hillel. *Rema* writes that, according to some authorities (*Rabbenu Tam* and *Rosh*), all the woman's *tzon barzel* property remains in the presumptive possession of the husband's heirs, and we do not take such property away from them if it is already in their possession (*Ran*). These laws apply only if we do not compel the brother-in-law to perform *ḥalitzah.* But if we compel the brother-in-law to perform *ḥalitzah,* the woman is treated as an ordinary widow, and so the brother-in-law does not succeed to any of her property." (*Rambam, Sefer Nashim, Hilkhot Ishut* 22:10; *Sefer Mishpatim, Hilkhot Nahalot* 3:9; *Shulḥan Arukh, Even HaEzer* 160:7.)

TRANSLATION AND COMMENTARY

The late **husband's heirs divide** the woman's property **with the** widow's heirs — her father if he is still alive, or the **father's heirs,** her brothers. [1]**Bet Hillel** disagree and **say: The** woman's *tzon barzel* **property remains in its presumptive state,** in the hands of the party who has presumptive possession of it (see notes). [2]**The** woman's **ketubah** settlement **remains in the possession of the husband's heirs,** for it is his property, that had been mortgaged to guarantee his wife's ketubah. After the husband's death the property that had been mortgaged to his wife's ketubah settlement passes into his heirs' possession, for the widow of a childless man cannot collect her ketubah settlement from her late husband's estate until after her brother-in-law performs *ḥalitzah* and releases her from the levirate tie. If she died while bound to her brother-in-law by the levirate tie, the property from which her ketubah would have been collected remains in the possession of the husband's heirs.

נְכָסִים [3]**The usufruct property that is brought** to the marriage by the wife **and is taken away by her** when she is divorced or widowed [4]**remains in the possession of the** woman's **father's heirs,** for the principal of that property remained in her possession while she was married.

הִנִּיחַ אָחִיו מָעוֹת [5]If the brother-in-law chooses to perform *ḥalitzah,* he receives no more than a brother's share of his late brother's estate, and the widow becomes entitled to collect her ketubah settlement from that estate. If the brother-in-law chooses to take his brother's widow in levirate marriage, he inherits his brother's entire estate. All of the property which the *levir* inherits from the deceased is mortgaged to guarantee his wife's ketubah settlement, which she collects if she becomes widowed a second time or divorced. Thus, the *levir* may not sell or give away the property he inherited from his brother. He may, however, enjoy the usufruct of the property, and if it does not bear fruit, it is converted into fruit-bearing property, so that the husband can enjoy the usufruct without disturbing the principal. Thus, **if the** *levir*'s **brother left** him **money,** [6]**land must be bought with** the money, so that the principal of the estate will remain intact, [7]**and the** *levir* **enjoys the usufruct.**

יַחְלְקוּ יוֹרְשֵׁי הַבַּעַל עִם יוֹרְשֵׁי הָאָב. [1]וּבֵית הִלֵּל אוֹמְרִים: נְכָסִים בְּחֶזְקָתָן, [2]וּכְתוּבָּה בְּחֶזְקַת יוֹרְשֵׁי הַבַּעַל. [3]נְכָסִים הַנִּכְנָסִים וְהַיּוֹצְאִים עִמָּהּ [4]בְּחֶזְקַת יוֹרְשֵׁי הָאָב. [5]הִנִּיחַ אָחִיו מָעוֹת — [6]יִלָּקַח בָּהֶן קַרְקַע, [7]וְהוּא אוֹכֵל פֵּירוֹת.

LITERAL TRANSLATION

The husband's heirs divide [them] with the father's heirs. [1]And Bet Hillel say: The property [remains] in its presumptive state, [2]and the ketubah [settlement remains] in the possession of the husband's heirs. [3]The property that comes in and goes out with her [4][remains] in the possession of the father's heirs. [5][If] his brother left money — [6]land must be bought with it, [7]and he eats the fruit.

RASHI

ובית הלל אומרים נכסים – דצאן ברזל בחזקתן. ובבבא בתרא בפרק "מי שמת" (קנח,ב) מפרש בחזקת מי הם מוחזקין; אי בחזקת יורשי הבעל, הואיל ואחריותן עליו, או בחזקת יורשי האשה שהיו שלה. הכי גרסינן: **כתובתה בחזקת יורשי הבעל** – מנה מאתים, ותוספת שראויין לבא לה משל בעל – בחזקת יורשי הבעל. **ילקח בהן קרקע** – לפי שכתובתה על נכסי בעלה הראשון, כדקתני לקמן. לפיכך נכסי המת אחראין לכתובתה, אלא שהיבם אוכל פירות, אם מייבם אותה. וקסבר: מטלטלי משתעבדי לכתובה.

NOTES

נְכָסִים בְּחֶזְקָתָן **The property remains in its presumptive state.** Our commentary follows *Rashi* and others who understand that Bet Hillel divide the woman's estate into three categories: (1) Her own property, known as her *tzon barzel property,* which remains in its presumptive state (as will be explained below); (2) her entire ketubah settlement; and (3) the property that comes with her at the time of her marriage and goes out with her when she is widowed or divorced, i.e., her *melog* property.

Elsewhere (*Bava Batra* 158a-b), the Mishnah records a dispute between Bet Shammai and Bet Hillel similar to the dispute found in our Mishnah. There the Tannaim disagree about what is to be done with a woman's property if both she and her husband died, but it is not known who died first. There, too, Bet Hillel rule that the woman's *tzon barzel* property remains in its presumptive state, and the Gemara discusses who has presumptive possession of the woman's *tzon barzel* property: The woman's heirs, because it was her property which she brought to the marriage; or the husband's heirs, because the husband was responsible for the value of the property, and so it was considered as his; or both the woman's heirs and the husband's heirs, for they both have a valid claim. According to *Rashi,* Bet Hillel's ruling in our Mishnah is subject to the same dispute.

Rabbenu Tam disagrees with *Rashi,* arguing that everyone agrees that, according to Bet Hillel's ruling in our Mishnah, the deceased widow's *tzon barzel* property remains in the presumptive possession of her late husband's heirs, for the *tzon barzel* property was in the *levir*'s presumptive possession from the moment that his brother died.

Rashba, Ritva and others agree with *Rabbenu Tam,* and suggest that our Mishnah should be revised to read: "Bet Hillel say: The property [remains] in its presumptive state: The ketubah settlement [remains] in the possession of the husband's heirs. The property that comes with her when she marries and goes with her when she is widowed or divorced [remains] in the possession of the father's heirs." According to this reading (which deletes the copulative ו,

TRANSLATION AND COMMENTARY

פֵּירוֹת הַתְּלוּשִׁין [1]If the *levir* inherited from his brother **produce that was detached from the ground,** he may not consume it, because whatever grew during his brother's lifetime is mortgaged to guarantee the widow's ketubah settlement. Thus, the produce must be sold, [2]**land must be bought with** the proceeds of the sale, [3]**and the** *levir* **enjoys the usufruct.** [4]If the *levir* inherited from his brother **produce which was** still **attached to the ground,** [5]**Rabbi Meir says:** Since the produce grew during the brother's lifetime, it is mortgaged to guarantee his widow's ketubah settlement. In order to determine its value, **we assess how much** the land **is worth** together **with the produce,** [6]**and how much** the land **would be worth without the produce.** [7]**The difference** between the two assessments reflects the present value of the produce, which is mortgaged to guarantee the woman's ketubah settlement. [8]**Land** worth that amount **must be bought** by the *levir*, the land remains mortgaged to the woman's ketubah settlement, **and the** *levir* **enjoys the usufruct.** [9]**The Sages disagree** and **say: The produce that was** still **attached to the ground** at the time that the *levir* inherited the property **belongs to the** ***levir***. [10]But regarding the produce **that was** already **detached from the ground** when the brother died, [11]**whoever seized** the produce **first** — whether the *levir* or the widow — **acquired it,** for the Sages maintain that a husband's movable property is not mortgaged to guarantee his wife's ketubah settlement. [12]Thus, **if the** *levir* **seized** the produce **first, he acquired it**. [13]But **if the woman seized** the produce **first** during her husband's lifetime, the produce became mortgaged to guarantee her ketubah settlement. [14]In such a case, the produce must be sold, **land must be bought** with the proceeds of the sale, [15]**and the** *levir* **enjoys the usufruct** of the property.

[1]פֵּירוֹת הַתְּלוּשִׁין מִן הַקַּרְקַע, [2]יִלָּקַח בָּהֶן קַרְקַע, [3]וְהוּא אוֹכֵל פֵּירוֹת. [4]הַמְחוּבָּרִין בַּקַּרְקַע — [5]אָמַר רַבִּי מֵאִיר: שָׁמִין אוֹתָן כַּמָּה הֵן יָפִין בְּפֵירוֹת, [6]וְכַמָּה הֵן יָפִין בְּלֹא פֵּירוֹת, [7]וְהַמּוֹתָר — [8]יִלָּקַח בָּהֶן קַרְקַע, וְהוּא אוֹכֵל פֵּירוֹת. [9]וַחֲכָמִים אוֹמְרִים: פֵּירוֹת הַמְחוּבָּרִין בַּקַּרְקַע שֶׁלּוֹ. [10]הַתְּלוּשִׁין מִן הַקַּרְקַע — [11]כׇּל הַקּוֹדֵם זָכָה בָּהֶן. [12]קָדַם הוּא, זָכָה. [13]קָדְמָה הִיא, [14]יִלָּקַח בָּהֶן קַרְקַע, [15]וְהוּא אוֹכֵל פֵּירוֹת.

LITERAL TRANSLATION

[1]Produce which is detached from the ground, [2]land must be bought with it, [3]and he eats the fruit. [4][Produce] which is attached to the ground — [5]Rabbi Meir said: We assess how much it is worth with the produce, [6]and how much it is worth without the produce, [7]and the difference — [8]land must be bought with it, and he eats the fruit. [9]And the Sages say: Produce attached to the ground is his. [10]That which is detached from the ground — [11]whoever comes first acquires it. [12][If] he came first, he acquired [it]. [13][If] she came first, [14]land must be bought with it, [15]and he eats the fruit.

RASHI

שמין אותם — דקסבר כל מה שגדל ברשות המת אחראין לכתובה. **וחכמים אומרים פירות המחוברין לקרקע שלו** — בגמרא פריך עלה. **כל הקודם בהן זכה** — קסבר: מטלטלי לכתובה לא משתעבדי, אלא אם כן תפסה. ומחיים דבעל בעינן תפיסה, כדלקמן ב״הכותב״ (פד,ב). והוא הדין נמי דפליגי אכספים — דמאי שנא כספים מפירות תלושים.

NOTES

"and," preceding the words "the ketubah"), Bet Hillel issued a comprehensive ruling that the woman's entire estate remains in its presumptive state. It can be divided into two categories: (1) Her full ketubah settlement, as well as her *tzon barzel* property, which remains in the presumptive possession of the husband's heirs; and (2) the *melog* property that comes with her when she marries and goes with her when the marriage ends, which remains in the presumptive possession of her father's heirs.

HALAKHAH

פֵּירוֹת הַתְּלוּשִׁין **Produce which is detached from the ground.** "If a man died without offspring, leaving detached produce or other movable goods, and the *levir* took the man's widow as his wife, the property is sold, land is acquired with the proceeds, and the *levir* consumes the usufruct (following Rabbi Meir, for by Geonic enactment a woman may collect her ketubah settlement from her husband's movable goods; *Rif* and others). According to some authorities (*Rambam*), the *levir* may do as he pleases with the detached produce, movable goods, and money (for the Geonic enactment does not prevent the *levir* from conducting business with the movable goods he inherited from his late brother). If, however, the husband had expressly mortgaged his movable goods to his wife's ketubah along with his land, and he died without offspring, all agree that the movable goods are sold, land is bought with the proceeds, and the *levir* enjoys the usufruct." (*Rambam, Sefer Nashim, Hilkhot Ishut* 22:13; *Shulḥan Arukh, Even HaEzer* 168:5.)

הַמְחוּבָּרִין בַּקַּרְקַע **Produce which is attached to the ground.** "If a man died without offspring, leaving produce which was still attached to the ground, and the *levir* took the man's widow as his wife, the produce is sold, land is bought with the proceeds of the sale, and the *levir* consumes the usufruct," following Resh Lakish's reading of the Sages (below, p. 82a). (*Rambam, Sefer Nashim, Hilkhot Ishut* 22:12; *Shulḥan Arukh, Even HaEzer* 168:4.)

כְּנָסָהּ [1]If the *levir* **married** his brother's widow, **she is like** an ordinary **wife in every respect**, [2]**except that** her **ketubah** settlement **serves** as a lien **on the property** which the *levir* inherited **from** the woman's **first husband,** and not as a lien on the *levir*'s own property.

לֹא יֹאמַר לָהּ [3]If the *levir* married his brother's widow, **he may not** set aside money for the payment of her ketubah and **say to her:** [4]**"Your ketubah rests** before you **on the table,** and the rest of the property that I inherited from my brother I will sell or give away." [5]**Instead all the property** that the *levir* inherited from his brother **is mortgaged to** guarantee the woman's **ketubah** settlement, and the *levir* may not sell or give away the property. [6]**A similar** law applies in general, that **a man may not** set aside a sum of money for the payment of his wife's ketubah settlement and **say to her:** [7]**"Your ketubah rests** before you **on the table."** [8]**Instead, all of his property is mortgaged to guarantee her ketubah** settlement. Although the lien that a wife has on her husband's assets does not prevent him from selling his property, if she is divorced or widowed and her husband or his estate cannot cover her ketubah settlement, she can collect it from the immovable property that her husband transferred to others.

גֵּירְשָׁהּ [9]If the *levir* marries his brother's widow, and later **divorces her,** [10]**she has only her ketubah** settlement. After the *levir* divorces her, he is permitted to sell the rest of the property that he inherited from his brother. But as long as she remains his wife, he cannot sell any of it, for the entire estate is mortgaged to guarantee her ketubah settlement. [11]**If the** *levir* marries his brother's widow and then divorces her, and then **he marries her again** without writing a new marriage contract and before she collects her ketubah settlement, [12]**she is** treated **like any other woman** in that situation. She is assumed to have been remarried on the basis of her original ketubah. Thus, if she is divorced again or widowed, she collects the ketubah settlement that had been stipulated at her first marriage. [13]Here, too, the *levir*'s wife is **only entitled to her** original **ketubah** settlement, which the *levir*'s brother wrote for her when he first married her. Thus, the settlement falls as a lien on the property the *levir* inherited from his brother, and not as a lien upon the *levir*'s own property. Hence, the *levir* is still forbidden to sell or give away any of the property he inherited from his brother, for it is all mortgaged to his wife's ketubah.

[1]כְּנָסָהּ, הֲרֵי הִיא כְּאִשְׁתּוֹ לְכָל דָּבָר, [2]בִּלְבַד שֶׁתְּהֵא כְּתוּבָּתָהּ עַל נִכְסֵי בַעְלָהּ הָרִאשׁוֹן.
[3]לֹא יֹאמַר לָהּ: [4]"הֲרֵי כְּתוּבָּתֵיךְ מוּנַּחַת עַל הַשֻּׁלְחָן", [5]אֶלָּא כָּל נְכָסָיו אַחֲרָאִין לִכְתוּבָּתָהּ. [6]וְכֵן, לֹא יֹאמַר אָדָם לְאִשְׁתּוֹ: [7]"הֲרֵי כְּתוּבָּתֵיךְ מוּנַּחַת עַל הַשֻּׁלְחָן" [8]אֶלָּא כָּל נְכָסָיו אַחֲרָאִין לִכְתוּבָּתָהּ.
[9]גֵּירְשָׁהּ, [10]אֵין לָהּ אֶלָּא כְּתוּבָּה. [11]הֶחֱזִירָהּ, [12]הֲרֵי הִיא כְּכָל הַנָּשִׁים, [13]וְאֵין לָהּ אֶלָּא כְּתוּבָּה בִּלְבַד.

LITERAL TRANSLATION

[1][If] he married her, she is like his wife in every respect, [2]except that her ketubah settlement [falls] on the property of her first husband.
[3]He may not say to her: [4]"Your ketubah settlement rests on the table," [5]but rather all his property is mortgaged to her ketubah. [6]And similarly, a person may not say to his wife: [7]"Your ketubah settlement rests on the table," [8]but rather all of his property is mortgaged to her ketubah.
[9][If] he divorced her, [10]she only has [her] ketubah settlement. [11][If] he remarried her, [12]she is like all the women, [13]and she has only [her] ketubah settlement.

RASHI

הרי היא כאשתו – מפרש בגמרא. **כל נכסיו** – שירש מאחיו. **גרשה** – ליבמתו לאחר שכנסה. **אין לה אלא כתובה** – אבל כל זמן שלא גרשה, היו כל הנכסים משועבדים לה – ואינו רשאי למכור. **הרי היא ככל הנשים** – דתנן בפירקין דלקמן: המגרש את אשתו והחזירה – על מנת כתובה הראשונה החזירה. ובגמרא פריך: למה לי לאשמועינן ביבמה?

NOTES

הֲרֵי כְּתוּבָּתֵיךְ מוּנַּחַת עַל הַשֻּׁלְחָן **Your ketubah rests on the table.** *Rashi*, below (p. 81b), explains that we are dealing here with a moneychanger who places the money that he set aside for his wife's ketubah settlement on the table at which he conducts his business transactions. *Arukh*, basing himself on the Baraitot cited at the end of the chapter

HALAKHAH

כְּתוּבָּתָהּ עַל נִכְסֵי בַעְלָהּ הָרִאשׁוֹן **Her ketubah settlement falls on the property of her first husband.** "A widow's ketubah settlement serves as a lien on her late husband's estate, both while she is waiting for her brother-in-law to take her as his levirate wife and after he does so. Thus, the *levir* may not sell any of the property of his late brother's estate. If he sold property, or gave it away as a gift, or divided the property with his brothers — whether before or after he took the widow as his levirate wife — the transaction is void." (*Rambam, Sefer Nashim, Hilkhot Ishut* 22:11; *Hilkhot Yibum* 1:1; *Shulhan Arukh, Even HaEzer* 166:4; 168:3.)

גמרא [1]אִיבַּעְיָא לְהוּ: [2]שׁוֹמֶרֶת יָבָם שֶׁמֵּתָה, [3]מִי קוֹבְרָהּ? [4]יוֹרְשֵׁי הַבַּעַל קָבְרֵי לָהּ, [5]דְּקָא יָרְתֵי כְּתוּבָּה, [6]אוֹ דִלְמָא יוֹרְשֵׁי הָאָב קָבְרֵי לָהּ, [7]דְּקָא יָרְתֵי נְכָסִים הַנִּכְנָסִין וְהַיּוֹצְאִין עִמָּהּ?

[8]אֲמַר רַב עַמְרָם: תָּא שְׁמַע, [9]דְּתַנְיָא: ״שׁוֹמֶרֶת יָבָם שֶׁמֵּתָה, [81A] [10]יוֹרְשֶׁיהָ, יוֹרְשֵׁי כְתוּבָּתָהּ, [11]חַיָּיבִין בִּקְבוּרָתָהּ״.

LITERAL TRANSLATION

GEMARA [1]It was asked of them: [2][If] a widow waiting for levirate marriage dies, [3]who buries her? [4][Do] the husband's heirs bury her, [5]for they inherit the ketubah settlement, [6]or perhaps the father's heirs bury her, [7]for they inherit the property that comes in and goes out with her?

[8]Rav Amram said: Come [and] hear, [9]for it was taught: "[If] a widow waiting for levirate marriage dies, [81A] [10]her heirs, the heirs of her ketubah, [11]are obligated [to pay for] her burial."

TRANSLATION AND COMMENTARY

GEMARA אִיבַּעְיָא לְהוּ [1]**The Sages raised the following problem:** [2]**If a widow dies while waiting for** her brother-in-law to take her in **levirate marriage** or to perform *ḥalitzah,* [3]**who** is liable to bear the costs of **burying her?** [4]Do we say that **the husband's heirs are liable** for her burial, [5]**for they inherit her ketubah** settlement? [6]**Or** do we perhaps say that her **father's heirs are liable for her burial,** [7]**for they inherit the** woman's usufruct **property that comes with** the woman at the time of her marriage **and goes with her** as it stands when she is widowed or divorced from her husband?

אֲמַר רַב עַמְרָם [8]**Rav Amram said: Come and hear** a resolution of the matter, [9]**for it was taught** explicitly in a Baraita: **"If a widow dies while waiting for** her brother-in-law to take her in **levirate marriage** or to perform *ḥalitzah,* [81A] [10]**her heirs,** i.e., **the heirs of her ketubah** settlement, [11]**are obligated to bear the costs of her burial."** Thus, we see that the obligation to bury a woman who dies while she was bound by the levirate tie falls upon her husband's heirs, who inherit the ketubah settlement.

RASHI

גמרא **מי קוברה** – משום דיש לה שני יורשין קמבעיא לן. **יורשי הבעל קברי לה דקא ירתי כתובתה** – ותניא בפרק ״נערה שנתפתתה״ (כתובות מז,ב): קבורתה תחת כתובתה. **יורשיה יורשי כתובתה** – אותן יורשים שיורשין כתובתה, חייבין בקבורתה.

NOTES

(p. 82b), understands that the Mishnah means that the husband may not designate for his wife's ketubah utensils which are used at the table. According to *Rabbenu Ḥananel,* the Mishnah teaches that the husband may not place the ketubah money in the woman's safekeeping at the time of her marriage, as though it were resting before her on the table.

מִי קוֹבְרָהּ **Who buries her.** This question makes the most sense if we follow the opinion of those Rishonim who understand that, according to Bet Hillel, the husband's heirs inherit the woman's *tzon barzel* property (see above, note s.v. בחזקתן נכסים). Are the husband's heirs liable for the woman's burial, because they inherit her ketubah settlement, including the *tzon barzel* property she brought into her marriage as her dowry, and the Rabbis enacted that a husband is liable for his wife's burial in exchange for her dowry (see *Ketubot* 47b)? Or do we say that the father's heirs are liable for the woman's burial, because they inherit her *melog* property, and the Rabbis would not have imposed an obligation upon the husband or his heirs to bury a woman if her own heirs succeed to her *melog* property? But according to *Rashi,* who understands that, according to one Talmudic opinion, it is the wife's heirs who succeed to her *tzon barzel* property, we must understand that the Gemara is arguing that the husband's heirs should be liable for the woman's burial, because they inherit her full ketubah settlement. As *Tosafot* and others point out, this creates a problem, for the Gemara states elsewhere (*Ketubot* 2a), that a man is not liable for his betrothed bride's burial because he does not inherit *tzon barzel* property from her. *Tosafot* distinguishes between a widow who dies while waiting for levirate marriage and a woman who dies while she is betrothed to her husband. The widow is viewed as having brought the *levir* a dowry, for she brought him the lien on her late husband's estate in favor of her ketubah settlement. Hence, if the ketubah settlement must be paid, it will not be paid from the *levir*'s assets. Thus, she is different from a woman who dies while betrothed, for she did not bring her husband anything at all. *Ritva* distinguishes between the two women, arguing that the *levir* must bury his sister-in-law, even though he does not inherit her dowry, just as her husband would have been required to do had she died during his lifetime, even if she had not brought a dowry into the marriage; for once the Rabbis enacted that a husband is liable for his wife's burial in exchange for her dowry, it makes no difference whether or not she actually had a dowry. But a man whose wife dies while she is betrothed to him is not liable for her burial, for a betrothed woman never has a dowry, and the Rabbis did not impose the obligation to bury her upon the man to whom she was betrothed.

HALAKHAH

יוֹרְשֶׁיהָ, יוֹרְשֵׁי כְתוּבָּתָהּ **Her heirs, the heirs of her ketubah settlement.** "If a woman dies while she is waiting for levirate marriage, her late husband's heirs, who succeed to her ketubah settlement and half of her *tzon barzel* property, are liable for her burial," following the Gemara's conclusion. (*Rambam, Sefer Nashim, Hilkhot Ishut* 22:10; *Shulḥan Arukh, Even HaEzer* 160:7.)

[1]אֲמַר אַבַּיֵי: אַף אֲנַן נַמִי תָּנֵינָא: [2]״אַלְמָנָה נִיזּוֹנֶת מִנִּכְסֵי יְתוֹמִין, [3]וּמַעֲשֵׂה יָדֶיהָ שֶׁלָּהֶן, [4]וְאֵין חַיָּיבִין בִּקְבוּרָתָהּ. [5]יוֹרְשֶׁיהָ, יוֹרְשֵׁי כְתוּבָּתָהּ, [6]חַיָּיבִין בִּקְבוּרָתָהּ״. [7]וְאֵיזוֹהִי אַלְמָנָה שֶׁיֵּשׁ לָהּ שְׁנֵי יוֹרְשִׁין? [8]הֱוֵי אוֹמֵר: זוֹ שׁוֹמֶרֶת יָבָם. [9]אֲמַר רָבָא: וְלֵימָא: [10]אָח אֲנִי יוֹרֵשׁ; [11]אִשְׁתּוֹ אֵין אֲנִי קוֹבֵר! [12]אֲמַר לֵיהּ אַבַּיֵי: [13]מִשּׁוּם דְּבָאִין עָלָיו מִשְּׁנֵי צְדָדִין: [14]אִם

TRANSLATION AND COMMENTARY

אֲמַר אַבַּיֵי [1]**Abaye said: We too have taught** a Baraita which gives the same ruling: [2]**"A widow is entitled to maintenance from the property** of her husband's estate which passes to **his sons.** She is entitled to be maintained from her late husband's property and to continue living in his house unless she collects her ketubah settlement. Just as the husband was entitled to his wife's handiwork while he was supporting her, [3]so are her late husband's sons **entitled to** the widow's **handiwork** while she is being supported from his estate. Although it is the husband's duty to bear the costs of his wife's burial if she dies during his lifetime, [4]his sons who inherit his estate **are not obligated to** bear the costs of **burying** his widow. [5]Instead, **her heirs, the heirs to her ketubah** settlement, [6]**are obligated to** bear the costs of **her burial."** How do we know that this Baraita refers to a woman who died while she was waiting to be taken in levirate marriage? Because it speaks of "her heirs, the heirs of her ketubah settlement," implying that she has other heirs who do not inherit her ketubah settlement. [7]Now, **which widow has two** sets of **heirs?** [8]**Say: This is a woman who** died while she **was waiting for levirate marriage,** whose estate is divided between her husband's heirs, who inherit her ketubah settlement, and her father's heirs, who do not. The former must bury her.

אֲמַר רָבָא [9]**Rava said: But let** the *levir* who inherits the woman's ketubah settlement **say:** When I inherit the ketubah settlement, [10]it is from **my brother**'s money that **I inherit.** [11]But **I should not** be obligated to **bury** my brother's **wife,** for the obligation to bury one's wife is a duty imposed by marriage, and I was never married to her!

אֲמַר לֵיהּ אַבַּיֵי [12]**Abaye said to** Rava: The obligation to bear the costs of burying the woman falls upon the *levir*, [13]**because we come to him from two sides:** Before he actually marries his sister-in-law, the *levir*'s position can be seen in two ways. Either he stands in his brother's place or he does not. [14]**If,** when the

LITERAL TRANSLATION

[1]Abaye said: We too have also taught: [2]"A widow is maintained from the property of the orphans, [3]and her handiwork is theirs, [4]and they are not obligated to bury her. [5]Her heirs, the heirs of her ketubah, [6]are obligated [to pay for] her burial." [7]And which is the widow who has two heirs? [8]Say: This is a widow who was waiting for levirate marriage.

[9]Rava said: But let him say: [10][From my] brother I shall inherit; [11]his wife I shall not bury!

[12]Abaye said to him: [13]Because we come to him from two sides: [14]If

RASHI

ואין חייבין בקבורתה — דהא בעי למיתב כתובתה ליורשיה. **שיש לה שני יורשים** — דאיצטריך לתנא למיתני אותן יורשין שיורשין כתובתה, שמע מינה — איכא יורשים אחריני בהדייהו, דלא ירתי כתובתה. **אח אני יורש** — כתובה זו שאני יורש — אין כאן מנדוניית אביה כלום, אלא מאתים ותוספת שכתב לה אחי. ואין אני יורש אותה אלא אחי.

NOTES

אָח אֲנִי יוֹרֵשׁ From my brother I shall inherit. The Rishonim note that this argument is well understood according to those authorities who maintain that the husband's heirs are entitled to his wife's ketubah settlement, but not to her *tzon barzel* property. But according to *Rabbenu Tam* and others (see note, p. 80b, s.v. נכסים בחזקתן) who maintain that the woman's *tzon barzel* property remains in the possession of her husband's heirs, this argument is problematic, for the *levir* inherits that property from the widow and not from his brother! Therefore, *Tosafot* explains the argument as follows: Let the *levir* say: I inherit my brother's privileges (his right to the woman's ketubah settlement and her *tzon barzel* property), but I shall not inherit his obligations (his duty to bury her). *Ritva* adds that the *levir* can argue that he should inherit the property, because he succeeds his brother by Torah law, but he should not be obligated to bury his brother's wife, because that duty was imposed by Rabbinic enactment, and only upon the woman's husband. Some Rishonim suggest that the *levir* does not mean to free himself entirely from the obligation to bury his brother's widow, but argues that the obligation should be divided up among her heirs (see *Ramban*, *Rashba* and *Rivash*).

מִשּׁוּם דְּבָאִין עָלָיו מִשְּׁנֵי צְדָדִין Because we come to him from two sides. Some Rishonim explain the passage as follows: Rava first argued that the *levir* can claim that he should inherit the money from his brother, but he should have no obligation to bury his brother's widow to whom he has never been married. Abaye countered by saying that the woman's heirs can argue that, upon the husband's death, his widow became entitled to receive her ketubah settlement. If, as the *levir* wishes to say, he has no obligation to bury the woman, he should pay her heirs the settlement that had been due her. Rava then clarified his position, explaining that the *levir* can indeed argue that he should inherit the money from his brother, but he should

אָחִיו יוֹרֵשׁ [1]יִקְבּוֹר אֶת אִשְׁתּוֹ. [2]אִם אֵינוֹ קוֹבֵר אֶת אִשְׁתּוֹ, [3]יִתֵּן כְּתוּבָּתָהּ.
[4]אֲמַר לֵיהּ: הָכִי קָא אָמִינָא: [5]אָח אֲנִי יוֹרֵשׁ; [6]אֶת אִשְׁתּוֹ אֵין אֲנִי קוֹבֵר. [7]וְאִי מִשּׁוּם כְּתוּבָּה, [8]לֹא נִיתְּנָה כְּתוּבָּה לִגָּבוֹת מֵחַיִּים.
[9]מַאן שָׁמְעַתְּ לֵיהּ דְּאִית לֵיהּ מִדְרַשׁ כְּתוּבָּה? [10]בֵּית שַׁמַּאי. [11]וְשָׁמְעִינַן לְהוּ לְבֵית שַׁמַּאי

LITERAL TRANSLATION

he inherits [from] his brother, [1]he must bury his wife. [2]If he does not bury his wife, [3]he must give her ketubah.

[4]He said to him: Thus I said: [5][From my] brother I shall inherit; [6]his wife I shall not bury. [7]And if because of the ketubah, [8]the ketubah was not given to be collected during the [husband's] lifetime.

[9]Who have you heard that accepts [the validity of] interpreting the ketubah deed? [10]Bet Shammai. [11]And we have heard Bet Shammai

TRANSLATION AND COMMENTARY

levir inherits the widow's ketubah settlement, he is seen as **inheriting** from **his brother** and not from his brother's widow, it must be that the *levir* is viewed as taking his brother's place. Consequently, the ketubah settlement could not yet have been collected by the brother's widow. Now, if that is the case, [1]**the *levir* must bury his** brother's **wife,** since he retains the money that would have been disbursed as the ketubah settlement, he is subject to the concomitant obligations. [2]But **if** the *levir* **is not required to bury his** brother's **wife,** it must be that the *levir* is not seen as standing in his brother's place. If that is the case, [3]then we should say that **the *levir* must** already **have given** his brother's widow **her ketubah** settlement, and so he should not now inherit her property.

אֲמַר לֵיהּ [4]Rava **said to** Abaye: **This is what I said:** Let the *levir* who inherits the woman's ketubah settlement say: [5]It is **my brother** from whom **I inherit.** [6]But **I should not** be obligated to **bury** my brother's **wife,** for the obligation to bury one's wife is a duty imposed by marriage, and I was never married to her. [7]**And if** you argue that I should be liable for the woman's burial **because of the ketubah** settlement that I inherit, [8]**the ketubah was not given to be collected during the** husband's **lifetime.** So, this sum of money never belonged to the wife.

מַאן שָׁמְעַתְּ לֵיהּ [9]The foregoing statement is based on an interpretation of the wording of the ketubah deed, which reads: "When you marry another man, you shall collect what is written for you." That clause implies that, while her husband is alive, she cannot collect her ketubah settlement because she cannot remarry while he is alive. Now **which** Tanna **have you heard accepts the validity of interpreting** the text of **the ketubah deed** in the manner that Halakhic texts are interpreted, so that it can serve as a source of the law? [10]It is **Bet Shammai,** as we have learned elsewhere in the Mishnah (see *Yevamot* 117a). [11]**But** surely

RASHI

יקבור את אשתו — כמו שהיה הוא קוברה אם מתה בחייו, ואפילו לא הכניסה לו כלום. **יתן כתובתה** — שהקבורה באה תחתיה. **לגבות מחיים** — כל זמן שהבעל חי. ואני במקום בעל עומד, שהייתי מצפה לכונסה. **מאן שמעת ליה דאית ליה מדרש כתובה** — שדורש לשון הכתובה, שכתוב בה "לכשתנשאי לאחר תטלי מה שכתוב ליכי" דמינה דייקת: לא ניתנה כתובה לגבות מחיים, דהא אינה יכולה לינשא לאחר. **בית שמאי היא** — ביבמות בפרק "האשה שהלכה", דקאמרי בית שמאי: והלא מספר כתובה נלמד "לכשתנשאי לאחר תטלי מה שכתוב ליכי" והואיל והיא נישאת על פי עצמה, שבאה ואמרה מת בעלי — אף כתובתה גובה על פי עצמה. **ושמעינן להו לבית שמאי** — שמי שיש לו שטר חוב על חבירו, הוא מוחזק בנכסי הלוה יותר ממנו.

NOTES

not be obligated to bury the widow. As for the woman's ketubah settlement, the *levir* can argue that he had been ready to take his brother's widow as his levirate wife, in which case she would not have been entitled to receive her ketubah. But now that she has died, he should bear no further obligation towards her.

דְּאִית לֵיהּ מִדְרַשׁ כְּתוּבָּה **That he maintains that there is the exposition of the ketubah.** According to some Rishonim, Bet Hillel do not at all accept the validity of interpreting the text of the ketubah deed so that it can serve as a source of the law. Thus, whenever Bet Hillel accept a law which the Gemara bases on the interpretation of the text of the ketubah deed, it cannot be on the basis of that interpretation, but rather for some other reason. *Rabbenu Tam* maintains that Bet Hillel do not interpret the ketubah deed as precisely as do Bet Shammai, but at times they agree that the text of the ketubah deed can serve as a source of the law (see *Tosafot,* s.v. והא). *Tosafot* argues (s.v. מאן) that, according to the Gemara's conclusion, Bet Hillel might not disagree with Bet Shammai about the validity of interpreting the text of the ketubah deed.

HALAKHAH

לֹא נִיתְּנָה כְּתוּבָּה לִגָּבוֹת מֵחַיִּים **The ketubah settlement was not given to be collected during the husband's lifetime.** "A woman's ketubah settlement is similar to a debt which is due at a specified date, for it can only be collected after her husband dies or grants her a divorce." (*Rambam, Sefer Nashim, Hilkhot Ishut* 16:3; *Shulḥan Arukh, Even HaEzer* 93:1.)

דְּאָמְרִי: [1]שְׁטָר הָעוֹמֵד לִגָּבוֹת כִּגְבוּי דָּמֵי.
[2]דִּתְנַן: [3]"מֵתוּ בַּעֲלֵיהֶן עַד שֶׁלֹּא שָׁתוּ, [4]בֵּית שַׁמַּאי אוֹמְרִים: נוֹטְלוֹת כְּתוּבָּה [5]וְלֹא שׁוֹתוֹת. [6]וּבֵית הִלֵּל אוֹמְרִים: אוֹ שׁוֹתוֹת אוֹ לֹא נוֹטְלוֹת כְּתוּבָּה".
[7]"אוֹ שׁוֹתוֹת"?! [8]"וְהֵבִיא הָאִישׁ אֶת אִשְׁתּוֹ אֶל הַכֹּהֵן" אָמַר רַחֲמָנָא, [9]וְלֵיכָּא!
[10]אֶלָּא מִתּוֹךְ שֶׁלֹּא שׁוֹתוֹת,

LITERAL TRANSLATION

that they say: [1]A bill [of indebtedness] which stands to be collected is considered collected.
[2]For we have learned: [3]"[If] their husbands died before they drank, [4]Bet Shammai say: They take the ketubah [5]and do not drink. [6]And Bet Hillel say: Either they drink or they do not take the ketubah."
[7]"Either they drink!?" [8]"And the man shall bring his wife to the priest," the Torah (lit., "the Merciful") said, [9]and there is not!
[10]Rather, since they do not drink

RASHI

כגבוי דמי – והנכסים בחזקתה, הלכך מינה קא ירית. מתו בעליהן – אכל הנשים שבעולם קאי. שקינאו להן בעליהן ונסתרו, ולא הספיק להשקותה עד שמת. ולא שותות – דבעינן "והביא האיש את אשתו".

TRANSLATION AND COMMENTARY

we have heard that Bet Shammai also **maintain:** [1]**A bill of indebtedness which stands to be collected is considered collected,** so that the creditor is viewed as having presumptive possession of the debtor's property that was mortgaged to the debt. Thus, it follows that while a woman cannot collect her ketubah settlement during her husband's lifetime, it is considered collected, so that she is viewed as having presumptive possession of her husband's property which was mortgaged to guarantee the ketubah settlement. Hence, the *levir* should not be able to argue that he inherited his brother's widow's ketubah settlement from his brother, for the property mortgaged to guarantee it was already in the woman's presumptive possession.

דִּתְנַן [2]To clarify the difference between Bet Shammai and Bet Hillel regarding a wife's presumptive possession of the ketubah settlement, **elsewhere** (*Sotah* 24a) **we have learned** in a Mishnah dealing with a woman suspected of marital infidelity (see Numbers 5:11-31): If a man has doubts about his wife's fidelity, he must warn her in the presence of witnesses against being alone with the specific man about whom he is suspicious. If she disobeys this warning and is observed alone with that man, she and her husband can no longer live together as man and wife until she has undergone the following test to determine whether she has committed adultery. The woman is taken to the Temple in Jerusalem and questioned about her behavior. If she takes an oath that she has been faithful, a scroll is brought on which are written the curses mentioned in the Torah passage dealing with a woman suspected of adultery. If she still does not admit that she has committed adultery, the scroll is submerged in a vessel filled with water, and the scroll's writing is dissolved in the water. She is then forced to drink the water. If she is guilty of adultery, her belly will swell, and she will die. If she is innocent, the water will bring her blessing and she is permitted to resume normal marital relations with her husband. [3]"**If the husband** warned his wife against being alone with a specific man, and she was later observed alone with him, but her husband **died before she drank** of the bitter water, so that the question of her guilt or innocence was not resolved, [4]**Bet Shammai say:** The widow **may collect her ketubah** settlement **from** her husband's estate, for a bill of indebtedness which stands to be collected is considered collected [as will be explained below]. [5]**And she does not drink** the bitter water, for the verse states [Numbers 5:15]: 'And the man shall bring his wife to the priest.' Only her jealous husband may bring her to the priest, and here the husband is dead. [6]**Bet Hillel** disagree and **say: Either she drinks** the bitter water **or she may not collect her ketubah** settlement."

אוֹ שׁוֹתוֹת [7]Before analyzing Bet Shammai's position, the Gemara asks: Do Bet Hillel really say: **"Either** the woman **drinks** the bitter water or she may not collect her ketubah settlement!?" How can the woman drink the bitter water? [8]Surely **the verse states: "And the man shall bring his wife to the priest,"** [9]**and** here **there is no** husband to bring the woman to the priest!

אֶלָּא [10]The Gemara answers: **Rather, since** the woman **cannot drink** the bitter water — for her dead husband

NOTES

אֶלָּא מִתּוֹךְ שֶׁלֹּא שׁוֹתוֹת **Rather, since they do not drink.** *Rivash* notes that the Gemara does not mean to revise the text

HALAKHAH

מֵתוּ בַּעֲלֵיהֶן עַד שֶׁלֹּא שָׁתוּ **If their husbands died before they drank.** "If a man warned his wife against being alone with a specific man, and she was later observed alone with him, and the husband died before she drank the bitter water, she may not drink the water, nor may she collect her ketubah." (*Rambam, Sefer Nashim, Hilkhot Sotah* 2:7; see *Shulḥan Arukh, Even HaEzer* 178:1.)

[1] לֹא נוֹטְלוֹת כְּתוּבָּה.
[2] בֵּית שַׁמַּאי אוֹמְרִים: [3] ״נוֹטְלוֹת כְּתוּבָּה וְלֹא שׁוֹתוֹת״. [4] וְאַמַּאי? [5] סְפֵיקָא הוּא, [6] סָפֵק זְנַאי, [7] סָפֵק לָא זְנַאי. [8] וְקָאָתֵי סָפֵק [9] וּמוֹצִיא מִידֵי וַדַּאי!
[10] קָסָבְרִי בֵּית שַׁמַּאי: [11] שְׁטָר הָעוֹמֵד לִגָּבוֹת כְּגָבוּי דָּמֵי.
[12] וְהָא בָּעֵינַן: [13] ״כְּשֶׁתִּנָּשְׂאִי

LITERAL TRANSLATION

[1] they do not take the ketubah.
[2] "Bet Shammai say: [3] They take the ketubah and do not drink." [4] And why? [5] It is [in] doubt, [6] perhaps she committed adultery, [7] perhaps she did not commit adultery. [8] And the doubt comes [9] and takes away from the certain!
[10] Bet Shammai maintain: [11] A bill [of indebtedness] which stands to be collected is considered collected.
[12] But surely we need: [13] "When you marry

RASHI

ספק זנאי — והפסידה כתובה. **מידי ודאי** — מידי יורשי הבעל, שהן ודאין בירושה. **בגבוי דמי** — והיא מוחזקת בנכסים יותר מהן, ואין כאן מוציא מידי ודאי. **והא בעינן לכשתנשאי כו׳** — אלעיל פריך: סוף סוף, היאך כתובה ניגבת מחיים, שנוכל לבא עליו משני צדדים? והא בעינן כו׳.

TRANSLATION AND COMMENTARY

cannot bring her to the priest — [1] she also **may not collect her ketubah** settlement. The burden of proof that she has been faithful and is entitled to the settlement falls upon the woman, for it is she who wishes to collect the money from her husband's heirs. Since she cannot drink the bitter water and thus establish her innocence, she also cannot collect her ketubah settlement.

בֵּית שַׁמַּאי אוֹמְרִים [2] By contrast, **"Bet Shammai say:** [3] The woman **may collect her ketubah** settlement, **and she does not drink** the bitter water." [4] The Gemara asks: **Why** may the woman collect the settlement? [5] Surely **there is a doubt about** her right to it, [6] for **perhaps she committed adultery** when she was alone with the man whom she had been warned to stay away from, [7] or **perhaps she did not commit adultery** with him. There is, however, no doubt about the right of the husband's heirs to his estate. [8] **And** nevertheless Bet Shammai maintain that **the** woman's claim to her ketubah settlement, which is in **doubt,** [9] allows her to **come and take** money **away from** her husband's heirs, whose right to the property of the estate is **certain!** This violates a general rule that a plaintiff in a civil suit cannot take money away from a defendant who is presumed to have rightful ownership of the property in his possession, unless the plaintiff can prove his claim, and here the woman is unable to prove her claim.

קָסָבְרִי בֵּית שַׁמַּאי [10] The Gemara explains: **Bet Shammai maintain:** [11] **A bill of indebtedness which stands to be collected is considered collected,** so that the creditor is viewed as having presumptive possession of the debtor's property that was mortgaged to the debt. This principle also applies to the ketubah settlement. Hence, a woman who had been suspected of infidelity, and whose husband died before she drank from the bitter water, may collect her ketubah settlement, for she is presumed to have rightful ownership of the property mortgaged to guarantee it, and her husband's heirs who wish to deny her the settlement are seen as seeking to take money from her with the doubtful claim that perhaps she committed adultery.

וְהָא בָּעֵינַן [12] The Gemara now raises an objection against Abaye, who argued that the obligation to bear the costs of burying a widow who had been waiting to be taken in levirate marriage should fall upon the *levir* because we come to him from two sides: How can it be argued that the *levir* should be seen as having inherited his brother's widow's ketubah settlement from her, and not from his brother? **But surely** the woman had never been entitled to collect her ketubah settlement, for in order for a woman to collect it, the terms of the ketubah deed had to be fulfilled. The ketubah deed reads: [13] **"When you marry another man, you**

NOTES

of the Mishnah, but rather to explain it. Bet Hillel maintain that the woman must either drink the bitter water, or forfeit her right to collect her ketubah. And since her husband is dead, and she cannot drink the bitter water, she may also not collect her ketubah.

קָסָבְרִי בֵּית שַׁמַּאי שְׁטָר Bet Shammai maintain: A bill of indebtedness. *Rosh* asks: Why does the Gemara understand Bet Shammai's rationale as it does, and not as follows? The widow's claim that she did not commit adultery was put forward with certainty, and the heirs' claim that she was guilty of adultery was not put forward with certainty. Since there is a general rule that if one party put forward his claim with certainty, and the other party did not, we accept the claim that was put forward with certainty, and Bet Shammai rule that we accept the woman's claim and allow her to collect her ketubah settlement. But *Rosh* answers that that rule does not apply in our case. The widow's certain claim is defective, since she knows that it cannot be refuted by her husband's heirs, and the heirs' uncertain claim is particularly strong, because the widow had secluded herself with a man despite her husband's warning.

וְהָא בָּעֵינַן כְּשֶׁתִּנָּשְׂאִי But surely we need: "When you marry." If the Gemara assumes that Bet Shammai's position is correct, it has already demonstrated that Bet Shammai maintain that a bill of indebtedness which stands to be collected is considered collected, and so a woman is viewed as having presumptive possession of her ketubah

לְאַחֵר, תִּטְלִי מַה שֶּׁכָּתוּב לֵיכִי״, [1] וְלֵיכָּא!
[2] אֲמַר רַב אַשִׁי: יָבָם נַמִי כְּאַחֵר דָּמֵי.
[3] שְׁלַח לֵיהּ רָבָא לְאַבַּיֵי בְּיַד רַב שְׁמַעְיָה בַּר זֵירָא: [4] וּמִי נִתְּנָה כְּתוּבָּה לִגָּבוֹת מֵחַיִּים?
[5] וְהָתַנְיָא: [6] ״רַבִּי אַבָּא אוֹמֵר: שָׁאַלְתִּי אֶת סוּמָכוֹס: [7] הָרוֹצֶה שֶׁיִּמְכּוֹר בְּנִכְסֵי אָחִיו, [8] כֵּיצַד

LITERAL TRANSLATION

another man, you shall take what was written to you," [1] and there is not!

[2] Rav Ashi said: The *levir* is also considered as another man.

[3] Rava sent to Abaye in the hand of Rav Shema'yah bar Zera: [4] But is the ketubah given to be collected during the [*levir*'s] lifetime?

[5] But surely it was taught: [6] "Rabbi Abba says: I asked Summakhos: [7] [If] someone wishes to sell his brother's property, [8] how

RASHI

יבם נמי כאחר דמי – וכיון שהתירתה מיתת הבעל לינשא ליבם – מאותה שעה זכתה בנכסים. **שלח ליה רבא לאביי** – לאחר שהשיבו על שאלתו, ואמר: ניתנה כתובת יבמה לגבות מחיים של יבם. **ביד רב שמעיה** – הוא היה שליח בתשובה זו. **ומי נתנה** – כתובת יבמה לגבות מחיים דיבם. **שימכור בנכסי אחיו** – לאחר שכנס את יבמתו, ואמרן לעיל: כל נכסיו אחראין לכתובתה.

TRANSLATION AND COMMENTARY

shall collect what was written for you," [1] and this **was not** fulfilled. The woman had been bound by the levirate tie, and unable to marry another man!

אֲמַר רַב אַשִׁי [2] **Rav Ashi said:** Regarding this matter, **the *levir* is also considered "another man."** So, since her husband's death permitted the woman to marry her brother-in-law, she was entitled to her ketubah settlement. Thus, the *levir* inherits the widow's ketubah settlement from the widow herself, and not from his late brother, and therefore he should pay her burial expenses.

שְׁלַח לֵיהּ [3] Some time afterwards, **Rava sent** the following question **to Abaye by way of Rav Shema'yah bar Zera:** [4] **But is a** levirate wife's **ketubah** settlement really **given to be collected during the *levir*'s lifetime,** so that if she dies, the *levir* should be seen as inheriting her ketubah settlement from the woman herself?

וְהָתַנְיָא [5] **But surely it was taught** otherwise in a Baraita: [6] **"Rabbi Abba says: I asked Summakhos:** [7] **If the** *levir* married his brother's widow and now **wishes to sell his brother's property,** but is barred from doing so because all the property is mortgaged to guarantee his wife's ketubah settlement, [8] **what should he do?**

NOTES

settlement even before it is collected. Thus the question appears to be unnecessary. And if the Gemara adopts the view of Bet Hillel, we have already said that Bet Hillel do not accept the validity of interpreting the text of the ketubah deed in the manner that Halakhic texts are interpreted! Thus, what position does the Gemara's question represent? The Rishonim suggest that the Gemara accepts the position of Bet Hillel. Bet Hillel do not accept the validity of interpreting the text of the ketubah deed in order to strengthen a woman's claim to her ketubah settlement when she was permitted to remarry on the basis of her own declaration that her husband was dead, but they might indeed accept the validity of interpreting the ketubah deed in order to free the *levir* from the duty of burying her. Alternatively, the Gemara might accept the position of Bet Shammai. Even though Bet Shammai maintain that a bill of indebtedness which stands to be collected is considered collected, that principle can only be applied in the case of the woman who had been suspected of adultery or the like, whose husband died, and who was permitted to remarry, so that her ketubah settlement could be considered as having been ready for collection. But here, in the case of the widow who died while she was waiting to be taken in levirate marriage, the clause of the ketubah, "When you marry another man, you shall take what was written to you," was not fulfilled, and so the settlement was never about to be collected (*Tosafot, Rivan, Ritva*).

יָבָם נַמִי כְּאַחֵר דָּמֵי The *levir* is also considered as another man. The Rishonim ask: Elsewhere (*Kiddushin* 13b), regarding the verse (Deuteronomy 20:7): "And another man take her," the Gemara argues that the *levir* is not considered "another man." *Tosafot* argues that the Biblical term "another man" does not apply to a *levir*, but the identical Rabbinic term does indeed apply to him. *Meiri* explains that the Gemara in *Kiddushin* does not mean that the *levir* is not considered "another man," but rather that the verse, "And another man take her," should not be understood as referring exclusively to the *levir*. *Ramban* suggests that the Gemara in *Kiddushin* means that the verse, "And another man take her," cannot be referring to a *levir*, for that verse is trying to discourage a bridegroom from going out to war, lest he die and another man take his wife, and, on the contrary, the bridegroom will be encouraged to go out to war if he knows that his brother will take his widow as his levirate wife, and his name will not be wiped out. *Ramat Shmuel* argues that the *levir* is indeed considered "another man," but the expression, "And another man take her [יִקָּחֶנָּה]," implies that that verse refers not to the *levir*, but to another man who takes the woman in ordinary marriage.

הָרוֹצֶה שֶׁיִּמְכּוֹר בְּנִכְסֵי אָחִיו If someone wishes to sell his brother's property. According to our Gemara's conclusion, the *levir* may not sell any of the property that he inherited from his brother, for it is all mortgaged to guarantee his widow's ketubah settlement, and if he sold any of the property, the sale is void. But an ordinary husband is not restricted in the same way. He may sell the property, and if he did not leave himself enough to pay his wife's ketubah settlement, if she is widowed or divorced, she can seize the property that her husband sold. *Rashi* and others

SAGES

רַבִּי אַבָּא Rabbi Abba. A Geonic tradition asserts that the "Rabbi Abba" (or "Rav Abba," according to some texts) mentioned here is the Babylonian Amora Rav. This stands to reason, chronologically, since Summakhos was an outstanding disciple of Rabbi Meir and a contemporary of Rav's teacher, Rabbi Yehudah HaNasi. The Baraita refers to Rav by his real name, Rabbi Abba, rather than by the term "Rav," as he was called in Babylonia. This also conforms with the Gemara's statement elsewhere that "Rav is a Tanna, and he disagrees" with other Tannaitic teachings, since the Rabbi Abba quoted here is a Tanna, albeit a relatively late one.

הוּא עוֹשֶׂה? [1]אִם כֹּהֵן הוּא, [2]יַעֲשֶׂה סְעוּדָה וִיפַיֵּיס. [3]אִם יִשְׂרָאֵל הוּא, [4]מְגָרֵשׁ בְּגֵט וְיַחֲזִיר״. [81B] [5]וְאִי סָלְקָא דַּעְתִּין נִתְּנָה כְּתוּבָּה לִגָּבוֹת מֵחַיִּים, [6]נְיַיחֵד לָהּ שִׁיעוּר כְּתוּבָּה, [7]וְהַשְּׁאָר לִיזְבִּין! [8]וּלְטַעֲמִיךְ, [9]וְלוֹתְבָהּ מִמַּתְנִיתִין:

LITERAL TRANSLATION

should he act? [1]If he is a priest, [2]he should prepare a banquet and appease [his wife]. [3]If he is an Israelite, [4]he should divorce her with a bill of divorce and remarry her." [5]And if we think [that] the ketubah is given to be collected during the [husband's] lifetime, [6]let him designate [property] in the amount of the ketubah, [7]and the rest he can sell!

[8]And according to your opinion, [9]let him ask from our Mishnah:

TRANSLATION AND COMMENTARY

[1]Summakhos answered: **If** the *levir* **is a priest,** who is forbidden to take his wife back after he divorces her (for a priest is forbidden to marry a divorcee, even his own), [2]**he should prepare a** special **banquet** in his wife's honor, **and persuade her** to grant him permission to sell a portion of his brother's estate which will not be needed to cover her ketubah settlement. [3]And **if** the *levir* **is an** ordinary **Israelite** who is permitted to divorce his wife and then take her back again, [4]**he should divorce** the woman **with a bill of divorce, and** then **remarry her.** The *levir* is barred from selling his brother's property because it is all mortgaged to guarantee his wife's ketubah settlement. But if he divorces her and then takes her back as an ordinary wife, he may sell the property that he inherited from his brother, just as any other husband is permitted to sell his property, even though it is mortgaged to guarantee his wife's ketubah settlement." [81B] [5]**And if we think that the** widow's **ketubah** settlement **is given to be collected during the** *levir*'s **lifetime,** why should it be necessary for the *levir* to divorce her in order to sell his late brother's property? [6]**Let him designate property in the amount of the** woman's **ketubah,** [7]**and** then **he should be able to sell the rest** of the property!

וּלְטַעֲמִיךְ [8]Abaye sent back the following answer: **According to your opinion,** Rabbi Abba's ruling that the *levir* must first divorce his wife if he wishes to sell his brother's property proves that the woman's ketubah settlement is not to be collected while she is married to the *levir*. But why seek a solution in Rabbi Abba's ruling in the Baraita? [9]**Ask from our Mishnah, where** we learned: "If the *levir* married his

RASHI

אם כהן הוא — שאם יגרשנה לא יוכל להחזירה. **יעשה לה סעודה** — יפה, לפתותה במשתה היין. **ויפייס** — הימנה, שתתן לו רשות למכור את העודף על כדי כתובתה. **ואם ישראל הוא** — שמותר להחזיר גרושתו. **מגרשה בגט** — ומגבה את כתובתה, ומוכר מה שירצה, ומחזירה על מנת כתובתה הראשונה. או אפילו רצה להחזירה מיד — מוכר כל זמן שירצה. שאין מעכבת מלמכור אלא יבמה, לפי שאין היבם כותב לה כתובה, ולא כתב לה "דקנאי ודקנינא" ואין כתובתה אלא על הראשון. ומשום הכי מעכבא בכולהו — דלמא משתדפי הני דמייחד לה. ואף על גב דאמר לקמן (כתובות נה,ב) אישתדוף בני חרי טרפא ממשעבדי — מכל מקום אמרה: איני רוצה לטרוח לבית דין. אבל כתב לה כתובה כשמחזירה, וכתב לה "דקנאי ודקנינא" — לא מציא מעכבא. והא דתנן (גיטין נה,ב): לקח מן האיש וחזר ולקח מן האשה — מקחו בטל, אוקמינן באותן שלש שדות: אחת שכתב לה בכתובתה, ואחת שייחד לה בכתובתה, ואחת שהכניסה לו שום משלה. **ולטעמיך** — דאמרת טעמא משום דלא ניתנה כתובה ליגבות מחיים, אמאי מהדרת אדרבי אבא לאותובי מברייתא — אותיב ממתניתין! ומשני: ממתניתין לא מותיבנא, דמתניתין איכא לשנויי: דלאו דינא קתני אלא עצה טובה, שלא תאבד כתובתה.

NOTES

explain that the Rabbis were more stringent with the *levir* because he does not guarantee his brother's widow a ketubah settlement from his own property. Thus, the widow may prevent him from selling any of her late husband's property, for she is afraid that the remaining property might be ruined and she will be unable to collect her ketubah settlement. Even though she, too, can seize her late husband's property from the buyer, she does not want to go to court to collect her ketubah settlement. And even though the Gemara concludes (below, p. 82b) that if the woman does not have a ketubah deed from her first husband, she can collect her ketubah settlement from her second husband? This ruling does not apply if her husband left property but it was sold. Moreover, if she collects from her late husband's property, she is entitled to two hundred dinars, but if she collects from the *levir*'s property, she may collect only a hundred dinars (*Ritva;* see note, below, p. 82b, s.v. איה לה משני). An ordinary wife may not prevent her husband from selling property, for the husband mortgaged all his property in the woman's favor, including what he will buy in the future. Hence the woman is not afraid that she will be unable to collect her ketubah settlement.

מְגָרֵשׁ בְּגֵט וְיַחֲזִיר He should divorce her with a bill of divorce. How does it help if the *levir* divorces his wife, and then remarries her? When the *levir* takes the woman back as his wife, he takes her back on the basis of what she was guaranteed in her first ketubah! The Rishonim explain: The Baraita means that the *levir* may sell some of the property of his brother's estate while he is divorced. But once he takes her back as his wife, he may indeed no longer sell the property, for he remarried the woman on the basis of her original ketubah deed. Alternatively, the Baraita means that the *levir* should divorce his wife and pay her her ketubah (or obtain a receipt from the woman

TRANSLATION AND COMMENTARY

brother's widow, [1]**he may not** set aside money and **say to her:** [2]**'Your ketubah** settlement **rests** before you **on the table,** and I will sell or give away the rest of the property that I inherited from my brother,' [3]**but rather all of the property** that the *levir* inherited from his brother **is mortgaged to** guarantee the woman's **ketubah** settlement."

הָתָם עֵצָה טוֹבָה [4]The Gemara rebuts this argument: Rava could not have asked on the basis of our Mishnah. **There** the Mishnah does not mean to say that the *levir* may not set aside money and say to his brother's widow: "Your ketubah settlement rests before you on the table," but rather **it advises** the levir not to do so. [5]**For if you do not say** that the Mishnah means to offer advice rather than issue a prohibition, [6]then a difficulty arises with respect to **the next clause** of the Mishnah, **which states:** [7]**"A** similar law applies in general, that **a person may not** set aside a sum of money and **say to her:** [8]**'Your ketubah** settlement **rests** before you **on the table,'** [9]but rather all of his property is mortgaged to her ketubah." [10]For is it possible to say that **here, too,** if the husband **wishes to sell** some of his property which is mortgaged to guarantee his wife's ketubah settlement, **he may not do** so? Surely the lien that a woman has on her husband's assets in favor of her ketubah settlement does not prevent him from selling his property! [11]**Rather,** we must understand that this clause of the Mishnah **advises** him not to designate money as his wife's ketubah settlement. [12]If so, then **here, too,** regarding the levirate wife, we may understand that the Mishnah **advises** the *levir* not to set aside money for the woman's ketubah settlement, but it does not mean to imply that doing so is forbidden.

LITERAL TRANSLATION

[1]"He may not say to her: [2]'Your ketubah lies on the table,' [3]but rather all of his property is mortgaged to guarantee her ketubah."

[4]There it teaches us sound advice. [5]For if you do not say thus, [6]the last clause which states: [7]"And similarly, a man may not say to his wife: [8]'Your ketubah lies on the table,' [9]but rather all of his property is mortgaged to guarantee her ketubah" — [10]if he wishes to sell, here, too, may he not sell? [11]Rather, it teaches us sound advice. [12]Here, too, it teaches us sound advice.

[1]"לֹא יֹאמַר לָהּ: [2]'הֲרֵי כְתוּבָּתֵיךְ מוּנַחַת לִיךְ עַל הַשֻּׁלְחָן', [3]אֶלָּא כָּל נְכָסָיו אַחֲרָאִין לִכְתוּבָּתָהּ"! [4]הָתָם עֵצָה טוֹבָה קָא מַשְׁמַע לָן. [5]דְּאִי לָא תֵּימָא הָכִי, [6]סֵיפָא דְּקָתָנֵי: [7]"וְכֵן לֹא, יֹאמַר אָדָם לְאִשְׁתּוֹ: [8]'הֲרֵי כְתוּבָּתֵיךְ מוּנַחַת לִיךְ עַל הַשֻּׁלְחָן', [9]אֶלָּא כָּל נְכָסָיו אַחֲרָאִין לִכְתוּבַּת אִשְׁתּוֹ" — [10]אִי בָּעֵי לֵיהּ לְזַבּוּנֵי, הָכָא נַמִי, דְּלָא מָצֵי מְזַבֵּין?! [11]אֶלָּא, עֵצָה טוֹבָה קָמַשְׁמַע לָן. [12]הָכָא נַמִי עֵצָה טוֹבָה קָמַשְׁמַע לָן.

RASHI

עַל הַשֻּׁלְחָן — הֵן מָעוֹת שֶׁהוּא מִשְׁתַּמֵּשׁ בָּהֶן, אִם הוּא שׁוּלְחָנִי. הָכִי נַמִי דְּלָא מָצֵי מְזַבֵּין — בִּתְמִיהַּ. הָא אוֹקִימְנָא לְהָהִיא בְּאוֹתָן שָׁלֹשׁ שָׂדוֹת. אֲבָל מִי שֶׁלֹּא כָּתַב וְלֹא יִחֵד — מוֹכֵר הַכֹּל, וְאֵינָהּ יְכוֹלָה לַעֲכֵב עָלָיו. וְטַעֲמָא — מִשּׁוּם דְּכָתַב לָהּ "דִּקְנַאִי וּדְקָנֵינָא". וּמִיהוּ, כְּשֶׁיָּמוּת אוֹ יְגָרְשֶׁנָה — טֹרְפָה לְקוּחוֹת. עֵצָה טוֹבָה — שֶׁמָּא יֹאבְדוּ הַמִּטַּלְטְלִין, וְנִמְצֵאת בְּלֹא כְתוּבָּה, וְצָרִיךְ לִכְתּוֹב כְּתוּבָּה אַחֶרֶת.

NOTES

that the ketubah has been paid out; following the Tosefta and the Jerusalem Talmud). He should then remarry her, writing her a new ketubah in favor of which he mortgages all of his property. Since the woman received her original ketubah settlement, and all of the *levir's* property is mortgaged to guarantee her new ketubah settlement, the *levir* may sell his brother's property, just as any other husband is permitted to sell his property (see *Rashi, Rivan,* and *Talmidei Rabbenu Yonah*).

הָתָם עֵצָה טוֹבָה **There it teaches us sound advice.** The Rishonim disagree about how to understand this "sound advice." Our commentary follows *Rashi* (which is also *Ritva's* second explanation), who understands that the Mishnah advises the husband not to set aside property for his wife's ketubah settlement, for the property might get lost and he will have to set aside other property in its place. *Tosafot* points out that this is only valid according to Rabbi Meir, who maintains that a man may not keep a

woman as his wife if she does not have a ketubah. *Tosafot* therefore suggests (as does *Rivan*) that the Mishnah means to advise the husband not to set aside property for his wife's ketubah settlement, so as not to make it easy for him to divorce her. *Rabbi Shimshon of Sens* suggests that the Mishnah advises the husband not to designate property for his wife's ketubah, because he would then be barred from selling it. But as long as there is a general lien on all of his property in favor of his wife's ketubah, he can sell any part of the property he wishes. *Shittah Mekubbetzet* notes that this last explanation is only valid with respect to a regular wife, but not to a levirate wife, for the *levir* can never sell any of his brother's property, all of it being designated for his widow's ketubah settlement. He adds that this explains why the Mishnah discusses separately the law regarding the levirate wife and that concerning the regular wife, for they are based on different principles.

TRANSLATION AND COMMENTARY

אֶלָּא [1] The Gemara now returns to Rava's question: **Rather,** the Baraita that cites the position **of Rabbi Abba is problematic** according to Abaye! For Rabbi Abba would surely not advise the *levir* to divorce his wife, unless there were no other way for him to sell his late brother's property. If, indeed, Rabbi Abba rules that the *levir* must divorce the woman if he wishes to sell the property, it must be that he may not designate property in the amount of her ketubah and then sell the rest of the estate! Hence it follows that the woman's ketubah is not to be collected during the *levir*'s lifetime, against Abaye!

דְּרַבִּי אַבָּא [2] The Gemara answers: **Rabbi Abba's** ruling **is also not problematic** for Abaye. Rabbi Abba does not suggest that the *levir* designate property for his wife's ketubah settlement because it is not to be collected while she is married to him. Rather, the *levir* may not designate property for the payment of his wife's ketubah settlement, [3] **because of the enmity** between the husband and the wife to which that action will give rise: She will suspect that he plans to divorce her, and so their relationship will sour. But if the *levir* divorces his wife and then takes her back, their relationship will not be affected, for she will understand that he divorced her only in order to sell his brother's property.

הַהוּא גַּבְרָא [4] It was related that **there was a certain man** living **in the** city of **Pumbedita before whom came a woman for levirate marriage,** he being the eldest brother of a man who died childless, and therefore the one obliged to carry out levirate marriage or *ḥalitzah*. [5] The *levir*'s younger **brother wished to disqualify** the woman **to him by** forcing upon her **a bill of divorce.** The Rabbis decreed that if a widow has received a bill of divorce from one of her late husband's brothers, she becomes disqualified for levirate marriage to any of his other brothers. [6] The *levir* who wished to marry his sister-in-law **said to** his brother who wished to disqualify her to him: **"What is on your mind?** [7] Are you envious of me **on account of the property** I will inherit if I marry her? For if I take her in levirate marriage, I will inherit our brother's entire estate, whereas if you give her a bill of divorce, thus making *ḥalitzah* necessary, the estate will be divided evenly among the brothers! If this is your consideration, you have nothing to worry about. Let me take our brother's widow as my levirate wife, and [8] **I will share** our brother's **property with you."** The *levir* then took

[1] אֶלָּא, דְּרַבִּי אַבָּא קַשְׁיָא!
[2] דְּרַבִּי אַבָּא נַמִּי לָא קַשְׁיָא: [3] מִשּׁוּם אֵיבָה.
[4] הַהוּא גַּבְרָא דְּנָפְלָה לֵיהּ יְבָמָה, בְּפוּמְבְּדִיתָא. [5] בָּעֵי אֲחוּהּ לְמִפְסְלָהּ לָהּ בְּגִיטָּא מִינֵּיהּ. [6] אֲמַר לֵיהּ: "מַאי דַּעְתֵּיךְ — [7] מִשּׁוּם נִכְסֵי? [8] אֲנָא

LITERAL TRANSLATION

[1] Rather, that of Rabbi Abba is difficult!

[2] That of Rabbi Abba is also not difficult: [3] Because of enmity.

[4] [There was] a certain man before whom fell a woman for levirate marriage in Pumbedita. [5] His brother wished to disqualify her to him with a bill of divorce. [6] He said to him: "What is on your mind — [7] because of the property? [8] I

RASHI

אלא דרבי אבא קשיא — אלמגרש לה — נייחד לה, שהרי גירושין גלאי הן לשניהם. אלא ודאי טעמא — דלא ניתנה כתובה להגבותה מחיים. **משום איבה** — המייחד לאשתו או קרקע או מטלטלין — נותן איבת עולם ביניהם, דסברה: עיניו נותן בגירושין. אבל זה שמגרש על מנת שיחזיר — ידעה דלא עשה אלא למכור, ופקעה לה איבה. **דנפלה ליה יבמה** — דמלוה בגדול לייבם. **בעא אחוה** — הקטן ממנו. **למיפסלה בגיטא** — לזרוק לה גט, ולאסרה על כל האחין, כדאמרינן בפרק קמא דיבמות. **משום נבסי** — קשה בעיניך שאכניסנה, שלא אזכה בנכסי אחי, כדתנן (יבמות מ,א): הכונס את יבמתו — זכה בנכסי אחיו.

NOTES

מִשּׁוּם אֵיבָה **Because of enmity.** According to *Tosafot* (and apparently *Rashi* as well), this explanation regarding enmity applies to all women, a levirate wife and a regular wife. *Rabbenu Crescas Vidal* understands that the argument of enmity applies only to the levirate wife. Since the *levir* does not write the woman a ketubah from his own property, she starts off already feeling insecure about her marriage. If the *levir* designates property for the payment of her ketubah settlement, she will constantly suspect that he did so because he plans to divorce her, and their relationship will be adversely affected.

נָפְלָה לֵיהּ יְבָמָה **Before whom fell a woman for levirate marriage.** When the deceased is survived by several brothers, the obligation of levirate marriage or *ḥalitzah* falls upon the eldest brother. If he does not want to take his sister-in-law in levirate marriage, or to perform *ḥalitzah*, each of the other brothers in descending order of age is asked whether he is willing to marry the widow. If none of the brothers want to marry her, the eldest brother can then be compelled to perform *ḥalitzah*, if he still refuses to marry her.

The Rabbis disqualified the woman for levirate marriage, because they were concerned that people might mistakenly conclude that, just as a bill of divorce has no effect, so too does *ḥalitzah* have no effect, and the *levir* might have sexual intercourse with the woman after *ḥalitzah* has been performed.

בְּנִכְסֵי פָּלֵיגְנָא לָךְ״. [1]אֲמַר רַב יוֹסֵף: כֵּיוָן דַּאֲמוּר רַבָּנַן לָא לִיזְבֵּין, [2]אַף עַל גַּב דְּזַבֵּין, לָא הֲוָה זְבִינֵיהּ זְבִינֵי.

[3]דְּתַנְיָא: ״מִי שֶׁמֵּת וְהִנִּיחַ שׁוֹמֶרֶת יָבָם, וְהִנִּיחַ נְכָסִים בְּמֵאָה מָנֶה, [4]אַף עַל פִּי שֶׁכְּתוּבָּתָהּ אֵינָהּ אֶלָּא מָנֶה, לֹא יִמְכּוֹר, [5]שֶׁכָּל נְכָסָיו אַחֲרָאִין לִכְתוּבָּתָהּ״.

[6]אֲמַר לֵיהּ אַבַּיֵי: [7]וְכָל הֵיכָא דַּאֲמוּר רַבָּנַן לָא לִיזְבֵּין, [8]אַף

LITERAL TRANSLATION

will share the property with you." [1]Rav Yosef said: Since the Rabbis said not to sell, [2]even if he sold, his sale is not a sale.

[3]For it was taught: "[If] someone died and left a widow waiting for levirate marriage, and he left property worth a hundred maneh, [4]even if her ketubah is only a maneh, he may not sell, [5]for all of his property is mortgaged to guarantee her ketubah."

[6]Abaye said to him: [7]And wherever the Rabbis said not to sell, [8]even

TRANSLATION AND COMMENTARY

the widow as his wife, but once he was married he refused to share the estate with his brother. [1]The matter was brought before **Rav Yosef,** who **said: Since the Rabbis said that** the *levir* may **not sell** any of the property of his brother's estate — neither before he takes his brother's widow as his wife, nor afterwards — [2]**even if he sold** the property, **the sale would be void.**

דְּתַנְיָא [3]**For it was taught** in a Baraita: **"If someone died** childless **and left a widow** who was now **waiting for levirate marriage, and** the deceased **left property worth a hundred maneh,** [4]then **even if** the woman's **ketubah** settlement **is only a maneh,** the *levir* who inherits his brother's estate **may not sell** any of the property, [5]**for all of the property** the *levir* inherited from his brother **is mortgaged to** guarantee the woman's **ketubah** settlement." Now, the *levir*'s promise to share property is no better than a sale, and so the agreement reached between the two is null and void.

אֲמַר לֵיהּ אַבַּיֵי [6]**Abaye** questioned Rav Yosef's ruling and **said to him:** Granted that the Baraita teaches that the *levir* may not sell any of the property of his brother's estate, but does it follow necessarily that if he sold the property, the transaction is null after the fact? [7]Is it really true that **whenever the Rabbis said that** a person **may not sell property** because it is subject to a lien, [8]**even if that** person **sold** the

RASHI

פליגנא לך – כאילו אני חולך לה, ולא אטול אלא כמוך. כיון דאמור רבנן – שומרת יבם – אין היבם רשאי למכור, כדאמרינן לקמן בשמעתין: מי שמת והניח שומרת יבם כו׳. אף על גב דזבין כו׳ – ומה שעשה זה שהתנה עמו לחלוק לו וקנו מידו – הרי הוא כמוכר.

NOTES

פָּלֵיגְנָא לָךְ **I will share with you.** *Rivan* and *Rid* understand that after the *levir* promised to share his late brother's estate with his other brother, a valid act of acquisition was performed to confirm the agreement. *Ritva* argues that no such act was performed. The Rishonim raise a question according to the view that the agreement was ratified with a valid act of acquisition: At the time that the *levir* concluded the deal with his brother, he had not yet acquired his late brother's estate. How, then, could he have transferred ownership to him by means of an act of acquisition when the property did not yet belong to him? *Meiri* answers that, indeed, the act of acquisition that was performed had no legal validity. But after performing such an act of acquisition, the *levir* would have kept his word and shared the estate with his brother, had he not been later informed that he was not permitted to do so. *Ran* explains that the act of acquisition was not performed in order to effect a transfer of ownership, for the *levir* cannot transfer property that does not belong to him. But, rather, here we are dealing with a case where the *levir* and his brother were the late brother's only heirs, and the *levir* performed an act of acquisition waiving his right to inherit half of his late brother's estate. As we learned in *Bava Batra*, such a waiver is only valid if it was performed before the estate came into the heir's possession.

לָא הֲוָה זְבִינֵיהּ זְבִינֵי **His sale is not a sale.** The Aharonim propose various explanations regarding Rav Yosef's position that the *levir*'s sale of the property of his brother's estate is void. Some suggest that Rav Yosef follows the position of Rava in tractate *Temurah*, that if a person does something which he is forbidden to do, his act has no validity. According to this, we well understand why Abaye disagrees with Rav Yosef, for Abaye also disagrees with Rava and says that even when a person violates a prohibition, his actions have legal validity. (Some Aḥaronim raise an objection that here we are not dealing with an act that is forbidden in the same sense as the acts under discussion in *Temurah*; see *Kovetz Shiurim*.) Others explain that here the Rabbis added a special reinforcement to the law, declaring the sale null and void. *Ayelet Ahavim* offers

HALAKHAH

כֵּיוָן דַּאֲמוּר רַבָּנַן **Since the Rabbis said.** "A widow's ketubah settlement becomes a lien on her late husband's estate, both while she is waiting for her brother-in-law to take her as his levirate wife and after he does so. Thus, the *levir* may not sell any of his late brother's estate, either before he takes his widow in levirate marriage, or afterwards. If he sold property, or gave it away as a gift, or divided the property with his brothers — either before or after he took the widow as his levirate wife — the transaction is void," following Rav Yosef. (*Rambam, Sefer Nashim, Hilkhot Ishut* 22:11; *Hilkhot Yibbum* 1:1; *Shulḥan Arukh, Even HaEzer* 166:4; 168:3.)

עַל גַּב דְּזַבֵּין לָא הֲוָה זְבִינֵיהּ זְבִינֵי? [1]וְהָתְנַן: [2]"בֵּית שַׁמַּאי אוֹמְרִים: תִּמְכּוֹר. [3]וּבֵית הִלֵּל אוֹמְרִים: לֹא תִּמְכּוֹר. [4]אֵלּוּ וְאֵלּוּ מוֹדִים שֶׁאִם מָכְרָה וְנָתְנָה, קַיָּים"!

[5]שְׁלַחוּהָ לְקַמֵּיהּ דְּרַבִּי חֲנִינָא בַּר פַּפִּי. [6]שְׁלָחָהּ: כִּדְרַב יוֹסֵף. [7]אֲמַר אַבַּיֵי: אַטּוּ רַבִּי חֲנִינָא בַּר פַּפָּא כֵּיפֵי תָּלָה לָהּ?

[8]שְׁלַחוּהָ לְקַמֵּיהּ דְּרַב מַנְיוּמֵי בְּרֵיהּ דְּרַב נַחוּמֵי. [9]שְׁלָחָהּ: כְּדְאַבַּיֵי. [10]וְאִי אָמַר בָּהּ רַב יוֹסֵף טַעְמָא אַחֲרִינָא, [11]שִׁלְחוּ לִי. [12]נָפַק רַב יוֹסֵף, דַּק, וְאַשְׁכַּח, [13]דְּתַנְיָא: "הֲרֵי שֶׁהָיָה נוֹשֶׁה בְּאָחִיו, וּמֵת, וְהִנִּיחַ שׁוֹמֶרֶת יָבָם: [14]לֹא יֹאמַר: 'הוֹאִיל וְשֶׁאֲנִי יוֹרֵשׁ, הֶחְזַקְתִּי'.

LITERAL TRANSLATION

if he sold, his sale is not a sale? [1]But surely we have learned: [2]"Bet Shammai say: She may sell. [3]And Bet Hillel say: She may not sell. [4]These and these agree that if she sold [the property] or gave [it] away, it is valid!"

[5]They sent it before Rabbi Ḥanina bar Pappi. [6]He sent: In accordance with Rabbi Yosef. [7]Abaye said: Did Rabbi Ḥanina bar Pappi hang jewelry on it?

[8]They sent it before Rav Manyume the son of Rav Naḥume. [9]He sent: In accordance with Abaye. [10]And if Rav Yosef says about it another reason, [11]send [it] to me. [12]Rav Yosef went out, investigated, and found, [13]for it was taught: "[If] he lent money to his brother, and died, and he left a widow waiting for levirate marriage, [14][the *levir*] may not say: 'Since I inherit, I will hold on to [the money that I owe].'

RASHI

כיפי = נזמים. כלומר: כמה ייפה והנאה את דבריו, ומה טעם נתן בה כששלחה? **שלחה כדאביי** — דהיכא דזבין — זביניה זביני. **ומת** — הנושה המלוה. **לא יאמר** — היבם המחויב המעות. **הואיל ואני יורש** — שאכניס את אשתו ואזכה בנכסים. **החזקתי** — בחוב זה, ולא אשלמנו עוד.

TRANSLATION AND COMMENTARY

property, **the sale is void?** [1]**But surely we have learned** in the first Mishnah of this chapter (above, p. 78a): "If a woman inherited property or received it as a gift after she was betrothed to her husband, [2]**Bet Shammai say: She may sell** the property or give it away while she is only betrothed to her husband. [3]**And Bet Hillel say: She may not sell** or give away the property even while she is only betrothed. [4]However, **both** Bet Shammai and Bet Hillel **agree that if** indeed **she sold the** property **or gave it away,** the transaction **is valid."** Here, too, then, perhaps the *levir* is barred from selling any of the property inherited from his brother, but if he sold it, the transaction might indeed be valid after the fact!

שְׁלַחוּהָ [5]The question was then **put to Rabbi Ḥanina bar Pappi, who sent** back the following ruling: [6]The law is **in accordance with Rav Yosef's** view. [7]When he heard Rabbi Ḥanina's decision, **Abaye said: Did Rabbi Ḥanina bar Pappi adorn** his ruling with **jewelry?** In other words, did he offer a persuasive rationale for his determination, so that I should feel compelled to accept it?

שְׁלַחוּהָ [8]The question was then **put before Rav Manyume the son of Rav Naḥume,** [9]**who sent** back the following ruling: The law is **in accordance with Abaye's** view. [10]**And if Rav Yosef offers another reason** why the sale should be void, [11]**send it to me** and I will look into the matter again. After Rav Manyume's decision was received, [12]**Rav Yosef went out, investigated** the Tannaitic traditions concerning the matter, **and found** support for his ruling, [13]**for it was taught** in a Baraita: **"If someone lent money to his brother, and** then **died** childless, **and he left a widow** who was now **waiting for her brother-in-law** to take her in levirate marriage or free her from the levirate tie by means of *ḥalitzah,* [14]the *levir* **may not say: 'Since I will inherit** my brother's estate when I marry his widow, **I will hold on to the** money I owe him. If one day the money is needed to cover her ketubah settlement I will pay back the

NOTES

a suggestion why this reinforcement was necessary: The *levir*'s rights regarding his brother's property were restricted, because the *levir* can marry his brother's widow against her will, and the Rabbis were concerned that he might take her as his levirate wife only in order to gain control of her late husband's estate.

אֵלּוּ וְאֵלּוּ מוֹדִים These and these agree. *Ritva* asks: How can Abaye bring proof from the first Mishnah of our chapter? The law in that Mishnah might be an exception to the rule, for Bet Hillel state explicitly that if the woman sold the property or gave it away, the transaction is valid. But in all other cases where the Rabbis said that a person may not sell property, the law might be that the transaction is void! *Ritva* answers that Bet Hillel themselves only said that the widow may not sell the property or give it away. It was Rabbi Yehudah HaNasi who added that Bet Hillel nevertheless agree that if the widow sold the property the sale is valid after the fact. Thus, Abaye was right to conclude that the Mishnah supports his position that the *levir* may not sell any of the property of his brother's estate, but if he sold property, the sale is valid.

הוֹאִיל וְשֶׁאֲנִי יוֹרֵשׁ Since I inherit. The Rishonim comment: We learned elsewhere in the Gemara (*Ketubot* 85b) that if a creditor sold a bill of indebtedness drawn in his favor, and then the creditor released the debtor from his obligation to repay the debt, the release is valid. Not only the creditor himself but even his heir can release the debtor from his obligation to repay the debt. Why, then, can the *levir* who inherits the debt from his brother not release himself from repaying the debt? *Tosafot* answers that, since

[1]אֶלָּא מוֹצִיאִין מִיָּבָם, [2]וְיִקַּח בָּהֶן קַרְקַע, [3]וְהוּא אוֹכֵל פֵּירוֹת״.

[4]אֲמַר לֵיהּ אַבַּיֵי: [5]דִּלְמָא דְּטָבָא לֵיהּ עָבְדוּ לֵיהּ?

[6]אֲמַר לֵיהּ: תַּנָּא תָּנֵי: ״מוֹצִיאִין״, [7]וְאַתְּ אָמְרַתְּ: דְּטָבָא לֵיהּ עָבְדוּ לֵיהּ?

[8]הֲדוּר שְׁלָחוּהָ קַמֵּיהּ דְּרַב מַנְיוּמֵי בְּרֵיהּ דְּרַב נַחוּמֵי. [9]אֲמַר לְהוּ: הָכִי אֲמַר רַב יוֹסֵף בַּר מַנְיוּמֵי אֲמַר רַב נַחְמָן: [10]זוֹ אֵינָהּ מִשְׁנָה.

[11]מַאי טַעְמָא? [12]אִילֵימָא מִשּׁוּם דְּהָווּ לְהוּ מִטַּלְטְלֵי, [13]וּמִטַּלְטְלֵי לִכְתוּבָּה לָא מִשַּׁעְבְּדִי, [14]דִּלְמָא רַבִּי מֵאִיר הִיא, [15]דְּאָמַר:

LITERAL TRANSLATION

[1]But rather we take [the money] away from the *levir*, [2]and he buys with it land, [3]and he eats the fruit."

[4]Abaye said to him: [5]Perhaps what is good for him they did for him!

[6]He said to him: The Tanna taught: "We take away," [7]and you say: What is good for him they did for him?

[8]They sent it again before Rav Manyume the son of Rav Naḥume. [9]He said to them: Thus said Rav Yosef the son of Manyume in the name of Rav Naḥman: [10]This is not a Mishnah.

[11]What is the reason? [12]If you say because they are movable goods, [13]and movable goods are not mortgaged to guarantee the ketubah, [14]perhaps it is Rabbi Meir, [15]who said:

TRANSLATION AND COMMENTARY

loan. But until then I will keep it, for if I pay it back now, it will just be returned to me as part of my brother's estate.' The *levir* may not put forward such an argument. [1]**Instead we take the money away from him,** [2]**land is bought with** it, it becomes subject to the woman's ketubah, [3]**and the** *levir* **enjoys the usufruct."** Rav Yosef argued as follows: If we take away the money that the *levir* owed his late brother, even though that money was in the *levir*'s possession during his brother's lifetime, all the more so should the *levir*'s sale be void if he sold property from his brother's estate which came into his possession only after his brother's death.

אֲמַר לֵיהּ אַבַּיֵי [4]**Abaye said to** Rav Yosef: You cannot prove your position from the Baraita dealing with the *levir* who had borrowed money from his brother, [5]for **perhaps** the Rabbis **did for** the *levir* **what is good for him.** Perhaps they only meant to recommend that it would be to his advantage to invest the money in land.

אֲמַר לֵיהּ [6]Rav Yosef **said to** Abaye: The wording of the Baraita does not allow for such an interpretation: **The Tanna taught this** regulation, using the formula, **"We take** the money **away from** the *levir*." [7]How, then, can **you say** that the Rabbis **did for** the *levir* **what was good for him?** Thus, indeed, the Baraita supports my position that if the *levir* sold property he inherited from his brother, the sale is void.

הֲדוּר שְׁלָחוּהָ [8]The matter was **once again sent** for comment **to Rav Manyume the son of Rav Naḥume,** who wished to be informed if Rav Yosef had adduced support for his position that the *levir*'s sale of property inherited from his brother was void. After reexamining the issue, [9]Rav Manyume **said to them: Thus said Rav Yosef the son of Manyume in the name of Rav Naḥman:** [10]**This is not a Mishnah.** The Baraita cited in support of Rav Yosef's view is not authoritative, and hence no proof may be adduced from it.

מַאי טַעְמָא [11]The Gemara asks: **What is the reason** that Rav Naḥman declared the Baraita unreliable? [12]**If you say** that Rav Naḥman rejected the Baraita **because** the money that the *levir* borrowed from his brother falls under the category of **movable goods,** [13]**and** the husband's **movable goods are not mortgaged to guarantee** his wife's **ketubah** settlement, this is not sufficient reason to reject the Baraita. [14]**For perhaps** the Baraita follows the position of **Rabbi Meir,** [15]**who said:** Not only the husband's land, but even his

RASHI

דטבא ליה עבדו – עלה טובה: שיהיה הקרקע קיים לו עולמית, ולא יוציא המעות בהוצאה. **תנא תני מוציאין** – דמשמע: על כרחו. **אינה משנה** – לא נשנית משנה זו בבית המדרש של חכמים, ולא סמכינן עלה במידי. **דלמא רבי מאיר היא** – במתניתין, דקתני גבי כספים ופירות תלושין: ילקח בהן קרקע, ואפילו לא תפסה. אלמא – משעבדי לכתובתה, ואפילו לא קיימא לן כרבי מאיר בהא, מיהו גבי מוציאין – ליכא מאן דפליג אי מקרקעי נינהו, ולעולם משנה היא.

NOTES

the *levir* only inherits his brother's estate because he takes his widow as his levirate wife, he cannot waive the debt to her detriment. Alternatively, the *levir* can indeed waive the debt, but he would have to compensate his brother's widow for her loss, for the law is in accordance with the view of Rabbi Meir that a person is liable for damage caused in an indirect manner (see *Ketubot* 86a). *Ramban* argues that a person can release someone else from a debt owed to him, but he cannot waive a debt which he owes to himself. He also suggests that if the *levir* is shrewd, he can indeed waive the debt, but most people do not realize that such a waiver is possible.

דִּלְמָא רַבִּי מֵאִיר הִיא **Perhaps it is Rabbi Meir.** *Ritva* explains that the expression, "This is not a Mishnah," implies that the Baraita does not follow any Tannaitic tradition. Thus, in order to rebut the objection, it suffices to demonstrate that the Baraita can be explained in accordance with the view of a Tanna, even if the law does not follow that view.

מְטַלְטְלֵי מִשַּׁעְבְּדִי לִכְתוּבָּה. [1]וְאֶלָּא מִשּׁוּם דַּאֲמַר לָהּ: [2]״אַתְּ לָאו בַּעֲלַת דְּבָרִים דִּידִי אַתְּ.״ [82A] [3]דִּלְמָא רַבִּי נָתָן הִיא דְּתַנְיָא, [4]״רַבִּי נָתָן אוֹמֵר: מִנַּיִן לְנוֹשֶׁה בַּחֲבֵירוֹ מָנֶה, וַחֲבֵירוֹ בַּחֲבֵירוֹ, [5]מִנַּיִן שֶׁמּוֹצִיאִין מִזֶּה וְנוֹתְנִין לָזֶה? [6]תַּלְמוּד לוֹמַר: ׳וְנָתַן לַאֲשֶׁר אָשַׁם לוֹ׳״.

LITERAL TRANSLATION

Movable goods are mortgaged to guarantee the ketubah. [1]But rather because he can say to her: [2]"You have no claim against me." [82A] [3]Perhaps it is Rabbi Natan, [4]as it was taught: "Rabbi Natan says: From where [do we know] that if someone is owed a maneh by his fellow, and his fellow by his fellow, [5]from where [do we know] that we take from this one and give to that one? [6]The verse states: 'And he shall give [it] to him against whom he has trespassed.'"

TRANSLATION AND COMMENTARY

movable goods are mortgaged to guarantee his wife's **ketubah** settlement, as we learned in our Mishnah (above, p. 80b) that Rabbi Meir disagrees with the Sages and says that the money and detached produce that the *levir* inherited from his deceased brother are mortgaged to his widow's ketubah. Thus, there is no reason to assume that the Baraita does not reflect a reliable tradition. [1]**But rather** you must say that Rav Naḥman rejected the Baraita **because** the *levir* **can say to** his brother's widow: [2]**"You have no claim against me,** for I did not borrow any money from you, but only from my brother." The woman has a claim against her late husband, and the late husband has a claim against his brother, but the woman has no claim against her husband's brother. Thus, the *levir* cannot be compelled to pay back the loan and purchase land with the money. [82A] But this, too, is not sufficient reason to reject the Baraita: [3]For **perhaps** the Baraita follows the position of **Rabbi Natan,** [4]**as it was taught** in another Baraita: **"Rabbi Natan says: From where do we know that if someone is owed a maneh by someone else, and** this **other person** is owed a similar sum **by yet another person** — [5]**from where do we know that** in such a case the court **takes** the money **from** the ultimate debtor **and gives it to** the ultimate creditor, without involving the middlemen at all? [6]**The verse states** [Numbers 5:7]: **'And he shall give it to him against whom he has trespassed.'"** Rabbi Natan understands the phrase לַאֲשֶׁר אָשַׁם לוֹ (translated here as "against whom he has trespassed") to mean "to whom the trespass [i.e., the principal of the debt] belongs." Hence, the court may take the money from the ultimate debtor and give it to the ultimate creditor, and that debtor cannot argue that that creditor has no claim against him. Perhaps, then, our Baraita follows the view of Rabbi Natan, and so it rules that the court may take away the money the *levir* owed to his late brother and compel him to buy land with it. Thus, there is no reason to assume that the Baraita does not reflect a reliable tradition.

RASHI

אלא – להכי איכה משנה, וטעות היה מי ששנאה. **משום דמצי אמר לה:** לאו בעלת דברים דידי את, ממך לא לויתי אלא מאחי. **דלמא** – בהא נמי לא טעה דרבי נתן היא דמוציאין מזה ונותנין לזה. **לאשר אשם לו** – לאשר הקרן שלו, ולא כתיב לאשר נושה בו.

NOTES

Rashi adds that not only does the Baraita follow a reliable tradition, but proof can be brought from the Baraita in support of Rav Yosef's ruling. For even if the law is not in accordance with the view of Rabbi Meir, that the husband's movable goods are mortgaged to guarantee his wife's ketubah settlement, there is no reason to reject the principle underlying the Baraita's ruling, that we remove the property that is mortgaged to guarantee the *levir*'s sister-in-law's ketubah settlement. Thus, the Baraita supports Rav Yosef's ruling, for there the *levir* from Pumbedita wished to give away land which all agree was mortgaged to guarantee the widow's ketubah settlement.

מִנַּיִן לְנוֹשֶׁה...? From where do we know that if someone is owed...? It would appear from the Gemara that, according to the Sages who disagree with Rabbi Natan, a creditor cannot collect his debt from someone who owes money to his debtor. *Ritva* begins his explanation of their position by asking: If a creditor can seize property sold to a third party by his debtor, why can he not collect his debt from the person to whom his debtor lent money? *Ritva*

HALAKHAH

מְטַלְטְלֵי מִשַּׁעְבְּדִי לִכְתוּבָּה Movable goods are mortgaged to the ketubah. "If someone died childless, leaving detached produce or other movable goods, the property is sold, land is acquired with the proceeds, and the *levir* consumes the usufruct. Even if the *levir* owed money to his late brother, the money is removed from the *levir*, land is bought with the money, and the *levir* enjoys the usufruct. According to some authorities (*Rambam*), the *levir* may do what he pleases with the detached produce and other movable goods. If, however, the husband had expressly mortgaged his movable goods to guarantee his wife's ketubah settlement along with his land, and he died childless, all agree that the movable goods are sold, land is bought with the proceeds, and the *levir* enjoys the usufruct." (*Rambam, Sefer Nashim, Hilkhot Ishut* 22:13; *Shulḥan Arukh, Even HaEzer* 168:5.)

נוֹשֶׁה בַּחֲבֵירוֹ מָנֶה If someone is owed a maneh by his fellow. "If a debtor owes money to somebody, and the creditor owes money to someone else, we take the money from the debtor and give it directly to the creditor's

TRANSLATION AND COMMENTARY

אֶלָּא [1] **Rather,** Rav Naḥman dismissed the Baraita because **we do not find** any **Tanna who maintains both stringencies with respect to the ketubah** — the stringency of Rabbi Meir that the husband's movable goods are mortgaged to guarantee his wife's ketubah settlement, and the stringency of Rabbi Natan that a woman may collect her settlement from someone who owed money to her husband. [2] **But rather** we only find authorities who agree **either with Rabbi Meir or with Rabbi Natan.** Now, since the Baraita assumes both stringencies, and we do not find a Tanna who combines them, the Baraita cannot be authoritative. The Tanna who taught the Baraita could not have received it from a reliable source, and so no proof may be adduced from it.

אָמַר רָבָא [3] **Rava said: If so, this** explains **what I heard Abaye say:** [4] **"This is not a Mishnah,"** [5] **and I did not understand** at the time **what he meant.**

הַהוּא גַּבְרָא [6] The Gemara now relates an anecdote similar to the one reported above: **There was a certain man** living in the city of **Mata Meḥasya to whom it befell to enter into a levirate marriage.** [7] The *levir*'s younger **brother wished to disqualify** the woman from marriage **to his brother by** forcing upon her **a bill of divorce.** [8] The *levir* **said to** his younger brother: **"What is on your mind** that you wish to prevent me from marrying our brother's widow? [9] **If** it is **on account of the property** that I will inherit if I marry her, let me take our brother's widow as my levirate wife, [10] and **I will share the property** of his estate **with you.** [11] The younger brother **said to** the levir: **"I fear**

[1] אֶלָּא, לָא אַשְׁכַּחַן תַּנָּא דְּמַחְמִיר תְּרֵי חוּמְרֵי בִּכְתוּבָּה, [2] אֶלָּא — אִי כְּרַבִּי מֵאִיר, אִי כְּרַבִּי נָתָן.

[3] אֲמַר רָבָא: אִם כֵּן, הַיְינוּ דְּשָׁמַעְנָא לֵיהּ לְאַבַּיֵי דַּאֲמַר: [4] ״זוֹ אֵינָהּ מִשְׁנָה״, [5] וְלָא יָדַעְנָא מַאי הִיא.

[6] הַהוּא גַּבְרָא דְּנָפְלָה לֵיהּ יְבָמָה בְּמָתָא מְחַסְיָא. [7] בְּעָא אֲחוּהּ לְמִיפְסְלָהּ בְּגִיטָּא מִינֵּיהּ. [8] אֲמַר לֵיהּ: ״מַאי דַּעְתֵּיךְ? [9] אִי מִשּׁוּם נִכְסֵי, [10] אֲנָא בְּנִכְסֵי פָּלֵיגְנָא לָךְ״. [11] אֲמַר לֵיהּ: ״מִסְתַּפֵינָא

LITERAL TRANSLATION

[1] Rather, we do not find a Tanna who is stringent with two stringencies regarding the ketubah, [2] but rather, either like Rabbi Meir, or like Rabbi Natan.

[3] Rava said: If so, this is what I heard that Abaye said: [4] "This is not a Mishnah," [5] and I did not know what it is.

[6] [There was] a certain man to whom fell a woman for levirate marriage in Mata Meḥasya. [7] His brother wished to disqualify her to him with a bill of divorce. [8] He said to him: "What is on your mind? [9] If on account of the property, [10] I will share the property with you." [11] He said to him: "I fear

RASHI

אלא — להכי אינה משנה, וטעה התנא ששנאה; דלא אשכחן תנא דאית ליה תרי חומרי בכתובה, שהרי היא מדברי סופרים, חדא — דמטלטלי משתעבדי לה, וחדא — דגביא מבעל חובו של מת מדרבי נתן. אלא חדא מהנך חומרי הוה ליה למיתני בה, אי כרבי מאיר אי כרבי נתן. וכיון דתנא תרוייהו — לא קבלה מרבו כן, ומאליו שנאה מי שסידר הברייתא, ולא סמכינן עלה במידי. **ולא ידענא מאי היא** — לא הייתי יודע טעם בדבר; אמאי אינה משנה.

NOTES

answers that, if the debtor expressly mortgaged his money and movable goods to his creditor along with his land, the creditor can indeed collect his debt from the person who borrowed money from his debtor. He must, however, first take an oath that the debtor has not already repaid his loan, just like any other creditor who wishes to implement his right of seizure.

לָא אַשְׁכַּחַן תַּנָּא דְּמַחְמִיר תְּרֵי חוּמְרֵי **We do not find a Tanna who is stringent with two stringencies.** *Tosafot* and others discuss whether or not there actually is a Tanna who maintains the two stringencies. *Ra'ah* and others emphasize that the Gemara does not mean to say that there are no Tannaim who maintain two stringencies with respect to a ketubah, but rather that we do not find any Tanna who maintains these two particular stringencies — the stringency of Rabbi Meir and that of Rabbi Natan. Thus, the Baraita cannot be authoritative, for it can only be understood if we assume both stringencies.

זוֹ אֵינָהּ מִשְׁנָה **This is not a Mishnah.** Even though the Gemara concludes that the Baraita is not authoritative, *Rif* records the Baraita as the final law, but *Ra'avad* questions it. *Ramban, Ritva* and others support *Rif,* arguing that the Gemara only says that we do not find any Tanna who maintains the stringencies of both Rabbi Meir and Rabbi Natan. But since the law follows the view of Rabbi Natan, and after the Geonic enactment the law in effect follows the view of Rabbi Meir, we do indeed maintain the two stringencies, and so the Baraita's ruling is law. *Rambam* rules that, while the Geonim enacted that a woman's ketubah settlement can be collected from her late husband's movable goods, that enactment is not strong enough to prevent the *levir* from conducting business with the movable goods that he inherited from his late brother.

HALAKHAH

creditor, regardless of when the two loans were made. This law applies regardless of whether the debt arose as a result of a loan (either a verbal loan or a loan committed to writing), a sale, unpaid wages, or any other factor," following Rabbi Natan. (*Rambam, Sefer Mishpatim, Hilkhot Malveh VeLoveh* 2:6; *Shulḥan Arukh, Ḥoshen Mishpat* 86:1.)

דְּעָבְדַתְּ לִי כִּדְעָבֵיד פּוּמְבְּדִיתָאָה רַמָּאָה״. [1] אֲמַר לֵיהּ: ״אִי בָּעֵית, [2] פְּלוֹג לָךְ מֵהָשְׁתָּא״.
[3] אֲמַר מָר בַּר רַב אַשִׁי: [4] אַף עַל גַּב דְּכִי אֲתָא רַב דִּימִי אֲמַר רַבִּי יוֹחָנָן: [5] הָאוֹמֵר לַחֲבֵירוֹ: ״לֵךְ וּמְשׁוֹךְ פָּרָה זוֹ וְלֹא תְּהְיֶה קְנוּיָה לְךָ אֶלָּא לְאַחַר שְׁלֹשִׁים יוֹם״, [6] לְאַחַר שְׁלֹשִׁים יוֹם קָנָה, [7] וַאֲפִילּוּ עוֹמֶדֶת בַּאֲגַם. [8] הָתָם — בְּיָדוֹ, [9] הָכָא — לָאו בְּיָדוֹ.

LITERAL TRANSLATION

that you will do to me as did the Pumbeditan swindler." [1] He said to him: "If you wish, [2] take your share now."
[3] Mar the son of Rav Ashi said: [4] Even though when Rav Dimi came, he said [in the name of] Rabbi Yoḥanan: [5] [If] someone says to his fellow: "Go and pull this cow, but it shall not be acquired by you until after thirty days," [6] after thirty days he acquires [it], [7] even if it is standing in a meadow. [8] There — it is in his hand, [9] here — it is not in his hand.

TRANSLATION AND COMMENTARY

that you will do to me what that Pumbeditan swindler did to his brother. Once you have married our sister-in-law, you could refuse to hand over my share of the estate." [1] The *levir* **said to his brother:** "I have no intention of cheating you, but **if you wish,** [2] **take** possession **now** of that **share** of our brother's estate which I promised you. Even though you will not acquire the property until I take the widow as my wife, take possession of your share of the property now, so that it will become yours as soon as I inherit the estate."

אֲמַר מָר בַּר רַב אַשִׁי [3] The Gemara raises a question about the validity of such a course of action. **Mar the son of Rav Ashi said:** Even if the brother takes possession of that part of the estate which was promised him by the *levir*, does he in fact acquire the property when the *levir* takes the widow as his wife and inherits the estate? [4] **Even though when** Rav Dimi **came** to Babylonia from Eretz Israel, he reported a ruling in the name of Rabbi Yoḥanan which at first glance supports the brother's claim to the property, it becomes clear upon closer examination that a comparison cannot be drawn between the two cases. For **Rav Dimi reported** the following ruling **in the name of Rabbi Yoḥanan:** [5] **If someone said to another person: "Go** now **and pull this cow** of mine into your possession, **but it shall not be yours until thirty days have passed,"** and the other person pulled the cow into his possession, [6] **he does** in fact **acquire** the cow **after thirty days** have passed, [7] **even if** at the end of that thirty day period the cow **was standing in a meadow which** did not belong to the buyer. An act of acquisition — such as *meshikhah,* drawing an article into the buyer's possession — is valid, even if it was stipulated that ownership would not be conferred on the buyer upon his performance of the act of acquisition, but only later. In the case of *meshikhah,* the transaction is valid even if the object of the sale was no longer in the buyer's physical possession when the acquisition was to take effect. Now, at first glance these two situations seem similar, so that the *levir*'s brother should acquire the property that he took into his possession, even though the acquisition cannot be completed until the *levir* marries his sister-in-law and inherits his late brother's property. But the cases are not really comparable. [8] For **there,** the seller **has the authority** to sell the cow, [9] but **here,** the *levir* **does not have the authority** to transfer the property of his late brother's estate before he marries his widow and the estate enters into his possession.

LANGUAGE

פּוּמְבְּדִיתָאָה רַמָּאָה Pumbeditan swindler. This derogatory expression reflects the Pumbeditans' bad reputation, as the residents of this city were considered thiefs and cheats. Cf. also *Ḥullin* 127a: "If a Pumbeditan accompanies you, change your lodging" (so he won't know where you are staying, lest he steal from you).

RASHI

פומבדיתאה רמאה — שאחרי כן חזר בו. פומבדיתא — קרי להו רמאה כדאמרינן בעלמא (חולין קכז,א): גרשאה נשקיך — מני ככיך, פומבדיתאה לוייך — שני אושפיזיך. (וב״חזקת הבתים״ (בבא בתרא מו,א) כמו כן: תא ואחוי לך רמאי דפומבדיתא). **פלוג מהשתא** — החזק בחלקך מעכשיו, ואף על פי שאינה עכשיו קנויה לך עד שאכנוס או שאחלוק. לכשאכנוס ואזכה בכולן — זכה אתה בחלקך על פי שהחזקתיך מעכשיו. **קנה לאחר שלשים** — במשיכה זו. **ואפילו עומדת באגם** — שאינה ברשות הלוקח. **התם** — הוא דקונה לאחר שלשים — משום דבידו היה להקנותה לו משעת משיכה. הלכך מהניא משיכה לכשיתקיים התנאי שימלאו יום. **הכא לאו בידו** — לחלקם לו מעכשיו ולהקנות לו אם ירצה. הלכך, אי אמר ליה נמי: לכשאכנוס זכה מעכשיו לאו מידי הוא, דקיימא לן כרב יוסף, כדקבעינן הלכתא כוותיה לקמן בשמעתין. ואפילו אית לן יבם ואחר כך חילק, מה שעשה עשוי — השתא מיהת לאו בידו.

NOTES

פּוּמְבְּדִיתָאָה רַמָּאָה The Pumbeditan swindler. The Rishonim ask: Of what deception was the Pumbeditan *levir* guilty? Surely it was Rav Yosef who annulled the deal which the *levir* had arranged with his brother! Why, then, is he called a swindler? *Rivan* and *Tosafot* answer that the *levir* himself violated his agreement and broke his promise to share the property of his late brother's estate. The fact that the transaction was indeed illegal does not mitigate the *levir*'s fundamental intentions. *Meiri* argues that while the Pumbeditan *levir* did not actually practice any deception, he gained the reputation of being a swindler, because people thought he had deceived his brother. It would appear from *Rashi* that Pumbeditans in general were reputed to be dishonest.

הָכָא — לָאו בְּיָדוֹ Here, it is not in his hand. Mar bar Rav Ashi argues that since the *levir* is not authorized to transfer

HALAKHAH

מְשׁוֹךְ פָּרָה זוֹ וְלֹא תְּהְיֶה קְנוּיָה Go and pull this cow, but it shall not be acquired. "If someone said to another person: 'Pull this cow into your possession, but you shall not acquire it until after thirty days,' and that other person

TRANSLATION AND COMMENTARY

וְהָא כִּי אֲתָא [1]The Gemara now points out that there is a direct contradiction between two statements made by Rabbi Yoḥanan: **But surely when Ravin came** to Babylonia from Eretz Israel, **he reported the** following ruling **in the name of Rabbi Yoḥanan:** If someone said: "Go and draw my cow into your possession, but it shall not become yours until thirty days have passed," and the other person drew the cow into his possession, [2]**he does not acquire** the cow even after the thirty days have passed. This contradicts Rabbi Yoḥanan's ruling on the very same matter as reported above by Rav Dimi, that in such a case the buyer indeed acquires the cow at the end of the thirty-day period!

לָא קַשְׁיָא [3]The Gemara resolves the apparent contradiction between the two rulings: **There is** really **no difficulty,** for the two statements refer to two different cases. [4]The ruling reported by Rav Dimi refers to the owner of a cow who **said to** the buyer: "Go now and draw my cow into your possession, and **acquire it** after thirty days retroactively **from today."** In such a case, the buyer does acquire the cow, for ownership of the cow is transferred retroactively. [5]The ruling reported by Ravin refers to an owner who **did not say to** the buyer: "Go now and draw my cow into your possession, and **acquire it** after thirty days retroactively **from today."** The buyer does not acquire the cow immediately, because the owner stipulated that the transfer of ownership should only take effect after thirty days, and he does not acquire it after thirty days, for then no act of acquisition is performed, and the act of acquisition performed earlier is no longer relevant.

[1]וְהָא כִּי אֲתָא רָבִין אָמַר רַבִּי יוֹחָנָן: [2]לָא קָנֵי! [3]לָא קַשְׁיָא. [4]הָא, דַּאֲמַר לֵיהּ: ״קְנֵי מֵעַכְשָׁיו״. [5]הָא, דְּלָא אֲמַר לֵיהּ: ״קְנֵי מֵעַכְשָׁיו״.

LITERAL TRANSLATION

[1]But surely when Ravin came, he said [in the name of] Rabbi Yoḥanan: [2]He does not acquire [it]. [3]It is not difficult. [4]This, where he said to him: "Acquire [it] from now." [5]This, where he did not say to him: "Acquire [it] from now."

RASHI

והא כי אתא כו׳ – גבי משיכת פרה קאי, ופריך דרבי יוחנן אדרבי יוחנן. **קני מעכשיו** – לאחר שלשים, כשיגיעו – תהא קנויה לך מעכשיו.

NOTES

his late brother's property to his surviving brother before he marries the sister-in-law, he can also not tell his brother to take possession of the property now, so that it should be acquired by him as soon as the *levir* marries and inherits their brother's estate. *Rivan* infers from this that, according to Mar bar Rav Ashi, after the *levir* marries his brother's widow, he may indeed sell the property. Thus, Mar bar Rav Ashi disagrees with Rabbi Abba, who said (above p. 81a) that the *levir* may not sell his brother's property even after marrying his widow, but must divorce her and then take her back as his ordinary wife, and only then may he sell the property. According to Mar bar Rav Ashi, the *levir* is only forbidden to sell his brother's property before the marriage, as is implied by the Baraita cited earlier (p. 81b): "If someone died and left a woman waiting for her brother-in-law...he may not sell." Alternatively, Mar bar Rav Ashi agrees with Rabbi Abba that the *levir* may not sell his brother's property, even after he marries his widow, but he understands that if the *levir* did sell the property, the sale is valid.

קְנֵי מֵעַכְשָׁיו Acquire it from now. According to *Rambam,* when the owner of the cow says to the buyer: "Go and pull my cow into your possession, and acquire it after thirty days retroactively from today," he is viewed as having sold him the cow from "today," on condition that thirty days pass. *Rashba* and *Ritva* explain that we understand that the buyer means to say: "Acquire the cow itself today, but the benefit that you may derive from the cow you will acquire only after thirty days." These Rishonim all agree that after the thirty days have passed, the buyer acquires the cow with the original act of acquisition. Thus, argue *Rashba* and *Ritva,* Rabbi Yoḥanan's formulation, that the transaction is valid after thirty days, even if the animal is standing in a meadow, is imprecise, for the transaction is valid even if the animal is standing in the public domain, for no additional act of acquisition is required. According to *Meiri,* however, the transaction is only valid if at the end of the thirty-day period the animal is standing in a meadow or an alleyway. But if it is standing in the public domain, where the act of acquisition would not be valid, the transaction is void.

Ra'avad and *Ritva* note that, if the animal is standing on the buyer's secured private property at the end of the thirty-day period, so that the animal could be acquired then by way of the buyer's "courtyard," the transaction is valid, even if the buyer did not add the words "retroactively from today." According to *Meiri,* if the owner told the buyer to draw the cow into his possession, but that he would acquire it for thirty days, then even if the animal is standing in the buyer's house at the end of the thirty-day period, the sale is not valid.

HALAKHAH

pulled the cow into his possession, he does not acquire the cow. But if the owner of the cow said: 'Acquire the cow from now and after thirty days,' that other person acquires the cow at the end of the thirty-day period, even if the cow is then standing in a meadow," following Rabbi Yoḥanan. (All the more so does the buyer acquire the cow if at the end of the thirty-day period it is standing on his property or on property which he owns jointly with the seller, but he does not acquire the cow if it is standing in the public domain; *Sema.*) (*Rambam, Sefer Kinyan, Hilkhot Mekhirah* 2:9; *Shulḥan Arukh, Ḥoshen Mishpat* 197:7.)

[1]בָּעוּ מִינֵּיהּ מֵעוּלָּא: יִבֵּם [2]וְאַחַר כָּךְ חִילֵּק מַהוּ? [3]לֹא עָשָׂה וְלֹא כְלוּם. [4]חִילֵּק, וְאַחַר כָּךְ יִבֵּם, מַהוּ? [5]לֹא עָשָׂה וְלֹא כְלוּם. [6]מַתְקִיף לָהּ רַב שֵׁשֶׁת: [7]הָשְׁתָּא יִבֵּם וְאַחַר כָּךְ חִילֵּק, [8]לֹא עָשָׂה וְלֹא כְלוּם, [9]חִילֵּק וְאַחַר כָּךְ יִבֵּם מִבָּעֲיָא?!

[10]שְׁנֵי מַעֲשִׂים הָווּ.

[11]כִּי אֲתָא רָבִין, אָמַר רֵישׁ לָקִישׁ: [12]בֵּין יִבֵּם וְאַחַר כָּךְ חִילֵּק, [13]בֵּין חִילֵּק וְאַחַר כָּךְ יִבֵּם, [14]לֹא עָשָׂה וְלֹא כְלוּם. [15]וְהִלְכְתָא: [16]לֹא עָשָׂה וְלֹא כְלוּם.

[17]״וַחֲכָמִים אוֹמְרִים: פֵּירוֹת הַמְחוּבָּרִים לַקַּרְקַע שֶׁלּוֹ״.

TRANSLATION AND COMMENTARY

בָּעוּ מִינֵּיהּ [1]**Ulla was asked** the following question: If the *levir* first **performed levirate marriage,** [2]**and afterwards he divided the property** of his late brother's estate with his other brother, **what is the law?** Is the transaction valid or not?

לֹא עָשָׂה [3]Ulla answered: The *levir* **did not accomplish anything, for** the property is mortgaged to guarantee his wife's ketubah settlement, and any attempt on the part of the *levir* to transfer ownership of that property is void.

חִילֵּק [4]Ulla was also asked a second question: **If** the *levir* first **divided the property** of his late brother's estate with his younger brother, **and afterwards performed levirate marriage, what is the law?** Is the transaction valid or not?

לֹא עָשָׂה [5]Ulla responded to this question with the same answer: The *levir* **did not accomplish anything.**

מַתְקִיף לָהּ [6]**Rav Sheshet strongly objected to** the order of presentation of these two questions to Ulla: [7]**Now if** the *levir* first **performed the levirate marriage and only afterwards divided the property** with his other brother, [8]and Ulla ruled that the *levir* **did not accomplish anything,** [9]**was it necessary to ask for a ruling when** the *levir* first **divided the property** of his late brother's estate with his other brother, **and afterwards performed levirate marriage?** If the *levir* cannot transfer ownership of the property of his brother's estate when it is in his possession, then surely he cannot transfer ownership of that property before the estate becomes his!

שְׁנֵי מַעֲשִׂים הָווּ [10]The Gemara answers: Indeed, once Ulla answered the first question, there was no need to ask the second one. But the two questions were not posed to Ulla as theoretical issues. Rather, **two actual incidents were** were brought before him on separate occasions.

כִּי אֲתָא רָבִין [11]**When Ravin came** to Babylonia from Eretz Israel, **he said in the name of Resh Lakish:** [12]**Whether** the *levir* first **performed levirate marriage and** only **afterwards divided the property** with his other brother, [13]**or** the *levir* first **divided the property** of his late brother's estate, **and** only **afterwards performed levirate marriage,** [14]**he did not accomplish anything,** because the property is mortgaged to guarantee his wife's ketubah settlement, and any attempt on the part of the *levir* to transfer ownership of that property is void.

וְהִלְכְתָא [15]The Gemara concludes: **And the** final **law is:** If the *levir* transferred any property from his late brother's estate at any time, [16]**he did not accomplish anything.**

וַחֲכָמִים אוֹמְרִים [17]We have learned in our Mishnah: **"The Sages say:** If the *levir* inherited from his late brother **produce which was** still **attached to the ground,** the produce **belongs to the *levir*** and is not

LITERAL TRANSLATION

[1]They asked Ulla: [If] he performed levirate marriage, [2]and afterwards he divided [the property], what [is the law]?

[3]He did not do anything.

[4][If] he divided [the property], and afterwards he performed levirate marriage, what [is the law]?

[5]He did not do anything.

[6]Rav Sheshet strongly objected to this: [7]Now [if] he performed levirate marriage and afterwards he divided [the property], [8]he did not do anything, [9]was it necessary [to ask for a ruling when] he divided [the property] and afterwards he performed levirate marriage?!

[10]They were two incidents.

[11]When Ravin came, he said in the name of Resh Lakish: [12]Whether he performed levirate marriage and afterwards he divided [the property], [13]or he divided [the property] and afterwards he performed levirate marriage, [14]he did not do anything.

[15]And the law is: [16]He did not do anything.

[17]"And the Sages say: Produce which is attached to the ground is his."

RASHI

שני מעשים הוו — ומי ששאל זו לא שאל זו, ולא שמע האחרון את הראשונה. שלא נשאלו יחד בבית המדרש לגירסא בעלמא, אלא על פי מעשים שאירעו נשאלו.

HALAKHAH

בֵּין יִבֵּם וְאַחַר כָּךְ חִילֵּק **Whether he performed levirate marriage and afterwards divided the property.** "The *levir* may not sell any of his late brother's estate at any time. If he sold property, or gave it away as a gift, or divided up the property with his brothers — whether before or after he took the widow as his levirate wife — the transaction

[1]אַמַּאי? [2]וְהָא כָּל נְכָסָיו אַחֲרָאִין וְעַרְבָאִין לִכְתוּבָּתָהּ!
[3]אֲמַר רֵישׁ לָקִישׁ: תְּנֵי: [4]״שֶׁלָּהּ״.
[5]״כְּנָסָהּ, הֲרֵי הִיא כְּאִשְׁתּוֹ״.
[6]לְמַאי הִלְכְתָא?
[7]אָמַר רַבִּי יוֹסֵי בְּרַבִּי חֲנִינָא: [8]לוֹמַר שֶׁמְּגָרְשָׁהּ בְּגֵט [9]וּמַחֲזִירָהּ.
[10]״מְגָרְשָׁהּ בְּגֵט״, [11]פְּשִׁיטָא!

LITERAL TRANSLATION

[1]Why? [2]But surely all his property is mortgaged and serves as surety for her ketubah!

[3]Resh Lakish said: Teach: [4]"Is hers."

[5]"[If] he married her, she is like his wife." [6]For which law?

[7]Rabbi Yose the son of Rabbi Ḥanina said: [8]To say that he divorces her with a bill of divorce [9]and he may remarry her.

[10]"He divorces her with a bill of divorce," [11]this is obvious!

TRANSLATION AND COMMENTARY

subject to the widow's ketubah." [1]The Gemara asks: **Why** should the produce not be mortgaged to guarantee the woman's ketubah settlement? [2]**Surely all** her late husband's immovable **property is mortgaged and serves as surety for her ketubah** settlement, and produce which was still attached to the ground when the *levir* inherited his brother's estate is considered immovable property!

אֲמַר רֵישׁ לָקִישׁ [3]**Resh Lakish said:** The text of the Mishnah must be slightly revised, so that it **teaches** as follows: "If the *levir* inherited from his brother produce which was still attached to the ground, [4]the produce **belongs to the woman, i.e.,** it is mortgaged to guarantee her ketubah settlement." The Sages do not disagree with Rabbi Meir about produce which grew during the husband's lifetime and which was still attached to the ground when the *levir* inherited his estate, but only about produce which was detached from the ground and about money.

כְּנָסָהּ [5]We have learned in a later clause of our Mishnah: **"If the** *levir* **married** his brother's widow, **she is like** an ordinary **wife."** [6]The Gemara asks: **Regarding which laws** was this stated?

אָמַר [7]**Rabbi Yose the son of Rabbi Ḥanina said:** A levirate wife is like an ordinary wife in two ways: First, if the *levir* wishes to end the marriage, [8]**he must divorce** her **with a bill of divorce.** And second, if the *levir* so desires, [9]**he may remarry her** after a divorce.

מְגָרְשָׁהּ בְּגֵט [10]The Gemara asks: Was it necessary for the Mishnah to teach us that the *levir* **must divorce** his wife **with a bill of divorce?** [11]Surely **this is obvious!** How else should the *levir* terminate the marriage if not with a bill of divorce?

RASHI

והא קתני כל נכסיו של מת אחראין לכתובתה — והמחובר לקרקע כקרקע. ולא דמו למחוברין דנכסי מלוג, דהתם פירא תקינו ליה רבנן היכא דאיכא קרן קיים. והני נמי פירי נינהו, דגמרי ברשותיה. אבל הכא — קרנא ופירא דידיה הוא, ושיעבודא הוא דאית לה עלייהו. ומאי דאישתעבד לה מחיים דבעל — לא אמרינן פירא הוא לאפקועי שיעבודא. **תני שלה** — ולא פליגי רבנן עליה אלא אתלושין ואכספים, ולמימר: דלא משעבדי מטלטלי לכתובת׳. **שמגרש׳ בגט ומחזירה** — תרי מילי אשמעינן: מגרשה בגט ואינה צריכה חליצה. ואשמעינן שאם רצה להחזירה — מחזירה כשאר אשה.

NOTES

תְּנֵי: ״שֶׁלָּהּ״ Teach: "Is hers." We learned in an earlier Mishnah (p. 79a) that, according to the Sages, if a married woman inherited land together with the produce that was attached to the ground, the produce belongs to the husband, for it is regarded as usufruct to which the husband is entitled. Now if the Sages maintain that the husband is entitled to the produce that is attached to land belonging to his wife, why should the *levir* not be entitled to the produce that is attached to land which he inherited from his late brother? *Rashi* explains that the husband is entitled to the produce attached to property inherited by his wife, because the Sages entitled the husband to all the usufruct of his wife's property, provided that his wife's principal remains intact, and attached produce is indeed regarded as usufruct. But the *levir* may not consume the produce attached to property inherited from his brother, because the property itself, together with the produce attached to it, was mortgaged to guarantee the woman's ketubah settlement during her husband's lifetime, and the *levir*'s right to the produce does not cancel that mortgage. *Rid* adds that the husband's right to the usufruct of his wife's property stems from a Rabbinic enactment, and the Rabbinic entitlement includes the produce that is attached to property she inherited. But the *levir* is entitled by right — and not just by Rabbinic enactment — to the usufruct of the property he inherited from his brother. However, he may not consume the produce that was attached to the property he inherited from his brother, for the produce together with the land to which it is attached is subject to a lien in favor of the woman's ketubah settlement.

HALAKHAH

is void," following the Gemara's conclusion. (*Rambam, Sefer Nashim, Hilkhot Ishut* 22:11; *Shulḥan Arukh, Even HaEzer* 168:3.)

שֶׁמְּגָרְשָׁהּ בְּגֵט וּמַחֲזִירָהּ That he divorces her with a bill of divorce and he may remarry her. "After the *levir* takes his brother's widow in levirate marriage, she is like an ordinary wife, so that if he wishes to end the marriage, he may divorce her with a bill of divorce, and if he wishes, he may remarry her after having divorced her." (*Rambam, Sefer Nashim, Hilkhot Yibum* 1:15; *Shulḥan Arukh, Even HaEzer* 168:1.)

LITERAL TRANSLATION

[1]Lest you say: "And he shall perform levirate marriage," the Torah (lit., "the Merciful") said, [2]and still the original levirate marriage is upon her, [3][so that] a bill of divorce shall not suffice for her, but rather *ḥalitzah* [is necessary]. [4]It teaches us.

[5]"He may remarry her," [6]this is obvious! [82B] [7]You may say: [8]The obligation that the Torah (lit., "the Merciful") cast upon him he performed, [9]and now she stands before him with the prohibition of one's brother's wife. [10]It teaches us.

[11]And say so indeed!

[12]The verse states: [13]"And he shall take her as his wife," [14]once he takes her, she becomes as his wife.

[15]"Except that her ketubah [falls] on the property of her first husband." [16]What is

GEMARA

[1]מַהוּ דְּתֵימָא: ״וְיִבְּמָהּ״ אָמַר רַחֲמָנָא, [2]וַעֲדַיִין יִבּוּמִין הָרִאשׁוֹנִים עָלֶיהָ, [3]לָא תִּיסְגֵּי לָהּ בְּגֵט, אֶלָּא בַּחֲלִיצָה. [4]קָא מַשְׁמַע לָן.

[5]״מַחֲזִירָהּ״ [6]פְּשִׁיטָא! [82B] [7]מַהוּ דְּתֵימָא: [8]מִצְוָה דִּרְמָא רַחֲמָנָא עֲלֵיהּ עֲבָדָהּ, [9]וְהַשְׁתָּא תֵּיקוּם עֲלֵיהּ בְּאִיסּוּר אֵשֶׁת אָח. [10]קָא מַשְׁמַע לָן.

[11]וְאֵימָא הָכִי נַמִי?

[12]אָמַר קְרָא: [13]״וּלְקָחָהּ לוֹ לְאִשָּׁה״, [14]כֵּיוָן שֶׁלְּקָחָהּ נַעֲשֵׂית כְּאִשְׁתּוֹ.

[15]״בִּלְבַד שֶׁתְּהֵא כְּתוּבָּתָהּ עַל נִכְסֵי בַּעְלָהּ הָרִאשׁוֹן״. [16]מַאי

RASHI

עדיין יבומין הראשונים עליה — אף על פי שלקחה, דהכי כתיב "ולקחה... ויבמה". **קא משמע לן** — דנעשית כאשתו, ומ"לאשה" דרשינן ליה לקמן. והאי "ויבמה" דרשינן לבעל כרחה, ביבמות (ח,ב). **נעשית כאשתו** — דכתיב "לאשה", קרא יתירא.

TRANSLATION AND COMMENTARY

מַהוּ דְּתֵימָא [1]The Gemara answers: It was necessary for the Mishnah to teach us this in order to prevent us from reaching an erroneous conclusion. For **you might have said: The Torah says** (Deuteronomy 25:5): **"And he shall** take her as his wife and **perform levirate marriage,"** from which it might have been inferred that even after the *levir* marries his brother's widow, [2]she is **still governed by** the laws that had applied to her when she was **first** bound to the *levir* by the **levirate tie.** [3]Were that the case, **a bill of divorce would not suffice** by itself to terminate **her marriage, but rather *ḥalitzah*** would be necessary in addition to the bill of divorce to sever the levirate tie. Therefore, [4]the Tanna of the Mishnah **teaches us that** the law is in fact otherwise and that *ḥalitzah* is unnecessary.

מַחֲזִירָהּ [5]The Gemara now asks: Was it necessary for the Mishnah to teach us that the *levir* **may remarry** his levirate wife? [6]Surely **this is obvious!** [82B] [7]The Mishnah taught us this to avoid another erroneous conclusion. For **you might have said:** [8]**The obligation that the Torah cast upon** the *levir*, **he already performed** when he took his brother's widow as his wife. [9]**Now** that he has divorced her, **she should** once again **be forbidden to him as his brother's wife.** The Torah prohibits sexual relations with one's brother's wife, even after the brother's death. An exception to the prohibition is made in the case of a widow whose husband died without offspring. The brother of the deceased is not only permitted to marry the woman, but is even obligated to do so by Torah law. But you might have said that if the brother took the widow as his levirate wife, and then divorced her, she should once again be forbidden to him as his brother's wife. [10]Therefore, the Tanna of the Mishnah **teaches us** that the law is not so. Once he took her as his levirate wife, the prohibition against engaging in sexual relations with her because she is his brother's wife was permanently canceled.

וְאֵימָא [11]The Gemara raises an objection: **Say indeed** that the *levir* must perform *ḥalitzah* if he wishes to terminate his marriage with his brother's widow, and that if he divorces her, he is forbidden to take her back as his wife!

אָמַר קְרָא [12]The Gemara answers: **The verse states** (Deuteronomy 25:5): [13]**"And he shall take her as his wife."** The words "as his wife," which seem to be superfluous, [14]teach us that **once** the *levir* **takes** his brother's widow in marriage, **she becomes to him as** an ordinary **wife**. Thus, she may be divorced with a bill of divorce, and he may remarry her after the divorce.

בִּלְבַד [15]The Mishnah continues: "If the *levir* married his brother's widow, she is like an ordinary wife, **except that** her **ketubah** settlement **imposes** a lien **on the property** that the *levir* inherited **from the** woman's **first husband,** and not as a lien on the *levir*'s own property." [16]The Gemara asks: **What is the reason**

NOTES

מַהוּ דְּתֵימָא? **What is the reason?** *Rivan* and others understand that the Gemara is asking why the woman's ketubah settlement imposes a lien on the property the *levir* inherited from the woman's first husband, and not as a lien upon the levir's own property. *Ra'ah* and *Ramban* explain the Gemara's question differently: Why is the woman not entitled to two settlements, one from her first husband and one from the *levir*? In other words, why should she not collect

TRANSLATION AND COMMENTARY

for this? The Gemara explains: The *levir* did not choose to take his sister-in-law in marriage, [1]but rather **it is Heaven that gave** her to **him** as **a wife.** Since the marriage was imposed upon the *levir* by Torah law, he is not required to mortgage his own property to guarantee her ketubah settlement.

וְאִי לֵית לַהּ [2]The Gemara adds: **And if** the woman **does not have** a ketubah settlement **from her first husband,** because he did not leave enough property, [3]**she has** a ketubah settlement **from her second husband.** [4]The Rabbis made that provision **so that** the *levir* **not consider it a trivial matter to divorce her.** As the Gemara explained earlier in the tractate (*Ketubot* 11a), the Rabbis imposed a financial penalty on divorce in order to deter a man from arbitrarily divorcing his wife. If the widow's ketubah could only be collected from her late husband's property, the *levir* would have no financial reason to think twice before divorcing his wife.

לֹא יֹאמַר לָהּ [5]We learned in the next clause of the Mishnah: "If the *levir* married his brother's widow, **he may not** set aside money and **say to her:** [6]**'Your ketubah** settlement **rests** before you **on the table,** and the rest of the property that I inherited from my brother I will sell or give away.' Rather, all the property that the *levir* inherited from his brother is mortgaged to guarantee his sister-in-law's ketubah settlement, and the *levir* is prohibited from transferring it. The Mishnah also states that a similar law applies in general, and the Gemara asks: [7]**What** does the Mishnah mean to teach us when it speaks of **"a similar** law"? Is it not obvious that the same law should apply in all cases?

מַהוּ דְתֵימָא [8]The Gemara answers: Had the Mishnah only taught the law with respect to a levirate wife, **you might have said:** Only **there,** in the case of a levirate wife, **is it so,** [9]**because he does not write her** a ketubah from his own property, [10]pledging **that** property **which he** has already **bought, as well as that** property **which he will buy in** the future. Since he does not pledge his own property to the ketubah settlement, designating money for the payment of the woman's ketubah settlement will cause marital strife, for the

טַעְמָא? [1]אִשָּׁה הִקְנוּ לוֹ מִן הַשָּׁמַיִם.
[2]וְאִי לֵית לַהּ מֵרִאשׁוֹן [3]אִית לַהּ מִשֵּׁנִי, [4]כְּדֵי שֶׁלֹּא תְּהֵא קַלָּה בְּעֵינָיו לְהוֹצִיאָהּ.
[5]״לֹא יֹאמַר לָהּ: [6]׳הֲרֵי כְּתוּבָּתֵיךְ׳״. [7]מַאי ״וְכֵן״?
[8]מַהוּ דְתֵימָא: הָתָם הוּא [9]דְּלָא כָּתַב לַהּ [10]״דִּקְנַאי וּדְקָנֵינָא״.

LITERAL TRANSLATION

the reason? [1]A wife was given to him from Heaven. [2]And if she does not have from the first [husband], [3]she has from the second [husband], [4]so that she not be easy in his eyes to divorce.

[5]"He may not say to her: [6]'Your ketubah [rests on the table].'" [7]What is "and similarly"?

[8]You may say: There it is so [9]because he did not write her [10]"That which I bought and which I will buy."

RASHI

אשה הקנו לו — ליבם זה מן השמים, אין עליו לכתוב לה שטר נישואין. **מאי וכן לא יאמר** — פשיטא, מי גריעה אשתו מיבמתו? **התם הוא** — גבי יבמתו קאמרינן שלא ייחד לה מעות לפני שולחנו. **דלא כתב לה** — כתובה האי יבם, דליכתוב בה נכסים. **דקנאי** — כבר. **ודקנינא** — שאני עתיד לקנות. **הלכך איכא איבה** — דלא סמכה דעתה שלא יאבדו המעות.

NOTES

the settlement from her first marriage, like an ordinary widow, and then enter into the new marriage with a new ketubah?

אִית לַהּ מִשֵּׁנִי **She has from the second husband.** The Rishonim ask: What difference does it make whether the woman collects her settlement from the property of her late husband's estate or from the *levir*'s own property? The *levir* inherits his brother's property, and so, practically speaking, the woman always collects the settlement from the *levir*! *Tosafot, Ramban,* and others answer that, since the woman's ketubah settlement only imposes a lien on the *levir*'s own property if her first husband's estate was inadequate, if the husband left sufficient property to guarantee the settlement, and the *levir* sold his own property, and afterwards the property of his brother's estate was struck by a natural disaster, the wife cannot collect her ketubah settlement from the buyer of the *levir*'s property, for it was not mortgaged to guarantee her ketubah settlement. *Rambam, Rashba, Ritva* and others maintain that, if the woman collects her ketubah settlement from her first husband's property, she is entitled to two hundred dinarim (the ketubah of a virgin), but if she collects from the *levir*'s property, she is only entitled to a hundred dinarim, for she was a widow when he married her. *Ra'ah* and *Rivash* maintain that the woman can collect two hundred dinarim even from the *levir*, for the Rabbis enacted that she has the same ketubah settlement from her second husband as she had from her first husband.

מַאי ״וְכֵן״? **What is "and similarly"?** *Rivan* explains that the Gemara argues that there was no reason for the Mishnah to teach this law, for it is obvious that the same law applies to an ordinary wife. *Shittah Mekubbetzet* (following *Rashbam*

HALAKHAH

אִי לֵית לַהּ מֵרִאשׁוֹן **If she does not have from the first husband.** "If the *levir* takes his brother's widow as his levirate wife, and she did not have a settlement from her late husband (or she waived it), the *levir* must write her a

[1]אֲבָל הָכָא דִּכְתַב לָהּ [2]״דִּקְנַאי וּדְקָנֵינָא״, [3]אֵימָא סָמְכָה דַּעְתָּהּ. [4]קָא מַשְׁמַע לָן.

[5]״גֵּרְשָׁהּ, אֵין לָהּ אֶלָּא כְּתוּבָּתָהּ״. [6]גֵּרְשָׁהּ — אִין, [7]לֹא גֵּרְשָׁהּ — לָא, [8]קָא מַשְׁמַע לָן כִּדְרַבִּי אַבָּא.

[9]״הֶחֱזִירָהּ, הֲרֵי הִיא כְּכָל הַנָּשִׁים וְאֵין לָהּ אֶלָּא כְּתוּבָּתָהּ״. [10]״הֶחֱזִירָהּ״, [11]מַאי קָא מַשְׁמַע לָן? [12]תָּנֵינָא: ״הַמְגָרֵשׁ אֶת הָאִשָּׁה וּמַחֲזִירָהּ, [13]עַל מְנָת כְּתוּבָּה רִאשׁוֹנָה מַחֲזִירָהּ״!

LITERAL TRANSLATION

[1]But here since he wrote her [2]"That which I bought and which I will buy," [3]say that she relies [on his guarantee.] [4]It teaches us.

[5]"[If] he divorced her, she has only her ketubah." [6][If] he divorced her — yes; [7][if] he did not divorce her, no. [8]It teaches us like Rabbi Abba.

[9]"[If] he remarried her, she is like all the wives, and she has only her ketubah." [10]"[If] he remarried her," [11]what does it teach us? [12]We learned: "[If] a man divorces his wife and remarries her, [13]on the basis of the first ketubah deed he remarries her"!

TRANSLATION AND COMMENTARY

woman will be concerned that the money might get lost and she will be unable to collect her ketubah. [1]**But here,** in the case of an ordinary wife, the husband pledges his own property, [2]**which he** has already **bought, as well as that** property **which he will buy** in the future. [3]Thus **you** might have **said** that the husband may indeed designate money for the payment of his wife's ketubah settlement, for **she relies** on his guarantee. If the money is lost, she will be able to collect her settlement from the rest of her husband's property. [4]Thus, the Mishnah comes and **teaches us** that this is not so.

גֵּרְשָׁהּ [5]Our Mishnah continues: **"If** the *levir* married his brother's widow, and later **divorced her, she has only her ketubah** settlement. After the *levir* divorces her, he is permitted to sell the property he inherited from his brother." The Gemara draws the following conclusion: [6]The Mishnah implies that **if** the *levir* **divorced** his brother's widow, he may **indeed** sell the property he inherited from his brother, [7]but **if he did not divorce her,** he may **not** sell the property, for the entire estate is mortgaged to guarantee the woman's ketubah settlement. [8]Thus, the Mishnah **teaches us** the position of **Rabbi Abba** cited in the Baraita above (p. 80b), that if the *levir* married his brother's widow, and now wishes to sell his brother's property, he must divorce the woman and then take her back as his ordinary wife, and only then may he sell the property that he inherited from his brother.

הֶחֱזִירָהּ [9]We learned in the last clause of our Mishnah: **"If** the *levir* married his brother's widow and later divorced her, and then **married her again** before she collected her ketubah settlement, and he did not write her a new ketubah deed when they remarried, **she is** treated **like any other woman** under these circumstances. Thus, **she is only entitled to her original ketubah** settlement, which the *levir*'s brother had written for her when he first married her." The Gemara wonders whether this clause of the Mishnah is superfluous: [10]When the Mishnah states that **if** the *levir* **remarried** his brother's widow after divorcing her, she is treated like any other wife, [11]**what is it** trying to **teach us?** [12]**We have** already **learned** elsewhere in the Mishnah (*Ketubot* 99b): **"If someone divorced his wife and** then **remarried her** before she collected her ketubah settlement, and he did not write her a new ketubah deed, [13]we assume that it was **on the basis of** what was written for her in **her first ketubah** that **he remarried her.** Why, then, was it necessary for the Mishnah to repeat this law with respect to a levirate wife?

RASHI

גירשה אין — הוא דאמרינן: אין לה אלא כתובה, ואם בא למכור מן השאר — ימכור. **לא גירשה** — לא ימכור כלום. **קא משמע לן כדרבי אבא** — דלעיל; אם ישראל הוא — מגרשה בגט ומחזירה. ואם תאמר: מרישא שמעינן לה, דקתני: כל נכסיו אחראין! התם עלה טובה הוא, דהא גבי אשתו נמי תנן הכי. אבל מהך משנה יתירא שמעינן: דווקא גירשה. דאי לא — למאי קתני לה? אי משום היא גופה — פשיטא דאין לה אלא כתובתה. אלא ודאי לדיוקא דיליה תנייה, למידק: הא לא גירשה — לא. **מ מאי קא משמע לן** — ביבמה. **תנינא** — לה באשתו, ומאי אולמיה דיבמתו, דאיצטריך למיתנייה?

NOTES

in *Bava Batra*) understands that the term "and similarly" implies that there is some novelty in the second regulation which goes beyond that which was taught in the first regulation. Thus, the Gemara wishes to clarify the novelty of the second regulation.

HALAKHAH

ketubah of a hundred zuz when he takes her as his wife, and all his property is mortgaged to guarantee it." (*Rambam, Sefer Nashim, Hilkhot Ishut* 22:14; *Shulḥan Arukh, Even HaEzer* 168:8.)

גֵּרְשָׁהּ אֵין לָהּ אֶלָּא כְּתוּבָּתָהּ **If he divorced her, she only has her ketubah settlement.** "If the *levir* divorced his levirate wife, and then remarried her before paying her settlement, she is treated like any other woman in that situation, and so she has only one ketubah." (*Shulḥan Arukh, Even HaEzer* 168:2.)

עַל מְנָת כְּתוּבָּה רִאשׁוֹנָה מַחֲזִירָהּ **On the basis of the first ketubah he remarries her.** "If a woman produces two bills

[1]מַהוּ דְּתֵימָא: אִשְׁתּוֹ הוּא, [2]דְּאִיהוּ כָּתַב לָהּ כְּתוּבָּה מִינֵּיהּ. [3]אֲבָל יְבִמְתּוֹ, דְּלָא אִיהוּ כָּתַב לָהּ — [4]הֵיכָא דְּגֵרְשָׁהּ וְאַהַדְרָהּ, [5]אֵימָא כְּתוּבָּתָהּ מִינֵּיהּ. [6]קָא מַשְׁמַע לָן.

[7]אָמַר רַב יְהוּדָה: בָּרִאשׁוֹנָה הָיוּ כּוֹתְבִין לִבְתוּלָה מָאתַיִם וּלְאַלְמָנָה מָנֶה. [8]וְהָיוּ מַזְקִינִין וְלֹא הָיוּ נוֹשְׂאִין נָשִׁים.

LITERAL TRANSLATION

[1]What you might say: It is [regarding] his wife, [2]for he wrote her a ketubah from his [property]. [3]But [regarding] his levirate wife, since he did not write her [a ketubah] — [4]where he divorced her and remarried her, [5]say that her ketubah is from him. [6]It teaches us.

[7]Rav Yehudah said: At first, they would write for a virgin two hundred [dinarim] and for a widow a maneh. [8]And they would grow old, and they would not marry women.

TRANSLATION AND COMMENTARY

מַהוּ דְּתֵימָא [1]The Gemara answers: The Mishnah had to restate the law with respect to a levirate wife because otherwise **you might have said** that the Mishnah's ruling applies only to a man's ordinary **wife,** [2]**for whom he wrote a ketubah from his** own **property.** [3]**But regarding a levirate wife, since** the *levir* **did not write** the woman **a ketubah** from his own property when he married her the first time, [4]**if** he **divorced** her **and** then **remarried her,** [5]you might have **said that** she is entitled to a second **ketubah** settlement **from** the *levir*'s own property. [6]Thus, the Mishnah **teaches us** that this is not so.

אָמַר רַב יְהוּדָה [7]**Rav Yehudah said: At first,** the Rabbis enacted that a man **should write** his wife a ketubah settlement of **two hundred dinarim** if she was **a virgin** at the time of her marriage, **and** if she was **a widow** or a divorcee, he should write her a settlement of **a maneh** (one hundred dinarim, or half the amount of a virgin's settlement). However, they did not require husbands to mortgage their property to guarantee the settlement, and women were reluctant to assume the financial risk of being left with no settlement. [8]As a result, many men **would**

RASHI

דלית לה כתובה מיניה — אלא על נכסי בעלה הראשון. **היו כותבין כו׳** — ולא היו משעבדים נכסיהן לאחריות הכתובה. **ולא היו נושאין נשים** — שלא היו רוצות לינשא להם, אמרו: לכשימות או יגרש — לא נמצא לגבות כלום שהיורשין יצניעו מעות של ירושה.

NOTES

אֲבָל יְבִמְתּוֹ But regarding his levirate wife. *Tosafot* asks: The Mishnah (*Ketubot* 99b) that teaches the law regarding a divorcee who remarried her first husband before collecting her ketubah is superfluous, for the law pertaining to such a woman could have been inferred from our Mishnah, which deals with a levirate wife in a similar situation! *Rosh* answers that one might have argued that, since the *levir* did not mortgage his property to guarantee his wife's ketubah settlement when he married her the first time, he also did not do so when he remarried her. Thus she is only entitled to her original ketubah settlement, which had been a lien on her late husband's property. But the law regarding an ordinary wife might be different. Since the husband guaranteed her a ketubah settlement from his own property when he first married her, he may have meant to entitle her to a second ketubah settlement when he married her again.

הָיוּ כּוֹתְבִין לִבְתוּלָה They would write for a virgin. The Rishonim disagree about the details concerning the original enactment of a woman's ketubah. *Rabbenu Ḥananel* writes that, at first, the husband would guarantee his wife a ketubah and place the money in the woman's safekeeping at the time of marriage. Most Rishonim understand that the husband would obligate himself to pay his wife a settlement upon the dissolution of their marriage, and he would set aside money for that purpose, but he would not mortgage all his property to the ketubah. Thus, if the money that had been set aside for the settlement was lost or spent or hidden away, the woman would not be able to collect it. *Ritva* notes that the law takes the view that the omission of a clause accepting responsibility for an obligation is considered a scribal error, so that even when such a clause is absent, it is viewed as having been explicitly mentioned in the document. Therefore we must understand that, originally, the husband would include a clause in the ketubah deed stating explicitly that he was not accepting responsibility for the settlement. According to *Re'ah,* the husband would stipulate that in the event that the marriage came to an end, he would pay his wife a settlement, but he would not undertake the obligation from the time of marriage. Thus, she would not be able to collect the settlement from property which the husband sold during their marriage.

וְהָיוּ מַזְקִינִין And they would grow old. Most Rishonim understand that, since the husband would not mortgage his property to guarantee his wife's ketubah settlement, many women were afraid that they would be unable to collect it should the marriage come to an end. Thus, many men were forced to remain bachelors all their lives. According to *Rabbenu Ḥananel,* men did not have enough ready money for the ketubah, and therefore found themselves unable to marry.

HALAKHAH

of divorce and a single ketubah, she can only collect one settlement, for if a person divorces his wife, and then remarries her without writing her a new ketubah, we assume that he remarried her on the basis of the first one." (*Rambam, Sefer Nashim, Hilkhot Ishut* 16:30; *Shulḥan Arukh, Even HaEzer* 100:15.)

עַד שֶׁבָּא שִׁמְעוֹן בֶּן שָׁטַח[1] וְתִיקֵּן: כָּל נְכָסָיו אַחְרָאִין[2] לִכְתוּבָּתָהּ.

תַּנְיָא נַמִי הָכִי:[3] ״בָּרִאשׁוֹנָה[4] הָיוּ כּוֹתְבִין לִבְתוּלָה מָאתַיִם וּלְאַלְמָנָה מָנֶה. וְהָיוּ מַזְקִינִין,[5] וְלֹא הָיוּ נוֹשְׂאִין נָשִׁים. הִתְקִינוּ שֶׁיְּהוּ מַנִּיחִין אוֹתָהּ[6] בְּבֵית אָבִיהָ. וַעֲדַיִין, כְּשֶׁהוּא[7] כּוֹעֵס עָלֶיהָ, אוֹמֵר לָהּ: ׳לְכִי[8] אֵצֶל כְּתוּבָּתֵיךְ׳. הִתְקִינוּ[9] שֶׁיְּהוּ מַנִּיחִין אוֹתָהּ בְּבֵית חָמִיהָ. עֲשִׁירוֹת[10] עוֹשׂוֹת אוֹתָהּ קְלָתוֹת שֶׁל כֶּסֶף וְשֶׁל זָהָב. עֲנִיּוֹת[11] הָיוּ עוֹשׂוֹת אוֹתָהּ עָבִיט שֶׁל מֵימֵי רַגְלַיִם.

LITERAL TRANSLATION

[1] Until Shimon ben Shetaḥ came and enacted: [2] All his property is mortgaged to her ketubah.

[3] It was also taught thus: [4] "At first they would write for a virgin two hundred [dinarim] and a widow a maneh. [5] And they would grow old, and they would not marry women. [6] They enacted that they should place it in her father's house. [7] But still, when he was angry with her, [8] he would say to her: 'Go to your ketubah.' [9] They enacted that they should place it in her father-in-law's house. [10] Wealthy women would make it into baskets of silver and gold. [11] Poor women would turn it into a utensil for urine [lit. 'feet water']."

RASHI

בבית חמיה – בבית בעלה. עשירות – שכתובתן מרובה. קלתות – כמין סל שמנחת על ראשה, ונותנת בה פלכיה, לאחר שנתמלא הפלך טווי. עביט – למימי רגלים.

TRANSLATION AND COMMENTARY

grow old and not get married, because they could not find women to accept them under these circumstances. [1] This was the situation **until Shimon ben Shetaḥ enacted** that [2] **all the husband's property is mortgaged to** guarantee his wife's **ketubah** settlement.

תַּנְיָא נַמִי הָכִי [3] A similar ruling **was also taught** in a Baraita which influenced the provisions that were ultimately adopted. [4] **"At first,** the Rabbis enacted that a man **should write** his wife a ketubah in the amount of **two hundred** dinarim if she was **a virgin** at the time of her marriage, **and** if she was **a widow** or a divorcee he should write her a ketubah in the amount of **a maneh.** But since the husband would not mortgage his property to guarantee the settlement, many women were reluctant to accept such an arrangement, [5] and as a result many men **would grow old and not** find women who were ready to **marry** them. [6] The Rabbis then **enacted that** at the time of marriage the husband **should deposit** money designated for his wife's settlement **in her father's house.** In that way the woman could feel secure that she would receive the money. [7] **But still** there was a problem, for **when** the husband **was angry with** his wife, [8] **he would say to her: 'Go** back **to** your father's house and take **your ketubah** settlement.' Once he had deposited money designated for his wife's settlement in her father's house, the deterrent effect of the ketubah was greatly diminished. [9] Thus, the Rabbis **enacted that** at the time of marriage the husband **should deposit** money designated for his wife's ketubah settlement **in her father-in-law's house,** so that if he divorced her, he would have to part with something. [10] **A wealthy woman** whose settlement was very large **would convert the** money **into baskets of silver and gold.** [11] **A poor women** whose settlement was more modest **would convert** the ketubah money **into a receptacle for urine.** In that way the woman could feel confident about receiving the settlement should

NOTES

מַנִּיחִין בְּבֵית חָמִיהָ **They should place it in her father-in-law's house.** *Tosafot* explains that when the husband set aside money in his own house for his wife's ketubah settlement, and she converted the money into some utensil, the husband would think twice about divorcing her, for whenever he needed money he could borrow the utensil from his wife for the purpose of pawning it. Thus, the deterrent value of the ketubah was greater when the settlement was kept in the form of a utensil in the husband's house than when it was deposited in cash in the wife's father's house.

עוֹשׂוֹת אוֹתָהּ עָבִיט שֶׁל מֵימֵי רַגְלַיִם **They would turn it into a receptacle for urine.** *Rashi* comments that the receptacle mentioned here was used for urine, indicating that his text of the Gemara did not include the words "for urine." *Ritva* objects to that reading and to *Rashi's* explanation, arguing that even the poorest woman in Israel receives a settlement of one or two hundred dinarim, much more than required for a receptacle for urine. *Talmidei Rabbenu Yonah* explain that a poor woman would convert the settlement into simple utensils, such as a receptacle for urine. According to *Tosafot* and others, the Baraita reads simply: "A utensil," or "a copper utensil," and refers to a large utensil which was used for collecting and carrying fruit.

HALAKHAH

שִׁמְעוֹן בֶּן שָׁטַח **Shimon ben Shetaḥ.** "The Sages enacted that all of a person's property is mortgaged to guarantee his wife's ketubah settlement. Even if the husband did not record the lien in his wife's ketubah deed, she can still collect her settlement from all of his property." (*Rambam, Sefer Nashim, Hilkhot Ishut* 16:10; *Shulḥan Arukh, Even HaEzer* 100:1.)

TRANSLATION AND COMMENTARY

she be divorced or widowed. [1]**But still** there was a problem, for **when** the husband **was angry with** his wife, [2]**he would say to her: 'Take your ketubah** settlement **and leave.'** If the wife converted the money into some utensil which would be left untouched to guarantee her settlement, her husband would not suffer any real financial loss if he divorced her. Thus, the ketubah would not serve its purpose of protecting the woman from arbitrary divorce. [3]This was the situation **until Shimon ben Shetaḥ enacted that** the husband must **write** in his wife's ketubah: [4]**'All my property is mortgaged to your ketubah.'"**

[1]וַעֲדַיִין, כְּשֶׁכּוֹעֵס עָלֶיהָ, [2]אוֹמֵר לָהּ: 'טְלִי כְּתוּבָּתֵיךְ וּצְאִי'. [3]עַד שֶׁבָּא שִׁמְעוֹן בֶּן שָׁטַח וְתִיקֵּן שֶׁיְּהֵא כּוֹתֵב לָהּ: [4]'כָּל נְכָסַי אַחֲרָאִין לִכְתוּבָּתָהּ'".

הדרן עלך האשה שנפלו

LITERAL TRANSLATION

[1]But still, when he was angry with her, [2]he would say to her: 'Take your ketubah and leave.' [3]Until Shimon ben Shetaḥ came and enacted that he write for her: [4]'All my property is mortgaged to her ketubah.'"

RASHI

טלי כתובתיך וצאי — לפי שהיתה מיוחדת לכך. **כל נכסי אחראין** — ולא ייחד לה כתובה במטלטלין.

הדרן עלך האשה שנפלו

NOTES

כָּל נְכָסַי אַחֲרָאִין All my property is mortgaged. The Jerusalem Talmud formulates Shimon ben Shetaḥ's enactment differently: "That a person should conduct business with his wife's ketubah." Since the husband was henceforth permitted to conduct business with the money that earlier would have had to be set aside for his wife's ketubah settlement, it became more difficult for him to grant his wife a divorce. *Ritva* writes that, even after Shimon ben Shetaḥ's enactment, the husband was permitted to designate money or property for his wife's ketubah settlement, provided that he mortgaged all his property to guarantee it. Our Mishnah (80b) records a later enactment, according to which the Sages ordained that a person not designate any specific property for his wife's ketubah settlement, so that it would not be a trivial matter for him to divorce her.

Conclusion to Chapter Eight

It was concluded that, according to all opinions, a woman who is bound to her brother-in-law by the levirate tie retains full control over any property which comes into her possession. She is permitted to alterate such property and the *levir* may not raise any objections. A betrothed woman who inherited property during the period of her betrothal may not in the first instance sell the property or give it away as a gift, but after the fact the transaction is valid. A married woman may not sell or give away her usufruct property, and if she does, her husband may reclaim it from the buyer or recipient. These rules apply to property which was known to the husband, i.e., which was in the woman's possession at the time of the marriage. But if she inherited property in a distant land, she is permitted to sell it or give it away.

If a woman inherited money or received money by way of a gift while she was married to her husband, land must be bought with the money, the principal remains in the woman's possession, and the usufruct belongs to her husband. If the woman has property which produces fruit, but does not restore itself, the husband may enjoy the usufruct even though the principal will be totally depleted. If the woman has property which does not bear fruit, it must be sold, and fruit-producing property is purchased in its place.

If a married woman inherits produce which is still attached to the ground, the produce belongs to her husband, but if he divorces her before it is harvested, the produce belongs to the woman. The reverse is true with respect to produce which is already detached from the ground. If a married woman inherits such produce, it belongs to her, but if the woman has such produce in her possession at the time of her divorce, it belongs to her husband.

A man is not entitled to any compensation for expenses he incurred with respect to his wife's usufruct property. Whatever he spent was spent, and whatever benefit he derived was enjoyed. An exception is made if the husband had expenses, but did not derive any benefit at all. In such a case he may take an oath concerning the sum of money he spent, and then collect that sum from his wife.

There are differences between the lien an ordinary woman exercises over her husband's property and the lien a woman taken in levirate marriage exercises over the property that the *levir* inherited from her late husband. Regarding an ordinary woman, the Sages enacted that her husband should not designate movable goods for her ketubah, but rather all of his property is mortgaged to cover that obligation. Both the husband and the wife benefit from this arrangement, for the husband is permitted to sell all his property, and the woman can recover her ketubah from the buyers. The law is different in the case of a levirate wife. All of the property that had belonged to the woman's late husband is designated for her ketubah, and therefore the *levir* may never sell any of it.

List of Sources

Aḥaronim, lit., "the last," meaning Rabbinic authorities from the time of the publication of Rabbi Yosef Caro's code of Halakhah, *Shulḥan Arukh* (1555).

Arba'ah Turim, code of Halakhah by Rabbi Ya'akov ben Asher, b. Germany, active in Spain (c. 1270-1343).

Arukh, Talmudic dictionary, by Rabbi Natan of Rome, 11th century.

Avnei Nezer, novellae on the Talmud by Rabbi Avraham Bornstein of Sokhochev, Poland (1839-1908).

Ayelet Ahavim, novellae on *Ketubot* by Rabbi Aryeh Leib Zuenz, Poland, 19th century.

Ba'al HaMa'or, Rabbi Zeraḥyah ben Yitzḥak HaLevi, Spain, 12th century. Author of *HaMa'or,* Halakhic commentary on *Hilkhot HaRif.*

Ba'er Hetev, commentary on *Shulḥan Arukh, Ḥoshen Mishpat,* by Rabbi Zeḥaryah Mendel of Belz, Poland (18th century).

Baḥ (Bayit Ḥadash), commentary on *Arba'ah Turim,* by Rabbi Yoel Sirkes, Poland (1561-1640).

Bereshit Rabbah, Midrash on the Book of Genesis.

Bertinoro, Ovadyah, 15th century Italian commentator on the Mishnah.

Bet Aharon, novellae on the Talmud, by Rabbi Aharon Walkin, Lithuania (1865-1942).

Bet Shmuel, commentary on *Shulḥan Arukh, Even HaEzer,* by Rabbi Shmuel ben Uri Shraga, Poland, second half of the 17th century.

Bet Ya'akov, novellae on *Ketubot,* Rabbi Ya'akov Lorberboim of Lissa, Poland (1760-1832).

Bet Yosef, Halakhic commentary on *Arba'ah Turim* by Rabbi Yosef Caro (1488-1575), which is the basis of his authoritative Halakhic code, *Shulḥan Arukh.*

Birkat Avraham, novellae on the Talmud, by Rabbi Avraham Erlinger, Israel (20th century).

Bnei Ahuvah, novellae on *Mishnah Torah,* by Rabbi Yehonatan Eibeschuetz, Poland, Moravia, and Prague (c. 1690-1764).

Derishah and *Perishah,* commentaries on *Tur* by Rabbi Yehoshua Falk Katz, Poland (c. 1555-1614).

Eliyah Rabbah, commentary on *Shulḥan Arukh, Orah Ḥayyim,* by Rabbi Eliyahu Shapira, Prague (1660-1712).

Eshel Avraham, by Rabbi Avraham Ya'akov Neimark, novellae on the Talmud, Israel (20th century).

Even HaEzer, section of *Shulḥan Arukh* dealing with marriage, divorce, and related topics.

Geonim, heads of the academies of Sura and Pumbedita in Babylonia from the late 6th century to the mid-11th century.

Giddulei Shmuel, by Rabbi Shmuel Gedalya Neiman, novellae on the Talmud, Israel (20th century).

Gra, by Rabbi Eliyahu ben Shlomo Zalman (1720-1797), the Gaon of Vilna. Novellae on the Talmud and *Shulḥan Arukh.*

Hafla'ah, novellae on *Ketubot,* by Rabbi Pinḥas HaLevi Horowitz, Poland and Germany (1731-1805).

Haggahot Mordekhai, glosses on the *Mordekhai,* by Rabbi Shmuel ben Aharon of Schlettstadt, Germany, late 14th century.

Halakhot Gedolot, a code of Halakhic decisions written in the Geonic period. This work has been ascribed to Sherira Gaon, Rav Hai Gaon, Rav Yehudah Gaon and Rabbi Shimon Kayyara.

Ḥatam Sofer, responsa literature and novellae on the Talmud by Rabbi Moshe Sofer (Schreiber), Pressburg, Hungary and Germany (1763-1839).

Ḥaver ben Ḥayyim, novellae on the Talmud by Rabbi Ḥizkiyah Ḥayyim Ploit, Lithuania, 19th century.

Ḥelkat Meḥokek, commentary on *Shulḥan Arukh, Even HaEzer,* by Rabbi Moshe Lima, Lithuania (1605-1658).

Hokhmat Manoaḥ, commentary on the Talmud by Rabbi Manoaḥ ben Shemaryah, Poland, 16th century.

Ḥoshen Mishpat, section of *Shulḥan Arukh* dealing with civil and criminal law.

Ittur, Halakhic work by Rabbi Yitzḥak Abba Mari, Provence (1122-1193).

Iyyun Ya'akov, commentary on *Ein Ya'akov,* by Rabbi Ya'akov bar Yosef Riesher, Prague, Poland, and France (d. 1733).

Kesef Mishneh, commentary on *Mishneh Torah,* by Rabbi Yosef Caro, author of *Shulḥan Arukh.*

Korban HaEdah, commentary on the Jerusalem Talmud by Rabbi David ben Naftali Frankel, Germany (1707-1762).

Kovetz Shiurim, novellae on the Talmud by Rabbi Elḥanan Wasserman, Lithuania (1875-1941).

Leḥem Mishneh, commentary on the Mishneh Torah by Rabbi Avraham di Boton, Salonica (1560-1609).

Magen Avraham, commentary on *Shulḥan Arukh, Oraḥ Ḥayyim,* by Rabbi Avraham HaLevi Gombiner, Poland (d. 1683).

Maggid Mishneh, commentary on *Mishneh Torah,* by Rabbi Vidal de Tolosa, Spain, 14th century.

Maharal, Rabbi Yehudah Loew ben Betzalel of Prague (1525-1609). Novellae on the Talmud.

Maharam of Rotenburg, Rabbi Meir of Rotenburg, Tosafist and Halakhic authority, Germany (c. 1215-1293.)

Maharam Schiff, novellae on the Talmud by Rabbi Meir ben Ya'akov HaKohen Schiff (1605-1641), Frankfurt, Germany.

Maharsha, Rabbi Shmuel Eliezer ben Yehudah HaLevi Edels, Poland (1555-1631). Novellae on the Talmud.

Maharshal, Rabbi Shlomo ben Yeḥiel Luria, Poland (1510-1573). Novellae on the Talmud.

Meiri, commentary on the Talmud (called *Bet HaBeḥirah*), by Rabbi Menaḥem ben Shlomo, Provence (1249-1316).

Mekhilta, Halakhic Midrash on the Book of Exodus.

Melekhet Shlomo, commentary on the Mishnah by Rabbi Shlomo Adeni, Yemen and Eretz Israel (1567-1626).

Melo HaRo'im, commentary on the Talmud by Rabbi Ya'akov Tzvi Yolles, Poland (c. 1778-1825).

Mishnah Berurah, commentary on *Shulḥan Arukh, Oraḥ Ḥayyim,* by Rabbi Yisrael Meir HaKohen, Poland (1837-1933).

Mishneh LeMelekh, commentary on *Mishneh Torah*, by Rabbi Yehudah ben Shmuel Rosanes, Turkey (1657-1727).

Mitzpeh Eitan, glosses on the Talmud by Rabbi Avraham Maskileison, Byelorussia (1788-1848).

Mordekhai, compendium of Halakhic decisions by Rabbi Mordekhai ben Hillel HaKohen, Germany (1240?-1298).

Nimmukei Yosef, commentary on *Hilkhot HaRif,* by Rabbi Yosef Ḥaviva, Spain, early 15th century.

Or Sameaḥ, novellae on *Mishnah Torah,* by Rabbi Meir Simḥah HaKohen of Dvinsk, Latvia (1843-1926).

Oraḥ Ḥayyim, section of *Shulḥan Arukh* dealing with daily religious observances, prayers, and the laws of the Sabbath and Festivals.

Perishah, see *Derishah.*

Pitḥei Teshuvah, compilation of responsa literature on the *Shulḥan Arukh* by Rabbi Avraham Tzvi Eisenstadt, Russia (1812-1868).

Pnei Moshe, commentary on the Jerusalem Talmud by Rabbi Moshe ben Shimon Margoliyot, Lithuania (c. 1710-1781).

Pnei Yehoshua, novellae on the Talmud by Rabbi Ya'akov Yehoshua Falk, Poland and Germany (1680-1756).

Porat Yosef, by Rabbi Yosef ben Rabbi Tzvi Hirsch, novellae on tractate *Ketubot* (19th century).

Ra'ah, see *Rabbi Aharon HaLevi.*

Ra'avad, Rabbi Avraham ben David, commentator and Halakhic authority. Wrote comments on *Mishneh Torah.* Provence (c. 1125-1198?).

Rabbenu Gershom, commentator and Halakhic authority, France (960-1040).

Rabbenu Ḥananel (ben Ḥushiel), commentator on the Talmud, North Africa (990-1055).

Rabbenu Shimshon (ben Avraham of Sens), Tosafist, France and Eretz Israel (c. 1150-1230).

Rabbenu Tam, commentator on the Talmud, Tosafist, France (1100-1171).

Rabbenu Yeḥiel, French Tosafist (d. 1268).

Rabbenu Yehonatan, Yehonatan ben David HaKohen of Lunel, Provence, Talmudic scholar (c. 1135-after 1210).

Rabbenu Yeruḥem, Rabbi Yeruḥem ben Meshullam, Halakhist, Spain, 14th century. Author of *Toledot Adam VeḤavah.*

Rabbenu Yonah, see *Talmidei Rabbenu Yonah.*

Rabbi Aharon HaLevi, Spain 13th century. Novellae on the Talmud.

Rabbi Akiva Eger, Talmudist and Halakhic authority, Posen, Germany (1761-1837).

Rabbi Avraham ben Isaac of Narbonne, French Talmudist (c. 1110-1179).

Rabbi Benyamin Musafiya, Italy and Amsterdam (c.1606-1675). Author of *Musaf Arukh.*

Rabbi Cresdas Vidal, Spanish Talmudist and commentator, 14th century.

Rabbi Elḥanan Wasserman, Talmudic scholar and Halakhic authority, Lithuania (1875-1941).

Rabbi Moshe the son of Rabbi Yosef of Narbonne, French Talmudist of the twelfth century, France and Eretz Israel.

Rabbi Shlomo of Montpellier, French Talmudist of the thirteenth century.

Rabbi Shmuel HaNagid, Spain (993-1055 or 1056). Novellae on the Talmud found in *Shittah Mekubbetzet.*

Rabbi Ya'akov Emden, Talmudist and Halakhic authority, Germany (1697-1776).

Rabbi Yosef of Jerusalem, French Tosafist of the twelfth and thirteenth centuries, France and Eretz Israel.

Rabbi Zeraḥyah ben Yitzḥak HaLevi, Spain, 12th century. Author of *HaMa'or*, Halakhic commentary on *Hilkhot HaRif.*

Radbaz, Rabbi David ben Shlomo Avi Zimra, Spain, Egypt, Eretz Israel, and North Africa (1479-1574). Commentary on *Mishneh Torah.*

Rambam, Rabbi Moshe ben Maimon, Rabbi and philosopher, known also as Maimonides. Author of *Mishneh Torah,* Spain and Egypt (1135-1204).

Ramban, Rabbi Moshe ben Naḥman, commentator on Bible and Talmud, known also as Naḥmanides, Spain and Eretz Israel (1194-1270).

Ran, Rabbi Nissim ben Reuven Gerondi, Spanish Talmudist (1310?-1375?).

Rash, Rabbi Shimshon ben Avraham, Tosafist, commentator on the Mishnah, Sens (late 12th- early 13th century).

Rashash, Rabbi Shmuel ben Yosef Shtrashun, Lithuanian Talmud scholar (1794-1872).

Rashba, Rabbi Shlomo ben Avraham Adret, Spanish Rabbi famous for his commentaries on the Talmud and his responsa (c. 1235-c. 1314).

Rashbam, Rabbi Shmuel ben Meir, commentator on the Talmud, France (1085-1158).

Rashbatz, Rabbi Shimon ben Tzemaḥ Duran, known for his book of responsa, *Tashbatz,* Spain and Algeria (1361-1444).

Rashi, Rabbi Shlomo ben Yitzḥak, the paramount commentator on the Bible and the Talmud, France (1040-1105).

Rav Aḥa (Aḥai) Gaon, author of *She'iltot.* Pumbedita, Babylonia and Eretz Israel, 8th century. See *She'iltot.*

Rav Hai Gaon, Babylonian Rabbi, head of Pumbedita Yeshivah, 10th-11th century.

Rav Natronai Gaon, of the Sura Yeshivah, 9th century.

Rav Sherira Gaon, of the Pumbedita Yeshivah, 10th century.

Rema, Rabbi Moshe ben Yisrael Isserles, Halakhic authority, Poland (1525-1572).

Remah, novellae on the Talmud by Rabbi Meir ben Todros HaLevi Abulafiya, Spain (c. 1170-1244). See *Yad Ramah.*

Ri, Rabbi Yitzḥak ben Shmuel of Dampierre, Tosafist, France (died c. 1185).

Ri HaLavan, French Tosafist (12th century).

Ri Migash, Rabbi Yosef Ibn Migash, commentator on the Talmud, Spain (1077-1141).

Rid, see *Tosefot Rid.*

Rif, Rabbi Yitzḥak Alfasi, Halakhist, author of *Hilkhot HaRif,* North Africa (1013-1103).

Rishonim, lit., "the first," meaning Rabbinic authorities active between the end of the Geonic period (mid-11th century) and the publication of *Shulḥan Arukh* (1555).

Ritva, novellae and commentary on the Talmud by Rabbi Yom Tov ben Avraham Ishbili, Spain (c. 1250-1330).

Rivan, Rabbi Yehudah ben Natan, French Tosafist, 11th-12th centuries.

Rivash, Rabbi Yitzḥak ben Sheshet, Spain and North Africa (1326-1408). Novellae on the Talmud mentioned in *Shittah Mekubbetzet.*

Rosh, Rabbi Asher ben Yeḥiel, also known as Asheri, commentator and Halakhist, German and Spain (c. 1250-1327).

Sefer HaYashar, novellae on the Talmud by Rabbenu Tam. France (c. 1100-1171).

Sefer Mikkaḥ U'Mimkar, by Rav Hai Gaon. Treatise on the laws of commerce.

Sha'ar HaTziyyun, see *Mishnah Berurah.*

Shakh (Siftei Kohen), commentary on the *Shulḥan Arukh* by Rabbi Shabbetai ben Meir HaKohen, Lithuania (1621-1662).

She'iltot, by Aḥa (Aḥai) of the Pumbedita Yeshivah, 8th century. One of the first books of Halakhah arranged by subjects.

Shittah Mekubbetzet, a collection of commentaries on the Talmud by Rabbi Betzalel ben Avraham Ashkenazi of Safed (c. 1520-1591).

Shulḥan Arukh, code of Halakhah by Rabbi Yosef Caro, b. Spain, active in Eretz Israel (1488-1575).

Sifrei, Halakhic Midrash on the Books of Numbers and Deuteronomy.

Sukkat David, by Rabbi David Kviat, novellae on tractate *Ketubot,* America (20th century).

Talmidei Rabbenu Yonah, commentary on *Hilkhot HaRif* by the school of Rabbi Yonah of Gerondi, Spain (1190-1263).

Taz, abbreviation for *Turei Zahav.* See *Turei Zahav.*

Terumot HaDeshen, responsa literature and Halakhic decisions by Rabbi Yisrael Isserlin, Germany (15th century).

Tiferet Yisrael, commentary on the Mishnah by Rabbi Yisrael Lipshitz, Germany (1782-1860).

Tosafot, collection of commentaries and novellae on the Talmud, expanding on Rashi's commentary, by the French-German Tosafists (12th and 13th centuries).

Tosafot Yeshanim, one of the editions of the *Tosafot* on the Talmud, 14th century.

Tosefot Rosh, an edition based on *Tosefot Sens* by the *Rosh,* Rabbi Asher ben Yeḥiel, Germany and Spain (c. 1250-1327).

Tosefot Rid, commentary on the Talmud by Rabbi Yeshayahu ben Mali de Trani, Italian Halakhist (c. 1200-before 1260).

Tosefot Sens, the first important collection of *Tosafot,* by Rabbi Shimshon of Sens (late 12th-early 13th century).

Tosefot Yom Tov, commentary on the Mishnah by Rabbi Yom Tov Lipman HaLevi Heller, Prague and Poland (1579-1654).

Tur, abbreviation of *Arba'ah Turim,* Halakhic code by Rabbi Ya'akov ben Asher, b. Germany, active in Spain (c. 1270-1343).

Turei Zahav, commentary on *Shulḥan Arukh* by Rabbi David been Shmuel HaLevi, Poland (c. 1486-1667).

Yoreh De'ah, section of *Shulḥan Arukh* dealing mainly with dietary laws, interest, ritual purity, and mourning.

Zuto Shel Yam, by Rabbi Moshe Leiter, glosses on the Aggadah in the Talmud (20th century).

About the Type

This book was set in Leawood, a contemporary typeface designed by Leslie Usherwood. His staff completed the design upon Usherwood's death in 1984. It is a friendly, inviting face that goes particularly well with sans serif type.